1st July 1916
Officer Roll of Honour
With Portraits

Dennis,

Hope you enjoy the book

Trevor Harkin

Trevor Harkin

1st July 1916
Officer Roll of Honour
First Edition 2021

Published by War Memorial Publications

For a copy of this publication email trevorharkin@btinternet.com

Contents

Abbreviations

BEF	British Expeditionary Force
Bn	Battalion
CCS	Casualty Clearing Station
CiC	Commander In Chief
CWGC	Commonwealth War Graves Commission
CO	Commanding Officer
Coy	Company
DCM	Distinguished Conduct Medal
DSO	Distinguished Service Order
GOC	General Officer Commading
GSW	Gun Shot Wound
LRB	London Rifle Brigade
MC	Military Cross
MGC	Machine Gun Corps
MIC	Medal Index Card
OTC	Officer Training Corps
RAMC	Royal Army Medical Corps
RFA	Royal Field Artillery
RFC	Royal Flying Corps
RMC	Royal Military College
UVF	Ulster Volunteer Force
VC	Victoria Cross

Preface

The origins of this book began back in 2006 whilst I was researching my ancestors. Three of my granny's uncles were killed in the Great War. Lance Corporal Daniel Doherty, 14679 fell on the first day of the Battle of the Somme with the 11th Bn., Royal Inniskilling Fusiliers. Corporal James Doherty 14680, who enlisted

with Daniel thus the consecutive service numbers was killed on the 16th August 1917 with B Coy., 11th Bn., Royal Inniskilling Fusiliers whilst attached to 109th Trench Mortar Battery. The final brother to be killed was Company Quartermaster Sergeant John Doherty MM, 5758, 1st Bn., Royal Inniskilling Fusiliers who was killed on the 22nd March 1918 (pictured right). John, the eldest brother enlisted prior to 1897 and was awarded the Military Medal in June 1917. At this point he had seen twenty years' service with 'The Skins' and had fought through the South African Campaign and in the Dardanelles. From the family photograph only William survived the war and Maurice and Eliza Doherty would receive thanks from the King and Queen for the role the family played in the War. Daniel was killed on the 1st July 1916 although his death was not confirmed to his parents until mid-July 1917 having been posted as 'missing since the 1st July'. His obituary read; 'He was a very fine type of British soldier and was the first man in the Letterkenny unit of the UVF to volunteer for active service on the formation of the gallant Ulster Division.' News of the death of James appeared locally in 'The Northern Whig' on the 27th August 1917. John was killed in the German advance that began on the 21st March 1918. All the brothers are commemorated on memorials.

I also researched my great-grandfather John Gibson who was married to Tessie Gibson. John served in the Great War as Private John Gibson, 15205, Royal Inniskilling Fusiliers and a note in his Bible reveals he served on the Somme. John never spoke about the war. From this research I began to write local history books. Various projects presented themselves. A book in 2011 centred around a link to the Battle of the Somme entitled Thiepval Memorial; 330 Coventry Men Day by Day. Whilst writing 'Polo and the Great War' when I struggled to find a photo of Lieutenant Leslie Terrett Day, Royal Field Artillery. He was killed on the 1st July 1916 and with the Centenary Anniversary of the start of the Battle of the Somme looming I questioned whether it was possible to get a photograph of every officer killed on the 1st July 1916.

The number of photos of fallen soldiers for for 'Polo and the Great War' and for 'City of Coventry; Roll of the Fallen' were both higher than I expected so I aimed to find as many as I could for this book. However with so much material available and more and more being loaded to the internet every week this book took longer than planned to finish and with only self-imposed deadlines, the objective of as many photos as possible became key. Sadly, I have not managed to get a photo of every officer killed on that fateful day, but what I have uncovered is the stories and the backgrounds of those who died. For example, one officer left specific instructions that no photographs were to appear after his death, whilst a portrait of another officer Second Lieutenant Madders once hung in the council offices at Hendon.

It should be pointed out that this book does not address the strategy nor the tactics used by the British Army on the 1st July 1916 and for this I would recommend reading Martin Middlebrook's The First Day of the Somme 1 July 1916, first published in 1971. Another work that should be mentioned written before computers and databases is Ernest Bell's 'Soldiers killed on the First Day of the Somme' from 1977 that provides basic information on all ranks that were killed. In 2004 a biographical database was set up by Pam & Ken Linge and this has been available at the Thiepval Visitor Centre for the Fallen commemorated at the Thiepval Memorial.

It has taken almost 50 years to add over 850 photographs to these two original works by Martin Middlebrook and Ernest Bell. An appendix covers the men whom were given an official date of death being the 2nd July 1916. In some cases there is evidence to suggest that an officer died on the 1st July rather than a differing date and I have added the biography to the 1st July and noted the reason. Evidence comes from Medal Index Cards, war diaries, letters to the families, officer ervice records and newspapers.

Acknowledgements

This project would not have even started if I was not assisted by Neil Clark and access to his pictorial database of fallen officers and clues as to where to find officer photographs by regiment or region. This gave me the start I need and encouragement to carry on. In the latter stages of the book, I began to communicate with Jonathan Porter author of the excellent 'Zero Hour Z Day 1st July 1916 XIII Corps Operations between Maricourt and Mametz' and 'Zero Hour Z Day XV Corps Operations between Mametz and Fricourt', I would like to thank him for access to files from the National Archives and for knowledge sharing. Over 275 National Archives records were consulted for the Fallen officers and the number of the file can be seen after the after the officer's entry. This code starts with WO and is the War Office: Officers' Services, First World War, personal files series. This contains records and correspondence for officers with temporary commissions and Territorial Army officers who served in the First World War. In some cases photographs were mentioned in the personal effects of the fallen officer they were returned to the family and from the 275 files only one photograph was found in the associated paperwork. This does however give some hope that for those officers who do not currently have a photo that at one point a photo existed and was returned to the relatives. Information has also been added if the officers signed the visitor's book to Talbot House, Poperinge, Belgium and thanks need to go to Mr. Jan Louagie, Hon. Secretary Talbot House Association. This book as always would not have been produced without the support of my wife, and two children when I would 'pop' into the local archives from Edinburgh to St. Ives.

Contact with relative of the Fallen always enhance the documented records and I need to thank the following; Philip and Lynn Andrade ((2nd Lieutenant Harold Asser); Mark Heath (2nd Lieutenant William Huxby Heath); Frances Hoskins (Lieutenant Cyril Hoskins); Geoff Huntriss (Captain Cyril John Huntriss MC); Jim Elliott (2nd Lieutenant Philip Maurice Elliott) and Gaye Woods (2nd Lieutenant Henry Bastick Pilgrim).

This book would not have been possible without the assistance of the following people and I apologise if I have inadvertently missed anyone of the list. The list ranges from school archivists to volunteers at hockey clubs and they are from a variety of institutions and museums. Names are in alphabetically order by surname with the brackets covering main area of interest, associated institution.

Richard Aldrich, (Ruthin School); Peter Allen, School Archivist, (Cranbrook School); Ruth Ainley, Head, (Read School); Penelope Baker, College Archivist, (Exeter College, Oxford); Tom Barclay, Local Studies Librarian, (South Ayrshire Library); Allan Barker (Author of Bagnalls of Stafford: Builders of Locomotives for the World's Railways: the Firm and Its Folk); Julie Barker, Secretary, (Bramcote Junior School); Shirley Baxter, Volunteer, (Sheffield Grand Cemetery Trust); Sophie Bell, School Archivist, (King's College School, Wimbledon); Stephen Benson, (Cheshire County Memorial Project); Dr. Charlotte Berry, College Archivist, (Magdalen College); Steven Bevan, (Cheshire County Memorial Project); David Birchall, (Anfield Bicycling Club); Geoffrey Bisson, (Queens College); Mark Bone, Head of IT, (Copthorne Preparatory School); Pat Bracken, (Northern Ireland Cricket Research); Nigel à Brassard (Sports Historian); David Woodd, Chief Executive, (Hurlingham Polo Association); Dr Robin Brooke-Smith, Taylor Librarian and Archivist, (Shrewsbury School); Miss Kerry Brown, Development and Alumni Relations Manager, (St. Lawrence College); James Buchanan, (Rutlandremembers.org); Rob Buckett, (Oriel College; Andrew Burt, (Thameside Library); Jonathan Cable, Archivist, (The Institution of Engineering & Technology); Caroline Carr, (Donegal Museum); Peter Catherall, Honorary Secretary & David Birchall, Club Archivist, (Anfield Bicycling Club); Harriet Cheng Alumni and Development Officer, (University College); Richard & Rosemary Christophers, Hon Archivists, (Ripley Court School); Charlotte Clare, Project Researcher, (British Jews in the First World War. We were there too); Mike Clifford, (Ballard School); Sarah Cobb, Office Administrator, (Ampleforth Abbey & College); Mandy Cochrane, (Wincanton Window); George Cogswell, (Trafford War Dead & Marden

High School); Jes Cooban, (Bexley Local Studies); Helen Cooper, (Packwood School); Paul Cooper, (Harrogate Roll of Honour); Mike Cordell, (Kent County RFC); John Cornwell, School Archivist & Historian, (King Edward's School); Caroline Covan, Curator, (Royal Irish Fusiliers Museum); Kelvin Dakin, (Bramford Great War Project); Claire Daniel, Duty Archivist, (University of Glasgow); Peter Daniels, Education Officer, (Westminster Archives); Dr. Robin Darwall Smith FSA FRHistS, Archivist, (University College, Jesus College, Oxford); Bev Davidge, Curator and Archivist, (Hilton College); Christopher Dawkins & Jules Wallis, Archivists, (Felsted School); Ian Diamond, Vice Commodore, (Royal Mersey Yacht Club); Peter Donnelly, Curator, (King's Own Royal Regiment Museum); Dr. Alexander du Toit, Archive Cataloguer, (Goldsmiths); Stuart Duncan, (Storrington Local History Group); John Eagle; Daniel Edwards, Heritage Librarian Assistant, (Cathays Library, Cardiff); Michael Eighteen (Southend 1914 1918); Henry Ellwood, (Farnham Fallen); Elizabeth Ennion-Smith, Archivist, (St. Catherine's College, Cambridge); Edwina Fahlqvist, (British Library); Yvonne Fenter, (WW1 Lives); Euan Ferguson, Headteacher, (Isleworth & Lyon School); Richard A. Flory for searching his database; Ann Fox, (Bromley War Memorial); Gerald Frykman, School Archivist, (Warwick School); Dawn Galer, Collections Officer, (Redbridge Museum & Heritage Service); Kevin Gallagher, (Burton Grammar School); Samantha Gautama, Alumni Manager, (Forest School); Sally Gilbert, Archivist, (Merchant Taylors' School); Vincent Gillen, Social History, (Inverclyde, McLean Museum & Art Gallery); Amanda Goode, (Emmanuel College, Cambridge); Alex van Goethem, Cataloguing Archivist, (Jesuits in Britain Archives); Amanada Green, Archivist, (High School of Glasgow); Philippa Green, Alumni Relation Officer, (Royal Grammar School); Dr. Stacey Harmer, Archivist, (Brentwood School); John Hartley, (Stockport 1914 1918); Rachel Hassall, School Archivist, (Sherborne School); David Hedges, Les Herbert, (Old Wandsworthians Trust); Laurie Holmes, (Colchester Royal Grammar School); Joanne Honeyford, (Coleraine War Memorial); Nick Hooper, (Bradford Grammar School and the Old Boys Association); Julia Hudson, (Highgate School); Linda Hutton, (Barnsley Historian); Jane, (WW1photos); Susannah Jarvis, Deputy Curator, (Royal Hampshire Museum); Jaymer Javier, Editorial, (Journal of the RAMC); Hannah Jenkinson, School Archivist, (Rossall School); Martin Kay, Honorary Secretary, (Pleasington Golf Club); Jean Kent-Sutton, College Librarian, (St. Columba's College, Dublin); John Kimbell, School Archivist, (Lambrook School); Lesley Koulouris, School Archives, (Berkhamstead School); Mrs Alison Lainchbury, Librarian & Archivist, (The Leys, Cambridge); Rory Lalwan, Senior Archivist & Local Studies Officer, (City of Westminster Archive Centre); Elizabeth Langsdale, Archivist, (Oundle School); Phil Lapage, (Shrewsbury School); Liz Larby, School Archivist, (Gresham's School); Simon Last (Author of Aldeburgh War Memorial The Story Behind the Names 1914 1918); Alec Lavender, (Bromley RFC); Anthony Lee, (Margate Local History Society); Christine Leighton, College Archivist, (Cheltenham College); Justin Levy; Roger De H Llewellyn, Director & Keith Cheyney, Honorary Archivist, (Haberdashers' Aske's Boys' School); Monika Ligocka, Digital Services, (Surrey Libraries); William Lynn, Archivist, (Foyle College); Neil Lyon, Foundation Director, (Wellingborough School); Susan Madden-Grey, Museum Curator, (Otago Boy's High School, New Zealand); Mrs J. Malloney, Head of Humanities, (Farnborough Academy); Elizabeth Manterfield, (Epsom College); Ian D. Martin, (Kings Own Scottish Borderers Regimental Museum); Una Mathewson, (Donegal Central Library); John McCarthy; Charlotte McColl, Archives, (Sydney Grammar School); Jennifer McEnhill, (Eaton House School); Suzy McGarel, Principal Secretary & Angela Campbell, Librarian, (Larne Grammar School); Mark McNally, President & Philip Tarleton, (Birkenhead Park Rugby Club); Nick Metcalfe (Author of Blacker's Boys); Imogen Middleton, Project Officer, (Surrey in the Great War); Heather Millard, Social History Curator, (Cliffe Castle Museum); Steve and Pam Mills, (The Judd School); Ursula Mitchell, Archive Officer, (Queen's University, Belfast); Liz Moloney, (Eastbourne History); Elizabeth Monterfield, (Epsom College Archives); Dr. R. Montgomery, Archivist, (Foyle College); Carol Morgan, Archivist, (Institution of Civil Engineers); Dean Moss, (Kingscolonials.com); Rachel Muir, Assistant Archivist, (Bank of England Archive); Chris Nathan, Archivist, (St. Edwards' Oxford); Su Orrey, (The King's School); Lesley Overton, (Bishop Vesey's Grammar School); Mary Painter, Librarian, (Blackburn Central Library); Jo Parker, Archivist, (Waltham Forest Archives); Caroline Parkes, (Barnsley MBC); Harriet Patrick, Archivist, (The King's School, Worcester); Hugh

Pattenden, Archivist & Lisa Friel, Librarian, (King Edward VI Grammar School); Stuart P. Pearson, Michael Pegum (Author of Our Fallen Members The War Casualties of the Kildare Street and Dublin University Clubs); Simon Perkin, (South African College); Gordon Phillips, Archivist, (King's School) and for a copy of Sons of Cambridge; Mike Pike, (Wilson's School); Fiona Platten, Enquiry Monitoring, (Institute of Chartered Accountants England and Wales); Dominic Price, (Merton Court Preparatory School); Gill Punt, (Chigwell School); Peter Reder, (Kilburn Grammar School); Bill Richards, (Christ's Hospital); Miss J. S. Ringrose, Hon Archivist, (Pembroke College, Cambridge); Michael Riordan FSA, Archivist, (St. John's and The Queen's Colleges, Oxford); Nicholas Rogers, Archivist, (Sidney Sussex College, Cambridge); Mary-Louise Rowland, (Hurstpierpoint College); Mike Sampson (Blundells School); Niall Sisson, (Wesley College); D. Smart, (King Edward's School, Aston); Ian Smith, Cricket Manager & Jim Hindson, Managing Director, (Cricket Archive); Malcolm Smith, Honorary Archivist, (Latymer Upper School); Geoff Spender (Assistant Curator, Imperial War Museum); Elizabeth Stazicker, Archivist, (King's Ely); Paul Stevens, Librarian and Archivist, (Repton School); Catherine Sunderland MA (Cantab) MSc, Deputy Librarian, (Magdelene College); Emma Sutcliffe, Assistant Curator, (Museum of Farnham); Marion Taggart, Admissions Registrar, (King William's College and The Buchan School); Philip Tardif (North Irish Horse); Justine Taylor, Archivist, (Honourable Artillery Company); Judy Teather, Development Director, Shrewsbury House Academic Tutor, (Denstone College); Paul R. Ternent, (Northumberland Archives); Kate Thaxton, Curator, (Royal Norfolk Regimental Museum); Gary Thomson, (Dundee Roll of Honour); Pauline Thornton, (Inniskillings Museum); Lucy Tipler, Steve & Pam Mills, (The Judd School); Sally Todd, Archivist, (St. John's School, Leatherhead); Cyril Trust, (Farnham Grammar School); Karen Tudor and Ian Quickfall (Malvern College); Linda Turner, (Chelmsford City Museum); June Underwood, (Buckinghamshire Remembers); Barbara Vesey, Archivist, (Society of the Sacred Heart); Ainsley Vinall, Assistant Curator, (William Morris Gallery and Vestry House Museum); Nicola Waddington, School Archivist, (Alleyns School); Gina Warboys, (Old Bedfordian Club); Karen Ward, (Bradfield College); Susan Webb, Records and Information Manager, (Jesus College); Elizabeth Wells, Archivist, (Westminster School); Abigail Wharne, (Brighton College); Stephen White, (Carlisle Library); Kate Wiggins, (Aysgarth School Trust); Jackie Wilkie, Admin, (Aldenham School); Peter Wilkinson, Assistant Head, (Scarborough College); Major Peter Williamson, Chairman of the Trustees, (Essex Regimental Museum); David Woodd, Chief Executive, (Hurlingham Polo Association); Frances Woodrow, Archivist, (John Gray Centre, East Lothian); Liz Woolley, (66 Men of Grandpoint 1914 1918); Catherine M. Worsley MBA ACIB, Development Director & Elaine Merckx, (Wakefield Grammar School Foundation).

Anonymous librarians and archivists from the following also assisted; Archives & Collection, University of Strathclyde, Brooklyn Historical Society Library, History Centre Surrey County Council, Auckland Museum, Torquay Cricket Club, Essex Records Office, Lincolnshire Archives and Cathedral School. I also need to thank members of the Great War Forum for supplying information and identifying sources of photographs. Copies of book were supplied to me free of charge and I need to thank the following; Gordon Phillips, Archivist, King's School for a copy of 'Sons of Cambridge'; Dominic Price, (Merton Court Preparatory School) for a copy of 'A Century in the Life of Merton Court School, Sidcup 1899 – 1999.'

The Evidence

Throughout this book various resources have been compiled to build a history of those who fell on the 1st July 1916, the main sources of reference were the Commonwealth War Grave Commission (CWGC) and Officers Died in the Great War. About one third of the Commission's records show no details for next of kin. This is because not all the "Final Verification" forms sent to the last known address of a casualty's next of kin were returned. War diaries for June & July 1916 have also been consulted for the battalions involved, not just the 1st July as appendices often appeared that listed all officers in the appendices at the end of the month.

A download into Microsoft Excel from the Commonwealth War Graves (www.cwgc.org) for date of death, 1st July 1916 is relatively easy to do, however application of additional filter for cemeteries and memorial in the vicinity of the Somme would have ruled out the following two officers; Major James Leadbeater Knott, DSO buried in Belgium and Lieutenant Colonel Denis Daly Wilson, DSO commemorated Neuve Chapelle Memorial, France. Major James Leadbitter Knott DSO was killed in action leading his men forward, and originally buried in Row B. Grave 14. Fricourt New Military Cemetery however his brother, Captain Henry Basil Knott was killed on the 7th September 1915 and was buried near where he fell. Both brothers are buried next to each other in Ypres Reservoir Cemetery and the headstones inscriptions read 'Devoted In Life In Death Not Divided'.

Lieutenant Colonel Wilson DSO was attached to the 1/5th Sherwood Foresters from the 17th Indian Cavalry and is commemorated at Neuve Chapelle. I have made additional inclusions to the CWGC download. One of these is Second Lieutenant Sydney Raymond Allen, 16th Bn., Manchester Regiment reported killed at Montauban, on the 1st of July, 1916, reports suggest that he was killed instantaneously when leading a bombing party towards the German lines. Officially his date of death is the 12th July 1916 with Commonwealth War Grave Commission however conflicting records including a report in his local paper on the 12th July state he was killed on the 1st July 1916.

From the CWGC the Grave Registration Unit (GRU) records were also checked for all officers that fell in the month of July 1916 as the date of death sometimes varies from the GRU date and the published CWGC date. Over 275 files of the officers that fell have been accessed via the National Archives. In addition over 400 files of officers that were involved were also accessed from the National Archives to check any inaccuracies in date of death. These files did highlight the location of original graves and some of the graves were subsequently lost during the latter parts of the war. In some cases the files contained reports from prisoners of war as to the circumstances of death of particular officers, with the confusion of the battle these accounts do not always match. Towards the end of the file is a list of returned personal effects and these have been included in the biographies where possible. Via Ancestry.co.uk I have checked all the Medal Index Cards and these revealed some useful information, address, next of kin and in some cases a date of death.

A copy of a letter from one of the officer files after an enquiry from a relative in 1994 reveals an explanation as to why some files are very sparse in content; 'I regret that the file is very meagre of content as it was custom during the inter-war period and particularly during the 1930's to 'weed' officers personal files and extract from them documents not considered necessary for retention. This was instigated mainly to save storage space due to the large number of files and documents held. Over the passage of time and because of numerous weeds, many files were destroyed'.

To the information obtained from the CWGC and National Archives I have added obituaries, school, college records etc. from various Rolls of Honour in an abbreviated form. Typically these included, ranks, how and where they fell, where born, employed, resided, education, marital status, pastimes, rank, regiment, address, birth details, occupation and in some cases employer. It has not been possible to include all the details from all sources for example an entry in the British Roll of Honour could extent to three A4 pages and one particular case from The National archives had over thirty A4 pages. The amount of detail on each entry varies. Papers and publication of the time often provided a photograph with only an accompanying name and no date of death so these had to be compared to the list of fallen officers. The photographs used came from different time periods, some have been extracted from school photos, group photos, and others appeared as a result of promotion, or when the death was announced.

The example below covered the deaths of four members of the Ayre family from Newfoundland, in a post war publication.

Two brothers and two cousins fell in France on the 1st July 1916. From left to right they are Captain Eric S. Ayre, Newfoundland Regiment; Captain Bernard P. Ayre, Norfolk Regiment; Second Lieutenant Wilfred D. Ayre and Second Lieutenant Gerald W. Ayre of the Newfoundland Regiment.

Whilst the Belfast Telegraph on the 22nd July 1916 covered the fate of the three Hewitt brothers.

In isolated cases I have included examples of letters that were send back to relatives from Commanding Officers and brother officers. A few examples of last letters home have also been included. Headstone inscriptions have been included at the end of the officer's text, these being highlighted in bold.

I have set the format very similar to the original Roll of Honour published by Marquis de Ruvigny's in honour of those soldiers who would gave their lives for their country. In its final published form, the Roll of Honour records the biographies of more than 25,000 men from the British Army, Navy and Royal Air Force, with nearly 7000 of the entries being accompanied by a photograph. Modern copies are easily obtainable.

The difficulties of compiling a Roll were summed up in July 1918 by J. Trant Bramston, St. Nicholas, Winchester College; 'I have tried in this edition to record the dates of death of those who have fallen in the War, but I am uncertain about many of them, and probably inaccurate, and shall welcome any certain information at this point'.

Various sources have been used to compile the biographies and compile the photographic database. The main sources are listed here; The Sphere, The Graphic, War Illustrated, The Great War I Was There, Illustrated London News, Illustrated War News, The Tatler, Baily's Magazine, Sporting & Dramatic News, Navy and Army Illustrated, Lloyds Bank Roll of Honour, De Ruvigny's Roll of Honour, Harrow School Memorial Book, Cheltenham College Roll of Honour, Malvern College Roll of Honour, Brighton and Hove Graphic, British Roll of Honour, St. Bee's Roll of Honour, University of Edinburgh Roll of Honour, Glasgow Academy Roll of Honour, British Jewry Book of Honour, Stock Exchange Memorial Record Roll of Honour, The Times, Argentina and The Great War, The Era, Northern Assurance Roll of Honour and The Polo Monthly.

A number of papers are available on line and many are viewable via Findmypast; Daily Record, Yorkshire Evening Post, Staffordshire Advertiser, Liverpool Post, Burnley News, Lincolnshire Chronicle, Bury Free Press, Liverpool Echo, Western Times, The Mirror, Western Mail, Aberdeen Evening News, Hull Daily Mail, Walsall Observer and South Staffordshire Chronicle, Birmingham Mail, Manchester Evening News, Aberdeen Evening Express, Shield Daily Gazette, Lancashire Daily Post, Bath Chronicle and Weekly Gazette, Cornish Man and Cornish Telegraph, Larne Times, Edinburgh Evening News, Sevenoaks Chronicle and Kentish Advertiser, Fifeshire Advertiser, Birmingham Gazette, Grantham Journal, Surrey Mirror, Derby Advertiser and Journal, Dorking and Leatherhead Advertiser, Dundee Evening Telegraph, Derbyshire Advertiser and Journal, Lancashire Daily Post, Berwickshire News and General Advertiser, Kirkcaldy Guardian, Daily Record, Dundee's People Journal, Leeds Mercury, Gloucester Journal, Yorkshire and Leeds Intelligencer, Auckland Star, Ballymena Weekly Telegraph, Belfast Evening Telegraph, Brisbane Courier, British American Tobacco 'house' magazine, British Medical Journal, Buxton Advertiser, Buxton Herald, Cardiff Times, Daily Mercury, Daily Record, Fermanagh Times, Manchester Evening News, Newbury Weekly News, Newcastle Daily Chronicle, The Accountant, The New York Times, Kent and Sussex Courier

 Some deaths were falsely reported, two examples are citied. One of these appeared in the Kent & Sussex Courier on the 14th July 1916. Lieutenant Frederick Robert Benson Jowitt of Harehills, Leeds was reported as killed in action, grandson of Mr. R. Benson Jowitt JP of Tunbridge Wells and the son of Mr. J. H. Jowitt of New Zealand. The War Office with the announcement of his death, made a mistake he was wounded and in hospital in London. Lieutenant Jowitt served with the West Yorkshire Regiment.

The second being Captain Arthur T. B. de Cologan, of Strathbran, Ross-shire, was reported missing, believed killed, on July 1st, he held on with his men in a hot spot until surrounded. The captain had some lengthy obituaries published; "The only son of Mrs. Herbert Maddick and the Marquis de Torre-Hermosa. Captain de Cologan was twenty-five, and the adopted grandson of the late Sir Arthur Bignold, to whose Ross-shire estates of Achanalt and Strathbran he succeeded last year. He was educated at the Oratory School (1904-09) and at Queen's College, Oxford (1909-12); and entered the Territorial Force as Second-Lieutenant, Unattached List, in 1910, going into the Oxford OTC six months later. He joined the London Rifle Brigade in 1913 ; and in the following July he was seconded for service as Assistant District Commissioner in the Somaliland Protectorate. He acted as District Commissioner for five months, and was then attached to the Camel Corps. In May, 1915, he was permitted to return to England, and he re-joined the London Rifle Brigade in France in July. He obtained his captaincy on

August 9. Captain de Cologan rowed in the Queen's Eight at Oxford in 1911-12". Captain de Cologan was from boyhood a first-class deer-stalker, rifle shot, and angler.

His Commanding Officer wrote: "No one could have behaved more gallantly, as I hear on all sides. He was with Harvey and Somers Smith, and all were splendid. Your son's company would, have followed him anywhere, and did follow him yesterday magnificently." The other officers referred to were Captain Bernard Sydney Harvey and Captain John Robert Somers-Smith both of whom were confirmed as killed on the 1st. On the 15th August 1916 he was reported officially as a prisoner of war. Through the influence of the King of Spain, (as his father was a foreign Count) he was sent to Holland for internment.

Men throughout the world returned to their native countries to take up arms. With the French Army, Professor Eugene Bourdon B.A who was killed on the 1st July 1916 and was well-known in Glasgow. He was appointed Director of Architectural Studies and Professor of Architectural Design at the Glasgow School of Architecture in 1904. Immediately after the declaration of war he re-joined the French Army of which he was a staff captain. His courage and exceptional ability in his military duties earned him great distinction and he received the Croix de la Legion d'Honneur, the French Croix de Guerre with three citations in army orders and the British Military Cross.

The logistics and training required meant that a number of accidental deaths would occur also occur on this fateful day and two examples are below, one with the 12th Bn., South Wales Borderers and one with the 10th Gordon Highlanders.

NEWMAN, Lieutenant, Alfred. He was a bombing officer and was putting A Coy through the practice of throwing live bombs when one of the men hit the back of the trench and dropped the bomb, he picked up the bomb and went to throw it out of the trench when he slipped and it fell into the trench killing him and wounding others, 1st July 1916. 12th Bn., South Wales Borderers. Aged 23. Son of M. J. and W. N. Newman, of 51 Dora Road, Small Heath, Birmingham. Educated Camp Hill Grammar School and at the outbreak of war was employed at the Birmingham Education Office. Joined the 1st Battalion as a private and rose to be corporal. Granted a commission and rose to lieutenant. Memorial Ref. X. F. 9., Lapugnoy Military Cemetery, France.

RIDDEL, Second Lieutenant, Robert Mackie. On 1st July 1916 he was instructing a class on the action of bombs, when the bomb exploded in his hands and killed him and twenty men were wounded. Born Kintore, 7th March 1892. Educated at Kintore H. G. Public School, where he served as a pupil teacher; student in Arts, Aberdeen University, 1912-14. He enlisted in the 6th Gordons on 5th October 1914. In November of the same year he was drafted to France, and a month later was invalided home. Returning to France in May 1915, he distinguished himself at the Battle of Loos, and for gallantry was recommended for a commission. He received his commission in December 1915 and was attached to the 10th Gordon Highlanders. His Commanding Officer wrote : "He was an excellent officer in every way and had proved himself of great value in the field on many occasions. . . . I shall find it hard to fill his place in the Battalion.". 10th Bn., Gordon Highlanders. Aged 24. Son of John and Elizabeth Riddel, of Townhead, Kintore, Aberdeenshire. The pipes and the drummers and a large party from his company attended his funeral. Memorial Ref. P. 4., Sailly-Labourse Communal Cemetery, France.

The Royal Field Artillery recorded the deaths of sixteen officers on the 1st July 1916, one of these is Second Lieutenant Sternberg with the remaining fifteen in the main Roll of Honour.

STERNBERG, Second Lieutenant, Rupert Oswald. Died of wounds, 1st July 1916. 83rd Bty., Royal Field Artillery. Aged 23. Second son of Siegfried and Louise Sternberg, of Manchester. Born 18th June 1893. Educated Charterhouse (Girdlestoneites, 1906 – 1911) and Clare College, Cambridge. His older brother also died in 1916 on the 16th October, Second Lieutenant Edgar Adolph Joseph Sternberg. Memorial Ref. II. A. 38., Boulogne Eastern Cemetery, France.

A number of deaths occurred on the 1st July 1916 and are not associated with the Battle of the Somme for example officers and men of the King Royal Rifle Corps with two further examples below. One from the 2nd/5th Bn., Royal Warwickshire Regiment and one from the 1st Bn., Devonshire Regiment. The list of valid battalions and regiments has been checked against the appendix entitled 'Order of Battle of British Infantry Units, 1 July 1916 in 'The First Day on the Somme' by Martin Middlebrook.

TRUMAN, Lieutenant, D. G. H. Killed in action, on his way back from a meeting at headquarters and in the trenches of his own company when he was hit by a shell, killed painlessly and instantaneously, 1st July 1916. 2nd/5th Bn., Royal Warwickshire Regiment. Resided Oakdale, Olton. Educated King Edwards' Grammar School and Birmingham University, joining the OTC there. Gazetted second lieutenant, November 1914 and lieutenant August 1915. Memorial Ref. I. J. 2., Rue-Du-Bacquerot No.1 Military Cemetery, Laventie, France.

TWINING, Second Lieutenant, Richard Wake. He had been buried by a shell during a "dummy" attack at Vailley (Wailly) south of Arras. The British Army sent up smoke shells and the enemy anticipating an attack started a barrage of fire. A private said that his body was dug out the same day and a tablet was put up. Private Rees, No. 8276 also thought he had seen 2nd Lieutenant Twining killed somewhere to the right of Arras. Killed with two other ranks, 1st July 1916. 1st Bn., Devonshire Regiment. Aged 21. Only son of Dr. Vincent Wing Twining and his wife Kate née Nelson of Salcombe, Devon. Enlisted August 1914. Gazetted 101st Dragoon Guards 24th November 1914, exchanged to Devonshire Regiment, August 1915. Born at The Knoll in Salcombe, Devon on 8th May 1895. Richard started in Epsom College's Lower School, Fayrer House on 1st May 1908 and progressed to Carr House in the Upper School. He gained a second division pass in the London Matriculation exam in 1912. He was also keen on rugby and played a three-quarter position in the school's first XV 1911-12 and 1912-13 seasons. He won his second hockey colours in 1913. In July 1913 he passed the first exam for a medical degree and went up to Emmanuel College, Cambridge in October. He had spent a year in the OTC at Epsom and joined a territorial unit, the Devon Yeomanry, as Private 2530 Trooper in C Squadron whilst at Cambridge. He served two and a half months before enlisting in Exeter on 29th September 1914. He was discharged to a commission as a temporary second lieutenant on the 19th November 1914 and served nine months in the 1st Reserve Cavalry from 23rd November stationed at Beaumont Barracks, Aldershot. He applied for the regular army on 28th July 1915 expressing a preference for Royal Field Artillery or the Cavalry. The University's Military Education Committee thought he would be well qualified to serve in either. He became second lieutenant, 1st Bn., Devonshire Regiment on the 24th September 1915. In January 1916 1st Bn., Devonshire Regiment became part of 95 Brigade, 5th Division. In March 1916, 5th Division took over a section of front line between St .Laurent Blangy and the southern edge of Vimy Ridge, near Arras. They moved south in July to reinforce The Somme. Richard went to France 4th April 1916. Emmanuel College War Memorial. Memorial Ref. I. C. 7., Wailly Orchard Cemetery, France.

Richard Twining Fifth from right middle row wearing a bow tie.
1913 Matriculation photo

 **EDMANSON,** Second Lieutenant, Joe. Killed in action, 2nd July 1916 Age 23. 7th Bn., attd. 13th Bn., Kings Own Yorkshire Light Infantry. Son of Benjamin and Maud Edmanson of 175 Spencer Place, Leeds. When war broke out he was a student at Leeds University and an articled clerk to Messrs. Sinclair and Atkinson, solicitors, Otley. Nephew of Mr. Alf Edmanson of Chapeltown, a former champion of the Leeds Board of Guardians. Aged 23. Mother applied for his medals. Grave Ref. I. J. 12. White House Cemetery, St-Jean-Les-Ypres, Belgium.

Behind A Frowning Providence He Hides A Smiling Face

CHASE, Second Lieutenant, Philip Hugh. Mentioned in Despatches. Died of wounds, 1st July 1916. He was send out on a raiding party on the night of the 30th June and when he returned to his trenches he found some of his men were missing, he went out to find them and was wounded on his return he found more men were missing and went out again this time he was severely wounded. He was send on by the RAMC with a wound to his lower body. D Coy 12th Bn., Middlesex Regiment. Aged 20. Son of Joseph James and F. Chase, of 150, Philip Lane, Tottenham, London. Born 19th October 1895. Tottenham Grammar School Roll of Honour (1904 -1908). Gazetted 27th November 1914. One time captain of the Merchant Taylors' rugby team, useful hand at boxing and a fine all round runner. In 1914 his last year at school he was prize winner in the 'half' and 'mile'. Member of Inns of Court OTC and Merchant Taylor's School, OTC. Enlisted 6th October 1914. Commemorated Merchant Taylors' School, Northwood. A private reported that 'Mr. Chase was a very good man for looking after his men, he always went out to look for the missing no matter who it was'. Originally buried Corbie Cemetery adjoining 21st Casualty clearing Station. Father applied for his medals. Memorial Ref. I. A. 18., La Neuville British Cemetery, Corbie, France. WO 339/1685

A Loving Son And Brave Soldier

Museum and local councils have also started their own databases and material has been taken from these sources. In numerous cases I have been contacted by members of the family and the information was received gratefully. It is important to note, however, that the cross-referencing of material has indicated anomalies, in particular order of forenames, middle names, rank, spelling, address etc. In the case of names I have gone with the majority. 'The London Gazette' has been used for citations and dates of commemorated. Original records should be consulted if required or further information is sought.

Roll of Honour

ADAM, Captain, Arthur De Bels, MC. Met his death whilst disposing of an enemy post, he was in charge of a bombing party and fatally wounded by sniper fire, also reported that although wounded he coordinated a reconnaissance of the German position until killed by a stick grenade. His job was to keep in communication with the 18th Division on the left flank. 1st July 1916. No. 3 Coy. 18th Bn., The King's (Liverpool Regiment). Aged 31. Son of John and Harriet Adam, of the Seven Sisters, Ellesmere, Salop. Born 23rd November 1884, Gateacre, Lancashire. Resided Belle Vale Cottage, Wambo Lane, Gateacre, Lancashire. **Arthur** had been engaged as partner in his father's firm, Messes. J. L. Bowes & Bro., wool brokers for whom he had travelled in the States and India at various times. He also took a practical interest in outdoor sport, and was keen on otter hounds. On three occasions he won the Cheshire Beagles point-to-point race in record time. Entered France on the 7th November 1915, with the "Pals", and in January 1916 was awarded the Military Cross for 'the manner in which he had organised his defences and handled his men during an attack by the Germans. The enemy made a bombing raid in strength, but Captain Adam and his men gave them such a warm reception that they retired badly beaten, having far heavier casualties than the 18th'. Private F. S. Haslam awarded the Military Medal on the 1st July 1916 for 'great bravery when acting as a runner to his captain who fell wounded within thirty yards of a hedge held by bombers and riflemen. Dashed forward and dressed Captain Adam's wound and continued to do so after being wounded himself. The enemy threw a bomb and killed Captain Adam and for the second time wounded Private Haslam'. Brother Lieutenant John Isabel Adam also fell on the 10th May 1918, Royal Field Artillery. Named on the Liverpool Exchange Newsroom Memorial. Memorial Ref. Pier and Face 1 D 8 B and 8 C., Thiepval Memorial, France. WO 339/24888

ADAMS, Lieutenant, Hugh Irving. Fell beyond the first line of trenches at about 8.15am, Beaumont Hamel on the 1st July 1916. 1st Bn., Hampshire Regiment. Born in India. Only surviving son of George Adams who worked for the Indian Civil Service and Mrs. Alice Adams of 8 Sydenham Villas, Cheltenham also The Rectory, Leighton Road, Hamerton, Huntingdonshire. Boarder at Cheltenham College from 1896 to 1899. After RMC Sandhurst he became an officer in the Indian Army, when he resigned in 1909 he was a lieutenant and a double company officer of the 5th Light Infantry. Married 29th October 1906 at Fatehgurh, United Provinces. Prior to enlisting worked in Canada in farming and returned to enlist receiving his commission in September, 1915. Joined unit in France, 5th April 1916. He left a widow, Aileen Adams (daughter of H. G. Arnott) in Burford, Ontario, Canada. Memorial Ref. I. H. 12., Sucrerie Military Cemetery, Colincamps, France.

ADAMS, Lieutenant, Ralph, MC and Bar. Last seen leading his men to the third enemy trench, Beaumont Hamel, 1st July 1916. 1st/8th Bn., Royal Warwickshire Regiment. Aged 23. Only son of John (secretary of the Birmingham Athletic Institute and headmaster of Birmingham City Road School) and Minnie Adams, of 301, Gillatt Road, Birmingham. Born 20th March 1893. Educated City-Road School, King Edward's High School, New Street and Birmingham University. Member of the brewing staff of Mitchells and Butlers. Entered France, 23rd March 1915. Military Cross awarded January 1916 in the New Year's Honours List. Bar to Military Cross, dated September 1916; "For conspicuous gallantry during a raid on the enemy's trenches. Under close fire he cut the enemy's wires with torpedoes, he then bombed his way along the enemy's trench killing three of the enemy himself and held a barricade until reinforced." His family received a letter from the War Office in February 1917 that due to the lapse of time since the 1st July 1916 regretfully constrained to conclude he died on or since that date. Body reported to be in No Man's Land about 100 yards further on from Lieutenant-Colonel Innes also killed 1st July 1916, remains found and subsequently buried. Walsall Roll of Honour. Memorial Ref. I. A. 33., Serre Road Cemetery No.1, France.

ADAMSON, Second Lieutenant, Maurice Leslie. Killed whilst leading his platoon, 1st July 1916. Royal Scots Fusiliers attached 10th Royal Irish Rifles. Aged 23. Born 3rd April 1893 in Myanmar Meiktila, Burma. Son of Sir Harvey Adamson, K.C.S.I., (Lieutenant Governor of Burma from 1910 to 1915, distinguished career in the Indian Civil Service as a soldier, judge, and legislator. He was an ordinary member of the Council of the Governor-General of India from 1906 till 1914) and Lady Adamson, of 36, Palace Gardens Terrace, Kensington, London. Grandson of the Reverend Alex Adamson, of Kinnermit. Educated at Tottenham Grammar School (1902-1903), Haileybury College (Highfield 1907-1911), King's College, London, and Pullman Agricultural College, Washington State, America. He sailed from Liverpool arriving in Quebec, Canada on the 13th September 1912. Previously employed Bank of Montreal. At the outbreak of the war he enlisted as private 17092, British Colombia Regiment, Canadian Contingent on the 23rd September 1914 in Valcartier, Quebec, Canada. After training at Valcartier came to England with the contingent where he received a commission. Went to France, on the 31st October 1915, and received a permanent commission in the Royal Scots Fusiliers, but continued to serve with his old regiment. Lieutenant Adamson was mentioned for gallantry. Memorial Ref. Pier and Face 3 C., Thiepval Memorial, France.

ADAMSON, Second Lieutenant, Travers Farrant. Died of wounds, 1st July 1916. Private Ralph Jones reported; 'he was wounded and the officer (Second Lieutenant Adamson) was wounded close to me but was sitting up and told me to carry on, I got back to our lines and saw no sign of him'. C Coy., X Platoon, 9th Bn., Devonshire Regiment. Aged 20. Son of Travers Patrick Muirhead Adamson (Cornish landscape painter) and Ethel Adamson, of Corleone, Longham, Wimborne. Born 2nd July 1895. Sergeant in the Hurstpierpoint OTC and discharged on leaving, December 1914. Entered France, 25th March 1916. Named on the Ferndown Roll of Honour, Dorset and Hurstpierpoint College. Originally buried Mansel Copse. Memorial Ref. A. 7., Devonshire Cemetery, Mametz, France. WO 339/4694

Fortiter Et Fideliter Grant Them O Lord Light And Peace

ADDISON, Lieutenant Colonel, Arthur Joseph Berkeley. Killed in attack on German Nordwerk, Thiepval, 1st July 1916. 9th Bn., York and Lancaster Regiment. Born 14th September 1866 in Cork, Ireland. Aged 49. Son of Gen. Thomas Addison, C.B., and Ellen Gillespie. Husband of Mildred Jeanne Addison (nee De Gilibert), of 18, Hans Road, Chelsea, London. Attended Haileybury College (Thomason, 1880 – 1882). He married Mildred Jeanne de Gilibert of 18 Hans Road, Chelsea, London in Ireland in 1901 and had one child, Marie Josephine de Gilibert born 1st November 1902. Entered France, 27th August 1915. His body lay where he fell until the 23rd September 1916 and his final words in a diary were "tell the regiment I hope they did well." Twice Mentioned in Despatches. Memorial Ref. I. W. 23., Becourt Military Cemetery, Becordel-Becourt, France.

Quis Separabit

AIRD, Second Lieutenant, James Gilbert. Reported to be killed by shrapnel just after 7.00am as the German artillery retaliated, led No. 8 platoon of B Coy., 1st July 1916. 13th Bn., attached 15th Bn., Lancashire Fusiliers. Aged 21. Born 20th September 1894 in Irvine, Ayrshire. Middle child of five and eldest son to Mr. and Mrs. Robert (Spirit Merchant) and Helen Aird, of 7, Winton Circus, Saltcoats, Ayrshire. Attended Colmonell and Girvan High School. A law student and had almost completed a course in Scots Law at Glasgow University. University of Glasgow's OTC. For several years he volunteered in the Town Clerk's office, Saltcoats, and prior to being gazetted was in the office of Messrs. G. H. Robb & Crosbie Solicitors, Glasgow. Applied for a commission 14th September 1915 and gazetted 1st October 1915. Entered France, 15th June 1916. Memorial Ref. Pier and Face 3 C and 3 D., Thiepval Memorial, France.

AKAM, Lieutenant, James Rhodes. Reported wounded and missing, at 8.40am, one platoon of 'B' Company reported to have reached the German parapet under Lieutenant Akam. Broke protocol and was seen to run, and seen to get through the German wire, 1st July 1916. 18th Bn., West Yorkshire Regiment (Prince of Wales's Own). Born 1893, Bradford. Only son of Mr. Benjamin Akam, (timber merchant, Bradford) and Martha Ellen Rotheray. Age 23. Educated Bradford Grammar School, 1902 to 1909. Timber merchant with his father. Enlisted as a private 16/631 in the 1st Bradford Bn. Appointed second lieutenant 14th March 1915 and promoted to lieutenant, 25th May 1915. Served overseas from 22nd December 1915 in Egypt. Memorial Ref. Pier and Face 2 A 2 C and 2 D., Thiepval Memorial, France.

ALEXANDER, Second Lieutenant, Henry Talbot. As soon as the troops left the front line, heavy machine-gun fire was brought to bear on them from all directions, casualties of officers amounted to 100%. Killed at Beaumont Hamel, 1st July 1916. 1st Bn., Hampshire Regiment. Son of Alfred Alexander and Susanna Alexander. Born 1889, Paddington, London. Resided 90 Fernhead Road, Paddington, London. Previous address listed as Cowley Road, Oxford. Joined the Civil Service in 1904 and employed General Post Office, Registry Assistant, Secretary's Office, Post Office, London. Formerly No. 222, corporal, 15th London Regiment. Commissioned June 1915. Entered France 27th January 1916. Brother, Lance Sergeant Alfred Reginald Alexander, 9th Rifle Brigade died 11th September 1915 and with no known grave is commemorated on the Menin Gate. Named on the Men of the Secretary's Office of the GPO War Memorial, Finsbury. Memorial Ref. C. 8., Redan Ridge Cemetery No.2, Beaumont-Hamel, France.

ALEXANDER, Second Lieutenant, Noel Legard. Killed in action at the head of the leading platoon, when his battalion attacked the German trenches near Fricourt, 1st July 1916. They left the sap at 7.25am and were to crawl as far as possible when they got 25 yards they were treated to a hail of machine-gun fire. No. 1 Platoon, A Coy., 9th Bn., King's Own Yorkshire Light Infantry. Born 24th December 1894. Aged 22. Son of Edward Disney Alexander, M.Inst. M.e., of Milton House, Northamptonshire. Attended Eastbourne College, member of the OTC, on leaving worked as a student at a fruit farm until the outbreak of war. Enlisted with the Royal Sussex Regiment, 7th September 1914 until receiving a commission, 21st September 1914 going to France, 23rd October 1915. Originally buried Fricourt Becourt Road, Map Ref. 574.X. 26.d.5.6. His brother, E. M. Alexander wrote to the War Office for information as he had heard unofficially he had been killed as official reports stated missing probably wounded. Memorial Ref. II. M. 10., Gordon Dump Cemetery, Ovillers-La Boisselle, France. WO 339/14817

ALEXANDER, Second Lieutenant, William Mercer. Killed in action, 1st July 1916. 17th Bn., Highland Light Infantry. Elder son of John H. Alexander, (agent of the National Bank of Scotland, Dundee). Aged 22. Born 27th December 1893. Educated at Glasgow Academy and Clifton Bank School Old Boy, St. Andrews. His name was forwarded for the Academical Contingent by the Hon. Secretary John MacGill on the 5th September 1914, as all the 1914-1915 matches were cancelled the Hon. Secretary forwarded 35 player names. Joined the Highland Light Infantry in September 1914, No. 15478 received his commission in January, 1915. Overseas 10th March 1916. Death reported 19th July 1916. His brother Lieutenant Ronald Ross Alexander MC served with the Royal Field Artillery. Value of Estate £104 to his father. Memorial Ref. Pier and Face 15 C., Thiepval Memorial, France.

ALISON, Captain, George Newdegate. Shot whilst giving direction to a machine-gun company, last words were "I'm hit go and tell Mr. Low to take command." 1st July 1916. 2nd Bn., Seaforth Highlanders attached 10th Bde., Machine Gun Company. Born in Bermuda on the 28th of November 1889. Aged 26. Second son of Sir Archibald Alison, 3rd Bart., former Colonial Secretary of Bermuda and of Lady Georgina Sarah Ann Alison, of "Possil House", Budleigh Salterton, Devon. Attended Hazelwood College, Malvern College and Cedar Court School and onto the RMC Sandhurst. He played cricket for the Incogniti Cricket Club and later for his battalion. Commissioned as a second lieutenant in the Seaforth Highlanders on the 11th December 1909 and promoted to lieutenant on the 9th April 1912. From the 29th of November 1913 to the 20th of October 1914 he served as Aide De Camp to Sir Henry May the Governor of Hong Kong.

Following this appointment he made his way with some difficulty via Petrograd and Archangel to England to rejoin his battalion at the front where he joined the 1st Battalion of his regiment in the field at Festubert along with one other officer and one hundred and fifty other ranks on the 20th of November 1914. On the 11th of December 1914 he was wounded by a bullet in the right buttock. He returned to France, was promoted to captain on the 28th of April 1915 and was wounded once again on the 24th of May 1915. On the 8th of December 1915 he was seconded for service as a brigade machine gun officer and on the 22nd of December he was attached to the 10th Machine Gun Company.

An account of his death is given in a letter to his parents written by the General Officer Commanding his Brigade:- "Your son was one of those daring, cool men, who were invaluable. His example was always splendid, his courage magnificent; in fact he was almost too courageous. Our division was ordered to attack the German lines on Saturday the 1st of July at 7.30am. The Seaforths were on the left and the Royal Dublin Fusiliers (2nd Battalion) were on the right, Alison's machine-gun in the centre, just in the rear of the two battalions. At about 9.15 the Machine-Gun Company were just between the English and German lines, in a heavy fire and one of the sections lay down in extended order. Alison strolled over to them with one hand in his pocket an attitude he was used to and told them to move on. Buckworth commanded that section. "Bucky, I think you had better get on", is what he said. He then rejoined his orderly, a man called Gould. The next thing was Alison was shot, a rifle bullet through, I think, the heart, for he merely said to Gould "I'm hit; go and tell Mr. Low to take command", but before Gould left him he was dead. Gould says he is quite sure that his captain could not have suffered, as he was perfectly quiet and cool, and died almost at once. Your son was one of the most remarkably plucky men I ever met. I was very fond of him, and often asked his opinion and advice on matters concerning the employment of his guns. I only wish I had him with me still. We recovered his body and buried him alongside about a hundred Seaforth Highlanders. I am sure he would prefer to be near them." Body was side by sided in a large British cemetery, 200 yards NW of the Sucrerie. Mentioned in Despatches. Memorial Ref. I. H. 36., Sucrerie Military Cemetery, Colincamps, France.

Loved Son Of Sir Archibald Alison 3rd Bart. Vincit Veritas

ALLARDICE, Lieutenant Colonel, Harry. Killed north of Fricourt, 1st July 1916. 36th Jacob's Horse, Indian Cavalry attached 13th Bn., Northumberland Fusiliers. Born at Mylemoney, Mysore, on 30th April, 1886, and was the fourth son of W. A. and Helen Allardice. Resided Green Street St Helier, Channel Islands. Attended Victoria College, Jersey entering in January, 1898, he got into the Football XV at the age of 14, and was in it for three years, 1900, 1901, and 1902. His last year, 1903, was his only year in the Cricket XI. In the same year he passed into RMC Sandhurst, and was gazetted to the Indian Army in 1905. In 1907 he became a lieutenant in the 36th Jacob's Horse, in which regiment he was captain and adjutant at the outbreak of the war. Polo player. Disembarked 7th November 1914. Later he served with the Royal West Surreys as temporary major. Grave Ref. I. F. 42. Dartmoor Cemetery, Becordel-Becourt, Somme, France.

ALLEN, Second Lieutenant, Geoffrey Austin. Killed 1st July 1916. He with his scouts had penetrated almost to the third German line when he was wounded in the right thigh by machine-gun fire. The wound was attended to and he was laid on the fire-step of the German trench as the regiment was outflanked on both sides and there were no reinforcements the order was given to retire and it was thought safer to leave Geoffrey where he was. His scout observer remained with him and says that he continued to give orders till at the last the Germans started bombing and it was then that Geoffrey was killed instantly. His scout was made a prisoner by the Germans. Scout officer, 2nd Bn., Essex Regiment. He was the son of Robert Allen of Greenstead Hall, Essex. He was educated at Aldenham School and St. John's College Cambridge, graduated 1905. One time assistant-master at Katherine Lady Berkeley's Grammar School, Wotton-under-Edge from 1909 to 1911 and afterwards at Milton Abbey School, Dorset. At the outbreak of war he was on the staff of a college (Blandford) at Dorset and immediately enlisted in the 2449, Artists Rifles. Entered France, 22nd January 1915. Commissioned second lieutenant, 24th July 1915. Memorial Ref. Pier and Face 10 D., Thiepval Memorial, France.

ALLEN, Second Lieutenant, Herbert. He was killed with a direct hit from a stick grenade as he tried to go forward with a group of men, grenades landed amongst them and caused heavy losses, 1st July 1916. 1st /5th Bn., South Staffordshire Regiment. Resided 70, Corporation Street West. Educated at Palfrey School and with a scholarship onto Queen Mary's Grammar School, Walsall (1903 – 1910). He left in 1910 going to Dudley Training College and prior to enlisting was a teacher at Croft Street Council School and Chuckery Senior School, Walsall. He joined as a private in the Territorial Force, September 1914 and after attaining the rank of quarter master sergeant was given a commission. Joined the battalion 13th May 1916. Commemorated Walsall Corporation Employees Memorial. Memorial Ref. Pier and Face 7 B., Thiepval Memorial, France.

ALLEN, Lieutenant, Humphrey Decius. He gallantly led his men into action and they took the German first line trench, he was slightly wounded in the neck and having bandaged the wound was on his way back when he was shot in the head and instantly killed, 1st July 1916. 10th Bn., West Yorkshire Regiment (Prince of Wales's Own). Aged 28. Son of Theophilus and Elizabeth Mary Allen, of Stanyards, Chobham, Surrey. Born 18th August 1887. Educated at Bradfield College 1902 to 1906 and a member of the OTC and gained the position of prefect and afterwards at King's College studying civil engineering for two years during which time he twice gained the Challenge Cup for the mile. Served in the RNVR (London) from 1907 to 1910. In 1911 he went to the Malay State and for over three years acted as assistant manager on the Sungei Krian Rubber Estate. Upon the outbreak of war he came home to offer his services. Enlisted 29th December 1914. Went to France, 13th July 1915. Reported missing believed wounded, his body was found three days after the attack and he was originally buried in Fricourt Cemetery Row B Grave 12. His brother Captain P. R. Allen served with the 10th Bn., West Yorkshire Regiment. Memorial Ref. C. 11., Fricourt New Military Cemetery, France. WO 339/17068

ALLEN, Second Lieutenant, Sydney Raymond. Reported killed at Montauban, on the 1st July, 1916, and that he was killed instantaneously when leading a bombing party towards the German lines. A brother officer stated he was shot dead through the head whilst crawling along the ground to see where the Germans were. Officially killed 12th July 1916 with Commonwealth War Grave Commission, differing records state 1st July 1916. 16th Bn., Manchester Regiment. Born 10th March 1894 at Seaforth, Liverpool. Son of Mr. George Thomas Allen Ada Eliza Allen, a provision broker, of 8 Alexandra Road, Claughton. Educated at the Great Crosby Merchant Taylors' School (1905 to 1909), he was apprenticed to Messrs. Alfred Dobell & Co., timber merchants. He joined the 6th King's (Liverpool Regiment) three days after was declared, No. 2003, and went out to France in March, 1915. Gazetted 1st April 1915, received training and went back to France in November 1915. Reported buried near Montauban. Effects returned were revolver, wrist watch, whistle, identity disc, pipe cleaner, nail file, note case & photos, card case, cheque book and advance book. His brother, Lieutenant Kenneth Harris Allen also fell on the 11th October 1918, 13th Bn., attd. 19th Bn., Manchester Regiment. Memorial Ref. Pier and Face 13A and 14C. Thiepval Memorial, Somme, France. WO 339/25468

ANDERSON, Captain, Archibald Joseph. Killed whilst advancing at Fricourt as the battalion were chosen to clear the woods, leading the company and had just reached the German parapet when he was killed, 1st July 1916. C Coy. 10th Bn., West Yorkshire Regiment (Prince of Wales's Own). Aged 23. Only son of Edward and Mary Anderson, of 302, Electric Railway Chambers, Winnipeg, Canada. Born Portage la Prairie, Manitoba, Canada on the 20th July 1893. Educated public schools; St. Boniface College, Manitoba and St. Thomas Military Academy. Law student. Volunteered and joined the Fort Garry Horse as a private, No.14789 in August 1914. Served in France from 13th July 1915 and given a commission January 1916 and captain, May 1916. Originally Grave Ref B. 2. Memorial Ref. C. 2., Fricourt New Military Cemetery, France. WO 339/25041

From Winnipeg, Canada

ANDERSON, Second Lieutenant, Arthur Furneaux Dalgaims. Reported missing and then killed, 1st July 1916. 4th Bn. attd. 1st Bn., Lancashire Fusiliers. Native of Australia Yamba, New South Wales. Born 1893. Aged 22. Son of Mr. A. W. H. and Florence E. Anderson, of 12, Park Avenue, Barrow-In-Furness. Apprentice Messrs. Vickers. Served in Gallipoli (landed in April 1915) and Egypt. One of two brothers who joined the Colours. Mother applied for medals, 17th September 1921. Memorial Ref. A. 6., Beaumont-Hamel British Cemetery, France.

ANDERSON, Second Lieutenant, Reginald Dudley Bawdwen. Killed with A Coy., 14th Bn. Private Burgess reported; "Only got 25 to 50 yards when we heard that a young lieutenant had been killed", 1st July 1916. 11th Bn., York and Lancaster Regiment. Aged 20. Youngest son of Reginald Gustavus Lincoln Anderson (headmaster of the academy, Wakefield) and Blanche Gertrude Anderson, of Ashfield House, 84 York Street, Wakefield. He attended St. Cuthbert's College between 1906 and 1908. Formerly a mining engineer. Served as a sergeant with the 10th Lincolnshire. Entered France, 14th September. Father appealed for any news from those who were in action with him. Brother Lieutenant Bernard Gordon Anderson MC, 10th Bn., Lincolnshire regiment died of wounds, 8th August 1916. Brother Lieutenant A. E. P. Anderson, Longshut Lane, Stockport applied for his brothers medals, 3rd March 1923. Memorial Ref. C. 4., Redan Ridge Cemetery No.2, Beaumont-Hamel, France.

Have Mercy Upon Him Lord And Let Perpetual Light Shine Upon Him

ANDERTON, Second Lieutenant, Frank Westall. Killed at Beaumont Hamel, 1st July 1916. 3rd Bn. attd. 1st Bn., Lancashire Fusiliers. Born 17th March 1895, Ashton-on-Ribble. Aged 21. Son of James (cotton manufacturer) and Alice Anderton, of Preston, Lancs, and Glenroyd, North Drive, St. Annes-on-Sea. Attended Mill Hill School, 1910 - 1912. Member of the OTC. Employed Wood Milne Ltd at the Ajax Rubber Works, Leyland. Private in Loyal North Lancashire Regiment, Commissioned March 1915. Appeal by parents, 13th July 1916. Named in the Memorial Chapel at St. Annes Parish Church and on the memorial in Ashton Gardens. His parents received a letter from his colonel confirming that he was missing which is reported in the St. Annes Express: "Lieut. Anderton bravely led his platoon to the attack and went over the top, where he was seen to be hit and fell. Search was made for him during three nights, but without results, and his fate, therefore, is in doubt." In his letter the colonel describes him as a very promising officer, and tenders the sympathy of the regiment. Medals applied for by his father. Memorial Ref. C. 33., Redan Ridge Cemetery No.2, Beaumont-Hamel, France.

ANDREW, Second Lieutenant, John. First reported wounded and missing and then killed in action, 1st July 1916. 3rd Bn. attd. 10th Bn., King's Own Yorkshire Light Infantry. Age 29. Born 16th April 1886. Fourth son of John W. and Georgina Andrew of, 47 Park Avenue, Hull and resided at 38, Westbourne Avenue, Hull. Old Hull Grammar School boy. Member of the Kingston Rowing Club, he trained the crew and acted as stroke in 1912 when the club won the competition on the 1st July 1912. Married 10th June 1915 to Dorothy Hyde and held a position in the accountant's department of the Hull and Barnsley Railway Company until he joined the army in March 1915, receiving his commission on the 29th May 1915 and entered France, 29th May 1916. Father in law wrote to the War Office having been informed he was wounded on the 2nd July, on the 23rd July he was reported wounded and missing on the 2nd August 1916 after enquires his whereabouts reported as 'unknown' by the 21st Division. Younger brother in the army. Kingston Rowing Club Roll of Honour. Memorial Ref. Sp. Mem. B. 8., Gordon Dump Cemetery, Ovillers-La Boisselle, France. WO 339/64499

ANDREWS, Captain, James Allfrey. As soon as the artillery lifted the captain got up and gave the order to advance hardly had the order been given when he was shot through the head, the four waves dashed for the German trenches, Ovillers-la-Boiselle, acting second in command, 1st July 1916. It was due to him, to a great extent, that the advance of the front line was carried out with such remarkable coolness and precision. D Coy., 2nd Bn., Devonshire Regiment. Born on the 20th April 1890 in Aldershot, Farnham, Surrey. Aged 26. Second son of Lt. Col. James Walker Andrews, and of Emily Andrews, of "Bantony," Robertsbridge, Sussex. Attended Eagle House School, Bradfield (1902 – 1905), Eastman's Naval Academy, Haileybury (Edmonstone, 1905 -1908) and RMC Sandhurst in 1908 after which he went to Egypt. Disembarked 6th November 1914. Wounded 21st December 1914 at Neuve Chapelle and treated at Voluntary Hospital, Wimereux when he badly shattered his arm and returned to France in May, 1915. Gunshot wounded in the left thigh in March 1916 and returned to France, May 1916 after being certified fit. Eldest brother served with the Australian Contingent. Father applied for medals, 12th July 1919 reply send 25th July 1920. December 1927 exhumed from map reference 57d. X.7.d.7.5 and identified by officers uniform and disc found in grave, moved to 57d.k.35.a.1.0. Found with Second Lieutenant Belcher, Corporal W. Howard, Private W. H. Hunt, Private K. Cody and Private F. Mitchell all killed on the 1st July. Memorial Ref. XV. B. 14., Serre Road Cemetery No.2, France. WO 339/7366

Son of Lt. Col. Andrews Devon Regt. of Bantony Roberts Bridge, Sussex

ANGUS, Second Lieutenant, Stewart. Killed in action near Gommecourt on the 1st July 1916 leading his men and trying to supervise the dig of a new communication trench. Killed alongside Lance Corporal Graham Hogg. 1st Edinburgh Field Coy., Royal Engineers. Born in Villa Rica, Paraguay on 7th July 1890. Aged 25. Elder son of Mary Wilson Angus, of 9, Muswell Road, London, and David Angus, M. Inst. C.E, BSc formerly of Chile. Educated at Edinburgh Academy (1901 – 1908) and at Edinburgh University from 1908, BSc in Engineering 1912, he served an apprenticeship to Messrs. D. and C. Stevenson, MM.Inst.C.E., becoming later their assistant. For an interval worked for a firm of engineers in Glasgow. Cadet in the Edinburgh University OTC. In 1913 he joined the staff of the Buenos Aires and Great Southern Railway, Argentina, returning for war service in November 1914. He was elected an Associate Member of the Institution of Civil Engineers, 11th January 1916. He came home to enlist as sergeant, 1160, Lothian and Border House and worked as an assistant to J. M. Adam and Co., Engineers, Glasgow until his commission, 2nd April 1915 in the Royal Engineers. Served in Egypt. Served in France from 24th April 1916. His younger brother aged 17, Private Archibald Angus, 1st/14th Bn., London Scottish was killed 1st November 1914. Legalee, Miss E. K. Kerr, 4 Rue de Metz, Croix, France. Body reported to be buried where he fell. Lance Corporal Hogg is buried in Serre Cemetery No. 1. Memorial Ref. Pier and Face 8 A and 8 D., Thiepval Memorial, France.

ANSTEE, Second Lieutenant, Joseph. Wounded in the chest in the big advance, he was being conveyed to a dressing station when a shell burst close by and fatally wounded him when he lay in the ambulance, 1st July 1916. Initially reported missing believed killed and on the 13th July as being killed. 2nd Bn., Lincolnshire Regiment. Aged 28. Younger son of Mr. and Mrs. William Albert Anstee, West Deeping, Peterborough. Born 18th March 1880. Educated privately. He received his training in the Inns of Court, OTC. Enlisted as a private 17th June 1915 and commissioned 6th October 1915. Went to France, April 1916. Member of the St. Guthlac's West Deeping Lodge of Freemasons. Memorial Ref. Pier and Face 1 C., Thiepval Memorial, France. WO 339/45226

APPLIN, Second Lieutenant, Geoffrey Walter Henry. Killed in action 1st July 1916. 1st Bn., Lincolnshire Regiment, war diary records 2nd Bn. Aged 23. Only son of Walter Coombs Applin and Ada Applin, of North View, Sidcup, Kent. Employed bank clerk, assistant in the cashier's department, Bank of England. 5th August 1914 granted 'War Leave'. Enlisted Honourable Artillery Company on the 19th September 1914. No. 658. Given a commission in the Lincolnshire Regiment in April 1915 and proceed to France with the 1st Bn., 25th April 1915, he came home wounded at the end of May, 1915 being wounded at Ypres on the 15th May 1915 by a rifle grenade and suffered bruising on the chest. Returned to the Front in October 1915. Medals applied for by father, 20th June 1919. Commemorated London Borough of Bexley. Memorial Ref. Pier and Face 1 C., Thiepval Memorial, France. WO 339/29451

ARKLE, Second Lieutenant, Norman Armitage. Posted as missing and later believed killed, 1st July 1916. 20th (Tyneside Scottish) Bn., Northumberland Fusiliers. Aged 21. Son of Frances Mary Arkle and William John Arkle of 17, Sandhill, Newcastle-on-Tyne. Born Low Fell, Gateshead on the 9th January 1895. Brother of Mrs. F. L. Wight, of Ravensworth, Stocksfield-on-Tyne, Northumberland. Resided Asbourne Gardens, Monkseaton, Northumberland. Clerk. Enlisted 5th September 1914 served as a private, 9th Bn., Northumberland Fusiliers. Temporary second lieutenant, December 18th 1914. Commemorated Commercial Exchange in Newcastle. Named on YMCA Memorial, Newcastle. Stocksfield Memorial Cross. Wesleyan Methodist Church, Low Fell, Durham. Memorial Ref. Pier and Face 10 B 11 B and 12 B., Thiepval Memorial, France. WO 339/17201

ARNAUD, Lieutenant, Frederick Cooper. 1st July 1916. 16th Bn., Northumberland Fusiliers. Aged 19. Son of John Frederick and Maria Arnaud, of "Fritzoe," of 13, Holwood Road, Bromley, Kent. He was educated at Holmcroft and Quernmore Schools in Bromley, and then Merchant Taylors' School before joining the staff of Messrs. Thomas Cook and Son. He was a trainee booking clerk. Second Class Air Mechanic, 5673, from RFC as a mechanic in May 1915, going to the Front, 12th June 1915 as a despatch rider to Northumberland Fusiliers. Commissioned 5th March 1916. Temporary second lieutenant to be transferred to the General List for duty with trench mortar batteries, 29th April 1916. Father applied for medals, 1922. Commemorated Merchant Taylors' School, Northwood. Memorial Ref. Sp. Mem. A.1., Lonsdale Cemetery, Authuille, France.

"His Last Letter "Only Doing His Little Bit" "God Bless You All"

My Darling Father and Mother,

This is just a short letter to say Goodbye in case anything happens – the Big Push is coming off in about a weeks' time, we go over the top first and of course 'accidents will happen', and I shouldn't like to get knocked out without leaving a note behind, hence this letter. We all feel very confident about 'The Day' and I think the Boche will get an awful shock, it might mean the beginning of the end of the war – Our Division and our Brigade in particular, have been given one of the most important points to take – I hope we do well at all events we are going to do our best. Stokes Mortars will be to the front if it is humanly possible to get them there, we are all hoping that we shall do great things – You mustn't be upset if I get knocked out, as I wouldn't be out of this for anything, after all we are only doing our bit, and not a very large one at that.

You are the very best Father and Mother a boy could have and I have had a very happy and jolly life – I am afraid I have done several things in the past that have annoyed you, but I daresay you will forgive me for these. It is Sunday today and has turned out quite warm and fine – the Church bells are ringing, you would hardly think that there was a war on………

Remember me to all my friends at home and anybody I know.

My very best love to all at home and especially to you dear Father and Mother

God Bless you all

Fred

'Just heard we are to be in the trenches and firing during the bombardment, as well as going over the top, it will be a pretty warm time for us, not much chance I am afraid'.

ARTHUR, Second Lieutenant, George Stuart. In charge of a bombing party they encountered fierce German resistance, he stayed behind with only his revolver to allow the men to retreat and was never seen again, killed after leading an attack on the Quadrilateral, 1st July 1916. Corporal H. Wolfenden saw him in the German front line when the Germans were following down the communication trench. Posted as missing. The Cheshire's were a pioneer battalion with the Westminsters who had lost all their officers, so Lieutenant Arthur took charge of the Westminster's bombing party. By 8.20pm the officers consisting of Captain Somers-Smith, (London Regiment), Lieutenant Petley, (London Rifle Brigade), Captain Leys Cox (Queen Victorias Rifles), Second Lieutenant Arthur, (Cheshire Regiment), Captain Harvey (London Rifle Brigade) and Second Lieutenant Bovill (Queens Westminster Rifles) admitted they would be forced to return to the British lines and provided covering fire for the men. Making a run for the nearest shell holes, the only officer who returned was Lieutenant Petley, five officers being killed. A Coy. 5th (Pioneer) Bn., Cheshire Regiment. Aged 32. Second son of Samuel and Louisa Arthur, of 24, Heath Crescent, Halifax formerly Rhodesia Avenue. Born Clifton, Bristol on the 24th August 1883. Educated Heath Grammar School. Well-known in Halifax. Manager of shop, S. Arthur and Sons, Drapers. Joined the army as a private, 2388, at the outbreak of war and granted a commission, 6th March 1915. Entered France, 18th July 1915. Joined the battalion, 5th June 1916 from No. 4 Entrenching Battalion. Remains linked to the discovery of a unknown second lieutenant of the Cheshires and officially changed by the CWGC on the 10th June 1996 and confirmed August 1996 as special memorial, previous map reference K.10.A.60.80. Memorial Ref. III. C. 15. (Spec. Mem.)., Gommecourt British Cemetery No.2, Hebuterne, France.

OFFICERS OF THE 2/5TH BATTALION, CHESHIRE REGIMENT

From left to right are: Back row—2nd Lieut. L. Harper, 2nd Lieut. A. J. Allmand, 2nd Lieut. J. G. Crawford, 2nd Lieut. J. H. Rowlands, 2nd Lieut. L. K. S. Laugharne, 2nd Lieut. E. S. Heron, 2nd Lieut. H. R. P. Fennell, Lieut. A. Abrahams (Quartermaster); third row—2nd Lieut. W. Cullimore, 2nd Lieut. G. S. Arthur, Lieut. L. Hinton, Lieut. R. H. Haslam, 2nd Lieut. G. Booth, Lieut. W. F. Lindsell, Lieut. T. F. Robertson, 2nd Lieut. J. L. W. Bles; second row—Captain W. Vernon, Captain G. Hatt-Cook, Captain Cecil Oakes (adjutant), Major H. J. Mothersill, Lieut.-Colonel D. Abercrombie (T.D.), Brigade-Major J. P. Jackson, Major H. Watts, Captain A. B. M. Lake, Captain E. S. Bourne; front row—2nd Lieut. F. T. Vernon, 2nd Lieut. W. E. Davies, 2nd Lieut. A. B. Seale, 2nd Lieut. E. B. Petty

ASHER, Second Lieutenant, Kenneth John Penrith. Struck down in the first hour, reported that when mounting the parapet he was shot through the head and killed at once, 1st July 1916. 10th Bn., King's Own Yorkshire Light Infantry. Only son of George Willis Penrith Asher and Esther Fallon of 56 Hindes Road, Harrow. Born 4th February 1896 in Algiers, Africa and moved to England. Attended John Lyon School, becoming house captain and left at 17 to join the army. Served as a cadet with Middlesex Regiment and as private, 1869 in the 9th Bn., Middlesex Regiment. Commissioned in the King's Own Yorkshire Light Infantry, 28th November 1914. War Office wrote to the family in March 1918 and confirmed he was killed on the 1st July 1916. Commemorated St John The Baptist, Greenhill and St. Peter's Church, Harrow & Harrow on the Hill. Memorial Ref. I. B. 87A., Norfolk Cemetery, Becordel-Becourt, France. WO 339/3650

ASHLEY, Second Lieutenant, Claude. He gloried in the opportunity of leading his men forward and they were proud to follow him even to the inferno of La Boiselle, reported to be killed near the German third line, 1st July 1916. 15th Bn., Northumberland Fusiliers. Aged 21. Only son of Frederick Ashley (Singer Company, Queens Street, Belfast), and Annie Ashley of 65, Wandsworth Road, Belfast. Resided Westland Road, Belfast. Attended Queens University, Belfast. Member of the Training Corps. Received his commission on the 20th July 1915. Went out to the company, 23rd March 1916. Father applied for medals, 21st November 1921. Memorial Ref. Pier and Face 10 B 11 B and 12 B., Thiepval Memorial, France.

ASHTON, Second Lieutenant, Edward Deakin. Killed leading an assault against the German redoubt of Thiepval, northeast of Amiens 1st July 1916. 9th Bn. attd. 19th Bn., Lancashire Fusiliers. Aged 27. Only child of H. D. and Louisa Ashton (mill owners), of "Ellerslie," Darwen. Born 27th October 1889. Educated at Horton School, Sedbergh School (1903 – July 1908) and Balliol College, Oxford. Intended to move into the family business. Entered theatre of war, 21st October 1915. Served at Suvla Front and after receiving treatment for frost bite returned to the Front in France, April 1916. Next of kin, sister; Mrs. A. A. Buit, 54 Garsende, Terrace, Murrayfield, Edinburgh. In his last letter written on Friday; "Just a line to say we are going into action tomorrow and that there is naturally a chance that this maybe the last letter I can write. I shall be taking No. 1 platoon over the top and thus should be right ahead of the battalion. I have every confidence I am going to get through alright and we all have the same feeling as to the success of our offensive of which of course we are only a small part. We'll goodbye and my dearest love to you both. Don't be downhearted if I am taken". Memorial Ref. F. 38., Aveluy Communal Cemetery Extension, France.

ASSER, Second Lieutenant, Harold Edward. He was shot through the head and killed instantaneously, this whilst most gallantly leading his men forward into the attack on the 1st July 1916. 1st Bn., 16th Bn., Middlesex Regiment. Son of Edith Marian and Arthur Edward Asser, of 65, Windsor Road, Ealing, London. Born 2nd February 1895, St. Margaret's, Middlesex. Architects Clerk. Assistant scout master at St. Mellitus's Boy Scouts. Member of Crusader Class and an old 'Cedars' boy. Member of Ealing Rugby Club and Ealing Swimming club. Joined the 9th County of London Regiment on the 2nd September 1914. Fought as a rifleman, 2856, went out with a draft, 22nd January 1915 and fought at Hill 60. Commissioned 29th August 1915. Wounded in the left shoulder at the Battle of Loos. Admitted 1st October 1915 to Queen Alexandra's Military Hospital at Millbank discharged 22nd October 1915 and whilst home for a month recruited at Harrow. A letter from Lieut-Col. J. Hamilton Hall stated "he is officially 'reported as missing believed killed because we have not been able to recover his body; but I am very sorry to have to state that their cannot be any hope of him being alive or even wounded". Commemorated Ealing Memorial Gates. His mother was awarded a special allowance on his death. Memorial Ref. Pier and Face 12 D and 13 B., Thiepval Memorial, France.

ATKINSON, Second Lieutenant, Arthur Wilfrid. Killed by machine-gun fire, before reaching the German front line, near Maricourt, 1st July 1916. Commanded No's 11 and 10 Platoon, 19th Bn., Manchester Regiment. Aged 35. Youngest son of Fenton G. and Rosalie Helena Elizabeth Atkinson, of the Corner House, Bowdon, Cheshire. Born 26th April 1882, Bowdon, Cheshire. Educated Bowdon College and connected with Messrs. Atkinson and Co. yarn merchants, St. Ann's Square, Manchester. Enlisted private, 20th Bn., Royal Fusiliers. Entered France, 6th March 1916. St. John's (Altrincham) Memorial and Altrincham & District Roll of Honour. Memorial Ref. Pier and Face 13 A and 14 C., Thiepval Memorial, France.

C Coy., Platoon No. XI. Second Lieutenant Atkinson, second row middle.
In the photo and also killed on the 1st July 1916 but not identifiable are Private Norman Labrow Dawes, Corporal George Holt, Private Thomas Ward, Private Ernest Eaton Jones, Private Alfred Johnson and Private Fred Bannister.

ATKINSON, Major, Thomas Joyce. Company penetrated three Germans lines and a small body of men reached Beaucourt Station but were unable to hold the position due to a lack of support, 1st July 1916. B Coy. 9th Bn., Royal Irish Fusiliers. Born 1878. Aged 38. Only surviving son of Wolsey Richard and Alice Atkinson. MA, LL.B., T.C.D., Eden Villa, Portadown. He was educated at Scarborough, Rathmines, and Trinity College, Dublin, of which he was MA and L.L.B. (graduated 1898); called to the Irish Bar in 1901, admitted a solicitor in 1906, when he became a member of the firm of Carleton, Atkinson and Sloan, Church Place, Portadown. Thomas organised the signing of the Ulster Covenant in Seagoe Parish Church on Ulster Day, 28th September 1912. He also played a prominent role in the UVF and was second in command to Major Stewart Blacker, commanding officer, of the Portadown Battalion, UVF. On the outbreak of war volunteered for service, was given a commission in the 9th Bn., Royal Irish Fusiliers, 36th Ulster Division, subsequently being promoted Major. He had been on active service in France since 5th October, 1915. Headstone inscription selected by Miss G. E. Atkinson, Eden Villa, Portadown. Memorial Ref. VIII. A. 5., Ancre British Cemetery, Beaumont-Hamel, France.

A Son of Ulster Your Memory Hallowed In The Land You Loved

ATTENBOROUGH, Second Lieutenant, John Haddon. Led repeated attempts to dislodge the enemy from Montauban Alley, Second Lieutenant J. A. Gundry White achieved a breakthrough but Second Lieutenant Attenborough and Company Sergeant Major Jeremiah Coe were killed before it was captured, 1st July 1916. Led C Coy., when Captain J. Hall had been wounded. 8th Bn., Norfolk Regiment. Aged 24. Son of George William and Elizabeth Sarah Attenborough, of South Ockendon, Essex. Resided South Ockendon. Entered France exactly one year earlier on the 1st July 1915. Gazetted 8th January 1916 from the Honourable Artillery Company, No. 2434. Thurrock Roll of Honour. Memorial Ref. Pier and Face 1 C and 1 D., Thiepval Memorial, France.

AUDAER, Second Lieutenant, Ernest Clifford. Led platoons of D Coy., and the first of its officers to be killed at about 8.00am at Hammer Top Sap near Albert, killed by shrapnel, 1st July 1916. 15th Bn. formerly 13th Bn., Lancashire Fusiliers. Born 14th July 1892 at 212 Tong Road, Armley, Leeds. Aged 24. Only son of Mr. Walter Walker (assistant dentist) and Mrs. Clara Audaer, of James' Crescent, Tong Road, Armley, Leeds. He was associated with his father's business. Attended Leeds University and a member of the OTC. In the army soon after the declaration of war. Applied for a commission 25th October 1915. Entered France, 15th June 1916 and joined the battalion a week before. In his will left his items to his sisters and darling Doris McInnes of Leeds. His father sought confirmation of the circumstances of his son's death in April 1920 to the War Office. Medals send to his father. Commemorated St Bartholomew within St. Mary Church, Armley, West Yorkshire. Memorial Ref. Pier and Face 3 C and 3 D., Thiepval Memorial, France.

AVERY, Second Lieutenant, William Ernest. 1st July 1916. B Coy. 16th Bn., Northumberland Fusiliers. Aged 26. Son of Mr. and Mrs. Richard Ernest and Mary Ann Louisa Avery, of 2, London Lane, Bromley, Kent. M.E., M.I.M.E. Resided at Toft Hill Cottage, Birtley. Mechanical Engineer and Member of the Institute of Mining Engineers from 8th June 1907. Under-manager of Bewicke Maine Colliery, Durham. Enlisted September 1914, commissioned 24th March 1915. Went to France, 22nd November 1915. Memorial Ref. Pier and Face 10 B 11 B and 12 B., Thiepval Memorial, France.

AYRE, Captain, Bernard Pitts. Killed leaving Bund Support Trench, just after 8.00am, started the attack smoking his pipe and leading his men with his stick, 1st July 1916. 8th Bn., Norfolk Regiment. Born St John's, Newfoundland on 28th November 1892. Aged 24. Son of Robert Chesley Ayre and Lydia Gertrude Ayre, of Brookdale, St. John's, Newfoundland. Educated at Methodist College and Leys School, Cambridge. Took a Honours Degree in medicine at Jesus College, Cambridge matriculated in 1911 having spent the previous five years at the Leys School. He graduated in 1914 with a 3rd in Natural Sciences I. An excellent lacrosse player and attained a lacrosse blue within his first year, one of four Jesuans in the University XII that year and he took up rugby. His brother Captain Eric Ayre and two cousins all joined the Newfoundland Regiment. All died on the 1st July 1916. A territorial he joined up immediately with the Norfolk Regiment. Upon his death a fellow officer wrote that his company had led the attack "magnificently… due entirely to his fine leadership". A brother officer despatched a signet ring, silver flask and watch from France but they were not received by his family, the family also wrote to the War Office requesting information on these items and additionally the whereabouts of his revolver and field glasses. Memorial Ref. D. 10., Carnoy Military Cemetery, France. WO 339/20790

AYRE, Captain, Eric Stanley. The advance was made direct over the open from the rear trenches known as St John's Road and Clonmel Avenue. As soon as the signal for advance was given the regiment left the trenches and moved steadily forward. Machine gun fire from the right front was at once opened up and then artillery fire also. The distance to the objective varied from 650 to 900 yards. The enemy's fire was effective from the outset but the heaviest casualties occurred on passing through the gaps in the front wire where the men were mown down in heaps. Many more gaps in the wire were required than had been cut. Killed 1st July 1916. D Coy., 1st Bn., Newfoundland Regiment. Aged 27. Son of Robert Chesley Ayre and Lydia Gertrude Ayre, of St. John's, Newfoundland. Husband of Janet Ayre (formerly Miller), of St. John's, Newfoundland. Educated at Methodist College and Leys School, Cambridge from 1905 and went into West House. He was a champion gymnast, twice a member of the Bisley VIII and won First Colours at football. On leaving school, he worked in the family business in St. John's, Newfoundland, and was enthusiastic member of the local church and Boys Brigade. Sailed on the SS Stephano on March 20th 1915. Gazetted captain, 26th January 1915. His brother Captain Bernard Pitts Ayre also fell on the same day and two cousins. Original map reference where grave found 57d.Q.16.b.8.4. Memorial Ref. II. E. 12., Ancre British Cemetery, Beaumont-Hamel, France.

AYRE, Second Lieutenant, Gerald Walter. The advance was made direct over the open from the rear trenches known as St John's Road and Clonmel Avenue. As soon as the signal for advance was given the regiment left the trenches and moved steadily forward. Machine gun fire from the right front was at once opened up and then artillery fire also. The distance to the objective varied from 650 to 900 yards. The enemy's fire was effective from the outset but the heaviest casualties occurred on passing through the gaps in the front wire where the men were mown down in heaps. Many more gaps in the wire were required than had been cut. 1st July 1916. 1st Bn., Newfoundland Regiment. Aged 25. Son of Frederick William and Mary Julia Ayre, of St. John's. Educated at Methodist College and Rossall College. Commissioned 23rd August 1915 and acting adjutant, 27th October 1915. Three cousins also died on the same day. Brother, Lieutenant C. R. Ayre. Father received a cable from the King and Queen who sympathised with his loss. No formal burial as his revolver and ID disc were discovered at No. 29 Casualty Clearing Station having been removed by a wounded soldier. Memorial Ref. Beaumont-Hamel (Newfoundland) Memorial, France.

AYRE, Second Lieutenant, Wilfrid Douglas. The advance was made direct over the open from the rear trenches known as St John's Road and Clonmel Avenue. As soon as the signal for advance was given the regiment left the trenches and moved steadily forward. Machine gun fire from the right front was at once opened up and then artillery fire also. The distance to the objective varied from 650 to 900 yards. The enemy's fire was effective from the outset but the heaviest casualties occurred on passing through the gaps in the front wire where the men were mown down in heaps. Many more gaps in the wire were required than had been cut. 1st July 1916. 1st Bn., Newfoundland Regiment. Aged 21. Son of Charles P. and Diana Ayre, of St. John's, Newfoundland. Born in 1895 in Newfoundland. Educated at Methodist College and attended The Leys, Cambridge in 1909 at the age of 14 and went into North A House. On leaving school, he worked in the family business in St. Johns, Newfoundland, before returning to England to study for his preliminary Chartered Accountant examinations. Commissioned 26th October 1915. Transferred to 1st Bn., March 11th 1916 and left Ayr for the Front a few days later. Killed alongside his cousins, Bernard, Gerald and Eric. Memorial Ref. B. 10., Knightsbridge Cemetery, Mesnil-Martinsart, France.

BADDELEY, Second Lieutenant, John Frederick. Killed between Montauban and Carnoy from either machine-gun fire or shell fire about 7.30am, 1st July 1916. Initially reported wounded and confirmed killed on the 12th July. Private Robert Cude wrote his memoirs; "as far as my eyes can see, I can see rows of dead. Poor Newcombe, Sergeant McCluskey, Sergeant Whipps, Lieutenant Baddeley, and most of my old platoon where there and would not rise again. Have lost my old Pals today". These men were 7th Bn., The Buffs (East Kent Regiment). Born 1894, Wimbledon. Aged 21. Son of Charles Edward and Amelia Mary Baddeley, of 33, Merton Hall Road, Wimbledon, London. Promising medical student at King's College, London. University of London, OTC. Commissioned December 1914. Effects were cheque book and advance book. Original burial map reference 62C.A.8.c.8.9 with four other officers also killed on the 1st July, Lieut. Cloudesley, Lieut. Goss, Lieut. Saltmarshe and Captain Scott. The soldiers mentioned by Private Cude have no known grave and all are commemorated on the Thiepval Memorial; Lance Sergeant Herbert McCluskey, Sergeant Alfred Whipps and Private Harold Victor Newcombe. Memorial Ref. Originally buried in the battlefield, reburied in VIII. R. I., Dantzig Alley British Cemetery, Mametz, France. WO 339/5267

BAGNALL, Second Lieutenant, Richard Gordon. Killed in action, 1st July 1916. 114th Heavy Bty., Royal Garrison Artillery. Aged 31. Son of William Gordon Bagnall and Jessie Bagnall, of 69, Overstrand Mansions, Prince Of Wales Road, Battersea, London and later Bannut Tree Farm, Castle Morton, Worcestershire. Native of Stafford. Born 25th May 1885. Educated Warden House, Upper Deal. Attended Charterhouse. Previously employed Divisional Manager, Merlimau Estate Rubber Estate, Malacca Straits Settlements, Malaysia. Entered France 18th December 1915. Mother received pension payment. Memorial Ref. I. A. 9., Bouzincourt Communal Cemetery Extension, France.

BAIRD, Captain, Charles Edward. Majority of the casualties especially those of the officers occurred during the first two hours of fighting, 1st July 1916. 2nd Bn., Seaforth Highlanders. Aged 21. Eldest son of Brigadier General Edward W. D. Baird and Millicent Bessie Baird, of Kelloe, Edrom, Berwickshire, and Forse, Caithness also 108, Lancaster Gate, London. Educated Eton (under H. F. W. Tatham) and on to RMC Sandhurst. Commissioned October 1913. Formerly stationed in Shorncliffe. Disembarked 23rd August 1914. Suffered gunshot wound to the arm, admitted 16th October 1914 to Queens Alexandra's Hospital at Millbank transferred to 18 Cadogan Gardens and discharged 17th October 1914, wounded in April 1915. Returned to the Front, February 1916. Gazetted temporary captain, 27th February 1916. Father applied for medals and confirmed eligible for the 1914 Star. Landwade Church Memorial. Memorial Ref. I. K. 21., Serre Road Cemetery No.2, France.

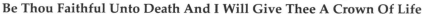

Be Thou Faithful Unto Death And I Will Give Thee A Crown Of Life

BAKER, Second Lieutenant, James Henry. 1st July 1916. 8th Bn., York and Lancaster Regiment. Aged 19. Born 1897. Son of James Henry and Charlotte Isabella Baker, of Friern Lodge, Friern Lane, Whetstone, London. Entered France, 9th February 1916. Still posted as missing 22nd July 1916. Map reference where body found, 57d.R.32.c.1.6 also found with 21869, Private W. Lindley, 8th Bn., York and Lancaster and buried next to him in plot. G. 3. Memorial Ref. VIII. G. 2., Lonsdale Cemetery, Authuille, France.

BAKER, Captain, Tom. Killed in action at La Boisselle, 1st July 1916. 10th Bn., Lincolnshire Regiment. Aged 34. Third son of Fredrick Steane Baker and Susan Baker, of Combe, Woodstock, Oxon previously resided 8 Holywell, Oxford. He was a master at Wolverhampton Grammar school during the years 1910-1912, leaving School in the latter year to take up a Modern Language post at Hymer's College, Hull. Officer in the school OTC. Gained a commission in the Lincolnshire Regiment, September 1914. Originally buried SE of La Boisselle in map reference 57d.X.20.c with six unknown British soldiers. Memorial Ref. II. L. 6., Bapaume Post Military Cemetery, Albert, France. WO 339/15871

Res Non Verba His Name Liveth For Ever

BALKWILL, Second Lieutenant, Charles Vince. Killed at Gommecourt, 1st July 1916. 1st /5th Bn., London Regiment (London Rifle Brigade). Son of Francis (fruit merchant) and Mary Vince Balkwill, of 6, Garlies Road, Forest Hill, London. Born 17th April 1885. Educated Mr. J. O. Boyes and St. Dunstan's, Catford. 1907 part of the Kent team that beat Surrey, 9 to 3 whilst playing for Catford Bridge later Bromley RFC. On the outbreak of war in 1914 he enlisted in the ranks of the 5th London Regiment, No. 125. He went to France with the 1st Battalion of the unit, 4th November 1914 and was promoted sergeant in the following month. On 26th April 1915 he fought with his unit at Wieltje and Neuve Chapelle, during the battle of Ypres, and was severely wounded. He was invalided home with a shattered right shoulder, but his fitness and his stay at the London Hospital led to a good recovery and by the end of the year he was playing rugby for his regiment. He underwent a course of officer training, and was commissioned into the 3rd Bn., of the 5th London Regiment on 8th December 1915. A few months later he was passed fit and joined the 1st Battalion in France on 27th May 1916. Brother Second Lieutenant John Balkwill killed on same day. Named on the Catford Bridge Memorial. Memorial Ref. Pier and Face 9 D., Thiepval Memorial, France.

Catford Bridge First Team 1913 1914
Middle row second from right, C. V. Balkwill

BALKWILL, Second Lieutenant, John. Reported killed, 1st July 1916. A Coy, 6th Bn., Royal Warwickshire Regiment. Aged 33. Son of Francis (fruit merchant) and Mary Vince Balkwill, of 6, Garlies Road, Forest Hill, London. Resided Dorridge, Knowle. Educated privately at J. O. Boyes, Forest Hill and onto St. Dunstan's, Catford. He was a member of Catford Bridge Football Club. Worked for the Northern Assurance Company Ltd, Birmingham. He entered company service in the London office in May 1899. He was transferred to Birmingham as a surveyor in July 1908 and volunteered for active service in September 1914, Private, 6/2481. Entered France, 22nd March 1915. He was commissioned on 19th September 1915 in the Royal Warwicks. Brother Second Lieutenant Charles Vince Balkwill killed on same day. Named on the Catford Bridge Originally buried at map reference 57d.K.35.a.5.2 with two privates of the 6th Bn., Royal Warwicks, Private F. Patrick and Private R. Green, these men also fell on the 1st. John was formally identified by his officer's khaki, boots, Royal Warwickshire collar badges a watch and a piece of waterproof sheet marked 'Lieut. Balkwill, A Coy, Warwick Regt'. Mr. T. J. Balkwill of 136 & 137, Upper Thames Street, EC4 choose his inscription. Memorial Ref. III. E. 36., Pargny British Cemetery, France.

Albam Exornat

BALLINTINE, Captain, Joseph. Posted as missing 1st July 1916. 11th Bn., Royal Inniskilling Fusiliers. Son of Mr. Joseph Ballantine. Born 23rd December 1872, Derry. **Educated** Foyle College. Wife Mrs. J. Ballintine, Clarence Avenue, Londonderry and they had three children; Joseph Robert Terence, Richard James Matterson and Dorothy Joan. Partner in the firm of Messrs. J. & J. Ballintine, Ltd., builders, Londonderry and a took a deep interest in the UVF movement, and when the call for men was made he was one of the first to answer. Member of Masonic Lodge of St John, No. 196, Londonderry. Took a commission in the Donegal and Fermanagh Battalion on the promotion of the Ulster Division. Entered France, 6th October 1915. Still being reported missing, 20th April

1917. Medals applied for by his wife. Original map reference for burial R.20.C.1.7 with five other soldiers from a variety of regiments reburied. Londonderry (Derry) War Memorial. Memorial Ref. XIV. D. 10., Mill Road Cemetery, Thiepval, France.

BAMBER, Lieutenant, John Walton. Killed in action instantly by a rifle bullet, to the left of a machine gun pit in the German front line, 1st July 1916. 10th Bn., King's Own Yorkshire Light Infantry. Born October 16th, 1887, in Ladysmith, Natal, South Africa. Aged 29. Seventh child of William and Bessie Bamber, of 128, Pietermaritz St., Pietermaritzburg, Natal, South Africa. Attended Maritzburg College in Pietermaritzburg. He worked in the Natal Civil Service, as a clerk in the Treasury Department, resigned in 1912 to study for the ministry. Natal Cadets 1896 to 1902 and Natal Militia Reserve 1906 to 1912. At the outbreak of the war he was a student at St Augustine's College, Canterbury, preparing for Holy Orders. On December 4th, 1914, he joined the army. Entered France, 1st October 1915. Mother received pension benefit. Memorial Ref. Believed to be buried in this cemetery. Sp. Mem. B. 12., Gordon Dump Cemetery, Ovillers-La Boisselle, France. WO 339/17207

Their Glory Shall Not Be Blotted Out

BARBER, Second Lieutenant, William Geoffrey Wright. Reported missing, killed at Gommecourt, 1st July 1916. Went over with Officer Commanding D Coy., Captain A. B. Naylor. No. 15 Platoon,, William was in the third wave and left the British line at Zero -2. He fought in a fire bay with Captain Naylor, Second Lieutenant Dornton and a few other men they threw bombs until the supply was exhausted, they were then subjected to an intense attack and those that could move were forced to leave the injured Dornton and Wright behind. 1st /5th Bn., Sherwood Foresters (Notts and Derby Regiment). Aged 20. Son of William and Emily Sarah Barber, of Duffield, Derby. Born 13th September 1896. He was 6 foot 7 inches in height. Educated at Rossall School until Christmas 1914 and in the OTC receiving a commission two months later. He had been in France just less than a year, 12th July 1915. In 1922, father applied for his medals. Memorial Ref. Pier and Face 10 C 10 D and 11 A., Thiepval Memorial, France.

BARKER, Lieutenant, Harold William. Died of wounds, 1st July 1916. 16th Bn., Middlesex Regiment. Father, W. H. Barker, 1 Hamblet Road, Clapham. Commissioned 19th March 1915. Entered France, 10th February 1916. Memorial Ref. Pier and Face 12 D and 13 B., Thiepval Memorial, France.

BARNES, Second Lieutenant, Francis Frank. Killed after 7.36am by machine gun fire, 1st July 1916. 22nd Bn., The King's (Liverpool Regiment). Aged 29. Eldest son of Frederick William and Hannah Thurston Barnes, of 9, Kinglake St. Edge Hill, Liverpool. Educated Holt School and Oulton Training College entering scholastic profession under Liverpool Education Committee. Formerly a master at St. Mary's, Frog Lane, Lichfield for five years. Member of the Lichfield Miniature Rifle Club being an excellent shot. Billiard player and member of Lichfield Cricket and Bowling Club. Upon leaving Lichfield entered the accountancy department of the British American Tobacco Company and appointed as representative in Constantinople and Trebizond. Shortly before war broke out transferred to Liverpool office. Enlisted 2nd September 1914. Rose through the ranks, commissioned 13th August 1915 and went to France, 16th April 1916. Reported to be wounded 24th June 1916 but stayed on duty. Letters to the War Office seeking more information from his fiancée, Miss Mary Hand. Original map reference where body found 62C.A.9.b.7.8 with ten other soldiers. Memorial Ref. II. O. 8., Dantzig Alley British Cemetery, Mametz, France. WO 339/36352

Be Thou Faithful Until Death And I Will Give Thee A Crown Of Life

BARNETT, Second Lieutenant, Phillip. Took part in the attack on the village of Fricourt situated to the east of the town of Albert. 'A' and 'B' Companies moved forward into No Man's Land five minutes prior to Zero Hour, and both were immediately subjected to enemy machine-gun fire which forced their withdrawal. At 7.29am a fresh attack was mounted, and although devoid of any of their officers, approximately forty other ranks managed to reach the German line and a sunken road beyond. 'C' and 'D' Companies similarly suffered heavy casualties whilst attempting to cross No Man's Land. Attack halted at Lozenge Wood. Officially died 2nd July 1916. Concentration of grave and burial return states date of death as 1st July 1916. Reports suggest killed by a shell that also killed Sergeant Frank Millwood and Sergeant Walter James Prosser, both of these men also given a date of death as 1st July. 4th Bn., Middlesex Regiment. Aged 25. Son of Hyam and Kate Barnett, of London. Born 24th March 1890. Resided The Crown, College Street, Lambeth. Husband of Violet Ethel May Barnett, of 34, Maison Dieu Road, Dover married 20th September 1913. Son in law of Mr. A. B. Evans of Shifnal. Enlisted 24th August 1908. Served in the ranks of the RGA, RFA and West Yorkshire Regiment and went to the Front in November 1914 as platoon sergeant. Commission for gallantry in the field. Joined Bn., 9th May 1916. Gazetted 29th May 1916. Originally buried angle of Empress Trench and new communication trench sht 26. Contour 110., 57d.X.27c.6.4 and later transferred to grave IV.K.5. Memorial Ref. IV. K., Gordon Dump Cemetery, Ovillers-La Boisselle, France. WO 339/61644

Eternal Honour Give To Those Who Died That We Might Live

BARRATT, Lieutenant, Kenneth Franklin. 1st July 1916. 3rd Bn., Essex Regiment attd. Machine Gun Corps. A number of officers had been attached from other Essex battalions. Aged 21. Born 4th March 1895. Younger son of Thomas James Barratt and Mrs. Barratt of Bell-Moor, Hampstead Heath, London. Gazetted lieutenant in January 1915. Memorial Ref. Pier and Face 10 D., Thiepval Memorial, France. The Battle of the Somme 1916, Souvenir and Roll of honour includes a poem under his entry;

Heedless and careless still the world goes on
And leaves us broken. Our son, our sons,
They, too, loved life, but loving dared not save themselves
Lest those they loved should pay the price;
Sunshine and youth and laughter, all they gave in sacrifice.

BASS, Lieutenant, Philip Burnet. Killed at Gommecourt when he had reached the German second-line trench, and assumed to be killed in action on or about that date. He went over behind the assaulting troops, 1st July 1916. No. 4 Platoon, A Coy. 5th Bn., Cheshire Regiment. In the second line trench he went to report to Captain Cox, Queen Victoria's Rifles and on return gave orders make a fire step in a trench, some bombers not the 5th Cheshires came past and dropped a bomb and seriously wounded Lieutenant P. B. Bass in the eye. Private John Clifford offered to take him back and both were posted as missing, 1st July 1916. Born on 11th January 1895 in St. Helier, Jersey. Aged 21. Eldest son of Colonel Philip de Salis. Bass, C.M.G., and Mrs. Frances Edith Bass, of 8, Madeley Road, Ealing, London. After attending Winton House, Aldershot the Imperial Service College, Windsor, where he was a member of the OTC. Philip matriculated at Pembroke College, Oxford in 1913 on a King Charles I Scholarship where he was again a member of the OTC. Second Lieutenant 20th November 1914 and went to France, 3rd May 1915. Promoted lieutenant, 1st March 1916. Memorial Ref. Pier and Face 3 C and 4 A., Thiepval Memorial, France.

BATES, Second Lieutenant, Alfred Neville. Killed whilst a member of a carrying party, 1st July 1916. B Coy., 5th Bn., Sherwood Foresters (Notts and Derby Regiment). Aged 23. Son of Arthur John (tailor) and Emily Bates, of 44, Midland Avenue, Lenton, Nottingham. Formerly a student at Mundella School and Nottingham University College where he took both pass and Honours degree in the London University Examinations, Modern Languages, First Class. Prior to entering the local contingent of the OTC under Captain Trotman and securing a commission on the 1st December 1915 in the Sherwoods, previously engaged as an assistant master at Bootle Secondary School. Entered France, 30th May 1916. Student teacher as was his twin, Albert John. Memorial Ref. I. B. 22., Foncquevillers Military Cemetery, France.

I Will Fear No Evil For Thou Art With Me

BAXENDINE, Second Lieutenant, John Young. Died at Beaumont Hamel, 1st July 1916 and originally buried a 100 yards from where he fell. Went over the top from the support line, and over the first line, the bridges over the front trench having being ranged by the German machine-gunners the day previously meet with heavy losses, while crossing these bridges and passing the lanes out in the wire, he died leading his men in the most gallant manner in the face of terrible fire. Reported missing believed killed, 1st July 1916. 5th Royal Scots attd. 1st Bn., Border Regiment. Aged 22. Eldest son of Andrew (bookseller and publisher) and Alice Baxendine, of 10, McLaren Road, Edinburgh. Born 17th November 1893, Edinburgh. Attended George Watson's College, 1899 - 1907. On leaving school he entered his father's business as bookseller and publisher. Member of the Edinburgh University OTC. Received his commission in April 1915. Entered Gallipoli, 7th October 1915, taking part in the Suvla Bay landing. Invalided from the Peninsula due to dysentery, he subsequently served in Egypt and France. Buried 100 yards from where he fell. Brother, Private Andrew Richard Baxendine died of pneumonia 11th December 1918 with the 1st Bn., Seaforth Highlanders. Father applied for his medals. Memorial Ref. B. 42., Hawthorn Ridge Cemetery No.2, Auchonvillers, France.

Greater Love Hath No Man Than This

BAYLY, Second Lieutenant, Erskine Cochrane. Reported to be shot in the head near Carnoy at about 7.00am, 1st July 1916. 6th Bn., Royal Berkshire Regiment. Born 16th February 1886. Resided 7 Ganely Place, London. Attended Bradfield College, 1900 to 1903, listed as William Erskine Cochrane Bayly. Attested 21st October 1914. Officers of the Training Corps to be Temporary Second Lieutenants gazetted 19th November 1914. Next of kin, sister Mrs. Allgood, Hermitage, Hexham, Northumberland. Memorial Ref. Q. 23., Carnoy Military Cemetery, France. WO 339/1596

1900 Bradfield College in the Greek Theatre

BEACALL, Second Lieutenant, Arthur. 1st July 1916. 10th Bn. attd. 11th Bn., East Lancashire Regiment. Born 17th August 1895. Aged 20. Son of Thomas (schoolmaster at Quedgeley School) and Eleanor Rebecca Beacall, of 44, Podsmead Road, Gloucester. Educated Crypt and King's School, Gloucester entered 1906 on a scholarship. After leaving school, he worked for Lloyds Bank and played as a forward for Stroud Rugby Club. Married Edith Brewer, June 1916. Enlisted as a private, No. 10463, 6th Somerset Light Infantry and promoted through the ranks being promoted second lieutenant, 26th November 1915. Entered France, 21st May 1915. Memorial Ref. I. D. 6., Euston Road Cemetery, Colincamps, France.

In Christ Shall All Be Made Alive

BEAL, Second Lieutenant, Arnold James. Reported missing, 1st July 1916. B Coy. 12th Bn., York and Lancaster Regiment. Aged 22. Son of Arnold James and Laura Angwin Beal, of Ranmoor Cliff, Sheffield. King Edward VII School, Sheffield. Previously a student at Sheffield University. Employed Messrs. J. and J. Beal, Red Hill, Sheffield. Enlisted private, No. 41, York and Lancasters. Commissioned 17th February 1915. Embarked 20th December 1915. He went into the attack with his younger brother, Temporary Lieutenant Frank Beal whom was wounded with the 94th Trench Mortar Battery. A statement by Private Michael Rooney who was taken a prisoner of war stated he was killed at Serre. Father applied for medals. Memorial Ref. E. 39., Queens Cemetery, Puisieux, France.

BEATSON, Lieutenant, Roger Stewart Montresor. He was killed in the late afternoon about 5.30pm while leading his men into action near Fricourt when all the officers of the battalion who went into action were either killed or wounded, officially 2nd July 1916. 6th Bn. attd. 10th Bn., King's Own Yorkshire Light Infantry. Born at Rangoon, on July 20th 1890. Aged 25. Eldest son of Mr. William Gordon Beatson (East India Merchant), and Mrs. Constance Mary Beatson of Shortlands, Kent. Attended Rugby School. He was in the Rugby Eleven cricket team in 1907, when he took twenty-three wickets for 13.30 runs each, heading the averages. Subsequently he played for the Burrard Cricket Club and the public school team of Vancouver, where he was regarded as one of the best batsmen in British Columbia. On leaving Rugby School he spent two years in the Capital and Counties Bank, Godalming, and three years in the Canadian Bank of Commerce, Vancouver, B.C. On the outbreak of war, in August, 1914, he enlisted in the Seaforth Highlanders of Canada No. 28966, and came to England with the First Canadian Contingent. He obtained a commission in the 6th Bn., King's Own Yorkshire Light Infantry in December, 1914, and went to the Front in May, 1915. He was wounded at Hooge, 31st July 1915 with a shrapnel wound below the right knee about the size of a sixpence and returned to England. Discharged 8th September 1915. He left for the Front again in March, 1916. Grave Registration document has the 1st/2nd July 1916 against a list of eight officers, Lieutenant Beatson was the only one given a date of death of the 2nd July 1916 and his National Archive file has the 2nd July crossed through and the 1st July added. Mother applied for his medals. Memorial Ref. Sp. Mem. B. 6., Gordon Dump Cemetery, Ovillers-La Boisselle, France. WO 339/5268

The Lord Bless Thee And Keep Thee

BEAVON, Second Lieutenant, John Leonard. Killed in action, leading his platoon 1st July 1916. 26th (Tyneside Irish) Bn., Northumberland Fusiliers. Born in 1889. Son of Mr. and Mrs. Thomas Beavon. Resided at 35 Merridale Street West, Wolverhampton. Enlisted in the 20th Hussars in 1907 (No. 1806). At the outbreak of the war, John Beavon was a sergeant and serving with his regiment at Colchester. Embarked for service on the 17th August 1914. Mentioned in Despatches, October 1914. Commissioned in Northumberland Fusiliers, 5th March 1916. His pension was granted to his mother until she died in July 1918 and then onto his father. Thomas Beavon applied for medals. Memorial Ref. Pier and Face 10 B 11 B and 12 B., Thiepval Memorial, France. WO 339/56460

BEDDOW, Second Lieutenant, Cecil Victor. Involved in the attack at Ovillers Spur, 1st July 1916 and fell fighting in the great advance. 2nd Bn., Devonshire Regiment. Aged 19. Younger and second son of Josiah (doctor) and Grace Mary Beddow, Of Mullion, Ballard Estate, Swanage, Dorset. Born 25th September 1896, Hackney. Attended King's School Worcester, (May 1909 to 1911) and Blundell's School (1912 – 1913). He joined "F" Company Inns of Court OTC on 10th December 1914 and served with them for 107 days (during which time he was promoted to lance corporal) until 26th March 1915. He was discharged to a commission in the Devonshire Regiment in March 1915. He was sent to the front on 20th May 1916. King's School Memorial, Worcester and Thorverton Memorial, Devon. Brother Leslie, also served. Original map reference 57d.x.7.d.7.5 where the body was found and marked as an unknown British officer, and later changed in 1927 to Cecil as means of identification were officer's uniform, buttons, boots size 8 Norwegian pattern and officers advance pay book. Memorial Ref. XV. A. 5., Serre Road Cemetery No.2, France. WO 339/37152

And They Rise To Their Feet As He Passes By Gentlemen Unafraid

BEDFORD, Second Lieutenant, Seaton Hall. He went over with the assault, leading his platoon in the attacking companies. Soon after he got over our parapet and beyond our wire bits of shell got him in the arms, he got on and pushed forward until he reached the enemy's barbed wire when his legs were knocked under him by a shell, he was in the act of rising again when a bullet struck him, 1st July 1916. A young private, Private Williams put him on a waterproof sheet and dragged him back through the grass to the wire but he died shortly afterwards. C Coy., 2nd Bn., Royal Berkshire Regiment. Aged 27. Son of Henry Hall Bedford and Lucy Bedford, of Sharrow Hurst, Sheffield. Solicitor. LLB., Cambridge. Attended Uppingham School in the OTC and in the Cambridge University OTC. Darlington and Denton Solicitors, Sheffield. On the outbreak of hostilities he was accepted as a private in the Honourable Artillery Company, and was sent to France with the first contingent of his regiment, 18th September 1914. Wounded April 1915 but did not require hospital treatment. Commissioned 7th May 1916. Captain J. Bedford, 4th Bn., York and Lancaster Regiment appealed to the War Office in August 1916 for more information, as the quartermaster-sergeant had send his belongings to the family via Messrs. Cox & Co. Confirmed killed as a result of a special enquiry on the 27th October 1916. Father applied for his medals, with the Victory Medal being returned for a replacement that was send 27th October 1920. Memorial Ref. Pier and Face 11 D., Thiepval Memorial, France. WO 339/62156

BEEVER, Captain, William Henry. Officially reported as wounded and missing, killed on 1st July 1916, at the head of his company, close to the German third line. B Coy., 1st Bn., Rifle Brigade. Aged 21. Elder son of Major Henry Holt Beever and Mrs. Catherine Leonide Beever, of Littleton House, Blandford, Dorset. Attended Harrow. RMC Sandhurst, 1913 and won the Riding Prize. William was gazetted to the Rifle Brigade in August, 1914. He joined the 3rd Battalion in France, 6th October, 1914, and a year later was transferred to the 1st Battalion. In December, 1915, he was gazetted temporary captain. Younger brother also died in the war, Lieutenant Jonathan Holt Beever, G Battery, 17th Brigade, Royal Horse Artillery died on the 25th March 1918. His father applied for his medals. Memorial Ref. Pier and Face 16 B and 16 C., Thiepval Memorial, France.

BEGGS, Captain, Henry Parker. Initially reported missing and confirmed killed in action, 1st July 1916. B Coy. 8th Bn., Royal Irish Rifles. Aged 26. Youngest son of Samuel and Minnie Beggs, of Chestnut Villa, Dunmurry, Co. Antrim. Employed by Messrs. Richardson, Sons and Owden (with which his father's firm was also associated) at their Glenmore works. Commercial Clerk for Silversmith. A member of Lisburn and Cliftonville Cricket Clubs and Cliftonville Hockey Club he also belonged to the UVF. Commissioned in 1914, and promoted to captain in early 1916. Entered France, September 1915. Sergeant R. Stitt who was taken a prisoner of war stated Captain Beggs was killed on the 1st. Mother applied for his medals. Memorial Ref. Pier and Face 15 A and 15 B., Thiepval Memorial, France.

BELCHER, Second Lieutenant, Basil Henry. His platoon ran into heavy machine-gun fire and was seen to fall after about 100 yards, 1st July 1916. 2nd Bn., A Coy., 2nd Platoon, Royal Berkshire Regiment. Born 3rd August 1894 in Newbury, Berkshire. Aged 22. Youngest child of William Belcher (solicitor) and Mary Belcher of Donnington Square, Newbury. Attended Brighton College (1905 – 1911, Junior and Chichester Houses), one of four men to die from Brighton College on the 1st July 1916. After leaving school studied in Paris and when war broke out was about to travel to Russia. Solicitor's clerk. Enlisted in the 18th Bn., Royal Fusiliers, and later commissioned in the Royal Berkshire Regiment, 16th May 1915. Prisoner of war transcript states killed 1st July 1916. Brother, Second Lieutenant W. B. Belcher, 2nd Royal Berkshire Regiment appealed for further information from the Graves Commission and contacted as many of the platoon as possible. In view of the lapse of time and with no further information death assumed to be 1st July 1916, dated 25th April 1917. Original map reference where body found 57d.X.7.d.7.5, 1927 believed to be Second Lieutenant Belcher identified by officers uniform, boots size 7 and buttons. Found with Second Lieutenant Andrews, Corporal W. Howard, Private W. H. Hunt, Private K. Cody and Private F. Mitchell all killed on the 1st July. Memorial Ref. XV. B. 13., Serre Road Cemetery No.2, France.

BELL, Captain, Eric Norman Frankland, VC. He started back to fetch more shells when he was shot through the body and died in a few moments without suffering, his servant, Private Stevenson stayed with him to the end, 1st July 1916. Trench Mortar Battery officer, 9th Bn., Royal Inniskilling Fusiliers. Native of Enniskillen, Ireland. Aged 20. Youngest son, three soldier sons of Captain E. H. Bell, of 22, University Road, Bootle, Liverpool. Student, Liverpool School of Architecture. Father also rejoined at the outbreak of war and served in Egypt. Eric went to France, 5th October 1915. Received his commission originally in the Tyrone Volunteers and attached to a Trench Mortar Battery. On his death the family received a letter from Colonel Ricardo. Awarded the Victoria Cross for most conspicuous bravery; 'He was in command of a Trench Mortar Battery and advanced with the infantry in the attack. When our front line was hung up by unfailing machine-gun fire, Captain Bell crept forward and shot the machine-gunner. Finally he was killed rallying and re-organising infantry parties which had lost their officers. All this was outside the scope of his normal duties with his battery. He gave his life in his supreme devotion to duty'. Two brothers also served. Father applied for medals. Memorial Ref. Pier and Face 4 D and 5 B., Thiepval Memorial, France.

BELL, Second Lieutenant, Norman Henderson. As soon as the troops left the front line, heavy machine-gun fire was brought to bear on them from all directions, casualties if officers amounted to 100%, killed at Beaumont Hamel, 1st July 1916. 3rd Bn. attd. 1st Bn., Hampshire Regiment. Age 19. Son of Mr. and Mrs. W. Henry Bell of Woolston, Southampton. Educated at King Alfred's School, Wantage from May 1908 to July 1914. Prefect, prominent athlete and a fine actor as well as captain of the football and cricket teams. He had been working for the Naval Paymasters Examination but after the outbreak of war he obtained a nomination to RMC Sandhurst, December 1914 to May 1915. Gazetted to the Hampshire Regiment. Death regretted by all 'Old Alfredians'. Grandson of Captain R. W. Evans R.N, J.P, and a nephew of Mr. Richard Bell. Memorial Ref. Pier and Face 7 C and 7 B., Thiepval Memorial, France.

BEMROSE, Second Lieutenant, Karl. News received by the family from Captain Kerr stating that he had made all enquiries and seemed no doubt he had been taken prisoner on the night of the attack. It was thought unwounded though it transpired that his orderly, Kelly died of wounds by his side, 1st July 1916. Prisoner of War records from Corporal Reynolds stated he was wounded in front of a German trench and possibly killed and Private J. W. Sharratt stated he was killed. Second Lieutenant Bemrose went over with the fourth wave and was killed. 1st /5th Bn., Sherwood Foresters (Notts and Derby Regiment) seconded to 139th Trench Mortar Battery. Aged 23. Son of Henry Howe Bemrose, Sc.D., J.P., and Nellie Bemrose, of Ash Tree House, Derby formerly Ormaston Road, Derby. Born 8th August 1893. Educated at Abbotsholme, Rocester, Derbyshire. Master printer. Private, Royal Fusiliers. Commissioned 1st January 1915. Entered France, 12th July 1915. Brother Second Lieutenant Roderick Henry Bemrose MC, Royal Field Artillery died 7th November 1918 with pneumonia. Memorial Ref. Pier and Face 10 C 10 D and 11 A., Thiepval Memorial, France.

BENNS, Second Lieutenant, Arthur Lionel. 1st July 1916. C Coy., 1st /5th Bn., London Regiment (London Rifle Brigade). Born 1891 and lived at 45 Brusfield Street, New Cross. Son of Roger William and Eliza Benns. He was educated at Christ's Hospital and Haberdashers' Aske's, Hatcham School. Shipping clerk, Commonwealth and Dominion Line. He enlisted in 'P' Company of the London Rifle Brigade on the 28th April 1910, No. 9148. Disembarked 4th November 1914. He was wounded in the Second Battle of Ypres in March 1915 and appointed lance corporal. He was commissioned into the 3/5th Bn., London Regiment on 27th September 1915 and on 5th March 1916 he was transferred to 'C' Company of the 1/5th Londons. Mrs. E. Benns of 62 Burnt Ash Hill applied for his medals. Memorial Ref. Pier and Face 9 D., Thiepval Memorial, France.

Reading from the back row to the front from left to right; 2nd Lt W. G. Perrin,
2nd Lt. D. McOwen, 2nd Lt. A. L. Benns

BENT, Second Lieutenant, Percy Temple. Killed as he led his men, 1st July 1916. 12th Bn. attd. 1st Bn., King's Own Scottish Borderers. Aged 21. Son of Captain Percy Salisbury Bent, MC. Born Japan. Attended Marlborough College. Served as a private, No. 11168 in the South Wales Borderers, 1914-1915, in China. Took part in the fall of Tsing Tau. Entered theatre of war, 23rd September 1914. Gazetted in 1915. Memorial Ref. Pier and Face 4 A and 4 D., Thiepval Memorial, France.

BERNARD, Colonel, Herbert Clifford. At 7:10am, as the battalion reached the position known as 'Ross Castle'. Killed in action at Thiepval Wood by a shell splinter whilst leading his men into the battle, he went forward with the Lewis guns and was seen near the German parapet instructing his men, 1st July 1916. Commanding 10th Bn., Royal Irish Rifles. Born at Cheltenham in 1865. Aged 50. Only surviving son of Robert Bernard, M.D., R.N., Deputy Inspector General of Hospitals and Fleets and Honorary Surgeon to the Queen, and Sarah Augusta Clifford. Educated at Llandovery School and at Derby Grammar School. He passed through RMC Sandhurst as Queen's cadet, was gazetted to the 67th (Hampshire) Regiment in 1884, joined the Indian Army and served in Burma when he joined Rattray's (45th Sikhs) as second in command. He commanded this regiment from 1909 to 1914. His war service included the Burmese Expedition (1885-89), Manipur Expedition (1891), Burmese War (1889-92), and the Chinuk Expedition (1901). On the outbreak of war he was given command of a battalion of the Royal Irish Rifles. He was well respected by all the officers, NCO's and other ranks whom he commanded and his death, being witnessed by many of the men as they followed his lead, came as an overwhelming blow. Rifleman James Smyth, who was alongside his Colonel when he died, told of how the Colonel was leading his platoon, his Webley pistol drawn, when the fateful shell-burst decapitated Bernard. The momentum of his charge propelled him forward for a number of yards, giving the impression to his men that although fatally wounded, he was still advancing. Colonel Bernard may have survived the Somme offensive had he obeyed orders, and remained with Battalion Headquarters in the rear echelon. He chose to lead the Belfast men the way he had led his native Indian Regiment – from the front. As a result, he paid the ultimate sacrifice, along with many of the men he led. Of his death, his close friend Lieutenant Colonel Crozier (author of 'A Brass Hat in No Man's Land') wrote "the adjutant of the 10th tells me Colonel Bernard is no more. The Colonel and half his men walked into a barrage of death during the advance. All died behind him as he resolutely faced the edge of the wood in an impossible effort to walk through a wall of raining iron and lead, which had lifted for us that brief five minutes." Brass plaque, at Saint Bridget's Parish church, Bridstow. His sister, L. M. Davies applied for his medals and decided his inscription. Memorial Ref. I. A. 16., Martinsart British Cemetery, France.

Miles Generosus Comitate Fidelitate, Virtute Pariter Iusiguis

BEVES, Captain, Trevor Howard, MC. Went over the top from the support line, and over the first line, the bridges over the front trench having being ranged by the German machine-gunners the day previously meet with heavy losses, while crossing these bridges and passing the lanes out in the wire, killed, 1st July 1916. 1st Bn., Border Regiment. Aged 25. Son of Lieutenant Colonel Edward Leslie and Clare Beves, of Brighton. Educated Wellington College (Talbot House 1905 – 1909) and whilst there was a prefect. In 1909 he went into the Infantry Company at RMA Woolwich. Gazetted to the Border Regiment October 1910. Lieutenant 1914, captain May 1915. Disembarked 5th October 1914. He was wounded at the first battle of Ypres in October 1914, gunshot wound to the left leg admitted 29th October 1914 and discharged 1st November 1914 and twice at the Battle of Neuve Chapelle in March 1915 when he was awarded the Military Cross for exceptional good work, 11th March 1915. Suffered gunshot wound to the nose, admitted to hospital, 4th August 1915 and discharged 6th September 1915, Queen Alexandra's Hospital, Millbank. He led his men with great ability in attack and was twice wounded. Major R. C. Mieklejohn wrote "the late Col. G. F. Broadrick who was his Company Commander absolutely swore by him, and I remember him telling me what an excellent officer he considered your son to be in, even in the early days. He was always considered to have won the VC at Neuve Chapelle." Father applied for his medals and decided his inscription. Memorial Ref. II. C. 2., Auchonvillers Military Cemetery, France.

Faithful Unto Death

BIBLE, Second Lieutenant, Geoffrey Roskell. Killed whilst gallantly leading his section forward, 1st July 1916. 101st Coy., Machine Gun Corps (Infantry). Aged 23. Son of Henry Bible, of 50, Grosvenor Road, Rathmines, Co. Dublin, and Lucinda Bible. Enlisted September, 1914 with 7th Bn. Royal Dublin Fusiliers, 15852. Entered France, 20th April 1916. Lieutenant Bible was attached to the machine-gun company of the Royal Sussex Regiment, and the gallant conduct of the machine-gun corps earned a special tribute of admiration from the Brigadier-General. Memorial Ref. Pier and Face 5 C and 12 C., Thiepval Memorial, France.

BICKERSTETH, Lieutenant, Stanley Morris. In May 1916 he received command of a company while still a subaltern, and it fell to him to lead his men in the attack against Serre, he was killed with his captain, 1st July 1916. Stanley went over the parapet with the last wave, but did not get more than thirty yards before he was killed by a high-explosive shell. His last words before going over were 'Come on, lads! Here's to a short life and a gay one', after going over his platoon was mixed with the wounded and the dead of the prior platoons, he gave the order to lie down. Private Beatson provided the details as he was wounded and asked the lieutenant to sign a 'chit' so he could return to the line for treatment, just after signing he looked around to see if any support was coming from the trenches when a shrapnel bullet struck him in the back of his head and he was struck again by another bullet that exited his forehead. Beatson confirmed he was killed and stayed with the officer for five minutes. Commanding, B Coy. 15th Bn., West Yorkshire Regiment (Prince of Wales's Own). Born 1st June 1891 at The Vicarage, Belvedere, Kent. Aged 25. Fifth son of the Reverend Samuel Bickersteth, D.D., Vicar of Leeds (afterwards Canon of Canterbury), Chaplain to The King, and of Ella, his wife, daughter of Sir Monier Monier-Williams, KCIE. He was grandson of Edward Henry, Bishop of Exeter, and of Sir Monier Monier-Williams, KCIE, DCL, Boden Professor of Sanscrit in the University of Oxford. Educated at St David's, Reigate and Rugby. After studying in Germany for six months, he went up to Christ Church, Oxford, and took his degree in February, 1914. When the war broke out, he was in Bulawayo, South Africa, on his way home from a visit to Australia. He returned at once to England, and in September, 1914, was gazetted lieutenant.

In December, 1915, he proceeded with his battalion to Egypt, where they spent three months strengthening the defence of the canal. In February, 1916, his regiment was ordered to France. Commemorated Sons and Daughters of the Anglican Church Clergy. He left a letter with his brother to be opened in the event of his death, to his Mother and Father. ' I just wanted to tell you that I do not fear death except in so far as everyone must fear it, viz, undergoing some experience which one has never had before….Don't forget that I shall be loving you both at the moment that you are reading this, just as dearly as I do now while writing it. Ever your own loving son, S Morris Bickersteth. He met with his brothers on June 29th, Julian and Burgon at the Front. Memorial Ref. E. 19., Queens Cemetery, Puisieux, France.

Fifth Son Of Dr. Bickersteth Vicar Of Leeds & Ella His Wife "Content"

BINNS, Second Lieutenant, Clement Stanley. Reported as missing believed, killed, 1st July 1916. Reported to have either been shot by the German first line or killed by a shell with four or five other men. Prisoner of war reported he was last seen in the German third line. 20th (Tyneside Scottish) Bn., Northumberland Fusiliers. Resided Fern Bank, Dore. Youngest son of George Binns of Sheffield and a member of the firm, Newson and Binns, Solicitors, Cambridge Street. Born 5th October 1884. Married to Ruth Victoria Binns on the 14th May 1914 and had two children; George and Lorraine. Served with the Sheffield Volunteer Defence Corps. Mrs. R. V. Binns makes appeal for medals in respect of the services of the late Second Lieutenant Binns on the 15th December 1919 of Albourne, 8 Blackwater Road, Eastbourne. Wife applied for his medals and received his pension from 2nd July 1916. Memorial Ref. Pier and Face 10 B 11 B and 12 B., Thiepval Memorial, France. WO 339/5248

BLACKBURN, Captain, Geoffrey Gaskell. Killed whilst leading his men into action, 1st July 1916. 10th Bn., West Yorkshire Regiment (Prince of Wales's Own). Aged 27. Second son of Henry Gaskell Blackburn, F.C.A., and Elizabeth Blackburn, of Bank House, Horsforth, Leeds. Attended Harrow where he shot in the Eight at Bisley and Trinity Hall, Cambridge. B.A. Trinity Hall, Cambridge, 1910. Member of the firm H. W. and J. Blackburn, Accountants, Leeds and was a brother of Flight Lieutenant Vivian Gaskell Blackburn. He joined the West Yorkshires at the beginning of the war. Entered France, 12th July 1915. Talbot House visitors book, page 39, dated 11th February 1916. Father applied for medals. Memorial Ref. C. 14., Fricourt New Military Cemetery, France. WO 339/13171

BLACKWELL, Second Lieutenant, Cyril. Killed in action, one of the sacrifices in the great thrust forward, 1st July 1916. 16th Bn., attd 2nd Bn., Royal Fusiliers. Aged 33. Son of John Blackwell (Bengal & North Western Railways, Bengal, India) and Marion Whelan Blackwell, of Fairfield House, North Avenue, Salisbury, Rhodesia. Born Goa, India Marmagoa. Bedford Modern School. Before going to Rhodesia, Lieutenant Blackwell had passed the entrance examination for RMC Sandhurst. He had been in the Civil Service of Rhodesia since 1901 and had experience in four different departments. When he left he was Native Commissioner at Bikita, in the N'Danga district. He was one of an eager band of Rhodesians determined to serve their country. Members of the Currie Cup football team in 1906 with his friend, Hadge Almond. Served in Dardanelles and Egypt from 4th December 1915. Second Lieutenant Henry Tristram Blackwell, 3rd Bn., Gordon Highlanders attd 54th Machine Gun Coy died 31st March 1916. Mother applied for his medals from Rhodesia. Memorial Ref. Pier and Face 8 C 9 A and 16 A., Thiepval Memorial, France.

BLACKWOOD, Second Lieutenant, Miles Harry. Majority of the casualties especially those of the officers occurred during the first two hours of fighting, killed while gallantly leading his men, Beaumont Hamel, 1st July 1916. 2nd Bn., Seaforth Highlanders. Aged 19. Only son of Captain Harry Officer and Isla Jessie Blackwood, of Kincurdie, Rosemarkie, Ross-Shire and Arthur's St. James's, London. A grandson of Mr. MacKenzie of Farr and a nephew of Mrs. Davidson of Tulloch. Educated Stone House, Broadstairs and Harrow. Represented the school in boxing. Straight from school, joined the Special Reserve of the 5th Bn., Royal Fusiliers in September, 1914, after serving with them at Dover he went to RMC Sandhurst in February of the following year. He obtained a commission in the 2nd Bn.,Seaforth Highlanders in July, 1915 with whom he served at Nigg and Cromarty He went to the Western Front in June, 1916. Body was side by sided in a large British cemetery, 200 yards northwest of the Sucrerie. 'A most promising and very popular young officer, to all of whom, as well as his many friends, his death will come as a severe blow'. Memorial Ref. I. H. 21., Sucrerie Military Cemetery, Colincamps, France.

Son of Isla And Harry Blackwood For Ever With The Lord

BLAKE, Captain, Francis Seymour. Killed in action near Y Ravine, 1st July 1916. Reported missing believed killed attached C Coy., 2nd Bn., South Wales Borderers, 15th Bn., The King's (Liverpool Regiment). Aged 38. Son of Mr. Blake (stationery salesman). Husband of Florence Blake, of 31, Newstead Road, Lee, London. Attended Wilson's Grammar School, Surrey as did his brother, two of the 120 old boys killed in the Great War. Member of the Faculty of Actuaries and Institute of Actuaries 1906. Before the war he had worked in the Comptroller's Department, London County Council. He had been in the 15/Londons, No.398 commissioned from sergeant into the Liverpools, was promoted to captain in the Liverpools, and transferred to 2nd Bn., South Wales Borderers in time to take part in the Helles Landings. Entered Gallipoli, 11th August 1915. Brother of Captain Charles Stanley Blake, 10th Bn., South Lancs (attd. 6th Bn) who was killed in action on 7th August 1915. Both men therefore fought at Gallipoli. Widow, Florence applied for his medals and posted to Avondale Road, Nottingham. His wife and children, Alan, Gwedoline and Sybil received his pension from the 24th October 1916 when his death was accepted for official purposes. The pay was back dated to the 2nd July 1916 and payable to his daughters until they were 21 and until his son was 18. Memorial Ref. Pier and Face 1 D 8 B and 8 C., Thiepval Memorial, France.

BLAND, Captain, Alfred Edward. Killed instantaneously by machine-gun fire from Dantzig Alley, gallantly leading his men, 1st July 1916. A Coy formerly B Coy., 22nd Bn., Manchester Regiment. Born 5th March 1881 in Kidderminster, Worcestershire to Alice M. and Joseph Bland he was their third son. Age 35. Went from Kidderminster Grammar School to Christ's Hospital and thence to Queen's College, Oxford where he obtained high Honours. Married Violet Amy Ellis in 1905. Two children, Lawrence Millward Bland born in 1911 and Christopher Bland born in 1909. Lived in Knoll Road, Bexley. He joined the Civil Service and was at the Public Records Office when war broke out. Published economic history textbooks. Entered France, 11th November 1915. Just before going over, Captain Bland borrowed a watch from Sergeant R. H. Tawney, and that was the last the sergeant saw of his captain. The local newspaper reported that his wife, Violet, had been told that "he died instantaneously and was reverently buried amid the grief of his fellow officers and men… His loss is irreparable to his wife and family." Reburied 1920, originally burial map reference F.5.d.4.2. Widow applied for his medals. Commemorated London Borough of Bexley. Memorial Ref. IX. B. 6., Dantzig Alley British Cemetery, Mametz, France. WO 339/19222

Includes Bland, Mellor, Gomersall. Taken at Heaton Park 1915.

BLATHERWICK, Second Lieutenant, Robert Hugh. Killed near Fricourt village, 1st July 1916. 10th Bn., West Yorkshire Regiment (Prince of Wales's Own). Aged 22. Youngest son of George Harry and Mary Ellen Blatherwick, of Cropwell Road, Radcliffe-on-Trent. Born 11th April 1891. He attended Mundella Preparatory School, Nottingham from January 1906 to August 1908. Nottingham. University College. Nottingham OTC. Quantity surveyors pupil, learning to be an architect and surveyor. Student in father's office. Enlisted 14th July 1915. Entered France, May 21st 1916. His brother, Private George Henry Blatherwick also fell on the 8th May 1915. Both were Freemasons. Father applied for their medals. Original grave reference Fricourt Row B. Grave 4. Memorial Ref. C. 5., Fricourt New Military Cemetery, France. WO 339/38240

BOAS, Second Lieutenant, Ernest George. Reported to have been hit by hand grenades and last seen lying in a communication trench between the 2nd and 3rd trenches, 1st July 1916. 5th Bn. attd. 13th Bn., Royal Irish Rifles. Born 14th June 1897. Aged 19. Only son of May L. Boas, and Ernest A. Boas of 31, Sans Souci Park, Belfast, and 7 College Gardens, Belfast. Educated at Belfast Royal Academical Institution, Campbell College, Belfast, and Clifton College, Bristol. At these schools he was a member of the OTC, and later on of the Queen's University, Belfast OTC, whence he obtained his commission in the Special Reserve of Officers in June, 1915. Worked in his father's linen business, the Loopbridge weaving factory, Belfast, when he enlisted. He joined the 5th Royal Irish Rifles and was sent to the front in May, 1916, where he was attached to another battalion of the same regiment. Only at the Front three weeks when the offensive began. Medals went to his father. Commemorated First Presbyterian Church, Belfast and the Belfast Academical Institution also Queen's University, Belfast. As his father was secretary of the Ulster Hospital, Ernest also has a plaque located at the hospital. Memorial Ref. Pier and Face 15 A and 15 B., Thiepval Memorial, France.

BOBBY, Second Lieutenant, Sidney Fitzgerald. Reported killed in command of a light trench mortar battery, at 8.26am when Bleneau Sap (Sap A) was blown in by a shell and the guns were put out of action, 1st July 1916. In this action he was replaced by Second Lieutenant Prickett. 18th Bn., Durham Light Infantry attd. 93rd Trench Mortar Battery. Aged 22. Son of William Thomas and Elizabeth Bobby, of 7, Wellesley Road, Leytonstone, London. Educated Davies Lane School, Leyton. Joined the Civil Service in 1910 as a boy clerk. Formerly private, 132, 1st Bn., Honourable Artillery Company. Disembarked 20th September 1914. Temporary second lieutenant April 25th 1915. Commemorated London Joint City and Midland Bank, Canary Wharf. Father made application for his medals, c/o Ide & Christie, Product Brokers, East Finchley. Memorial Ref. Pier and Face 14 A and 15 C., Thiepval Memorial, France.

BOLTON, Captain, Henry Albert. Missing, believed, killed 1st July 1916. Private William Dodds reported to his father in an interview at hospital that he was killed by a shell in advance of Albert on 1st July. Private Dixon also seen him fall but couldn't stop as they had orders to go on. 23rd (Tyneside Scottish) Bn., Northumberland Fusiliers. Aged 22. Son of Charles Augustus and Clara Bolton, of 69, New River Crescent, Palmer's Green, London formerly Manor House Road, Jesmond, Newcastle. Born 21st January 1893. Employed actuarial department of the Commercial Union Assurance Company before the war in the Fund Department at the head office of the Liverpool Victoria Life. Appointed sergeant with the 18th Bn., Northumberland Fusiliers, 7th December 1914. Commissioned with the 23rd Bn., 15th December 1914. Entered France, 9th January 1916. His brother, Charles made an enquiry into his personal effects; bayonet, compass, watch, revolver and binoculars. Concern was expressed the revolver was an item in his will and the binoculars made by Hunt of Scarborough & Hull were lent by his sister-in-law, value £6. A chaplain reported he was buried with Captain Joseph Berkeley Cubey also killed 1st July 1916. The Adjutant replied that the battalion moved away on the 4th July and the bodies were buried between the 8th and 10th and no effects were recovered. There are unknown soldiers of the 23rd Bn., buried in Ovillers Military Cemetery. Medals to his father. Memorial Ref. Pier and Face 10 B 11 B and 12 B., Thiepval Memorial, France. WO 339/17244

BOLTON, Lieutenant, William Curtis, MC. 1st July 1916. 8th Bn., York and Lancaster Regiment. Aged 26. Oldest son of William Henry and Emily Bolton, of Lidgett House, Edwinstowe, Notts formerly 52, Westgate, Mansfield. Born Norwich. A student with The Society of the Sacred Mission at Kelham Theological College, Newark training for the priesthood attended for two years. Previously had been a draper's assistant for Messrs. Cook's in London. Member of St Peter's Men's Class and Choir. Agreed with his fellow students to enlist with the men as a private in the 8th Sherwood Foresters, 16278 and not accept a commission and promoted through the ranks. Temporary second lieutenant gazetted 4th June 1915. Went to France, 27th August 1915. Military Cross gazetted March 1916; 'Carried out a piece of scouting work when he led a reconnoitering patrol under the enemy's wire to obtain information. He was subjected to machine-gun fire and one of his men was wounded and bought back in. His commanding officer described as a fine performance'. Medals to his father. Memorial Ref. Pier and Face 14 A and 14 B., Thiepval Memorial, France.

BONCKER, Second Lieutenant, Barry Robert. Fell at Fricourt, shortly after going over, 1st July 1916. 9th Bn., attd, 1st Bn., East Yorkshire Regiment. Born at 23 Farquhar Road, Upper Norwood, Croydon on the 26th August, 1897 also recorded as born Pretoria, South Africa 24th June 1896 as his mother had come to England when he was one or two years of age. Aged 19. Son of Frederic and Violet Boncker, of 35, Whitworth Road, South Norwood, London. Educated Ardingley College, Hayward's Heath and a member of the OTC. Clerk, National Bank of South Africa. Resided 12 Upper Grove, South Norwood. Enlisted 1st September 1914 as a private, No. 2314, 4th Bn., Royal West Surrey Regiment. Served in India. Commissioned 16th November 1915 and went to France, 15th June 1916. His wallet (letters and four photos), identity disc, cheque book, ring and a stamp were returned to his mother. Army ruled his mother was not dependent on his pension. Originally buried 1000 yards NW of Fricourt. Medals to his mother. Memorial Ref. Pier and Face 2 C., Thiepval Memorial, France. WO 339/47635

BONHAM-CARTER, Captain, Arthur Thomas. Killed whilst company commander near Beaumont Hamel. As soon as the troops left the front line, heavy machine-gun fire was brought to bear on them from all directions, casualties of officers amounted to 100%. Killed Beaumont Hamel, 1st July 1916. 3rd Bn. attd. 1st Bn., Hampshire Regiment. Born May 24th, 1869, in London. Third son of John Bonham-Carter M.P. J.P. D.L. (Fellow of Winchester College, 1901 to 1906), of Adhurst St. Mary, Petersfield, and his second wife, the Hon. Mary Baring, daughter of Lord Northbrook of 17, Chesham Street, London. Educated St George's Preparatory School, Ascot & Winchester College onto Trinity College, Cambridge, admitted as pensioner at Trinity, May 30th 1887. Taking his BA degree in 1890. Called to the Bar in 1894. Obtained a commission in the 1st Volunteer Company of the Hampshire Regiment on the outbreak of the South African War and held various judicial appointments in the Transvaal and British East Africa to 1914. When war broke he organised a defence force and was Director of Military Supplies, Mombasa Town Guard. Commissioned 22nd July 1915. Returning to England posted to the 1st Battalion, Hampshire Regiment going to France on February 8th 1916. Cousin Guy Bonham-Carter was killed in action on 14th May 1915. Medals to Mrs. Lubbock, St. Mary, Petersfield. Originally buried at map reference 57d.Q.5.a.08.25 as an unknown British officer and in 1927 reinterned identified by uniform, buttons and boots. Memorial Ref. XVI. D. 13., Serre Road Cemetery No.2, France.

BOOTE, Lieutenant Colonel, Charles Edmund. "A good officer and a very gallant gentleman", killed 1st July 1916 as was his adjutant, Lieutenant Robert Ramsay Stuart Shaw. Private B. Morris received a hand to get out of the trench by Lieutenant Colonel Boote and him and Second Lieutenant Ewers disappeared in to the smoke as one of the leading waves. The Lieutenant Colonel was not seen again. Second Lieutenant Ewers survived the war. 5th Bn., North Staffordshire Regiment killed with the 1st/6th. Aged 41. Youngest of three sons of Richard and Sarah Anne Boote, of Shallowford, Staffs. Attended Shrewsbury School, from 1887, he left in 1891 and in 1892 he joined up and after promotion served in South Africa (Hon. Captain) with the Volunteer Service Co. and awarded the South African Medal. Later became Managing Director of his family firm. Husband of Gertrude Ethel Boote, of 62, St. Michael's Road, Bedford. He went to France, 15th May 1915 as Major, 5th North Staffords and was promoted to command. Suffered from influenza in October 1915 and was released from hospital after three days. His widow applied for his medals, although his rank had to be re-engraved in 1923. Three children received gratuity payment, Mollie, Isabel and Charles. Originally map reference for burial 57d.E.28.a.5.0 and late reburied in Gommecourt Wood, original grave was marked with a cross. Memorial Ref. II. B. 12., Gommecourt Wood New Cemetery, Foncquevillers, France.

BOOTH, Lieutenant, Harold Stanley. Died 1st July 1916. 11th Bn. attd. 8th Bn., York and Lancaster Regiment. Previously corporal, West Yorkshire Regiment. Entered France on the 29th May 1916. Medal application by Mrs. Martha Booth, 41 Shipley Fields Road, near Bradford. Pension paid to Martha for Harold but also Second Lieutenant Herbert Booth killed 3rd May 1917 with the West Yorkshire Regiment. Memorial Ref. Addenda Panel, Pier and Face 4 C., Thiepval Memorial, France.

BOOTH, Second Lieutenant, Major William. Fighting was hard and shelling heavy, machine-gun fire was intense, killed in action 1st July 1916 near La Cigny, France. Another cricketer, Abraham 'Abe' Waddington was wounded by shrapnel and took shelter in a crater with Second Lieutenant Booth whom would die in his arms. Private Fleming was tending to a wounded soldier when Major Booth came up behind him and said "what are you doing? Come on it doesn't matter about him onward you go, come on, get hold." Fleming's account states "there was two shell holes open, one was on the right, in the wire, and one was on the left. He made for one shell hole and I made for another and there was a shell burst." D Coy., 15th Bn., West Yorkshire Regiment (Prince of Wales's Own). Born 10th December 1886, Pudsey, Yorkshire. Aged 29. Son of James and Louise Booth, of Town End House, Pudsey, Yorks. Educated Fulneck and played his early cricket with Pudsey St Lawrence. He moved to Wath, South Yorkshire Cricket Club in the winter of 1908/09 when work took him to a local colliery in South Yorkshire. By then he had already represented Yorkshire at first-class level although it took him a further two years to cement a regular place. His batting first grabbed the headlines in 1911 with a double century at Worcester. He returned home from a MCC tour of South Africa to find himself selected as one of Wisden's five cricketers of the year in the 1914 edition. Professional cricketer - played for Yorkshire. A fine punishing batsman. Booth was also a tall medium fast bowler who was in his prime as a cricketer. After joining up, No. 136, alongside his fellow Yorkshire colleagues Dolphin and Roy Kilner he had been commissioned as a second lieutenant and first served in Egypt, 22nd December 1915 before being assigned to the Western Front. Second Lieutenant Booth having Yorkshire's proud President Lord Hawke summed up the county's loss: "England lost one of the most promising and charming young cricketers it was ever my lot to meet." Second Lieutenant's Booth body lay on the battlefield until it was recovered in Spring, 1917. Medals applied for by his brother, J. C. Booth who also specified his headstone inscription. Memorial Ref. I. G. 14., Serre Road Cemetery No.1, France.

In Proud & Loving Memory Of Our Dear Brother

Three Yorkshire County Cricketers. Second Lieutenant Booth (middle) later promoted,
Corporal Roy Kilner injured and Private A. Dolphin

BOOTH, Second Lieutenant, Percival Edward Owen. In command of a machine-gun detachment, commanded No. 11 and 10 gun teams killed in action, Albert, 1st July, 1916 before the front line trench. 93rd Machine Gun Company, attd from 14th Bn., Middlesex Regiment. Born 8th April, 1892, at Cricklewood, Middlesex. Aged 24. Son of Walter Scott (railway accountant) and Ruth Booth, of 7, Haslemere Road, Winchmore Hill, London. Educated at The Haberdashers' Hampstead School, The Enfield Grammar School, and matriculated at London University. Entered the service of the Commercial Bank of Canada, 3rd February, 1913. Enlisted, 18th November, 1914, from London, in King's Royal Rifle Corps, with the rank of rifleman. Transferred to 14th Middlesex Regiment, attached to Machine Gun Corps. Promoted second lieutenant, 16th March, 1915. Father applied for medals and specified headstone inscription. Memorial Ref. I. B. 2., Euston Road Cemetery, Colincamps, France.

Faithful Unto Death

BOSANQUET, Brevet Major, Graham Bromhead, MC. About 300 yards from the sunken road, Major Bosanquet went over the open ground towards Crucifix Trench unfortunately a German machine-gun was brought into action at this moment, Graham and several men were hit. Killed on the Fricourt-Contalmasion Road leading the advance of the 64th Brigade, 1st July 1916 as Brigade Major. 1st Bn., Gloucestershire Regiment. Born 17th November 1885 in Liandinabo, Herefordshire. Aged 30. Chevalier of the Legion of Honour. Only son of Admiral Sir Day Bosanquet, GCVO, KCB Governor of South Australia and Mary Butthe. 23rd February, 1910 married Flora MacDonald Lindsay Stewart in the Parish Church of Brompton, London. February 1905 he was promoted second lieutenant in 3rd Bn., Suffolk Regiment. Joined the Gloucesters on 30th October 1914 joining the regiment at Zillebeke on the 7th November 1914. On the 21st December 1914, as a captain, his battalion reached Bethune and were ordered to re-take the trenches at Festubert where he was wounded along with five other officers. He returned to the regiment on 27th March 1915 at Neuve Chapelle. On the 9th May 1915 Graham was wounded a second time in the area of Rue du Bois. Gazetted June 1915 as having been Mentioned In Despatches and having received the Military Cross. Rejoined his regiment on the 18th August 1915. November 1915 awarded the Legion of Honour 'Croix de Chevalier' after having taken part of the Battle of Loos along with French troops. Promoted to Brevet Major 21st April 1916. Commemorated on Llanwarne War Memorial. Twice Mentioned in Despatches. Originally buried north of Fricourt, map reference, 57d.22.d.3.3, reinterred 1919. His father applied for his medals on behalf of his widow and decided his headstone inscription. Memorial Ref. IV. H. 10., Gordon Dump Cemetery, Ovillers-La Boisselle, France. WO 339/6698

The Lord Your God Hath Given You Rest Joshua 1.13

BOSWELL, Second Lieutenant, Percy George. Over half of the second wave of the attack was cut down as they crossed the 320 metres of No Man's Land. 1st July 1916. 8th Bn, King's Own Yorkshire Light Infantry. Aged 22. Son of Lewis Charles and Caroline Boswell, of 26, Norfolk House Road, Streatham, London. Attended Alleyn's School, Dulwich. Banker's clerk. Enlisted 3rd September, 1914 as No. 421, London Rifles. Entered France, 6th June 1915. Promoted temporary lieutenant 3rd October 1915. Effects returned were letters, note book, cheque book, photos and some clothes. His father wrote to the War Office enquiring to the whereabouts of his field glasses, shaving mirror, watch, two revolvers, flask, cigarette case, pocket knife, fountain pen and compass. Father applied for his medals. Memorial Ref. Pier and Face 11 C and 12 A., Thiepval Memorial, France. WO 339/44267

30.06.16 BEF

Dear Father

I am just writing you a short note which you will receive only if anything has happened to me during the next few days. The Hun is going to get consummate hell just in this quarter and we are going over the parapet tomorrow when I hope to spend many hours in chasing the Boche all over the place. I am absolutely certain that I shall get through all right, but in case the unexpected does happen I shall rest content with the knowledge that I have done my duty – and one can't do more.

Good Bye with the Best of Love to you all from

Percy

BOVILL, Second Lieutenant, Edward Henry. On the 1st July he was wounded in the nose the moment he got out of our trenches in the early morning, but continued to lead his men the whole day and was one of the last, if not the last, to leave the German trenches, out of which they were forced by sheer weight of numbers. His regiment was cut to pieces, and he was shot dead, he was killed on the parapet of our own trench, and was seen firing his revolver and throwing bombs, 1st July 1916. By 8.20pm the officers consisting of Captain Somers-Smith, (London Regiment), Lieutenant Petley, (London Rifle Brigade), Captain Leys Cox (Queen Victorias Rifles), Second Lieutenant Arthur, (Cheshire Regiment), Captain Harvey (London Rifle Brigade) and Second Lieutenant Bovill (Queens Westminster Rifles) admitted they would be forced to return to the British lines and provided covering fire for the men. Making a run for the nearest shell holes, the only officer who returned was Lieutenant Petley, five officers being killed. Edward was the last of the five to be killed. A Coy., 1st/16th Bn., London Regiment (Queen's Westminster Rifles). Born 13th April 1887. Aged 29. Elder and only surviving son of John Henry Bovill, and of Mary Constance Bovill, of Buckland, Betchworth,

Surrey. Attended Summer Fields, Oxford, Harrow & Pembroke College, Cambridge, BA, 1910 and afterwards in business. He had been at the Front with his regiment since 4th February 1916. His younger brother, Second Lieutenant Edward Bovill, was killed in France on the 23rd January 1916 and his cousin, Captain, Olaf Ranson Cuthbert also killed on the 1st July. Father applied for his medals. Memorial Ref. Pier and Face 13 C., Thiepval Memorial, France.

BOWEN, Lieutenant, Francis Moull Storer. Reported missing, 1st July 1916. 9th Bn., Queen's Own (Royal West Kent Regiment) attd 1st Bn., Royal Inniskilling Fusiliers. Aged 32. Second son of Henry Storer Bowen and Beatrice Bowen, of Littlebourne, Canterbury. Matriculated June 1900 from Brentwood Grammar School. Undergraduate London University. Called to the Bar, 1908 by Gray's Inn. Schoolmaster and assisted at Rempton School, Broadstairs. Entered France 28th February 1916. Received his commission originally in the Royal West Kent Regiment but had been serving with the Royal Inniskilling Fusiliers since the beginning of March 1916. Commemorated Gray's Inn Memorial and Littlebourne, Kent. Original map reference where body found 57d.Q.18.a, his grave was marked with a cross and he was buried in this location with nine other soldiers. Mother applied for his medals and stated his headstone inscription. Memorial Ref. VII. D. 44., Ancre British Cemetery, Beaumont-Hamel, France.

I Look For The Resurrection Of The Dead

BOWES, Second Lieutenant, Cyril Hulme. Killed with No. 4 Coy., 1st July 1916. 2nd Bn., Duke of Wellington's (West Riding Regiment). Aged 24. Only child of George Henry Poynter (teacher) and Lilian Bowes. Educated Wolverhampton and Bradford Grammar School. Returned from business in Paris to enlist in the 9th Bn., West Riding Regiment as a private, 13204. Entered France, 15th July 1915 and was promoted in France, 12th March 1916. Body identified in May 1917 and buried. Memorial Ref. II. B. 15., Serre Road Cemetery No.2, France.

BOWYER, Second Lieutenant, George Henry. Reported missing, killed at Beaumont Hamel, 1st July 1916. 2nd Bn., South Wales Borderers attd 87th Machine Gun Coy. Born 16th August 1890. Aged 26. Son of W. S. Bowyer, of "Heathcote", 36, Christchurch Road, Streatham Hill, London. Dulwich College 1903 -1907. On leaving school went into father's business. Joined the Honourable Artillery Company in 1909. Mobilized, August, 1914, proceeded to Egypt, 8th April, 1915. After actively serving 15 months with the Honourable Artillery Company, No. 171, as shoeing smith, he joined the School of Instruction, Zeitoun in November 1915. Gazetted 5th December, 1915 with the 2nd Bn., South Wales Borderers. Went to France, February 1916. Served in the machine-gun section. Father applied for his medals. Memorial Ref. Pier and Face 4 A., Thiepval Memorial, France.

BOYD, Captain, George Vallance McKinlay. Killed leading a charge at the head of his company, 1st July 1916. B Coy., 17th Bn., Highland Light Infantry. Born May 1880. Aged 36. Son of George Vallance Boyd and Helen Landale Symington Boyd, of Landale, Troon, Ayrshire. Educated Loretto School, (1896 to 1898). Partner in the firm, Boyd and Dunn, Stockbrokers, 86 St. Vincent Street, Glasgow. Fine golfer, member Royal and Ancient, Troon and Prestwick Clubs. 1912 won the South of Ireland championship. Granted a commission with B Coy., on its formation. Death reported 11th July 1916. Memorial Ref. Pier and Face 15 C., Thiepval Memorial, France.

BRADFORD, Second Lieutenant, Frederick Reith Campbell. At 7:30 am on 1st July attacked the German lines near Gommecourt, designed as diversionary manoeuvre to draw German troops away from the main attack. Battalion was responsible for new trench construction and supplying the front-line trenches. C Coy., 1st /4th Bn., London Regiment (Royal Fusiliers). Born 21st July 1896. Aged 19. Eldest son of Archibald Campbell Bradford and Clara Sophia Bradford, of "Alverstoke", 68, Derby Road, Woodford, Essex. Attended Bancroft's School as a day boy between 1906 and 1908 living at 68 Derby Road, South Woodford and later at St. Saviour's School, Ardingly where he was in the OTC. He took up a position in the London County & Westminster Bank. Enlisted September 1914 in the 4th Bn., Royal Fusiliers, No. 2924. By 15th October he had been promoted corporal, then acting sergeant in January 1915, being commissioned second lieutenant aged 18 in the same month. Initially deployed to Malta, saw service in Egypt and Gallipoli in January 1915 moved to the Western

Front. Arrived on the front line near Hebuterne on the 7th May 1916. Commemorated in Chingford Mount Cemetery. Father applied for medals. Memorial Ref. Pier and Face 9 D and 16 B., Thiepval Memorial, France.

BRADSHAW, Lieutenant, Richard Edward Kynaston. Originally posted as missing, 1st July 1916. A Coy., 1st /12th Bn., London Regiment (The Rangers). Born April 9th, 1895, at Parndon Hall, Essex. Aged 21. Son of William Graham Bradshaw and Dora Sophia Bradshaw, of Down Park, Crawley Down, Sussex. Educated Copthorne Preparatory School, Warre House School, Eton College. Admitted at Trinity College, Cambridge, June 25th 1914. Member of the OTC. Entered France, 20th September 1915. Father applied for his medals. Commemorated Copthorne School, Sussex. In view of the lapse of time death assumed to be 1st July 1916, dated 25th April 1917. Memorial Ref. Pier and Face 9 C., Thiepval Memorial, France.

BRAITHWAITE, Lieutenant, Valentine Ashworth, MC. Reported to have fallen at Serre on 1st July 1916, while in command of one of the leading platoons of the 11th Infantry Brigade. He and seventeen other officers were all shot as they left their trench. Date of death officially 2nd July 1916, battalion history states 1st July 1916. 1st Bn., Somerset Light Infantry. Aged 20. Son of Gen. Sir Walter Pipon Braithwaite, KCB, ADC, and Lady Braithwaite, of 35, Sloane Gardens, Westminster, London. Attended Winchester College, 1910 to 1912 from Wyford School, rowed at Winchester and a good racquets player. After leaving school he worked for a year for an insurance company, then applied to enter RMC Sandhurst obtaining his commission in the 1st Bn., Somerset Light Infantry in August 1914 and went to France the following month, 26th September 1914 seeing action almost immediately at Le Ghers after which he received the Military Cross for gallant conduct and "for services rendered in connection with Operations in the Field" for defending a barricade during a sustained attack. He was also Mentioned in Despatches. Shortly after this he became ill with influenza and was not fit again until the end of November. On Boxing Day 1914 he reported to the regimental surgeon with swollen feet and numb toes. He was suffering from frostbite and given ten days sick leave. Although he saw several medical boards he was away from his regiment for the next three months. Soon after being declared fit again he went to the Dardanelles as ADC to his father, the Chief of the General Staff, and was again Mentioned in Despatches. In 1916 he resigned his appointment as ADC in order to rejoin his battalion in France. Suffered from German measles being treated at the 39th Casualty Clearing Station Hospital and returned to duty, 5th June 1916. His father purchased land in France where they erected a cross in his memory at the approximate position where he was seen to fall. Father applied for medals to be sent to Army & Navy Club, Pall Mall, London. Memorial Ref. Pier and Face 2 A., Thiepval Memorial, France.

BRAMBLE, Second Lieutenant, Gerald Henry Joseph. As soon as the troops left the front line, heavy machine-gun fire was brought to bear on them from all directions, casualties if officers amounted to 100%. Killed at Beaumont Hamel, 1st July 1916. 3rd Bn. attd. 1st Bn., Hampshire Regiment. Aged 21. Son of John and Rose Bramble, of "Avon", Christchurch, Hants. Enlisted as a private in the Grenadier Guards, No. 18376, September, 1914. Gazetted 25th March 1915 and went to the Front, January 1916. Whilst his father was seeking accurate information on Gerald, his eldest son, Bombardier John Bramble belongings (identity disc, watch and ring) arrived in the post as he was killed on the 3rd July 1916, 109th Heavy Battery, 6th Artillery Brigade and is buried in Vlamertinghe Military Cemetery. Father applied for Gerald's and John's medals. Memorial Ref. Pier and Face 7 C and 7 B., Thiepval Memorial, France.

BRANCH, Second Lieutenant, Albert. Private Barclay, 9285 stated that Lieutenant Branch was shot dead by rifle fire, he rolled off the parapet into the German first line and a further report indicates this was about 8.45am, 1st July 1916. 4th Bn., Middlesex Regiment. Son of Albert and Elizabeth Branch of 118 Clarence Road, Lower Clacton formerly 119 Elderfield Road, Lower Clacton. Age 26. Employed as a leather dresser. Joined with the 5th Lancers on the 20th February 1908 and moved to the 12th Lancers, 17th February 1909. Served in India and Africa. Promoted lance corporal 16th February 1913, corporal 1st July 1914 and sergeant 10th April 1915, No 969 having had 7 years' service. Embarked for France, 16th August 1914. Awarded DCM for conspicuous gallantry on the 1st November 1914, Wytschaete when he went forward voluntarily and succeeded in killing eight of the enemy himself. On the 17th October near Houthem, he took control of a patrol after the officer had been killed and brought his men back under difficult circumstances. 16th October 1915 recommended for a commission by Lieutenant Colonel

Commanding 12th Lancers as 'exceedingly capable and reliable NCO' and granted commission 28th October 1915. Joined the Middlesex on the 16th November 1915. He was treated for sickness at 21 Casualty Clearing Station on the 31st May 1916 and returned to duty 12th June 1916. Initially buried at the angle of Empress Trench and a new communication trench sht 26. Sq D Contour 110. Reburied in a collective grave with eleven fellow officers of the 4th Bn., Middlesex whom were killed on the 1st July 1916. Father applied for his Mons Star, plaque and medals. Memorial Ref. IV. K., Gordon Dump Cemetery, Ovillers-La Boiselle, France. WO 339/47898

B Coy., 4th Bn., Middlesex Regiment photographed 26th June 1916
2nd Lt A.H. Winn-Sampson (killed 1st July 1916), 2nd Lt W. John Wood (killed 1st July 1916), 2nd Lt. A. A. Johnston (killed 2nd July 1916), 2nd Lt. A.F. C Paxton (killed 1st July 1916), Lt. D. Cutbush (killed 10th April 1917), Lt. H.M. Williams, 2nd Lt. A. Branch killed 1st July 1916, Captain O.R. F. Johnston Centre (killed 1st July 1916)

BRAND, Second Lieutenant, Geoffrey Jermyn. Met his death by artillery fire leading his men into action, 1st July 1916. General List attd 101st Trench Mortar Battery. Aged 22. Born Walsall in 1893. Youngest son of Suffolk-born Charles Skinner Brand (spelter manufacturer) and his Staffordshire-born wife, Annie. Resided Wayside, Dorridge and Ardindine, Troon, Scotland. Educated at Arden House School, Henley in Arden and at Rossall where he was a member of the OTC. On leaving school he entered the office of Messrs. George Smith & sons, Bothwell Street, Glasgow. Joined the 20th Bn., Royal Fusiliers as a private, 6139, in November 1914 before being commissioned as second lieutenant with the Royal Scots in September 1915, and then being transferred to the General List and attached to the 101st Trench Mortar Battery shortly after reaching France. Commemorated Arden House School Memorial and parent's grave. Father applied for medals. Memorial Ref. Pier and Face 4 C., Thiepval Memorial, France.

BREENE, Lieutenant, Thomas Frederick. Captain Burrill wrote that two men who were in the same section and survived the battle reported the young officer was shot through the heart whilst gallantly leading his men up to the German front line, 1st July 1916. 1st Bn., Royal Warwickshire Regiment attached 87th Machine Gun Corps. Born Belfast on 17th May 1888. Aged 28. Son of Thomas John (Custom and Excise Department) and Mary Breene, of 99, Fitzroy Avenue, Belfast. 1906, joined Northern Bank in Head Office. Transfers followed to Balbriggan (1908), Londonderry (1910) and Kingscourt (1911). Member of the Queen's University, Belfast, Training Corps. He obtained a commission in the Warwickshire Regiment in May 1915, theatre of war entered 20th November 1915 and had been serving at the Front some time with the South Wales Borderers. One brother Reverend R. S. Breene was a Chaplain to the Forces. Father applied for medals. Memorial Ref. Pier and Face 9 A 9 B and 10 B., Thiepval Memorial, France.

BROCKBANK, Captain, Charles Norman. Fell at the forefront of his men, twice wounded by machine-gun fire near Brick Lane Trench but continued to cheer his men on, shouting "go on – number one", killed about 7.30am, 1st July 1916. Wounded got up and then hit in the throat. 1 Coy., 18th Bn., The King's (Liverpool Regiment). Aged 32. Only child of Marion Annie Brockbank, of "Ulverscroft," 19, Adelaide Terrace, Waterloo, Liverpool, and Robert Henry Brockbank. Born 14th September 1884. Educated Merchant Taylors' School, 1894 to 1898, and then to Malvern College, 1899 - 1901. Travelled to Canada and the USA, he came home to enter on a commercial career, and it was two years afterwards that he went out to India for Messrs. Forbes, Forbes Campbell & Co., a London firm of East India merchants at Karachi. Coming back again after five years, (1906 – 1911) he became a partner in his father's firm, Messrs. William Porter & Co., general brokers of African produce in Liverpool. Enlisted at the outbreak of war. Entered France, 7th November 1915. Wounded 11th January 1916 by a rifle grenade. Captain, March 1916. Originally buried between Carnoy and Montauban at map reference 62C.A.9.a.3.central with 20339, Private Hough, 15th Bn., Cheshires also killed 1st July and remains next to him in grave 9. Mrs. Brockbank applied for medals. Memorial Ref. V. U. 8., Dantzig Alley British Cemetery, Mametz, France. WO 339/65375

"That Life Is Long That Answers Life's Great End" Duty & Love Rest In God

BROCKLEHURST, Captain, Thomas Pownall. Killed in action, near Mametz, gallantly made the supreme sacrifice making his way to the junction of Dantzig Alley and Fritz Trench, 1st July 1916. B Coy., 2nd Bn., The Queen's (Royal West Surrey Regiment). Born in 1887 in Horley. Aged 29. Third son (two elder brothers and a sister) of Edward and Katharine L. Brocklehurst, of Kinnersley Manor, Reigate, Surrey. Attended Malvern College, 1900 - 1904. Trinity Hall, Cambridge, BA, studied law and became a solicitor. He joined the Artists Rifles in 1914, No. 1821 and went to France, 24th October 1914 and subsequently given a commission being posted to Queen's Royal West Surrey Regiment, 25th May 1915. Promoted captain, 20th August 1915. Wounded in action at Loos, 25th September 1915, gunshot wound right hand treated at No. 2. Field Ambulance, wounded 28th September 1915 with gunshot wound to the right buttock and treated at No. 3 General Hospital. Returned to England where an unsuccessful attempt was made for removal and rejoined his battalion, 15th February 1916. Originally buried Mametz-Montauban Road, sht 62d. sq.F.6.a and reinterred 1920. Father applied for his medals. Memorial Ref. II. D. 9., Dantzig Alley British Cemetery, Mametz, France. WO 339/804

BROMILOW, Major, John Nesbit. Commanding 1st Bn., King's Own Regiment. Killed at Hebuterne, 2nd July 1916 originally reported as missing. Body found August 1917. The 93rd Brigade had failed on the left and the 29th Division on the right, the Germans came down from either flank and the King's Own and Essex were practically missing, Major Bromilow not heard of since. Second Lieutenant Hudson and Weatherhead also went missing and were given a date of death as the 1st July 1916. Prisoner of War records also give a date as the 1st July 1916. Born in 1887. Youngest son of Henry and Editha Bromilow, of Rann Lea, Ramhill, Lancs. Educated Eastbourne College and RMC Sandhurst. A well-known hunting man, steeplechase rider, and polo player being handicapped at two goals. He served for a time with the home battalion at Colchester and later in Jersey. He then joined the foreign service battalion and proceeded to India. On the outbreak of war he was home and was ordered to join the 6th (Service) Battalion of his regiment to assist in training them. He became adjutant for a time, and was then appointed staff captain to the 38th Brigade, 13th Division, with which he proceeded to Gallipoli in 1915. There he was badly wounded. On recovery, after a spell of home service, he was ordered to France to take command of his regiment's 1st Battalion in April 1916. Grave Ref. I. B. 51. Serre Road Cemetery No. 1. Pas de Calais, France.

BROOKE, Lieutenant, Charles Berjew, DSO. In command of a company and leading it to the assault when he was shot, 1st July 1916. A Coy., 2nd Bn., Yorkshire Regiment. Aged 21. Only son of Charles Berjew Brooke (manager in British Xylonite Company) and Maud Gwenddolen Brooke, of Colne House, Brantham, Suffolk. Born 7th March 1895. For two years a boarder in Schoolhouse and attended Colchester Royal Grammar School, Bilton Grange, Rugby and Bradfield College, September 1909 to 1st July 1913. Gazetted to the Suffolks and was sent to France attached to the Queens in December 1914 and rose to the rank of captain. Seriously wounded on the 25th September 1915 in the Battle of Loos. Mentioned in Despatches and awarded the DSO; 'whilst in command of B Company he was over the parapet like a shot and took three lines of German trenches quite quickly. Nearly every officer was killed or wounded, Brooke was wounded in the face, he carried on the fight with wonderful endurance and courage. No bombs were left and the situation became desperate, Captain Brooke was injured in the chest, he withdrew the remainder of the men and was one of the last to leave, he personally accounted for a few Germans with revolver, rifle and bayonet.' In January 1916 gazetted to the Yorkshire Regiment. Home on leave in April 1916. Original map reference where body was found 62c.A.14.b.5.4. with nine other soldiers all of whom who had a date of death as the 26th/27th August 1918. Memorial Ref. IV. H. 7., Peronne Road Cemetery, Maricourt, France.

Montauban Formerly Captain, Suffolks Attached 1st The Queen's

BROOKS, Second Lieutenant, Frank Smith. He was hit a few yards into No Man's Land near Bois Francais and his body was bought in by his fellow officers, 1st July 1916. 20th Bn., Manchester Regiment. Born in Northenden on 8th August 1892. Aged 23. Eldest child of Arthur Percy and Edith Brooks, of "Redcot," Bramhall Lane, Stockport. Resided 186 Northenden Road, Gatley. Frank had been educated at Stockport Grammar School and studied law at Manchester University entering in 1912. Articled to the family practice and in partnership, Smith and Brooks with offices at St. Peters Chambers, 39 St. Petersgate, Stockport and 12 Exchange Street, Manchester. Applied for a commission on 27th November 1914, stating he was a member of the Special Reserve with the 4th Battalion, North Staffordshire Regiment mobilised on the outbreak of war. When he became a second lieutenant, he was posted the 20th Battalion and took command of No. 14 Platoon, in "D" Company. He left for France with the battalion, 9th November 1915. In early May 1916, Frank returned home for a brief period of leave but then returned to his regiment. He was buried with his commanding officer and other brother officers in a grave in the German trench they died trying to capture and later reinterred, south of Fricourt and three miles ESE of Albert Sht. 62.F.q.d.o.8. Original map reference where body was found 62d.F.9.d.9.7 with fellow 20th Bn officers, Eaton, Lord, Kemp and Ross the grave marked with a cross. A Mr. W. H. Clarke wrote to Mr. Arthur Percy Brooks and explained that his son Frank Clarke also with the Manchesters, was near Second Lieutenant Brooks as him and another man rushed out and carried his body into the lines. Silver cigarette case, identity disc and silver flask returned to family. Record of service of Solicitors and Articled Clerks with H. M. Forces 1914-1919 – Law Society. Father applied for his medals. Memorial Ref. V. I. 9., Dantzig Alley British Cemetery, Mametz, France. WO 339/17246

There Is A Corner Of A Foreign Field That Is For Ever England

Second Lieutenant F. S. Brooks 2nd Row middle.
Also killed in the photograph on the 1st July 1916 but location unknown;
Corporal H. Joyce, Private G. Humphreys, Private Frank Hackett and Private W. Widdeson.

BROOM, Second Lieutenant, Frederick. Jordan. Killed in same engagement as his friend, Second Lieutenant James Harvey, 1st July 1916. 2nd Bn., Seaforth Highlanders. Native of Greenock. Son of John Broom, ship surveyor. Employed Messrs. Fleming, Reid & Co., Merino Mills, Greenock. Enlisted 1st Dragoon Guards, Private, No. GS/3655. Entered France, 16th June 1915. Body was side by sided in a large British cemetery, 200 yards northwest of the Sucrerie. Mother, Mrs. J. Broom of 15 Forsyth Street, Greenock applied for his medals. Memorial Ref. I. H. 20., Sucrerie Military Cemetery, Colincamps, France.

BROPHY, Second Lieutenant, Ernest Gordon. Reported missing and then as killed, body seen lying in the German front line, at a place called 'Sausage Valley', 1st July 1916. No. 9 Platoon, 2nd Bn., West Yorkshire Regiment (Prince of Wales's Own). Aged 27. Son of Edward and Julia Brophy, of 11 Glenarm Road Clapton, London formerly 29 Westminster Road, Edmonton. Born Islington. Captain of St. Mark's Dalston Company, London Diocesan Church Lads Brigade. Audit clerk. Entered France, 12th March 1915. Suffered a gunshot wound to the scalp on the 6th June 1915 and rejoined his unit on the 8th June 1915. On the 24th June 1915 whilst with B Coy., 1/7th Middlesex, No. 2479 he wrote to his sister at Lower Edmonton; "The other night some of our chaps had some fun. They went out to the front line and captured two German flags and 300 yards of their barbed wire. A party went out with a bell tied around some bushes and this was stuck in the ground near the German trench. Attached to the bell was a wire from our trench and at frequent intervals we would ring the bell and shout 'Waiter!'". 27th November 1915 to be temporary second lieutenant from Middlesex Regiment to West Yorkshires. Brother G. R. Brophy applied for his medals. Effects returned were pocket book, letters and photos, cheque book and advance book. Memorial Ref. I. E. 1., Bouzincourt Communal Cemetery Extension, France. WO 339/50505

Loving And Beloved He Lives In The Hearts Of Those He Has Left

BROUGH, Second Lieutenant, James Lindsay. Reported missing and then killed, 1st July 1916. 15th Bn., Royal Scots. Only son of David Brough (Manager of the Inveresk Paper Mills), The Cottage, Inveresk, Musselburgh. Born 20th March 1894. Employed Edinburgh Architect and began his military career as a private No. 17036, 15th Royal Scots, sergeant 21st November 1914 receiving a commission in the course of a few months, 14th January 1915. Entered France, 1st January 1916. Connected with various organisations in Musselburgh. Reported as missing on the 2nd July and as being killed on 4th July. Items returned cheque book, advance book, wrist watch and strap with broken glass, sliver match box and identity disc. Father applied for his medals. Memorial Ref. Pier and Face 6 D and 7 D., Thiepval Memorial, France. WO 339/23127

BROWN, Second Lieutenant, Andrew Cranstoun. Killed in action, in the foremost line of the advance, at Fricourt, on July 2nd, 1916. He appears to have taken a trench, and then to have been engaged on clearing it to the right. C Coy. 8th Bn., South Staffordshire Regiment. Aged 21. Only son of Katharine Brown, of Springfield, Downton, Salisbury, and James Brown, M.B., of Harvieston, Tring, Herts. Attended Rugby School from 1908 to 1911 and went to Queen's College, Oxford, in order to qualify for his father's profession. When war was declared he enlisted as a private, but obtained a commission in the South Staffordshire Regiment in September, 1914. He went to France, 8th March, 1916, attached to the 8th Battalion of his Regiment. His captain wrote :- "I was in command of C Company, and all the time your son was with me I found him one of the most fearless and utterly reliable officers I have ever met. He was one of the most popular men in the regiment, and his men were ready to follow him anywhere. I shall always remember him as one of my best friends, and for the noble, fearless way in which he fought and met his death." Grave Registration dates as 1st July 1916 and concentration of graves records. Original map reference where body was found 62D.F.3.a.5.8, with eleven other soldiers whom had a date of death as 1st/2nd July. Mother applied for his medals. Memorial Ref. V. N. 9., Dantzig Alley British Cemetery, Mametz, France.

"Rejoice In The Lord"

BROWN, Captain, Colin Selwyn. He was reported missing, believed wounded in the leg, in front of the Leipzig Redoubt on 1st July 1916. 'C' Company, 11th Bn., Border Regiment. Born in Highgate. Aged 26. Born 5th October 1889. Son of Colin and Adela J. Brown, of Old Meadow, South Zeal, Okehampton, Devon formerly 55 Fitz James Avenue, Fulham. On completion of his training as an engineering student and graduating BSc (London), he was appointed assistant engineer on the Beira and Mashonaland and Rhodesia railways under Mr. Charles Corner M. Inst. C.E. At the outbreak of war he received a commission with the Royal Engineers proceeding to France at the end of 1915. Associate Member of the Chartered Institute of Engineers, 12th January 1915. Mother applied for his medals. Memorial Ref. II. F. 17., Lonsdale Cemetery, Authuille, France.

Dulce Et Decorum Est Pro Patria Mori

BROWN, Second Lieutenant, Ralph Adair. Killed at Gommecourt on the 1st July 1916, originally reported missing. A Coy. 1st/14th Bn., London Regiment (London Scottish). Aged 21. Son of George T. and Mary A. Brown, of Manor Hurst Palmerston Road, Bowes Park, London formerly Arbroath. On the staff of Messrs. Gutbrie & Co., East India Merchants, London. He joined the army in September 1914 as a private in the London Scottish (Territorial Force), and passed through all grades of non-commissioned rank, in accordance with the traditions of that distinguished corps. In 1915 he was promoted second-lieutenant in his own battalion. Went to France, 25th May 1916. His twin brother Second Lieutenant Lindsay J. Brown also took part in the fighting at the Somme, a third brother was severely injured in the eye on the eve of coming home for his commission and a fourth brother was a surgeon in the navy. The fifth brother was Mr. J. Hamilton Brown, marine insurance broker, Leith. Father applied for medals. Memorial Ref. Pier and Face 9 C and 13 C., Thiepval Memorial, France.

BROWN, Second Lieutenant, Robert Stanley. Battalion simply mown down by machine-gun and rifle fire, 1st July 1916. Leading up on the left, B Coy., 16th Bn., Highland Light Infantry. Born on 5th August 1894. Aged 21. Son of Thomas Stark Brown (writer) and Annie Murray Brown, of 162, St. Vincent St., Glasgow. He was the fourth of five children. Attended Glasgow Academy. Member of the OTC, Glasgow University from 1910 to 1914. Gazetted second lieutenant, 2nd September 1914. Father was a partner with Mr. Gemmill whom also lost his son on the 1st July 1916, (Second Lieutenant J. A. Gemmill) the firm being Messrs. Brown, Mair, Gemmill & Hislop, 162 St. Vincent Street, Glasgow. Entered France, 23rd November 1915. Death reported 11th July 1916. Father applied for medals. Original map reference where found 57D.R.31.a.2.3 with a cross on his grave, at least five other soldiers were also at this location. Memorial Ref. III. L. 1., Lonsdale Cemetery, Authuille, France.

BROWN CONSTABLE, Lieutenant, John Cecil. Relieved Captain Anderson as Officer Commanding and was to go over the top in the second wave with No. 14 Platoon. Killed in the vicinity of Farmyard Trench, the German first line. Went over with D Coy., and by his skill got a footing in the German line, and his men continued to bomb there way up to Fall Trench suffering severely by rifle fire but progress was made by bombers getting out and rushing them over the open. By 10.15am no messages were received from 'D' as they had lost all officers and NCO's and ceased to exist as a separate unit. John had gone over with his walking stick, and was killed being hit in the right side of the head by a piece of shrapnel. 1st July 1916. D Coy., 14th Bn., London Regiment (London Scottish). Born Allahabad, India. Aged 26. Son of the Reverend Albert Edward (Chaplain to Indian Forces) and Clara Emily Brown Constable, of "Greet," Mottingham, London. Attended University Engineering College, Johannesburg. Worked in Pretoria prior to the outbreak of war in the Public Works Department. Formerly private 2890, London Regiment. Theatre of war, France from 15th September 1914. Resided Frant Road, Tunbridge Wells. Commissioned 31st December 1914. The night before the attack examined the enemy wire and found it broken up. Sir William Borlase's Grammar School Memorial. His mother was still writing to the War Office for further information in March 1917 and she was to have some of her questions answered when information came that he had died instantly and was buried in a shell hole. Original map reference where found K.2.3.4.9.10.11 and identified by a cross, thirteen other graves in this location as a result his headstone is inscribed 'believed to be'.

This ties in with the account from a German soldier who writing to Major Low of the London Scottish Regiment stated he buried a British officer whom was carrying a walking stick. His mother applied for his medals and payments. Memorial Ref. II. G. 26., Gommecourt British Cemetery No.2, Hebuterne, France.

BROWNE, Captain, Dominick Augustus. Killed near Albert, 1st July 1916. Adjutant, 1st Bn., Royal Irish Rifles. Born June 28th 1888. Aged 28. Eldest son of Frank and Mary Browne, of Killadreenan, Newtownmount-Kennedy, Co. Wicklow. Attended Marlborough College and passed into RMC Sandhurst. Entered the Royal Irish Rifles in September 1908, promotion came in March 1910. Entered France, 5th November 1914 and in March 1915 he was appointed adjutant and in the following May gazetted captain. Suffered a fractured fibula on the 24th April 1915 and spent 29 days in hospital, medical board at Beaufort War Hospital, Bristol found he recovered 23rd August 1915. Miss Lucy Dominick Browne (Aunt) from Marlborough Buildings, Bath applied for his medals. Memorial Ref. Pier and Face 15 A and 15 B., Thiepval Memorial, France. WO 339/7134

BRUCE, Major, John Russel. Killed in action, La Boisselle, 1st July 1916. 15th Bn., Royal Scots. Aged 33. Born 10th December 1883. Second son of James Bruce (Writer to the Signet), of 58 Gt. King Street, Edinburgh. Attended Edinburgh Academy and University of Edinburgh. Student of Law MA, 1907, LLB 1910. Advocate 1911. In 1907 joined the University OTC Infantry Unit and had been commanding the same since 1910. Member of the Scottish Bar before the war. Passed all the Territorial Force examinations for promotion to major. Commissioned 9th October 1914. Promoted major, December 1914. In March 1916 had slight pleurisy and was discharged to duty 21st April 1916. Brother Captain Alexander Charles Arbuthnot Bruce was killed in Egypt, 23rd April 1916. Effects returned were field glasses, revolver and set of chess men. Mother applied for his medals. Memorial Ref. Pier and Face 6 D and 7 D., Thiepval Memorial, France. WO 339/55464

BRUNT, Second Lieutenant, William Edward. Instantly killed by a machine-gun, 1st July 1916, seen lying dead in long grass at about 9.00am, killed about 100 – 200 yards in front of Dantzig Alley and the southern section of Fritz Trench. B Coy., 22nd Bn., Manchester Regiment. Aged 22. Eldest son of Joseph and Mary Alice Brunt, of 4, Dale Terrace, Buxton, Derbyshire. Reporter working for the Buxton Herald. Enlisted in the Oxford and Bucks Light Infantry, 10th September 1914 and entered France on the 22nd July 1915. Promoted to second lieutenant, 20th June 1916 with the Manchester Regiment and gazetted after his death on the 18th August 1916. Buxton War Memorial. Originally buried Mametz Montauban Road, map reference where found 62D.F.6.c.1.8 with eleven other soldiers. Effects returned were only a wrist watch. Memorial Ref. II. F. I., Dantzig Alley British Cemetery, Mametz, France. WO 339/65925

Dead - Yet Liveth

BRUNTON, Second Lieutenant, Hereward. Killed in action, 1st July 1916. 17th Bn., Highland Light Infantry. Aged 32. Only son of Mr. and Mrs. William N. Brunton, of 15, Regent Terrace, Edinburgh. He took evening classes at the University of Strathclyde's antecedent institution, the Royal Technical College (RTC) of Glasgow from session 1911-12 to session 1913-14. The RTC student registers record his address as 6 Berkeley Terrace, Charing Cross, Glasgow, and his occupation as 'Engineer'. In session 1911-12, he enrolled for Inorganic Chemistry Course I; Practical Inorganic Chemistry Course I (a laboratory class, for which he gained a second-class certificate of merit), and Mathematics Course I (for which he gained a first-class certificate of merit). In session 1912-13, he enrolled for Mechanics Course IIa: Strength of Materials, and Mathematics Course II. Finally, in session 1913-14, he again enrolled for Mechanics Course IIa: Strength of Materials and Mathematics Course II. Enlisted as a private in the Lovat Scouts, No. 2418. Temporary second lieutenant gazetted 24th September 1915. Entered France, 10th March 1916. Death reported 11th July 1916. Listed on the Roll of Honour of the Royal Technical College of Glasgow and University of Strathclyde. Sister, Edith applied for his medals. Memorial Ref. Pier and Face 15 C., Thiepval Memorial, France.

BRYAN, Second Lieutenant, Sydney Arthur. Reported missing up to 22nd July 1916 and then killed, 1st July 1916. His commanding officer wrote; "met his death calmly and gallantly at the head of his men under terrific fire." Attacking Ovillers shot down by machine-gun fire from Thiepval Spur. 9th Bn., York and Lancaster Regiment. Aged 21. Adopted son of John Barham Bryan (Chief Officer of Leigh Coastguard) and Agnes Emma Bryan, of 9, Oakleigh Park Drive, Leigh-on-Sea, Essex. Old boy of Southend High School for boys (1909 to 1913). Enlisted in the Civil Service joining the Territorial Force and became a private in the 15th London Regiment, No. 1774, going to France, 17th March 1915. Commissioned with the 9th Bn., York and Lancaster Regiment, December 1915. Father applied for his medals. Memorial Ref. Pier and Face 14 A and 14 B., Thiepval Memorial, France.

BUCHANAN, Second Lieutenant, David. Majority of the casualties especially those of the officers occurred during the first two hours of fighting, killed while leading his men with the utmost gallantry, the second lieutenant was quite prepared to make the supreme sacrifice, 1st July 1916. 2nd Bn., Seaforth Highlanders. Second and younger son of William Buchanan (Member of the board of Port and Harbour Commissioners and Principal of the firm of Buchanan Bros., Ltd., Londonderry). Born 4th March 1893. Resided Alt-na-Aros, Northland Road, Londonderry. Educated at Foyle College from 4th September 1906 and belonged to First Derry Presbyterian Church. Director in the firm of Buchanan Brothers. Joined the Colours at the outbreak of war the 6th Black Watch in November 1914, in training at Dundee as a private, No. 2533 before going to the Front, 2nd May 1915. He obtained his commission in the field, 14th August 1915 and was attached to the Seaforth Highlanders with whom he was at the Front ever since. Wrote a letter to the family of Lieutenant H. A. J. Lennox informing them of the death of their son whom was killed in action, February 1916. The bodies of Captain Alison, Second Lieutenant's Williamson, Broom, Buchanan and Blackwood with 25 others were side by sided. Brother applied for his medals. Londonderry (Derry) War Memorial. Memorial Ref. I. H. 35., Sucrerie Military Cemetery, Colincamps, France.

BUCKWORTH, Lieutenant, Charles Raymond. Attached to the 10th Brigade, Machine Gun Coy, came up and reported that he had a machine-gun and one stokes gun in action just south of point 92. From there he was able to enfilade the Germans in their front line trenches north of point 87. It was soon after this that he was severely wounded and last seen, wounded and missing believed killed, 1st July 1916. The objective was the ridge between Grandcourt and Puisieux-au-Mont. 2nd Bn., Seaforth Highlanders. Aged 19. Only son and child of Mr. and Mrs. Buckworth, of Ardgay, Ross-Shire formerly Gruinards, Ross-Shire. At Wellington he was in the Talbot House, 1910-13, and entered RMC Sandhurst the following year. Joined September 1914 and received his commission in 1914, wounded June 1915. Seconded to the Brigade Machine Gun Company, 22nd December 1915. Listed in the Wellington College Roll of Honour in January 1917. Father applied for medals. Mr. L. M. Buckworth choose the headstone inscription. Memorial Ref. I. K. 22., Serre Road Cemetery No.2, France.

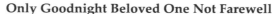

Only Goodnight Beloved One Not Farewell

BURGE, Major, Montague. Fell before he got across No Man's Land, fell after a few yards, 1st July 1916. 23rd (Tyneside Scottish) Bn., Northumberland Fusiliers. Aged 40. Son of C. Burge of 2, Winshull Court, London. Attended Marlborough College, 1888 to 1892. Served in the Boer War with the Imperial Yeomanry. Lieutenant Montague Burge, half-pay list, is placed on the retired list, under the provisions of Article 486 of the Royal Warrant for Pay and Promotion, 1909. Dated 13th July, 1913. Disembarked 11th September 1914. Previously lieutenant, 3rd Hussars to be captain dated 12th November 1914. His brother applied for his medals. Memorial Ref. Pier and Face 10 B 11 B and 12 B., Thiepval Memorial, France.

BURLURAUX, Lieutenant, John Rene Cornelius. Reported missing believed wounded, 1st July 1916. D Coy., 27th (Tyneside Irish) Bn., Northumberland Fusiliers. Aged 25. Born 1891, Newcastle-on-Tyne. Son of Eugene (basket maker) and Helene Burluraux (née Wehrle), of Germany of 28, Campbell St., Newcastle-on-Tyne. Old boy of St. Cuthbert's Grammar School. First boy in the county to receive the King's Crown Badge for scouts. Journalist by profession, and was prominently identified with the Boy Scout movement in his district, 1st Elswick Troop. On the editorial staff of a Newcastle newspaper. At the time of the 1911 census, Burluraux was working as an assistant librarian while living with his family at 116 Buckingham Street. Enlisted as a private in the 18th, Northumberland Fusiliers at the outbreak of war and granted a commission, temporary second lieutenant 28th May 1915. Mother applied for his medals. Original map reference 57d.X.20.c and marked with a regimental cross, two unknown soldiers also found in this location. Memorial Ref. III. H. 6., Ovillers Military Cemetery, France.

Greater Love Than This No Man Hath R.I.P.

BURTON, Second Lieutenant, Cyril Henry. Hit in thigh before the attack began and refused to retire. A small party of bombers, under the Battalion Bomb Officer Burton, worked their way along a communication trench and advanced beyond the German 2nd line, bombing several dug-outs on the way, and accounting for a number of Germans, this party however had to fall back eventually. He was hit again just in front of a shell hole occupied by his men and wounded managed to get refuge in the shell hole with a number of men. His men dressed his wound and he left the shell hole for one of two reasons either to get help or for medical assistance, and was never seen again. Reported as missing, 1st July 1916. Wounded prior to the attack but refused to go back. C Coy., 1st/7th Bn., Sherwood Foresters (Notts and Derby Regiment). Born 16th July 1988. Son of Edward Henry and Matilda Burton of Brandon, Suffolk. Attended Thetford Grammar School and King's College, London. He was a student of the Evening School of History at U.C.L. from 1911 to 1914, when he took his Diploma, and was awarded the Gilchrist Medal. Entered the Civil Service (Board of Education). In the spring of 1915, 5th May 1915 he enlisted in the No, 3787, Artists' Rifles, The London Regiment and on October 9th, 1915, he was gazetted second lieutenant, 7th Sherwood Foresters. Mother applied for his medals. Memorial Ref. Pier and Face 10 C 10 D and 11 A., Thiepval Memorial, France.

BUTLER, Captain, Charles Kingstone. Commanding A Coy., gallantly led a bombing attack from a communication trench leading from the hostile support line to the reserve line, he was killed by a bullet wound through the head, 1st July 1916. Adjutant, 10th Bn., attached 2nd Bn., King's Own Yorkshire Light Infantry. After his death Lieutenant M. H. Garland did excellent work. Eldest son of Mr. and Mrs. Charles William and Helen Gordon Butler of Standen Manor, Hungerford. Born 16th April 1891. Aged 25. Educated St. Vincent's, Eastbourne and Wellington College 1905 to 1908. Received his commission in 1910, promoted August 1914 and the following month made adjutant. Promoted to captain, 24th April 1915. Reported wounded 25th September 1915, shot in the face. Struck on the left side of the lower lip by a bullet that passed through and knocked out four off his teeth, one tooth being driven under the surface of his tongue. This required further work by a dentist and a stay at Lady Islington's Hospital for five days. Mentioned in Despatches, January 1916. Memorial plaque in All Saints Church, Eastbourne and the Ascham Memorial Arch. His Colonel wrote :" He was the life and soul of us all, and had the two chief virtues of a soldier, indomitable courage and unfailing cheerfulness; added to that he was a disciplinarian and got the best out of his men." Private Carl was given his watch and letters before the advance and gave them to a chum who was not advancing. His watch engraved C.K.B and Halfhunter No 2901279 were returned to the family. His father wrote to the War Office as to the whereabouts of his revolver, field glasses and compass but was reminded there was no record of recovery of the body and he probably took these into battle. Father applied for his medals. Memorial Ref. Pier and Face 11 C and 12 A., Thiepval Memorial, France. WO 339/7715

BUXTON, Second Lieutenant, Bertie Reginald. He died at the head of his men leading them to the attack, sent forward about 2.00pm, 1st July 1916. 1st /2nd Bn., London Regiment (Royal Fusiliers). Aged 24. Born 1st December 1891, Hanley, Staffordshire. Son of Henry Samuel and Harriet Buxton. Brother of G. H. Bush of Wadhurst, Fleetwood Avenue, Westcliff, and a prominent member of the Westcliff Operatic Society enlisted in the 4th Seaforth Highlanders, No. 287 in September 1914, went to France with them on November 5th obtained his commission in November 1915 and went out again in early February 1916. His Commanding Officer wrote; "He died very gallantly at the head of his man…leading them into the attack…a good officer, a leader of men and a cheery comrade." Mrs. M. Bush, his sister claimed his medals. Memorial Ref. Pier and Face 9 D and 16 B., Thiepval Memorial, France.

BUXTON, Second Lieutenant, Jocelyn Murray Victor. Still being reported wounded and missing, August 1916 died 1st July 1916, behaved with great gallantry in the action. Officially reported as killed on that date, the 21st April 1917. Jocelyn's servant, Private Rycroft wrote to the family to clarify that he had been wounded and had not brought in the body of the second lieutenant, and confirmed his last words to him were "Are you ready, Rycoft?" followed by "Come on, follow me." 6th Bn., Rifle Brigade, attd. 6th Bn, Machine , Gun Corps (Infantry), attached 25th Company. Aged 20. Fourth son of Sir Thomas Foxwell Victor Buxton, 4th Bart., and of Lady Anne Louisa Matilda Buxton, of "Warlies", Waltham Abbey, Essex. Born April 1st 1896. Educated at Broadstairs and Marlborough from 1910 to 1914. Gained a history exhibition at Trinity College, Cambridge admitted 1914. Went to France, 22nd October 1915. Lady Buxton applied for his medals. Memorial Ref. Pier and Face 16 B and 16 C., Thiepval Memorial, France.

BYRNE, Second Lieutenant, Louis Frederick. On the field of battle he was found dead with his prayer-book open in his hand, 1st July 1916. In his kit was found a letter addressed to his parents in the event of his death. He said he had been to Holy Communion on the previous Sunday, and had no fear of death, and hundreds of thousands of others had died willingly in the same cause. Informant stated he was seen lying wounded in right thigh at point of death between the front line and support trenches at about 9.00am. 24th (Tyneside Irish) Bn., Northumberland Fusiliers. Only son of Mr. and Mrs. Frederick Byrne, of 62, Eldon Place, Newcastle-on-Tyne. Age 21. Born 17th August 1894, Dublin. Educated at Ratcliffe College, Leicester, and Bruge, Belgium. Subsequently articled to a firm of Newcastle solicitors, Messrs. Avery (Ltd.). He was in Italy when war broke out and had also travelled to Belgium. Attested 11th November 1914, Belfast joined the Leinster Regiment. He received a commission in the Tyneside Irish Brigade soon after its formation, 25th December 1914 and left with the battalion from Salisbury Plain for Flanders.

Writing from France, his commanding officer says :—" The whole regiment join with me in sending you our deepest sympathy. I cannot express to you how very deeply I feel Louis' loss. He was always so bright and cheerful, keen in all his duties, and took such an interest in his men. His example was a noble one, and will ever live in the memory of those who are left."

Father George McBrearty, chaplain to the Tyneside Irish, writes to Mrs. Byrne :—"Please accept my deepest sympathy with you all for Louie's death. Such a charming boy—always bright and happy. We are all sad at his loss. What must your mother's sorrow be! On the night before the battle, I was hearing confessions in the lines of the 24th Northumberland Fusiliers. Louie was one of those who came to me. 'I have just come for your blessing, Father,' he said. I gave it to him with all my heart and what was to be a final absolution. He was found dead with his prayer-book open in his hand.' Nephew of the Louis F. Byrne who forms the central figure in Lady Butler's painting of Rorke's Drift. Moved to Gordon Dump Cemetery, December 1919. Original map reference 57d.X.20.c found with Second Lieutenant T. S. Charlesworth, (grave 8) 25th Bn., Northumberlands and Private Arthur Graves, 11th Bn., Suffolk Regiment (grave 10) both were killed on the 1st July. Mother, Mrs. L. M. Byrne applied for his medals. Memorial Ref. X. S. 9., Gordon Dump Cemetery, Ovillers-La Boisselle, France. WO 339/15322

Requiescat In Pace

Northumberland Fusiliers 24th Battalion Officers
Included Byrne, Sutcliffe, Thompson, MacKenzie, Horrox and Howard

CADDICK, Major, Alfred Armstrong War diary states; "7.30am, advance begins. Enemy first line reached and passed very quickly also was the second. Only in one or two cases were any enemy seen in these two lines. Having plenty of casualties from machine-gun fire in enemy third and fourth lines. At the third line we were temporarily held up my machine-gun fire but took it by rushes. From this point the fighting was all with bombs along trenches. We reached our objective probably 35-40 minutes from zero hour (7.30am) and at once commenced consolidating and cleaning rifles under the direction of Captain Martin and Second Lieutenant Turner. By this time the next battalion was arriving but had had so many casualties that they could not go through us so helped consolidating. This happened with all battalions following us. Many times we were bombed from this position and regained it until bombs ran out. We had to retired to their third line parapet and hold on with machine and rifle fire. Parties were detailed to collect as many bombs as could be found (both English and German) and when we had a good store we again reached our objective. No supply of bombs coming from rear so could not hold on and returned again. Enemy machine-guns and snipers were doing a great amount of damage all the while. Enemy artillery opened but fortunately their range was over. Held on to this position until relieved by a battalion from the rear. All through the action no troops were seen on our right or left. This had a great deal to do with the inability to push past our objective." Major Caddick was killed in the assault on the Quadrilateral, Beaumont-Hamel reported that he stepped on a man-trap in the first line German trenches, July 1st 1916 but posted as missing for nearly one year before death conceded. 8th Bn., Royal Warwickshire Regiment. Aged 44. Eldest son of Alfred Caddick (solicitor and for many years Town Clerk of West Bromwich) and Annie Jessie Caddick of The Firs, Ockford Road, Godalming, Surrey formerly Glenfield, Manor Road, Sutton Coldfield. Admitted to the Bar, July 1894. The Major was well known in the West Bromwich district where he practices as a solicitor, member of Caddick & Walker. Entered France, 23rd March 1915. Mentioned in Despatches. Mother made newspaper appeals for news of her son. Father applied for his medals. Memorial Ref. Pier and Face 9 A 9 B and 10 B., Thiepval Memorial, France.

CALDER-SMITH, Second Lieutenant, Raymond Alexander. 10.10am Heavy barrage put up by enemy whilst trying to dig communication trenches, causing numerous casualties, Hebuterne, posted as missing 1st July 1916. 3rd Bn., London Regiment (Royal Fusiliers). Aged 26. Son of Robert Calder-Smith, of Manila Philippine Islands and Mrs. Ramona Calder-Smith, of Madrid, Spain. Attended Ampleforth College. Played cricket for the Old Amplefordians. Gazetted to be second lieutenant, 7th September 1914. Entered France, 24th April 1916. Mother of Winchester Road, Swiss Cottage applied for his medals. Memorial Ref. Pier and Face 9 D and 16 B., Thiepval Memorial, France.

CALLAGHAN, Second Lieutenant, Joseph Patrick Aloysious. A letter from his' captain reports that he fell just after climbing over the parapet to advance with his men :—"He showed great pluck" (the officer writes), "but a shell burst near him and blew him back into the trench and killed him." 1st July 1916. 64th Bde., Machine Gun Corps (Infantry). Fourth son of Thomas J. Callaghan, Esq., J.P., and of Mrs. Callaghan of Dame Street, Dublin. He was educated at Clongowes Wood College, Co. Kildare, and subsequently went to Montreal, Canada, where he was when war broke out. Returning to Ireland from Montreal, he applied to a commission and came home in May, 1915 and was attached to the 5th Leinster Regiment. After training for a time with the regiment he volunteered for service with the newly-formed Machine Gun Corps, and went out to France with his company, 25th February 1916 when he had spent most of his time in the trenches. Brother applied for his medals. Memorial Ref. Pier and Face 5 C and 12 C., Thiepval Memorial, France.

CALLARD, Second Lieutenant, William Kingsley. A new attack was ordered for 3.30pm with artillery and a smoke screen, meanwhile the enemy's artillery was still active and Second Lieutenant Callard was killed by enemy shellfire near Gommecourt, along with Company Sergeant Major Frank Johnson of C Company, 1st July 1916. 5th Bn., Leicestershire Regiment. Aged 19. Born March 13th 1897 in Leicester, baptised at Bishop Street Methodist Church on the 18th April 1897. Son of William Thomas (baker and confectioner) and Fannie Callard, of 122, London Road, Leicester. Grandson of Mr. W. Callard JP of St. Leonard's, Torquay. Educated Wyggeston Grammar School, 1905 to 1915. He taught in the Sunday School at Bishop Street, was a local Methodist preacher and intended to become an ordained minister. He had one brother and one sister, Annie Maud. In 1915 he was awarded a scholarship in science by University College, Oxford and then signed up. Entered France, 4th June 1915. Father William Thomas Callard died unexpectedly in September 1916 following two operations. Mother applied for his medals and decided his inscription. Memorial Ref. I. L. 15., Foncquevillers Military Cemetery, France.

He Gave His Life For His Country

CALLOW, Second Lieutenant, Donald. Last seen in the German second line trench, he set off to find men of the 5th Bn. and was not seen again, 1st July 1916. D Coy., No 16 Platoon, 1st /5th Bn., Sherwood Foresters (Notts and Derby Regiment) formerly 1/14th London Regiment. Aged 19. Youngest son of J. M. and Mrs. Callow, of Ashbourne, Derbyshire. Entered France, 15th September 1914. Wounded October, 1914. Commissioned 10th July 1915. On the 14th July 1916 Mrs. Callow of Green Road, received notification that her son Lieutenant Donald Callow of the Sherwood Foresters was missing. Callow, who joined the London Scottish Regiment as a private, 2028 had fought in several engagements in France and was wounded. Once recovered, he was gazetted into the Sherwoods as a second lieutenant, 10th July 1915. A prisoner of war, a lieutenant in the Sherwoods stated he was last seen in the German trenches alive, believed to be killed. Mother applied for his medals. Memorial Ref. Pier and Face 10 C 10 D and 11 A., Thiepval Memorial, France.

CAMBIE, Lieutenant, Edward Maurice Baldwin. Those who saw him in the battle say that his courage, skill and resource were extraordinary, reported missing and then killed, 1st July 1916. Private Firth saw him die, between the German front line and their wire, "he ran on for a few yards and then fell dead, this was about 8 o'clock. I saw him again later when we were returning and quite sure he was dead." Another witness stated he was wounded in a shell hole when the lieutenant fell into the shell hole and died with a wound in his neck, he knew it was the lieutenant as he checked his identity disc. 8th Bn., King's Own Yorkshire Light Infantry. Aged 22. Only surviving son of the Reverend Dr. Cambie (Vicar of Otley formerly Vicar of St. Saviours, Brixton Hill) and Mrs. S. R. Cambie, of Saxlingham Rectory, Norwich. Born at Gorsley Vicarage, Gloucester on the 7th August 1894. Educated Dean Close School (1904 to 1913), Cheltenham and Hertford College, Oxford. Corporal in the OTC. When war broke out enlisted in the Public Schools Brigade and received a commission, 30th October 1914. He was promoted in November 1914. Left for France on the 24th March 1916. Captain Bryant wrote to his father and stated he died gallantly leading his men and this was received prior to official notification from the War Office. Commemorated Sons and Daughters of the Anglican Church Clergy. Father applied for his medals. Memorial Ref. Pier and Face 11 C and 12 A., Thiepval Memorial, France. WO 339/20197

CAMPBELL, Lieutenant, Lawford Burne. Heavy machine-gun fire caused high casualties, 1st July 1916. C Coy. 12th Bn., Royal Irish Rifles. Aged 20. Son of Robert Garrett Campbell and Alicia Anna Campbell, of Coolgreany, Fortwilliam Park, Belfast. Educated Wellington College. In business with his father's firm the well-known thread manufacturer, of Mossley. He had been in the Central Antrim Regiment nearly since its formation. Entered France, 5th October 1915. Home on leave just prior to his death. Father applied for his medals. Commemorated St. Anne's Cathedral, Donegal Street, Belfast and Carnmoney Churchyard. Memorial Ref. Pier and Face 15 A and 15 B., Thiepval Memorial, France.

Officers of the Royal Irish Rifles (Central Antrims)

Top row; Lieutenants 6th from left Lawford Campbell (1st July 1916), T. G. Haughton (1st July 1916). Second row; Lieutenants 6th from left Captain Griffiths (1st July 1916), Lieutenants W. McCluggage (1st July 1916), Third row; 8th from left Captain J. E. Jenks (wounded 1st July died 4th July 1916).

CAMPBELL, Second Lieutenant, Robert Alexander Rankine. He was last seen to fall wounded leading his platoon forward in support, shot through the head, 1st July 1916. Second Lieutenant Campbell had been sent back for more support to 'clean' the trench and whilst Captain Freeman was rendering support, Robert was shot and fell. B Coy. 2nd Bn., West Yorkshire Regiment (Prince of Wales's Own). Aged 23. Born 19th February 1893, Terravallur, India. Son of Robert Lewis and Alice Elizabeth Campbell, of 5 Barnaby Road, Bromley, Kent. Educated at Berkhamsted School, Herts, and forestry student at Toronto University, Canada. Canadian Expeditionary Force, No 77475 and previously in the Berkhamsted OTC. Entered France, 16th May 1915. Injured by a shell in June 1916 and returned to duty. Written by Commanding Officer: "during the bombardment prior to the attack in which he was killed he had carried out several daring reconnaissance's and had he survived I should have forwarded his name for reward." Body found and buried two weeks later with no location. His father, Robert wrote to the War Office asking for further details as the chaplain might know the location, he had also spoke to Captain Freeman who drew up a map of the possible location near Mash Valley. Father applied for his medals. Memorial Ref. Pier and Face 2 A 2 C and 2 D., Thiepval Memorial, France. WO 339/39759

CAMPBELL, Second Lieutenant, Samuel McDonnell. Killed in action as he fired guns around Hawthorn Ridge crater, 1st July 1916. 13th Bn., Lancashire Fusiliers attached to 86th Trench Mortar Battery. Born 16th October 1882. Second son of Mr. Robert M. Campbell, Dungiven. A brilliant musician. Joined Northern Bank on 26th March 1900 in the Head Office and was cashier in the Larne branch of the Northern Banking Co. previous to joining the army. Signed the Ulster Covenant. Commissioned 7th May 1915. Known as 'MacCampbell'. He served for some time in Egypt and was subsequently sent to France. His two brothers also served in the army, one with the Australian Forces and the other in the North Irish Horse. Mother applied for his medals. Memorial Ref. B. 52., Beaumont-Hamel British Cemetery, France.

CAMPBELL, Second Lieutenant, William MacKenzie. He was killed in action, gallantly fighting at close quarters in hand to hand fighting, 1st July 1916. 9th Bn., Royal Irish Rifles. Younger son of Councillor W. M. and Mrs. Campbell of Dacre-Hill Rock Ferry. Belonged to Dacre Hill, Birkenhead. Chartered Accountant, Deloitte, Griffith & Co., Buenos Aires. Articles with Hilditch and Wood, Liverpool. Accepted a five year appointment in the office of Sir John Plender & Co of London commencing in April 1914. Former captain of the Bebington Hockey Club and took part in an international match in Buenos Aires. Obtained a commission 12th May 1915. He assisted in quelling the Dublin rebellion. Welcomed back in the battalion a few days earlier. Memorial Ref. Pier and Face 15 A and 15 B., Thiepval Memorial, France.

CANE, Second Lieutenant, Reginald Shapland. As soon as the troops left the front line, heavy machine-gun fire was brought to bear on them from all directions, casualties if officers amounted to 100%. Killed whilst leading his men, Beaumont Hamel, 1st July 1916. 1st Bn., Hampshire Regiment. Aged 34. Second son of John James and Annie Cane, of 18, Byron Road, Ealing, London and nephew of Mr. T. Cane, Dunsden. Honorary Secretary and Treasurer of the Ealing Swifts F.C. On the staff of London and Western Bank at the Acton Branch. Passed the Institute of Bankers Final Examination, in April 1914. Formerly Rifle Brigade, Private, 2888. Served in France from 18th May 1915. Engaged to Miss Violet Bedford. Journal of the Institute of Bankers - Roll of Honour. Memorial Ref. Pier and Face 7 C and 7 B., Thiepval Memorial, France.

CAREY, Second Lieutenant, Leonard Arthur. Accounts state he was first wounded in the upper left arm not far from the first line of German trenches, wounded again by a shell after leaving the second line of trenches, and spotted on his side in the third enemy trench, 1st July 1916. During the last ten minutes of the intense bombardment A and B Coy had left New Trench and advanced to about 100 yards of the enemy's trenches, Lieutenant E. G. Roberts was badly wounded by shell fire leaving the front line and about the same time Second Lieutenant Carey, A Coy., was killed. 2nd Bn., Devonshire Regiment. Aged 24. Born at Finchley on December 3rd 1891. Father Ernest Edward Carey and mother, Mary Carey, 33 High Holburn. Occupation farmer. A good wicket-keeper and useful batsman, he played for Christ College (Finchley), the Finchley Cricket Club and the King's County Cricket Club of Brooklyn. Enlisted as No. 1288 a private in the 2nd King Edward's Horse, on the 23rd December 1914. Entered France, 4th May 1915. In May 1915 he suffered from German measles. He had been wounded in October, 1915 with a gunshot wound to the left hand. Commissioned second lieutenant 23rd April 1916 in the 2nd Devons. Left the whole of his property and effects to his mother, some article of her choice to his father, sister and two brothers and also to the following Miss Ruth Scott and Miss Audrey Wyatt. Father applied for his medals. His mother applied for retirement payment for officers for both Leonard and his brother, Second Lieutenant Mansel Ernest Carey killed 30th November 1917, Royal West Kent Regiment. Memorial Ref. Pier and Face 1 C., Thiepval Memorial, France. WO 339/59701

CARPENTER, Second Lieutenant, John Neilson, MC. Killed in action on the 1st July, 1916, in an attack upon the Leipzig Redoubt. 17th Bn., Highland Light Infantry. Aged 21. Born 1894. Younger son of Mr. Thomas F. and Mrs. T. F. Carpenter, of 36, Falkland Mansions, Hyndland, Glasgow. Educated Hillhead High School, Glasgow Academy and Glasgow University. His outstanding ability in Mathematics and Science pointed to engineering as a suitable sphere of activity, and he became indentured with Messrs. Yarrow & Co., Scotstoun, shipbuilders. Playing member of the Glasgow Academy Rugby Football Club and resided with his mother at Northcote, Bearsden. In August, 1914, joined the Chamber of Commerce Battalion as a private. Awarded a commission in his own battalion. With them he proceeded to France in November, 1915. On the 23rd April, 1916, his company carried out a singularly successful raid upon the German trenches, taking back with them many prisoners and several machine-guns. For conspicuous gallantry in this raid and for showing great dash in hand-to-hand fighting, he was awarded the Military Cross. Gazetted 30th May 1916. 'Second Lieutenant Carpenter, strong, athletic, fearless, was not only an excellent soldier, but looked the part. His men were all deeply attached to him, and greatly mourned his death.' Death reported 19th July 1916. Mother applied for medals. Memorial Ref. Pier and Face 15 C., Thiepval Memorial, France.

CARR, Second Lieutenant, Eric Marcus. Fell leading his men, 1st July 1916. D Coy., 12th Bn., York and Lancaster Regiment. Aged 20. Only son of Mr. Marcus and Mrs. Constance Carr, Sheffield. Resided 120 Millhouses Lane. Born 30th June 1896 died one day after his 20th birthday. King Edward VII School, Sheffield. Played cricket in 1913 and photographed with Second Lieutenant Howard Morley Hibbert also killed 1st July 1916. Commissioned in the battalion in which he enlisted, 27th June 1915. Commemorated St Peter and St. Oswalds Church, Abbeydale. Mother applied for his medals. Memorial Ref. Pier and Face 14 A and 14 B., Thiepval Memorial, France.

CARSON, Second Lieutenant, William John White. Wounded and missing in action near Thiepval, in the third line of the German trenches, 1st July 1916. 14th Bn., Royal Irish Rifles. Aged 29. Only son of William McRobert Carson (Estate Agent on the Ormeau Road, Belfast) and Sarah Carson, of Tareen House, Old Cavehill Road, Belfast. Born in County Down. Student at the Royal School, Dungannon between 1900 and 1902. Took his degree in surveying at London College and went into business with his father. Enlisted with the 14th (Young Citizens) Battalion of the Royal Irish Fusiliers. Still posted as missing 26th December 1916. Father applied for his medals. Memorial Ref. Pier and Face 15 A and 15 B., Thiepval Memorial, France.

CARTLAND, Captain, George Trevor. He fell between Serre and Beaumont-Hamel, killed 1st July 1916. Adjutant, 1st Bn., Rifle Brigade. Aged 23. Son of George and Lilian Cartland, of Bevere Cottage, near Worcester. Attended St. Ronan's and Winchester College, 1906 to 1911 from Reverend P. Crick's School at Worthing being an enthusiastic member of Archaeological Society. In 1911 he entered RMC Sandhurst, where he had a distinguished career, passing out at the head of the list and receiving the King's Sword and Gold Medal. He played cricket for the Greenjackets and in regimental matches and may have been a member of Worcester County Cricket Club since a T. Cartland is commemorated on the club war memorial. He was gazetted in September 1912 to the 1st Battalion Rifle Brigade and went to France with them 23rd August 1914, taking part in the retreat from Mons and the Battle of the Marne. After a few months' service on the Personal Staff, he rejoined his regiment, was appointed adjutant and shortly afterwards was Mentioned in Despatches. Copy of General Sir Aylmer Hunter-Weston's letter received 11th July, 1916; "I cannot tell you how deeply I sympathise with you in the terrible loss that not only you and your husband, but I his friend, and the country, have incurred by the death of that capable officer and gallant gentleman, your son Trevor. He was killed with his Colonel in the centre of the great attack on the German position, between Beaumont-Hamel and Serre, where the 1st Rifle Brigade covered themselves with glory by their discipline, courage, and determination. It was a magnificent attack. The fine training and discipline of the 1st Bn., Rifle Brigade, were not a little due to the work and example of your gallant son." Father applied for his medals and wrote inscription. Original map reference where body found 57D.K.35.a.4.1, identified by disc and officer's uniform, buried with six soldiers all of whom were killed on the 1st July. Reburied 1927. Memorial Ref. III. E. 14., Serre Road Cemetery No.2, France.

He Fought The Good Fight

CARVER, Second Lieutenant, George Sholto Douglas. Reported, wounded and missing, and then killed near Wailly, 1st July 1916. His orderly reported he was wounded in the first German trench and a returning soldier reported seeing him lying dead about 20 yards in front of our own line and thought the body had been picked up. 3rd Bn. attd. 2nd Bn., Devonshire Regiment. Aged 29. Born 17th November 1886, Coleraine. Son of Lieutenant Colonel William Edward and Beatrice Enuna Elizabeth Carver, of "Southstoke," Exmouth. Former pupil of Oxenford House School, St. Lawrence, Jersey. Enlisted as a private, 7th September 1914. Second lieutenant 16th January 1915. Wounded 5th June 1916 and rejoined his battalion on the 13th June. Still missing believed killed 25th August 1916. His identity disc was returned to the family in June 1917 and his father questioned the War Office as to where it had come from only to be informed it was received with a consignment of men's effects. Father applied for his medals. Memorial Ref. Pier and Face 1 C., Thiepval Memorial, France. WO 339/31056

CARY, Second Lieutenant, Richard Harry. Died at Gommecourt, 1st July 1916. B Coy., 1st/9th Bn., London Regiment (Queen Victoria's Rifles). Aged 22. Son of Henry Cary and Ellen Cary, of 3, Darlington Road, Knights Hill, West Norwood, London. Born 6th March 1894. Educated Western High School, Washington DC. Commercial traveller. Enlisted September, 1914 with the 13th Bn., London Regiment, No. 2857. Entered France, 11th February 1915. Gazetted second lieutenant, 19th November 1915. Served for 22 months. Commemorated St. Luke's Church, West Norwood. Mother applied for his medals and received a parents' pension. Memorial Ref. Pier and Face 9 C., Thiepval Memorial, France.

CASSELS, Captain, Robert Wilson. Died 1st July 1916. 17th Bn., Highland Light Infantry. Aged 31. Son of Robert (ironmaster, Glasgow and Marion Cassels, of Huntly Lodge, Moffat, Dumfriesshire). Native of Glasgow. Educated Kelvinside Academy Fettes College, Glencorse House from 1900. Employed chartered accountant with M'Clelland, Ker & Co., St. Vincent Street. Commissioned lieutenant on 10th September 1914. Appointed to 'D' Company on the formation of the 17th Highland Light Infantry (Glasgow Chamber of Commerce Battalion) in September 1914. In January 1915 promoted captain. Trained for a year at Gailes and Troon, Ayrshire, Prees Heath, Shropshire, Wensleydale, North Yorkshire, Totley Rifle Ranges, Derbyshire and finally Codford St. Mary on Salisbury Plain before crossing to France, 22nd November 1915. Death reported 19th July 1916. Left £2,419 in his will. Mother applied for his medals. Memorial Ref. II. F. 20., Lonsdale Cemetery, Authuille, France.

Photo of the battalion officers as they left Troon, 13th May 1915

CATMUR, Lieutenant, Harry Albert Frederick Valentine. 1st 1916. 3rd Bn., Royal Sussex Regiment. Son of Mr. A. V. Catmur, of 8, Park Road, Beckenhun, Kent. Private, 1346, 18th Bn., Royal Fusiliers onto commission 3rd Bn., Royal Sussex, May 1915 and then Machine Gun Corps (Infantry). Entered France, 11th March 1916. Mentioned in Despatches. Father applied for his medals. Memorial Ref. Pier and Face 7 C., Thiepval Memorial, France.

CECIL, Second Lieutenant, Rotheram Bagshawe. Killed near Mametz, 1st July 1916. Reported to have reached third line trenches and fought until bombs ran out, this officer was reported to be struck by a bomb and killed, apparently refused to surrender. This was when he was in a small party of men and they ran into a German bombing party coming the other way. D Coy., 1st /5th Bn., Sherwood Foresters (Notts and Derby Regiment). Aged 21. Younger son of Rotheram Cecil and Henrietta Jervis Cecil, of Manor House, Dronfield, Derbyshire. Attended Rottingdean School and Tonbridge. At the school 1909-12 (Park House). Entering the School in May 1909, left at Christmas 1912, having become a lance-corporal in the OTC. Working in Earl of Wiltons Estate Agent. Gazetted a second lieutenant in the Sherwood Foresters July 21st 1915, and after a comparatively short period of training sailed on January 8th 1916. In March 1916, his company were holding a trench within twenty yards of the German trenches, and he was at the time in command of the firing line when the Germans exploded a large mine under a portion of the trench that by good fortune was unoccupied at the moment. Some thirty Germans, who crawled over to occupy the crater, were wiped out by machine-gun fire, and Second Lieutenant Cecil was himself the first to gain and occupy the edge of the crater.

Another party of Germans who attempted to rush the crater met with the same fate as the first, and, after his Company Commander had arrived and taken command, Cecil did some effective shooting from the edge of the crater. He is stated to have been specially recommended to the General for his services on this occasion. His Company Commander testified to his conspicuous bravery and services on many occasions, and added: - "He has been an ideal platoon commander, zealous in doing his duty, and always most concerned as to the feeding and general comfort of the men whom he was proud to command as they were to obey him." Some of his men who were talking of him were heard to say that he was "one of the right sort-no nonsense about him. Off with his coat and do the job"; and a brother officer wrote: - "I do hope you have good news of your son. He was so popular with all of us and such a good officer." Elder brother, Private F. R. Cecil joined the Artists Rifles in 1916, but died on the 21st December 1916 being buried at St. John the Baptist Church, Dronfield. Memorial Ref. Pier and Face 10 C 10 D and 11 A., Thiepval Memorial, France.

CHALMERS, Second Lieutenant, John Robert Thorburn. Killed instantaneously gallantly leading his men in the assault, 1st July 1916. Also reported that he had just gone over the top and turned around to talk to his men helping them over and forming them up when he was hit in the back in two or three places, undaunted, he still issued orders until forced into our own trench by his men where he died half an hour later. 8th Bn., Somerset Light Infantry. Aged 28. Born 30th March 1887. Second son of Peter and Jessie Chalmers, of Alburne, Bearsden, Glasgow. Educated Peebles High School. He was travelling in the East at the outbreak of war. Keen athlete, enthusiast in hockey. Member of the Western Club, Glasgow. Scottish Manager for the Sceptre Life Association Ltd. Attested 9th October 1914. Served with the 81st Brigade, Royal Field Artillery promoted from gunner to corporal, No. 23203. Commissioned 27th April 1915. Entered France, 29th May 1916. Effects returned were half franc note, penny, identity disc, letter, fountain pen, compass, pair cuff links, coin and writing pad. Memorial Ref. Pier and Face 2 A., Thiepval Memorial, France. WO 339/41195

CHAMBERS, Second Lieutenant, Anthony Gerald. 1st July 1916. 4th Bn., Middlesex Regiment. Aged 21. Fourth son of Dr. Anthony Bernard Chambers and Julia Chambers, of Barnley House, Brayton Road, Selby, Yorks. Native of Long Eaton, Nottingham. Born 12th March 1895. Educated at St. Mary's College, Chesterfield. Enlisted in the Public Schools Bn. Gazetted second lieutenant to 6th Bn., Middlesex on the 9th May 1915. Entered France, 29th May 1916. Three of his brothers served at the Front. Before the war he was on the editorial staff of The Standard. Joined his battalion, 2nd June 1916. Buried angle of Empress Trench and a new communication trench sht 26. Sq d. contour 110. Mother applied for his medals. Original grave reference 57d.X.27c.7.6 and buried as unknown officer, Middlesex Regiment, identified from collective grave and reburied in Row L. Memorial Ref. IV. L., Gordon Dump Cemetery, Ovillers-La Boisselle, France. WO 339/56804

CHAMBERS, Second Lieutenant, Edward Chandos Elliot. Leading the first wave of his men, he was hit by a machine-gun bullet and killed instantaneously; 'whilst gallantly leading his men in an attack on the German trenches, this was about 9.40am', Authuille Wood, 1st July 1916. A Coy., 19th (Service) Bn., Lancashire Fusiliers. Aged 20. Born Allwal North, Cape Colony on April 4th 1896. Only son of Richard Edward Elliot Chambers and Edith Frances Chambers of Lyme Regis, Dorset. Family held property in Co. Meath. Educated at Mr. Douglas's, Malvern Link (1905 – 1909), where he was captain of the school in his last term and Marlborough College (1909 – 1913). In Oxford, where he was an exhibitioner at St. John's College also studied in Paris. Played cricket although not in the Eleven at Marlborough, he was a useful cricketer and in 1913 was one of the Cock House team. Having been four years in the Marlborough College and Oxford University OTC, he was gazetted as a cadet from the latter corps. Gazetted June 15th 1915. Second lieutenant, 19th (Service) Battalion, Lancashire Fusiliers. Landed with his regiment, 22nd November 1915. In the trenches for the first time, 1st December 1915. He was buried on the 3rd July 1916. Medals to his mother and father in Lyme Regis. Memorial Ref. I. A. 13., Bouzincourt Communal Cemetery Extension, France.

Only Son Of R. E. Elliot Chambers Killed Near Authuille Wood Aged 20

CHAPMAN, Second Lieutenant, Arthur Donald. Reported wounded and missing, 1st July 1916. 1st/5th Bn., North Staffordshire Regiment. Aged 24. Son of Albert (commercial traveller), and Clara Chapman, of Ashby Road, Loughborough formerly of Burton Street, Loughborough. Trained in the boot and shoe trade. Educated at Loughborough Grammar School, and for some time had been in a good position in South Africa came back to England to join the army. Member of Longcliffe Golf Club. Married to Lizzie. Commissioned 13th August 1915. Entered France, 8th May 1916. His brother, Albert served and became a Major in the Machine Gun Corp. Two cousins died in the war, Captain John Chapman, 15th May 1915 and Lieutenant Hubert Chapman died March 1917. Father applied for his medals. Memorial Ref. Pier and Face 14 B and 14 C., Thiepval Memorial, France.

CHARLES, Second Lieutenant, Albert. Deceased 1st July 1916. Reported missing believed killed, C Coy., 1st/7th Bn., Sherwood Foresters (Notts and Derby Regiment). Son of Thomas Charles (smallholder). Resided Meadow View, London Colney, St. Albans. Attested, private, Inns of Court OTC. Lance corporal in the OTC, No. 3760. Commissioned 17th September 1915. By 1922 his widow had remarried, Mrs. Gaullard, Victoria Road, Netherfield and applied for his medals. Memorial Ref. Pier and Face 10 C 10 D and 11 A., Thiepval Memorial, France.

CHARLESWORTH, Second Lieutenant, Thomas Stephens. Officially reported killed 10th July 1916. 25th Bn., (Tyneside Irish) Northumberland Fusiliers. Grave Registration Unit and Concentration Burial Records both show date of death of the 1st July 1916. Reports in The Newcastle Journal also refer to date of death as the 1st July in his 21st year. Second son of Mr. and Mrs. Arthur Heyward (solicitor) and Eliza Charlesworth of Hotspur Street, Tyneside. Born Chorlton-cum-Hardy on the 29th October 1895. Educated Tynemouth School. Grandson of John Charlesworth, architect of Manchester. Awarded St. John's decoration certificate, May 1914. Enlisted as private 6505, 13th, Northumberland Fusiliers. Temporary second lieutenant, 4th March 1915. Moved to Gordon Dump Cemetery, December 1919. Original map reference 57d.X.20.c found with Lieutenant L. F. Byrne, (grave 9) 24th Bn., Northumberlands and Private Arthur Graves, 11th Bn., Suffolk Regiment (grave 10) both were killed on the 1st July. Commemorated St. John Ambulance Brigade No. V1 District Memorial under North Tyneside group. Memorial Ref. X. S. 8. Gordon Dump Cemetery, Ovillers La Boisselle, France.

CHARLTON, Captain, John MacFarlan. He was shot through the head by a bullet, while leading his company near La Boiselle, 1st July 1916. This was after they had taken the first and second lines of enemy trenches and when they were just about to charge the third. John's last reported words were to his orderly: "Is that you, B? For God's sake, push on, I'm done." The orderly stooped down and asked if there was anything he could do, but the captain was dead. Captain Charlton and Captain Herries lay in hollow ground and managed to get a machine gun up, John initially had success but when trying to take on a German strong-point the gun jammed and he was killed. 21st (Tyneside Scottish) Bn., Northumberland Fusiliers. Age 25. Born 1st July 1891, Middlesex. Son of John, (a renowned painter), and Kate MacFarlane Charlton, 6 William St, Knightsbridge, SW. Educated at Uppingham School, Rutland from September 1906 to July 1910 where he was secretary to the Natural History section of the school. In December 1910 he won a special bronze medal given by the Royal Society for the Protection of Birds and wrote many short articles in other journals and local papers. Skillful and artistic taxidermist. Attended Uppingham and Armstrong College (Newcastle University) and in the Uppingham Cadets Corps He joined the Northumberland Hussars Yeomanry in October 1914, received his commission in the Northumberland Fusiliers on 17th November 1914, and was promoted to captain in the 21st Bn., (2nd Tyneside Scottish) on the 21st September 1915. He entered France in February 1916 and was a transport officer at Division Head Quarters. Recommended for the Military Cross, the Germans made a raid on his section and he grabbed a few men and drove the Germans out. He personally shot dead the officers who led the raid. He was Mentioned in Despatches on the 13th November 1916. Brother, Second Lieutenant Hugh Vaughan Charlton, also died in the war, 24th June 1916. Their father, painted the two young men sat with their grandmother; while in another painting entitled 'The Brothers H.V.C. and J.M.C., Sandisdyke', two young men with their three dogs look up to the viewer. He also painted a posthumous portrait of John that was exhibited in the spring of 1917. Left an estate worth £5,757 and gave a of group of games in a large case to Uppingham School with a tablet thereon saying 'Presented by Captain J. M. Charlton, In memory of some of the happiest days of his life'. Aunt's address for his medal correspondence. Memorial Ref. Pier and Face 10 B 11 B and 12 B., Thiepval Memorial, France. WO 339/28849

CHESHIRE, Second Lieutenant, William Robert. Companies came under heavy artillery and machine-gun barrage immediately they appeared over the parapet causing heavy losses, 1st July 1916. 3rd Bn., attd. 1st Bn., Essex Regiment. Aged 27. Eldest son of Councillor William and Emma Jane Cheshire, of St. Botolph's Street and Meyrick Crescent, Colchester. Educated Colchester Royal Grammar School. Worked in Ceylon since 1911, assistant Colombo Stores Company Joined the Ceylon Planter's Rifles, F Company, No. 1 Section, No. 1748, private at the outbreak of war and went to Egypt, 17th November 1914 and onto Gallipoli where he contracted jaundice afterwards given a commission in the Essex Regiment. Before going to Gallipoli he trained the Australians in Egypt. Distinguished and fine all-round athlete and won many events. Medals to his father in Colchester. Memorial Ref. G. 18., Knightsbridge Cemetery, Mesnil-Martinsart, France.

Till We Meet Again

CHIPLIN, Captain, William Henry. Unofficial report stated he was seen at a dressing station and initially reported missing. 1st July 1916. 15th Bn., Royal Irish Rifles. Aged 30. Son of William John (telephone official) and Frances Annie Chiplin, "Rosenalea", Cyprus Gardens, Bloomfield, Belfast. Service of Ocean Accident and Guarantee Corporation Ltd, Belfast. Before obtaining his commission on the formation of the Ulster Division he was captain of St. Donard's Church Company of the Church Lads' Brigade, a member of the Church of Ireland Miniature Rifle Club and an officer in the East Regiment UVF. His manager wrote that he was: "a keen soldier and was regarded as an officer of high ability. It is hoped the worst has not happened and that he may be a prisoner." Entered France, 3rd October 1915. Medals to his mother in Belfast, she also applied for his pension payment. Memorial Ref. Pier and Face 15 A and 15 B., Thiepval Memorial, France.

CHOLMELEY, Lieutenant, Eric Randolph. Killed while crossing No Man's Land in Mash Valley towards Ovillers La Boisselle, reported wounded and missing, 1st July 1916. 2nd Bn., West Yorkshire Regiment (Prince of Wales's Own). Born 21st May 1895 in West Kensington, London. Son of Randolf Lucas and Clara Louise Cholmeley. Attended Twyford School (September 1903 to March 1906) and Haileybury (Batten 1909 – 1912). Bank clerk. Attended RMC Sandhurst from January 1913 to July 1914. Entered France on 5th November 1914. Expeditionary Force, November to July 1915. 23rd July 1915 suffered a shell wound to the right thigh and treated at King Edward VIII Hospital and declared fit for duty, 31st December 1915. Eric applied for Royal Flying Corps in the 11th March 1916 and was due to join them at Reading on the 5th June 1916 but these orders were cancelled. Father applied for his medals. Commemorated St. Mary's Church, The Boltons, Chelsea. Memorial Ref. Pier and Face 2 A 2 C and 2 D., Thiepval Memorial, France. WO 339/11155

CHOLMELEY, Lieutenant, Harry Lewin. Reported wounded and missing, the 1st Bn., Borders went into action with 23 officers and 809 other ranks, casualties were 20 officers and 619 other ranks. Reported wounded and missing, 1st July 1916. 3rd Bn. attd. 1st Bn., Border Regiment. Aged 23. Son of Lewin Charles and Elizabeth Maud Cholmeley, of 19, Hamilton Terrace, St. John's Wood, London. Educated Eton and Magdalen College, Oxon. Intended to take Holy Orders. Previously wounded with 2nd Bn., March, 1915. Memorial located in the Cloisters, Eton College reads; "To the beloved & ever honoured memory of Montague Aubrey Cholmeley Baronet, Capt. Grenadier Guards killed Festubert 24th December 1914 aged 38 and Hugh Valentine Cholmeley, Second Lieutenant Grenadier Guards killed Ypres 7th April 1916 aged 28 & Harry Lewin Cholmeley Lieutenant The Border Regiment killed Beaumont-Hamel 1st July 1916 aged 23. Be content/ no honour of age had been more excellent." Father applied for his medals. Memorial Ref. Pier and Face 6 A and 7 C., Thiepval Memorial, France.

CHURCHFIELD, Second Lieutenant, Sidney Percival. 1st July 1916. 63rd Trench Mortar Battery formerly 4th Bn., Middlesex Regiment followed behind the brigade attack and killed either crossing No Man's Land or within the enemy trenches. Aged 24. Son of James and Minnie Churchfield. Born 22nd January 1887. Attended Strand School, Brixton. Husband of Winifred Annie Churchfield, of 40, Eglantine Road, Wandsworth, London married 23rd January 1915. Formerly private, 28th Bn., London Regiment, Artists Rifles, No. 3272. Entered France, 9th May 1915. Commissioned second lieutenant 16th January 1916 to a Trench Mortar Battery on the 30th May 1916.

Last letter home from the trenches dated 28th June 1916;

"Darling when you get this you know I will have gone under & my object in writing this note before I go over the top is to let you know I have left no will but I want everything I have to go to you with the exception of one or two small trinkets. My watch chain I want to be given back to my mother and my gold ring to Jim & the gramophone if it ever reaches home to be given to Sister Ford at the B. H. for her gallery. Well Darling I want you to bear up and not grieve for remember I am but one of many who have given their lives in this great cause. My last thoughts dearest were of you & I want you to put a stout heart and face to the world.

Goodbye we shall met again. Hubby."

His widow, Winifred applied for his medals and claimed his pension of £100. Buried angle of Empress Trench and a new communication trench. Sht 26. Sq D contour 110 and reburied row L. Memorial Ref. IV. L., Gordon Dump Cemetery, Ovillers-La Boisselle, France. WO 339/54353

In Honourable And Glorious Memory

CLARK, Second Lieutenant, Charles Augustus. Missing believed killed, five miles south of Gommecourt, 1st July 1916. 5th Bn. attd. 1st Bn., Rifle Brigade. Aged 30. Born Matlock. Son of Arthur Clark and Mary Francis Clark of Derwent Terrace, Post Office, North Parade, Matlock Bath, Derbyshire. Baptised 25th November 1888 at Holy Trinity Church with his brothers. Accountant associated with the firm of Messrs. Derbyshire Bros & Co. Landed France 7th December 1915. Confirmed in rank, 1st April 1916. Brother Lieutenant Neville Arthur Clark, Coldstream Guards died 28th November 1917. Three brothers served as did his sister, Edyth with the Women's Army Auxiliary Corps (W.A.A.C). Father applied for his medals. Memorial Ref. Pier and Face 16 B and 16 C., Thiepval Memorial, France.

CLARK, Second Lieutenant, Eric Henry Lloyd. Liaison officer between the artillery and infantry for a diversionary attack on Gommecourt, killed whilst advancing, laying a wire, 1st July 1916. Killed with Lieutenant Trevor Arthur Manning Davies. 5th Bty., 3rd North Midland Bde., Royal Field Artillery. Aged 19. Born 19th May 1897. Son of Francis John and Lily L. Clark, of "Gulmarg", 12, Albemarle Road, Beckenham, Kent. He attended St. Lawrence College in Ramsgate from 1906 to 1915 and a member of the OTC. Hockey player. To be second lieutenant, October 14th 1915. Talbot House visitors book, page 53, dated 26th February 1916. Medal application by his father. Memorial Ref. Pier and Face 1 A and 8 A., Thiepval Memorial, France.

CLARK, Captain, William Spencley. Killed at the head of his men, by machine-gun fire, 1st July 1916 and left hanging on the wire. A Coy. 12th Bn., York and Lancaster Regiment. At 1.55am he reported our own wire cut on our front and tapes laid out in front of our line, laying of tape was completed at 12.30am. Aged 24. Youngest son of William (Director of Vickers Ltd.) and Margaret Kirkwood Clark, of Whiteley Wood Hall, Sheffield, later Annet House, Skelmorie, Ayrshire. After leaving Dollar Academy educated at Glasgow High School and an engineering pupil at Vickers. On the outbreak of war he hastened back from a holiday and joined the Sheffield University OTC. He took a part in forming the 12th York and Lancaster City Battalion, and was commissioned in that battalion in September 1914. He was promoted captain in November 1915. The battalion went to Egypt in December 1915, and returned to France early in March. Many of his comrades wrote to testify to his excellent qualities as a soldier. His colonel said that he "was a good, brave lad, worthy of the uniform he wore, and a credit and example to the Sheffield battalion." The senior Major wrote: "A braver or keener boy never lived." A brother officer told how "he was killed on the parapet of the German line, where he was first on, leading his men with cheerful and encouraging words". On the 16th June 1931 it was necessary to exhume the bodies of two unknown York and Lancaster officers from map reference 57d.K.29.b.4.4 Puisieux au Mont in an isolated grave. The effects found were a ring engraved W.S.C or S.W.C and dentures (found in grave near bodies), pieces of officer's tunics, Y & L buttons, two pairs of Bedford cord breeches, two officer ties, two pairs of G.S boots (size 9) and inside DORA, October 1914. The bodies were approximately 5'9" and 5'10". The upper parts of the bodies were so intermingled as to render separate exhumation impossible. The remains were reburied in one coffin with two graves spaces being allowed thus grave numbers 7/8. There are nineteen York and Lancaster officers killed on the 1st July 1916 with no known grave, there is also an unknown Yorks and Lancaster officer in grave 9. Memorial Ref. XXXIX. J. 7/8., Serre Road Cemetery No.2, France.

CLARKE, Second Lieutenant, Arundel Geoffrey. Fell at Serre, he was twice wounded while leading his bombers towards their objective, but continued to press on until struck by a shell and killed. Missing believed killed, 1st July 1916. One of the few to reach the German second line of wire. 5th Bn., Rifle Brigade attached 1st Bn. Aged 33. Younger son of the Reverend Arthur Edward Clarke (first Headmaster of the Oxford Preparatory School /Dragon School), of Oxford. Born at Oxford in 1883. Educated under Mr. C. C. Lynam at Oxford Preparatory School/Dragon School. Went to Dragon as a boarder in Mrs. Clarke's House, left in 1896. Geoffrey was a splendid all-round boy. He was in the Cricket XI and Football XV for two years. He had a beautiful voice and gained great reputation in the school concerts for singing and recitation. He won the School French Prize for three years, the School Prize for Classics, Latin Verse, and Mathematics, and Professor Wallace's prize for Latin in his last year, 1896. He finished as Head of the School and winner of the Gold Medal. Elected to the third scholarship at Winchester College, where he was Prefect of Hall in 1901 and 1902, and got into College XI under 16. He won a Scholarship at New College in October 1902 and got a Second Class in Honour Moderations, and a Third Class in Literature and Humanities in 1906. He represented the University at lawn tennis. In 1907 he went as assistant master to the Royal Naval College, Osborne and in 1912 was in Bethnal Green where he lived for the next two years. Here he made a study of social and economic conditions and in 1914 published "A Text Book of National Economy". He took great interest in national education, which he studied during visits to Germany, especially as regards the teaching of 'Civics', upon which he published a Manual for Teachers early in 1914. He helped to organise Bethnal Green Boys' Clubs, and always attended the Old Dragon dinners.

Soon after the outbreak of war he attempted to enlist but was rejected by the doctors and began a course of physical training, first for Home Service and shortly after for General Service in the Royal Fusiliers (Public Schools Brigade) eventually being passed fit and joining the ranks as a private soldier. Suffered a gunshot wound to the face, in August 1915 and spent 11 days in hospital. After serving sometime in the ranks, he was given a commission in the Intelligence Corps and proceeded to France in September 1915. He spent all his spare time working up his military subjects. In March 1916 he reverted at his own request to regimental duty with the Rifle Brigade, to get a more thorough knowledge of the work and requirements of the fighting troops, was appointed battalion bombing officer and placed on the list for employment on the General Staff. A brother officer writes: "He led his bombers well on to his objective under a heavy fire before he fell, wounded, into a shell hole. One of our bombers dressed his wounds, and Geoffrey continued to throw bombs into the enemy trench till he was killed by a Boche bomb. We had to leave him there when we were ordered to retire."

His Commanding Officer writes: "I had the privilege of knowing your brother very well indeed, and a more competent and energetic officer I never hope to meet. There was no officer who was more thoroughly liked and whose character commanded such general respect among his fellow officers and I am sure that none was loved by his men in quite the same way. I know that he fell, happy in the thought of his work well done, and himself prepared for anything." Brother, Major B. G. S. Clarke applied for his medals. Mr. D. A. Clarke, Lenwood, Northam, Devon decided the personal inscription. Original map reference of burial 57d.K.35.c.25.65 identified by his disc, officer's khaki, boots, disc and watch engraved 'A. G. Clarke.' He was originally buried with an unknown British soldier who lies next to him in grave 14. Memorial Ref. XIII. A. 13., A.I.F. Burial Ground, Flers, France.

R.I.P.

CLARKE, Second Lieutenant, James Henry Fisher. Killed at Fricourt, 1st July 1916. School magazine covered his death: "He had several bullet wounds. I was passing along the trench when he was dying. He did not recognise me, although I spoke to him. He had been leading the first assaulting platoon of his battalion. He was the first man therefore over the top. The objective was Fricourt village. You can understand it was no mean death, but of course we would rather have had him back alive. The attack took place very early in the Somme push." No. 7 Platoon, 7th Bn., Yorkshire Regiment. Son of Charles (colliery clerk) and Nellie Clarke. Born Nether Hoyland, Yorkshire in 1895. Boarded at St. Cuthberts College, Sparken Hill, Worksop and educated King Edward VII School, Sheffield, member of the OTC between 1908 - 1913 as a sergeant. Entered Edinburgh University, in the OTC between October and December 1914. Enlisted and served in the Yorkshire Hussars (Alexandra Princes of Wales Own Yorkshire Regiment). Second lieutenant 6th January 1915. Entered France, July 1915.

Wounded 28th July 1915 with a gunshot wound from a sniper's bullet to the left temple that left him stunned for a short time and after undergoing hospital treatment required two months recovery time. The following letter was received by his family: "The 7th Yorks were detailed to attack Fricourt, seize the village, and the wood beyond. The German front line ran almost parallel to our own at a distance alternating from 200 to 300 yards. The order of advance was three companies in the front line, with B Company in the centre Nos. 4 and 5 platoons of B Company were to push forward with No 6 in close support. No 7 platoon, commanded by Mr. Clarke, were in local reserve to the Company and were not to advance until the German front line was taken. As I expect you already know, the unexpected happened, and the first two platoons were no sooner over than they were met by a withering fire from the enemy machine-guns at close range. Mr. Hornsby, commanding No. 5 platoon, fell mortally wounded before they had advanced ten yards. No. 6 were now ready to advance and leave No. 7 in the trench. Mr. Hillman, command No. 6, climbed the parapet and ordered his platoon forward. He was shot immediately through the head. B Company were thus left without any officers to lead them. The captain was wounded, and the Officer Commanding No. 8 was too far away on the left to be in touch with the right and centre. On seeing this your son immediately climbed the parapet, saying, "Follow me B Company, I will lead ." But nothing could exist under that fire, and he fell before he reached our own wire about ten yards in front of our parapet. He was brought in immediately but was past all hope and died almost at once. I think he would not have felt any pain as the wounds would have rendered him unconscious immediately. We laid him side by side with Mr. Hillman on the fire step, and I told his servant to collect his things and send them to headquarters. Where he was buried I could never find out, but I think that they must have both been taken away and buried behind the line. In conclusion I should like to say that no gentleman gave up his life for his men more gallantly than he did. On his own initiative he went forward to certain death because he saw the men left without a leader. He was mourned by all those who were left, as not only an officer, but also a true comrade to all his men, and I think he left a void which will never be entirely filled. Only the day before, his platoon sergeant was mortally wounded, and he accompanied him all the way to the dressing station, comforting him as far as possible. When we left, the sergeant asked Mr. Clarke to kiss him, as he had lost both arms. I know how deeply he felt that loss of his sergeant. We had little thought when he rejoined us how soon we were to lose him again. Always kind and considerate to all, he still combined it with the soldierly instinct, which made him a true type of British officer and gentleman. Now I must close, Sir, knowing how deeply you must mourn. I tender my deepest sympathy in which I am joined by the entire Company.
Hoping this letter will in some way appease your natural desire for information, I will close Sir, with best wishes. Yours sincerely,
Private E. Greenwood.
P. S. - Sir, on enquiry from the Regimental Sergeant Major, I was told that your son was buried with Mr. Hillman, near the railway which ran between the opposing trenches. The grave is marked by a white cross."

Mr. Hillman is Lieutenant, Harold Alexander Moore Hillman killed 1st July 1916. Items returned were letters, pipe, tobacco pouch, canvas ammunition case, electric torch, whistle and lanyard, cheque book, advance book and block notes. 1920 relatives informed he was re-buried from Fricourt Cemetery. Original map reference for burial 62d.f.9.c.3.9 with three other soldiers. Father applied for his medals. Memorial Ref. II. I. 9., Dantzig Alley British Cemetery, Mametz, France. WO 339/5477

CLEGG, Second Lieutenant, Alexander. Led No. 4 Platoon of A Coy., wounded in the head about half way to the German lines, last seen getting into a shell hole, 1st July 1916. 15th Bn., Lancashire Fusiliers. Born 24th March 1892 at Halliwell, Bolton. Son of Samuel and Ellen Clegg of 20 Cobden Street, Halliwell, Bolton. He attended Derby Street Congregational School in Bolton, and in 1911 enrolled at Manchester University completing a BSc in 1914 and a teaching certificate in 1915. He was a member of the Manchester University OTC being an NCO from October 1911 to June 1915 when he was gazetted second lieutenant in the 13th (Service) Bn., Lancashire Fusiliers. For a short while he became an assistant teacher at Cork Grammar School, when he applied for a commission in 1915 his address was 48 Great George Street, Cork. He had been at the Front a few months since 23rd March 1916. Mother applied for his medals and parents pension. Memorial Ref. Pier and Face 3 C and 3 D., Thiepval Memorial, France.

CLEGG, Second Lieutenant, Percy. Killed leading his men over a German trench in 1st July 1916. 1st Bn., King's Own (Royal Lancaster Regiment). Aged 21. Son of Robert and Margaret A. Clegg, of Higher Lomax, Heywood, Lancs. Formerly, private in the Royal Fusiliers. Commissioned 4th December 1915. Entered France, 1st June 1916. Body recovered from the battlefield. Father applied for his medals. Mother applied for parents pension. Memorial Ref. I. H. 3., Sucrerie Military Cemetery, Colincamps, France.

Until the day breaks

CLESHAM, Second Lieutenant, Thomas Henry. He fell just as he led his men over the parapet and was killed instantly, 1st July 1916. 17th Bn., Manchester Regiment. Aged 34. Eldest son of the Reverend T. Clesham, MA, Incumbent of Aasleagh, Co. Mayo, and Isabella Clesham, of Caherduff, Cong, Claremorris, Co. Mayo. Attended Portora School. He graduated at Trinity College, Dublin, and subsequently went to South Africa to take up an important post in the mining fields. On the outbreak of the war he joined the forces of General Botha as a trooper, with the Natal Light Horse. and took his full share in the campaign, on the termination of which he hurried home to take his part in the Western field. He was gazetted to a lieutenancy in the Manchester Regiment and joined the Flying Corps until he became a fully qualified aviator. Lieutenant Clesham was a splendid type of officer and beloved by his comrades. Medals to his mother in Co. Mayo. Memorial Ref. Pier and Face 13 A and 14 C., Thiepval Memorial, France.

CLIFFORD, Lieutenant, Hugh Gilbert Francis. Reported missing, believed killed on the 1st July 1916. 2nd Bn., Lincolnshire Regiment. Aged 19. Only son of Sir Hugh Clifford, G.C.M.G., G.B.E. (Governor of the Gold Coast) and Minna Clifford. Born 20th January 1897. Grandson of Major-General the Hon. Sir Henry Hugh Clifford, VC., Educated at Downside School, 1908 to 1913 and Wimbledon College 1913 to 1914. Passed into RMC Sandhurst in August, 1914 and received his commission in the following December. Entered France, 7th March 1915. Wounded May, 1915, at Fromelles. Suffered from stomatitis an inflammation of the mouth and lips in February 1916 to March 1916, and returned to the Front in April 1916. After his death the results of a special enquiry were revealed. Several reports were received, that Hugh was killed trying to get back to our own lines, he was shot through the head and was seen lying dead in a German first line trench. Address for medals was His Excellency Sir High Clifford, Governor & Commander in Chief, Nigeria. Original map reference for burial 57d.X.7.b with thirteen fallen soldiers. Memorial Ref. IX. M. 9., Ovillers Military Cemetery, France. WO 339/23626

Only Son Of Sir Hugh Clifford G.C.M.G. Governor Of Nigeria

CLODE-BAKER, Lieutenant, George Edmund. He was seen lying about 50 yards from the German trenches shot through the wrist and eye, 1st July 1916. 5th Bn., London Regiment (London Rifle Brigade). Aged 22. Eldest son of George and Winifred Clode-Baker, of Holmfields, Reigate, Surrey. Born in London. Educated at Uppingham. Inns of Court OTC, private, 2455. Resided The Chestnuts, Croydon Road, Beddington. At the outbreak of war enlisted in the London Rifle Brigade, gazetted second lieutenant in February 1915 and promoted to lieutenant in May. Joined the battalion in France, 24th December 1915. Wallington War Memorial. Correspondence on medals to his father. Body recovered in Spring 1917 when the Germans retreated. Memorial Ref. Sp. Mem. Believed to be buried in this cemetery. C. 6., Gommecourt British Cemetery No.2, Hebuterne, France.

Their Glory Shall Not Be Blotted Out

CLOUDESLEY, Lieutenant, Hugh. At 7.30am the battalion assaulted the German trenches to the front of left half of A1 subsector on a front of about 400 yards – After 12 hours fighting the final objective west of Montauban was reached and consolidated on a front of about 280 yards, killed in No Man's Land or close to Breslau Trench, 1st July 1916. 7th Bn., The Queen's (Royal West Surrey Regiment). Youngest son of John Leslie Cloudsley, Brightlands, Reigate, and grandson of James Cloudsley, White Hart Hotel, Arbroath. Born 1884. Attended Berkhamsted School and Caius College, Cambridge where he took a Law Tripos. Called to the Bar 1906 (Inner Temple) and joined the Midland Circuit, barrister-at-law. Member of Thames Hare and Hounds. Joined the Inns of Court OTC at the outbreak of war in which he had previously served four years and was gazetted in November 1914. Active service since 27th July 1915 and had served as a bombing officer. Medals to his family home in Reigate. Original burial map reference 62C.A.8.c.8.9 with four other officers also killed on the 1st July, Second Lieutenant Baddeley, Lieutenant Goss, Lieutenant Saltmarshe and Captain Scott. Memorial Ref. VIII. R. 2., Dantzig Alley British Cemetery, Mametz, France.

CLOUGH, Captain, Alan. Fell mortally hurt at the head of his men, making it into No Man's Land near Serre, 1st July 1916. 'Sent a message at 8.00am D Coy. Advancing – casualties unknown. In front of Bradford Trench'. Wounded in No Man's Land probably in the left wrist appeared to try to move backwards and was reported hit again. He took command when Major Guyon was mortally wounded. D Coy., 16th Bn., West Yorkshire Regiment (Prince of Wales's Own). Aged 21. Third son of Henry Smith Clough, and Elizabeth Clough, of Redbolt, Keighley. Educated Horton School, Ickwell Bury and at Tonbridge (1909 -1913) at the point of proceeding to Trinity College when war broke out. The year 1913-14 he spent in his father's business (Messrs. Robert Clough of Bradford and Keighley) spinning and weaving, learning that portion of it which involves most drudgery, and working with the men exactly as if he had been an apprentice. Admitted as pensioner at Trinity, 1914. His elder brother, Major John Clough, DSO, MC, served with the Tank Corps. Applying for a commission like his brother not long after the outbreak of war, he was gazetted as a temporary lieutenant in the 16th (1st Bradford) Bn., West Yorkshire Regiment, 23rd September 1914. He was promoted captain, December 16th 1914, when he was still only nineteen. 24th December, 1915, he went out to Egypt, and was for a time in the Syrian Desert. In April, 1916, the Battalion went to France.

The Major, second in command, wrote of Captain Clough; "I think the regiment, officers and men, miss him more than anyone else in the battalion. I personally miss him more than I can say. . . . When things were at their worst, he always had a laugh and a solution. His saying, 'Life is one great scream,' was practically a motto with us. He was an extraordinarily capable and lovable lad. He was killed, where one would expect, gallantly leading his men." A captain wrote : "Of all our many friends whom we have lost, there is none who is more regretted. He was such a cheery little chap, and in the bad times we had before the 1st of July, if the little man came in, things brightened up immediately. . . . The Major will have told you what a good soldier he was. There was nobody in whom the men had greater confidence, and the whole regiment was, and is, proud of him." Medal correspondence to his father. Memorial Ref. Pier and Face 2 A 2 C and 2 D., Thiepval Memorial, France.

COATES, Second Lieutenant, Harold Brearley. At 2.30pm they rose from the trenches to push the attack and were met with heavy machine-gun fire, 1st July 1916. Battalion bombing officer. 7th Bn., Yorkshire Regiment. Aged 20. Only son of Henry and Julia Coates, of 15, Sutherland Avenue, Johannesburg, South Africa and grandson of Thomas Coates of Harrogate, Yorkshire. Born Barnsley, 10th January 1896. Entered Oundle (Dryden House) School in September 1909, leaving in December 1914, member of the Oundle OTC. His intention had been to study medicine although he won a place at Caius College, Cambridge, he did not go up. He obtained a commission in the Yorkshire Regiment, 26th December 1914. Entered France 13th July 1915. On hearing that Second Lieutenant Coates had been killed two bombers left the line in attempt to take revenge by the killing of a German, the first got ten yards the second got within twenty yards of the German line, before he too was also killed. The District Staff Officer, No. 8 Military District, Johannesburg made an application on behalf of his mother for his medal entitlement. Original map reference for burial 62d.F.9.c.3.9 buried with three other soldiers including Second Lieutenant G. H. F. Clarke killed on the 1st July. Memorial Ref. VI. G. 2., Dantzig Alley British Cemetery, Mametz, France. WO 339/4696

COCKCROFT, Second Lieutenant, Arthur Clarence. Reported to be shot through the head, as soon as he left the dug-out and the first off the company to fall, 1st July 1916 locally reported as the 3rd July 1916. B Coy., 11th Bn. attd. 10th Bn., King's Own Yorkshire Light Infantry. Aged 24. Elder son of Mr. George Henry and Mrs. Ellen Cockcroft, of Chapel Street, Knottingley, Yorks. Born May 1892, Hull. Educated King's School, Pontefract from 1904 to 1910. Professional rugby league player for Wakefield. Trinity 1913-1914. Enlisted as a private, 20071 in the Grenadier Guards at Leeds and commissioned January 1915. Entered France, Christmas Day 1915, accidentally wounded taking a German trench 25th January 1916 and returned to duty 1st March 1916. In his last letter headlined 'To be send home in case I fall' dated 29th June 1916, Arthur wrote; 'Well goodbye and please don't mourn my loss but comfort yourselves with the fact I have given my life for King and Country.' Father applied for his medals. Memorial Ref. Sp. Mem. B. 9., Gordon Dump Cemetery, Ovillers-La Boisselle, France. WO 339/4245

"Honoris Causa"

COE, Second Lieutenant, George. Battalion advanced from assembly trenches at 8.00am and came under very heavy machine-gun fire, 1st July 1916. 1st Bn. attd. 11th Bn., Border Regiment. Aged 30. Eldest son of George John and Rosa Coe, of 2, Westgate Terrace, formerly Lodge Farm, Long Melford, Suffolk. Formerly sergeant 1367 in the Ceylon Planters Rifle Corps, having held an important position in Colombo. He was one of the best tennis players in Ceylon and won the Biddulph Cup for shooting. At the outbreak of war he volunteered for active service and went to Egypt, 17th November 1914 where he was engaged in training the Australians and New Zealanders. Commissioned 19th April 1915, 1st Border at the request of Sir George Birdwood, served at Gallipoli, where he took part in the battles of 21st August 1915. Contracted dysentery, and was invalided home to the Palace Hotel. After a time at his own home, he again took up duty at Shoeburyness, Clapham and Conway. On 18th March 1916 he was attached to 11th Border Regiment going out to France. An officer of the regiment wrote; ' It is with great regret that I have to inform you of the death of your son, who was killed on the morning of the 1st during our attack on the German lines. When I tell you that there were only three officers and about a third of the men left you will have some idea of how we suffered. Your son, who had only been in our company for a short time, was shot in the head whilst leading his platoon into action. As soon as the battalion left the trenches the Germans opened a terrific machine-gun fire, which caught our men in the cross-fire. The only consolation I can offer you is that death was instantaneous and he died as all of us would wish to, namely, at the head of his men. Though only in the company for such a short time, he had gained the full confidence of his men, and was very popular with the officers.' His brother Second Lieutenant W. Coe, Border Regiment was reported missing April 1918 and survived the war. Medal correspondence to his father. Memorial Ref. Pier and Face 6 A and 7 C., Thiepval Memorial, France.

COLDWELLS, Second Lieutenant, Francis Baker. Wounded and missing, 1st July 1916. No. 16 Platoon, D Coy., 3rd Bn. attd. 2nd Bn., Devonshire Regiment. Son of Joseph George Coldwells, FSAA (accountant) and Elizabeth Coldwells of Sutton, Surrey. Born 25th November 1891. Attended Whitgift School where he was captain of the school in 1910 and gained a scholarship to Wadham College, Oxford achieving a First in the Classics. Instructor, Oxford OTC. He was a member of the hockey team and the debating society. Enlisted in the 20th Bn., Royal Fusiliers 12th September 1914, PS/4685, at Croydon and was commissioned 11th July 1915.' In May 1916 he went to France and joined the Devons. 'A fine scholar and a modest man.' Two brothers fell, Private Leonard George Coldwells, 31st October 1914 and Second Lieutenant Charles Albert Coldwells, 28th September 1915. Sutton War Memorial. Reported to be buried southwest of Pozieres after being badly wounded in front of our trenches. The War Office send some effects to the father for identification a notebook, which contained a roll of men of the company, photographs and letters and asked him to identify them formally, he confirmed they were his sons, returned the roll and asked for more information where the items had come from, he was simply told they had been forwarded from the lines. Correspondence to his brother, Captain E. G. Coldwells. Memorial Ref. Pier and Face 1 C., Thiepval Memorial, France. WO 339/32420

COLEMAN, Second Lieutenant, Arthur. Originally reported as missing, 1st July 1916, official notification received 20th July 1916. 20th (Tyneside Scottish) Bn., Northumberland Fusiliers. Aged 24. Son of Patrick and Agnes Coleman, of 23, Albert Road, Consett, Co. Durham. Educated at St. Cuthbert's Grammar School, Newcastle-on-Tyne, and was a schoolmaster by profession. Teacher at Sunderland, teaching at St. Joseph's Roman Catholic School. Joined the Durhams in the ranks, corporal, 2213, prior to commission. He had been at the Front about four months from 8th March 1916. His Will left his estate jointly to his mother and his fiancée, Edith Cordner. Medals to his mother. Memorial Ref. Pier and Face 10 B 11 B and 12 B., Thiepval Memorial, France. WO 339/36597

COLES, Captain, Lionel George. He led C company over the parapet near Contalmaison, and was killed 1st July 1916 at about 11.00am near Sausage Redoubt, he was seen to fall beyond German first line trenches. 16th Bn., Royal Scots. Aged 27. Only son of Walter George Coles, F.S.I., (Chief Surveyor, Board of Agriculture, Edin.), of Barntyles, Oxted, Surrey. Born 20th October 1889, and entered George Watson's College in 1899. A member of the Queen's Edinburgh, Mounted Rifles. In 1910 he took a commission in the 3rd Border Regiment, but resigned in 1911 to take up a post in the rubber industry in the Malay States. On the outbreak of war, he returned to a commission in the 16th Royal Scots and his ability soon won him his captaincy. His servant, Private John Bird from Edinburgh was also killed trying to assist the dying officer. His sister served in France, Miss D. K. M Coles with the 58th General Military Hospital. About a week after the attack his body was found by the Tunnelling Coy., Royal Engineers assigned to the salvage company, they buried Captain Coles, Captain Ross, Sergeant Curry and Private Wattie in the third line of German trenches of the La Boisselle Road. Original map reference where found 57d.X.22.b with thirteen other soldiers. Private Henry Wattie, 16th Bn., and Lieutenant George Munro Ross have no known grave and commemorated on the Thiepval Memorial and both died 1st July 1916. Lionel was re-interred in 1919. Memorial Ref. V. E. 5., Gordon Dump Cemetery, Ovillers-La Boisselle, France. WO 339/23539

COLLEY, Second Lieutenant, Harold. Platoon Commander and an intelligence officer for the attack on Serre, 1st July 1916. Reported that about 8.30am Lieutenant Colley, was lying on the top of a shell hole, bleeding badly in the back. He asked for a drink of water, and was carried to our front line trench. Then word came that the battalion were to retire; and when soldiers passed back over the place where they laid him, he couldn't be found. It was noted there were no stretcher bearers to take anyone down and due to intensive shelling he may have been blown to pieces or buried. D Coy., 18th Bn., West Yorkshire Regiment (Prince of Wales's Own). Born in Bradford on 3rd March 1891, family home was at 879 Moor Park Terrace, Bradford. Educated Ermysted's Grammar School. Graduated from the University of Liverpool in 1913 with an Arts Degree, Harold took up a position as English lecturer at Posen in Poland. In June 1914 he came home for a holiday leaving all of his possessions in the care of friends as he intended to return to his post in September. In the meantime war broke out. He decided to join the army and while he was waiting for enlistment took a temporary job at Skipton Grammar School. He was soon asked to teach French and German to the officers at the camp and was promised a commission by Colonel Muller. He trained for this through the Inns of Court. Harold joined the 18th Bn., West Yorkshire Regiment on 17th August 1914 and went to Egypt, 22nd December 1915. The regiment returned to France in 1916 by which time he had been promoted to second lieutenant from the 1st April 1915. Medals to his father. Memorial Ref. Pier and Face 2 A 2 C and 2 D., Thiepval Memorial, France.

COLLEY, Captain, William Arthur. Commander of C Company, "went down to his fate like a brave English gentleman", one of the first out of the trenches and killed by a shell, 1st July 1916. 12th Bn., York and Lancaster Regiment. Aged 47. Son of Francis William and Sarah Colley, of Sheffield. Attended Uppingham School. Resided Collegiate Crescent with his brother. Commissioned into the Royal Engineers (Volunteers) in 1896 and subsequently to Captain, 1908. He had experience in the Sheffield Engineers and in the early days of the war joined one of the new battalions. Former member of Sheffield City Council, a steel and cutlery manufacturer and director of John Kenyon and Co. In France from January 1916. Medals to his brother, John Herbert Colley in Sheffield. Memorial Ref. Pier and Face 14 A and 14 B., Thiepval Memorial, France.

COLLOT, Second Lieutenant, Thomas Alexander. Killed before reaching Pommiers Trench, although dressed as an ordinary soldier he was identifiable in the advance, 1st July 1916. A Coy., 6th Bn., Royal Berkshire Regiment. Aged 22. Son of Henry (auditor in the exchequer) and Margaret A. Collot, of 37, Woodville Gardens, Ealing, London. Born 4th February 1894. Attended Plymouth College, 1904-1908. Attended Sherborne School (School House) September 1908 - July 1912. Attended the sixth form and in the 2nd XI cricket team and 2nd XV rugby football team. Attended Gonville and Caius College, Cambridge. Took French as an additional subject. Whilst at Caius College, he was a dresser for the Red Cross Society from 31st October 1914 to 20th November 1914. Attested for the Inns of Court OTC in November 1914. Gazetted a second lieutenant in the 6th Bn., Dorset Regiment and transferred to the Royal Berkshire Regiment. Moving to Romsey in May 1915, the regiment sailed to Boulogne on the 14th July 1915. Medals applied for by his father. Memorial Ref. Q. 22., Carnoy Military Cemetery, France.

They Never Fail Who Die In A Great Cause

COLMER, Second Lieutenant, Arthur Cecil Reported to be killed assisting men in No Man's Land, 1st July 1916. "A" Bty. 96th Bde., Royal Field Artillery. Aged 23. Born in 1893 in London. Son of Arthur May Colmer (tailor and outfitter) and Annie Letitia Colmer, of Restormel House, Southwood Avenue, Bournemouth. Native of Liskeard, Cornwall. Resided Hannafore, Headland Road, Newquay. Tailor cutter. Enlisted at the outbreak of war and posted to the Duke of Cornwall's Light Infantry, 15839, entered the theatre of war on the 14th November 1914. Royal Engineers as a corporal, then went to the Royal Horse Artillery & Field Artillery as a second lieutenant on 10th September 1915. Newquay War Memorial. Queen's College, Taunton Roll of Honour. Sister, D. M. Colmer applied for his medals. Memorial Ref. I. F. 44., Dartmoor Cemetery, Becordel-Becourt, France.

He Gave His Life For Another

CONNER, Second Lieutenant, Frederic Attenborrow. Majority of the casualties especially those of the officers occurred during the first two hours of fighting, 1st July 1916. 2nd Bn., Seaforth Highlanders. Aged 21. Son of James Conner (Sheriff Clerk), of 58, Gladstone Place, Aberdeen. Born Aberdeen, 20th February 1895. Educated at Aberdeen Grammar School matriculated in agriculture in 1913. At Aberdeen University he was a well-known and popular figure. His career in agriculture was highly successful and he looked forward to specializing in forestry. As an athlete and sportsman he was recognized as a brilliant all-round man. He was a valued member of the Grammar F.P.'s Rugby team and a prominent member of the Aberdeenshire Cricket Club, and as a hobby his greatest pleasure was plying the rod and tackle. As a member of the Grammar School Company of the 4th Gordons he was mobilized on the outbreak of war. He went to France with his unit, 19th February 1915 and rose to the rank of sergeant, No. 1215. In August 1915, while still abroad, he was commissioned to the Seaforths and proved himself an ideal soldier and officer. Father applied for his medals. Memorial Ref. Pier and Face 15 C., Thiepval Memorial, France.

COOPER, Second Lieutenant, Howard Frank Byrne. Hit a few yards over the front line trench and killed immediately, detailed to lead the company, and had to go out into the open from a trench in the rear under heavy artillery and machine-gun fire, 1st July 1916. A Coy. 1st Bn., King's Own Scottish Borderers. Aged 19. Born Mussoorle, India, 15th May 1897. Elder son of Captain Frank Alexander (Government Educational Service) and Mabel Ellen Cooper, of Aligarh, United Provinces, India. Educated Bedford School and RMC Sandhurst. Gazetted 16th March 1915. February 1916 stationed in Alexandria where he joined the 1st Bn. Entered France, 22nd April 1916. Originally buried 1000 yards south-southeast of Beaumont Hamel, original grave reference, 57d.Q.18.a with nine other soldiers. Father applied for his medals. Memorial Ref. VIII. D. 44., Ancre British Cemetery, Beaumont-Hamel, France.

"In Thy Light Shall We See Light" Psalm XXXVI.9

COOTE, Second Lieutenant, Arthur Eyre. Official wire states although missing, he must not be presumed wounded or dead, 1st July 1916. 8th Bn., Royal Irish Rifles. Aged 19. Son of Captain Albert Augustus Eyre Coote (3rd Bn., Royal Irish Fusiliers) and Mrs. Mary Emily Coote, of 1, Victoria St., Armagh. Born Armagh. Queen's University, Belfast, Faculty of Medicine 1914-1915. Eighteen months service in the Ulster Division most of which has been spent in the East Belfast Regiment. Entered France, 4th January 1916. Still missing 26th December 1916. Mother applied for his medals. Memorial Ref. Pier and Face 15 A and 15 B., Thiepval Memorial, France.

COPE, Lieutenant, George Eric. Killed in action, 1st July 1916. 20th (Tyneside Scottish) Bn., Northumberland Fusiliers. Aged 18. Son of George and Elizabeth Beatrice Cope, of Windyridge, Devauden Green, Chepstow, Monmouthshire formerly 43, Corn Street, Bristol. Born 18th April 1896. He was at Cheltenham College from 1911 until war broke out. Enlisted in the 12th Gloucesters on the 1st October 1914 and was quickly promoted, corporal, 14634 30th January 1915 and commissioned 15th May 1915. Went to France, January 1916. Father applied for his medals. Memorial Ref. Pier and Face 10 B 11 B and 12 B., Thiepval Memorial, France. WO 339/29740

CORBETT, Captain, Alfred Edward. Killed whilst leading his company in an attack that was met by terrific gun fire, 1st July 1916. D Coy., 11th Lonsdale Bn., Border Regiment. Younger son of Joseph and Emmeline Corbett. F.R.I.B.A., H.M.I. (Technical Schools). Born Broughton Salford, Lancashire in 1873. Studied at Manchester Technical College and became an architect. Became a partner in Woodhouse Corbett and Dean Architects of, 100, King Street, Manchester, working in Manchester and London. The firm were most famous as the architects of St George's House (formerly the YMCA), Peter Street, Manchester. His designs were exhibited a number of times at the Royal Academy and he eventually returned to Manchester Technical College as a lecturer on architecture and building. Served in the volunteers and on the outbreak of the war aged 41 he joined the 16th (Public Schools) Battalion, Middlesex Regiment as a private, 838. In early 1915 he was commissioned into the 11th (Lonsdale) Bn., Border Regiment. He went to France with the battalion in November 1915, and after a course at Royal Staff College, Camberley he returned to his unit and was promoted to captain in command of "D" Company. Royal Academy War Memorial. Brother, H. Corbett applied for his medals. Memorial Ref. Pier and Face 6 A and 7 C., Thiepval Memorial, France.

CORMACK, Second Lieutenant, Reginald Ormiston. Reported missing and then killed in action, 1st July 1916, confirmed as killed, 16th December 1916. 15th Bn., Durham Light Infantry. Aged 23. Son of William O. and Edith Cormack, of Hammer Vale House, Haslemere, Surrey. Born 23rd August 1895. Educated Kirkdale School, Leytonstone, 1900 to 1908. Enlisted 10th August 1914 as private, 55570 in the Army Service Corps. Went to France, 12th October 1914, returned home 2nd August 1915, back to France 15th November 1915. Temporary second lieutenant, 16th November 1915. Brother killed with RAF, Second Lieutenant P. F. Cormack, 27th October 1918. Father applied for his medals. Originally buried near Shelter Wood in X22c. Sht 57d. S.E. Memorial Ref. Pier and Face 14 A and 15 C., Thiepval Memorial, France. WO 339/47208

COSTELLO, Lieutenant, Edward William. He fell whilst gallantly leading his men in an attack on the German trenches, and while preparing for a further advance he was shot through the head and killed instantly, 1st July 1916. 3rd Bn., Royal Inniskilling Fusiliers. Attached 87th Machine Gun Corps. Aged 19. Eldest son of Mr. and Mrs. T. D. Costello, of 55, Pembroke Road, Ballsbridge, Dublin and Bank House, Tullamore. Educated at St. Vincent's College, Castleknock. He received his commission in December, 1914 at Derry, and went to the Dardanelles in August, 1915, and after the evacuation of Gallipoli he served in Egypt. In March, 1916, he went to France. Father applied for his medals. Memorial Ref. Pier and Face 4 D and 5 B., Thiepval Memorial, France.

COTTON, Second Lieutenant, John. Reported to have died from wounds, wounded by German counter battery fire, 1st July 1916 which killed Major John F. Graham. Sergeant Gregory was awarded the Military Medal for gallantry in attending to Second Lieutenant Cotton when wounded. "A" Bty., 150th Bde., Royal Field Artillery. Aged 29. Elder son of Lawrence (Chairman of Blackburn Rovers FC) and Frances Eleanor Cotton. Husband of Margaret Cotton, of "The Pines," Clayton Green, Chorley and had one child. Native of Blackburn. He was identified in the textile trade as a salesman for the firm in which his father, Mr. L. Cotton and his uncle, Mr. Clement Cotton are the principals. Popular member of the Pleasington and Wilpshire golf clubs and Longshaw Tennis club. When war broke out he joined the artillery as a ranker, No. 1343 and was subsequently given a commission in the County Palatine Artillery. He had been at the Front since November 1915 and from time to time wrote letters descriptive of life in the trenches. Letter home in February 1916 stated that a shell had landed a yard away just as they had finished firing. His cousin, Private Arthur Cotton (Uncle Clement's son) was killed in Gallipoli on the 21st June 1915. Widow applied for his medals. Memorial Ref. II. B. 24., Dive Copse British Cemetery, Sailly-Le-Sec, France.

The Memory Of The Just Is Blessed

COURAGE, Second Lieutenant, Godfrey Michell. Killed in action, 1st July 1916. Ordered forward by Captain Harold Longhurst to take control of the remnants of B Company, known as Beer company. 6th Bn., Royal Berkshire Regiment. Aged 20. Only son of Lieutenant Godfrey Mitchell Courage, R. N and Evelyn Agnes Courage, of Heckfield Heath House, Basingstoke formerly Snowdenham Hall, Bramley and Leigham, Devon. Born Holmbury St. Mary, Dorking, Surrey. Educated at Cheam, Osborne and Dartmouth Colleges. Served as a midshipman in His Majesty's Ship, Dominion leaving the Navy at his own request he volunteered at the outbreak of war and was gazetted to the Royal Berkshire in October 1914. Mentioned in Despatches, 25th June 1916. Mother applied for his medals. Memorial Ref. Q. 20., Carnoy Military Cemetery, France.

The Lord Preserveth The Faithful

COURTICE, Second Lieutenant, Reginald Leyster. Lead his platoon across the open ground towards the German trenches which were swept all the time by machine-gun fire, he led them as far as the German second line trench when he was hit in two places the head and the stomach, he died immediately. 2nd July 1916. Stated as being killed on the 1st July in the war diary. Informant stated between 8am and 9am in the advance we reached the 1st and 2nd line German trenches, I was about seven yards away when a shell burst quite close to him and he was blown to pieces, I was covered in mud. Medal Index Card states killed in action between the 1st and the 3rd July 1916. A Coy., 8th Bn., Lincolnshire Regiment. Elder son of Mr. Leyster and Mrs. Laura Maria Courtice of 69, Forest Drive West, Leytonstone. Born St. Pancras. Stockbrokers' clerk. Enlisted Honourable Artillery Company, private, 1782. Entered France, 23rd January 1915. Commissioned into the Lincolnshire Regiment, 15th January 1916. Mother applied for his medals. Memorial Ref. Pier and Face 1 C., Thiepval Memorial, France. WO 339/54326

COWIN, Second Lieutenant, Henry Hampton. Reported to be shot by a bullet through the heart, 1st July 1916. B Coy., 21st Bn., Manchester Regiment. Aged 31. Son of Henry and Mima Cowin, of "Neston," Selborne Drive, Douglas, Isle Of Man. Born Isle of Man. Employed Bank Clerk, Lloyd's Bank. Enlisted 11th September 1914 with 19th King's Liverpool and promoted lance corporal, 21476, 6th August 1915. Entered France, 7th November 1915. Commissioned 20th June 1916 to 21st Manchesters. Original burial map reference 62d.f.5.d.1.4 and marked with a cross, in 1920 remains moved to Dantzig Alley. Father applied for his medals. Memorial Ref. II. C. 9., Dantzig Alley British Cemetery, Mametz, France. WO 339/65241

A True Manx Gentleman And Loved By All Who Knew Him

COX, Captain, Harold Edward Leys. Reported to be hit in No Man's Land returning from the German front line trench, missing believed killed following the attack on Gommecourt, 1st July 1916. By 8.20pm the officers consisting of Captain Somers-Smith, (London Regiment), Lieutenant Petley, (London Rifle Brigade), Captain Leys Cox (Queen Victoria's Rifles), Second Lieutenant Arthur, (Cheshire Regiment), Captain Harvey (London Rifle Brigade) and Second Lieutenant Bovill (Queens Westminster Rifles) admitted they would be forced to return to the British lines and provided covering fire for the men. Making a run for the nearest shell holes, the only officer who returned was Lieutenant Petley, five officers being killed. Officer Commanding C Coy., 1st/9th Bn., London Regiment (Queen Victoria's Rifles). Aged 29. Younger son of Edward William Cox, of 28, Madeley Road, Ealing, London. Educated St. George's School, Windsor Castle and St. Paul's School. Second lieutenant to lieutenant, March 1911. Went to the Front, 4th November 1914 and took part in the Battle of Ypres and Hill 60. Medals to his home address. Memorial Ref. Pier and Face 9 C., Thiepval Memorial, France.

COXON, Second Lieutenant, Herbert Archibald. Killed seconds before going over the top at Hebuterne. His last words were "fix bayonets". He took a direct hit from a German shell which killed him instantly. 1st July 1916. B Coy., 1st/14th Bn., London Regiment (London Scottish). Aged 32. Born 5th May 1884. Attended St. Lawrence College, Ramsgate, Kent. Quantity surveyor. Returned from Victoria, British Columbia. Enlisted with the London Regiment, No. 3115, 3rd September 1914, acting sergeant. Commissioned 18th November 1915. Entered France 3rd April 1916. His sister, Mrs. P. Lovell of Manor House, Worthing applied for his medals also identified as his next of kin. Memorial Ref. Pier and Face 9 C and 13 C., Thiepval Memorial, France.

CRAGG, Second Lieutenant, John Francis. Detailed to attack German positions in front of the village of Fricourt, the first to go over and one of the first to be killed by machine gun fire, killed just after 7.45am, 1st July 1916. 8th Bn., Lincolnshire Regiment. Aged 28. Third son of Captain William Alfred Cragg and Mrs. Adelaide Alexander Cragg of The Hall, Folkingham Road, Threekingham, Lincs. Born 21st June 1888 at Threekingham. He was educated at Lancing College where he was in Seconds House from May 1900 to July 1906. He was a member of the Shooting VIII in 1906 and was a member of the OTC. On leaving school he became a motor engineer and by the outbreak of war he was Works Manager for the Lincoln Printing Works and was living at 8 North Parade, Lincoln. On the 29th June 1914 he enlisted at Lincoln as private, 2184 in the 4th Bn., Lincolnshire Regiment. He was promoted to corporal on the 29th of August 1914 and on the 12th of September 1914 he signed a document agreeing to overseas service if required. On the 4th of December he applied for a commission and was discharged from the 4th battalion on the 26th of December 1914 being commissioned as a second lieutenant in the Lincolnshire Regiment on the 30th of December 1914 where he served as a battalion machine-gun officer. Entered France, 10th September 1915, and wounded in this month at Loos. Lancing Register entry 1857, father also attended Lancing his entry being 775. His brother Lieutenant Noel Henry Cragg RN of HMS Victory (Naval Siege Guns) died on the 20th of September 1915. His father applied for his medals. Memorial Ref. Pier and Face 1 C., Thiepval Memorial, France. WO 339/5166

CRAIG, Second Lieutenant, John Arnott Taylor. Officially reported missing, 1st July 1916. D Coy. 11th Bn., Royal Inniskilling Fusiliers. Aged 21. Eldest son of James and Rosie Craig, of Glen House, Helen's Bay, Co. Down. Educated at Mourne Grange, Kilkeel and St. Edward's School, Oxford and was a member of the UVF obtaining his commission on the 25th September 1914. Born in Belfast on 29th December 1894 and he was the eldest son of James and Annie Rosina (Rosie) Craig (nee Taylor) who were married on 6th December 1893. James Craig worked as a merchant with a firm of linen manufacturers and bleachers in Belfast – McCrum, Watson & Mercer Ltd., Linenhall Street. Commemorated on the North of Ireland Cricket Club Memorial Plaque. Unusually the Medal Index Card had written on it 'no issue to be made until estate settled'. Original burial map reference 57d.R.25.a.4.9 with a cross being found on the grave. Memorial Ref. IV. A. 5., Connaught Cemetery, Thiepval, France.

Till The Dawn Break

CRAVEN, Second Lieutenant, Brian Thornthwaite. Killed in action, Carnoy, 1st July 1916, Royal Field Artillery. Trench Mortar Battery. Born 1886, Jamaica. Son of Mr. Percival Craven and Ellen Craven of Norbury. Employed by Messrs. Robert Schwarzenbach of Aldermanbury. Warehouseman Silk merchant. Enlisted as a private in the London Scottish, 4368, January 1915. Temporary second lieutenant 28th July 1915. Commissioned August 1915. Memorial Ref. J. 31., Carnoy Military Cemetery, France.

CREES, Second Lieutenant, William. At about 9.50am 'A' and 'C' Companies were advancing towards Dantzig Alley to the East of Mametz when they came under enemy machine-gun fire. There were a good many casualties, 1st July 1916. 2nd Bn., The Queen's (Royal West Surrey Regiment). Aged 34. Fifth child of Charles (farm labourer) and Harriett Crees of Church Norton. Born in Selsey in 1881. 3rd September 1900 enlisted in the 1st Battalion of the Queen's (Royal West Surrey) Regiment with No. 6574, He served in India and Aden, and in 1910 returned to Selsey as a lance corporal. In 1910 married Lucy of 6, South View, East Road, Selsey, Sussex and had three children, Dulcie, William and Vera. Promoted to sergeant and embarked for France on 16th December 1915. A few months later he was given a battlefield commission and was gazetted as a second lieutenant on 16th April 1916. Killed having served for 16 years. Originally buried field near ridge to right of Mametz, Sht 62d. Sq. F.5. Widow applied for his medals. Memorial Ref. Sp. Mem. B. 7., Peronne Road Cemetery, Maricourt, France. WO 339/60960

The Lord Knoweth Them That Are His

CROMBIE, Second Lieutenant, William Lauder. Originally reported as wounded. A soldier had picked up his notebook in the field and stated it was lying next to a body, he assumed the officer had been shot in the ankle and was treating the wound with his pocket book when he was shot in the heart and died. Killed at La Boisselle, 1st July 1916. 3rd Bn., Royal Scots recorded as attached 4th Bn. Killed with the 16th Bn., A Coy. Born in 6th October 1888, the son of Mr. George B. Crombie, Leven Street, Edinburgh. He attended James Gillespie School, George Watson's College 1900-4 when he joined the staff of the Bank of Scotland. Enlisted 2nd August 1908 and served with the Queen's Rifles Volunteer Corps. Mobilised in the Bankers' Company, 4th Royal Scots, No. 111, he served in Gallipoli as a sniper till invalided home in 1915. Commissioned 8th February 1915. In June 1916 he was sent to France. His father looked for more accurate information as his son's name appeared in the wounded list, the lady he was engaged too also received a letter implying he had been wounded and this gave her hope he was still alive. J. A. C. Fife from Edinburgh made an application for his medals. Memorial Ref. Pier and Face 6 D and 7 D., Thiepval Memorial, France. WO 339/52800

CROSSLEY, Second Lieutenant, Cyril. Killed almost immediately, undergoing a terrible bombardment, 1st July 1916. 15th Bn., Lancashire Fusiliers. Son of Agnes Crossley. Born 27th February 1891 in 30 Bolton Road, Pendleton. He went to Manchester Grammar School (1905 – 1907) on the Classical side and worked as an insurance clerk before enlisting on 8th January 1915 in a Public Schools Battalion, 19815, 16th Royal Welsh Fusiliers. He was posted to France on the 22nd November 1915, became a lance corporal 4th March 1915 and commissioned 7th August 1915. Cyril had been connected with the Hankinson St Mission, was secretary of the Salford and District Scout Association and also of St Thomas Scouts. The Reverend Fosbrooke said of him; "He possessed a most lovable disposition, and was a general favourite with his boys. They were looking forward to his return with great expectations, but God has ruled it otherwise." Mother who was residing in Blackpool applied for his medals and officers parents' pension. Memorial Ref. Pier and Face 3 C and 3 D., Thiepval Memorial, France.

CROZIER, Lieutenant, William Magee. Missing, believed killed, 1st July 1916. Killed in action hit twice before he reached the German wire, he was seen to try to take cover in a shell hole, after which no more is known of his movements. 9th Bn., Royal Inniskilling Fusiliers. Aged 42. Second son of the Francis Rawdon Moira Crozier (solicitor), and Catherine Sophia Magee of Carrickbrennan, Monkstown and St. Stephen's Green, Dublin. Born 5th December 1873 at Roebuck Hall, Dundrum, Dublin. In cricket he was in the Repton Eleven in 1892, when he made 113 runs with an average of 7.53 and is commemorated on the Repton School Memorial leaving Repton in 1886. Educated Dublin University.

A barrister-at-law, a popular member to the Irish Bar since 1898. Keen golfer. Enlisted August 1914. Lieutenant 10th October 1914. Entered France, 5th October 1915. Still posted as missing 26th December 1916. Application from his father for his sons, three medals. Memorial Ref. Pier and Face 4 D and 5 B., Thiepval Memorial, France.

CRUICKSHANK, Captain, Philip. Fell in action during the offensive, 1st July 1916. 9th Bn., Royal Inniskilling Fusiliers. Aged 34. Son of Colin Allan Cruickshank and Ann Bennett Cruickshank. Native of Aberdeen, he joined the editorial staff of the Aberdeen Journal and onto the Derry Standard. He inaugurated the Boys Brigade in Omagh and was captain until war broke out. Secretary of the Mid-Tyrone Unionist Club and commander of the 2nd Mid-Tyrone Battalion UVF. Prior to the outbreak of the war, editor of the "Tyrone Constitution", and a well-known and popular figure in Unionist circles in the North of Ireland. He was a journalist of much ability and a talented writer. On the outbreak of the war he at once volunteered. He served with the Tyrone battalion, and was soon promoted captain. He went to the front 5th October, 1915, and had, previous to the action in which he fell, been twice wounded. Medals to a Miss Cruickshank, Bellingham Road, Catford. Memorial Ref. Pier and Face 4 D and 5 B., Thiepval Memorial, France.

CRUM, Second Lieutenant, Stewart Alexander. Majority of the casualties especially those of the officers occurred during the first two hours of fighting, met his death in the most gallant and splendid way, 1st July 1916. 2nd Bn., Seaforth Highlanders. Aged 19. Son of J. L. Crum. Educated at Aldeburgh Lodge, Wellington College and RMC Sandhurst. Gazetted in September 1915. A senior officer, writing of him, says : "He was killed while leading his men with the utmost gallantry. Nothing possible could have exceeded his coolness and devotion to duty, and in dying such a splendid and heroic death he in every way proved himself worthy of the traditions and records of the Seaforth Highlanders." Aldeburgh War Memorial. Father of Park Road, Swanage applied for his medals. Memorial Ref. I. C. 32., Serre Road Cemetery No. 2, France.

CUBEY, Captain, Joseph Berkeley. Recorded that he was killed commanding 'A' Company before they had travelled 100 yards, reported missing, believed killed, 1st July 1916. Witnessed by Private Dixon and Young and Second Lieutenant Daggett who all confirmed he was shot just after he had said 'Come on boys!'. Fell before he reached the British wire. 23rd (Tyneside Scottish) Bn., Northumberland Fusiliers. Aged 32. Born 2nd May 1884. Son of Thomas and Elizabeth Mary Cubey, of 25, Osborne Avenue, South Shields. Prior to the war he held an appointment in the Government Land Valuation Department. Member of the Westoe Rugby Football Club. Received his commission as a second lieutenant in 1914 and joined the Northumberland Fusiliers, promoted to the rank of captain. In France since 9th January 1916. A pocket book was forwarded by a chaplain but personal effects were collected by a party from the 34th Division. Effects returned were compass (damaged), waterproof sheet, notes and two mirrors. Original burial map reference 57d.X.14. Mother applied for his medals. Memorial Ref. XI. D. 1., Ovillers Military Cemetery, France. WO 339/17248

Beloved Son Of Thos. & Elizabeth M. Cubey Of South Shields

CUMMINS, Second Lieutenant, Leslie. Lead A Coy., he paused to track a wounded comrade to cover in a shell hole as he straightened up he was killed instantly having been shot through the heart by machine-gun fire, he gallantly led what few men he had left until 30 yards in front of the German trench, 1st July 1916. 10th Bn., Lincolnshire Regiment. Aged 24. Eldest son of George Valentine (draper) and Mary Cummins, of 22, Macaulay St., Grimsby. Born 30th April 1892 in Grimsby. Educated locally. On October 1st 1909, at the age of 17, Leslie began work as a laboratory assistant at the Municipal College, Grimsby, earning an annual salary of £20. In 1912, Leslie moved to Haverhill to take up a teaching position at the Haverhill Board School on September 23. Played football for the Rovers and attended the Old Independent Church. Joined the 1st Lincolns as a private, 19th September 1914, No. 166 and gained a commission, 5th January 1915. Entered France, 8th January 1916. Father applied for his medals. Memorial Ref. Pier and Face 1 C., Thiepval Memorial, France. WO 339/17900

CUNDALL, Lieutenant, Hubert Walter. The Medal Index Card confirms date of death as 1st July 1916 and unusually has Hebuterne as place of death written underneath the date. 1st Bn., London Regiment (Royal Fusiliers). Aged 24. Son of Florence and John Hubert Cundall. Civil Service Commission for registration as temporary boy clerk, 3rd July 1908. To be second lieutenant from the 6th (City of London) Battalion, 19th February 1915. Theatre of war, Egypt & Gallipoli entered September 1915. His mother applied for his medals asking them to go to Messrs. C. R. Randall & Sons, 4 Capthain Buildings, EC2. Memorial Ref. Pier and Face 9 D and 16 B., Thiepval Memorial, France.

CUNNINGHAM, Second Lieutenant, James. He had been on the line for six weeks and fell as the battalion went into action for the first time, one of two officers killed, 1st July 1916. Reported to have been hit by a splinter from a shell piercing his heart, he also had a broken arm. 9th Bn. attd. 7th Bn., Bedfordshire Regiment. Born 7th September 1880. Aged 35. Son of James Cunningham, of Ashfield, Craigmore, Rothesay. Formerly lieutenant with Transport and Remount Department, West African Forces. Served for 2 years and 2 months in the Boer War with the Imperial Yeomanry and 5 years and 11 months in the Johannesburg Mounted Police. Awarded King's and Queen's Medal. Arrived in the battalion on the 25th May 1916. Effects returned were 5 Franc note, note case, cheque book and papers. Buried on the 4th July 1916 at reference Sq. A.2.D. Central Maurepas trench map, one mile NW of Carnoy and 1,000 yards east of Mametz. The chaplain who buried him was killed a few days later. Memorial Ref. Pier and Face 2 C., Thiepval Memorial, France. WO 339/49146

CUNNINGHAM, Captain, Robert William. Missing believed killed, 1st July 1916. The final objective was an area known as the 'Quadrilateral' and in order to get to this the battalion had to take shelter in a sunken road, however this could be fired into from the Germans and a machine gun bullet killed Robert. Officer Commanding A Coy., 1st/9th Bn., London Regiment (Queen Victoria's Rifles). Aged 24. Son of Robert and Mary Cunningham. Government clerk and resided King's Road, Kingston Hill. Attested in the East Surrey Regiment in 1909. Enlisted 13th London Regiment, Lance sergeant, No. 779. Disembarked 4th November 1914. Commissioned 3rd January 1915. Mrs. A. M. Cunningham, his mother from Durham Road, Finsbury Park applied for his medals. Memorial Ref. Pier and Face 9 C., Thiepval Memorial, France.

CURROR, Second Lieutenant, William Edwin Forrest. Missing 1st July 1916 afterwards reported killed in action. The platoon had pushed on to their final objective and fierce hand to hand fighting took place. No. 8 Platoon, B Coy., 14th Bn., London Regiment (London Scottish). Parents, John Curror (commission agent) and Annie Forrest Curror of Chancellor Road, West Dulwich. Born 2nd January 1882 in Dorking. Attended Dorking High School 1894-97 (Ashcombe School) and received a 5th Form prize. In 1902 gained one of the 'Whitworth'(engineering) Scholarships awarded by the Board of Education, scholarship £50 becoming an engineer draughtsman. Enlisted into the 14th (County of London) Battalion (London Scottish). Disembarked on the 3rd April 1916 to France. His body was later found, identified by his disc at map reference K.12.d.80.60 (approx) with thirteen other soldiers. Dorking War Memorial. His mother applied for his parents' pension but she died on the 27th April 1919 which explains why the application for medals was made by his cousin, Miss H. O. B. Laing, Neill Road, St. John's Wood, NW8. Memorial Ref. V. C. 1., Gommecourt British Cemetery No.2, Hebuterne, France.

CUTHBERT, Captain, Olaf Ranson. Hit by machine-gun fire near Avallon Trench whilst between the trenches during an attack, 1st July 1916. 8th Bn., York and Lancaster Regiment. Aged 25. Youngest son of Goymour (architect and surveyor) of Brook Meadow, Holmwood and Marion Cuthbert, of Palace Mansions, London. Born 10th February 1891 and was baptised in Marylebone, London. Two year's farm pupil with Mr. Leslie Pogson at Anwick and made a number of friends in Sleaford. Educated at Dover College (1905 to 1907) and St. John's College, Oxford. He was in the University Officers' training Corps for two years. He volunteered on 4th August 1914 as a private (No. 1265) in 25th Battalion, London Regiment, which was a territorial cyclist battalion. He was embodied the following day and became a motor cyclist. He was commissioned as a temporary second lieutenant in the infantry in October 1914. He was promoted to temporary lieutenant in January 1915 in the 8th Bn.,York and Lancaster Regiment. Went to France, 27th August 1915, with the battalion, landing at Boulogne. Captain in October 1915. On 25th November 1915 he was married Millicent Frances Cuthbert, of Elmhurst,

Dorking, Surrey and made his will two days later. Cousin Second Lieutenant Edward Henry Bovill killed on the same day. Medals applied for by his widow. Memorial Ref. V. C. 5., Blighty Valley Cemetery, Authuille Wood, France.

At The Going Down Of The Sun And In The Morning We Will Remember Them

DAGGE, Second Lieutenant, Albert Lima. Killed 1st July 1916 after five months of active service he was hit on the head by a shell splinter. "B" Bty., 68th Bde., Royal Field Artillery. Trench Mortar Battery. Aged 32. Third son of Walter Hickie Dagge and Mary Thereza Isabel Dagge of Nogueira, Mogadouro, Portugal. Born in 1884. Educated at Clapham College and at Wye Agricultural College, Ashford, Kent. After several years spent in farming in Portugal, he went to Mexico just before the revolution broke out. He spent three years working as a mining engineer. In July, 1915, he threw up an appointment in Brazil to join the army. Obtaining a commission in the Royal Field Artillery on the 27th October 27, 1915, he was sent to the front 16th January 1916. His commanding officer writes: "He was detailed by the artillery commander as 'liaison officer' to accompany the infantry in their advance. Shortly after the attack was made, communication with a portion of a battalion was lost, and he determined to cross a fire-swept zone with two telephonists to restore it. I was not on the spot myself, but from the accounts of men who were, I am convinced that few men would have made the attempt. He was killed instantaneously shortly after starting, being hit on the head by a splinter of a shell. . . . He was a most gallant officer and a splendid companion. The saddest part of it was that even his magnificent courage must have failed to accomplish the task he considered it his duty to attempt. . . . I feel that nobody can fill the place he occupied." Sister Miss H. Dagge applied for his medals. Original burial map reference 57d.Q.36.b.1.9 and identified by his disc, burial return has TMB next to his name for Trench Mortar Battery, buried with six other fallen. Memorial Ref. XIII. D. 7., Connaught Cemetery, Thiepval, France.

Son Of Walter Hickie Dagge And Mary Lima Dagge Of Nogueira, Mogadouro Portugal. R.I.P.

DALBY, Second Lieutenant, Herbert Charles. Killed in action near La Boisselle, 1st July 1916. 11th Bn., York and Lancaster Regiment. Eldest son of Major Herbert Ernest Dalby and Molly Edith of Valetta, Babbacombe, Torquay. Born London, 30th April 1897. Educated Launceston and Havre subsequently studying to take up medicine. Joined the York and Lancaster, 1st January 1915. Gazetted May 1915. Served in France from 9th February 1916 being attached the Light Trench Mortar Battery and given command of four guns, 28th June 1916. Reported to be buried in Aveluy Wood, near Albert. Mother applied for his medals. Memorial Ref. Pier and Face 14A and 14B., Thiepval Memorial, France.

DALRYMPLE, Second Lieutenant, Hew (Norman). Killed in the glorious offensive, 1st July 1916. 8th Bn., Somerset Light Infantry. Aged 31. Elder son of Hon. David Hay Dalrymple and Effie Margaret Dalrymple, of "Harbury", 39, Acland St., South Yarra, Melbourne, Australia formerly Hamilton, Brisbane. Born 15th February 1885. His father died of a heart attack in September 1912 and he was heir in his will but as he resided outside of jurisdiction, left to Marion Dalrymple (spinster). Hew was a dental student in Philadelphia, crossed over from America to volunteer in England and enlisted 7th October 1914. Went into King Edward's Horse and then into the Sportsman's Battalion, 23rd Bn., Royal Fusiliers, and placed in the 8th Somersets, receiving a commission, 10th June 1915. Went to France, 25th December 1915. Probate granted to John Hamilton Dalrymple, (dentist) Queensland and Marion Colman, Brisbane. Medals application by Mrs. Dalrymple, Brisbane. Memorial Ref. Pier and Face 2A., Thiepval Memorial, France. WO 339/2818

DANDRIDGE, Second Lieutenant, George Sidney. Killed in No Man's Land or close to Breslau Trench by machine gun fire, 1st July 1916. 7th Bn., The Queen's (Royal West Surrey Regiment). Aged 22. Only son of Major Charles C. W. Dandridge (35th King's Own Scottish Borderers) and Mrs. Dandridge of The Ridges, 82, Westcourt Road, Worthing and nephew of the Reverend G. Dandridge, rector of St. Nicolas, Guildford. Educated Royal Grammar School, Guildford where he was a member of the OTC at the outbreak of war he joined the 5th Hampshire, Royal Field Artillery. Received a commission start of 1915 and went to the Front in December serving as a transport officer. Father applied for his medals. Original burial map reference, 62c.A.8.b.4.7 with nine other men from the 7th Bn., Queens including Second Lieutenants R. C. Herbert and F. J. Miller all of whom were killed on the 1st July. George was identified by his wallet and photos. Memorial Ref. III. O. 3., Dantzig Alley British Cemetery, Mametz, France.

DARLEY, Second Lieutenant, Desmond John. Killed in action near La Boisselle, 1st July 1916 a false sighting at a Casualty Clearing Station meant his family originally thought he survived. 11th Bn., Suffolk Regiment. Born 31st January 1895 in London, son of Major Henry Read Darley, DSO, OBE and Emily Vereker. Aged 21. He was educated at Summer Fields, Oxford, Eton and Kings College, Cambridge and was a promising classical scholar and musician. Matriculated Cambridge 1914. Cambridge OTC. He obtained a commission in April 1915 and served in the expeditionary forces in Flanders from March 1916 after an arrival in France on 8th February 1916.

He was a keen sportsman and promising classical scholar with great musical talent. His uncle, Captain Joseph Watkins William Darley of the 4th Dragoon Guards was killed in action on 17th January 1885 at The Battle of Abu Klea during the Egyptian campaign with General Gordon and his father served with distinction in the Boer War and World War 1. Desmond wrote home, 2nd April 1916; "Dear Father, The present scene is the garden of a farmhouse about a mile from the front trenches. Blazing sun absolute stillness except for an aeroplane of ours heading ......We are all sorting out .....and writing letters......we are (worn) out after a tour of five days. The sensation of getting into pyjamas and bed after so long in is indescribable. I slept for 12 hours without a break." His father applied for his medals, asking for them to go to the Secretary's Office, Cavalry Club, Piccadilly. Memorial Ref. Pier and Face 1C and 2A., Thiepval Memorial, France. WO 339/21739

DART, Captain, Hugh. Battalion headquarters had been shelled out of two shelters and on the second occasion, Captain Dart was wounded by shrapnel and died of wounds in a field hospital, 1st July 1916. 13th Bn., York and Lancaster Regiment. Aged 34. Third son of Richard Dart (JP for the city of Liverpool) and Ellen Dart, of 28 Aigburth Drive, Sefton Park, Liverpool. Born September 4th 1881, at Toxteth, Liverpool. Attended Harrow. Admitted at Trinity College, Cambridge matriculated 25th June 1900. BA, 1903. MA, 1907. In 1904 he went to work for Parr's Bank and worked at its London Cavendish Square and Kensington branches before being appointed to the Head Office Metropolitan Inspection Staff in March 1912. Enlisted as a private, Middlesex Regiment. Captain Dart was given a commission in the York and Lancaster Regiment in September, 1914. In the beginning of 1916 he was sent to Egypt, and two months later, in March, 1916, he was transferred to France. He received his captaincy in June 1916, and had also been appointed adjutant of his regiment. Brother applied for his medals. Memorial Ref. Plot 1. Row E. Grave 15., Bertrancourt Military Cemetery, France.

M.A. Cambridge Killed In Action At The Battle Of The Somme

DAVEY, Second Lieutenant, William Roy. Killed in the attack at Gommecourt, D Coy., 1st July 1916. The left company (D) were held up by uncut wire in front of the German line and came under enfilade machine-gun fire on their left, attempts were made to get through the wire during which 2nd Lieutenant Davey was killed. 12th Bn., London Regiment (The Rangers). Aged 19. Oldest son of William Henry (tailor's cutter) and Jessie F. L. Davey of Albert Road, Hendon. Born 14th June 1897. From private, 2478, County of London Yeomanry to be second lieutenant, 8th December 1915. Proceeded to France, May 1916. Educated at the Drayton School and Acton and Chiswick Polytechnic. Bank clerk. His body not located until May 1921. Original grave location 57d.K.10.b.9.5, the only grave in this location and identified by his uniform and disc. Father applied for his medals although his will suggested his sweetheart, Dorothy Alice Glover could have any medal to which he was entitled. Memorial Ref. VI. A. 1., Gommecourt British Cemetery No.2, Hebuterne, France.

This Corner Of A Foreign Field That Is For Ever England

DAVID, Second Lieutenant, Lionel Adolf David. Killed in the attack on Fricourt, 1st July 1916. A Coy. 7th Bn., Yorkshire Regiment. The attack was due to happen later in the day, but they attacked at 8.20am under orders of Major Kent and were wiped out. A message got back that Major Kent and Second Lieutenant David were lying in front of the wire. Aged 25. Eldest son of Alexander and Beatrice Marian David, of Claremont, Monk Bridge Road, Headingley, Leeds formerly 161, Victoria Road. Native of Kensington, London. Born 30th April 1892. Member of the Willaston School from 1903 to 1906 and was head of the school in his last year. Member of the Leeds University OTC. Employed by Messrs. Paul Hirsch and Joseph, Jun., Cookridge Street, Leeds when the war broke out. Went to France, July 1915. Slightly wounded in February. Brother, Eric was an officer in the King's Own

Yorkshire Light Infantry. Originally buried south of Fricourt, map reference 62d.F.9.a.8.8 and buried with six unknown British soldiers. Father applied for his medals. Memorial Ref. VI. E. 2., Dantzig Alley British Cemetery, Mametz, France. WO 339/663

He Hath Awakened From The Dream Of Life He Hath Outsoared
The Shadow Of Our Night

DAVIDSON, Captain, James Samuel. Shot dead by a German sniper at 3.20pm he was helped back across No Man's Land by two of his men, he was seriously wounded defending a communication trench despite being virtually surrounded, 1st July 1916. Attached 108th Brigade, Machine Gun Officer from, 13th Bn., Royal Irish Rifles. Aged 39. Only son of Samuel Cleland Davidson, of Seacourt, Bangor, Co. Down. Born Belfast, 9th March 1877. Educated at Belfast Royal Academical Institution attended Campbell College, Belfast and afterwards spent a year in Paris to acquire the French language. On 1st January 1895 he commenced his apprenticeship in the Sirocco Engineering Works, and passed through the various departments. Five years later he became works manager, and remained in this capacity until May 1902, during which time he had under his charge the construction of machines for all the various processes in tea manufacture, and also the manufacture of centrifugal fans, propeller fans, drying machines, and other general engineering work and personally brought out several improvements, including the Sirocco enclosed type of tilting tray drier. In June of the same year he became general manager and a director of the firm, which, at the outbreak of the war, was employing about 750 men his father was the founder. Accompanied his father to the 1904 St. Louis World Fair to promote the company and from October 1910 to July 1911, undertook a world trip to evaluate and sell Sirocco machinery. Member of the Institute of Mechanical Engineering (Graduate 1900; Associate Member 1903; Member 1907), and served as a volunteer with the 1st Bn., North Down Regiment of the UVF for two years. Keen tennis player and motorist, he was a member of the Ulster Club, Ulster Reform Club and Royal North of Ireland Yacht Club, and a governor of Belfast Royal Academical Institution.

He was amongst the first to answer his country's call and applied for a commission on 26th September 1914 in the County Down Battalion, Royal Irish Rifles, and was quickly promoted captain. As brigade machine-gun officer, he had been held in reserve when the initial assault began at 7.30am. He and his men were sent out shortly after 8.00am in response to a request from Captain Matthew, a fellow director of Davidson and Co. He had sent a report back at 10.20am, reporting "Am in B line and have got up two Vickers guns, am consolidating both. Cannot say how many infantry are in line, but in this part, there are only about 30 men of 13th, 11th and 15th Royal Irish Rifles. We cannot possibly advance and reinforcements, ammunition and bombs most urgently needed." A co-director, Captain G. W. Matthew was wounded in the same action.

Two hours later, James, now wounded in the knee, sent a further message requesting urgent reinforcements. "I am holding the end of a communication trench in A line with a few bombers and a Lewis gun. We cannot hold much longer. We are being pressed on all sides and ammunition almost finished." One survivor wrote: "the Germans were keeping up a very hot fire and it was open ground we had to cross, and the Germans could see anyone between our front line and theirs. We just got twenty yards from the wire when the captain got shot through the head - he just fell and never spoke or moved. He died instantly - there was no hope."

On 3rd July, James' family received a letter from him: "Only a few minutes to tell you that I am well. The dawn of tomorrow will be the critical time for us but I hope good luck will attend us. Mother dearest, I don't want you to be too anxious about me but if I should have bad luck, will you give Eileen any of my little personal things she would like to have. I will send a postcard just as soon as I can if all goes well." Captain B. Spender, General Staff Headquarters, in writing to Mr. Davidson on the death of his son states: "I am told your son fell after gallantry which deserved the Victoria Cross. Though badly wounded he had insisted in carrying on, and was killed when his men had at last persuaded him to consent to letting them carry him back." His brother in law made the application for his medals on behalf of his sister, Mrs. F. E. M. Binns. Originally buried map reference, Thiepval 57d.Q.24.d.15.45 and marked as unknown British officer of the Machine Gun Corps exhumed 7th November 1929. Approximately 6'0" high and found with a compass stamped J. S. Davidson, 1914, 13th Batt, R.I.R, tie pin & stud, officers uniform, MGC collar badges and buttons and boots subsequently formally identified. Commemorated Holywood First Presbyterian Church, Mountpottinger, Campbell College and Royal Academical Institution and Bangor War Memorial. Memorial XXX. E. 7. Serre Road Cemetery No.2, France.

Son Of Samuel Cleland Davidson Of Seacourt Bangor, Co. Down Ireland

DAVIDSON, Second Lieutenant, Robert Henry Walter. Fell whilst leading his men, in the assault on a German trench in the Battle of Mametz, 1st July 1916. 8th Bn., Devonshire Regiment. Aged 31. Elder son of Frederick Gerald and Mary Davidson of Suez, Egypt and of Birley, Prideaux Road, Eastbourne. Born Singapore on 3rd August 1884 and educated at St. Andrew's School, Eastbourne and won a classical scholarship to Tonbridge. At Tonbridge from September, 1899, he left in July, 1902, from the Modern Sixth, having previously been in the Scientific Sixth, after starting on the Classical side. Member of the OTC. He was in the XI in 1901 and 1902, and became a sergeant in the cadet corps in his last term, and a house praepostor in his last year.

Shortly after leaving school he went out to Singapore, became a planter in Ceylon, 1908-9, and then returning to the Federated Malay States, went first to the Damansara Estate, Selangor, and later to Perak. He was well advanced in his career as a planter, and threw up an important appointment in order to come home and serve his country.

He was gazetted to a temporary commission, dated 26th August 1915, in the Devonshire Regiment, and after training at Oxford, Wareham, and Swanage, he went to France on March 24th, 1916, to join the 8th Battalion at the Front. "He was a hard-working, conscientious officer, and always did his duty under all circumstances" so wrote his Commanding Officer, whilst one brother officer wrote: "He is a great loss to the regiment and to all who knew him, but he died in a great victory, which by his sacrifice he helped to win." Brother Lieutenant G. L. Davidson, MC died of wounds nine days later on the 10th July 1916 before he could learn that he had been awarded the Military Cross. Medals to his sister, Miss H. W. Davidson, Southampton. Memorial Ref. 2., Devonshire Cemetery, Mametz, France. WO 339/40009

Late Of The Malay States Elder Son Of Gerald Davidson Suez, Egypt

DAVIDSON, Lieutenant, Roland Cooper. Initially reported wounded and missing and later confirmed that he had been killed on the 1st July 1916. 20th (Tyneside Scottish) Bn., Northumberland Fusiliers. Aged 25. Elder son of Robert (London Joint Bank Ltd, Bank House, North Shields) and Annie Isabel Davidson, of Kenner's Drive, Tynemouth. Bank clerk. Joined the Duke of Wellingtons as a private when war broke out, 14976 on the 27th August 1914. Four months later he received a commission and went to the Front on New Year's Day. Reported locally the family suffered great anxiety as rumours swept through the town, these rumours would have been via letters home or returning wounded soldiers. Effects returned were revolver, cheque book, note case, identity disc, letters, bill and photos. Father applied for his medals and they were to go to London Joint Bank Ltd, Bank House, North Shields. Memorial Ref. Pier and Face 10B 11B and 12B, Thiepval Memorial, France. WO 339/17203

DAVIES, Captain, Cyril Thomas Morris. Reported to have fell mortally wounded while leading his men against the German trenches at Serre, which the Warwicks took but had to relinquish later on in the day, and so his body was not recovered. Missing believed killed 1st July. 6th Bn., Royal Warwickshire Regiment. Aged 31. Fourth son of Morris and of Mary Anne Elizabetha Davies. Entered Rugby School in 1898 and left in 1902. Shortly after leaving he entered the office of Messrs. W. and F. Cuthbert, Stockbrokers, of Birmingham, and remained with them until the outbreak of war. Although he never filled a prominent place in games while in the school, he became a good golfer after leaving, winning from scratch the Birmingham Stock Exchange Challenge Cup on three occasions, and developed into a first-class hockey player. He formed one of the Warwickshire County Hockey Team from 1905 onwards, was its secretary and captain for some years, and, in 1913, was elected as its vice-president; he concurrently captained the powerful Midlands team, and represented Wales as an international in twelve out of the last fifteen matches prior to the outbreak of war. In 1909 he was elected a member of the Warwickshire County Cricket Executive Committee. Early in September, 1914, he enlisted as a private, 2809, in the Warwickshire Regiment. Stationed at first in the Eastern Counties, he crossed over to France in March, 1915, and entered the trenches between Fouquevillers and Hebuterne, on Easter Sunday, April 4th, and there remained until the end of June, 1916 . Commissioned 18th September 1915. Although prominent as an athlete, it is for the qualities which he displayed in every-day life that he will be best remembered by the very large and varied circle of friends that he possessed, he was true to type to his death While serving in France he rose step by step until as captain and assistant adjutant. Memorial Ref. Pier and Face 9A 9B and 10B., Thiepval Memorial, France.

DAVIES, Lieutenant, Frank Arnold. Two platoons under Lieutenant Davies and W. F. Smith were to fix boards bearing new names in the captured German trenches. Frank went over in front of his platoon but was killed instantly by machine-gun fire soon after he entered No Man's Land over the parapet, 1st July 1916. He was shot through the head whilst leading his men, the leading men of the platoon were also killed or wounded. B Coy., 5th Bn., Cheshire Regiment. Sixth son and second to be killed of William Davies (cotton salesman) of Mountfield, Lower Bebington. Born 20th December 1892. Attended Wallasley Grammar School and Storrington College. Played for the Sefton Park Cricket Club. Employed J. M. Edmiston, shipping agents, Liverpool as a clerk. Served his time with Mr. J. Hoult. Lieutenant Davies received his commission in January 1916 from being a private in the King's (Liverpool Regiment), 2092, and had only been at the Front since 24th February 1915. Joined the battalion, 30th May 1916. Brother also killed, R. E. Davies, King's Liverpool in April 1915. Father applied for his medals. Original reference where body found, B.K10.A.70.90 with eight other soldiers all of whom were identified by individual crosses. Memorial Ref. III. B. 7., Gommecourt British Cemetery No.2, Hebuterne, France.

DAVIES, Second Lieutenant, Harry Noel. Deceased 1st July 1916. 10th Bn. attd. 11th Bn., East Lancashire Regiment. Aged 21. Son of John and Louisa Elizabeth Davies, of 12, Whitegate Road, Southend-on-Sea formerly Twickenham. Born 29th September 1894 at Croydon, lived at 16 Seymour Gardens, Twickenham. University of London OTC. Life insurance clerk. Appointed second lieutenant 10th Bn., East Lancashire Regiment, 10th June 1915. Entered France, 19th April 1916. Joined 11th Bn., East Lancashire Regiment, 23rd April 1916. Father applied for his medals. Memorial Ref. Pier and Face 6 C., Thiepval Memorial, France.

DAVIES, Lieutenant, Trevor Arthur Manning. Attached to the 1/5th Sherwood Foresters as a liaison officer between the artillery and infantry for a diversionary attack on Gommecourt, killed whilst advancing and laying a wire, 1st July 1916. Killed with Second Lieutenant Eric Henry Lloyd Clark. North Midland Div. Ammunition Column, Royal Field Artillery. Aged 23. Elder son of Arthur Manning Davies (wholesale coal business) and Ada Rose Davies, of Hafod, Llandudno, Caernarvonshire previously Aragon House, Sutton Coldfield. Born in Walsall, Warwickshire in 1893. Scholar, King Edward's School, Birmingham also attended Clifton College, Bristol (1909-1912) where he was head of Barff's House and proceeded to Corpus Christi College, Cambridge (senior classical scholar). Member of the College OTC. On 29th August 1914, gazetted as a second lieutenant in the 4th North Midland (Howitzer) Brigade, Royal Field Artillery, Territorial Force. Went to France, 24th February 1915. Served initially in the Ypres Salient, La Bassee, Arras. Commemorated Memorial Chapel of Holy Trinity Church, Llandudno and two large wooden candlesticks, were presented to the Church. Original burial map reference 57d. K10.A70.90. Memorial Ref. II. H. 26., Gommecourt British Cemetery No.2, Hebuterne, France.

DAVIS, Second Lieutenant, Charles Stewart. Reported wounded and missing followed by killed in action, 1st July 1916. 5th Bn. attd. 2nd Bn., Middlesex Regiment. Aged 29. Son of R. J. C. Davis, of Highgate, 32, Pembury Road, Clapton, London. Born 9th February 1887. Educated Merchant Taylor's School from 1899 to 1903. Formerly employed Stock Exchange and Lloyds in Alberta, Canada. Gazetted 23rd June 1915. Treated for influenza, March 1916. Father asked for specific burial details from the War Office and it was only confirmed after a special case review that he was buried by a burial party of the 34th Division. Items returned to father were a mirror, note book, advance book and revolver. Commemorated Merchant Taylors' School, Northwood. Mrs. H. Davis of Pembury Road choose his inscription. Believed to be buried in this cemetery. Memorial Ref. Sp. Mem. 20., Ovillers Military Cemetery, France. WO 339/66843

Their Glory Shall Not Be Blotted Out

DAVIS, Second Lieutenant, Walter Arthur Bernard. His behaviour was fine and his men followed him well, 1st July 1916. Last seen lying wounded against the German barb wire, badly wounded in the chest. 11th Bn., Sherwood Foresters (Notts and Derby Regiment). Aged 27. Son of John and Omelia Davis, of 25, Wilton Street, Old Basford, Nottingham. Educated at Stanley Road Higher Grade School and in 1913 proceeded to America. On the outbreak of war he returned home and enlisted in the Hussars receiving a commission in the Sherwoods in April 1915. His commanding officer wrote in October 1916 your son's body was found and buried being identified by his disc. Reported missing in July and reported killed in October. Commemorated Aidan's Book of Remembrance, Nottingham. Memorial Ref. II. I. 6., Blighty Valley Cemetery, Authuille Wood, France.

Duty Nobly Done

DAWSON, Lieutenant, Gerald Moore. Killed in action, 1st July 1916. 18th Bn., The King's (Liverpool Regiment). Aged 23. Second son of Dr. and Mrs. T. Moore Dawson of West Oakfield, Hooton, Cheshire. At school a member of the OTC. Thorough sportsman and good athlete. Educated at Liverpool College, and left in 1912. He then went into the office of Messrs. Bushby & Son and Beazley, cotton and colonial produce brokers and subsequently entered the employment of Henry Tate and Sons., Ltd, sugar refiners. At the outbreak of war joined the army, stationed at Knowlsey and trained recruits at Hooton Hall. Obtained a commissioned and went to France, 18th April 1916. Medals to his mother, Mrs. Jane Dawson, Hooton. Memorial Ref. Pier and Face 1 D 8 B and 8 C., Thiepval Memorial, France.

DAWSON, Lieutenant, Sydney. It was reported that his last words were, "We will carry on a bit longer". Commanding officer was killed and Lieutenant Dawson took over command of the battalion. Wounded in the capture of the German first line trenches he met his death in the third, 1st July 1916. Adjutant, 8th Bn., York and Lancaster Regiment. Aged 22. Fourth son of John William (brush manufacturer) and Annie M. Dawson, of 189, Hyde Park Road, Leeds. Attended Leeds Boys Modern. Sydney left school to become an articled pupil with a chartered accountants, he won the Fletcher Memorial prize in 1913 for being first place in the Intermediate Examination of the Institute of Chartered Accountants. In August 1914 Sydney joined the Leeds University OTC and in October of that year he was granted a commission in the Yorkshire and Lancaster Regiment. In the June of 1915 he was promoted to lieutenant, and in the January of 1916 he became the battalion's adjutant writing the battalion diary. Entered France 27th August 1915. Leeds University Roll of Honour. Father applied for his medals. Memorial Ref. V. C. 36., Blighty Valley Cemetery, Authuille Wood, France.

Somehow It Seemed To Me That God Somewhere Has Just Relieved A Picket

DAY, Lieutenant, Leslie Terrett. Royal Field Artillery attd. Trench Mortar Battery, killed in action, 1st July 1916. Second Lieutenant Hobbs was killed by a machine gun positioned at the end of a straight section of Fritz Trench, in trying to take the gun, Lieutenant Leslie Terrett Day, Second Lieutenant Gill and Lieutenant Gomersall were all killed, 1st July 1916. Age 30. Enlisted in the Royal Engineers having returned from Chile in April 1914 where he was employed on business and obtained a commission in the Royal Armoured Car Branch of service and served in France. He returned home and then went out again to command a Trench Mortar Battery in September 1915. Keen cricketer, golfer and polo player. Eldest son of Mr. and Mrs. Terrett Day of Ross. Captain H. J. F. Day applied for his brothers medals on behalf of his father. Mother, Isabel Elsie Day applied for parents' pension, c/o Kelly & Son, Ross, Hertfordshire. Memorial Ref. Pier and Face 1A and 8A. Thiepval Memorial, Somme, France.

DEAN, Second Lieutenant, Rosser Fellowes Marriott. Killed by a shell, immediately on leaving the assembly trenches, this was about 8.10am, 1st July 1916. 4th Bn., Royal Warwickshire Regiment attd 93rd Machine Gun Company. Aged 33. Son of Frederick John and Constance Mary Dean, of Enderby, Branksome Hill Road, Bournemouth. Educated at Wellington College and Oriel College, Oxford. Acted as intelligence officer in Kenya Colony in 1914. Returned to England, invalided with Malaria. Rejoined in 1915. From August 1914 to February 1915 served with the British East Africa Field Force afterwards joining the special reserve of the Warwickshires from which he was seconded to duty with the Machine Gun Corps. Father applied for his medals. Memorial Ref. I. D. 14., Euston Road Cemetery, Colincamps, France.

The Best Of Sons And He Nobly Did His Duty To The Last

DEAN, Second Lieutenant, William. Missing, killed in action, 1st July 1916. 3rd Bn. attd. 10th Bn., Royal Irish Rifles. Aged 30. Son of Joel Frederick Dean and Thomisina Dean, of Beachworth, Town Lane, Woodhey, Rock Ferry, Cheshire. Born on 23rd April 1886 at Babington, Cheshire. He had formerly served as 118061, Private William Dean with the Canadian Cavalry Brigade, being attested on the 1st February 1915 at Pincher's Creek. Unmarried. Previously employed as a rancher in the Lundbreck area. Obtained his commission in the Special Reserve of the Royal Irish Rifles at Belfast in December, 1915, and was serving at the front with the South Belfast Volunteers. Commemorated in Canada's Great War Book of Remembrance. Mother applied for his medals. Memorial Ref. Pier and Face 15A and 15B., Thiepval Memorial, France.

DENMAN, Second Lieutenant, Percy Darrell. At 6.00am he was in Headquarters, Avenue Trench with A Company of 2nd Battalion. At 7.30am A Company went over the top with B Company, followed three minutes later by companies C and D. As the front line advanced towards the village of Montauban, it came under intense fire from heavy machine-guns on their left front. All the officers were hit, Lieutenant Denman being one of three officers killed in the advance, 1st July 1916. 2nd Bn., Yorkshire Regiment. Parents were Staff Sergeant William Darrell Denman and Letitia Anderson. Born Lancaster on 4th November, 1874. Aged 41. Percy was the youngest in the family of four children. Resided Abalon, Harcourt Road, Uckfield formerly St. Hilda's, Whitby Avenue, York. Attended St. Thomas' School. Previously telegraphist. Enlisted 21st May 1896 drafted to India, served with the Punjab Command in 1897 and 1898 as lance corporal, 5192. Awarded medals for the Punjab Campaign and Tirah. In 1906 he was sent to South Africa where he married on the 30th April 1908 to Catherine Kerr at King's Hill, South Africa. Sent to France, arriving on 18th April 1915. Sergeant major with 4th Bn., The Green Howards (Princess Alexandra's Own Yorkshire Regiment). Wounded at Givenchy in June and again at Hulluch in September 1915. He was recommended for officer training and was gazetted second lieutenant on 29th September, 1915. Transferred to the 2nd Bn., Yorkshire Regiment. Awarded the Croix de Guerre (First Class) and mentioned in a despatch dated 30th November 1915 'for gallant and distinguished conduct in the field'. Effects were identity disc, chain with coin and wheel. Originally buried 500 yards east of Carnoy, Talus Boisa British Cemetery at grave map reference 62c.A.14.b.5.4 with nine other soldiers. His wife applied for his medals. Two children received pension payment, Letitia and Percy Darrell. Memorial Ref. IV. H. 35., Peronne Road Cemetery, Maricourt, France. WO 339/45777

DERWENT, Second Lieutenant, Robert Ivor. Reported wounded and later officially killed on that date, 1st July 1916. He had been wounded above the groin and bled for some hours before it was dressed and died. 18th Bn., West Yorkshire Regiment (Prince of Wales's Own). Aged 26. Third son of Henry Casaubon Derwent, JP. (general manager of the Yorkshire Observer) and Ann Maria Derwent, of Nearcliffe, Bradford, Yorks. Editorial staff, Bradford Telegraph. Sergeant, 827, West Yorkshire Regiment, entered France, 16th April 1915. Temporary second lieutenant 8th December 1915. Wounded in the leg and whilst recovering acted as a recruiter. Brother, Rifleman Norman Derwent died June 18th 1917. Father applied for his medals. Memorial Ref. I. B. 27., Euston Road Cemetery, Colincamps, France.

Son Of Mr. And Mrs. H.C. Derwent Bradford, Yorkshire

DEWHURST, Lieutenant, George Charnley Littleton. Missing believed killed, 1st July 1916. 1st Bn., Rifle Brigade. Aged 24. Only son of Mrs. Annie M. Jones (formerly Dewhurst) and George Littleton Dewhurst of Aberuchill, Comrie, Perthshire, Born December 23rd, 1891 at Knutsford, Cheshire. Attended Eton. Admitted as pensioner at Trinity, Cambridge June 25th 1910. Known in Cheshire hunting circles. Member of the firm Messrs. G. and R. Dewhurst, cotton spinners, Preston. Entered France, 27th January 1915 and was twice wounded. George left estate in England and Scotland to the value of £110,749 and generously he left six months wages to each of his servants. Four uncles serving with the Colours. Weaverham War Memorial Cheshire. Plaque in St. Serf's Episcopal Church, Comrie. Mother applied for his medals. Memorial Ref. I. G. 38., Serre Road Cemetery No. 2, France.

And How Can Man Die Better Than Facing Fearful Odds

DICKIE, Second Lieutenant, William. Fell whilst leading his platoon in action, at Beaumont-sur-Ancre, 1st July 1916. 9th Bn. attd. 1st Bn., King's Own Scottish Borderers. Transferred to the Border Regiment but had yet to make the move when he was killed. Father William Dickie (editor, Dumfries and Galloway Standard) and his mother, Jane of Mirtlewood, Albert Road, Maxwelltown. Born 1892 at Laurieknowe, Maxwelltown, Troqueer. Aged 24. He was dux of Dumfries Academy in 1910 and proceeded to Edinburgh University in preparation for ministry of the United Free Church. At the entrance exam he won the John Welsh classical bursary and the Lanfine and C. B. Black scholarships. In 1913 after an arts course he graduated with an MA (Hons. Classics) first class. In the open scholarship he obtained the Bible Clerkship of Oriel. He was then a scholar of Oriel College, Oxford until 1914. He joined the OTC, and was gazetted 22nd October 1914. On the 6th September 1915 he landed at Gallipoli, and was part of the evacuation and went to Egypt were he appreciated the classical elements, going to France and landing on the 26th March 1916. On the night of his last leave he occupied the pulpit of St. George's Church, Dumfries. Named on the Maxwelltown/Troqueer War Memorial and on the St. George's Church Memorial in Dumfries. Edgar P. Dickie, his brother applied for his medals in respect of the services of his late brothers. Memorial Ref. Pier and Face 6 A and 7 C., Thiepval Memorial, France.

DICKINSON, Second Lieutenant, Thomas Arthur. Killed in action, 1st July 1916. 1st /6th Bn., South Staffordshire Regiment. Aged 22. Son of Alderman Thomas William (Wolverhampton) and Sarah Elizabeth Dickinson, of Palmer's Cross, Tettenhall, Staffs. Born on 21st July 1893 at St. Mark's Road, Wolverhampton. Deceased was educated at Tettenhall College and was secretary to the Old Boys' Association. Articled law clerk, and at some point he worked for Messrs. May and Court, solicitors of Wolverhampton. Enlisted 26th July 1915, 5071, Inns of Court OTC. Given a commission 8th November 1915. Entered France, 17th April 1916. Tettenhall College War Memorial. His father applied for his medals. Memorial Ref. Pier and Face 7 B., Thiepval Memorial, France.

DICKSON, Lieutenant Colonel, Arthur. Died of wounds, leading his battalion, 1st July 1916. 1st Bn., South Lancashire Regiment attd. 10th Bn. West Yorkshire Regiment (Prince of Wales's Own). Aged 41. Son of Arthur Dickson (solicitor) and Mary Dickson, of Montrose. Attended Fettes College. Sheriff-substitute of Forfarshire. He took part in operations in the Transvaal and on the Natal frontier. Also served in India. Correspondence on medals to his uncle, J. Burness, Charlotte Square, Edinburgh. Memorial Ref. C. 12., Fricourt New Military Cemetery, France.

DINES, Second Lieutenant, Percy John Francis. Nearly all casualties occurred just by the Magpie's Nest, reported to have died of wounds, 1st July 1916. 9th Bn., Devonshire Regiment. Aged 24. Son of Mr. Tom P. (commercial traveller) and Mrs. Bertha H. Dines, of Berwyn, 91, Lansdowne Avenue, Leigh-on-Sea, Essex formerly Fern Lodge. Born 29 St Mary's Road, Fulham on the 23rd January 1892. Old boy of Southend High School for boys (1906 to 1908). Employed as abstractor, Board of Trade, Patent Office. Resided 3 Percy Circus, Lloyd Square, London. Civil Service Cadet Corps. Joined the territorials, 20th March 1910 and enlisted in August 1914, 15th Bn., London Regiment, private, No. 1204, C Company, No.10 Platoon. Went to France with the 1st Bn., Civil Service Rifles on 17th March 1915. Commissioned with the 11th Devonshire Regiment, 11th May 1915. Joined the 9th Bn., for duty on the 24th May 1916. Reported missing and death reported 12th August 1916, confirmed to his parents on the 5th August 1916. Buried Carnoy Cemetery Sht 62c. Sq. a.13.d Medal application made by his father. Commemorated on the Patent Office Memorial 1914-1918, scroll within the Civil Service Rifles Memorial at Somerset House, London. Memorial Ref. Sp. Mem. 8., Carnoy Military Cemetery, France. WO 339/30256

To Memory Dear

DINSDALE, Second Lieutenant, Frank. Reported wounded and missing and then officially killed, 1st July 1916. 12th Bn., York and Lancaster Regiment. Son of Mr. James and Sarah Dinsdale. Born High Abbottside, Yorkshire. Leeds University OTC from where he received his commission, October 1915 and went to France, June 1916. Medals to brother, H. Dinsdale Esq., Showcote, Yorks. Memorial Ref. C. 20., Queens Cemetery, Puisieux, France.

DIXON, Captain, James Evelyn Bevan. Attacked towards the village of Serre, Captain Dixon was badly wounded in the original assault and had to be left behind as his men retired in the face of a German counter-attack, reported killed, Beaumont Hamel, 1st July 1916. 6th Bn., Royal Warwickshire Regiment. Aged 22. Born October 25th, 1893, at 3 Augustus Road, Edgbaston, Birmingham. Younger son of Mr. and Mrs. Arthur Stansfeld Dixon, of Deddington, Oxon. Entered Oundle School in 1907 and left in 1913, played full back for the XV in 1911 and 1912. Admitted as pensioner at Trinity College, Cambridge, June 25th, 1913. He received a commission with the Royal Warwickshire Regiment in October 1914 and went with them to France, 23rd March 1915. He was promoted lieutenant a year later and captain just a few days before his death. One of his fellow officers later wrote of him: "He showed the greatest bravery, and, after being wounded, carried on for some time before receiving the wound which proved fatal. He was one of the officers I placed the greatest reliance on in getting men out of a tight corner." Dixon's Major wrote simply that "He had a great moral effect on the men, who always saw him absolutely composed." Father applied for his medals, resided at Broad Street, Birmingham. Memorial Ref. I. K. 7., Serre Road Cemetery No.2, France.

DODD, Second Lieutenant, Neville. 1st July 1916. 1st /6th Bn., West Yorkshire Regiment (Prince of Wales's Own). Aged 32. Youngest son of Arthur and Alice Dodd of Tulse Hill, London. Born on 28th August 1884. Educated Eastbourne College. On leaving school he went into his father's business as a diamond merchant. He joined the London Scottish in September 1914 and served as quartermaster sergeant until early in 1915 when he received a commission. He went to France, 2nd November 1915 and was assistant adjutant of his battalion until he was killed. At the Front, nine months. Medals to his father in Hampstead. Mrs. Laura C. Dodd, Furtherside, Woldingham, Surrey choose his inscription. Map reference where body found 57d.Q.30.d.75.90 and formally identified by his disc. Memorial Ref. XX. E. 12., Serre Road Cemetery No.2, France.

Love, Remembrance, Hope

DODINGTON, Lieutenant, Thomas Marriot. Reported missing 1st July officially date of death, 2nd July 1916. Battalion history states 1st July. 1st Bn., Somerset Light Infantry. Eldest son. Father, a lieutenant colonel in the West Somerset Yeomanry. Educated at Marlborough College. From Marlborough he went to RMC Sandhurst in 1913. Commissioned 16th December 1914. Served in the 1st Bn., Somerset Light Infantry and was wounded at Ypres on 13th May 1915 by a piece of shrapnel casing in his upper left thigh. Most of his muscle was torn away and one of his tendons chipped. Declared fit on the 13th December 1915. Private Fox of the Somerset Light Infantry wrote; "on July 1st near Colincamps Lieutenant Dodington was leading our platoon and I saw him fall at the enemy's fourth line trench. He fell on the parapet of the trench and was then shot through the head". Private Martin, reported that "on July 1st during an attack on Hamel, I saw Mr. Dodington lying wounded not far from the parapet perhaps 10 to 20 yards. I myself was wounded about 6 to 8 yards from the parapet and succeeded in crawling back into our trench. He was lying 10 yards to the left of me". Memorial Ref. Pier and Face 2 A., Thiepval Memorial, France.

DON, Second Lieutenant, David Fairweather. On the first day of the great advance he led his platoon in the assault they were met by murderous fire and he was hit by a shell half way across No Man's Land and died on the parapet to which his servant dragged him, 1st July 1916. Attached to the 2nd Bn., South Wales Borderers from 14th Bn., Sherwood Foresters (Notts and Derby Regiment). Aged 22. Youngest son of Surgeon General, Dr. William Gerard Don and Jean Ann Don, of Caufield Gardens, West Hampstead. University College School, Hampstead (1908-11). Bank clerk, National Bank of India. Member of the Bisley team. Disembarked for Mudros, 22nd November 1915 a note on the Medal Index Card states HMS Olympic. Enlisted in the Honourable Artillery Company and got his commission and went to France with the South Wales Borderers. Memorial Ref. Pier and Face 10C 10D and 11A., Thiepval Memorial, France.

DONALDSON, Second Lieutenant, John James. He was killed by a shell very soon after leaving the trenches at La Boisselle, he was left on the ground as he was dead and there was no time to bury him, 1st July 1916. 20th (Tyneside Scottish) Bn., Northumberland Fusiliers. Aged 28. Son of Robert and Elizabeth Donaldson, of 10, Albury Park Road, Tynemouth and 105 Park Crescent, North Shields, Northumberland. Attended Armstrong College (Newcastle University). Born 10th December 1887, Tynemouth. Employed as a clerk at Borough Accountant Office. Enlisted 4th November 1914 and commissioned on 21st April 1915. Medals applied for by his mother. Memorial Ref. Pier and Face 10 B 11 B and 12 B., Thiepval Memorial, France. WO 339/30491

DONCASTER, Second Lieutenant, Robert Ivan. Reported that his company commander was wounded so Ivan leapt on to the parapet in charge of the company saying "Come on lads". A hail of machine-gun fire was opened on them but he was unharmed until within 12 yards of the Bosch trench when he was hit on the wrist by a bullet. He sat down to bind it up when he was hit by another through the head and never seen again. 1st July 1916. C Coy., 13th Bn., attached 15th Bn., Lancashire Fusiliers. Born in Sandiacre Noel Street, Nottingham on the 19th December 1897. Eldest son of Robert, (director of a screw manufacturing company) and Gertrude Louisa Doncaster, of The Grange, Sandiacre, Derbyshire. Educated Long Eaton Secondary School and went to Nottingham University. In December 1913 he went to work for Crompton & Evans' Union Bank at its Buxton Branch, the bank was acquired and he worked for Parr's Bank. Enlisted in March 1915 into the Leicestershire Regiment, 13th Battalion attached 15th Bn. and applied for a commission 29th June 1915 whilst still in the OTC, commissioned in the 13th Bn., on the 22nd July 1915. Entered France, 12th May 1916. Medals applied for by his father. Originally grave map reference R.31.a.10.8 with eight other soldiers, believed to be R. I. Doncaster. Memorial Ref. VI. V. 8., Lonsdale Cemetery, Authuille, France.

DORE, Second Lieutenant, Alfred Clarence. Killed in action, 1st July 1916. 101st Bn., Machine Gun Corps formerly York and Lancaster Regiment. Aged 22. Son of Alfred George and Edith Dore, of "Thaxted," Devonshire Avenue, Sutton, Surrey. Entered France, 26th April 1916. Sutton War Memorial. His mother applied for his medals. Original burial map reference 57d.26.a. Memorial Ref. VIII. N. 2., Gordon Dump Cemetery, Ovillers-La Boisselle, France.

He Died And Left So Dear A Memory

DORNTON, Second Lieutenant, Harold Shafto. Bombing officer, reported missing after the attack on Gommecourt, 1st July 1916 in a raid on the German trenches. The third wave caught up with the second wave in the advanced trench and on arrival, Harold informed them they were 45 seconds to early, the third and second wave waited and they were then informed that they could go over. He fought in a fire bay with Captain Naylor, Second Lieutenant Barber and a few other men they threw bombs until the supply was exhausted, they were then subjected to an intense attack and those that could move were forced to leave the injured officers; Dornton and Wright behind. No. 13 Platoon, D Company, 1st/5th Bn., Sherwood Foresters (Notts and Derby Regiment). Son of Alfred Shafto Duff Dornton and Ann Clara, 29 Woodville Gardens. Born in Hendon, Middlesex, 1896. Age 20. 5th London Regiment, Private, No. 83. Disembarked on the 4th November 1914 and had been in the fighting line since that month. Commissioned to Notts and Derby on the 23rd March 1915. Captain Arthur B. Naylor, Officer Commanding, D Company wrote to the family on the 5th July 1916; 'I am very strongly of opinion that your son is a prisoner in the hands of the enemy. A party of six of us, attacked a German trench and cleared three bays of the enemy, killing many. Revolvers then becoming useless and we used bombs. Soon, however our supply ran out and no support was forthcoming. Now we were attacked by both sides by the enemy and bombs falling around us and amongst us, one of these slightly wounded your son, myself and Lieutenant Barber. When we decided we must withdraw, and crawled towards some shell craters for cover, it was here in the thick smoke I lost sight of your son, but I feel sure he would be captured that night by an enemy patrol and you will hear from him shortly through the American Embassy. His valise and kit are being looked after and will be returned to you shortly'. His father applied for his war medals but had to return the Victory Medal and it was reissued. Memorial Ref. Pier and Face 10 C 10 D and 11 A., Thiepval Memorial, France.

DOUGAL, Second Lieutenant, John Braes. Killed in action, 1st July 1916. 15th Bn., Royal Scots. The younger son of Mr. W. Dougal, JP, Linlithgow. Born 31st January 1891, and received his early education at Linlithgow Academy. Attended George Watson's College (1900-06), and on leaving entered the firm of Messrs. A. Dougal and Sons, brick manufacturers, Winchburgh. Married 22nd February 1916 to Barbara Mary Alexander. Enlisting in 1915 in the Royal Engineers as a despatch rider, No. 78778, he received a commission in April 1915 in the 15th Royal Scots. He was for some time bombing officer of the battalion and ongoing to France in April 1916 was attached to a Trench Mortar Battery. Keen huntsman. On receipt of death notification on the 7th July 1916, father sought more details from the War Office. His wife, Mrs. E. Cooper applied for his medals. Memorial Ref. Pier and Face 6 D and 7 D., Thiepval Memorial, France. WO 339/39446

DOUGAL, Lieutenant, Robert Joseph. Killed in action, 1st July 1916. 21st (Tyneside Scottish) Bn., Northumberland Fusiliers. Aged 21. Youngest son of Susan Dougal, of 34, May Street, Belfast, and Hugh Dougal. A member of Andrew Dougal & son, (carting contractors), Belfast. Member of the Queen's University, Belfast OTC, 1914. Commissioned in October 1914. Entered France, 13th May 1916. His mother applied for his medals and parents' pension. Memorial Ref. Pier and Face 10 B 11 B and 12 B., Thiepval Memorial, France.

DOUST, Second Lieutenant, Charles Bowden. Killed at Gommecourt, 1st July 1916. He emerged from the smoke screen and was shot by Gerfreiter Frederick Fuchte the commander of No. 8 gun, 73rd Machine Gun Marksmen Section, Fuchte was killed shortly after this by a grenade thrown by one of the Second Lieutenant Doust's team. 1st /5th Bn., London Regiment (London Rifle Brigade). Oldest son of Mr. and Mrs. Charles Henry and Laura Doust of Inglehurst, Shortlands, Kent. Born 26th October 1887. Dulwich College (1900-1903) and in the Cadet Force. After Dulwich he went to Germany working in a textile factory and went to Paris employed in a commercial house. Finished his education prior to going to joining his father's business as a Colonial Merchant Assistant. At the outbreak of war enlisted with his younger brother in the 5th London Rifle Brigade, private, 9871, and went to Flanders, 4th November 1914, being wounded in May 1915 in the second Battle of Ypres. Gazetted in August 1915 and after training went to the Front joining as an officer 14th March 1916. Charles's brother, Norman Shellibeer Doust died of pulmonary tuberculosis on the 20th June 1918 having left the London Rifle Brigade to join the Royal Flying Corps being discharged on the 8th August 1917. Application made for Charles's medals by his father. Memorial Ref. Pier and Face 9D., Thiepval Memorial, France.

DRINKILL, Lieutenant, Frederick Maurice. Died of wounds, 1st July 1916. 5th Bn., attd 2nd Bn., Royal Fusiliers. Aged 24. Only son of Richard and Ellen Rosanna Drinkill, of 43, Walton Street, Chelsea, London. Educated at Keble House School, Ostend and at King's College, London. Frederick was a valued member of the Guild of St. Gregory attached to Westminster Cathedral, and a lover and keen student of the liturgy. He obtained his commission through the London University OTC in November, 1914, and was promoted a year later before going to France. Served in Egypt and Gallipoli, Mudros. Mother applied for his medal and officer pensions. Memorial Ref. II. F. 1., Auchonvillers Military Cemetery, France.

God Bless Thee "Boy" Whereso'er Thou Art In His Great Universe R.I.P.

DRURY, Lieutenant, Harold Strickland. Killed in action, Authuille Wood, 1st July 1916. 3rd Bn. attd. 8th Bn., King's Own Yorkshire Light Infantry. Aged 19. Eldest son of Frank James and Clara Drury, of St. Anne's Place, Manchester and 89, Promenade, Southport. Born 27th October 1886. He had been at the Front about a month. Commissioned on his 18th birthday. In business with his father, Frank Drury Ltd. Educated Southport University School and Southport College. Member of the Southport Cadets. Went to France, 4th June 1916. Wounded men from the King's Own were being treated at Southport and his parents managed to find further information by visiting the nearby Cottage Hospital. A soldier relayed that Lieutenant Drury had reached the parapet of the first line of German trenches when he was shot above the knee and crawled back to a shell hole occupied by the soldier, a wounded captain and a wounded stretcher bearer. The four men must have been spotted as the Germans continued to throw bombs. Lieutenant Drury dressed his leg and against advice tried to get help but was shot as he got to the top of the small crater and rolled back he tried to move on his elbows but fell back and did not move again. The captain tried to do the same and was shot as was the stretcher bearer, the wounded soldier managed to climb out and was shot at but managed to get into another shell hole when he was picked up by the Field Ambulance. Father applied for his medals. Memorial Ref. Pier and Face 11 C and 12 A., Thiepval Memorial, France. WO 339/48393

DUNN, Second Lieutenant, Ralph Ellis. Missing believed killed 1st July 1916. 13th Platoon, H Coy., 1st Bn., Somerset Light Infantry. Aged 20. Son of Mrs. H. Ellis Dunn, of Myre Cottage, Clatworthy, Wiveliscombe, Somerset, and Reverend Henry Ellis Dunn, Vicar of Upton. Joined as trooper in 2nd King Edward's Horse, January 1915, private, 1413 went to France 4th May 1915. Obtained his lieutenancy 3rd March 1916. Commemorated Sons and Daughters of the Anglican Church Clergy. Reverend Dunn made the application for his medals. Memorial Ref. Pier and Face 2A., Thiepval Memorial, France.

DUNSTAN, Second Lieutenant, Guy Peirce. Killed in action July 1st 1916 carrying a despatch from Brigade HQ to the front line. A Company, 11th Bn., Border Regiment Attached 97th Brigade. Aged 23. Son of Kenneth J. and Alice Adams Dunstan, of 279, Russell Hill Road, Toronto, Ontario. Born July 9th 1892. Educated Model School Upper Canada College, University College 1911-15 BA. (Member of the OTC). In May 1915 enlisted in 2nd Universities Company and went overseas in June. Received his commission and joined 11th Borders and then appointed to HQ Staff, 97th Brigade. Original burial grave map reference 57d.X.1.b.3.6, grave marked with an individual cross and buried in this location with fourteen other men all of which were killed on the 1st July, fourteen men were from the 11th Bn. Memorial Ref. VI. X. 9., Lonsdale Cemetery, Authuille, France.

DUSSEE, Second Lieutenant, Arthur Norman. Killed leading his men, Leipzig Redoubt near Thiepval, 1st July 1916. 4th Bn. attd. 19th Bn., Lancashire Fusiliers. Aged 26. Son of Arthur Wilmot Dussee and Eleanor Frances Dussee, of Lee Terrace, Blackheath, London. Born Blackheath, 27th January 1890. Colfe's Grammar School, Lewisham. Clerk in the London County & Westminster Bank. Played cricket with the Bedford United Banks Team and member of Bedford Thursday Hockey Club. Enlisted September 1914 in Public School Corps. Gazetted May 1915. Entered France, 13th May 1916. Father applied for his medals, from Lewisham Hill, Lewisham. Memorial Ref. I. A. 11., Bouzincourt Communal Cemetery Extension, France.

When Good Men's Bodies Die Their Souls Go Winging To God

EAMES, Second Lieutenant, Arthur Horwood. At about noon, information having been received by the brigade, that parties of Germans still remained in the trench network on the immediate left, which were endangering our communications, the East Yorkshire Regiment were detailed to despatch a bombing party to reconnoitre the ground and clear up the situation. This party was despatched under Second Lieutenant A. H. Eames. A superior number of Germans was encountered and it was while dealing with this situation that Lieutenant Eames was killed. In consequence however of his reconnaissance, a strong party of the East Lancashire Regiment were sent up to clear out the enemy and fighting took place in the network which lasted throughout the day and resulted in the killing and capturing of all the enemy who had occupied it. Officially 1st July 1916, evidence shows the 2nd July. 1st Bn., East Yorkshire Regiment. Aged 21. Born at Pulborough, Sussex on November 24th 1894. Son of Mr. L. H. Eames of Upper Nash, Pulborough, Sussex. Attended Cranleigh School and in the OTC. Enlisted as a private, No. 1681 with the 28th London Regiment, Artists Rifles. Entered France, 26th October 1914. After officer training he was commissioned into the Yorkshire Regiment in April of 1915 and joined the 2nd Battalion in France just after the battle of Neuve Chapelle. He saw action with the battalion at Festubert and Givenchy in the early summer of 1915 . On the 13th June 1915 he received a shrapnel wound to the left temple and returned home being treated in Birmingham for three weeks. In August was transferred to the 1st Battalion of the East Yorkshires. Possessions of a wallet with letters and photos, wrist watch, map tracer, safety razor, pocket diaries, trench dagger, regimental buttons and badges along with his advance book were returned to the family. Pulborough War Memorial. War Diary and Medal Index Card has 2nd July 1916. Father applied for his medals. Memorial Ref. Pier and Face 2 C., Thiepval Memorial, France. WO 339/28245

EASON, Lieutenant, Raymond Praed. Killed near the mine crater at La Boiselle, reported to be hit by machine-gun fire at the German first line, he was found in a shell hole as if he was asleep reported to be one of the first men over, 1st July 1916. A Coy. 10th Bn., Lincolnshire Regiment. Aged 21. Born 4th April 1895. Only son of J. W. Eason, JP, (former mayor of Grimsby) and Elizabeth Praed Eason, of Scartho House, Grimsby. Member of the Cadet Corps and University of London, OTC. Attested August 1914 but his application seems to have been lost reapplied 17th September 1914, Lincolnshire Regiment, Sergeant, No. 150. Gazetted 27th November 1914. Reinterred 1919, originally buried south of La Boiselle at reference 57d.X.20.c with thirteen other men. Effects returned were revolver, waterproof bag, identity disc, electric torch and compass in case. Medal Index Card implies died of wounds. Father applied for his medals. Memorial Ref. VI. F. 6., Gordon Dump Cemetery, Ovillers-La Boisselle, France. WO 339/15682

He Is Not Here But Is Risen

EAST, Captain, John. Killed in action, 1st July 1916. 15th Bn., Durham Light Infantry. Aged 28. Son of John and Louisa East, of Auckland, New Zealand. Husband of Marguerite East (nee Jacquet), of 33, Hatherley Road, Sidcup, Kent and father to a two month old child. Resided 53 Exeter Street, Strand, London. Hotel employee at the Carlton Hotel. Enlisted in Poplar, London 4th August 1914, No. 1637, 18th Bn., London Regiment. Promoted to interpreter 23rd October 1914. Entered France, 11th September 1915. 26th May 1916 promotion to captain. Left an estate valued at £262. At the point of his death his wife was residing at Au Plait, Le Brevil, Allier, France where she received her telegram. His brother also asked the War Office for details on his death. Widow applied for his medals. Memorial Ref. Pier and Face 14 A and 15 C., Thiepval Memorial, France. WO 339/29823

EATON, Second Lieutenant, James Willcox. Killed whilst leading his men, though wounded twice, he still fought on with just his revolver, until he eventually fell mortally wounded, 1st July 1916. 20th Bn., Manchester Regiment. Aged 24. Only son of James Morley Eaton (cotton goods merchant) and Alice Annie Eaton, Sandymount Hale, Altrincham. Born at Sharston, Northenden, Cheshire. Educated at Ackworth School, Pontefract and at the Bowdon College. Employed as salesman, cotton goods merchant. Commissioned in the Manchester Regiment in November 1914 and drafted to the front on the 18th February 1916. Joined battalion, 12th March 1916, A Coy., Platoon No II. Commemorated Hale Cenotaph, St. Peter's Memorial (Hale), Wadham House School (Hale), Altrincham & District Roll of Honour. Originally buried south of Fricourt, Sht 62.F.9.d.99.10 also listed as 62.F.9.d.9.7 with fellow officers killed on the 1st, Second Lieutenants Lord, Kemp, Brooks and Ross where the grave was marked by a memorial cross. Returned items in two packages, coins, cigarette case, flask, cheque book and wallet. His mother applied for his medals. Memorial Ref. VI. I. 5., Dantzig Alley British Cemetery, Mametz, France. WO 339/66160

Platoon No.II. Also killed on the 1st July in the photograph, Private John William Ashton, Private E. Bowyer, Private Joseph Hughes, Private R. A. Hall, Private A. Horridge, Private F. T. Lever, Private B. Sheehan, Private T. Thorneycroft and Private Eric James Woodhead.

EDINGBOROUGH, Second Lieutenant, Noel Duncan. Teams 1, 2, 3 and 16 under their officers Lieut. H. Hewitt and Second Lieut. N. Edinborough were completely wiped out in No Man's Land. At the time they were heading for a position known as Lisnaskea Trench, whilst he was gallantly directing the fire from his machine-guns he was hit by a bullet and killed instantaneously, 1st July 1916. Machine Gun Corps attached 15th Bn., Middlesex Regiment. Born Hendon. Third son of Thomas and Frances Mary Edingborough. Educated Dagmar House School, University College School, Hampstead. Student, electrical engineering. Member of the Institute of Electrical Engineering. Apprenticed July 1913 to British Westinghouse Electric and Manufacturing Company. Freemason, Salisbury Lodge. Volunteered to serve in Machine Gun Corps. Entered France, 23rd June 1916. Joined the company on the 30th June 1916. Father applied for his medals. Memorial Ref. Pier and Face 12 D and 13 B., Thiepval Memorial, France.

EDMOND-JENKINS, Major, William Hart. He went out of the trench with one knee on the parapet when a bullet struck him just above the knee coming out by the hip - a terrible wound. Reported to have died of wounds on the 2nd July 1916 officially 1st July 1916. Locally reported succumbed to wounds on the 1st July 1916. 25th (Tyneside Irish) Bn., Northumberland Fusiliers. Aged 35. Eldest son of Captain William Henry (shipping agent) and Katherine Barbara Edmond Jenkins, Swansea. Born Argaty, Sketty, 20th January 1881. Educated Swansea by private tutors and at the Normal College. Joined 1897 as a private and obtained a commission. He served through the South African campaign as a volunteer. On his return he went through a course of civil engineering and later District Superintendent of Police in Uganda. On his return became a captain in 1911. He went to Canada settling in Graham Island, Queen Charlotte Island. On the outbreak of war he rejoined the army and offered his services. Gazetted Major 4th February 1915 and went to France, January 1916. War Gratuity of £135 12s 2d claimed by his sister, Mrs. Helen Moffat as father Captain W. H. Jenkins died 5th September 1921 and William was unmarried. Father had applied for his medals prior to his death. Memorial Ref. I. C. 30., Albert Communal Cemetery Extension, France. WO 339/9625

I Thank My God Upon Every Remembrance Of You

EDMUNDSON, Captain, Charles Robert Ewbank, MC. On the 21st July reported to have been killed 1st July 1916. Gallantly led his men through a terrible fire and even when all his men were shot down he continued the attack. 8th Bn., York and Lancaster Regiment. Aged 24. Only son of Charles Francis Peter and Mary Eleanor Edmundson, of Masham and Ripon, Yorks. Husband of Grace Maude Edmundson, of 14, Cathcart Hill, Tufnell Park, London and had one son. Attended Marlborough College admitted February 1914. Enlisted September 1914 as a private, Middlesex Regiment and given a commission and attached to the 8th Bn., Yorks and Lancashire Regiment. Captain July 1915 and went to France, 27th August 1915. Awarded a posthumous MC; 'He led his company forward in face of heavy shell and machine-gun fire, and after most of his men were shot down and he himself badly wounded he collected the remainder and again led them to the assault. He was again severely wounded'. Mrs. Edmundson from Eastbourne applied for his medals. Daughter Grace Elizabeth was born on the 10th September 1915 and received pension payment. Original map reference, 57d.X.1.d.7.8 and identified by his name on a ground sheet and prismatic compass, buried with an unknown British soldier. Memorial Ref. VIII. K. 15., Adanac Military Cemetery, Miraumont, France.

EGLINGTON, Captain, Ferdinand. In the seventh wave and shot by machine-gun fire, twenty yards from the German wire, Gommecourt, reported he died bravely and very gallantly, cutting the barbed wire when he was struck by a bullet, officially 2nd July 1916. A Coy., 1st/5th Bn., South Staffordshire Regiment. Sergeant Major E. Martin stayed with the officer for an hour until he died, making date of death as the 1st. Aged 31. Born 14th March 1885. Elder son of Edward H. (bit, spur and stirrup manufacturer of Walsall) and Lucy Eglington, of Hammerwich, Lichfield. Old boy of King Edward's School, Birmingham and a noted rugby player. Keen cricketer and member of Lichfield Cricket Club and for some years captain of Hammerwich Cricket Club. Joined Walsall Territorial Company after the outbreak of war, private, 558, and obtained a commission. Entered France, 25th February 1915. On Easter Monday 1915 he was severely wounded in the head by shrapnel and needed an operation also wounded in 1916. October 1915 gazetted as a temporary captain. Member of Walsall and District Chamber of Commerce. Member of the Walsall Hockey team. Father applied for his medals. Memorial Ref. Pier and Face 7 B., Thiepval Memorial, France.

EKIN, Second Lieutenant, James. Missing 1st July 1916. 8th Bn., York and Lancaster Regiment. Aged 19. Born 1897. Son of James and Josephine Alice Ekin, of De Walden Court, Eastbourne. Native of Sydney, Australia. His brother Second Lieutenant Leslie Montrose Ekin also fell on the same day. Previously private, Rifle Brigade, 2/2845. Epitaph reads 'Now heaven is by the young invaded'. Medal Index Card has theatre of war as 'missing'. Father applied for medals, two addresses; Queensborough Terrace, Hyde Park and Redcliffe Square, SW10. Original map grave reference R.31.a.6.3 the grave being marked with a cross and five other men found in this location. Memorial Ref. VI. O. 1., Lonsdale Cemetery, Authuille, France.

Now Heaven Is By The Young Invaded

EKIN, Second Lieutenant, Leslie Montrose, MC. Seriously wounded, Leslie managed to hold his line of advance with his machine-gun team, then taking control of the Lewis gun himself before he was cut down. For his bravery he was awarded the Military Cross. 1st July 1916. 8th Bn., York and Lancaster Regiment. Aged 22. Born 1894. Son of James (property owner) and Josephine Alice Ekin, of De Walden Court, Meads, Eastbourne. In 1911 the family resided at 5 Redcliffe Square, South Kensington. Native of Australia. His brother James also fell on the same day. Educated at Sydney Grammar School and had returned to England with his parents, selecting law as his profession. He was a member of the Middle Temple and was going to Oxford University when war broke out. He joined the Inns of Court OTC, 1365 and received his commission, 17th December 1914. Attended Manor House School, Clapham. Probate; £1079 18s 2d was left to James Ekin, father. Medals applied for by his father. Memorial Ref. V. C. 13., Blighty Valley Cemetery, Authuille Wood, France.

The Farewell Lies Behind But The Meeting Lies Before

ELAM, Lieutenant, Charles. At 3.45am reported battalion in position in the assembly trenches. Led a party through the wire into the German front line where they fought in vain to hold on to the hard-won ground, reported wounded and missing, Serre, 1st July 1916. Last seen to be wounded in the neck. A Company, 12th Bn., York and Lancaster Regiment. Aged 21. Born 17th January 1895 at 96 Manor Road, Stoke Newington. Son of Dr. and Mrs. George Elamand Ethel Elam, of Edenthorpe, 41, Wickham Road, Beckenham, Kent. Steelworker. Applied for a commission in the territorials, joined the 12th Bn. York & Lancaster Regiment as a private (12/1423) on 10th September 1914. Eight days later he was appointed to a commission in the battalion with the rank of second lieutenant. Promotion to full lieutenant followed on 5th December as the battalion moved to Redmires Camp. Father applied for his medals. Originally buried at map reference 57d.29.b.4.1 and marked as on unknown British officer later identified by a disc, York and Lancaster buttons, and regimental badge. Buried with an unknown British officer and an unknown British soldier. Memorial Ref. XII. M. 2., A.I.F. Burial Ground, Flers, France.

ELDER, Second Lieutenant, Alexander. Initially reported wounded on the 2nd July 1916 later as killed on the 1st July 1916. 15th Bn., Royal Scots. Aged 26. Elder son of Hugh and Madge Elder, of 89, East Trinity Road, Edinburgh. Born 5th January 1890. Known in athletic clubs of Daniel Stewarts College and Royal High School (1902). Employed coffee essence manufacture. He joined the rank as a private, 17075 at the outbreak of war with the Royal Scots, 28th September 1914. After serving for eleven months he received a commission, 9th August 1915 and later was appointed sniping officer. Entered France, January 1916. Medals to his parents address. Original grave reference 57d.20.c and buried as a unknown British officer of the Royal Scots and later identified. Memorial Ref. IX. M. 8., Gordon Dump Cemetery, Ovillers-La Boisselle, France. WO 339/38819

Till The Day Dawns

ELLIOTT, Second Lieutenant, Philip Maurice. Killed near La Boisselle and Ovillers, last seen with his servant handing him bombs, 1st July 1916. Reported he was shot in the head and shoulder whilst standing on the parados of a German front line trench. Survivors were forced to return to the German Front line and here they proceeded to consolidate their position until 9.15am when a small handful of unwounded men were forced to retire to the shell holes in No Man's Land. 3rd Bn., Middlesex Regiment. Aged 22. Fifth son of Henry John and Annette Elizabeth Mary Elliott, of Upperton, Crawley, Sussex. Born on 28th March 1894. Attended Eastbourne College. Enlisted in the 1420, Artists Rifles on 5th August 1914, and went to France with the 1st Battalion in October 1914. He next obtained a commission in the 3rd Bn., Middlesex Regiment on the 14th February 1915. On the 9th May 1915 he was wounded at the Second Battle of Ypres by shrapnel in the foot and invalided home, recovered 28th May 1915. He returned to France in December 1915, joining the 2nd Bn. Originally buried near La Boisselle. In a letter to his parents from Reverend H. B. Burnaby (Regimental Padre); "Thus he lies where the 2nd Middlesex so splendidly opened the great attack, buried close to his brother officers who fell with him, Captain Meeke, Captain Heaton and Lieut. Van den Bok". Brother of Captain Henry Elliott MC who died on the 2nd March 1919. His father from Eastbourne applied for his medals, had to be re-issued due to an incorrect surname. Original map reference 57d.X.14.a.4.3 and buried with six other soldiers. Memorial Ref. VII. H. 39., Adanac Military Cemetery, Miraumont, France. WO 339/27781

Loving All He Was Beloved By All

The seated figure is Captain Henry Elliott, MC of the Royal Garrison Artillery
Second Lieutenant Phillip Maurice Elliott stood behind

ELLIOTT, Second Lieutenant, Thomas Brignall. 1st July 1916. 10th Bn., Royal Irish Rifles. Aged 29. Son of Thomas and Annie Elliott, of Sandown, Chichester Park, Belfast formerly of Tremona, Knockdene Park, Knock, Belfast. Born 5th May 1887, Stockton-on-Tees. Educated at Belfast Royal Academical Institution. Attended Royal University of Ireland. He was working as a clerk when he enlisted as a private with the 8th Royal Irish Rifles on 8th September 1914, in Belfast. Thomas had previously served as a lieutenant with the Boys Brigade for three years, and was commissioned on 30th November 1914, in the East Belfast Battalion. He subsequently transferred to the South Belfast Battalion in March 1915. Accounts of his death vary, Chaplain the Reverend James Quinn, informed: "He fell leading his men on the morning of the 1st inst. It is hardly possible for him to have been left lying where he fell if the wound had not been mortal, as the ground has been frequently and fully searched. Of course, until his body has been found, there is just a slight chance for him, as wonderful and almost incredible instances of survivors are returned on such occasions, but up till this afternoon, there are no traces of him." Father applied for his medals. Memorial Ref. Pier and Face 15 A and 15 B., Thiepval Memorial, France.

ELLIS, Lieutenant, Clifford Walker. Killed in action at Fricourt, 1st July 1916. 3rd Bn. attd. B Coy., 9th Bn., King's Own Yorkshire Light Infantry. Aged 19. Second son of George and Elizabeth Ellis, of Easthorpe, Mirfield, Yorks. Born 6th October 1896 at Dewsbury, Yorks. Attended Batley Grammar School, Scarborough and Marlborough College. Articled to civil engineers. Commissioned 11th March 1915. Entered France, 1st November 1915. Father advised it is not possible to bring his body home as it is not allowed by the French Government. Items returned were a watch, cup, keys, buttons and an ammunition pouch. Brother of Second Lieutenant James Norman Ellis who also fell on the 1st December 1917. Father applied for his medals. Originally buried NW of Fricourt, map reference 57d.26b.5.4 and marked as unknown KOYLI officer, later changed to Lieutenant Ellis. Memorial Ref. V. N. 4., Gordon Dump Cemetery, Ovillers-La Boisselle, France. WO 339/47850

ELLISON, Second Lieutenant, Stanley John. Wounded close to the German wire, reported missing, afterwards presumed killed at Gommecourt 1st July 1916. 1st/5th Bn., South Staffordshire Regiment. Aged 19. Born on 4th October 1896. Son of John and Susannah Ellison, of Wyndhurst, Sutton Coldfield, Birmingham. Aged 21. Educated Sutton Coldfield Grammar School. Attended Bishop Vesey's Grammar School between 1906 and 1914. He was a prefect, librarian and sergeant of cadets. He played first team football, cricket and hockey during 1912-1914. He passed the Birmingham University Matriculation Examination and Oxford Senior Local Examination with Honours and was awarded the Eddowes Prize upon leaving school in 1914. Articled to John Ellison (father), of

Birmingham, firm of Edge and Ellison, Solicitors, Waterloo Street, Birmingham. Upon the outbreak of war he became a sergeant in the Birmingham University OTC and on 21st October 1915 he obtained a commission in the South Staffordshire Regiment. He went out to France in June 1916. Brother, Captain Douglas Hems Ellison. 95th Russell's Infantry attached to 1st/109th Indian Infantry died 14th January 1920. Commemorated on the Sutton Coldfield Memorial, King Edwards Square and St. Peters Church, Maney. Father applied for his medals. Original grave reference 57d.E.28.c.3.4, and identified by his clothing and disc. This area was behind German lines, he was seen to be hit and died in the hands of the Germans. Memorial Ref. III. B. 24., Bailleul Road East Cemetery, St. Laurent-Blangy, France.

He Died That Others Might Live

ELPHINSTONE, Lieutenant Colonel, Arthur Percy Archibald. Killed 1st July 1916. Commanding, 22nd (Tyneside Scottish) Bn., Northumberland Fusiliers. Aged 53. Born at Malligaum, Bombay, India, on the 22nd of July 1863. Son of Colonel Percy Augustus Elphinstone, Bombay Staff Corps. Husband of Augustine Chiappe. Passed through RMC Sandhurst with Honours, 1883. Gazetted to Warwickshire Regiment, 1884, transferred to 107th Pioneers, and later to 106th Pioneers. Served in the Burma (1885-9) Campaign (medal and two clasps) and Somaliland (1902-4) Campaign (medal and clasp). Retired from the Indian Army, on the 1st of September 1911. Arthur rejoined the army with the outbreak of war in August 1914. Appointed the Commanding Officer of the 22nd (Service) Battalion (3rd Tyneside Scottish), Northumberland Fusiliers on the 14th of December 1914. Entered France, July 1915. Mentioned in Despatches. Claim submitted by Mr. A. H. L. Elphinstone with the address changed from Notting Hill to Alliance Bank of Simla, Calcutta. Memorial Ref. Pier and Face 10 B 11 B and 12 B., Thiepval Memorial, France.

ELY, Captain, Dennis Herbert James. From the regimental history; "One incident in connection with this is worthy of note: Captain Ely, though wounded slightly in the foot, pressed on with his men towards Shelter Wood. He showed a magnificent example to his men and until his death by a sniper's bullet he was full of enthusiasm and courage. That sniper's time was short. One of our men, Private J. Jolley, saw him. They saw each other and fired. The German's bullet grazed Jolley's nose, Jolley's bullet struck fair and square in the head," killed in Sunken Road near Fricourt, 1st July 1916. 15th Bn., Durham Light Infantry. Born 27th February, 1896 at Langside. Only son of George Herbert and Francis Ely of Haling Park Road, Croydon. Educated Ayr Academy and attended Whitgift School. Whitgift OTC. Attested 2nd September 1914 at Westminster, No. 314. Commission 31st October 1914 in the Durham Light Infantry. Went to France 18th October 1915. Slightly injured but remained on duty 11th February 1916. Originally buried near Fricourt, his father received information that he was killed between Crucifix Trench and Shelter Wood. The effects returned were clothes and trifles and his father wrote that 'nothing he had on him when he was killed has been returned; watch, compass, binoculars, and revolver. Granted these articles were worth stealing but not his writing case that he would not have taken into battle with him, it is worthless article but invaluable to my family'. He was in regular contact with his mother's friend, Mrs. Bourne who supplied socks, cake and woollen items originally to his platoon but then organised for the whole company. Dennis's last letter to her is dated 16th May 1916 and his mother wrote to her on the 10th July advising 'My dear and much loved soon has been killed'. As a tribute a book was published full of his letters and his biography in 1916 'Dennis Ely, Captain, Durham Light Infantry'. His last letter home to his father was dated 30th June 1916; 'Mother tells me you have spent hours at home readjusting the pictures….I am just going off to a company's commanders conference with the C.O, so cheerio!'. Memorial Ref. Pier and Face 14 A and 15 C., Thiepval Memorial, France. WO 339/30823

A photo in the book featuring Captain Ely

EMBERTON, Second Lieutenant, Percival Harvey. Killed in action, 1st July 1916. 1st Bn., South Staffordshire Regiment. Aged 28. Only son of William and Emily Jane Emberton, of 176, Sandon Road, Stafford. Educated Rowley Street Schools under Mr. G. Symcox (headmaster) proceeding later to Stafford Grammar School. Passed into Civil Service and for four years was at Somerset House, London. Entered King's College to continue his studies and passed the higher grade of the Civil Service. Since November 1907 he had been stationed in the office of the Irish Land Commission, Dublin. At the beginning of the war with his fellow clerks went into training with the Black Watch at Perth, private, 1406 and went to the Front. In April 1916 entered the officers' training school in France and was gazetted on June 14th to the South Staffs. In his last letter wrote 'After all it is a good finish for any man'. Originally buried east of Fricourt, SE of Albert map reference 62D.f.10.b and marked as 'unknown Sec. Lieut. South Staffs July 1916'. Medals to his parents. Memorial Ref. II. C. 7., Dantzig Alley British Cemetery, Mametz, France. WO 339/65217

Nature Might Stand Up And Say To All The World "This Was A Man"

ENGALL, Second Lieutenant, John Sherwin. The Vickers gun which accompanied A Coy., got as far as the junction of Etch, Feed and Feint trench and was brought into action by Second Lieutenant Engall who had only one of his team left with him, he fought the gun himself until he was killed at this spot being hit in the head, as he was firing from an exposed position, 1st July 1916. Corporal J. C. Bolwell was with him and managed to make it back to the trenches, the gun was put into action behind a bank at the side of the road. 1st/16th Bn., London Regiment (Queen's Westminster Rifles) attd. 169 Infantry Brigade, Machine Gun Coy. Aged 19. Born 25th July 1886. Son of John Benjamin Sherwin Engall and Edith Mary Engall, of 62, Goldsmith Avenue, Acton, London. Acton County School Old Boy. Enlisted six weeks after the outbreak of war in the Queens and had only recently left St. Paul's School. Member of St. Dunstan's Church, East Acton. Chartered accountant. Entered France, 31st December 1915. Gazetted 15th January 1915. Seconded to Machine Gun Corps, March 1916. Wrote 'A Subaltern's Letters: The Letters of Second-Lieutenant J. S. Engall 1915-16'. Last letter home 'I ask you that you should look upon it as an honour that you have given a son for the sake of King and Country…Fondest love to all those I love so dearly, especially yourselves'. Mother applied for his medals. Memorial Ref. Pier and Face 13 C., Thiepval Memorial, France.

EVANS, Captain, Charles William, MC. Crossed the German front trench, he jumped down and shot a German with his revolver, he lost his weapon and borrowed another revolver from an NCO and continued the attack. At the next traverse he was shot in the stomach and seen to be bleeding from his nose and stomach by a lance corporal who had to retire without him, 1st July 1916. 1st Bn. attd. 4th Bn., South Staffordshire Regiment died with D Coy., 1st/6th South Staffordshire Regiment a couple of weeks prior to the attack. Born 28th March 1891. Son of Henry and Florence Eliza Evans, The Lawn, Hagley, Worcestershire. Attended Shrewsbury School. Haydon's (Rigg's) from 1903 left in 1909 to enter Royal Military College. Promoted second lieutenant, 1st April 1910. Mentioned in despatches for valuable service. Promoted to be Lieutenant 9th April 1913 in South Africa with the 1st Bn., which he joined in 1910. Entered France, 7th October 1914. Wounded early in the war, November 1914 and at Richebourg on the 16th May 1915. Military cross awarded June 1915. Application for medals by Miss. Molly Evans in respect of her late brother whist working at the Queen Alexandria Hospital Headquarters, B.E.F. It was three years before she and the family accepted her brother's fate, she was in a good position to speak to wounded soldiers and try and understand the exact details of her brother's last moments. The family clung on to hope as long as possible. Memorial Ref. Pier and Face 7 B., Thiepval Memorial, France.

Officers of the 1st Battalion, South Staffordshire Regiment. India 1914
Back row; Lt. H. W. MacGeorge, Lieut. D. C. Twiss, Lt. C. R. Limbery (killed 1st July 1916), 2nd Lt. C. R. C. Bean.
Second Row; Lt. V. G. Olive, Lt. C. W. Evans (Killed 1st July 1916), Lt. L.C. Moor-Radford, 2nd Lt. C. E. C. Bartlett.
Middle Row; Lt. W. A. P. Foster, Capt. C. H. Green, Capt. Barber, Lt. C. M. Morris, Lt. F. L. Holmes (k), Capt. C. G. Rainsford. Front Row; Capt. S. Bonner (adt), Capt. R. W. Morgan, Major J. F. Loder-Symonds, Gen. Sir Reginald Hart, Lt. Col. R. M. Ovens, Major A. C. Buckle, Major S. C. Welchman, Capt. J. F. Vallentin, Capt White.

EVANS, Lieutenant, Humphrey Pennefather. Reported missing believed killed, within twenty minutes off zero the battalion were virtually wiped out, 1st July 1916. 2nd Bn., South Wales Borderers. Son of Granville Pennefather Evans (Commissioned Indian Army officer, Lieutenant Colonel) and Grace Woodburn Evans. Born India. Attended Rossall School, named on the memorial board. Had two brothers. Gazetted April 1915. Went to France, 16th July 1915. Father, Lt. Col. Evans applied for his medals with the address of c/o Messrs. Thomas Cook & Son, P.O Box 46, Bombay, India. Memorial Ref. Pier and Face 4 A., Thiepval Memorial, France.

EVANS, Second Lieutenant, Tudor Eglwysbach. Known to be killed by 7.50am in fierce fighting in No Man's Land, 1st July 1916. B Coy. 8th Bn., East Surrey Regiment. Aged 24. Younger son of the Reverend John Evans and Clara Kate Evans of Newstead, Minehead. Born 12th August 1891. Educated at Cardiff University College, BA (Hons). No. 2637, sergeant, 21st Royal Fusiliers commissioned to East Surrey, 13th May 1915. Entered France, 5th January 1916. Brother, E. R. Evans, Westbourne Road, Glamorgan applied for his medals. Memorial Ref. E. 30., Carnoy Military Cemetery, France.

EVERED, Second Lieutenant, Henry Robert Hastings. Fell at the head of his men, 1st July 1916. 27th (Tyneside Irish) Bn., Northumberland Fusiliers. Attended Denstone College. He was in the OTC and joined the Norfolk (Cyclist) Regiment in September, 1914. In a month he was promoted lance-corporal and corporal in six months, No. 1239. In August, 1915, he received a commission in the Northumberland Fusiliers. He left England and entered France, 13th May 1916. Father applied for his medals. Memorial Ref. Pier and Face 10 B 11 B and 12 B., Thiepval Memorial, France.

EVERITT, Second Lieutenant, John Paxman. Fighting was hard and shelling heavy, machine-gun fire was intense, died of wounds, part of the 2nd wave, 1st July 1916. 15th Bn., West Yorkshire Regiment (Prince of Wales's Own). Aged 19. Born. August 16th 1896, London. Son of Charles (clergyman) and Elizabeth E. Everitt, of 12, Inglis Road, Colchester. In 1910, aged 13, entered Malvern College (1910-1914), becoming a school prefect. Member of the OTC. During his time there, played for his college in both the football and cricket elevens. On the 14th December 1914, at the age of 17, he accepted a commission in the 10th Bn., Kings Own Yorkshire Light Infantry. Served in Egypt. On the 12th June 1915, he was posted to the West Yorkshire Regiment as a second lieutenant and given command of 14 Platoon, D Coy., Leeds Pals. A private wrote "I am proud to be able to say that he was always kind, and a gentleman. I admired his principles. He was well liked and admired by his men and the few that them remain, join me in sending our deepest sympathy in your sad bereavement." The Malvern College Obituary reads: "His career here marked him out to be a leader of the first order and one cannot speak too highly of the splendid example he set to those over whom he was in authority. Full of grit, a thorough gentleman, with his ideals and with a cherished hope for the welfare of his school and House, he answered the call of his country in the same grand spirit that was characteristic of him throughout his school days." Commemorated St. Leonard at the Hythe Church. Left his personal estate to his father. Memorial Ref. Pier and Face 2 A 2 C and 2 D., Thiepval Memorial, France. WO 339/31115

EVERSHED, Lieutenant, Albury. Parents received a telegram with the addition of 'believed killed', confirmed to have been caught up in the wire and killed, Gommecourt, 1st July 1916. D Company, 1st /6th Bn., North Staffordshire Regiment. Aged 25. Youngest son of Sydney Herbert (director of brewing company, Marston, Thompson and Evershed) and Alice C. Evershed, of Albury House, Burton-on-Trent who had four children. Attended Burton Grammar School and Clifton College. Played rugby for Burton Football Club. Employed John German & Sons, Estate Agents, Ashby-de-la-Zouch he had passed all his examinations. Commissioned 26th November 1914, promoted to Temporary Lieutenant 1st July 1915 and went to France on the 30th October 1915. Medals to go to Albury House. Memorial Ref. Pier and Face 14 B and 14 C., Thiepval Memorial, France.

EWART, Captain, Cecil Frederick Kelso. As second in command of C Company he took command when Captain Samuels was wounded. Originally reported wounded and missing, 1st July 1916. C Coy. 11th Bn., Royal Irish Rifles. Aged 28. Born 14th November 1887. Second son of Frederick William and Maryanne Elizabeth Ewart, of Derryvolgie, Lisburn, Co. Antrim. Attended Winchester College, 1901 to 1903 from Hillside School, Godalming. Entered his father's business (William Ewart & Son Limited, flax spinners and linen manufacturers) at Belfast. He was commander of I Company of the 1st Lisburn Bn., UVF whom he supplied with rifles and ammunition and allowed to practice on his own private shooting range. On the outbreak of war, with his two brothers, he joined the new army. He embarked for France from Bordon Camp, as a second lieutenant in A Coy., 11th Bn., Royal Irish Rifles, in October 1915 and was promoted to captain early in 1916. Commemorated on a plaque in Christchurch, Lisburn. Father applied for his medals. Memorial Ref. Pier and Face 15 A and 15 B., Thiepval Memorial, France.

FAIR, Second Lieutenant, George Patrick Conroy. Missing believed killed 1st July 1916. 1st Bn., Somerset Light Infantry. Aged 20. Born 1896. Younger son of Mr. Thomas Conroy Fair and Catherine Fair, of Woodside, Walton-By-Clevedon, Somerset. Educated at Eastington, Clevedon at Lambrook, Bracknell and Uppingham. On the outbreak of war he left Uppingham and passed third into the RMC Sandhurst. He obtained his commission in early 1915 and had been at the Front since 17th July 1915. His elder brother, Second Lieutenant James Conroy Fair, Coldstream Guards was reported missing and wounded at Loos whilst trying to rescue a wounded man, subsequently reported as killed 27th September 1915. Commemorated Parish of Clevedon Saint John. Mother applied for his medals. Memorial Ref. I. H. 8., Sucrerie Military Cemetery, Colincamps, France.

In God's Keeping Till We Meet Again

FAIRLEY, Lieutenant, Duncan. Two platoons, under Lieutenant Fairley and Second Lieutenant Lowinsky in file along Nairne following A Coy., duty to file into Russian Sap, convert it into fire trench facing north and hold it, Serre, they were held up by a block, and enfiladed by heavy fire that by 9.30am had almost annihilated them, 1st July 1916. Lieutenant Lowinsky badly wounded returned to report their heavy losses and request urgent help. A platoon from C Coy., went to the rescue but found the sap totally destroyed by fire and the two platoons wiped out. B Coy., 14th Bn., York and Lancaster Regiment. Aged 26. Son of Barker (Headteacher at St. John`s National School) and Charlotte Fairley, of 84, Ormonde St., Sunderland. Native of Barnsley. Locke Scholar at Barnsley Holgate Grammar School after which he studied at Manchester University from 1908 gaining his teaching diploma in 1912 then taking up a position as English master at a school in Scarborough. Member of Leeds OTC, 1907-1908, when the war began Duncan returned to Barnsley and on 1st May 1915 enlisted in the 14th (2nd Barnsley Pals) Bn., York and Lancaster Regiment. Commissioned and promoted to lieutenant. Memorial Ref. IV. S. 7., Euston Road Cemetery, Colincamps, France.

FALCONER, Lieutenant, Robert Whitfield. 1st July 1916. 16th Bn., Northumberland Fusiliers. Aged 31. Born in 1885, the only son of James William and Isabella Falconer (née Nixon), of 3, Roseworth Terrace, Gosforth, Northumberland. Educated at St. George's School in Gosforth where he won the Exam Prize and the Junior Cambridge Local Exam Prize in 1899 aged 14. In 1899 signed on as a seaman on the Linden, a cargo boat, and worked for 11 days. On leaving school he worked for several firms on Newcastle Quayside serving time as a shipbroker's clerk. Intended to take over the firm of Falconer Boss & Co., the family shipbuilding business. Interested in woodwork and volunteered at the W. J. Sanderson Orthopaedic Hospital in Gosforth teaching children wood carving, joinery and shorthand. Bell ringer at All Saints, Gosforth. He was one of the original members of the band at All Saints Gosforth, an honorary member of the Newcastle Cathedral Guild, a member of the Durham and Newcastle Diocesan Association, in which he held various offices, a member of the Yorkshire Association and became a member of the Salisbury Diocesan Guild while training with his regiment on Salisbury Plain. At the outbreak of war he joined the 16th Northumberland Fusiliers as a private but rapidly rose to sergeant and became instructor of musketry in his battalion. After nine months training he was offered a commission and went to France in the latter part of November 1915.

While there he was one of two picked from his division to instruct at the Telescopic Sight and Sniping School and rejoined his battalion just before the Battle of the Somme. Father applied for his medals. Memorial Ref. Pier and Face 10 B 11 B and 12 B., Thiepval Memorial, France.

FALKOUS, Captain, Robert. In D Company of the 27th Battalion, Captain Falkous was last seen encouraging and helping his men forward when he fell mortally wounded. His batman, Private Greaves, also wounded in the same burst, went to his aid but the captain refused assistance and implored the private to save himself. 1st July 1916. 30th (Tyneside Irish) Bn. attd. 27th (Tyneside Irish) Bn., Northumberland Fusiliers. Son of George Falkous, Low Feil. Aged 23. Born 1st May, 1892, Witton Gilbert, County Durham. Educated at the Friends School, Great Ayton, Wife and infant reside at 23, Peel Street, Sunderland. Served as a private with the 16th (Service) Battalion, Northumberland Fusiliers (Newcastle Commercials) at Alnwick. Posted to the 30th (Reserve) Battalion. Before embarkation, May 1916 he joined the 27th (Service) Battalion Northumberland Fusiliers (4th Tyneside Irish) in France. When Mrs. Falkous received the news of her son's death, she tried to obtain more information, writing several times to the Army Graves Registration and to the Red Cross. His widow applied for his medals. Memorial Ref. Pier and Face 10 B 11 B and 12 B., Thiepval Memorial, France.

FANGHANEL, Second Lieutenant, Frederick Charles. Reported missing 1st July 1916. He made it to the first line German trench but was hit as he passed the last line of German wire, six yards from the trenches, he collapsed unconscious and was dragged into the trench being mortally wounded in the stomach. The majority of the small party of men that had got that far were all wounded and with no other choice were forced to give themselves up. Second Lieutenant Fanghanel was carried to a nearby dugout and tied shortly afterwards, his ID disc, cigarette case and wallet were removed and given to Second Lieutenant Blunn whom along with the other men were taken away to become prisoners of war. A Coy., 1st/4th Bn., London Regiment (Royal Fusiliers). Aged 26. Son of Paul Gustav Adolf (general merchant) and Clara A. Fanghanel, of Ravendale, Shaa Road, Acton, London. Admitted to Latymer School in September 1900. The February 1915 edition of the School Magazine says that he joined the 16th Battalion of the Middlesex regiment as Private PS/415, September 1914 entered France in 1915. He was mentioned in the July 1916 edition and it was confirmed in the that he had been killed in the October edition. Father applied for his medals. Frederick's body was last seen in the dugout. Memorial Ref. Pier and Face 9 D and 16 B., Thiepval Memorial, France.

FARLEY, Second Lieutenant, Frederick Albert. Killed in action, having been under bombardment for nearly two hours he was one of the casualties, 1st July 1916. 1st/2nd Bn., London Regiment (Royal Fusiliers) attd. Support, D Coy., 1st/16th Bn., London Regiment (Queen's Westminster Rifles). Aged 25. Son of Arthur Albert and Frances Eleanor Farley, of 11, Warleigh Road, Brighton, Sussex. Born 19th January 1891. Educated at Rugby Road School, Brighton and Brighton Technical College. Trained as a fitter's apprentice, London, Brighton and South Coast Railway Company. Appointed King's Messenger and lived in Liverpool. Trooper, 1466, Sussex Yeomanry. Commissioned 8th September 1915. Entered France 5th June 1916. Member of Brighton Cruising Club. Mother applied for his medals and officers pension, Ditchling Road, Brighton. Memorial Ref. Pier and Face 9 D and 16 B., Thiepval Memorial, France.

FARROW, Second Lieutenant, Brian. Killed in No Man's Land on his way back, having been successfully in keeping the Germans back in the Quadrilateral, 1st July 1916. 4th Bn. attd. 2nd Bn., Lancashire Fusiliers. Aged 24. Son of Captain Jacob Frederick Farrow, MC. (RAMC), and Clara S. Farrow, of 248, Upper Chorlton Road, Manchester. Born at Cleckheaton, Yorks on the 5th January 1892. Educated Bradford Grammar School 1901 to 1904 and Manchester Grammar School. Hon. Secretary of the Hulme Rugby Football Club. Apprenticed to Charles Behrens & Co. Enlisted September 1914 in the 18th Royal Fusiliers and gazetted December 1915. Entered France, 7th May 1916. Body found and buried in March 1917. Medals applied for by his father. Memorial Ref. I. C. 6., Serre Road Cemetery No.1, France.

In God's Keeping Till We Meet Again

FAWCETT, Second Lieutenant, Frank Aldridge. Missing in action during an attack near Gommecourt, 1st July 1916. 1st/5th Bn., South Staffordshire Regiment. Resided Springfield Road, Kings Heath, Birmingham. Only child of Frederick and Eva Fawcett. Aged 19. Born 17th August 1896, Birmingham. On leaving school Frank worked as an accountant at Tyndall and Hall at 86 Colmore Row, Birmingham before joining the 1st Birmingham Pals, Royal Warwickshire Regiment in September 1914, private, 14/236. After a short spell in Egypt from 20th October 1915 went to France and worked as a battalion bombing officer. Commissioned 6th September 1915, joined the 1st/5th from the 2nd/5th South Staffordshire Regiment on the 24th October 1915. Recorded on the roll of King Edward's School, Birmingham as he attended between 1911 and 1913. Father, residing at Paternoster Row, Birmingham applied for his medals. Memorial Ref. Pier and Face 7 B., Thiepval Memorial, France.

FEARNLEY, Second Lieutenant, William. Killed in action, seen lying dead fifty yards in front of trench, 1st July 1916, killed by machine gun fire. No. 16 Platoon, 2nd Bn., Gordon Highlanders. Aged 37. Native of Headingley. Throughout the South African War he was with the Yorkshire Hussars. Promoted to sergeant major at the age of 23, being offered a commission in the Army Service Corps he accepted but relinquished after a short time and rejoined the Hussars. After a short spell he joined the 5832, Scots Guards and received the rank of sergeant. He went to Egypt and at the expiration of his service he held a civil post in the Sirdar's Office at Cairo. Recalled at the outbreak of war he was posted to the 2nd Gordons, No. 6442 and went to France with the first detachment, 7th October 1914. Married 26th October 1915 to Emily Elizabeth Ellen Fearnley, Vile Mead Cottage, Church Crookham, Fleet, Hants. Commissioned 8th June 1916. His wife received notification by telegram however his father wrote to the War Office enquiring about his death that appeared in the press. Originally buried 67 Support Trench, F.11.c.8.3. Effects returned sphinx collar badge, officer chevrons, identity disc, medal bar, cheque book, advance book and notes. Medal Index Card has correspondence of Rogan Street, Nyngan, New South Wales, Australia. Memorial Ref. A. 6., Gordon Cemetery, Mametz, France. WO 339/65134

FEATHERSTONE, Second Lieutenant, George Herbert. Succeeding in passing the German front line trench with four other officers, was hit later in the morning and died in the afternoon in Lozenge Alley, 1st July 1916. Signalling officer, 9th Bn., King's Own Yorkshire Light Infantry. Second son of Reverend Ralph John Featherstone, Vicar of St. Luke's, Thornaby. Age 26. Born 23rd August 1897. Educated at Stockton on Tees Grammar School and St. John's College, Oxford entered 11th October 1912 and it was intended that he should enter the Consular Service when he took his final degree in French. Obtained a commission and appointed to rank of second lieutenant, 29th June 1915 went to France, 25th December 1915. Resided 9 Walton Street, Oxford. Father received a letter stating he was killed on the 1st July 1916 and date of death corrected by the War Office from the 3rd July. Items send to next of kin, letters, photos, cheque book, advance book and note book. Commemorated Sons and Daughters of the Anglican Church Clergy. Ilkley War Memorial. Father applied for his medals. Memorial Ref. Pier and Face 11 C and 12 A., Thiepval Memorial, France. WO 339/33876

FENWICK, Second Lieutenant, Percival Fenwick. Forward Observation Officer, he was leading at the time when one of the signallers he was with got shot he went back to give a hand and was shot in the leg and managed to crawl back to a shell hole having managed to get 40 to 50 yards from his own parapet. Signallers left him with food and water, this was when he was last seen, death accepted as 1st July 1916. Royal Field Artillery. Aged 22. Son of P. B. Fenwick, of 31, Middle Head Road, Mosman, New South Wales. Husband of S. C. H. Fenwick, of Trefusis, Moree, New South Wales, Australia. Sent a telegram to his father in May 1915 saying he had been made second lieutenant left Australia two months prior on RMS Malwa on the 30th March 1915, he had forwarded his name for the King Edwards Horse. Entered France, 11th March 1916. Medals to his father in New South Wales. Original burial map reference 57d.k.29.b.0.4 an isolated grave and in 1925 identified as Second Lieutenant Fenwick through officer's khaki, collar, badge & boots but preliminary with cigarette case stamped 'P.F.F', field glasses, compass and flask. Memorial Ref. I. D. 17., Cerisy-Gailly French National Cemetery, France.

FERGUSON, Second Lieutenant, John Roy. 1st July 1916. D Coy., 1st Bn., Newfoundland Regiment. Aged 27. Son of Daniel (roadmaster) and Isabella Ferguson, of 39 Leslie Street, St. John's. A Copuar Angus boy who migrated early in life with his parents. Born in Dundee. Husband of Jeannette Ferguson, of Grand Falls. Auditor with A.N.D. Co., Grand Falls and Botwood. Left a son. Company sergeant major, 882 with the Newfoundland Regiment. Served in the Balkans from 19th September 1915. Commissioned 5th June 1916. Brother of Sergeant Stewart Small Ferguson also killed with the Newfoundland Regiment on the 1st July 1916. Jeanette found out about her husband's death through a friend and a list of killed officers from the paper, she had moved several times and the official telegrams never found their way to her. Memorial Ref. Beaumont-Hamel (Newfoundland) Memorial, France.

FIELD, Second Lieutenant, Henry Lionel. Reported killed, he had led his men forward and they had swept after him triumphantly over the first and second German trenches; he had called a laughing remark to a brother officer and was raising his hand as the signal for a further advance when a bullet struck him down, Beaumont Hamel, 1st July 1916. 6th Bn., Royal Warwickshire Regiment. Aged 22. Born 1894. Second son of Henry Cromwell Field and Ruth Field, of Courtlands, Edgbaston, Birmingham. Born Edgbaston, 2nd May 1894. From Marlborough he went to Oxford, and matriculated for Lincoln College, but instead of going there preferred to start at once on what he meant to be the real work of his life, and became a student at the Birmingham School of Art. Grandson of Right Hon. Jesse Collings. He was at a sketching school at Coniston, when the sudden outbreak of war brought him hurrying home to enlist and commissioned in September 1914 and joined the Warwicks, sent to France, 5th February 1916 at Foncquevillers.

For five months he was in the trenches, and wrote home saying he was enjoying himself; "I am much happier than I ever thought I should be in the army. After all, I am in my destined place, doing or about to do what I should be doing or about to do. In some way or another, home seems nearer, and thank God I don't flinch from the sound of the guns." On another occasion, he wrote about himself and his brother, who was also in the firing line, "It is our birthright to do something of this sort once in our lives. I honestly don't wish things otherwise, neither does Guy. I don't mean to talk about Spartan mothers, and that sort of thing. . . . But remember we are all part of each other, and think of it like this when we leave you, it is not so much you losing us as you fighting through the medium of your sons." Established war poet and wrote 'Carol for Christmas 1914'. Brother was Captain Guy C. Field. Father applied for his medals. Memorial Ref. II. C. 10., Serre Road Cemetery No.2, France.

The Everlasting Arms Are Wide

FIELDING, Second Lieutenant, Francis Willoughby (Jack). Fell leading his men against the line of enemy trenches, 1st July 1916. C Coy., 9th Bn., London Regiment (Queen Victoria's Rifles). Aged 22. Younger son of Harry (auctioneer) and Letitia E. Fielding, of Stoneleigh, Thame, Oxon. Born in Towersey on 8th October 1892. Attended Lord Williams's Grammar School, 1902 -1906 . After leaving school, Francis had moved to Coventry and begun work in the fledgling motor industry as a draughtsman. He enlisted in the Queen's Own Oxfordshire Hussars, corporal, 1522, and served in France from the 20th September 1914 as a despatch rider. In 1914 he was wounded by an exploding shell while carrying despatches 1914 and invalided home. He later returned to the front and transferred with a commission as second lieutenant gazetted from corporal, 24th April 1915 transferred to the 9th London Regiment. Resided 48 St. Patrick's Road, Coventry. His mother applied for his medals in 1928 from Stoneleigh, Thame, Oxon. Original grave map reference 57c.C.K.4.b.20.20 and marked as Unknown British Soldier (officer) and in 1920 formally identified. Buried in that location with three unknown officers also killed on the 1st July. Memorial Ref. III. D. 1., Gommecourt British Cemetery No.2, Hebuterne, France.

FIRTH, Captain, Ernest Hartley. Met his death whilst leading his men into action, 1st July 1916. 13th Bn., York and Lancaster Regiment. Aged 42. Fifth son of Francis Helme Firth, of Mounthill, Beckenham, Kent previously 5, Radnor Park Avenue, Folkestone. Served through the Boer War with the Kaffrarian Rifles and also through South West Africa. On the conclusion of that campaign he came to England, and was appointed to the Oxford and Buckinghamshire Light Infantry, transferred to the York and Lancaster Regiment. Gazetted second lieutenant 14th August 1915. His brother, Mr. C. M. Firth from Horne Cottage, Batcombe, Somerset applied for his medals and decided his inscription. Memorial Ref. Special Memorial. B. 16., Euston Road Cemetery, Colincamps, France.

Their Glory Shall Not Be Blotted Out

FISHER, Lieutenant, Thomas Edward Coney. At 7.28am, six leading platoons took up their position in No Man's Land, without loss. At 7.30am our front line pushed forward, they were met with very heavy artillery and machine-gun fire, some of A and B Coys who did make the German front line at 7.35am were surrounded and captured by the Germans. Reports vary to he was killed on the way across and also reported he was last seen in a German trench and it had been initially hoped that he would been reported as a prisoner, 1st July 1916. 1st Bn., East Lancashire Regiment. Aged 19. Son of Major Edward and Edith Mabel Fisher, of Braywick, Budleigh Salterton, Devon (formerly of La Guilaumerie, St. Saviour, Jersey). Born 14th January 1897. Educated at Victoria College, Jersey (1906 to 1910), Felsted (September 1910 – December 1914) and RMC Sandhurst. Commissioned 15th June 1915. Only in France, six weeks since 25th May 1916. Reported to be buried in Waggon Hill Cemetery, Beaumont Hamel. Report of a corporal in whose arms he died was accepted, and he was officially reported as killed on the 1st July 1916. Medals applied for by his father. Memorial Ref. Pier and Face 6 C., Thiepval Memorial, France.

FITZBROWN, Second Lieutenant, Eric. Colonel Trotter, told how this young leader was mortally hit nearly at the final objective after he and his men had carried it in irresistible style. He explained that the gallant young officer, who led his company, and was the first man to enter the enemy's front line trench, where he had emptied his revolver, seeing the situation, took two bombs in his hand, and attempted to bomb the position, but was hit in the head by a bullet from the enemy snipers, 1st July 1916. 18th Bn., The King's (Liverpool Regiment). Aged 21. Son of Mr. and Mrs. George Fitzbrown, (director of Broughton Copper Co.) of Shirley, Hunts Cross, Liverpool. Eric was educated at Rhos-on-Sea, and afterwards at Aldenham School, Hertfordshire. Apprenticed to a firm of metal brokers, but he interrupted his career joining the ranks of the 7th Norfolk Regiment. Early in 1915 he received his commission in the 18th King's (Liverpool) Regiment, and he formed many happy comradeships at Knowsley, Grantham, and Salisbury Plain. Went to France, 7th November 1915. His brother, Second Lieutenant Geoffrey Fitzbrown also fell, 24th October 1916. Medals applied for by his father. Memorial Ref. Pier and Face 1 D 8 B and 8 C., Thiepval Memorial, France.

FITZGERALD, Lieutenant, Gerald. Killed in action, 1st July 1916. C Coy. 26th (Tyneside Irish) Bn., Northumberland Fusiliers. Aged 26. Son of Alderman Sir John Fitzgerald, D.L., of (former Lord Mayor of Newcastle-on-Tyne), of Hillfield, Granger Park Road, Newcastle-upon-Tyne. Born 11th February 1889, Newcastle-upon-Tyne. Old boy of St. Cuthbert's Grammar School and St. Edmund's College (1903-1906), Old Hull, Hertfordshire. Held a responsible position in his father's business. Answered the Call at the start of the war. Captain F. Stephenson, of his battalion, referring to his death in a letter home, describes how Second-Lieut. Fitzgerald died shouting to his men, "Come on!" Effects returned were whistle, knife, identity disc, electric torch, purse, ring and charm. His father wrote to the Secretary, War Office in August 1916 and explained his sword, compass, watch and cigarette case were not returned. Originally buried half a mile west of La Boisselle Church, map reference 57d.X.19.a and marked with a regimental cross. Memorial Ref. II. N. 5., Bapaume Post Military Cemetery, Albert, France. WO 339/27343

FLATAU, Captain, A Theodore. Hand to hand fighting went on for a long time in the German trenches and news that Captain Flatau and Pearce were killed, leading their men to a German first line trench, 1st July 1916. He was killed before 9.30am after the 2nd line German trench had been taken. The bullet struck him and passed through to his chest. He fell back and was killed instantaneously. 8th Bn., East Surrey Regiment. A clever unconventional novelist. Son of Dr. J. M. Flatau of Sydney. Born in Sydney. Attended Sydney Grammar and the High Schools and proceeded to England and spent four years at Oxford University. Having learnt Arabic he went onto Cairo and edited a newspaper and returned to London to be the Editor of 'The World'. Entered France, 27th July 1915. Rejoined his battalion from sick leave, 23rd May 1916. The family made an enquiry into his silver cigarette case. The Lieutenant Colonel A. Irwin explained what happened. 'At about 8.30am a messenger came into Battalion Headquarters with a satchel that came from Captain Flatau and the contents were emptied onto the table it contained no message some other contents and a cigarette case. It was left in the Headquarters as me and the adjutant went to trenches at Montauban. Next day Captain Flatau's servant was send to retrieve the satchel and it was found to have been looted, the Divisional Police were regulating traffic so no-one was there to prevent this from happening. I severely regret that some effects were not recovered but all officers of the battalion were warned not to carry items of intrinsic value into action and knew that the casualties of all ranks would be heavy, and the chances of recovering items on the person would be small'. Medals applied for by his sister, Miss D. Flatau of Victoria Square, SW1. Memorial Ref. E. 30., Carnoy Military Cemetery, France.

FLAXMAN, Second Lieutenant, Alfred Edward. Leading a battalion of bombers, his group got caught between the wires. They were shot down by enemy fire while exposed in the open, 1st July 1916. Spent the night detonating his men's bombs so they could sleep before the attack. Bombing Officer, 1st /6th Bn., South Staffordshire Regiment. Aged 36. Son of Alfred Edward Flaxman, of 34, Grand Avenue, Southbourne, Bournemouth, and Harriet Jecks Flaxman. Born in Wombwell, South Yorkshire on the 1st October 1879. British track and field athlete who competed in the Summer

Olympics. In 1908, he participated in the discus throw competition, in the Greek discus throw event, in the freestyle javelin throw competition, and in the standing high jump event. Commissioned 18th June 1915. Student of music. Brother also served, Captain Samuel Christopher Reeve Flaxman, RAMC and later he had an opportunity to search the battlefield looking for the body of his brother but it could not be found. Medals to the Bournemouth address. Memorial Ref. Pier and Face 7 B., Thiepval Memorial, France.

THE OFFICERS OF THE 2/6TH BATTALION: ST. ALBANS, AUGUST 1915.

LIEUT. J. E. LATHAM; LIEUT. V. H. PINSON; LIEUT. C. F. GARDNER; LIEUT. P. H. HIGHFIELD JONES; LIEUT. H. F. MERRY; LIEUT. J. R. B. HERRON; 2ND LIEUT. W. H. HICKMAN; LIEUT. M. G. YOUNG; LIEUT. A. J. MULLINER (Q.M.); CAPT. W. A. JORDAN; 2ND LIEUT. M. S. BOSTOCK; LIEUT. A. L. JOYNSON; LIEUT. J. SHEPPARD; CAPT. P. S. BAYLISS; 2ND LIEUT. J. S. SNOWBALL; LIEUT. S. H. EVANS; 2ND LIEUT. A. F. BROWN; 2ND LIEUT. BOYES; 2ND LIEUT. A. E. FLAXMAN; CAPT. R. M. SHEPPARD; CAPT. A. G. C. SIMS; MAJOR F. HOLCROFT; LIEUT.-COL. H. TAYLOR; CAPT. WEBSTER (ADJT.); CAPT. N. G. HARRIES; CAPT. W. S. BERKELEY-FORRESTER.

To face p. 112

FLETCHER, Captain, Gilbert Harding. Last words reported to be 'The 5th North never retire! Come on!' and he was killed shortly afterwards. 1st July 1916. B Coy., 1st/5th Bn., North Staffordshire Regiment. Aged 39. Son of J. S. and Mary Fletcher, of Highfield, London Road, High Wycombe. Born Everton, Liverpool, 27th April 1877. Educated at Wellingborough. Went to learn about brewing at Messrs. John Joules and Sons Brewery, Stone. Left Stone in 1909 for an appointment at High Wycombe. Joined the battalion as a lieutenant, 9th September 1914. Gazetted in the North Staffordshire at the outbreak of war and was promoted to rank of captain in October 1915. Entered France, 5th March 1915. Nephew of Colonel J. Harding. Lieutenant in the old L Company of the North Staffordshire Volunteer Regiment, who had served in the South African War and awarded the South African Medal with three bars and was in the Lancashire Hussars. Miss S. H. Fletcher applied for his medals on behalf of her mother. Memorial Ref. I. L. 48., Foncquevillers Military Cemetery, France.

FLETCHER, Second Lieutenant, John Harwood Cash. He was posted as missing after operations in front of Gommecourt, where he was seen in the German second line, 1st July 1916. B Coy., 1st /7th Bn., Sherwood Foresters (Notts and Derby Regiment). Aged 30. Son of Mr. John Keyworth Fletcher, (lace manufacturer) Mary Ellen Fletcher of Arboretum Street, Nottingham. Born in 1887 in Heanor, one of four children. Boarder at King Edward VI Grammar School, Retford. Married 20th February 1912 at All Saints Church, Sawley, Derbyshire to Alice Maud Fisher and had two children, Vera Eileen and Silas Harwood. Prior to the outbreak of war he was in business with an uncle in Mansfield, Nottinghamshire. When war broke out he volunteered and resigned from an important position in High Wycombe. Having formerly held a commission, that he resigned on his marriage he once again volunteered for service, in 1916 and had only been on active service for five weeks. Entered France, 1st June 1916. Widow of Plough Hotel, Tewkesbury applied for his medals and pension payments. Memorial Ref. Pier and Face 10 C 10 D and 11 A., Thiepval Memorial, France.

FLINT, Second Lieutenant, Charles William. Killed in the attack on La Boisselle, 1st July 1916. 26th (Tyneside Irish) Bn., Northumberland Fusiliers. Aged 35. Son of William and Ellen Flint. Born 10th July 1881. Married 4th August 1910 to Marie Josephine and had three children. Wife resided Mayville, Sandwich, Rangoon, Burma. Resided 4 Bridge Avenue, Hammersmith, London. Previously served five years with Rangoon volunteers. Commissioned 6th January 1916 from 28th London Regiment, No. 4354, 2nd Artists' Rifles OTC where had served from 14th August 1915 to 5th January 1916. Notification of his death went his wife in Burma. His brother, Ernest Flint wrote to the War Office in December 1916 asking for news believing he was a prisoner of war and the War Office replied notification of death on the 2nd July 1916 had gone to his wife. His will left his estate to his mother, Ellen and Miss Lucy Mugridge his fiancée, 13 Kramer Mews, Earls Court. His widow who was remarried, Mrs. Craddock asked for his medals to go to Rangoon, Burma. Pension payments to children; Ruth Mary, Ellen Bernice and Rona Marie. Memorial Ref. Pier and Face 10 B 11 B and 12 B., Thiepval Memorial, France.

In a letter to Miss Mugride, 2nd Lieutenant Leslie E. Brown, A Coy., 26th Bn., wrote; "It is with deep regret that I have to perform this most unpleasant task. Your fiancé was killed on the 1st July leading his men. I don't know if you want details as far as I can give them. His platoon was the second to go over the parapet in this advance. His men loved him and would have gone to Hell with him if he would have led them. He had been lying in a shell-hole for about an hour when he got up yelling 'Come on men stick by me.' He hadn't gone far when a bullet got him right through the head. He died as he lived a clean and brave English gentleman. Forgive me and try to understand Charlie was my pal, we were together the whole time so naturally I am quite down. May God comfort you always, with sincere regret and deep sympathy." WO 339/52034

FLINT, Second Lieutenant, Wilfred Ernest. Reported missing believed killed during the attack on Gommecourt, 1st July 1916. B Coy., 1st/7th Bn., Sherwood Foresters (Notts and Derby Regiment). Aged 18. Son of Samuel Flint, JP, and Lillan Anna Flint, of Merridale, Stoneygate, Leicester. Born at Leicestershire, 9th September 1897. Attended Wyggeston Grammar School for Boys, Leicester between 1909 and 1914. Entered the army as private, 4825, in the Leicesters soon after the outbreak of war afterwards going to the Inns of Court OTC. Commissioned to the 1/7th Battalion, Sherwood Foresters Regiment, 15th September 1915. He went to France 8th May 1916 and joined B Company, 14th May 1916 at Calais, France. Wounded 29th June 1916 but remined on duty. His brother, Second Lieutenant Frank Carey Flint was also reported wounded in June 1916. Alderman Flint received a communication from the War Office that was published locally on the 10th March 1917 that he must be presumed to be dead. Extract from 1/7th Bn., War Diary, 12th March 1917 - "The bodies of 2nd Lieutenant W. E. Flint and Second Lieutenant Gamble who were killed in action on July 1st were brought in from the wire in front of Gommecourt and buried in Fonquevillers Cemetery by the Reverend W. A. Uthwaite, Chaplain to the Battalion." His family received notification from Colonel Toller on the 27th March his body had been found and buried in a cemetery and confirmed he died on the 1st July. Medals applied for by his father. Memorial Ref. III. E. 5., Foncquevillers Military Cemetery, France.

To Dear Wilfred

FOIZEY, Lieutenant, Harold Egbert. A fellow officer said he saw him tumble over the back of a trench, wounded in the thigh, he was made comfortable and had his wound dressed and placed in a small traverse in the back of the trench, soon afterwards a huge explosion took place throwing up the sandbags and earthworks and burying several men and Lieutenant Foizey underneath. His sister learned that Lieutenant Foizey's body was discovered by men who were repairing trenches. Another report suggests he went out with a section of bombers and over thirty yards they were cut down to four men and they took cover behind a small hillock, he went forward and was killed. Serre, 1st July 1916. 18th Bn., West Yorkshire Regiment (Prince of Wales's Own). Aged 31. Born 26th June 1885. Third son of Benjamin and Alice Foizey, of Tipton, Staffs. Educated at King Edward VI School, Birmingham. When the war broke out, he was a representative of Messrs. Stewart and Lloyds, steel manufacturers, Neville Street, Leeds. His sister was Miss Edith M. Foizey, of Leeds. He enlisted as a private with the Leeds Pals in September 1914. On the 24th May 1915 he was given a temporary commission as a lieutenant with the 18th Battalion West Yorkshire Regiment (2nd Bradford Pals) only eight months after enlisting. Trained in both the Colsterdale and Skipton (Bradford Pals) camps respectively, and served in Egypt and France. His sister married and became Mrs. E. M. Williams, Vine Street, Romford, Essex and wrote his inscription. Memorial Ref. I. D. 42., Euston Road Cemetery, Colincamps, France.

Jesu Mercy

FOLEY, Captain, John. Fell whilst gallantly leading his men, though severely wounded at the time, 1st July 1916. 25th (Tyneside Irish) Bn., Northumberland Fusiliers. Aged 29. Eldest son of David J. Foley, Newtown, Ballyhea, Charleville, Cork. Born Charleville, 1886. Studied at Sunderland Day College. Husband of Mona E. Foley, of 3, Belle Vue Crescent, Tunstall Road, Sunderland. Married 4th October 1915. Resided Ivy Cottage, Haswell. Attested 2nd November 1912, 7th Bn., Durham Light Infantry. At the outbreak of the war he was a teacher under the London County Council, but at once offered his services, and in January, 1915, he obtained a commission in the 2nd Bn.,. Tyneside Irish Brigade and soon afterwards was promoted captain, June 1915. He went to the front early in 1916. Initial telegram received by his wife stated he was wounded. Memorial Ref. Pier and Face 10 B 11 B and 12 B., Thiepval Memorial, France. WO 339/26003

FOORD-KELCEY, Second Lieutenant, John, Mordaunt. Killed at Mametz, by lead shrapnel along with men of his platoon whilst in the assembly trench, 1st July 1916. 2nd Bn., The Queen's (Royal West Surrey Regiment). Aged 22. Only son of William (Professor of mathematics at the Royal Military Academy) and H. I. Foord-Kelcey, of Brent House, Woolwich, London. Attended Tonbridge, 1908-11. In the employ of Cumberlege & Moss, tea brokers of 27, Mincing Lane. He joined the infantry of the Honourable Artillery Company, private, 703 in the Autumn of 1912, and volunteering on the outbreak of war with the 1st Bn., for foreign service, served with them in France from 20th September, 1914, until he was wounded in the leg by shrapnel at Messines on February 15th, 1915. On recovering from his wound he received a commission, dated July 22nd 1915, in 3rd Bn.. Queen's (Royal West Surrey Regt.), and joined the 2nd Bn. in France in November, 1915.

The head of his business firm wrote of him :— "He was an universal favourite and an example to all by his cheerful good nature and readiness to put his hand to anything, whether his own work or another's." The following are extracts from the letters of two General Officers:— "I saw him on his way out to his battalion, and I remember how delighted I was with the way he had developed into just the right stamp of young officer that one wants in these hard times." "Whenever I saw him in France he was doing his bit, and was proud to be doing it, and was doing it for all he was worth." The following from those of two of his brother officers:— "He was doing so well in the regiment and was generally popular. . . . I saw him before he went up to the trenches on the 1st and he was in the best of spirits and full of courage." "We miss him, as he was always in everything, football, fighting, or whatever was on. I wish we had more like him." His Commanding Officer also wrote :— "Your son was a most hard-working officer, who took the greatest interest in his work, and was liked by both officers and men." Buried ESE of Montauban Sht 62d Sq. F. 12./62d.f.11.d.5.5. with three other soldiers. Medals applied for by his father. Memorial Ref. VI. D. 2., Dantzig Alley British Cemetery, Mametz, France. WO 339/33773

Blessed Are The Pure In Heart For They Shall See God

FORD, Captain, Charles Clement. (Adjutant to Lieutenant Colonel John Thicknesse). Reports suggest killed before our trenches were passed 1st July 1916 this aligns with battalion history, officially died of wounds, 2nd July 1916 with CWGC. Medal Index Card has 1st July 1916. 1st Bn., Somerset Light Infantry. Son of Commander C. R. Ford, Royal India Marine. Born at Kirkee, Bombay, India on the 14th December 1894. Baptised at Kirkee, Bombay, India on the 5th of January 1895. Educated and a Boarder at United Services College, Windsor, Berkshire and RMC Sandhurst. Commissioned as a second lieutenant, 1st Bn., Prince Albert's Somerset Light Infantry Regiment on the 25th of February 1914. Posted to France, disembarking at Havre on the 22nd August 1914. Mother applied for his medals. Memorial Ref. I. I. 67., Sucrerie Military Cemetery, Colincamps, France.

FORD, Second Lieutenant, Lawton Stephen. Killed in action, crossing to Dantzig Alley, 1st July 1916. 2nd Bn., The Queen's (Royal West Surrey Regiment). Only son of Mr. Lawton Robert and Mrs. Catherine Ford of Esher, Surrey formerly 60 Haymarket, London. Aged 25. Born 30th August 1890. Educated at a private school at Bexhill and after passing the London Matriculation Examination trained at the Architectural Association school for the architecture profession. Resided Fairmile Avenue, Cobham. On the outbreak of war he joined the army (28th September 1914) as a private with the Army Service Corps (motor section), MT/217. Second lieutenant on probation 10th April 1915 with 3rd Bn., Royal West Surrey. Confirmed in rank as second lieutenant, 23rd October 1915. Entered France, 15th February 1916. Effects were compass, trench cooker, shaving stick tin, trench orders, part of periscope, handkerchief, medicine case, waterproof sheet and knapsack. Father applied for his medals. Memorial Ref. Pier and Face 5 D and 6 D., Thiepval Memorial, France. WO 339/30172

FORD, Captain, Reginald James. Killed while gallantly leading A Company of the battalion into action, (A Company forming the first wave), at Glatz Redoubt, Montauban, shot in the head and body by machine gun fire, 1st July 1916. 17th Bn., Manchester Regiment previously E Coy. Aged 28. Born Oxford, 5th May 1888. Eldest son of James and Lois Kate Ford, of Radcliffe, 36, Warwick Street, Oxford. Attended New College School and Queen's College, Oxford. Prior to the war was a science master at St. Bee's School, Cumberland where he was a captain in the school's OTC. Went to France 6th November 1915. Originally buried between Maricourt and Montauban at map reference 62c.A.9.a.8.9 with eight other men. Medals applied for by his father. Memorial Ref. V. W. 9., Dantzig Alley British Cemetery, Mametz, France. WO 339/19067

Blessed Are The Pure In Heart For They Shall See God

FORGE, Second Lieutenant, William Frederick. Reported to be shot through the throat and although mortally wounded managed to shake the hands of men around him. 1st July 1916. 2nd Bn., Middlesex Regiment. Aged 20. Son of Frederick W. and Mabel F. Forge, of 107, Hornsey Lane, Highgate, London. Pupil at Merchant Taylor School from 1910-1913, leaving in the fifth form to work as a clerk at the Port of London Authority. Enlisted in 1914 and served in the Middlesex Regiment. Old Merchant Taylors and School Staff War Memorial. Medals applied for by his father. Memorial Ref. Pier and Face 12 D and 13 B., Thiepval Memorial, France.

FORSDIKE, Lieutenant, Harold Brooke. B Coy., under Captain Houston, two platoons (Lieutenant Forsdike and Second Lieutenant Strong) in Copse Trench. Duty to follow second assaulting wave & clear first, second and third German trenches. Many casualties were caused by machine-gun and rifle fire to which A and B companies were much exposed owing to levelling of Nairne Trench etc. Seen to enter the first German trench, reported to have been leading a bombing party. 1st July 1916. 14th Bn., York and Lancaster Regiment. Aged 24. Son of W. D. Forsdike, of Parkfield House, Sheffield. Resided Norfolk Road, Sheffield. Educated Edward VII School, Sheffield. Employed Sheffield Simplex Motor Co. before the war joined the City Battalion as a private. Commissioned 11th March 1915. Brother Second Lieutenant L. Forsdike was wounded on 1st July 1916. Memorial Ref. Pier and Face 14 A and 14 B., Thiepval Memorial, France.

FORSTER, Captain, John Percival. Missing feared killed in action, Forster, McIntosh and Lamb got over with a party of men but the whole lot were gunned down by a machine gun, 1st July 1916. 22nd (Tyneside Scottish) Bn., Northumberland Fusiliers. Born 12th April 1888. Elder son of Mr. and Mrs. Forster, 37 Heaton Grove, Newcastle and joined shortly after the start of the war and trained with the 3rd Bn., Tyneside Scottish. Gazetted lieutenant and promoted to rank of captain in May 1915. Well-known in musical and political circles having been organist and choirmaster at St. Paul's Church, Whitley Bay and the secretary of the Tyne Habitation of the Primrose League. Assisted in his father's business and was married in August 1915. Wife resided New Redford Vicarage, Forest Road, Notts. Effects returned were gold ring, writing case and leather case with photos. Memorial Ref. Pier and Face 10 B 11 B and 12 B., Thiepval Memorial, France. WO 339/18932

FOUNTAIN, Second Lieutenant, John Alfred Arnott. He was commanding a platoon, manning trenches half-way between La Boisselle and Fricourt, 1st July 1916. On this part of the line the Germans had managed to get their machine-guns up when the bombardment ceased, Lieutenant Fountain was wounded in the thigh ten yards in front of the British trench and he passed away from blood loss, first reported wounded and then killed. 10th Bn., King's Own Yorkshire Light Infantry. Aged 23. Son of Dr. Edward Osborne Fountain and Isabella Maria Fountain, of Crossley House, King Edward's Road, Ruislip, Uxbridge, Middx. Native of Turnham Green, Chiswick, London. Born 30th January 1893. Educated Bradfield College, September 1906 to December 1910 and a member of the OTC, 1908 – 1910. Articled to C. F. Booth, of 4 Bedford Row, W.C. Joined November 23rd 1914, as private, 2146/6462, Royal Sussex Regiment. Gazetted second lieutenant, 10th Bn., King's Own Yorkshire Light Infantry, February 24th 1915. Entered France, 9th February 1916. Father applied for his medals. Memorial Ref. Sp. Mem. B. 5., Gordon Dump Cemetery, Ovillers-La Boisselle, France. WO 339/35576

Till The Shadows Break

FOX, Second Lieutenant, Francis Parker. Missing believed killed, he had led his platoon to the German line and was superintending the preparation of the trench to resist a counter attack when he was struck and killed instantly, 1st July 1916. 9th Bn., Royal Inniskilling Fusiliers. Aged 22. Son of Thomas Fox of the Inland Revenue Service. Native of Dublin educated at the grammar school, Burton-on-Trent. On the staff of the Royal Exchange Assurance, Dublin Branch. He was refused enlistment in Dublin owing to short vision but went to Belfast, offered his service there and was accepted, Royal Innsikillings, lance corporal, 21290. Received his commission 6th May 1915 and served with the 12th Bn., at Newtonards and the 3rd. Bn., in Derry before going to the Tyrone Volunteer Battalion at the Front, 20th April 1916. Brother was also at the Front. Aunt, Miss. F. Fox of Rathmines, Dublin applied for his medals. Memorial Ref. Pier and Face 4 D and 5 B., Thiepval Memorial, France.

FRADD, Second Lieutenant, Kingsley Meredith Chatterton. The 2nd Londons were held in reserve, lying in the open until 2.30pm on the afternoon of the 1st July. They were ordered to attack a German line known as Ferret Trench which lay slightly southeast of Gommecourt and within site of the formidable German strongpoint called The Quadrilateral. Three attempts were made to take Ferret Trench, each attempt was massacred by German artillery and machine-gun fire. During one of these attempts, he was killed, 1st July 1916. 2nd Bn., London Regiment (Royal Fusiliers) attached 169th Brigade Machine Gun Corps. Born 1897 in St. Pancras, London. Only son of Martin, (gun maker) and his wife Ada, his sister was Doris Mary. Kingsley was a pupil at All Saints' School, Bloxham between 1908 and 1914. He served as a sergeant in the school cadets, and on leaving school he went to Canada where he took a position as a clerk at the First National Bank of Ontario. He returned from Canada in 1915 and took a commission as a second lieutenant in the 2nd Bn., London Regiment. Memorial Ref. IV. A. 10., Hebuterne Military Cemetery, France.

FRASER, Second Lieutenant, Arthur William, DSO. Went over the top from the support line, and over the first line, the bridges over the front trench having being ranged by the German machine-gunners the day previously meet with heavy losses, while crossing these bridges and passing the lanes out in the wire, reported missing believed killed, near Beaumont Hamel, 1st July 1916. DSO for conspicuous gallantry in action he led his company to the enemy wire to a place where it had been uncut, though severely wounded twice by bombs and once by rifle fire he continued to direct the wire cutting until he lost consciousness. 8th attd. 1st Bn., Border Regiment. Aged 39. Son of Captain James Kemp Fraser (14th King's Hussars) and Mrs. Fraser of 39, Southdown Avenue, Brighton. Born 20th November 1876. Husband of Mary Ann Fraser. Served as trooper, King's Medal with two clasps and Queen's Medal, with three clasps in South Africa. Re-enlisted 11th September 1914, No. 23360, No. 4 Troop, B Squadron 3rd Hussars. Entered Gallipoli, 5th September 1915. Listed in St. Peters Memorial Book. Brighton War Memorial. His identity disc was returned to his mother and was confirmed to have been taken from his body. Although his mother could have accepted his DSO publicly by a General Officer Commanding on the King's behalf she choose to have it send to her address. Medals applied for by Mrs. L. G. Maynard whom also decided his inscription. Memorial Ref. A. 33., Hawthorn Ridge Cemetery No.2, Auchonvillers, France. WO 339/40134

Thy Will Be Done

FRASER, Captain, Donald. Possibly a member of a carrying party supplying sappers killed by a shell, 1st July 1916. Field Engineer, IV Corps, Royal Engineers. Aged 48. Son of William and Isabella MacDougall Fraser, of Annfield, Inverness. Trained an engineer in Inverness. Miss C. W. Fraser, 3 Berkeley Terrace, Glasgow decided his inscription. Memorial Ref. III. B. 1., Ecoivres Military Cemetery, Mont-St. Eloi, Pas de Calais, France.

He Gave All

FRASER, Second Lieutenant, Malcolm Goulding. He was sent on a most difficult reconnaissance with one sergeant and five privates from D Coy., patrolling, and as a result was able to send back a report to the General Staff which saved the lives of hundreds of men, shot by a sniper as he was returning, and body bought in that night, 1st July 1916. Due to the losses of the 2nd West Yorkshire the advance of the 2nd Scottish Rifles beyond the front line was stopped. 2nd Bn., Cameronians (Scottish Rifles). Aged 20. Son of Mary Lee Fraser, of 82, Stratheam Road, Edinburgh, and Harry Fraser (Glasgow and Valparaiso, Chile). Born June 19th 1896 at Watertown, New York, USA – his mother's home. Fraser moved to Santiago, Chile with his family as a youngster and was one of the founder members of the Everton Football Club established in Valparaiso in 1909. Fraser played in that club's very first fixture and was a key member of the team until he returned to the United Kingdom to attend university. He was educated at Colejio Aleman, Valparaiso and two years in the College Classique Cantonal, Lausanne, Switzerland and to George Watson's College in 1913. He proved an industrious and brilliant scholar, and won a bursary at Edinburgh University in 1915. Gazetted in August 1915 to the Scottish Rifles, he went to France, 27th May 1916. Nephew of Reverend Norman Fraser, Mount Pleasant Presbyterian Church, Liverpool. Mother applied for his medals. Memorial Ref. Pier and Face 4 D., Thiepval Memorial, France.

FRASER, Lieutenant, Patrick Neill. 2nd Line, Left, D Coy., under Lieutenant P. N. Fraser having two platoons in Albert Street from junction of Webb Street to the left. Two platoons in Wellington Redoubt. Killed 1st July 1916. D Coy., 11th Bn., North Staffordshire Regiment (attd D Coy., 2nd Bn., Border Regiment). Youngest and second son of Patrick Neill Fraser, (master letterpress printer) and Mrs. Margaret Neill Fraser, of 50, Grange Road, Edinburgh. Born in Edinburgh in 1879. Died age 37. Member of Murrayfield Golf Club. Educated Edinburgh Academy and was managing director of the printing firm, Neill & Company Limited. Well-known in musical circles and was accomplished player of the cello. Fellow of the Society of Antiquaries of Scotland. Enlisted private, 439, 23rd Bn., Royal Fusiliers. Commissioned 9th November 1914 as lieutenant shortly after the outbreak of war. Entered France, 15th August 1915. Sister Madge, an international golfer died of typhus fever after going to Serbia in the early part of the war at Kragujevatz, March 1915. Left £6568 in his estate. Mother applied for his medals. Memorial Ref. II. D. 10., Citadel New Military Cemetery, Fricourt, France.

FRASER, Captain, Rowland. Killed in action 1st July 1916. 6th Bn. attd. A Coy., 1st Bn., Rifle Brigade. Aged 26. Born January 10th 1890. Third son of J. M. Fraser Esq., (principal of firm, Messrs. MacDonald & Fraser) of Invermay, Forgandenny. Husband of Mary Dorothy Fraser, of Invermay, Forgandenny, Perthshire married in leave in June and following day left for the Front. Educated at Merchiston Castle School, Edinburgh, and Cambridge University (Pembroke). He was in the Merchiston Cricket Eleven in 1905 and three following years, in 1908 being second both in batting and in bowling. Subsequently he played for the Grange Cricket Club and Perthshire. Captain, Cambridge Rugby XV, 1910-11. Scottish international, 1912. He obtained his Blue at Cambridge for Rugby football, and was a Scottish International played against France, Ireland, Wales and England 1910-1911. B.A Cambridge 1911. Student of law, 1911 to 1914, equipping himself in Edinburgh office for the legal profession. A front-row forward for Edinburgh and captained Cambridge in 1910. Second lieutenant, August 1914. In France, 4th January 1915. Captain, November 1915. Society of Writers to His Majesty's Signet Roll of Honour recorded as apprentice. Widow applied for his medals. Memorial Ref. Pier and Face 16 B and 16 C., Thiepval Memorial, France.

FRASER, Lieutenant, Thomas. Killed in action, 1st July 1916. C Coy., 2nd Bn., Essex Regiment. Age 35. Third son of Mrs. T. Fraser of Homerton. Resided 42 Audrey Road, Ilford. Served in the South African War, 1901 and 1902 and subsequently in various parts of the country. Married to Miss Barber of Withem. She had been abroad with her husband for five years in Burma and India. Thomas had 21 years and 4 months service to his credit, having joined at Warley when he was 14 years old. Essex Regiment, acting sergeant major, 4461. Entered France, 13th May 1915. Brother, Joseph Fraser was killed in Gallipoli in June 1915. His widow was remarried and applied for his medals, Mrs. Ridgewell, Lovelace Gardens, Southend-on-Sea. Memorial Ref. Pier and Face 10 D., Thiepval Memorial, France.

FREEMAN, Second Lieutenant, Francis Basil. Reported wounded and missing, shot through the stomach whilst advancing between the German second and third line, shot by machine-gun fire, Beaumont Hamel, 1st July 1916. 1st/8th Bn., Royal Warwickshire Regiment. Aged 26. Born on 20th January 1890 at Hednesford, Staffs. Younger son of Albert Francis and Ellen Louise Freeman, of 71, King's Road, Bengeworth, Evesham, Worcs. Educated at Berkeley National and Evesham Grammar School and was appointed a pupil teacher at Bengeworth School from where he proceeded to Saltley College, Birmingham. On 5th January 1907, aged 16, he joined 2 Volunteer Bn., Worcestershire Regt. In October 1910 he transferred to the 8th Warwickshire Regiment with the No 1280 and was embodied for war service on 5th August 1914. At the outbreak of the war was working for the London County Council. At enlistment he stated that he was a school teacher employed by Worcestershire County Council. On 20th November 1914 Francis was promoted to corporal and on 21st March 1915 was drafted to France with his battalion. He was appointed lance sergeant in July 1915 and was promoted sergeant two months later. In April 1916 he was commissioned into 1/8th Warwickshire Regiment. Father applied for his medals. Original map reference for burial 57d.K.35.a.35.20 and identified by his disc and officer's tunic. Memorial Ref. II. G. 16., Cerisy-Gailly French National Cemetery, France.

Asleep Till Jesus Calls Him

FREEMAN, Second Lieutenant, Francis Hubert. Reported missing, 1st July 1916, the battalion made an attack, being in charge of No. 3 Platoon and was last seen leading a handful of men over the enemy trenches. A Coy., 19th Bn., Lancashire Fusiliers. Aged 23. Youngest son of George and Helen Freeman, of Wyche Cliff, Wyche Road, Malvern, Worcs formerly 407, Gillott Road, Edgbaston. Born at Edgbaston, Birmingham in 1892. Educated at King Edward's School, Five Ways. On leaving school he engaged in his father's business at Edwardian Works, New John Street West. He was interested in the Boy Scout Movement from its commencement and was a scout master of the 1st Midland Troop. Joined the 1st Birmingham City Battalion, Royal Warwickshire Regiment, private, 234, on its formation and afterwards took a commission in the Lancashire Fusiliers. Temporary second lieutenant 27th September 1915. Entered France , 11th March 1916. Death announced November 1916. Medals to his sister, Miss A. H. Freeman, Malvern, Worcs. Original map reference of burial, 57d.R.25.c.8.8 where his grave was marked by a cross and formally identified by a broken disc. Memorial Ref. XII. U. 2., Ovillers Military Cemetery, France.

FRENCH, Captain, St. George. Reported killed, immediately the lines appeared on the parapet, heavy machine-gun fire brought to bear, 1st July 1916. Attached 1st Bn., Royal Inniskilling Fusiliers. 15th Bn., The King's (Liverpool Regiment). Aged 25. Son of the Reverend Arthur Thomas William French and Magdalene Gibb, of 4066, Tupper St., Westmount, Parti Quebecois, Canada. Born at Montreal, Canada. Graduate in Arts, McGill University, Montreal. Undergraduate Trinity College, Oxford (1912). Original buried Y Ravine Cemetery QW17.a.4.9 and his grave was marked with a cross. His headstone has the cross of the King's Liverpool regiment and his inscription was changed from 'Killed at Beaumont Hamel Grad McGill Montreal Alum. Trin. Coll. Oxon Juvenes Vicistis Quoniam Fortes' to the text shown below. Memorial Ref. I. A. 13., Ancre British Cemetery, Beaumont-Hamel, France.

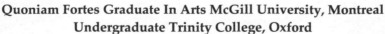

Quoniam Fortes Graduate In Arts McGill University, Montreal
Undergraduate Trinity College, Oxford

FROST, Second Lieutenant, Alfred Ingo. Wounded and missing, seen to fall being struck in the knee at a point between the first and second German lines, southwest of Ovillers-La Boisselle and north of the Albert-Pozieres road. Witness accounts state he was killed by 7.45am, 1st July 1916. The soldier that seen him fall was seriously wounded but the ground was subjected to a terrific bombardment and he was not found. 2nd Bn., Middlesex Regiment. Aged 33. Son of Joseph Ingo Frost and Honoria Frost. Attended St. Edmund's with his brother in 1895 to 1897. Enlisted 19th June 1899. Company sergeant major, Middlesex Regiment, No. 218. Entered France, 12th March 1915. Joined the 2nd Bn., 27th August 1915. Appeals for information to go to 19 Fitzwarren Gardens, Highgate. Officially in the view of the lapse of time, by March 1917 presumed death by the War Office. Medals application by his mother, Kingsbury Road, Erdington, Birmingham. Memorial Ref. Pier and Face 12 D and 13 B., Thiepval Memorial, France. WO 339/32928

FRYER, Second Lieutenant, James Whaley. Originally reported missing, 1st July 1916. Informant stated he fell after about 100 yards with a wound in the temple and he was turned over and found to be dead, he was then buried by a shell. 22nd (Tyneside Scottish) Bn., Northumberland Fusiliers. Aged 24. Only son of Edith Fryer, of Kingarth, 5, Moorside, Fenham, Newcastle-on-Tyne, and Major James Whaley Fryer. Attended Yorebridge Grammar School, Hawes, Giggleswick and Carlisle Grammar School for Boys. Articled clerk to Messrs. Dickinson, Millar and Turnbull, Solicitors, Newcastle. Entered France, 10th January 1916. On the 28th August 1916 the Officer Commanding wrote to his mother; 'the evidence of men returning from the operations of the 1st July is the 2nd Lieutenant J. W. Fryer was killed, presumably by shell fire, both his legs having been shot off'. His mother applied for his medals from Dean Park Lodge, Bournemouth. Memorial Ref. Pier and Face 10 B 11 B and 12 B., Thiepval Memorial, France. WO 339/25932

FURSE, Second Lieutenant, William Henry. 1st July 1916. 21st (Tyneside Scottish) Bn., Northumberland Fusiliers attd 102nd Trench Mortar Battery. Aged 25. Eldest son of Henry and Florence Mundy Furse, of 36, Salisbury Road, Moseley, Birmingham. Born 20th May 1891 at Hampstead, London. Educated Solihull Grammar School and Finchley College, London. Afterwards entered Lloyds Bank. Joined the City Battalion, 14th Bn., Royal Warwickshire Regiment, No. 399 on its formation 9th September 1914 and appointed sergeant, May 1915 and received a commission in the Northumberland Fusiliers, 18th October 1915. He married 3rd October, 1915, Miss Beatrice M. Law, Sunnyside, Cambridge Road, King's Heath, Birmingham. Originally reported buried in trench south of La Boisselle. His uncle wrote a letter to the Right Honourable Lloyd George in August 1916 asking for assistance as his letters were returned 'wounded location unknown'. A letter to the War Office in February 1917 from his wife's solicitors followed up from a previous letter enquiring about pension and explained that the expected child was still born and nothing further would need to be done with regards to pension. Medals applied for by his mother. Original grave reference 57d.X.19.d and buried with three other soldiers. Memorial Ref. II. F. 2., Bapaume Post Military Cemetery, Albert, France. WO 339/41091

FUSSELL, Lieutenant, James Gerald. Killed in action, Beaumont Hamel, 1st July 1916. 1st/8th Bn., Royal Warwickshire Regiment. Aged 23. Second son of Ada Fussell, of the Hincks, Lilleshall, Wellington, Salop, and H. S. C. Fussell. Educated Aston Grammar School. Employed Elkington and Co. Newhall Street. Commissioned 24th September 1914. Entered France, 23rd March 1915. His mother applied for his medals, Ashbourne Road, Derby. Memorial Ref. Pier and Face 9 A 9 B and 10 B., Thiepval Memorial, France.

Lieutenant Fussell second from right, centre row

GAFFIKIN, Major, George Horner. Hit by grenade shrapnel while standing on a parapet using a rifle in support of a bomb party, he was evacuated but died of wounds at a Casualty Clearing Station, 1st July 1916. When some of his men wavered, reported he removed his orange sash and shouted 'Come on, Boys! No surrender!' Prior to that he passed a fellow officer and shouted; "Good-bye, sir, good luck. Tell them I died a teetotaller. Put it on the stone if you find me." B Coy., 9th Bn., Royal Irish Rifles. At 9.40am reports came through that Major Gaffikin had been injured and Captain Montgomery was taking over. Montgomery later suffered a severe head wound. Aged 30. Only son of William and Georgina Gaffikin, of King's Castle, Ardglass, Co. Down. Educated at Uppingham and Clare College, Cambridge, and was a scholar both of this school and university. Organiser and Commander of the UVF in East Down. Member of the North of Ireland and Downpatrick cricket clubs. He entered the army at the outbreak of war, receiving his commission in the Ulster Division. He was a very able officer, gazetted captain, 23rd November 1914 and major in April 1916. Entered France, 21st October 1915. Mentioned in Despatches in June, 1916. The officers and men of D Coy., 1st Bn., East Down Regiment, UVF paid for a framed memorial and raised the sum of £13 10s. Mother applied for his medals. Memorial Ref. III. A. 22., Bray Vale British Cemetery, Bray-Sur-Somme, France.

Write Me As One That Loves His Fellow Men

GAGE, Second Lieutenant, John Stewart Moore. Reported missing, believed killed 1st July 1916. He had been wounded in the head on the 25th April, 1916, and had only just rejoined his battalion when killed. 9th Bn., Royal Inniskilling Fusiliers. Aged 23. Son of Dr. Francis Turnly Gage, M.D., and Katherine Gage (nee Stewart Moore) of Moyarget, Ballycastle, Co. Antrim and grandson of General Ezekiel Gage, of Rathlin Island. Educated at Rossall School, and subsequently went to Australia, but returned shortly before the outbreak of war and at once enlisted in the Despatch Riders' Corps. 8th January 1915, he received his commission in the Inniskilling Fusiliers, and was appointed intelligence officer to his battalion. Entered France, 5th October 1915. Father applied for his medals. Memorial Ref. Pier and Face 4 D and 5 B., Thiepval Memorial, France.

GALLIE, Lieutenant, Edward Archibald. 1st July 1916. D Coy. 17th Bn., Highland Light Infantry. Aged 19. Younger son of Edward and Jessie G. Gallie, of 7, Westbourne Terrace, Kelvinside, Glasgow. Educated Kelvinside Academy, Cargilfield and Fettes College. Left the college mid-term of 1914 to take a commission in the Highland Light Infantry. Enlisted November 1914. Entered France 1915. Death reported 11th July 1916. Originally buried R.31.c.5.3 with ten other men. Mother applied for his medals. Memorial Ref. IV. F. 1., Lonsdale Cemetery, Authuille, France.

He Had Done His Work And Held His Peace And Had No Fear To Die

GAMBLE, Second Lieutenant, Frank Burfield. Reported, wounded and missing 1st July 1916. 1st /7th Bn., Sherwood Foresters (Notts and Derby Regiment) attd. 139th Trench Mortar Battery. Aged 29. Son of Frank William and Sarah Ann Gamble, of 2, Ashleigh Road, Leicester. Born 8th July 1886. Attended Wyggeston Grammar School for Boys in Leicester between 1898 and 1904. Employed as a yarn agent. At the Front for about six months, trained with the Inns of Court OTC. Enlisted 7th June 1915 as private 4041 in the Inns of Court OTC. Gazetted to be second lieutenant from the Inns of Court OTC, 17th September 1915 along with other men killed on the 1st July; Lance Corporal Albert Charles, Private Frank Burfield Gamble, Private William Ernest Flint, Cadet Ernest James Peach from the Nottingham University College Contingent, Senior Division, OTC. Frank joined his battalion September 1915. Reported killed 5th October 1916 and was attached to the Trench Mortar Battery from 30th April 1916. Extract from 1/7th Bn., War Diary, 12th March 1917 - "The bodies of 2nd Lieutenant W. E. Flint and 2nd Lieutenant Gamble who were killed in action on July 1st were brought in from the wire in front of Gommecourt and buried in Fonquevillers Cemetery by the Reverend W. A. Uthwaite, Chaplain to the battalion." Memorial Ref. III. E. 4., Foncquevillers Military Cemetery, France.

GAMON, Captain, Maurice Partridge. Reported killed 1st July 1916. Intelligence Officer, 3rd Bn., attd 2nd Bn., Lancashire Fusiliers. Born 14th January 1885. Educated Kent College, Canterbury from 1899 to 1901. Secretary of Kent College Old Boys. Author of books for boys. Served 8 years with the Honourable Artillery Company, private, 440. Scoutmaster Wellington Troop, and Assistant Commissioner South London for Boy Scout Movement. Director of the firm, Routledge Publishers, Wimbledon. Enlisted 15th August 1914, commissioned, 24th August 1914 and entered France, 27th December 1914. Gassed and invalided home and married, Ethel Elisabeth Gamon. One son, Maurice Partridge Gamon born 2nd March 1916, he was subsequently killed in the Second World War on the 12th October 1940 onboard HMS Ajax. Medal application by his widow and officers pension. Memorial Ref. I. E. 35., Serre Road Cemetery No.2, France.

GARLAND, Captain, James Richard, BSc. Fell at the head of his company leading them in an attack in a very gallant manner, made a brave attempt to cross No Man's Land at 3.00pm but was killed by a rifle bullet, within a few yards of going over, 1st July 1916. A Coy., 1st /2nd Bn., London Regiment (Royal Fusiliers). Aged 23. Only son of Richard Edmund and Olive May Garland, of 162, All Souls Avenue, Willesden, London. Educated at Latymer School, where he won a scholarship at the age of 11. From there he went as a student teacher, and joined King's College and the London Day Training College. A member of the OTC, he was at camp when the war broke out. He immediately volunteered for active service and received a commission on August 29th 1914. Entered France, 11th July 1915. His colonel writes of him to his father thus- "He was a very good and competent officer and one in whom I found I could always repose confidence, which is a very valuable asset indeed, and his gallant death is a sad loss to his company and to the battalion besides being a great personal loss to me and his brother officers. The example he set us all during his life he maintained right up to his death which he met so gallantly." Medal application by his father. Original grave map reference A.K.10.a.60.80 and his grave was marked with a cross. Memorial Ref. III. H. 1., Gommecourt British Cemetery No.2, Hebuterne, France.

For Ever In Our Thoughts

GARTON, Lieutenant, Reginald William. Killed by shell fire in opening up communication trenches and saps, 1st July 1916. B Coy., 11th Bn., South Lancashire Regiment. Aged 19. Youngest son of Lieut-Colonel William G. A. and Mrs. Garton, of "Cragarhan", Reigate Road, Ewell, Surrey formerly Merton Hall Road, Wimbledon. Born 8th March 1897, Hanover Square, London. Educated at Christ's Hospital School, Horsham, Sussex being a member of the OTC. Clerk. Attested at Somerset House, London, on 10th August 1914 as private No. 2135, into the 15th (County of London) Bn., London Regiment (Prince of Wales's Own Civil Service Rifles). On 23rd February 1915, Reginald was granted a commission in the South Lancashire Regiment landed with the battalion at Le Havre on 7th November 1915. William Garton employed as an Admission Order Office, House of Commons and therefore Reginald is commemorated in House of Commons, Book of Remembrance. His brother Lieutenant A. R. Garton also fell in April 1915. Medals sent to his parents. Memorial Ref. Pier and Face 7 A and 7 B., Thiepval Memorial, France. WO 339/23885

Christ's Hospital House Photo 1912
Second from back row and seventh from the left R. W. Garton

GATRELL, Lieutenant, Reginald James Hurst, MC. Reported he was in an assembly trench at Fricourt Wood when he was mortally wounded with a bad wound in the chest from a shrapnel shell that landed in the trench and he died shortly afterwards, 1st July 1916. 3rd Bn. attd. 1st Bn., East Yorkshire Regiment. Born 7th April 1896. Aged 20. Younger son of Mr. Walter. H. and Mrs. E. M. L. Gatrell, of 19, Musgrave Crescent, Fulham, London. Educated St Mark's, Chelsea and Institution Bertrand, Versailles, France. Employed Bank of British North America. Enlisted 31st December 1914. Awarded the Military Cross for conspicuous gallantry near Vermelles on September 29th and 30th 1915, when he led a bombing party against the Germans, who had broken into the trenches of the battalion on the left. Lieut. Gatrell succeeded in forcing the enemy behind their barricades, but was severely wounded in the thigh with a gunshot wound. On his recovery he again joined the fighting line in April 1916. Unusually his Medal Index Card has 'wounded 30th September 1915' relating to the deed of his MC. Father applied for medals. Memorial Ref. Pier and Face 2 C., Thiepval Memorial, France. WO 339/43170

GEAKE, Lieutenant, Boyd Burnet. Exposed to devastating machine- gun fire from high ground ahead and killed. Posted as missing, believed to be wounded in the shoulder, Thiepval, 1st July 1916. 9th Bn., York and Lancaster Regiment. Aged 28. Only son of John Barnet Geake (draper) and Emily Geake, of Westcott, Surrey. Born in Westminster, London on 21st March 1888. He attended Ashton Grammar School, Dunstable, Eastbourne College and University College, London. University of London, OTC. After finishing his education Boyd became a motor car agent and soon after war was declared in 1914 he was commissioned second lieutenant into the 9th Bn., York and Lancaster Regiment. Husband of Dorothy May Geake (Nee Cutforth), of Normans Cottage, Newdigate, Surrey being married in 1915. Arrived in France, 27th August 1915 landing at Boulogne. Widow applied for his medals and Mrs. Dorothy M. Geake, Normans Cottage, Newdigate, Surrey decided his inscription. Memorial Ref. V. C. 33., Blighty Valley Cemetery, Authuille Wood, France.

Christ Watch You In Your Sleeping

GELIOT, Second Lieutenant, William Henry. Killed attacking Gommecourt, 1st July 1916. 4th Bn., Lincolnshire Regiment. Aged 26. Son of William Peter and Florence Louisa Geliot, of 73, York Road, Holloway, London. Name misspelt in war diary as 'Jelliott'. Born 30th September 1890. Educated Watford Grammar School. Clerk, Stock Exchange. 16th Bn., London Regiment, private, 3114. Entered France, 4th July 1915. Commissioned in the Lincolnshire Regiment, 2nd February 1916. Medals to Mrs. Whitehead, Montpelier Road, Upper Holloway Road, N19. Memorial Ref. I. G. 1., Foncquevillers Military Cemetery, France.

I Fear No Foe With Thee At Hand To Bless

GEMMILL, Second Lieutenant, John Adshead. Mown down on the left in support of A Coy., 1st July 1916. C Coy., 16th Bn., Highland Light Infantry. Aged 25. Eldest son of John Leiper Gemmill and Lily Russell Adshead Gemmill, of 16, Dargarvel Avenue, Dumbreck, Glasgow. Educated Glasgow Academy and Glasgow High School. Won the Glasgow High School Cup in 1907, good rugby player and keen shot. Entered the business of N. Adshead & Son, wholesale stationers and printers, Glasgow. Commissioned September 1914. Entered France, 23rd November 1915. Wounded start of 1916 and recovered to join his battalion. Father was a partner with his friend's father in the firm Messrs. Brown, Mair, Gemmill & Hislop, 162 St. Vincent Street, Glasgow. Second Lieutenant R. S. Brown who was also killed on the 1st July 1916. Death reported 11th July 1916. Medals applied for by his father. Original map reference for burial 57c.R.31.3.c.8. and a cross was on the grave. Memorial Ref. VI. C. 8., Lonsdale Cemetery, Authuille, France.

In Proud And Loving Memory Eldest Son Of Mr. & Mrs. J. Leiper Gemmill 16 Dargarvel Avenue, Glasgow Killed In Action Near Thiepval Loved One Death Is Not The End

GIBSON, Second Lieutenant, Albert Henry. Reported missing believed killed, led his platoon over the parapet, across No Man's Land and there the information stops, 1st July 1916. 12th Bn. attd. 9th Bn., Royal Inniskilling Fusiliers. Aged 19. Third son of Robert Gibson, J.P., and Mrs. Agnes E. M. G. Gibson, of Devonshire Villas, North Parade, Belfast and Grand Secretary of the County Grand Orange Lodge. Educated at the Methodist College and spent time in the office of Mr. Saunders Graham, chartered accountant and before enlisting in the Black Watch was in the service of D. D. Leitch & Son, flax merchants. After passing through the Belfast University Contingent of the OTC he got a commission in the 12th Royal Inniskilling Fusiliers, 22nd August 1915 being gazetted 25th November 1915. Previous lance corporal, 3136, 6th Royal Highlanders. Later transferred to the 9th Bn. Drafted to France, 15th June 1916. Two brothers also served. Lieut-Col. Ricardo wrote 'your lad was brought in the day before the advance to replace an officer wounded during the preliminary bombardment…was so delighted to get his chance.' Medals applied for by his mother and pension payment. Memorial Ref. Pier and Face 4 D and 5 B., Thiepval Memorial, France.

GIBSON, Second Lieutenant, Charles Sydney. Died 1st July 1916. He had instructed his men to move to a safer position and whilst leading his men into the open he was killed by machine gun fire. 2nd Bn., Royal Warwickshire Regiment. Serving with the 22 Company of the Machine Gun Corps. Aged 23. Son of Mr. and Mrs. Charles Sidney Gibson, of Aberdeen. Only brother of Mrs. D. J. B. Lacon. Private, 734, Royal Fusiliers. Commissioned 4th Bn., Royal Warwicks on the 10th April 1915. Entered France, 29th September 1915. Medals to his sister, Mrs. Lacon, c/o solicitor L. W. Taylor, 1 Newlan Buildings, Grays Inn. Presumably the same person a Mrs. Doris Lacon, 3 Ovington Square, London, SW3 decided his inscription. Memorial Ref. D. 10., Point 110 New Military Cemetery, Fricourt, France.

Dearly Loved Only Son Of C.S. Gibson And Adored Brother Of Doris Lacon

GIBSON, Second Lieutenant, William. Reported to be wounded in the fighting, posted as missing, 1st July 1916. 14th Bn. attd. 15th Bn., Royal Scots. Aged 21. Eldest son of William Gibson, J.P (golf iron head and club manufacturer) and Alison Gibson, of 12, MacDuff Crescent, Kinghorn, Fife. Born 14th July 1895. Educated at Kinghorn Public and Kirkcaldy High School. School athlete. He was studying law in Edinburgh previous to being called up for military service. Enlisted 18th September 1914. Commissioned 8th May 1915. He got his commission in 1915 and was transferred from the Kinghorn Company of the Forth Royal Garrison Artillery (T.F) in which for some time he was a private, No. 419. Presumed to have died, on the 1st July 1916, officially declared April 1917. His father received notification in August 1917 that his son's body had been found, on the 3rd December 1917 this was retracted as the grave was that of another officer with the same surname also in the Royal Scots. Father applied for his medals. Memorial Ref. Pier and Face 6 D and 7 D., Thiepval Memorial, France. WO 339/39912

GILES, Second Lieutenant, Geoffrey. 1st July 1916. 2nd Bn., Gordon Highlanders. Aged 28. Son of Urban Phillip and Margaret Giles, of Hillcrest, Arkley, Barnet. Native of Highbury, London. Born 1888. Stock Exchange member 1911 with Messrs. Hopkin & Giles. Enlisted with the Artists Rifles, 28th London Regiment, private, 1373. Disembarked for France, 26th October 1914. 16th May 1915 at Festubert suffered a shrapnel wound that on x-ray had hit no bones and quickly became septic, with no exit wound the entrance wound was enlarged and the fragment removed on the 21st May. Possessions were silver watch, identity disc, cheque book, officers chevrons and advance book. Commemorated Merchant Taylors' School, Northwood. Originally buried 67 Support Trench 62d.sq. F11.c.8.3. Father applied for his medals. Memorial Ref. A. 3., Gordon Cemetery, Mametz, France. WO 339/27917

GILL, Second Lieutenant, Charles Treverbyn. Killed in action at Mametz, with his revolver in his hand in when he was struck down and pitched over he is reported to have said 'I'm beat, push on.' Killed in the evening, in final assault on Fritz Trench, and more precisely killed in the vicinity of Fritz Trench and Bright Alley, 1st July 1916. 4th Bn. attd. 22nd Bn., Manchester Regiment. Aged 26. Youngest son of Thomas and Julia Gill, of 8, St. Quintin Avenue, North Kensington, London. Born 24th February 1890. Educated St. Paul's School and in the OTC 1906 to 1908, matriculated Exeter College Oxford in January 1908. Cricket player. Rowed for two years in the college eight, four in 1911 and stroke in 1912 and stroked the London Rowing Club Thames Cup Eight. Law student, articled to Messrs. Maples, Tweedale & Co. Entered service, September 1914 and served in the ranks with the 16th (Public Schools) Middlesex Regiment as private 904, prior to receiving his commission in April 1915. Arrived France, 1st June 1916 and joined his battalion, 7th June 1916. Commemorated St. Peter the Apostle Church, Treverbyn, Cornwall. Mother applied for his medals. Originally buried 400 yards East of Mametz, East of Albert, map reference 62c.F.5.8.3.8 Memorial Ref. Sp. Mem. Believed to be buried in III. B. 30., Peronne Road Cemetery, Maricourt, France. WO 339/45911

Dominus Illuminatis Mea Et Salus Mea Quem Timebo?

GILLIES, Second Lieutenant, James. Killed whilst leading his men, 1st July 1916. 2nd Bn., The Queen's (Royal West Surrey Regiment). Aged 30. Son of Mr. Peter James and Martha H. Gillies, of 1, Scott's Road, Leyton, London. Born 21st November 1885. Educated Plough Road Board School, Clapham. Carpenter. Joined the Royal West Surrey Regiment, 19th January 1903 and later became sergeant, 2/7750. Entered France, 4th October 1914. Promoted CQMS on the 9th October 1914. Served in Gibraltar and Bermuda prior to the war and had been 12 years in the army. 21st October 1914 suffered a wound in the groin by gun shot. Commissioned 20th May 1916. Mother applied for his medals. Originally buried 1 mile east-side of Mametz village, 6 miles east of Albert 62D.Sq.F.5. Memorial Ref. Sp. Mem. B. 6., Peronne Road Cemetery, Maricourt, France. WO 339/64249

Faithful Unto Death

GILSON, Lieutenant, Robert Quilter. Fatally wounded when he was leading his men out of the trenches, hit by a shell, La Boisselle, 1st July 1916. 11th Bn., Suffolk Regiment. Aged 22. Eldest son of Robert Cary Gilson (head master of King Edward's School, Birmingham), and Emily Annie Gilson, of Canterbury House, Marston Green, near Birmingham. Born October 25th 1893, at Harrow-on-the-Hill. Distinguished career at King Edward's, Birmingham, he passed on to Trinity College, Cambridge (Classical exhibitioner). June 25th, 1912. He was an undergraduate in his third year when war broke out, having taken first-class Honours in the Classical Tripos the previous year. Classical Exhibitioner 1914. BA 1915. He was gazetted in the early days of the war and was promoted to full lieutenancy in France. Lieutenant Gilson was a very good rifle shot, and was one of the shooting eight of the School OTC, and was later a member of the Cambridge University OTC. He was a skilled draughtsman, and did excellent work both in England and France in connection with trench construction. He was passionately devoted to architecture, and intended reading for that profession at Cambridge. Good friend of J. R. R. Tolkien. Hoped to be an architect and spent a good deal of time sketching out trench construction. Entered France, 8th January 1916. Father applied for his medals. Effects returned were canteen, whistle, pair of field glasses, haversack, pipe, tobacco pouch, identity disc, pencils, fountain pen, electric lamp, cheque book, advance book, notebooks, books, looking glass, field note book, cigarette case, purse, photographs, letter case with letters and periscope. Memorial Ref. I. R. 28., Becourt Military Cemetery, Becordel-Becourt, France. WO339/29720

Nec Propter Vitam Vivendi Perdere Causas

 GLASTONBURY, Second Lieutenant, Harold Mynett. Reported wounded and missing, 1st July 1916. Several reports that he had a wound in the leg dressed in a shell hole and was taken to a dressing station or tried to crawl back to the first line trench under shell and machine gun fire. Opposing reports suggest he was last seen in front of the parapet at Albert at around 7.40am, reported he fell back into the trench hit by a rifle bullet. 5th Bn. attd. 1st Bn., Royal Irish Rifles. For some years assistant master at Raynes Park School. He lived in Hartfield Road, Wimbledon. Previous London Regiment, acting sergeant, 2354, attested 1st September 1914. Obtained a commission in the Royal South Downs on the 8th May 1915 and entered France, 23rd June 1915, having been at the Front for several months. Information on his death to go to School House, Park Lane, Thatcham, this was the address of his widow, Mrs. Irene Lilian Glastonbury who also applied for his medals and officers pension. Commemorated St. Andrew's Church War Memorial, Puckington. Memorial Ref. Pier and Face 15 A and 15 B., Thiepval Memorial, France. WO 339/30831

GLENNIE, Second Lieutenant, John Herbert. Killed in action, 1st July 1916. 1st Bn., King's Own Scottish Borderers. Aged 22. Eldest son of David Graham Glennie and Jane Glennie of 22 Wellington St., Portobello, Midlothian. Entered France, 6th March 1915. Promoted from Scots Guards, lance sergeant, 8869, commissioned 20th June 1916. News received by his parents, 20th July 1916. Parents applied for his medals. Memorial Ref. B. 10., Knightsbridge Cemetery, Mesnil-Martinsart, France.

GLOVER, Captain, Ben Hilton. Reported killed in action, he was hit in the head by shrapnel as he went to see the commanding officer of The Buffs who were nearby, this was about 9.15am, killed in action, 1st July 1916. 7th Bn., Queen's Own (Royal West Kent Regiment) attached 55th Trench Mortar Battery. Aged 19. Second son of (Councillor) Edward A. and Gertrude Glover, of Brookside, Southover, Lewes. Educated Thanet College, Margate. Prior to the outbreak of war an articled pupil at Southdown and East Grinstead Brewery. At school he was a keen sportsman and appeared in several local hockey matches. 'Energetic and promising officer' who had been on active service for two years, at the age of 16 he joined the 5th Bn., Sussex Regiment, private, 5/1724. He left for France, 18th February 1915 and served with his regiment until 27th November 1915 when he received his commission. Gazetted 22nd December 1915. At the end of January 1916 transferred to a Trench Mortar Battery, in March he was given a place in charge of an up to date trench mortar battery, service with 55th Trench Mortar Battery, 29th May 1916. Received his promotion to captain on June 13th the day of his 19th birthday. His father was a member of the Military Service Tribunal and his colleagues expressed great sympathy in his loss. Brother, Second Lieutenant Brian Edward Glover, RFC killed on the 13th March 1916. Third son Lance Corporal Eric A. Glover of the Machine Gun Corps served. Named on the Lewes War Memorial which was dedicated in September, 1922.

Originally buried Carnoy-Montauban, grave reference 62C.A.8.b.2.2 with 14 other men whom were killed on the 1st July apart from Lieutenant E. J. Innocent whom was given an official date of death as the 3rd July (refer to entry). Reinterred 1920. Father applied for his medals. Memorial Ref. VIII. T. 3., Dantzig Alley British Cemetery, Mametz, France. WO 339/49362

Let All Try And Live As Nobly As He Did

GODFREY, Second Lieutenant, Harry Frederick. Went over in the second wave and was platoon commander of No. 9 Platoon, C Coy., 1st July 1916. He got through the wire to the German line with Major Wragg and at this point was killed. 1st/5th Bn., Sherwood Foresters (Notts and Derby Regiment). Born 5th August 1890. Son of Harry Charles and Emily Gemma Godfrey of 207 Banbury Road, Oxford. Educated Wesleyan Higher Grade School, Oxford. Member of the Lion Brewery, Oxford. Clerk. Enlisted 12th December 1914. To be second lieutenant 16th April 1915 from private 3559 the 4th Bn., Oxford and Buckinghamshire Light Infantry. Father applied for his medals. Memorial Ref. Pier and Face 10 C 10 D and 11 A., Thiepval Memorial, France.

OFFICERS OF THE 1/5TH BATTALION, THE SHERWOOD FORESTERS (T.F.)

From left to right are: Back row—Lieut. J. C. McInnes, Lieut. J. A. Gilchrist, Lieut. E. C. Villa, Lieut. E. B. Woodforde, Lieut. F. L. Bailey, Lieut. H. C. Dornton, Lieut. W. G. W. Barber, Lieut. H. F. Godfrey, Lieut. R. A. Cecil, Lieut. G. Nutt, Lieut. H. H. Lilley: middle row— Lieut. F. H. M. Lewes, Lieut. H. Rudgard, Lieut. H. C. Wollaston, Lieut. E. F. Ann, Captain H. Claye, Lieut. E. A. Crossley (Adjutant), Captain S. J. Aldous, Lieut. L. J. B. Harrison, Lieut. R. J. Case, Lieut. N. Howard, Lieut. A. Stone: front row—Captain J. L. Green, R.A.M.C. Captain L. H. Finch, Captain A. B. Naylor, Major F. Worgan (Quartermaster), Major J. H. F. Marsden, Brig.-General H. H. Campbell (Commanding Divisional Artillery), Lieut.-Colonel G. A. Lewis, C.M.G., T.D., Brig.-General C. T. Shipley, C.B. (Commanding Brigade), Major R. J. Wordsworth (Staff Captain), Major B. H. Checkland, Captain F. W. Wragge, Captain J. D. Kerr, Captain J. Hunter, Lieut. M. S. Fryer, and Jack, the regimental mascot

The following officers in the photograph were killed on the 1st July; Captain F. H. M. Lewes, Captain J. L. Green (RAMC), Major F. W. Wragg, 2nd Lieutenants H. S. Dornton, H. F. Godfrey, W. G. W. Barber, R. B. Cecil and J. E. McInnes. The following were wounded Captain H. Claye, Lieutenant E. A. Crossley, and Second Lieutenants E. C. Villa, E. F. Ann and J. A. Gilchrist. In addition the following were POW's, Lieutenant M. S. Fryer and Second Lieutenant H. H. Lilley.

GODFREY, Second Lieutenant, Hugh. Posted as missing, led the 5th Platoon, B Coy and seen to fall heavily as if killed after being hit by machine gun fire, 1st July 1916. 2nd Bn., Royal Berkshire Regiment. Aged 36. Son of Mr. and Mrs. Godfrey, of Bagshot, Surrey. Husband of Constance Maud Godfrey, of 4, Brunswick Villas, Station Road, Herne Bay. On his 18th birthday in November 1897, he joined the Royal Berkshire Regiment. Spend seventeen years in South Africa (1898-1902), Egypt (1902-1906) and India (1906-1914). He rose to the rank of colour sergeant during that period seeing action throughout the Second Anglo Boer War (1899-1902). Hugh Godfrey became the regimental sergeant major in November 1914, 5215 soon after the 2nd Bn., arrived on the Western Front, 6th November 1914. Sergeant Major Godfrey was wounded twice in 1915, at Neuve Chapelle in March and again at Bois Grenier in September. Both wounds were sufficient to return home. Married 20th October 1915 at Blean, near Canterbury to Clarence and left one child, Hugh Terrence born on the 1st August 1916. Returned to France in December was commissioned in the 2nd Battalion, 18th December 1915. Captain Alan Hanbury Sparrow wrote two letters to his widow; 'It is with the greatest regret that I am writing to you, to tell you that your husband has been killed. He fell whilst gallantly leading a charge against the German trenches on the 1st July. …He fell on an unsuccessful assault at Ovillers and we were unable to recover his body, the smoke and noise made it almost impossible to see what had happened to individuals.' Death presumed 22nd March 1917. Widow applied for his medals. Memorial Ref. Pier and Face 11 D., Thiepval Memorial, France. WO 339/53210

GODFREY, Second Lieutenant, Victor. Killed near Montauban, about 8.00am, 1st July 1916, although his death was not officially confirmed until the 4th August 1916. On the day of his death he was chosen, as an expert brigade wiring officer, to strengthen a difficult position, but neither he nor any of his 27 men returned. Reported that he was shot in the side and badly wounded at Triangle Point, a private dressed him but because of the seriousness of his condition he could not be moved and he could not move himself, his revolver was brought in from the field. The area was counter attacked, when the ground was reclaimed he could not be found. 2nd Bn., Royal Scots Fusiliers. Aged 20. Son of Sidney C. and Susan Godfrey, of the Crossways, Abinger Hammer, Surrey. Born on 14th December 1895. Educated Eastbourne College. He joined the Artists Rifles, 28th Bn., London Rifles, private, 1341 in August 1914 with his two brothers, and they all took their commissions after a few months' training in France. Disembarked 28th October 1914. Effects were pair field glasses, diary, notebook, eye glasses, writing case & photos, letters, cheque book and advance book. Mother and brother addressed given for correspondence on his medals, his brother's being Captain S. C. Godfrey, XIV Wing, Royal Flying Corps, Italy. Memorial Ref. Pier and Face 3 C., Thiepval Memorial, France. WO 339/27787

GODWIN, Second Lieutenant, Colin Harold. Killed in action, 1st July 1916. 15th Bn., York and Lancaster Regiment. Aged 22. Eldest son of Dr. Gerald Leith Godwin (physician and surgeon) and Susan Lilian Godwin, of "Dilkoosha", Clowne, Chesterfield. Born July 27th, 1893, in Clay Cross, Derbyshire. One of four children. Entered Oundle (Crosby House) in January 1909, staying until December 1911. He was in the elevens of 1910 and 1911. After leaving school he studied medicine at Sheffield University as a medical student and St Cuthbert's College, Sparken Hill, Worksop. When war broke out he enlisted in the Sheffield City Battalion, receiving his commission in the York and Lancaster Regiment a few months later. Gazetted 1st August 1915 to temporary second lieutenant in the 12th Bn., York and Lancaster Regiment. Entered France, 1916. Mother applied for his medals. Memorial Ref. Pier and Face 14 A and 14 B., Thiepval Memorial, France.

GOLDING, Second Lieutenant, Frank Alfred. Hit by shell fire in the head in the German line and died straight away, dead body confirmed in a shell hole, 1st July 1916. C Coy., IX Platoon, 9th Bn., King's Own Yorkshire Light Infantry. Aged 18. Son of Alfred and Gertrude Mary Golding, of 76, Cranbrook Road, Redland, Bristol. Born 2nd July 1897. Attended Bristol Grammar School (1909 to 1914) and Bristol University. Entered Bristol University OTC, August 1915. Commissioned November 1915. Entered France 21st June 1916 and only joined the battalion on this date. Father wrote to the War Office hoping his son was a prisoner in German hands and also asked for further information as only a fountain pen was returned and items were missing field glasses, walking stick, razor, ring etc. Originally buried north of Fricourt map reference 57D.27.b.5.7 from a burial return dated July 1919. His father applied for his medals. Memorial Ref. II. N. 4., Gordon Dump Cemetery, Ovillers-La Boisselle, France. WO 339/47645

GOLDS, Second Lieutenant, Gordon Brewer. Reported to have been shot through the head when he was half way up the ladder, 1st July 1916. 18th Bn., The King's (Liverpool Regiment). Born 9th August 1886 in Worthing. Resided Purley, Surrey. Clerk for Samuel Sanday & Co of Exchange Chambers, St Mary Axe. Enlisted 31st August 1914. Transferred to the 18th Bn. 7th April 1915 to be temporary second lieutenant 1915 formerly corporal, 27520. Married Christina Marjorie Gillanders in Croydon, September 1915. Entered France, 11th March 1916. Left £1,285 in his Will. Originally buried Vernon Street Cemetery, Carnoy his grave being destroyed in later battles. Mrs. James, his widow, Purley, Surrey applied for his medals. Memorial Ref. Mem. 2., Dantzig Alley British Cemetery, Mametz, France.

GOMERSALL, Lieutenant, William Ellis. In the afternoon took a small number of men over the open to charge two machine guns and was killed, Mametz, 1st July 1916. 22nd Bn., Manchester Regiment. Aged 21. Eldest son of Hubert (staff of the Sewing Cotton Company) and Jane Eliza Gomersall, of Newholme, 69, Queen's Road, Urmston, Manchester. Also nephew of Reverend W. J. Gomersall, curate of St. John's Kensal Green, London. Born at Hellifield, native of Craven. Educated at the Manchester Grammar School, he passed his Classical Matriculation in 1911 and was a member of the Grammar School OTC. He holds the certificates of the St. John Ambulance and The Royal Life Saving Society, and is a commissioned lieutenant in the Urmston Company of the Church Lads' Brigade. On leaving school he was articled to a Manchester firm of chartered accountants. Shortly after the outbreak of the war, he enlisted as a private in the University and Public Schools Brigade (Manchester Battalion), giving valuable help in the recruiting which was for several weeks conducted at the Manchester Grammar School. On the formation of the Manchester City Service Battalions, selected for a commission. Gazetted March 19th 1915 as temporary second lieutenant in the 23rd Service Battalion, Manchester Regiment. Selected for full lieutenancy in the D Coy., Platoon No. XV, 22nd Manchester Regiment. Received training at Morecambe, Grantham, and Salisbury Plain, and after being promoted to full lieutenant, (May 11th 1915), he entered a course at the Royal Staff College, Camberley, and eventually accompanied his regiment to France. Entered France, 11th November 1915. Engaged to his cousin May, the youngest daughter of the Reverend W. J. Gomersall. In his last letter home he wrote; "Tomorrow I am going to have the day of my life." Commemorated St. Clement's Church Lads Brigade (Urmston) & St. Clement's Church. His mother applied for his medals. Memorial Ref. Pier and Face 13 A and 14 C., Thiepval Memorial, France. WO 339/23785

Platoon No XV. Also killed on the 1st July; Sergeant William Reginald Lambert, Private Uttley Stansfield, Private William Wright, Private W. Chaloner, Private T. Hampson, Private F. Salisbury, Lance Corporal Daniel Clark, Private Herbert Hoyle, Private Thomas Cryne, Private Frederick Davey, Private G. Clark, Private A. Galley, Private Frank Therfall and Private William Jones.

GOODALL, Lieutenant, Albert James Gill. Hit by a shell and died shortly afterwards, whilst gallantly leading his men in the assault, 1st July 1916. Reported to be shot in the arm and through the lungs, died of wounds. 2nd Bn., Royal Berkshire Regiment. Aged 20. Eldest son of Albert William and Leah Goodall, of 28, Russell St., Reading formerly Queen's Road. Attended Queen Elizabeth's Grammar School, Ashbourne. Scholarship, Christ's Hospital, July 1907. Employed Huntley & Palmers Ltd., Reading in the Export Invoice Office. He enlisted immediately after the outbreak of war in the 4th Royal Berks, private, 2756, and within six months was grant a commission, being posted to the 9th Bn., April 1915 and made a full lieutenant. Entered France, 25th October 1915. Temporary lieutenant April 1916. June 1916 slightly wounded in the face but stayed on duty. The Chaplain stated in a letter to the family that he was buried not far from the firing line in a little village. All monies and belongings bequeathed to his father, who also applied for his medals. Effects returned were cheque book and officers advance book. On receiving these effects his father, Albert wrote to the Military Secretary of the War Office to apply for a commission for himself as he had served with the volunteers, he had lost one son and the other son was in hospital. Memorial Ref. F. 26., Aveluy Communal Cemetery Extension, France. WO 339/33446

Am Avimus Am Amus Am Abimus

GOODCHILD, Second Lieutenant, Stanley Cecil. Reported wounded and missing and then killed, 1st July 1916. A Coy., 2nd Bn., Essex Regiment. Resided 3 Cambridge Gardens, Notting Hill and formerly 36 Tavistock Road, Westbourne Park, London. He was fine rugby half having got his cap for Somerset and having played for the west of England. Engaged to be married to Miss Olga Baswitz of 39, Brompton Road, S. W. Enlisted in the 1476, Artists Rifles on the outbreak of war, entered France, 26th October 1914 and obtained his commission in the Essex Regiment, 15th August 1915 being promoted lieutenant 1st May. 'He was a most gallant officer and his end was a gallant one.' His Will arose on the 7th March 1917, with the executor being Percy William Clifford Goodchild. A Captain Goodchild applied for medals of his late brother. Mrs. O. Vincent, High Street, Kensington presumably his fiancé, now married received his medals, his Victory Medal had to be returned in 1920 for a replacement. Name appears on the Rosslyn Park FC Roll of Honour 1914-19. Memorial Ref. Pier and Face 10 D., Thiepval Memorial, France.

GOODFORD, Lieutenant, Charles James Henry, MC. As soon as the troops left the front line, heavy machine-gun fire was brought to bear on them from all directions, casualties if officers amounted to 100%. Beaumont Hamel, 1st July 1916. 1st Bn., Hampshire Regiment. Aged 20. Only child of Henry Frank (solicitor & councillor) and Katharine Goodford, of 69, Frances Road, Windsor. Educated Eton and Magdalene College, Cambridge. Attended Sandhurst and commissioned. Entered France, 20th January 1915. Wounded early in the war. Suffered from influenza and in hospital from the 12th February 1915 to the 2nd March 1915, Queen Alexandra's Hospital. His name was on the Honours List on January 14th 1916 as having been awarded the Military Cross and Mentioned in Despatches. Eton College Roll of Honour. Memorial at All Saints Church, Windsor. Father applied for his medals. Memorial Ref. I. H. 13., Sucrerie Military Cemetery, Colincamps, France.

Love Out Of A Pure Heart & A Good Conscience & Faith Unfeigned

November 1915 Taken on the first anniversary day the battalion left for France.
Middle row; Third from left Lt. Col The Hon L. C. W. Palk killed the 1st July 1916 and Front Row second from left Lt. C. J. H. Goodford.

GOODWIN, Lieutenant, Harold Desborough. Reported missing 1st July 1916, a chaplain wrote saying he was last seen wounded but the ground was searched by artillery fire for some time afterwards. Harold had shook the hand of Alf Damon prior to going over at 7.55am and when they crossed the head of the parapet a shell fell and killed Lieutenant Goodwin and a number of other men. 16th Bn., Middlesex Regiment. Aged 25. Born July 28th, 1890, at Ilfracombe, Devon. Son of Albert Frederick Goodwin, (Royal Watercolour Society & prolific artist), and Alice Goodwin. Bexhill-on-Sea Memorial. Mr. Beale's Preparatory School, Ellerslie. Charterhouse School. Admitted as pensioner at Trinity, June 25th, 1908. BA 1912. Entered France, 30th November 1915. Confirmed killed January 1917. Probate and medals to his sister, Olive Goodwin, Bexhill-on-Sea. Memorial Ref. A. 88., Hawthorn Ridge Cemetery No.1, Auchonvillers, France.

GOODWIN, Lieutenant, William 'Billy' Alexander Delap. Acting as signalling officer to his battalion at the time he was killed in action, Ovillers, 1st July 1916. 11th Bn., York and Lancaster Regiment. Aged 23. Only son of Singleton Goodwin (county surveyor, of Tralee) and E. K. Goodwin, of Westcott House, Rochbeare, Exeter. Native of Ballyroe, Tralee, Co. Kerry. Born 22nd December 1892. Educated at Bromsgrove School, Worcestershire and scholar and undergraduate of Corpus Christi College, Oxford (1912-1914) achieving 2nd Classics Moderations. Membership of the University Contingent of the OTC. He obtained a commission in the York and Lancaster, November, 1914, and was gazetted to the regiment in January, 1915. He went to the front, 22nd April, 1916. Father applied for his medals. Memorial Ref. V. F. 24., Blighty Valley Cemetery, Authuille Wood, France.

Son of Singleton And E.K. Goodwin Psalm L.V.5

GORDON, Second Lieutenant, Colin Graham. He was shot through the head leading his men gallantly, 1st July 1916. 3rd Bn., attd. 2nd Bn., Gordon Highlanders. Aged 25. Only son of Henry and Bessie Laura Gordon, of Coniston, Victoria Grove, Bridport, Dorset. Born 30th July 1889 at Bridport. Attended Wellington School and a member of the OTC. Enlisted 27th November 1911 as private No. 1550 in the London Scottish, entered France, 15th September 1914 and took part in the charge at Messines, October 1914. Commissioned 2nd July 1915. Married 6th July 1915 to Dorothy Mona Gordon and she claimed his widow's pension of £100p.a. and resided 28 Mayflower Road, Clapham. Originally buried at 67 Support Trench, 62d. F11.c.8.3 by the road near Mansel Copse leading to Mametz with five other men who died on the 1st July. Two photos and advance book returned to next of kin. Widow applied for his medals. Memorial Ref. A. 1., Gordon Cemetery, Mametz, France. WO 339/64133

SOME 2ND GORDONS—SOMEWHERE ABROAD

Left to right : Standing—Captain G. H. Gordon, 2nd Lieutenant G. Macdonald, Captain J. E. Fiennes, 2nd Lieutenant G. R. S. Cookson, Captain H. B. Brooke ; sitting—Captain and Qr.-Mr. J. Mackie, Captain D. R. Turnbull, D.S.O., Lieut.-Colonel B. G. R. Gordon (commanding), Major H. A. Ross, D.S.O.

Safe In The Arms Of Jesus

GOSNELL, Second Lieutenant, Harold Clifford. Company lost all its officers between 2.30pm and 3.00pm, 1st July 1916. C Coy. 1st /2nd Bn., London Regiment (Royal Fusiliers). Aged 26. Son of H. Clifford Gosnell, and Alice Augusta Gosnell, 54 Hornsey Rise London. Freemason. Born 6th January 1890. Educated Surrey House, Margate. Chartered accountant, Loriners' Company. Private, 1768, 7th Bn., London Regiment. Entered France, 18th March 1915. Wounded at Festubert and Loos. To be second lieutenant 15th November 1915. Masonic Roll of Honour. Miss A. Gosnell applied for the medals of her late brother. Memorial Ref. Pier and Face 9 D and 16 B., Thiepval Memorial, France.

GOSS, Lieutenant, Edouard Herbert Allan. The left-hand party entered the enemy trenches with only one casualty, the platoon commander Lieut. E. H. A. Goss, who was killed instantly by a shell whilst trying to secure Mine Trench, 1st July 1916. 7th Bn., The Buffs (East Kent Regiment). Aged 39. Second son of Louis Allan Goss and Marie Leonie Goss, of 5, Harvey Road, Cambridge (formerly of Clifton and Rangoon). Born 13th June 1877 at Rangoon, Burma. His early years were spent in India and Burma. Clifton College 1889-95. He joined Clifton Rugby Football Club in 1896. Gazetted December 1914 promoted in October 1915. Entered France, 10th October 1915. Well known in the Sevenoaks area as his parents lived in the town prior to Cambridge, he had been home on leave twice from the Front, making his headquarters in the Royal Oak Hotel. Last leave was May and he returned to France on the 16th. Several months stationed at Purfleet and was often over at his farm at Fig Street which was kept on under a manager. On his death his stock, living and dead was sold in October 1916. Member of the National Farmers Union, Sevenoaks Branch. A typical English gentleman. Originally buried just northeast of Carnoy in a crater on the Carnoy-Montauban Road. To try and find out what happened to him his family wrote to his friend, Captain Kenchington of the same battalion. Medals applied for by his father. Burial map reference 62C.A.8.c.8.9

with four other officers also killed on the 1st July, Lieut. Cloudesley, 2nd Lieut. Baddeley, Lieut. Saltmarshe and Captain Scott. Mentioned in Despatches Memorial Ref. VIII. R. 4., Dantzig Alley British Cemetery, Mametz, France. WO 339/20784

On Whose Soul Sweet Jesus Have Mercy Requiescat In Pace

GOTCH, Captain, Roby Myddleton. On July 1st 1916 under an intense barrage he was wounded in the wrist close to the German wire but went to the assistance of a runner who was struggling to lay a telephone wire. He was again wounded this time in the stomach or chest when a shell came and killed him, originally reported as wounded and missing, but in 1917 it was presumed that he was killed on July 1st 1916. C Coy., 7th Bn., Sherwood Foresters (Notts and Derby Regiment). Aged 26. Only son of John Alfred Gotch (architect), MA (Hons.) Oxon. F.S.A., F.R.I.B.A., J.P., and Annie Gotch, of Weekley Rise, Kettering. Born Kettering, 4th September 1889. His father was Fellow and Vice-President of the Royal Institute of British Architects, Fellow of the Society of Antiquaries, I.P. and Deputy Chairman of Quarter Sessions for the County of Northampton. Attended Cottesmore School, Hove and Rugby School in 1903 and had his Cap in 1907. He left in 1908 and went to New College, Oxford, taking his degree in Law with Second Class Honours in 1911, and passing in the following year for the Bachelor of Criminal Law with Third Class Honours. On leaving Oxford, he was articled to Messrs. Thorpe and Perry, Solicitors, of Nottingham. In 1913 he went to Messrs. Field and Roscoe, of London, and passed the Final Law Examination in 1914 with Second Class Honours. During the winter of 1913-14 he played for the Harlequins. Ongoing to Nottingham in 1912 he was mobilized with the 7th Sherwood Foresters and went to the Front, as lieutenant, with his battalion in February, 1915. He was promoted temporary captain and adjutant in July 1915, and to captain in July 1916. Mentioned In Despatches, January 1st 1916. Cousin, Lieutenant Philip Joseph Crook, Duke of Lancaster's Own Yeomanry, died 7th November 1917. Brigadier-General C. T. Shipley, C.B., wrote:- "He was such a splendid fellow-standing out as quite one of the best officers in the whole of my Brigade. His work as adjutant was most excellent, and he set all the young officers a wonderful example in devotion to duty." Father applied for his medals. Memorial Ref. Pier and Face 10 C 10 D and 11 A., Thiepval Memorial, France.

GOULD, Second Lieutenant, Eric Melville. Killed with his batman, in a very gallant but unsuccessful attack on some German trenches, led his men shouting; "Remember Belgium. Remember the Lusitania." 1st July 1916. In the advance, Private Cyril Jose had to take cover behind the bodies of Eric his batman until night fall. 3rd Bn. attd. 2nd Bn., Devonshire Regiment. Aged 23. Third son of Claude W. S. and Elizabeth S. C. Gould, of Pilton Abbey, Barnstaple, Devon. Born 9th March 1893. Attended All Hallows School, Honiton and a member of the OTC. Returned at the outbreak of war from Canada where he was farming and enlisted in the 11th Hussars on the 1st September 1914, No. 13610, and was given a commission in the Devons on the 7th April 1915. Went to France, 13th May 1916. Two brothers served, Second Lieutenant Ronald Gould in the machine-gun section and Major C. G. B. Gould in the Royal Flying Corps. Eric's will left all his possessions to Ronald. Father applied for his medals. Memorial Ref. Pier and Face 1 C., Thiepval Memorial, France. WO 339/55679

GOURLAY, Second Lieutenant, John Norman. Killed near Beaumont Hamel, 1st July 1916. Majority of the casualties especially those of the officers occurred during the first two hours of fighting, 2nd Bn., Seaforth Highlanders. Aged 20. Eldest son of Dr. Frederick and Mary Gourlay, of Rathmore, Elgin. Born 13th September 1895, Southend-on-Sea. Norman was a student. Member of the Elgin Golf Club in the Elgin Golf Club Membership Directory 1906, in the list of original members (boys, under 16). He enlisted at Elgin in October 1914. Gazetted 18th March 1916. Joined the battalion on the 14th June 1916. Commemorated on Elgin & Miltonduff War Memorials. Father applied for his medals. Original grave map reference 57d.k.35.a.45.10 formally identified by his disc and two watches. Memorial Ref. III. A. 41., Pargny British Cemetery, France.

Into Thy Hands

GOW, Second Lieutenant, James Lightfoot. At 2.00am C Coy., were in Buckingham Palace Road Trench, Second Lieutenant Gow killed whilst getting his men into position, 1st July 1916. 9th Bn. attd. 1st Bn., King's Own Scottish Borderers. Aged 26. Youngest son of Mr. David Gow (clothier) and Mrs. Gow, Glencairn Cottage, Dunfermline. Educated Dunfermline High School. Private, Royal Army Medical Corps, September 1914 to April 1915, 37737. Commissioned in April 1915. Went to Egypt, 25th January 1916, and remained there until April 1916 when he was drafted to France. His brother, Mr. A. Gow applied for his medals. Memorial Ref. C. 42., Knightsbridge Cemetery, Mesnil-Martinsart, France.

GRAHAM, Major, John Frederick. He fell in action whilst directing his battery, killed by German counter battery fire, Maricourt, Bray-sur-Mer, 1st July 1916. Killed when Lieutenant John Cotton was mortally wounded. "A" Bty., 150th Bde., Royal Field Artillery. Aged 38. Second son of Mary Graham and Robert Graham, MA (Trinity College, Dublin). Born Kingston, Co. Dublin on the 16th March 1878. Major Graham had a very distinguished Intermediate and University career. He was a senior moderator and gold medalist in Mathematics and Mathematical Physics, a Brooke Prizeman and Professor Woods' Prizeman in Political Economy. Entered Trinity in 1897. He obtained his BA in 1901 and MA Degree in Trinity in 1905. In 1908 he was appointed Assistant Accountant-General to the Government of India at Lahore, and later Accountant-General at Madras. He was subsequently appointed Accountant-General of the United Provinces, which appointment he held until he returned to Ireland on leave in September, 1915. He was Lieutenant-Colonel of the Madras Artillery Volunteers. Member of Indian Civil Service. In November, 1915, he was appointed Major, RFA, and afterwards went to France, June 1916. Left a widow and three sons. Mrs. H. M. Smyth, Highcroft, Godalming, Surrey applied for his medals. Original burial map reference 62C.A.21.a.2.9 with six other men including Second Lieutenant D. Rowatt also killed 1st July 1916. Mrs. F. M. Watt Smyth c/o Thos. Cook & Sons, Ludgate Circus, EC4 applied for his medals. Memorial Ref. II. E. 35., Peronne Road Cemetery, Maricourt, France.

Moving Unruffled Through Earth's War The Eternal Calm To Gain

GRAHAM, Captain, Percy Gordon. Killed by machine-gun fire whilst leading B Coy., 1st July 1916. 16th Bn., Northumberland Fusiliers. Aged 27. Educated Rutherford College, Newcastle. Qualified as an architect. Won the swimming championship seven years in succession, Newcastle Corporation Cup. International water polo player. Teacher of boys in a Sunday school. Jesmond Presbyterian Church. On the outbreak of war entered as a private. Medals applied for by J. C. Graham, Rectory Drive, Gosforth, Newcastle-on-Tyne. Memorial Ref. Pier and Face 10 B 11 B and 12 B., Thiepval Memorial, France.

GRAHAM CLARKE, Second Lieutenant, John Altham Stobart. Died gallantly leading his platoon into action, 1st July 1916. 9th Bn. attd. 1st Bn., King's Own Scottish Borderers. Aged 19. Only child of Captain F. Graham Clarke DSO and Mrs. Altham Graham Clarke, of Frocester Lodge, Stonehouse, Glos. Born Sheffield, 1894. Attended Wye College and Wellington College. Joined as a private with the 5th Royal East Kent, Regiment, No. 1570, in October 1914. Cousin of Sir Lionel Darell, Bart of Frocester Manor, Stonehouse and Glanrhos, Rhayader. He was wounded in 1915 when serving in Gallipoli and had been home on leave. On hearing the news on his death his mother went to stay with Sir Lionel. Original map reference for burial 57d.Q.16.b.4.d with a cross on his grave. Medals applied for by his mother. Memorial Ref. II. A. 26., Ancre British Cemetery, Beaumont-Hamel, France.

To Our Beloved Son "Thou Shalt Be Perfect With The Lord Thy God"
Deuteronomy 18ch. 13 V.

GRAINGER, Second Lieutenant, John Scott. Reported missing, 1st July 1916. C Coy., 1st /2nd Bn., London Regiment (Royal Fusiliers). Aged 27. Youngest of three soldier brothers, of Thomas Alexander and Marion Grainger of 122, Main St., Tweedmouth, Berwick-on-Tweed. Born 17th November 1889. Employed inspector Sun Insurance Company in Middleborough district. Enlisted as a private with the Queens Own Cameron Highlanders, No. 2019 and five months later took his commission with the London Regiment. Posted to Malta and went to Egypt and Gallipoli. Served since 24th April 1916 at the Front and was transferred to another battalion of the regiment in early June. He was a bright and courageous soldier who fought not for a love of fighting but because it was his sacred duty due to his God and County. Officially reported as killed on the 1st July in March 1917. Tweedmouth War Memorial. Father applied for his medals. Memorial Ref. Pier and Face 9 D and 16 B., Thiepval Memorial, France.

GRANT, Second Lieutenant, Henry Norman. During the advance, when about 40 yards from the enemy's line, witness saw Mr. Grant fall about 10 yards to his right, 1st July 1916. A Coy. 1st Bn., Lancashire Fusiliers. Aged 23. Eldest son of Henry Richard and Jane Victoria Grant, of 6, Castle Street, Hay, Breconshire. Educated Christ College, Brecon. Member of the staff of Hereford Branch of the United Counties Bank. Outbreak of war joined the Public School Battalion of the Royal Fusiliers, received training at RMC Sandhurst and became a machine-gun section officer with the East Lancashire Regiment. Entered France, 4th May 1916. Barclays War Memorial. Father applied for his medals. Memorial Ref. C. 31., Redan Ridge Cemetery No.2, Beaumont-Hamel, France.

O Lord Whose Mercies Are Infinite Give Him Eternal Rest R.I.P.

GRANT, Second Lieutenant, John. 1st July 1916. 15th Bn., Royal Scots. Aged 28. Son of Mr. and Mrs. John Grant, of 75, Finnart St., Greenock. Educated at Greenock Academy. Chartered account in London. Outbreak of war joined the 6th Cameron Highlanders, private, S/14813. Entered France, 14th April 1916. Father applied for his medals. Memorial Ref. Pier and Face 6 D and 7 D., Thiepval Memorial, France.

GREEN, Captain, John Leslie, VC. 1st July 1916. Royal Army Medical Corps attd South Staffordshire Regiment. Aged 26. Born 4th December 1888 at Buckden, Hunts. Son of John George and Florence May Green, of St. Mark's Lodge, Cambridge. Educated at Felsted School (September 1902 – December 1906) and Downing College, Cambridge (1907 – 1910 Third class Natural Science Tripos), and medical trained at Bartholomew's Hospital. While at Downing, he was a keen member of the boat club, rowing in the Lents and Mays between 1908 and 1910. On the outbreak of war he obtained a commission for the RAMC. He was at first attached to the 5th South Staffordshire Regiment, then to a field ambulance in France, entering France on the 2nd March 1915 and lastly to the Sherwood Foresters (5th Bn., Notts and Derby Regiment), with whom he was serving when he met his death. He was awarded the Victoria Cross in recognition of his bravery, described in the London Gazette of 4th August 1916: "For most conspicuous devotion to duty. Although himself wounded, he went to the assistance of an officer who had been wounded and was hung up on the enemy's wire entanglements, and succeeded in dragging him to a shell hole, where he dressed his wounds, notwithstanding that bombs and rifle grenades were thrown at him the whole time. Captain Green then endeavoured to bring the wounded officer into safe cover, and had nearly succeeded in doing so when he himself was killed." The wounded officer was Captain Frank Bradbury Robinson, brigade machine-gun officer who died on the 3rd July 1916. John's body was recovered in Spring 1917 and identified by his clothing. Brother, Second Lieutenant Edward Green killed at Loos, September 1915. Father applied for his medals. Memorial Ref. III. D. 15., Foncquevillers Military Cemetery, France.

GREEN, Second Lieutenant, William Osmond. Entrusted with the very important job of cutting the battalions wire, he very gallantly led his men through an awful fire, 1st July 1916. Reported missing then reported missing, believed killed. 10th Bn., Royal Irish Rifles. 69, Bridge Street, Portadown. Son of William John (merchant) and Elizabeth Green of Portadown. Aged 19. Attended Wesley College, Dublin. Student at Trinity College, Dublin with a view to taking Holy Orders with the Church of Ireland being a member of the University OTC. All-round athlete and great swimmer playing cricket. Received his commission on the 1st February 1916 and gazetted May 1916. He was attached to the 17th Royal Irish Rifles and send to the Queens University (Belfast) Officers' Training School. Father applied for his medals. Memorial Ref. Pier and Face 15 A and 15 B., Thiepval Memorial, France.

Wesley 1st XV 1914
Back; Harte, Kenny, Shier, Clegg, Rudd, Gillespie, Rev Irwin
Middle Burns, Notley, Mills, Irwin, Dart, Davies, Green. Front; Dowling, Maguire

GREENLEES, Second Lieutenant, Charles Fouracres. Assault began at 8.00am and barbed wire was cut every 40 yards the Germans had their machine-guns trained on these gaps and only a few men ever got through the wire, attached 1st Bn., Royal Dublin Fusiliers, killed in action, 1st July 1916. 9th Bn., The Queen's (Royal West Surrey Regiment). Aged 21. Born 1st June 1895. Second and only surviving son of Archibald and Jessie Mary Greenlees, of 198, Park Lane, Tottenham, London. Educated St. John's, Leatherhead, and was gazetted from the OTC University College, Oxford, November 1914. Entered France, 19th May 1916. Father applied for his medals. Memorial Ref. I. A. 4., Auchonvillers Military Cemetery, France.

In Sure And Certain Hope Of The Resurrection To Eternal Life

GREGG, Second Lieutenant, William Henry. Reported as missing, officially reported as killed 1st July 1916. Rifleman King and Corporal Beehan both reported him killed. He advanced in front of his men under heavy machine gun fire saw to fall as he turned to talk to his men, he fell lying on his side with blood oozing out of wound above his left eye and with no movement of his body. 14 Platoon, 5th Bn. attd. 1st Bn., Royal Irish Rifles. Born 25th August 1885. Son of John Gregg JP, and Margaret Wynne Gregg, of 10, Deramore Park South, Belfast formerly 3 Chichester Gardens, Belfast. He was educated at Rydal Mount, Colwyn Bay, and Clifton College, entered the business of the well-known firm of Gregg, Sons, and Phoenix, Belfast, of which his father was a partner. Employed as a traveler. Member of the Queen's University, Belfast, Training Corps, 1913 -1914. He endeavoured to enter the army when the Ulster Division was formed, and was rejected no fewer than five times owing to eye weakness, but he was ultimately given his commission in May, 1915. Brother Lieutenant A. L. Gregg lost an eye whilst serving in the Dardanelles, on the 16th August 1915. William went to the Front in early 1916. His brother wrote to the War Office on behalf of his ill father questioning the evidence and informed that as men were picked up by the stretcher bearers four to five yards passed where Second Lieutenant Gregg had fallen the inference in the reply being that his body would have been examined and found dead they would have passed on, to find someone whom was wounded. Father applied for his medals. Memorial Ref. Pier and Face 15 A and 15 B., Thiepval Memorial, France. WO 339/51794

GRIERSON, Second Lieutenant, John Livingston Hailes. Killed in action, led on after the 17th Manchesters, 1st July 1916. 3rd Bn. attd. C Coy., 2nd Bn., Royal Scots Fusiliers. Aged 35. Second son of the Colonel John Grierson (Indian Army), and of Ismena Evans Grierson, of Hostellerie Du Bonhomme, Chateau Thierry, France and of Polygon House, Southampton. Served in the South African Campaign. Gazetted October 1915. Father applied for his medals. Memorial Ref. Pier and Face 3 C., Thiepval Memorial, France.

GRIFFIN, Captain, George Edward. Killed in action, informants differ one says killed by a shell another shot by machine-gun fire after about 100 yards, 1st July 1916. D Coy., 9th Bn., King's Own Yorkshire Light Infantry. Aged 41. Son of William and Emma Passmore (formerly Griffin), of 52 Portland Avenue, Stamford Hill, London. Born 20th July 1875. Enlisted 16th December 1891. No. 3470 with the 1st Bn., Dorsetshire Regiment, Awarded the Indian Good Service Medal for work on the northwest frontier and the Africa Good Service Medal for work in Somaliland. Retired to Winnipeg, Canada and joined the Canadian Expeditionary Force. Attested 9th December 1914. Commissioned 24th March 1915. Entered France, 11th September 1915. Mrs. Passmore (mother) applied for his medals. Memorial Ref. Pier and Face 11 C and 12 A., Thiepval Memorial, France. WO 339/2439

GRIFFITHS, Captain, John. Killed in action whilst leading his company, 1st July 1916 he collected men from No. 9 and No. 12 platoons and gave the order to charge and was hit. 12th Bn., Royal Irish Rifles. Aged 34. Only surviving son of John (partner in the firm of Griffiths Brothers, Corn Merchants, Chester) and Jane Griffiths, of Chester. Native of Chester. Born 23rd August 1881. Educated Alun School, Mold. Captain Griffiths was a graduate of the University College of Bangor (North Wales), BSc. He became science master at Cleobury Mortimer College, on the outbreak of the war was science master in the grammar school, Larne for some six years and Larne Technical School. He was a leading member of the Ulster Volunteers, and on entering the army in January, 1915, joined the Ulster Division and obtained his commission in the 12th Royal Irish Rifles, where his soldierly ability gained him rapid promotion, captain August 1915. At one point he held a commission in the Territorials. Active service September 1915, wounded June 6th slight shrapnel wound in the face and home on leave June 13th, returning June 19th. His absolutely clean sportsmanship and high moral principles making for the good of everything in which he took part. Lieutenant McCluggage, from Ballyboley also killed on the 1st July 1916, had been taught science by Captain Griffiths at Larne Grammar School. The two men were reunited in the Larne 1st XV where they played together in the Towns Cup winning side of 1913-1914. Originally buried R.E.D Cemetery Q.17 Central with a cross on his grave and reburied. Headstone inscription chosen by Miss H. Griffiths, Lyndhurst, Christleton near Chester. Memorial Ref. I. D. 38., Ancre British Cemetery, Beaumont-Hamel, France. Mentioned in Despatches.

The Path Of Duty Is The Way To Glory

GRUNDY, Second Lieutenant, Ronald Edwin. Reported to have been shot through the throat by a sniper on the 1st July 1916 and died instantly whilst leading his platoon. 2nd Bn., Middlesex Regiment. Aged 20. Born 6th June 1895. Son of John F. E. Grundy, of 24, Buckingham St., Charing Cross, London formerly 33 St. James Road, Upper Tooting. Attended Emmanuel School and a member of the OTC. Attended Royal Military College, February 1915. Served with the Honourable Artillery Company. Entered France, 29th May 1916. Father of Buckingham Street, Strand applied for his medals. Originally buried 500 yards SW of Ovillers Communal Cemetery. Memorial Ref. Sp. Mem. 6., Ovillers Military Cemetery, France. WO 339/56437

Fell Whilst Leading His Platoon

GUEST, Major, Thomas Heald. Attack on village of Serre. At 7.40am B Coy. Under Major Guest followed the fourth wave with order to advance to the German fourth line. Major Guest and all his officers as well of those of the clearing party being killed or wounded before they reached the German 1st Line. Although this advance had to carried out in a tornado of fire all ranks advanced steadily as if on drill parade. Major Guest, Lieut. Heptonstall and three men of B Coy reached the German front line. Major Guest was shot in the right leg and never seen again, killed in action, 1st July 1916. The three men were killed. Lieut. Heptonstall wounded returned at nightfall. 13th Bn., York and Lancaster Regiment. Aged 41. Attended All Saints' School Bloxham, 1886-1889. He was the only son of Thomas Guest JP (of the firm Thomas Guest and Co. Ltd, Carruthers Street, Ancoats) of Manchester. He served in the army and in the South African War. Married Mabel Ellen Fountain on the 3rd October 1905. Connected with his father's business. Rejoined into the 13th Bn., York and Lancaster Regiment, and served in Egypt before being sent to France.

A letter from the Colonel to his wife stated: 'He was last seen leading his company into a German trench and was reported to have been hit in the leg just as he reached it. I gave him the choice of leading the company or remaining in reserve, and he chose the former. Our Brigadier, who has seen many fights, remarked that he had never seen anything more splendid than the way your husband led his men through the artillery barrage and intense machine-gun fire. He showed an example of bravery and devotion which has been unequalled." Final words of encouragement were "Now boys we have to uphold the honour of the old town and remember, I am the first over the top. Over boys and give them hell." Commemorated St. Peter's (Hale) Memorial, Altrincham & District Roll of Honour. Mother applied for his medals. Memorial Ref. Pier and Face 14 A and 14 B., Thiepval Memorial, France.

GUNNING, Second Lieutenant, Frank Douglas. The survivors of the platoon spoke about how he led them across No Man's Land in the face of heavy shell and machine-gun fire, a bullet took off one of his fingers and he was binding it up and refused to go to the dressing station, he went on until a shell extinguished his spirit, 1st July 1916. 6th Bn. attd. 11th Bn., Royal Inniskilling Fusiliers. Aged 22. Third son of Mr. and Mrs. Sinclair Gunning, of Wheatfield Gardens, Belfast also of Willoughby Place, Enniskillen. Educated Portora Royal School. Service of Ulster Bank prior to war from May 1912 and was working as bank clerk in Sligo when war broke out. His bank were reluctant to let him sign up. Enlisted in the 7th Bn., Royal Dublin Fusiliers, private, 14764, in September 1914 and left England for active service in July 1915. Invalided from the Dardanelles with dysentery on the 18th August 1915, entered the Balkans, 9th August 1915 subsequently obtaining a commission in the 6th Bn., on the 8th December 1915 and in June 1916 was sent to France with the 11th Bn. Younger brother in the Royal Navy. Bank of Ireland Roll of Honour. Mrs. K. Gunning, Wheatfield Gardens, Belfast applied for his medals. Memorial Ref. Pier and Face 4 D and 5 B., Thiepval Memorial, France.

GUYON, Lieutenant Colonel, George Sutherland. Left battalion HQ at five minutes to zero, had been at Sap A about two minutes when struck in the helmet by a bullet, bandaged by Lieutenant Ransome and Second Lieutenant Laxton, unconscious and apparently dying, they were obliged to leave him, killed at Serre, 1st July 1916. Appointed commanding officer of the Bradford Pals just 48 hours before the attack. 2nd Bn., Royal Fusiliers killed leading the 16th Bn., West Yorkshire Regiment. Aged 41. Born Hastings, Sussex on the 19th January 1875. Son of Major General Gardiner and Mary Guyon. Attended Brighton College (Mr. Wickham's House, 1886 -1891), one of four Old Brightonians lost on the 1st July 1916. Commissioned 1897. Fought in the Boer War and promoted to captain 1901 and major in 1912. Husband of Winifred and father of two boys. Wounded at Gallipoli in 1915, shot in the head in the landing at Cape Helles and returned to England being promoted to Lieutenant Colonel. His widow, Mrs. G. S. Guyon, Norfolk applied for his medals. Memorial Ref. Pier and Face 9 A, Thiepval Memorial, France.

HABLUTZEL, Second Lieutenant, George Rudolph. Killed in action, 1st July 1916. 1st Bn., King's Own (Royal Lancaster Regiment). Aged 39. Husband of L. A. Hablutzel, of Hatfield Road, Northallerton, Yorks. Eldest son of Mrs. H. Hablutzel, 11 Slade Hall Road, Longsight. Previously Warrant Officer II, 4600, Royal Lancaster Regiment. Served in the South African War and awarded Queen's Medal with two bars. Entered France, 24th August 1914. Commissioned 30th May 1916. Mrs. G. R. Hablutzel, applied for his medals. Memorial Ref. Pier and Face 5 D and 12 B., Thiepval Memorial, France.

HACK, Lieutenant, Adrian Henry. Killed in action, gallantly leading his men in the attack, 1st July 1916. 8th Bn., King's Own Yorkshire Light Infantry. Aged 25. Third and youngest son of Sydney John (retired civil engineer) and Ellen Hack, of The Knoll, Holmwood, Surrey. Born 23rd November 1890. Adrian was educated at the Pilgrim School, Sevenoaks and then from 1904 to 1909 at Bradfield College, Berkshire. Member of the Bradfield OTC. Apprenticeship, with Vigors & Co, 1909 to 1912. Surveyor. Enlisted 1st September 1914 in the 10th Royal Fusiliers. Received his commission January 1915 and went to France, 27th August 1915. Father applied for his medals. Memorial Ref. V. I. 18., Blighty Valley Cemetery, Authuille Wood, France. WO 339/31224

In Glad Thanksgiving For His Life & Proud Remembrance Of His Death

HADWEN, Captain, Noel Waugh. He was killed by a shell when leading his men into action with No. 2 Coy., between Serre and Beaumont Hamel. 1st July 1916. B Coy. 2nd Bn., Duke of Wellington's (West Riding Regiment). Aged 30. Second son of Frederick W. Hadwen and Anna M. Hadwen, of Kebroyd, Triangle, Yorkshire. Named after his grandfather. Attended Lockers Park and Harrow. Well known in Halifax. Architect, Associate of the Institute of British Architects 1910. Captain Hadwen joined the Duke of Wellington's Regiment in September, 1914, and went to France in April, 1915. He was in the engagement at Hill 60, where he was badly gassed, so badly indeed that he was being carried away to be buried, when he recovered. He returned to the Front in October, 1915. On June 30th he wrote his last letter home; "We go over to see the Boches at dawn tomorrow. I don't think the attack can fail, but at the present my head doesn't have room for any idea except for my own little company patch. I know they will do well and that's all that seems to matter after five days bombardment." Mother applied for his medals. Memorial Ref. Pier and Face 6 A and 6 B., Thiepval Memorial, France.

HALL, Second Lieutenant, John McRobb. Missing believed killed, 1st July 1916. 21st (Tyneside Scottish) Bn., Northumberland Fusiliers. Born 11th June 1896. Son of John Hall, (marine superintendent), of 28 Malvern Street, Newcastle-upon-Tyne formerly The Grove, Gosforth, Newcastle. Grandson of John McRobb of the Aberdeen Lime Company. Educated at Rutherford College, Newcastle and Robert Gordon's College. Lived with his grandfather at 79 Murray Terrace while at the college. He was a Gordon Highlander Territorial from the 27th March 1914, private 1659, and obtained a commission in the Northumberland Fusiliers in January 1916 when he went to the Front, 3rd February 1916. Named in the Aberdeen District Roll of Honour. Originally buried Albert, Sheet 62d. sq. E. 4. D.9. 9. Effects were cheque book, wallet with correspondence, holdall, advance book, ID disc, gold by Vickery, London, Map case, Sam Browne belt, prismatic compass (broken), cheque book and bottle. Father applied for his medals. Memorial Ref. Pier and Face 10 B 11 B and 12 B., Thiepval Memorial, France. WO 339/22996

HALL, Lieutenant, Warwick Died at Mametz, initially had his right arm blown off and subsequently reported to be hit in the stomach about 9.00am and there was little chance of him surviving, and died of his wounds, 1st July 1916. At 8.00am he had reported to Battalion HQ that he required reinforcements. D Coy., 1st Bn., South Staffordshire Regiment. Aged 20. Son of Dr. Walter and Frances Hall, of Hodnet, Salop. Born Southampton. Educated Denstone College and trained with the OTC, played in the Cricket XI. Entered at Sidney College, Cambridge when war broke out and volunteered he should of matriculated in 1914 intending to read Medicine. Gazetted August 1914 to France, 5th March 1915. Twice wounded in May 1915. Commissioned as a lieutenant in the 1st Bn., South Staffordshire Regiment. Twin brother Lieutenant Bruce Hall killed 25th September 1915 at the Battle of Loos. His father made application for his medals. Original burial map reference 62d.F.5.d.5.9, and buried as an unknown officer, as '1st S. Staff. R.' Memorial Ref. IX. A. I., Dantzig Alley British Cemetery, Mametz, France. WO 339/23581

Twin Son Of Walter And Frances Hall Thy Will Be Done

HAMILTON, Second Lieutenant, John Hamilton. Missing assumed to be killed, 1st July 1916. 11th Bn., Royal Inniskilling Fusiliers. He was a son of Mr. James Hamilton. Woodview, Strandtown, Belfast. Born 20th February 1886. Clerk in the Belfast Bank of Coleraine before he received his commission on the 19th April 1915. Previously lance sergeant, Royal Inniskillings, 14748. Still missing 26th December 1916. Reported presumed to have been killed dated 9th May 1917. His brother Lieutenant William Hamilton served in the Royal Engineers. Mrs. W. Storling, his married sister, applied for his medals from Denver, Colorado. Memorial Ref. Pier and Face 4 D and 5 B., Thiepval Memorial, France.

HAMILTON, Second Lieutenant, Robert Victor. Killed in action, 1st July 1916. 9th Bn., Royal Irish Rifles. Youngest son of James and Matilda Hamilton, of 7, Charnwood Avenue, previously 2 Glendarra, Charnwood Avenue, Belfast, Co. Antrim. Victor was born on 7th January 1892. He was educated at the Royal Academic Institution, Belfast. At the outbreak of the war he held a civil service appointment in the Treasury Department, Dublin Castle. He joined the army as a cadet in March, 1915 at Newcastle and after training, lance corporal, 17/98, Royal Irish Rifles was gazetted to the 9th Royal Irish Rifles, 23rd August 1915, and in March, 1916, went to the front. Medals applied for by his father, Memorial Ref. Pier and Face 15 A and 15 B., Thiepval Memorial, France.

HAMPSON, Lieutenant, Edgar. Missing, led platoons of D Coy in the 15th Bn., 1st July 1916. Reported by Lance Corporal Joseph Appleyard to have been shot in the stomach by machine-gun fire whilst in the German front line trenches and died at once. 15th Bn. attd. 16th Bn., Lancashire Fusiliers. Born on 23rd August 1895, he was the son of Edith and Peter (Borough Magistrate) of Millville House, 81, Camp Street, Broughton. His father was a Salford councillor and proprietor and editor of the Salford Reporter. His elder brother Captain Stuart Hirst Hampson was acting adjutant in the 20th Lancashire Fusiliers. Edgar went to Vernon House School, Broughton, Manchester Grammar School and Salford Technical Institute which he left join the army. He was a noted swimmer, footballer and cricketer. He attended the Church of the Ascension Lower Broughton, and was a Sunday school teacher. He trained with Manchester University OTC and was commissioned second lieutenant, September 1914, becoming a lieutenant a year later. Entered France, 22nd November 1915. Brother a captain in the same regiment. Private W. Hall wrote; "He always was a gallant officer, cool under the most trying ordeal and also very considerate to the men under his command – a thorough gentleman and not afraid of anything". Lieutenant Norman Blackett wrote confirming he had found the grave to The Salford Reporter, grave subsequently lost. His parents applied for his medals. Memorial Ref. Pier and Face 3 C and 3 D., Thiepval Memorial, France.

HAMPTON, Second Lieutenant, William Orr. Attacked the German lines on July 1st, in a most gallant manner, getting his men and two machine-guns forward under very heavy fire, 1st July 1916. 3rd Bn., Norfolk Regiment attached to the 70th Bn., Machine Gun Corps. Aged 28. Elder son of the Reverend William Henry (Vicar of Pondersbridge, Huntingdon) and Elizabeth Hampton. Born in Pakenham, Suffolk on 23rd July 1887. Attended The King's School, Peterborough from May 1900 to December 1900. From January 1901 to July 1906 he attended The King's School, Ely, winning a Bishop's scholarship in 1902 and the Potticary Medal in 1905. A fine athlete, he won Ely School's Champion's Cup in summer 1906. He later became a schoolmaster at St. Saviour's College, Ardingly. Sports Committee and playing for the Masters and Boys' football team. He was Honorary Vice-President of the Senior Debating Society. He was also Assistant Scoutmaster. He joined the 77th Field Coy., Royal Engineers as a sapper on 27th August 1914, No. 42022. He moved to the 79th Coy., in which he rose to sergeant. His commission as second lieutenant from 8th June 1915 with the 3rd Bn., Norfolk Regiment, seconded for duty with the Machine Gun Corps on 27th March 1916. He arrived in France on 4th June 1916 and posted to the 70th Coy., Machine Gun Corps, 8th Division. His father living at Cromwell Road, Bristol applied for his medals. Commemorated Ramsey War Memorial, The King's School, Ely and Pondersbridge Church Parish War Memorial, Originally buried about 1500 yards east-southeast of Authuille Church, map reference 57d.X.1.b.6.9 Memorial Ref. IV. A. 2., Lonsdale Cemetery, Authuille, France.

Rest Divine, Perpetual Light Remain To Him For Ever O Lord

Ardingley College Staff c1913. William is standing top right. Ardingly College magazine

HANDYSIDE, Captain, Percy James Alexander. 2.30pm, having moved up from communication trenches to the front line, attacked in line across the open but met with intense barrage, he was wounded about 15 yards from the front line but crawled forward encouraging the men until a shell burst over him and he was killed, 1st July 1916. C Coy., 1st/2nd Bn., London Regiment (Royal Fusiliers). Aged 37. Elder son of James Alexander Handyside of Petrograd. Born 10th December 1878, St. Petersburg, Russia. Educated privately in Stuttgart and in Bruges. Married 20th May 1916 at Pyrford Church to Dorothy Handyside (nee Hampshire), of Redcourt, Pyrforand, Surrey. Commissioned 7th October 1913 and to captain, 21st April 1915. Mrs. P. J. A. Handyside, C/o Messrs. Prince Vintcent, Mossel Bay, South Africa applied for his medals. Original burial map reference 57c.K.4.b.2.2 and his grave was marked with a cross. Buried near to an unknown officer of the London Regiment with a date of death as the 1st July 1916. Inscription chosen by his wife. Memorial Ref. II. L. 11., Gommecourt British Cemetery No.2, Hebuterne, France.

In Proud And Ever Loving Memory

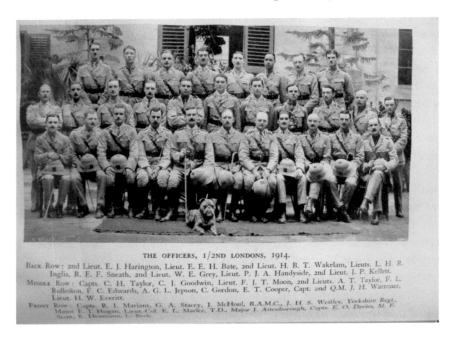

THE OFFICERS, 1/2ND LONDONS, 1914.

Back Row: 2nd Lieut. E. J. Harington, Lieut. E. E. H. Bate, 2nd Licut. H. B. T. Wakelam, Lieuts. L. H. R. Inglis, R. E. F. Sneath, 2nd Lieut. W. E. Grey, Lieut. P. J. A. Handyside, 2nd Lieut. J. P. Kellett.
Middle Row: Capts. C. H. Taylor, C. J. Goodwin, Lieut. F. J. T. Moon, 2nd Lieuts. A. T. Taylor, F. L. Rolleston, F. C. Edwards, A. G. L. Jepson, C. Gordon, E. T. Cooper, Capt. and Q.M. J. H. Warrener, Lieut. H. W. Everitt.
Front Row: Capts. R. L. Marians, G. A. Stacey, J. McHoul, R.A.M.C., J. H. S. Westley, Yorkshire Regt. Major F. J. Hogan, Lieut-Col. E. L. Marler, T.D., Major J. Attenborough, Capts. E. O. Davies, M. F. Scott, R. Heumann, L. Beck.

HARBORD, Lieutenant, George Alfred Lionel. Reported killed, immediately the lines appeared on the parapet, heavy machine-gun fire brought to bear, 1st July 1916. 3rd Bn. attd. 1st Bn., Royal Inniskilling Fusiliers. Aged 20. Youngest surviving son of the Reverend Richard Charles M. Harbord, BD., (from 1894 to 1903 Resident Canon of Christ Church Cathedral) and Margaret Grace Harbord, of Murragh Rectory, Enniskean, Co. Cork. Grandson of Colonel Richard Harbord, 7th Royal Fusiliers. In December, 1914, he received his commission in the 3rd Inniskilling Fusiliers at Londonderry and promoted lieutenant in November. He had been through the Gallipoli campaign, and attached to the 1st Bn. Served in France from January, 1916. Father applied for his medals. Memorial Ref. Pier and Face 4 D and 5 B., Thiepval Memorial, France.

HARDMAN, Second Lieutenant, Robert Taylor. Detailed to provide a smoke screen at Martinsart near Beaumont Hamel, they were to establish a mortar position on the enemy's side at zero plus 30, killed as soon as he went over the top with Second Lieutenant C. J. Sutton and Lieutenant Swann, 1st July 1916. 'C' Section, No. 1 Mortar Company, 5th Mortar Bn., Special Bde., Royal Engineers. Aged 27. Son of Robert Taylor Hardman and Alice Ann Hardman, of 32, Stockton Road, Chorlton-Cum-Hardy, Manchester. Born 23rd February 1889. Pupil of Bury Grammar School. Graduate of Manchester University, from 1907 gaining a BSc in 1910 and MSc in Chemistry in 1911. He went on to work in the USA as a research chemist in New York and engaged to lady from Pittsburgh, but was living on Rochdale Road, Bury on the outbreak of war. Member of the OTC, initially private, 4956, 20th Bn., Royal Fusiliers, commissioned in the King's Own Royal Lancasters, November 1914, and later transferred to the Royal Engineers. Mentioned in Despatches, July 1915 for patrol work. In December 1915 fell ill from exhaustion and shell shock and in April 1916 had the role with the Royal Engineers. Captain Robertson, the Company Commander wrote a detailed account of what happened in a letter to Robert's brother, Benjamin: 'Your brother, while fully realising the danger of advancing with his guns and detachment in the great advance during the main attack on July 1 1916, nevertheless, on the 107th Brigadier General's statement that it was most important that the guns should advance boldly, emerged from our trenches on the north-east edge of Thiepval Wood at the head of his detachment, notwithstanding heavy machine gun and other fire. After proceeding some distance and finding that a bomb-carrying party detailed to carry his bombs had failed to advance and that three of his small party (including an officer) had become casualties, and that it was obviously useless to advance without the bombs etc, he gave the order to retire. Under a rain of machine gun bullets, however, he attempted to succour a wounded comrade (2nd Lieut. C. J. Sutton, R.F.A) and in attempting to carry him back to our trenches was regrettably killed by machine gun fire. Sergeant W. W. Potts risked his life to succour your brother and 2nd Lieut. C. J. Sutton by crawling out from our trenches to the spot where these two officers lay. After ascertaining by careful observation that both were dead he returned to our trenches.'

Two men were both awarded the DCM for their role, Sergeant W. W. Potts and Corporal D. J. Gavin. Sergeant Potts; "For conspicuous gallantry and devotion. During a retirement which had become necessary owing to casualties, he remained to pick up, and ultimately carried back under heavy fire a wounded comrade. He also made a gallant effort to succour two officers (Second Lieutenant Hardman & Sutton) who unfortunately were found to be dead. Corporal Gavin; For conspicuous gallantry in endeavouring to assist a wounded officer during a retirement under very heavy artillery and machine gun fire. While so doing the officer was killed. Corporal Gavin then returned at great personal risk to the assistance of a wounded comrade". Father applied for Robert's medals. Memorial Ref. Pier and Face 8 A and 8 D., Thiepval Memorial, France.

HARKNESS, Captain, Percy Yarborough. He was in command of the two leading companies, and led them with great coolness right up to the enemy's trenches when he was killed by a shell, 1st July 1916. 2nd Bn., West Yorkshire Regiment (Prince of Wales's Own). Son of Reverend Henry Law Harknes of Hove, Brighton. Born 1884. He was captain of cricket at Malvern College, attended 1898 to 1900. Captain Harkness held a commission in the West Yorkshire Regiment at the outbreak of the war, and saw active service in the earlier engagements. Entered France, 11th February 1915. He was injured at Neuve Chapelle owing to a fall from his horse, and was invalided home. He had only recently rejoined his regiment when he fell in action on July 1st. To him and his fine example during the battle is greatly due the splendid reputation the battalion gained in this action. Father to two children Francis Warwick born 26th September 1908 and James Percy Knowles born 25th November 1916, they were entitled to pension payments. His widow, remarried, Mrs. Johnstone, Nettlecombe Avenue, Southsea applied for his medals. Effects returned were diary, letters, cap badge, advance book, cheque book and a pair of 'Pince-nez'. His brother, Captain H. L. Harkness wrote to request if any further information was available on his burial, but received reply saying it would be forwarded when available. Memorial Ref. Pier and Face 2 A 2 C and 2 D., Thiepval Memorial, France. WO 339/28607

HARLEY, Captain, Arthur Darent. He was in command of a platoon of his company in front of Gommecourt Wood. He advanced gallantly up the front line gallantly encouraging his men. Here he was wounded in the face and later to be seen fighting single handedly against three Germans including an officer and a warrant officer. Reported wounded and later killed, 1st July 1916. C Coy. 1st/6th Bn., South Staffordshire Regiment. Aged 21. Son of Mr. and Mrs. Percy Harley, of Rathlin, Northwood, Middx. Born 1895 at 71, Broadhurst Gardens, Hampstead. Resided 95 Fellows Road, South Hampstead. In 1908 he won a major scholarship to University College School, Hampstead and became a member of the OTC. In 1912 he was confirmed at St. Saviour's Church, Hampstead. BSc, University College with Honours in Chemistry. University of London, OTC. Commissioned September 1914 and to France, 20th July 1915. Gazetted to lieutenant 13th October 1915. He was wounded in an attack at Vermelles 28th December 1915 with a gunshot wound to the arm returning to England to recover, leaving hospital, 4th February 1916 transferred to Endsleigh Place. In June 1916 he was awarded a BSc War Degree. Promoted captain, 1st June 1916. Prisoner of war records indicate he was wounded, 'disparu et blesse' translated 'missing and hurt'. Father applied for his medals. Memorial Ref. Pier and Face 7 B., Thiepval Memorial, France.

HARLEY, Second Lieutenant, Benjamin Chapman. Prisoner of war records indicate missing, 1st July 1916. B Coy. 14th Bn., Royal Irish Rifles. Aged 22. Son of Mr. E. M. Harley and Mrs. Anne Letitia Harley, of "St. Cross", Copthorne Road, Croxley Green, Watford, Herts. Enlisted private, 3216, 12th Bn., London Rifles. Entered France 24th December 1914. Commissioned 6th June 1916. Mother applied for his medals, and officers' pension whilst residing Union Road, Wembley. Prisoner of war contact, brother Mervyn Harley, Copthorne Road. Memorial Ref. Pier and Face 15 A and 15 B., Thiepval Memorial, France.

HARRIS, Captain, Hamilton Snow. Instructed his comrades to leave him in a shell hole and do their duty, 1st July 1916. Seen in Quarry Bray Street back of Avelin Woods at about 10.00am, he was hit in the hips and legs and could not walk. His men tried to get him away but the shelling and machine gun fire was too heavy. A Coy., 13th Bn. attd. 11th Bn., Sherwood Foresters (Notts and Derby Regiment). Aged 25. Born 16th May 1889. Son of Mr. Graham Harris and Mrs. Frances Harris, of Little Court, 80, Grand Drive, Raynes Park, London. Native of London. Formerly with the Canadian General Electric Company. Enlisted 3rd Bn., Canadian Expeditionary Force, private, 2450. Gazetted lieutenant in August 1915 and promoted captain in March 1916. Reported killed 20th October 1916. Commemorated St. Thomas (Anglican) Church, Huron St., Toronto, Ontario. Medals applied for by his mother. Body exhumed 1919, originally buried 970 yards NW of Ovillers Church. Harold Watson wrote to his wife; "I should have written to you before but I wanted to wait until I had some definitive news on your son. I had parties on the ground trying to identify the dead lying where they fell ever since I got back in these parts. Today our chaplain came back and reported he had found the body of your son. He was buried closed to where he fell. We have found close on 50 of my missing men and four of the five missing officers. I enclose two notes which he wrote to you and were on his body". Memorial Ref. III. H. 2., Blighty Valley Cemetery, Authuille Wood, France. WO 339/34207

They That Love Beyond The World Cannot Be Separated By It

HARRISON, Second Lieutenant, Geoffrey. He was leading his section in No Man's Land, he received a wound in the thigh. He gave instructions to his NCO's to push on, when a shell burst and killed him. He fell at Contalmaison, 1st July 1916, Machine Gun Corps (Infantry). Aged 20. Younger son of Bernard Bowles Harrison and Elisabeth Anne Harrison, of Hurstmead, Pembury Road, Tunbridge Wells. Born Sevenoaks, 1896 he was educated first by Miss Webb in Granville Road then at Beechmont where he became captain of the school. Attended Rugby School. He entered the school in 1910 and left, in 1914, for University College, Oxford. On the outbreak of war he enlisted in the Public Schools Brigade, and obtained a commission, in December, 1914, in the 12th Bn., Hampshire Regiment, and later was transferred to the 13th Bn. In January, 1916, he was transferred to the Machine Gun Corps, and went to the Front, 26th April 1916. A brother officer wrote :- "He was greatly esteemed and respected both by officers and men, and there was not a more cheery fellow in the Company." And another wrote :- "Off parade and in Mess his classical allusions and quaint phrases kept us in constant good humour to the last. He was everybody's pal. On parade I can only say that his men loved him."

His father applied for his medals. Original burial map reference 57d. X.20.c. Memorial Ref. IV. G. 6., Ovillers Military Cemetery, France.

They Played Their Part For England

HART, Lieutenant, Andrew Chichester. Reported wounded, 1st July 1916. 109th Bn., Machine Gun Corps. Aged 34. Youngest son of William Edward Hart, MA and Mrs. B. L. Hart, of Kilderry, Co. Donegal. Husband of Mrs. Minnie Elizabeth Hart. He obtained a commission in the 11th Bn., Royal Inniskillings on the 25th September 1914 and transferred to the Machine Gun Corps in 1916. Entered France, 1915. Elder brother, Captain Henry P. Hart awarded the Military Cross. His medals and officers' pension were applied for his wife, Rossinuremore, Derry Gonelly, Co. Fermanagh, Ireland. His inscription was chosen by Lt. Col. J. G. Vaughan Hart, Kilderry, near Londonderry. His family had a long connection with Derry, one of his ancestors was the first Alderman in 1613, and another ancestors built the city walls and the cathedral. Londonderry (Derry) War Memorial. Memorial Ref. I. E. 28., Connaught Cemetery, Thiepval, France.

Youngest Son Of W.E.Hart Esq., M.A. Of Kilderry, Co. Donegal

HART, Captain, Cecil Lyon. Killed by a shell fragment, commanding No. 3 Company, 2nd Bn., 1st July 1916. 3rd Bn., Duke of Wellington's (West Riding Regiment). Only son of Mr. and Mrs. Moss Alexander Hart and Marguerite Hart of 12 Alexandra Mansions, West End Lane, Hampstead. He was born in Kimberley, Cape Colony. Received his education in Britain, attending University College School, Hampstead. He later passed his bar examinations and entered the Inner Temple as a law student. The outbreak of war in 1914 precluded his being called to the bar, belonged to the Jewish Lads' Brigade promptly enlisted and was commissioned as a second lieutenant in the 3rd (Reserve) Bn., The Duke of Wellington's (West Riding Regiment) and subsequently went to the Front, 7th December 1914. University of London, OTC. University College. Mentioned in Despatches, January 1, 1916. Jewish Book of Honour. Mother applied for his medals. Memorial Ref. I. H. 10., Sucrerie Military Cemetery, Colincamps, France.

HARTLEY, Lieutenant, William Ismay Spooner. All the men went calmly forward following the example set by the officer, reached the enemy's barbed wire when they came under the fire of three to four machine-guns, reported he died a true hero with a smile on his face, killed Ovillers La Boisselle, 1st July 1916. 8th Bn., King's Own Yorkshire Light Infantry. Aged 25. Son of the Reverend William Robert and Sarah Alice Ismay Hartley, of the Rectory, Barnburgh, Doncaster. Born 18th May 1891. Educated at King Edward VII School, Sheffield and at Queens College, Oxford where he graduated in the Honour School of Modern History, MA. After leaving university he held assistant mastership at Ovingdean Hall Preparatory School, South Cliff College (Filey) and King William's College (Isle of Man) resigning to enter the army. At the Front about a week before the Great Advance. His original CWGC cross is located in St Peter Church, Barnburgh, South Yorkshire his father having received permission to have it relocated. Body found and buried on the 20th September near Authville Wood. Effects were cheque book, advance book, knife, fork, spoon, eye glasses, prayer book, note book, pipe, keys and letters. King William's College Book of Remembrance, Castletown and commemorated Sons and Daughters of the Anglican Church Clergy. Memorial Ref. IV. H. 1., Blighty Valley Cemetery, Authuille Wood, France. WO 339/52056

HARVEY, Captain, Bernard Sydney. Reported to be hit in No Man's Land returning from the German front line trench, Gommecourt, 1st July 1916. By 8.20pm the officers consisting of Captain Somers-Smith, (London Regiment), Lieutenant Petley, (London Rifle Brigade), Captain Leys Cox (Queen Victoria's Rifles), Second Lieutenant Arthur, (Cheshire Regiment), Captain Harvey (London Rifle Brigade) and Second Lieutenant Bovill (Queens Westminster Rifles) admitted they would be forced to return to the British lines and provided covering fire for the men. Making a run for the nearest shell holes, the only officer who returned was Lieutenant Petley, five officers being killed. Officer Commanding C Coy., 1st /5th Bn., London Regiment (London Rifle Brigade). Aged 27. Younger son of Walter Sydney and Florence Harvey, of 9, Vale Court, Maida Vale, London. Born 1888. Attended Malvern College, 1903 to 1907 and Trinity College, Oxford (1907 -1910) obtaining an BA. Assistant master at St. Andrew's School, Eastbourne where he was a pupil prior to Malvern

College. Joined BEF as an officer 20th December 1914 when he entered France. Wounded 3rd May 1915 and rejoined 5th August 1915. His General writes: "One of my men says he was with Captain Harvey when he was hit in the shoulder, but he still continued to lead his men and cheer them on. He was wounded again, and in the evening when conducting the retirement he and others had to get through some wire; in doing so a noise was made that attracted the attention of the enemy, and the end came at once." His mother applied for his medals. Memorial Ref. Pier and Face 9 D., Thiepval Memorial, France.

HARVEY, Second Lieutenant, James. Majority of the casualties especially those of the officers occurred during the first two hours of fighting, 1st July 1916. 2nd Bn., Seaforth Highlanders. Aged 24. Third son of Jessie Harvey (draper in Greenock), of 47, Palatine Road, Douglas, Isle Of Man, and James Harvey, of Greenock. Employed Messrs. Robert Houston & Sons, woollen manufacturer, Greenock of which his uncle, Mr. James Robertson is a partner. Nephew of Chief Constable of Greenock. Enlisted 5th Dragoon Guards, lance corporal, GS/3654 with Lieutenant Broom who fell in the same engagement. Commissioned 9th March 1916. Entered France, 9th June 1916. Mentioned in a despatch from Lieutenant General Sir Percy Lake dated 17th August 1916. Medals to his home address. Memorial Ref. Pier and Face 15 C., Thiepval Memorial, France.

HASWELL, Captain, Gordon. Killed in action, 1st July 1916. B Coy., 9th Bn., King's Own Yorkshire Light Infantry. Aged 24. Eldest son of Robert and Jessie Haswell, of 27, Thornhill Gardens, Sunderland. Attended Armstrong College (now Newcastle University), gaining a BA. Born 17th May 1892. University's OTC. Assistant master at the Harrow County School teaching English and History when he enlisted on the 1st September 1914. Organist at Roxeth Parish Church, Harrow. He had a younger brother, Lieutenant Frederick Haswell who also served in the 3rd Bn., East Yorkshire Regiment, he died 23rd April 1915 aged 19. Entered France, 11th September 1915. On the 30th June 1916 All officers received a summons to go to Battalion HQ for a final drink before going into action, Haswell gave the toast, not to the health of the Commanding Officer Lynch but as follows; 'Gentlemen, I give you the toast of the King's Own Yorkshire Light Infantry, and in particular the 9th Battalion of the Regiment' – a slight pause – 'Gentleman, when the barrage lifts…'. Father applied for his medals. Memorial Ref. I. B. 92., Norfolk Cemetery, Becordel-Becourt, France. WO 339/20283

Dulce Et Decorum Est Pro Patria Mori

HATCH, Second Lieutenant, Nicholas Stephen. Reported missing after the advance, 1st July 1916 presumed to have fallen on that date. A Coy., 13th Bn., Royal Irish Rifles. Aged 20. Youngest son of Mark and Jemima Hatch, of Mill House, Duleek, Co. Meath. On the outbreak of the war joined the 13th Bn., Royal Irish Rifles, lance corporal, 19024. He subsequently received his commission, 10th April 1915 and was shortly afterwards sent to the front, 13th February 1916. His father applied for his medals. Original burial map reference 57d.Q.24.d.40.95 and marked as unknown British officer R.I.R and later identified as Nicholas by his cigarette case stamped N.S.H, gold ring, officer's khaki, boots (size 8) and collar badges. Memorial Ref. X. A. 1., A.I.F. Burial Ground, Flers, France.

Until The Resurrection Morn

HATT, Captain, Arthur Beach, MC. Mortally wounded, 1st July 1916. A Coy. 8th Bn., Somerset Light Infantry. Aged 27. Son of Sir Harry Hatt (Mayor of Bath) and Lady Hatt, of Sunnycroft, Bloomfield Park, Bath. Born 25th March 1889, Oxford. Educated Dean Close School (1900 to 1905), Holland and Germany. Farmer. Enlisted Royal Sussex Regiment, November 1914. Promoted Sergeant 18th December 1914. Gazetted second lieutenant, February 1915 from Royal Sussex Regiment to Somersets. Gazetted lieutenant July 17th 1915. Went to France 9th September 1915. Awarded Military Cross at Loos, 25th September 1915 for determination when he and a few of his men held a forward position when everyone else in the vicinity retired. Gazetted captain 29th September 1915. Mentioned in Despatches twice. Brother Captain Edward Beach Hatt killed 26th August 1916. His father applied for medals in respect of his two late sons. Original grave map reference 57d.X.26.d.5.5. Headstone inscription decided by Mr. H. H. Hatt, Sunnycroft, Bloomfield Park, Bath. Memorial Ref. II. M. 4., Gordon Dump Cemetery, Ovillers-La Boisselle, France. WO 339/36466

I Thank My God Upon Every Remembrance Of You

HAUGHTON, Lieutenant, Thomas Greenwood. Died like a hero leading his men in a grand charge for the German lines, 1st July 1916, wounded in the leg soon after leaving our front line but led his platoon on. He was wounded a second time during the retirement and killed. 12th Bn., Royal Irish Rifles. Aged 25. Son of Thomas Wilfred and Catherine Isabel Haughton, of Hillmount, Cullybackey, Co. Antrim. He was educated at Edgbaston Preparatory School, Birmingham, and St. Edmund's School, Oxford. At his coming of age on 2nd June 1912 the employees of the family firm, Messrs. Frazer and Haughton, Cullybackey, made him a presentation of a gold watch and chain as a token of the respect in which he was held. When war broke out he at once offered his services securing a commission in the Central Antrims, 12th Royal Irish Rifles and had been at the front since October, 1915. Lieut. Haughton was an able and enthusiastic officer and very popular with his brother-officers and men. He had been a popular and enthusiastic officer in connection with the Ulster Volunteers and was commander of E Coy., 1st Bn., North Antrim Regiment. His mother applied for his medals. Original burial map reference, 57d.Q.17.d.2.4. Memorial Ref. I. A. 15., Hamel Military Cemetery, Beaumont-Hamel, France.

And All That Hope Adored And Lost Hath Melted Into Memory

HAWKINS, Captain, Herbert Edwin. Reported to be killed by a shell, at the Brigade stores dump on the Carnoy-Montauban Road as the shell detonated very close to him, 1st July 1916. 10th Bn., Essex Regiment. Aged 21. Eldest son of Edwin James and Mary Susanna Hawkins, of 89, Coventry Road, llford, Essex. Born 26th April 1895. Educated County High School, Ilford. Worked as an accountants clerk and later in a barrister's office. Joined the Inns of Court OTC before the war started and was given a commission in the Essex Regiment. Promoted lieutenant November 1914 and captain May, 1915 just after his 20th birthday. Entered France, July 1915. Father applied for his medals. Memorial Ref. J. 34., Carnoy Military Cemetery, France. WO 339/30905

Out Of The Wilderness Into The Light

HAYCRAFT, Lieutenant, Alan Montague. Reported wounded and missing, 1st July 1916, 11 months later his body was found and identified by his cheque book. 6th Bn. attd. 2nd Bn., Royal Fusiliers. Aged 32. Worked for the Scottish Insurance Corporation Ltd in London as an insurance clerk. Friend of Mr. A. Hawkes of Hadleigh and associated with the Caravan Club. He enlisted in the Honourable Artillery Company at the outbreak of war as a private, 2324 and was commissioned in the Royal Fusiliers, 31st October 1914. He served at Gallipoli, Egypt and Khartoum and had spent four or five months in hospital at Alexandria prior to going to France. Entered France 26th March 1916. His commanding officer wrote that he was 'very popular a very good officer and one whom the country could ill afford to spare'. His father, L. H. Haycraft Esq., Rowe Lane, Sydney, New South Wales applied for his medals. Memorial Ref. B. 44., Hawthorn Ridge Cemetery No.2, Auchonvillers, France.

HAYNES, Second Lieutenant, Clifford Skemp. Wounded slightly in the arm and gallantly continued later meeting his death at the head of his men, being the only officer remaining in his company, 1st July 1916. B Coy., 15th Bn., Durham Light Infantry. Aged 25. Youngest son of the Reverend and Mrs. W. B. Haynes. Native of Caxton, Cambs. Attended Dudley Training College. Teacher under the Stoke-on-Trent Education Authority. Husband of Lizzie Abigail Haynes, of the Cabin, Grimsby Road, Louth, Lincs., being married 3rd April 1916. Enlisted with his brother with the outbreak of war in the Loyal North Lancashires on the 7th September 1914 as private, No 2536. Promoted to lance corporal 6th March 1915 and commissioned 15th January 1916. Entered France, 12th February 1915. On the 15th July 1916 his father wrote if it is possible we may definitely as to the fate as to disposal of the body, as letters had been returned before official notification came marked up 'Killed in action 1st July 1916'. Brother killed 17th June 1917, Corporal Henry Hillas Haynes with the Loyal North Lancashires. His widow applied for his medals. Memorial Ref. Pier and Face 14 A and 15 C., Thiepval Memorial, France. WO 339/54360

HEAD, Lieutenant, Albert Everest. Family received a telegram stating 'missing', he died a soldiers death, killed in action, most gallantly leading his men, later reported that he fell wounded near the German front line at about 7.30am, 1st July 1916. 20th (Tyneside Scottish) Bn., Northumberland Fusiliers. Aged 22. Eldest son of Mr. and Mrs. William John Head (manager of the Silvertown Rubber Company, Westgate Road, Newcastle), of 26, Park Parade, Whitley Bay, Northumberland. Native of Tottenham, London. Born 9th July 1893. Employed North British and Mercantile Insurance Company, Mosley Street, Newcastle. Attested 26th January 1914. Attached to the Territorial Battalion prior to the outbreak of war, No. 1866 Northumberland Fusiliers and received a commission, 1st December 1914. He got his second star for proficiency in scientific examinations relating to signalling and machine-guns, before going to France and soon after his arrival was given responsibility as a machine-gun officer. Educated at Armstrong College, Newcastle studying for an actuarial degree. Treated for rubella, April 1916. He was buried in the original German line, 500 yards south of La Boiselle church. His father applied for his medals. Memorial Ref. Sp. Mem. A. 1., Gordon Dump cemetery, Ovillers-La Boiselle, France. WO 339/15016

Willingly Gave His Life For His Country No Love Greater Than This

HEAD, Captain, Leslie Dymoke. The battalion advanced at 7.30am but immediately came under intense machine-gun fire with A and B companies suffering very heavy casualties, leading companies had crawled about 25 yards when the machine guns opened up, 1st July 1916. A Coy. 9th Bn., King's Own Yorkshire Light Infantry. Aged 28. Younger son of Dr. Percy T. (surgeon), and Louisa A. Head, of "The Gables," Staines, Middx. Husband of Annette Marris (Formerly Head), of Lucerne, Slinfold. Horsham, Sussex. Born in Eastbourne, 29th February 1888. He was educated at Eastbourne College from 1902 to 1903 and at Bradfield College from January 1904 to December 1905 where he served as a private with the 1st Berkshire Cadets for two years. On leaving school he went to work as a clerk for F.G.A. Povah Esq. and others at Lloyd's Royal Exchange E.C in 1907. Leslie applied for a commission in the 3rd (County of London) Bn., Royal Fusiliers on the 26th March 1909 and was commissioned as a second lieutenant in the battalion on the 19th April 1909. Following the outbreak of war, he applied for a commission in the infantry on the 21st August 1914 in an application which was supported by E. L. Richardson MA, assistant master and housemaster at Bradfield. Leslie was commissioned as a second lieutenant in the King's Own Yorkshire Light Infantry on the 22nd of September 1914, was promoted to lieutenant on the 31st October 1914 and was commanding officer of A Company. He was married at All Saints Church, Margaret Street, Marylebone on the 12th June 1915 to Caroline Annette (née Hind later Marris) later of Lucerne, Slinfold in Sussex. Leslie was promoted to captain on the 10th September 1915 and embarked for France with his battalion from Folkestone on board the SS St. Seriol on the same day, docking at Boulogne at 1.00am the following morning. Listed on the Lloyd's War Memorial. Originally buried Becourt-Fricourt Road, map reference 57d.26.d.1.6. His mother applied for his medals. Memorial Ref. X. A. 6., Gordon Dump Cemetery, Ovillers-La Boiselle, France. WO 339/14708

Living For Ever In Our Love Enshrined R.I.P

HEALD, Captain, Geoffrey Yates. Reported as missing and his body subsequently found and identified, Thiepval, 1st July 1916. Commanding B Company (support of A Coy who had taken up positions near Oblong Wood). He had led very bravely and was witnessed to shot three Germans with his revolver, he was then hit by machine-gun fire and killed instantly. 15th Bn., Lancashire Fusiliers. Aged 20. Younger son of William (worked for Williams Deacon Bank) and Sarah Ann Heald, of Northfield Urmston, Manchester. He had an elder brother Oliver and a sister, Miss Jessie E. Hadfield of 4 Old Hall Lane Worsley. He was born 16th November 1895. Geoffrey won a scholarship to Manchester Grammar School, where he was in the OTC and he became a sergeant in St. Clements Church Lads Brigade, Urmston. He was an actuarial clerk with the Refuge Assurance Co. Manchester. Probationer of the Faculty of Actuaries and Institute of Actuaries. Second Lieutenant under Lieutenant Abercrombie when he was nineteen. For gallantry in May he was recommended for promotion and gazetted in June 1916. Commemorated Memorial St. Clement's Church Lads Brigade (Urmston) and St. Clement's. Close friend of Lieutenant Clarence Harold Wright also killed on 1st July 1916. In his memory his mother organised a concert to raise funds for the Lancashire Fusiliers comforts fund.

Mother applied for his medals, c/o William Deacons Bank Ltd. St. Anne Street, Manchester. Mrs. Heald, Rockside Hydropathic Establishment, Matlock decided his inscription. Memorial Ref. V. E. 1., Lonsdale Cemetery, Authuille, France.

Farewell Loved Boy Sleep On And Rest Your Warfare Here Is O'er

HEALY, Lieutenant, John Frederick. Reported as killed Aveluy Wood, 1st July 1916, official date 2nd July 1916. 3rd Bn. attd. 9th Bn., Royal Irish Rifles. Aged 19. Elder son of George F. and Dorothea Healy, of Peafield, Blackrock, Co. Dublin. Born at Dublin. He was educated at Avoca School, Blackrock, from whence he went to Elstow (Bedford County) School, where he remained about five years, being in his time both house and school captain. He also served in the school OTC. He then entered Trinity College, Dublin, and joined the 3rd Royal Irish Rifles before he was 18 years old. He was attached to the 9th Bn., the West Belfast Regiment, April 1916 at the time of his death. Served about 16 months in the army, including nearly four months at the Front, since 15th March 1916. Father applied for his medals. Memorial Ref. Sp. Mem. 2., Mill Road Cemetery, Thiepval, France.

"Quis Separabit ?"

HEATH, Lieutenant, Henry James, MC. He was seen to be wounded, but still directed his men, reported missing and presumed to have died on the 1st July 1916. 16th Bn., Middlesex Regiment. Aged 39. Son of George and Eliza Barbara Heath. Born at Alton, Hants. Attended Farnham Grammar School and named on the school's war memorial. Educated Beauchamp College, Lyons. Went to Egypt to work for a large cotton firm. Sergeant, 988, Middlesex Regiment. Commissioned 28th January 1915. Military Cross awarded for commanding his platoon with great coolness and courage and when severely wounded he continued to urge his men on and issue instruction, Gazetted 25th September 1916. Medals to his parents at Waverley Road, Farnham. Memorial Ref. A. 84., Hawthorn Ridge Cemetery No. 1, Auchonvillers, France.

HEATH, Second Lieutenant, William Hutsby. Reported missing, went over with the third wave, hit in the stomach about fifty yards in front of the German wire, and died almost immediately, 1st July 1916. Lewis Gun Officer. 1st /6th Bn., North Staffordshire Regiment. Son of Robert Heath (police superintendent) of Burton Police and Eliza Ann Heath. Born 24th May 1893. Educated at Tamworth and Stafford grammar schools. He worked at the Royal Insurance Offices in Birmingham. He attested as private, No. 2847 on 4th September 1914 in the 6th South Staffordshire's and went to France on 3rd March 1915. He was commissioned into 3/6th North Staffordshire's on 6th September 1915. His older brother Corporal Horace Godfrey Heath served in Salonika. His father applied for his medals. Memorial Ref. Pier and Face 14 B and 14 C., Thiepval Memorial, France.

HEATON, Second Lieutenant, Eric Rupert. Killed in action, picked off before he got through the wire, last seen near Hawthorn Ridge crater shot in the leg, 1st July 1916. Remains recovered 1917. 14th Bn. attd. 16th Bn., Middlesex Regiment. Aged 22. Youngest son of Reverend Daniel Heaton (formerly superintendent of the Wesleyan Circuit and later Scunthorpe) and of Mrs. Heaton of Cressbrook, 46, Pembroke Crescent, Hove, Sussex previously Scunthorpe. Educated Guildford Grammar School and was with Messrs. Snell and Pomeroy, dentists of Woking when war broke out. Played cricket for Guildford Grammar School XI and Woking Cricket Club and football for the Melrose Club. Studying medicine at Birkbeck College, London University. Member of the OTC. Keen interest in the Wesleyan Church, of the Sunday School he was for some time secretary. Went to France, 8th February 1916. Reported missing 29th July 1916. Trench called Heaton Road Trench. Last letter, home wrote; 'If I fall, do not let things be black for you. Be cheerful, and you will living then always to my memory.' Reverend Heaton applied for medals in respect of his son. Memorial Ref. A. 89., Hawthorn Ridge Cemetery No.1, Auchonvillers, France.

Our Youngest Son "I Came Out Willingly To Serve My King And Country"

HELLARD, Second Lieutenant, John Alexander. Missing believed killed, 1st July officially 2nd July 1916. Battalion history suggests 1st July 1916. 3rd Bn. attd. 1st Bn., Somerset Light Infantry. Aged 34. Younger Son of Edwin (solicitor) and Alice Jane Hellard, of "The Knoll," Stogumber. Born at Stogumber, Somerset on the 20th March 1882. Educated at the King's School Canterbury from January 1896 to July 1900 where was granted a junior scholarship in July 1896 and a senior scholarship in July 1900. He was a keen sportsman and played for the Rugby XV in 1899 and the Cricket XI in 1900. He was a member of the OTC. He also played county cricket as a right hand batsman for Somerset on two occasions against Worcestershire in 1907 at Bath, where he scored fifteen runs, and in 1910 at Worcester. On leaving school he became a solicitor's clerk and was admitted as a solicitor in June 1906. He moved to Ceylon on the 8th of February 1913 and practiced law at 7 Prince Street, Colombo. He enlisted as a bombardier in the Artillery Company, Colombo Town Guard on the 4th January 1915. He applied for a commission in the Special Reserve of Officers for the Somerset Light Infantry on the 24th March 1915. His application was accepted and a telegram was sent to the Governor of Colombo instructing him to send John Hellard home subject to him being medically fit but by the time it arrived he had already left for England on the 25th March 1915 and was commissioned as a probationary second lieutenant in the Somerset Light Infantry on the 27th April 1915, being confirmed in that rank on the 12th August. He was attached to the 1st Bn., of his regiment in May 1916 and landed in France on the 21st of May 1916. An interview was undertaken with Corporal 11403 George Hibbard B Company; 'We reached the 3rd or 4th line of German trenches. I saw Lieutenant Hellard hit though the head by a bullet - he dropped beside me. I crawled to him, and he was dead - he was hit in the wire between the 3rd and 4th line .... I crawled back myself." His father applied for his medals. Memorial Ref. II. A. 1., Serre Road Cemetery No.2, France.

HEMING, Second Lieutenant, Maurice Ivory. Seen to fall in front of the barb wire at Albert on the 1st July 1916, he was shot through the head and killed outright he did not move. D Coy., 2nd Bn., Royal Berkshire Regiment. Aged 23. Son of Charles and Gertrude Heming, of 18, Rattray Road, Brighton, London formerly 22 Temple Row, High Wycombe. Enlisted 23rd Bn., London Regiment, private, 3111, 22nd September 1914. Entered France, 14th March 1915. Suffered a gunshot wound to the back on the 15th June 1915 and returned to England to the 31st August 1915. Treated for influenza 6th to the 18th November 1915. Commissioned 7th May 1916. Captain Cahill who was in command of Maurice described that he was with his platoon and was hit, Maurice shouted to his company 'Come on' and fell before he could reach Captain Cahill. The captain could see blood coming from his tunic and feared that 'no hope could be entertained'. By August 1916 Captain Cahill had visited Maurice's parents and confirmed the circumstances, lacking official information they in turn wrote to the War Office for a death certificate. His mother applied for his medals. Memorial Ref. Pier and Face 11 D., Thiepval Memorial, France. WO 339/62160

HENDERSON, Captain, Andrew William. He fell leading his men, 1st July 1916. 1st Bn., Rifle Brigade. Elder son of William Henderson of William Terrace, Glasgow. Born 13th June 1894. He entered Sunnyside, Winchester College, 1908 to 1913, from Mr. Bernard Rendall's School at Copthorne and in 1911 was appointed a Commoner Prefect; his last year he was Head of House, in senior division of Sixth Book, President of the Golf Club and a colour-sergeant in the OTC. Also educated Kelvinside Academy. Fine golf player. After a short period in Germany he went up in October 1913 to Balliol College, Oxford. August 26th 1914 received his commission. Entered France, 24th November 1914. Very early in the war he was gazetted to the 6th Bn., Rifle Brigade and at a later date obtained a regular commission in the 1st Bn. Rapidly promoted to captain. Brother of Captain Thomas Harvey Henderson, MC, Rifle Brigade, who fell on November 30th 1917. Miss Mary E. Henderson, Grosvenor Street, W1 applied for his medals. Memorial Ref. Pier and Face 16 B and 16 C., Thiepval Memorial, France.

HENEKER, Lieutenant Colonel, Frederick Christian. Killed 1st July 1916 by a shell before they had left the third line trenches, La-Boisselle. Leinster Regiment attached 21st Bn., Northumberland Fusiliers given command on the afternoon of the 30th June, 1916. Aged 43. Third son of Richard William (Mayor) and Elizabeth Tuson Heneker, of Sherbrooke, Quebec, Canada. Husband of Constance Heneker, of Berily House, Southlands Grove, Bickley, Kent. Brother, William in the Connaught Rangers. Entered France, September 1914. Recovered from a shrapnel wound he received in 1915, wound to the hand in hospital from 30th January to 4th February 1915. His wife, Mrs. C. M. Heneker Lynwood Avenue, Epsom applied for his medals and decided his inscription. Two children received payment on the compassionate list; Christian Lee born 5th April 1909 and Frances Constance born 6th June 1916. Original burial map reference 57c.X.20.a. Memorial Ref. III. A. 1., Ovillers Military Cemetery, France.

He Died The Noblest Death A Man May Die

HERAPATH, Second Lieutenant, Alfred Maltravers. Reported to be killed by a shell, 'he was seen just before a big shell exploded and then he was gone', Hebuterne, 1st July 1916. 8th Bn., York and Lancaster Regiment attd. Machine Gun Corps. Aged 28. Son of Major (Yorkshire Regiment) and Mrs. Edwin L. Herapath, of Homebush, Burnham, Somerset. Born Dublin, 24th August 1887. Educated Dean Close School, Cheltenham (1901 to 1905). Attended Harper Adams, 1905. Enlisted Royal Fusiliers and commissioned entering York and Lancaster. Brother, Second Lieutenant Norman Finnis Herapath killed 11th April 1917, 1st Bn., Somerset Light Infantry. Another brother John survived the war. Application for medals by his father. Memorial Ref. IV. S. 10., Euston Road Cemetery, Colincamps, France.

I Know That My Redeemer Liveth

HERBERT, Second Lieutenant, Ronald Crouch. At 7.30 am the battalion assaulted the German trenches to the front of left half of A1 subsector on a front of about 400 yards – After 12 hours fighting the final objective west of Montauban was reached and consolidated on a front of about 280 yards, killed in No Man's Land or close to Breslau Trench, 1st July 1916. 7th Bn., The Queen's (Royal West Surrey Regiment). Aged 20. Son of Harry Crouch Herbert. Registration as temporary boy clerk, gazette 4th July 1911. Husband of Annie Rosamond Herbert, of 248, Upland Road, Dulwich, London. Private, 2266, 15th Bn., London Regiment. Entered France, 17th March 1915. Commissioned Royal West Surrey's, 11th May 1915. Father applied for his medals. Original map reference for burial 62c.A.8.b.4.7 with other fallen casualties from the 1st July. Memorial Ref. III. O. 4., Dantzig Alley British Cemetery, Mametz, France.

HERDER, Lieutenant, Hubert Clinton. Died at Beaumont Hamel, seen lying dead at our own front line, 1st July 1916. 1st Bn., Newfoundland Regiment. Aged 25. Son of William James (proprietor, Evening Telegram) and Elizabeth Herder, of St. John's, Newfoundland. Born 29th July 1891, St John's, Newfoundland, Canada. Enlisted on October 1st 1914. He was rapidly promoted and served on the Western Egyptian frontier as transport officer. Commissioned April 1915. One of the advanced guards for the Dardanelles sailing on the transport Minewarka on the 18th August 1915. After rejoining his regiment he sailed for Marseilles in April 1916. Famous ball player and hockey player as well as one of the strongest men in the regiment. Brother Lieutenant Arthur Herder died of wounds 3rd December 1917. Correspondence on inscription to Lt. Col. T. Nangle, DGR&E, Newfoundland Contingent, 47 Victoria Street, SW1. Memorial Ref. C. 69., Y Ravine Cemetery, Beaumont-Hamel, France.

He Giveth His Beloved Sleep

HERDMAN, Second Lieutenant, George Andrew. He led his men, they say, with a smiling face, performing at the end a gallant action which his superior officer says saved many lives in the battalion, 1st July 1916. He went to the assistance of a party of bombers and was killed by a German grenade, conflicting accounts suggest blown to pieces by a shell. 18th Bn., The King's (Liverpool Regiment). Aged 20. Only son of Professor William Abbott Herdman (Zoology Department, University of Liverpool) and Mrs. Abbott Herdman, of Croxteth Lodge, Liverpool and grandson of Mr. Robert Herdman RSA of Edinburgh. Born September 28th 1895, in Liverpool. Educated Greenbank School and Clifton College, 1909 - 1914. Admitted as Entrance Scholar at Trinity, 25th June 1914. Cambridge OTC. Second lieutenant, gazetted January 1915. Entered France, 23rd August 1915. Father applied for his medals. Memorial Ref. Pier and Face 1 D 8 B and 8 C., Thiepval Memorial, France.

HERTSLET, Second Lieutenant, Harold Cecil. Reported as missing, believed killed, 1st July 1916. 6th Bn., attd 16th Bn., Middlesex Regiment. Aged 27. Son of Gerald and Ethel Hertslet. Husband of Helen Dorothy Hertslet, of Nosoton Heights, Conn., USA. Grandson of Sir Edward Hertslet, KCB of the Foreign Office. Educated at Merchant Taylors. Emigrated to New York 1906 and was a US citizen. Played cricket for Crescent Athletic Crick Club, Brooklyn, New York. A prominent member of the Crescent Athletic Club, New York, 1910 and 1911. Married 13th February 1912 in New York. At the outbreak of war was a partner in the firm of Messrs. Dowler, Forbes and Co. of New York. Returned to England to enlist. Wife and son, Victor Beardsley resided New York. Confirmed in rank, 4th April 1916. Commemorated Merchant Taylors' School, Northwood. Resided Thorpe Bay. Medals to Connecticut, USA and compassionate payments to his son. Memorial Ref. II. E. 21., Auchonvillers Military Cemetery, France.

Battle Of Somme 1916

HESLOP, Captain, George Henry. Killed within ten minutes of zero hour, Beaumont Hamel, shot between the British front line and Hawthorn Ridge crater, 1st July 1916. D Coy., 16th Bn., Middlesex Regiment. Aged 21. Born 1895. Son of George Henry Heslop MA, (Headmaster of Sevenoaks School) and Gertrude Heslop, of 41, The Park, Mitcham, Surrey. Born at Sandbach in Cheshire on the 10th April 1895. He was educated at Lancing College where he was in Olds House from September 1910 to July 1914. He was a member of the OTC where he achieved Certificate A. He was in the Cricket XI from 1911 to 1914 being captain in 1913 and 1914. Most promising all round cricketer, in the Lancing Eleven. Admitted as pensioner at Trinity College, Cambridge, October 1st 1914 but did not take it, due to the outbreak of war, choosing to join the army instead. Enlisted London. Commissioned September 1914. Wounded at Loos, September 1915. Wounded January 28th 1916. Father applied for his medals. His memory at Lancing College is honoured at Lancing in the award of the 'Heslop Bat'. Memorial Ref. B. 40., Hawthorn Ridge Cemetery No.1, Auchonvillers, France.

Pro Patria Pro Deo

HEWITT, Lieutenant, Holt Montgomery. Teams 1, 2, 3 and 16 under their officers Lieutenant H. Hewitt and 2nd Lieutenant N. Edinborough were completely wiped out in No Man's Land. At the time they were heading for a position known as Lisnaskea Trench, 1st July 1916. 109th Bn., Machine Gun Corps (Infantry). Aged 29. Third of four sons of James H. (manager in the Workshops for the Blind) and Jeannie D. Hewitt, of 97, Mornington Park, Bangor, Co. Down. Born in Belfast, Northern Ireland on the 11th June 1887. Educated at Belfast Royal Academical Institution he served an apprenticeship as an accountant and worked as a manager in a coal merchant, and played rugby half-back for Bangor and the North of Ireland Rugby Football Clubs. He was also a member of the UVF, serving two years with the North Down Battalion in Bangor. After enlisting in Bangor on 14th September 1914 with the 13th Battalion, Royal Irish Rifles, 17872 and being commissioned on 30th September 1914, he sailed to France on 4th October 1915. He subsequently transferred to the 9th Royal Inniskilling Fusiliers, alongside his brother, William, and then to the 109th Machine Gun Company on 24th January 1916. His brothers; Second Lieutenant William Arthur Hewitt killed 1st July 1916 and Lieutenant Ernest Henry Hewitt also fell on 15th/16th June 1915 and is commemorated on the Le Touret Memorial.

Holt is commemorated on the Bangor War Memorial and on a brass memorial tablet in St Comgall's Church, Bangor. Father applied for his medals. Original burial map reference 57d.R.25.a.2.10. Memorial Ref. XIX. D. 9., Mill Road Cemetery, Thiepval, France.

I Am The Resurrection And The Life

HEWITT, Second Lieutenant, William Lieutenant Colonel Ricardo reported that Wille led his platoon over the parapet, they got across to the German trenches in front of which they came across appalling machine-gun fire and Willie was hit. Sergeant Lally lay with him until he passed, 1st July 1916. 9th Bn., Royal Inniskilling Fusiliers. Aged 23. Youngest son of James H. (manager of workshop for the Blind, Royal Avenue, Belfast) and Jeannie D. Hewitt, of Altamont, Bangor, Co. Down. Educated at Belfast Royal Academical Institution. Members of the UVF and played Rugby for the North of Ireland Club. Joined the Belfast Banking Company and served in Markets Branch as a bank clerk. Entered France, 25th March 1916. His brothers; Lieutenant Ernest Henry Hewitt fell on the 15th June 1916 and Lieutenant Holt Montgomery Hewitt fell on the 1st July 1916. Commemorated on the Bangor War Memorial, on a brass memorial tablet in St Comgall's Church, Bangor. His father applied for his medals. Memorial Ref. Pier and Face 4 D and 5 B., Thiepval Memorial, France.

HEYGATE, Captain, Claud Raymond. A Colonel saw him killed and ordered some men to carry him to the rear, 1st July 1916. 2nd Bn. attd. 10th Bn., King's Own Yorkshire Light Infantry. Aged 29. Second son of Major and Mrs. William Howley Beaumont and Helen Francis Heygate, of Roecliffe Manor, Loughborough, Leicestershire and a member of the Heygate family, Londonderry. Born 27th July 1886, Edinburgh. Attended Saint Ronan's School and whilst their excelled at sport leaving in 1900. Educated at Radley and RMC Sandhurst, and received his commission in the 1st Yorkshire Light Infantry in August, 1906. He returned to St Ronan's in the Summer of 1902 to participate in the "past v. present" annual cricket match. In 1905 he passed into RMC Sandhurst, "35th on the list of successful candidates" and whilst there was a member of their hockey team. Played for Warwickshire Gentlemen at cricket. At the outbreak of war he was at the depot of the regiment and went out with a draft from Hull, 26th August, 1914. He was present at the battle of Marne, the Aisne, and the first battle of Ypres, when he was wounded at Lorgues in both legs by shrapnel on the 26th October 1914. He was then drafted to Hull and proceeded to France about a month before his death. He was originally buried by a party from the 34th Division. In the return of his effects, his father only received an empty case for field glasses, on receipt he immediately wrote to the War Office who subsequently advised they had been retrieved from a fallen officer, 2nd Lieutenant G. H. Gorton. who fell on the 10th July 1916. In reply Claud's father wrote again to the War Office pointing out he had received no ID disc or any other effects, apart from the empty case, and thought this extraordinary! In his letters he continued 'I am sorry to think he has been robbed by the stretcher bearers'. The War Office response was to advise a very large number of officers and men were interred some of whom were unrecognisable. His father applied for the medals. Memorial Ref. Sp. Mem. B. II., Gordon Dump Cemetery, Ovillers-La Boisselle, France. WO 339/6585

Grant Him O Lord Eternal Rest Let Light Perpetual Shine Upon Him

HIBBERT, Second Lieutenant, Howard Morley. Reported missing, Gommecourt, 1st July 1916. A Coy., 1st /5th Bn., Sherwood Foresters (Notts and Derby Regiment). Aged 21. Son of Charles Morley Hibbert and Evangeline Hibbert, of 68, Broomgrove Road, Sheffield. Born 8th January 1895. Educated King Edward VII School, Sheffield and Sheffield University being a member of the OTC. Enlisted 22nd January 1915 as a private, 2264, in the 12th Royal Sussex Regiment. Commissioned 4th May 1915. September 1915 developed a heart condition returning to his battalion, entered France, 9th May 1916. Father applied for his medals. Memorial Ref. Pier and Face 10 C 10 D and 11 A., Thiepval Memorial, France.

The 1913 KES Cricket Team

Back Row L to R John Scott the Master in Charge. Killed in 1916. William Taylor (team secretary) killed at Arras 1917. A. E. Budd won the Military Medal, survived. Robert Matthews killed on the Somme. J. J. Kay survived the war. Eric Carr killed 1st July 1916. A. E. Furniss survived. Mr. J. W. Wright, (coach). Middle Frederick Marrs killed on the Somme 1917. G. B. Hill survived. F. Ambler (captain) survived. Howard Hibbert Killed 1st July 1916. Front A. E. Bagnall won Military Cross, survived. Caryl Battersby Killed on the Somme 1916

HICKING, Second Lieutenant, Francis Joseph. Killed in action, 1st July 1916. 13th Bn. attd. 10th Bn., West Yorkshire Regiment (Prince of Wales's Own). Aged 19. Born 20th May 1896. Youngest son of Joseph William and Kate Florence Hicking, of Halsey House, Pittville, Cheltenham, formerly of Ruddington, Notts. Born Nottingham, 20th May 1896. Educated Bramcote School, Scarborough and Uppingham. In the Uppingham OTC for three years, 1911 to 1914. On leaving, 25th January 1915 he joined the Honourable Artillery Company, No. 3004, gaining his commission three months later on the 27th April 1915. Entered France prior to 11th December 1915. On 15th December 1915 wounded in the right thigh with a gunshot wound and returned to duty 30th March 1916. His brother, Lieutenant George Graham Hicking also fell on the 1st July 1916. Ruddington St. Peter's War Memorial. His father applied for his medals. In 1917 reported buried Fricourt Row B Grave 6. Memorial Ref. C. 4., Fricourt New Military Cemetery, France. WO 339/34251

His Duty Was Well Done

HICKING, Lieutenant, George Graham. Killed 1st July 1916. 6th Bn., York and Lancaster Regiment. Aged 22. Born 14th September 1893. Second son of Joseph William and Kate Florence Hicking, of Halsey House, Pittville, Cheltenham, Formerly of Ruddington, Notts. He was an articled clerk. Educated at Broadgate School, Nottingham, and Uppingham left in April 1910. Left Liverpool for Montreal on the 9th May 1913. When war was declared he was fruit farming in Canada, and immediately returned to England and joined the Public Schools Corps, and received his commission two months later. In September, 1915, he was sent out to the Dardanelles, and several months later invalided home with dysentery. Reported for duty on the 31st January 1916. His brother Second Lieutenant Francis Joseph Hicking also fell on the 1st July 1916. Ruddington St. Peter's War Memorial. Father applied for his medals. Memorial Ref. Addenda Panel, Pier and Face 4 C., Thiepval Memorial, France.

HICKMAN, Second Lieutenant, William Christie. Killed whilst serving as a forward observation officer, attd. 4th Bn., Northumberland Fusiliers, 1st July 1916. 175th Bde., Royal Field Artillery. Second son of Mr. Hickman, Trunkwell House, Beech Hill, Reading. Attended Marlborough College. Proceeded to Cauis College, Cambridge and then onto Canada returning at the outbreak of war. One brother was a prisoner of war in Germany the other in Turkey. His widow remarried, Mrs. Curwen, Market Street, Shepherd Market, W1 and applied for his medals. Original burial map reference 57d.X.20.a where his grave was marked with a cross. Memorial Ref. II. A. 1., Ovillers Military Cemetery, France.

HIGGINS, Second Lieutenant, Cuthbert George. Died of wounds, 1st July 1916. 6th Bn., West Yorkshire Regiment (Prince of Wales's Own). Son of William C. and Maud Ella Higgins, 64 Hamilton Terrace, London, NW8. Educated Eton College. March 1915 from the 5th Bn., to be second lieutenant. Went to France 10th August 1915. Parents applied for his medals. Unusually his Medal Index Card had the words; 'death assumed 1st July 1916'. Memorial Ref. Pier and Face 2 A 2 C and 2 D., Thiepval Memorial, France.

HILL, Captain, Barry. Killed whilst serving with A Company. Initially reported as wounded and missing, 1st July 1916. A Coy. 10th Bn., Royal Irish Rifles. Aged 30. Son of Squire and Sarah Hill, of Ballyclare, Co. Antrim. Resided University Street, Belfast. Former medical student and Queen's University, Belfast, Faculty of Medicine 1904-1907. Signed the Ulster Covenant at Saint Patrick's School, Jordanstown in 1912. Before the war, in practice as a dentist in University Street. He was a Company Commander in the South Belfast Regiment UVF, and joined the South Belfast Regiment on its formation. Entered France, September 1915. He was gazetted to captain, the appointment appearing in the Belfast Telegraph on the 27th March 1916. Still missing 26th December 1916. Commemorated by Queen's University, Belfast. His brother, S. Hill, Greenisland, Co. Antrim applied for his medals. Memorial Ref. Pier and Face 15 A and 15 B., Thiepval Memorial, France.

HILLMAN, Lieutenant, Harold Alexander Moore. The 7th Yorks were detailed to attack Fricourt, seize the village, and the wood beyond. The German front line ran almost parallel to our own at a distance alternating from 200 to 300 yards. The order of advance was three companies in the front line, with B Company in the centre Nos. 4 and 5 platoons of B Company were to push forward with No. 6 in close support. No. 7 platoon, commanded by Mr. Clarke, were in local reserve to the company and were not to advance until the German front line was taken. The first two platoons were no sooner over than they were met by a withering fire from the enemy machine-guns at close range. Mr. Hornsby, commanding No. 5 platoon, fell mortally wounded before they had advanced ten yards. No. 6 were now ready to advance and leave No. 7 in the trench. Mr. Hillman, command No. 6, climbed the parapet and ordered his platoon forward. He was shot immediately through the head. 1st July 1916. 11th Bn. attd. 7th Bn., Yorkshire Regiment. Aged 30. Son of Arthur Stock Hillman and Annie Marie Hillman of 12 Quadrant Road. Born 1st February 1885 at Wallington, Surrey. Educated High School, Croydon. Employed by Law Guarantee and Trust Society. Society entertainer. Enlisted in 19th Royal Fusiliers as a private, 490, September 1914. Second Lieutenant, James Henry Clarke, and Lieutenant's Hillman's bodies were laid together on the fire step they were taken away and buried behind the line, near the railway which ran between the opposing trenches. Original burial map reference 62d.F.9.a.8.8 Harold's sister, Miss L. L. Hillman applied for his medals and decided his inscription. Memorial Ref. VI. A. 3., Dantzig Alley British Cemetery, Mametz, France.

Beloved By All

HILTON, Captain, Clarence Stuart. Killed instantaneously whilst leading the company in an attack upon the front line of German trenches, 1st July 1916. 2nd Bn., Middlesex Regiment. Son of Mr. and Mrs. Ernest F. Hilton of 188, Cromwell Road, London. Born 1889. Educated King's College and entered Middlesex Regiment from RMC Sandhurst in 1909. Brother also fell, Captain Herbert Philip Hilton on the 14th February 1915. On the same day his brother was killed, Clarence was taken to hospital suffering from frostbite and spent four days under treatment. Medical records show five officers from the Middlesex Regiment suffered from frostbite on this day. In a letter to Second Lieutenant Philip Maurice Elliott's parents, the Reverend H. B. Burnaby (Regimental Padre) wrote; "Thus he lies where the 2nd Middlesex so splendidly opened the great attack, buried close to his brother officers who fell with him, Captain Meeke, Captain Hilton and Lieutenant Van den Bok". Mother applied for his medals. Memorial Ref. Pier and Face 12 D and 13 B., Thiepval Memorial, France.

HIND, Second Lieutenant, Ernest William Gayles. Lieutenant Hind fell in the advance on July 1st whilst gallantly leading his men in an attack on the German trenches, taking cover in a shell hole he raised his head to look for a gap in the wire and was shot in the head, he decided to go over with his men, 1st July 1916. At 7.00am left Advanced HQ and headed to the advanced trench were they would be ready to go over. 15th Bn., Royal Irish Rifles. Aged 22. Eldest son of William Edward and Adelaide Hind, of the Cottage, Holywood, Co. Down who had three other sons in the army. Member of the Bangor Rugby Football Club. On the outbreak of the war he was on the staff of Messrs. W. T. Graham and Co., accountants, Scottish Temperance Buildings, Belfast, but at once offered his services, Royal Irish Rifles, corporal, 17882, and obtained his commission in the Royal Irish Rifles, 31st December 1914. Enlisted 1st Co. Down Volunteers. Entered France, 3rd October 1915. Ernest was about to go into training with the RFC when he was killed. Father applied for his medals. Memorial Ref. Pier and Face 15 A and 15 B., Thiepval Memorial, France.

HIND, Lieutenant Colonel, Lawrence Arthur, MC. He got to the German wire and saw it intact, just after Captain Gotch was killed by a shell he took refuge in a shell hole, hiding behind a small bank he got on his hands and knees to get a better look, he was hit in the head by a single bullet and died, 1st July 1916. Reported missing believed killed, Gommecourt, C Coy., 1st /7th Bn., Sherwood Foresters (Notts and Derby Regiment). Aged 38. Son of Jesse and Eliza Hind, of Edwalton, Nottingham. Born Nottingham. Husband of Eliza Montgomery, of Ardara, Comber, Co. Down whom he married on 26th April 1906. He was educated at Lambrook, Berks, Uppingham School and obtained an Honours Law Degree at Trinity Hall, Cambridge in 1899 and was admitted to the Bar in December 1902. He practiced law in Nottingham with the firm Wells and Hind of Nottingham and of Hind Sons and Roberts, solicitors, of 33 Chancery Lane, London. Member of the Territorial Force some years before the war. Mobilised August 1914, as captain, 7th (Robin Hood) Bn., Notts and Derby Regiment (Sherwood Foresters), promoted Major 1915, became Lieutenant-Colonel, 18th May 1916 being battalion commander from the 1st May 1916. Went to the Front, 26th February 1915. Wounded at Hooge July 1915. Twice Mentioned in Despatches. Awarded the Military Cross, 3rd June 1916. His wife applied for his medals. Two children, Eileen and Edith on the compassionate list and received pension. Commemorated Comber Non-Subscribing Presbyterian Church, High Pavement Unitarian Church in Nottingham and Comber and District War Memorial. The latter being unveiled by his wife in April 1922. Memorial Ref. Pier and Face 10 C 10 D and 11 A., Thiepval Memorial, France.

HIRST, Second Lieutenant, Cecil Pollock. Killed in action at Fricourt, 1st July 1916. Shot through the head with No. 4 Company, D Coy whilst they were going through a machine-gun barrage. 8th Bn., Devonshire Regiment, war diary records with the 9th Bn., Devonshire Regiment. Born 26th April 1892. Keble College, Oxford. Entered college in Michaelmas Term, 1911. History Scholar. A member of the University Contingent of the Officers' Training Corps. A member of the 1st Hockey XI, 1912 - 1914 (captain in 1914). President of the Essay Club, 1914. 3rd History B.A., 1915. Commenced service in June 1915. Reinterred 1920. Original burial map reference 62d.F.10.d.7.3 Memorial Ref. IV. J. 4., Dantzig Alley British Cemetery, Mametz, France. WO 339/5494

HIRST, Second Lieutenant, William. A Coy., under Captain Roos with 2nd Lieuts. Hirst, Anderson and Kell in file in front end of Nairne Trench and along Traffic Trench from Nairne to John Copse. To proceed in file across No Man's Land immediately following assaulting waves. Many casualties were also caused by machine-gun and rifle fire to which A and B companies were much exposed owing to levelling of Nairne Trench etc. He met his death while gallantly leading his men in the face of a violent storm of shot and shell, 1st July 1916. Reported to have been shot in the head by a machine-gun bullet just after going over the top. A Coy. 14th Bn., York and Lancaster Regiment. Aged 30. Son of John and Jessie Hirst, of Wombwell, Yorks. Husband of Bertha Hirst nee Lockwood, of Wath-on-Dearne, Yorks married August 1915. Mine surveyor for the Wombwell Main Colliery and an instructor at the Sheffield University. Leader of the Wombwell Church Lads Brigade. On the 11th July locally reported wounded. Mrs. B. Tyler (widow remarried), Albert Bridge, Battersea Park applied for his medals and decided his inscription. Memorial Ref. Plot 1. Row E. Grave 16., Bertrancourt Military Cemetery, France.

All I Had I Gave

HITCHON, Lieutenant, James Foldys. Killed around 7.30am, just after going over the parapet he was shot in the abdomen and fell into a shell hole, 1st July 1916. Y Coy., 10th Bn. attd. 11th Bn., East Lancashire Regiment. Aged 21. Son of George Henry (Head of firm, Hitchon & Pickup, architects and surveyors, Burnley) and Margaret Hitchon, of the Grove, South Promenade, St. Anne's-on-the-Sea, Lancs. Native of Burnley but lived at Hoghton Bank last four to five years. Born 4th July 1894. Educated Sedbergh (1908 – July 1910), studied architecture and entered his father's firm. Was on the staff in England up to 1st June 1916. When he received orders for France. Enlisted 5th September 1914 as private, No. 2233, 4th Bn., The Loyal North Lancashire Regiment. Appointed second lieutenant, 10th Bn., East Lancashire Regiment, 20th January 1915. Appointed lieutenant, 27th October 1915. Entered France, 5th June 1916. Attached 11th Bn., East Lancashire Regiment, 17th June 1916. Father applied for his medals. Memorial Ref. A. 16., Queens Cemetery, Puisieux, France.

Of Burnley, Lancashire Son Of George Henry And Margaret Hitchon

HOARE, Captain, Richard Lennard. Left centre company, 'C' crossed the enemy line, though a large part of it under Captain Hoare was held up by uncut wire and its gallant leaders was annihilated with rifle and bomb fire, reported missing, killed by shrapnel, 1st July 1916. C Coy., 12th Bn., London Regiment (The Rangers). Aged 33. Third son of Laura Hoare, of Summerhill, Benenden, Cranbrook, Kent, and William Hoare. Born at Staplehurst, Kent. Educated Lambrook, Berkshire, Eton College and Sandhurst. He received his commission as second lieutenant, August 1914 in the London Regiment and was promoted to the rank of captain in May 1915. Entered the army at a young age, commissioned into the Royal West Kent Regiment in 1902 and left to join the British American Tobacco Company later moving to Hoare, Gothard and Bond, coal factors. Entered France, 24th December 1914. Wounded April 1915 and rejoined his regiment, March 1916. His cousin Major Vincent Robertson Hoare was killed 15th February 1915 and previously commanded the same company. Grandson of Sir J. Farnaby Lennard, Bart., of Wickham Court, West Wickham. Father applied for his medals. Memorial Ref. I. C. 1., Gommecourt British Cemetery No.2, Hebuterne, France.

" And The Leaves Of The Tree Were For The Healing Of The Nations " Rev.XXII.2

HOBBS, Second Lieutenant, Eric. Mortally wounded in the afternoon, (between 4.00pm and 4.51pm) at the time he was well ahead of the battalion bombing along Fritz Trench in a magnificent way, when he was killed by a machine gun positioned at the end of a straight section of trench, 1st July 1916. The same machine gun would also account for Lieutenant Leslie Terrett Day, Second Lieutenant Gill and Lieutenant Gomersall. 2nd Bn., The Queen's (Royal West Surrey Regiment). Aged 21. Youngest son of Ernest (wine merchant) and Louisa Marian Hobbs, of Lea Hurst, Newbury, Berks. Born in Alverstoke, Hampshire in 1893. Educated at Bedford House School in Folkestone, and then for three terms only at St. Edward's School, Oxford (1911-12). After school he joined Thomas Wilson Sons and Company as an apprentice (cadet in merchant service) and was in the service of the Wilson line. When war was declared in August 1914 Eric was in Norway. He returned to Hull and sought leave from his apprenticeship in order to serve his country. Permission was granted and on 3rd September 1914 he enlisted into the Public Schools Battalion, private, 1629, posted to the 18th Bn. Commissioned into the Queen's (Royal West Surrey Regiment) as a second lieutenant on 11th May 1915. Sent to France where he joined the 2nd Battalion of the Queen's, on 8th October joining B Company and became its bombing officer. Eric was buried near where he fell, in a makeshift cemetery west of Fritz Trench, towards Bunny Wood originally recorded as ESE Montauban Sheet 62 Sq F.5. later confirmed as 62d.F.5.a.4.5. Commemorated Newbury War Memorial and St Edward's, Oxford. Father applied for his medals. His mother applied for his pension and a note was made , 'another son, Air Force'. Memorial Ref. III. D. 10., Dantzig Alley British Cemetery, Mametz, France. WO 339/43015

Greater Love Hath No Man Than This R.I.P.

HODGKINSON, Lieutenant, Alan. Not called upon to act till about 2.30pm Killed while trying to capture a machine-gun, at Mametz, 1st July 1916. A few minutes before he was killed he had captured over 200 prisoners with the help of a sergeant and four men. They were fired upon by another well placed machine-gun, with a sergeant and a corporal, Alan advanced in order to locate it, he went on further, alone, and had just exclaimed, 'It is in that ruined barn, I see the smoke,' when he fell, riddled by bullets from the gun. 2nd Bn., Royal Warwickshire Regiment (Divisional Reserve). Aged 23. Born 22nd March, 1893. Second and youngest son of Alexander Hodgkinson, M.B., of The Grange, Wilmslow, Cheshire and Bradshaigh, Farnham, Surrey. The family left Wilmslow in 1913. He was Mentioned in Despatches of November 30th, 1915. Entered Rugby School in 1907 and left in 1910. In 1911 he went up to St. John's College, Oxford, to prepare for his father's profession. On the outbreak of war he obtained a commission in the Royal Warwickshire Regiment, and went to the Front, attached to the 2nd Battalion, at the end of December, 1914 and promoted the following February. He fought in the Battles of Neuve Chapelle, Festubert, and Aubers Ridge, and was invalided home in September, 1915. He returned to France in March, 1916, and was given command of a company, with the temporary rank of captain. His mother applied for his medals. Original burial map reference 62d.F.5.c.6.2 and grave marked with a cross. Memorial Ref. II. G. 10., Dantzig Alley British Cemetery, Mametz, France.

HODGSON, Lieutenant, William Noel, MC. Bombing officer and when taking a fresh supply of bombs was shot in the throat, 1st July 1916. 9th Bn., Devonshire Regiment. Aged 23. Fourth and youngest child of the Rt. Reverend Henry Bernard Hodgson, D.D., 1st Bishop of St. Edmundsbury and Ipswich, and Penelope Hodgson (nee Warren), of Churcher's College, Petersfield, Hants. One of the war poets. Author of "Verse and prose in peace and war". Born 3rd January 1893. 1905, educated Durham School on a King's Scholarship where he steered in the second crew in 1907. In the XI, 1910, 1911; and in the XV, 1910. He won the Steeplechase in 1909 and 1911. In July 1911 he came up to Christ Church as an Exhibitioner. He gained a first class degree in Classical Moderations in March 1913 and stayed on to read the 'Greats'. He was a member of the University Contingent OTC. On the outbreak of war, he joined the 9th Battalion of the Devonshire Regiment. He trained in England, before landing at Le Havre on 28th July 1915 and being sent to trenches near Festubert. He was at the Battle of Loos on 25th September and was Mentioned in Despatches and awarded the Military Cross, 14th January 1916 for 'holding a captured trench for 36 hours without reinforcements or supplies during the battle.' Promoted to lieutenant, he spent some time in England before returning to France with his battalion and was in the front line trenches at Fricourt in February 1916. William was bombing officer for his battalion during the attack, responsible for keeping the men supplied with grenades. Within an hour of the attack it is said that he was killed by a machine-gun positioned at a shrine whilst taking grenades to the men in the newly captured trenches. The bullet went through his neck, killing him instantly. His batman was found next to him after the offensive had ended. His body was retrieved that night and brought back into the British Front Line position, along with over 160 of his comrades. They were buried in the vicinity of Mansell Copse. A ceremony was held at the burial site on 4th July. William had been writing poetry since at least 1913, and started publishing stories and poems in periodicals at the beginning of 1916, under the pen name, Edward Melbourne. His posthumous volume 'Verse and Prose in Peace and War" which was published in London, by Murray in 1917, ran into three editions. His poem 'Before Action' was written two days before he died. Wrote for The Spectator and Yorkshire Post. Originally buried Mansel Copse. Commemorated Sons and Daughters of the Anglican Church Clergy. His mother applied for his medals. Memorial Ref. A. 3., Devonshire Cemetery, Mametz, France. WO 339/19422

HOLCROFT, Second Lieutenant, Raymond Boycott. Wounded in the leg and was stooping down helping a corporal when he was shot and killed, 1st July 1916. Lewis gun officer. 9th Bn., Devonshire Regiment. Aged 20. Elder son of Arthur and Ethel Holcroft, of Hill End, St. Albans, Herts. Native of Codsall, Staffs. Born 23rd August 1895. Educated Wergs Preparatory School. He had been in the Cricket Eleven at Warwick School and also a sergeant in the OTC. Outbreak of war he was engaged in farming at Mr. Guildings Farm, Bushley, Gloucestershire and attested 18th August 1914, entered France, 3rd October 1915 obtained a commission. Twice wounded in on the 10th and 17th March 1916. Well-known in Tewkesbury cricket circles. Originally buried Mansel Copse sht. 6d. sq.F. 11.c. Effects returned were small pocket case with photos, Ingersoll wrist watch, silver wrist watch with black dial (damaged), fountain pen, two pipes and advance book. His father applied for his medals. Memorial Ref. A. 1., Devonshire Cemetery, Mametz, France. WO 339/18678

HOLE, Lieutenant, William Arthur. Last seen heading a bayonet charge against a German counter attack, reported that the attack took four line of trenches and reached a fifth but had to return, a counter attack was launched but repulsed, missing in the region of Contalmaison, 1st July 1916. 15th Bn., Royal Scots. Aged 28. Born 12th March 1888. Youngest son of William Hole, RSA, and E. D. Hole, of St. Margaret's Tower, Strathearn Road, Edinburgh. Educated Edinburgh Academy. At the beginning of the war, 10th August 1914 he enlisted in the 4th Royal Scots No. 19149 and obtained a commission in another battalion of the same regiment early in 1915, promoted April 1916. Entered France, January 1916. Miss M. Stevenson wrote to the War Office asking for further details as well as his parents. His identity disc was found on the ground by a member of a salvage company belonging to the 1st Division, this was returned to the family. His mother applied for his medals. Any correspondence on prisoner of war transcripts to go Edinburgh and an address in Copenhagen. Memorial Ref. Pier and Face 6 D and 7 D., Thiepval Memorial, France. WO 339/16924

Officers of the 15th Battalion The Royal Scots
Lieutenant Hole seating third from left. Major Stocks standing fifth from left

HOLLYWOOD, Lieutenant, Arthur Carson. Killed in vicinity of German trench, 1st July 1916. A Coy., 9th Bn., Royal Irish Fusiliers. Aged 24. Son of Elizabeth Hollywood and James (property broker and insurance agent) Hollywood, of Bayswater, Princetown Road, Bangor and later of Red Gorton, Helen's Bay, County Down. Born on 29th December 1891 in Ballymacarrett, Belfast. Educated at Belfast Royal Academical Institution. Old scholar of Friend's School, Lisburn, from September 1903 to July 1906. He joined the Royal University of Ireland in September 1909, member of the Queen's University, Belfast, Faculty of Medicine 1909 -1910 and served as the company commander of F Company of the Willowfield Battalion of the UVF in 1913 and 1914. He was working in his father's business on the Albertbridge Road, Belfast, as a rent agent, and living in Helen's Bay, County Down, when he joined the 108th Field Ambulance, RAMC part of the 36th Ulster Division, on 12th September 1914, as staff sergeant, 41015. Arthur was commissioned into the Royal Inniskilling Fusiliers on 19th April 1915, and joined the 9th Bn., Royal Irish Fusiliers in January 1916, being posted to A Company. He was subsequently appointed lieutenant on 29th February 1916. Entered France, 4th March 1916. He had been recommended for conspicuous gallantry several months before for recovering the body of a brother officer. The telegram announcing his death arrived at his parents' house one day apart from that announcing the death of his brother, Second Lieutenant James Hollywood who also died on the 1st July 1916. Arthur's body was brought in, and reported that he was buried in the Hamel village graveyard. Commemorated on the Bangor War Memorial. Medals applied for by his brother, D. Hollywood as his father died 20th June 1919. Memorial Ref. Pier and Face 15 A., Thiepval Memorial, France.

HOLLYWOOD, Second Lieutenant, James. 1st July 1916. 18th Bn. attd. 12th Bn., Royal Irish Rifles. Aged 23. Son of Elizabeth Hollywood and James Hollywood. Born on 16th April 1893. Educated at Belfast Royal Academical Institution. As well as the Institution, he was a scholar of Friend's School, Lisburn from September 1904 to July 1906. He spent one year in the Young Citizen Volunteers, and six months in the UVF. He left employment with Ross Brothers Linen Merchants in Linenhall Street to join the 18th Royal Irish Rifles on 14th September 1914 as a corporal, being appointed company quartermaster sergeant, 17888 on 14th October 1914 and subsequently being gazetted second lieutenant with the 12th Battalion on 5th May 1915. Entered France, 28th February 1916. The telegram announcing his death arrived one day apart from that announcing the death of his brother, Lieutenant Arthur Carson Hollywood who also died on the 1st July 1916. His body was found later in the year by men of the 2nd Hants Regiment but was subsequently lost.

Commemorated on the Bangor War Memorial. Medals applied for by his brother, D. Hollywood as his father died 20th June 1919. Memorial Ref. Pier and Face 15 A and 15 B., Thiepval Memorial, France.

HOLMES, Second Lieutenant, Aubrey. He fell with his men just as they arrived at the German trench they were about to take, 1st July 1916. Officer in charge of carriers, 2nd Bn., Essex Regiment. Second son of Benjamin Holmes, and of his wife, Alice Holmes, of 80 Oakwood Court, London and brother of Lieutenant Cyril Holmes, who died of pneumonia at Mudros, on December 21st, 1915. Born 18th October 1880. Attended Harrow. Balliol College, Oxford, MA. Was admitted to the Bar and entered Lincoln's Inn. Lieutenant Holmes, on the outbreak of the war, enlisted in the Queen Victoria Rifles, 9th London Regiment, private, 2299, and with them went to the Front, 4th November, 1914. He was afterwards given a commission in the Essex Regiment, 25th May 1915. Mrs. M. F. Holmes applied for his medals. Memorial Ref. A. 50., Redan Ridge Cemetery No.1, Beaumont-Hamel, France.

HONE, Lieutenant, Nathaniel Frederick. Reported as missing, 1st July 1916. Private L. M. Richardson stated he last saw him on that day about 9.00am when he took charge of a bombing party. 3rd Bn. attd. 9th Bn., Royal Irish Rifles. Aged 18. Elder son of Nathaniel Mathew Hone and Lillian Gertrude Hone, of Glenbourne, Sandyford, Co. Dublin. Born in Ceylon (Sri Lanka) where his father was a tea planter. Left St. Columba's College in 1913. Originally buried map reference 57d.R.19.d.65.45 and marked as unknown British soldier until 1924 he was identified by khaki, boots, disc, pocket book, charm, flask marked N.F. Hone, Royal Irish Rifles. Carrickfergus Roll of Honour. Chapel Memorial, Dublin. Medals to Mrs. J. S. Dyas, Sandyford, Co. Dublin. Mrs. L. G. Dyas choose his inscription, possibly being his mother whom remarried. Memorial Ref. VIII. A. 10., Tincourt New British Cemetery, France.

Still The Race Of Hero-Spirits Pass The Lamp From Hand To Hand

HORNE, Captain, David Douglas. Killed whilst gallantly leading the company at La Boisselle, 1st July 1916 and fell in the original front line German trench at approximately 7.40am, being buried there. 29th (Tyneside Scottish) Bn., Northumberland Fusiliers. Eldest son of John (Director of Messrs., Cowan, Sheldon & Co., Ltd, Engineers, Carlisle) and Mary Horne. Born 22nd October 1875. Educated Grosvenor College, Carlisle. Electrical engineer, Newcastle representative of Messrs. Crompton & Co., Ltd of London and Chelmsford. Joined the 1st Cumberland Volunteer Artillery, 8th June 1901 as second lieutenant. Promoted lieutenant July 1903. Resigned commission 1912. Volunteered at outbreak of war and promoted to captain. Married to Mabel Brooke in 1902 and had two daughters, Isabel Mary and Mabel Brooke. Medals to Highland Gardens, Leonards-on-sea. Memorial Ref. Pier and Face 10 B 11 B and 12 B., Thiepval Memorial, France.

HORNE, Second Lieutenant, James Anthony. At 12.30pm 2nd Lieutenant Horne who had displayed the greatest gallantry during the whole morning, organising and directing men all along Fellow Trench and shooting with a Lewis gun when all the team had been knocked out, decided to withdraw to the next line of German trenches and it was during this withdrawal that he was hit and beyond doubt killed, 1st July 1916. A note in the war diary records; 'Acts of Gallantry Most gallant conduct and bearing who by his example and leading inspired and helped all who came within his reach, a recommendation for the Victoria Cross'. B Coy., 16th Bn., London Regiment (Queen's Westminster Rifles). Aged 23. Elder son of the Reverend Joseph White Horne (former Vicar of St. James's, Islington and Vicar at St. Mary Magdalene, Monkton, Kent and Chesham Bois, Buckinghamshire,) and Katherine Grace Horne, of 8, Stradmore Gardens, Kensington, London formerly Ivy House, High Street, Highgate, North London. Born on 3rd August 1892 and was baptised on 1st September 1892 by his father. James received his secondary school education at Highgate School which he entered in September 1904. He left in July 1910 having been awarded a Choral Exhibition to Christ's College, Cambridge. He studied there for four years gaining honours in both parts of the Theological Tripos and being awarded his BA Degree, preparing for the Holy Orders. He had a fine voice and he regularly performed as a member of a vocal quartet. He was an active member of the Musical Society and served on their committee. Both his father and his uncle were alumni of the University of Cambridge. Enlisted almost immediately on the outbreak of the war as private No. 2535 in the 2/28th Bn., London Regiment (Artists Rifles) and afterwards took a commission in the London Regiment and was at the Front nine months before the

Great Advance. Medal Index Card states initial theatre of war as being Ypres, November 1915. Application made by his father for his medals. Memorial Ref. Sp. Mem. C. 5., Gommecourt British Cemetery No.2, Hebuterne, France.

Their Glory Shall Not Be Blotted Out

Christ's College Cambridge Matriculation 1910. James Anthony Horne seated third from right

HORNSBY, Second Lieutenant, Harold Gibson. Attack on Fricourt, Mr. Hornsby, commanding No. 5 platoon, fell mortally wounded before they had advanced ten yards, Fricourt, 1st July 1916. 7th Bn., Yorkshire Regiment. Aged 28. Only son of Jane Hornsby, of 7, Fladgate Road, Leytonstone, London, and fourth son of Michael Hornsby, of Saltburn-By-The-Sea. Resided 20 Redbridge Lane, Wanstead. Educated at Middlesbrough High School. Served his articles with a solicitor. Mr. H. G. Stevenson, town clerk of Darlington. Admitted a solicitor in March 1910. On the solicitor's staff of His Majesty's Customs and Excise, Lower Thames Street, E.C. Soon after the war broke out enlisted September 20th 1914, as a private, Bristol Bn., Gloucestershire Regiment transferred to 20th Hussars January 1915. Gazetted second lieutenant 11th Bn., Yorkshire Regiment, 13th March 1915. Went to the Front, October 1915. Talbot House visitors book, page 59, dated 11th February 1916 and page 48 dated 20th February 1916. Well known in Cleveland as an amateur footballer and cricketer. Brother Second Lieutenant Charles Michael Hornsby wounded in the right eye, right ear and cheek in August 1916. Commemorated Middlesbrough School and Saltburn War Memorial. His father applied for his medals and mother, Jane applied for the officers pension. Memorial Ref. A. 29., Fricourt British Cemetery, France. WO 339/36975

Until The Day Breaks And The Shadows Flee Away

HORROX, Second Lieutenant, Henry Millalieu. He had been wounded and had come back to a dressing station when he was killed by shell fire, 1st July 1916. 24th (Tyneside Irish) Bn., Northumberland Fusiliers. Aged 19. Son of Edward and Alice Horrox, of 14, McLaren Road, Edinburgh. Born 7th February 1897. George Watson's College, 1905 to 1913. Student of Medicine, University of Edinburgh. Edinburgh University OTC. Second lieutenant, April 1915. Went to France, 16th June 1916. Effects were prayer book, comb, photos and letters. Father applied for his medals. Memorial Ref. Pier and Face 10 B 11 B and 12 B., Thiepval Memorial, France. WO 339/40407

HORSNELL, Second Lieutenant, Alick George. Killed in action, 1st July 1916. 7th Bn., Suffolk Regiment. Aged 34. Son of Charles Henry (market gardener) and Mary Ann Horsnell, of The Bungalow, Hull Green, Matching Green, Harlow, Essex. Born Chelmsford, 1881. Educated Victoria School, Chelmsford. Artist and architect under Frederick Chancellor, Chelmsford's first mayor. Prize winning architect. Served in the territorials with the Artists Rifles, 28th London Regiment, private, 3310 from February 1915 and entered France, 9th May 1915. Gained a commission into the Suffolk Regiment, 23rd October 1915. Wounded November 1915 and returned to France. His father applied for his medals. Memorial Ref. Pier and Face 1 C and 2 A., Thiepval Memorial, France.

HORWOOD, Second Lieutenant, Ronald Bentall. Companies came under heavy artillery and machine-gun barrage immediately they appeared over the parapet causing heavy losses, he got hit within 20 to 30 yards of the German trenches when he was hit after getting out of shell hole in which he had been sheltering with Lieutenant Chawner, 'he did his duty like a soldier and died like a hero', 1st July 1916. 3rd Bn. attd. 1st Bn., Essex Regiment. Aged 22. Born 10th April 1894 in Stebbing, Essex. Eldest son of Henry Samuel (draper) and Caroline Sarah Horwood, of Leighton House, Victoria Road, Colchester formerly 26, High Street, Colchester. Pupil at Layer Hall Farm. Educated Colchester Royal Grammar School. Enlisted in the Royal Irish Rifles in September 1914 and served six months as a private and corporal when he was gazetted as a second lieutenant in April 1915 with the Essex Regiment. Previously severely wounded at Gallipoli. 'A very nice officer and thought a lot of his platoon'. His father applied for his medals. Memorial Ref. V. C. 3., Ancre British Cemetery, Beaumont-Hamel, France.

Until The Day Break

Ronald outside his mother's house a few weeks before his was killed

HOSKINS, Lieutenant, Cyril. Killed Beaumont Hamel, 1st July 1916. 1st /8th Bn., Royal Warwickshire Regiment. Aged 25. Son of Mr. and Mrs. J. E. Hoskins, of the Limes, Yardley, Birmingham. Father's firm, Hoskins and Sewell Ltd. Attended King Edward VI School, Stratford-upon-Avon from May 1903. Cyril enjoyed rugby at school and was captain of the 1st XV for 1907-1908. Two of his four brothers also attended King Edward's. On leaving, Cyril served in the Territorial Force, RAMC reaching the rank of sergeant, he retired on February 14th 1914, he immediately applied for a Territorial Force commission and was made a lieutenant in the 1/8th Bn., Royal Warwickshire Regiment. Mobilized in August 1914. On March 22nd 1915 the battalion sailed from Southampton and disembarked the following day at Le Havre, entered the trenches at Steenbeek on April 16th. On April 30th, Cyril Hopkins was conducting instruction in the field in the use of hand grenades when one of them exploded. The conclusion was that the grenade had been defective, the accident had arisen in the course of duty and no blame was attached to any individual. Cyril had been wounded in the left ankle, seriously enough for him to leave his unit and return to England. On June 3rd the medical board at No. 1 General Hospital, Birmingham pronounced him fit for general service, and five days later he was back in France. Brothers served; Herbert Ronald Hoskins he became a major in the Royal Warwickshire Regiment; and Hugh Gilbert Hoskins served as a private in the 1/8th Royal Warwickshire Regiment and Peter was a lieutenant in the 3/8th Bn., Warwicks. His mother applied for his medals. Memorial Ref. Pier and Face 9 A 9 B and 10 B., Thiepval Memorial, France.

Left to right; Cyril Hoskins 1/8th Bn.; Captain Hoskins 1/7th Bn., Warwicks; Private Tommy Hoskins 14th Bn.; Lt. Peter Hoskins 3/8th Bn.

HOUGHTON, Captain, Philip Squarey. Fatally wounded, 1st July 1916. Officer Commanding B Coy., 1st/9th Bn., London Regiment (Queen Victoria's Rifles). Aged 23. Only son of Philip Arthur Houghton (surgeon) and Leonie Mabel Houghton, of Aldeburgh, Suffolk formerly Lindfield, Sussex. Born Hampstead, London, 11th April 1893, educated at Brunswick, Hayward's Heath, Charterhouse and University College, Oxford. Bachelor of Arts. (in absence). Matriculated 1912. He read Natural Science at University College, Oxford. Keen golfer. Resided Hook Hill Cottage, nr Woking. Gazetted second lieutenant, 26th August 1914 and went to the front in November 1914, being promoted lieutenant July 1915 and then captain. Wounded May 1915. In a letter Major Sampson adds: "The regiment has earned the thanks of the Colonel in Chief and everyone else. But the divisions on our flanks were held up and in the bend we had to come back to our trenches, what was left of us. Casualties of course are heavy. Phil Houghton, I am afraid, is certainly killed. He was hit and I fear there is no doubt". Aldeburgh War Memorial. Father applied for his medals. Memorial Ref. Pier and Face 9 C., Thiepval Memorial, France.

HOUSTON, Captain, Fredrick Neville, MC. B Coy., under Captain Houston, two platoons (Lieutenant Forsdike and 2nd Lieutenant. Strong) in Copse Trench with a number of B Company packed tight into Nairne Street. Duty to follow second assaulting wave and clear first, second and third German trenches. Many casualties were also caused by machine-gun and rifle fire to which A and B companies were much exposed owing to levelling of Nairne Trench etc. Worked to ensure that men could push on as quickly as possible and as a result the file commenced to move at a fair pace at 7.52am and at 7.58am. 1st July 1916. 14th Bn., York and Lancaster Regiment. Elder son of Mr. and Mrs. W. D. Houston, of Oriental Bay, Wellington, New Zealand. Born 2nd March 1890 at Dunedin, Otago. Otago Boys' High School, New Zealand. Received his primary education at St. Clair and went home to study for the army. Husband of Ellen Marie Houston, of Oakwood Lodge, Davigdor Road, Hove, Sussex formerly Kirkman. Second lieutenant, November 1911. To the York and Lancaster from the 3rd Bn., South Staffordshire Regiment, 3rd December 1912. May 1914 qualified as instructor at the school of musketry, Hythe, Kent. Appointed assistant adjutant of the 2nd Bn., York and Lancaster at Limerick, Ireland. Went to France, 9th September 1914. Wounded November 1914 with a gunshot wound in the shoulder and spent eight days in hospital. From the 15th July to the 31st July 1915 he spent another 15 days in hospital with a gunshot wound to the neck and shoulder. Promoted captain January 1916. Mentioned in Despatches. His wife applied for his medals and officers pension, however there was a delay as his death was not accepted for official purposes until 27th November 1916. Memorial Ref. Pier and Face 14 A and 14 B., Thiepval Memorial, France.

HOWARD, Lieutenant Colonel, Louis Meredith. On the 1st July 1916 Louis Meredith Howard was wounded, during the battle of the Somme. He succumbed to his wounds one day later, 2nd July 1916. The Officer Commanding the battalion filed the death as the 1st July and this was changed to died of wounds on the 2nd July 1916 with an amended casualty report on the 30th July 1916. However his pension that was payable to his children, Audrey Battye and Cyril Meredith was paid from the 2nd July 1916 implying he died on the 1st July. Burial return also states the 1st July 1916. 24th (Tyneside Irish) Bn., Northumberland Fusiliers. Aged 37. Born Manitoba, Canada, 21st May 1877. Son of Mrs. Howard, of Northview,"Queens Road, Tankerton-on-Sea, and Rice Meredith Howard (Barrister). Husband of Naomi Wycliffe Fortier (Formerly Howard), of 11, St. Mark's Court, Abercorn Place, St. John's Wood, London. Branch Manager from 1912, Equitable Life Assurance Society. Served in London Rifle Brigade, 1891-3 (cadet). Cape Mounted Rifles, 1893-8 (corporal). Natal Mounted Police, 1898-9 (trooper). Imperial Light Horse,1899-1902 (lieutenant and adjutant). Natal Border Police, 1902-03 (captain and adjutant). Northern District Mounted Rifles (Natal) 1903-08 (captain and adjutant). Naval Volunteer Reserve (Hammersmith) 1903 – 1910 (Organiser). 3rd Bn., Royal West Surrey Regiment (The Queen's) 1914 (captain). 15th West Yorkshire Regiment, 1914 (captain and adjutant), 1915 (Major second in command). Louis wrote to the Private Secretary Office on the 24th August 1914 volunteering as he was retired; 'an honour and pleasure to offer my services in any of the forces that you may select'. On November 19th 1914, whilst holding the rank of captain in the Royal West Surrey Regiment, he was gazetted into the Leeds "Pals" and was appointed their Adjutant.

He played an active part in the recruitment of the battalion and on many occasions would travel with the recruitment party on the recruiting tram. On battalion sports day, at Colsterdale Camp, on Wednesday 12th May 1915, Major Howard was to not only judge, but also present the trophy to the competitor who obtained the highest number of points. On the 28th August 1915, Major Howard left the battalion to take command of the 24th (service) Battalion (1st Tyneside Irish), Northumberland Fusiliers and left with the battalion from Salisbury Plain for Flanders. Medals and War Service; Jubilee 1897. Boer War. Queen's Medal, five clasps. King's Medal, two clasps. Natal Rebellion, 1906, one clasp. Body was removed from original map reference 57d.X.20.a and reburied in January 1920. Widow applied for his medals. Memorial Ref. II. D. 4., Ovillers Military Cemetery, France. WO 339/20453

HOWE, Second Lieutenant, Charles Kingsley. Reported to be killed by a bullet to the head about 7.00am, 1st July 1916. 6th Bn., Royal Berkshire Regiment. Aged 28. Fifth son of John Foster Howe and Caroline Howe, of 9, West Down Road, Seaford, Sussex. Born in Lewisham and studied at the Lewisham College of Art. Studied art for about ten years and travelled in Russia. The Sussex Downs were his special inspiration. Illustrated books. Exhibitor at the International Society of Sculptors, Painters and Gravers. Joined the Artists Rifles, 28th Bn., London Regiment in September 1914, private, 2754 went to France, 22nd January 1915 and 18th September 1915 received his commission and part of the engagement at Loos. On 25th October 1915 he was transferred from 5th Battalion to the 6th Battalion at La Boisselle and was posted to 'C' Company. Also known as Charlie and Ching. He was home on leave about ten days before his death. Commemorated at Goldsmiths College Art School, New Cross, where he had been employed in the teaching staff. Memorial Ref. Q. 21., Carnoy Military Cemetery, France. WO 339/43090

Amavimus-Amamus-Amabimus God Is Love

HOWLETT, Second Lieutenant, Charles Wilfred. Reported, missing and wounded, than as killed 1st July 1916. A Coy., 9th Bn., King's Own Yorkshire Light Infantry. Born 26th April 1892. Aged 24. Second son of Francis Robert (Under-sheriff for Kent) and Mary M. Howlett, of Toppesfield, Maidstone. Old Felstedian, educated at Felsted (May 1907 to July 1910, cricket XI, hockey XI) and grandson of Sir Arthur Howlett. Member of the Felsted OTC. When war broke out he was studying law. Articled clerk to his father, F. R. Howlett, of Maidstone. He entered the Public School Brigade in September 1914, private No. 1650, enlisted in Westminster and in December 1914 received a commission with the 9th Bn., King's Own Yorkshire Light Infantry, went to the Front, 11th September 1915 and fought in the Battle of Loos. From 23rd October 1915 to 29th December 1915 treated at the military hospital at Etaples. His mother applied for his medals. Memorial Ref. I. B. 88., Norfolk Cemetery, Becordel-Becourt, France. WO 339/4450

HOYLE, Lieutenant, John Baldwin, MC. After acting some time as Brigade Scout Officer, he was appointed Forward Observing Officer to his division, and while discharging these duties on the first day of the advance on the Somme he was reported missing, 1st July 1916. Killed in action at Fricourt. 7th Bn., South Lancashire Regiment. Aged 23. Third Son of Edward Lascelles Hoyle JP., for Cheshire and Margaret Hoyle, of Holme Hall, Bakewell, Derbyshire. Born at Knutsford, Cheshire on the 16th September 1892. Attended Rugby School, 1906 to 1911 onto Pembroke College, Cambridge where he took his degree with Classical Honours in May 1914. He enlisted in the University and Public Schools Corps in August, 1914, but received his commission in the following month, being promoted lieutenant in April, 1915. He went to France with his battalion in July. Early in 1916 he was specially commended by the Divisional General for" excellent reconnaissance work," and in June was awarded the Military Cross for his conduct in operations at Neuve Chapelle and for" daring reconnaissance on several occasions." What is known as to the manner of his death is told by the Staff Officer under whose orders he was :-"At a certain hour your son was to go forward into the German line with a telephone to a place hidden from us and report to me direct how things were going. As our troops rushed the German trenches opposite Ovillers, he followed on with an orderly. Half-way across 'No Man's Land' he sent the orderly back and went on alone. Meanwhile our troops received very heavy punishment from machine-guns and finally were forced back. Your son, who was seen to enter the German trenches, did not return with the survivors of the attack, and that is all we know. He certainly proved himself a most gallant gentleman in going forward by himself to a place where he thought he ought not to take others, yet himself went on according to his orders." John was awarded the Military Cross;- "On the night of the 27th/28th February 1916, he and Lance-Corporal Hill made a thorough examination of the enemy wire opposite Neuve Chapelle, crawling about for three hours. He accurately noticed the position and number of enemy sentries, and selected a suitable spot for making a gap in the enemy wire. After returning to our lines and making a report he guided the party to the selected spot and covered them whilst the arrangements were being made. On several occasions Lieutenant Hoyle has carried out daring reconnaissance's." His youngest brother, Lieutenant G. M. Hoyle, who also attended Rugby School was killed at Hooge on the 9th August 1915 whilst serving with the The Sherwood Foresters. John's body was recovered by a burial party. Father applied for his medals. Memorial ref. I. B. 15., Ovillers Military Cemetery, France.

He Asked Life Of Thee And Thou Gavest It Him

HUDLESTONE, Second Lieutenant, Harold Robert. Wounded at Carnoy and died on the stretcher on the way to medical assistance, officially the following day, 2nd July 1916. However the Grave Registration Report suggests the 1st July and he is buried alongside Private J. Smith and Private A. Weedon both also killed the 1st July. Mortally wounded by a shell whilst in a trench previously occupied by the Germans, as the Germans bombed their old trenches. 12th Bn. Attd from 14th Bn., Middlesex Regiment. Aged 33. Son of Robert William (solicitor) and Emmeline Belbin Hudlestone of 68, Parliament Hill, Hampstead. Born 3rd March 1883. Educated University College School, London. Admitted July 1908. Solicitor to London & North Western Railway Company, Euston Station. His connection with railway work exempted him from the services. At the outbreak of war joined the Golders Green Volunteer Training Corps and enrolled as a special constable. In January 1915 joined the anti-Aircraft Corps, RNVR and the Inns of Court, OTC. Obtained a commission 21st June 1915, a first class shot was employed as a musketry instructor served in France from May 1916. Mentioned in Despatches. Memorial Ref. G. 24., Carnoy Military Cemetery, France.

HUDDLESTON, Second Lieutenant, Maurice Louis. Fallen in action, missing believed killed, 1st July 1916. 15th Bn., Durham Light Infantry. Born 10th July 1891 in Kensington, London. Resided Loudoun Castle, Ayrshire. Educated at Douai Abbey Catholic School, Beaumont College and at Ushaw College, Durham. Clerical student. Received his commission in February, 1915; Entered France, 14th December 1915 and was wounded slightly 28th January 1916, additionally receiving a mention in Sir D. Haig's despatches in June. Commemorated on the plaque in St John's Seminary, Wonersh, Surrey and Digby Stuart College. Next of kin, sister Mrs. Greenish and brother, Edward, Earl of Loudoun Castle. Originally buried Fricourt and body moved in 1919. His brother, E. H. Huddleston applied for his medals via his solicitor in Ashby-de-la-Zouch. Original map reference for burial 57d.26.d.1.4. Memorial Ref. VIII. D. 2., Gordon Dump Cemetery, Ovillers-La Boisselle, France. WO 339/35950

HUDSON, Second Lieutenant, Arthur Henry William. Originally reported as missing. 1st July 1916. 1st Bn., King's Own (Royal Lancaster Regiment). Aged 19. Son of Arthur John Hudson and Hannah Hudson, of 341, Fairfax Drive, Westcliff, Southend. Born 9th May 1897. Attended Bancroft School. He began boarding at Bancroft's in 1909, and remained at Bancroft's until 1914, playing 1st XI cricket. He was a capable athlete, and was the chief exponent of the game of single-sticks. Singer, member of the school debating society, an active member of the newly formed school scout troop where he achieved the rank of patrol leader. Arthur was the vice-captain of the shooting team. Captain of the Scouts' football team and became proficient in signaling in Morse code taking part in various contests with other Scout troops. In 1913-14 Arthur was successful in matriculating from Bancrofts School. At the outbreak of war he exited for training in the Essex Regiment and then applied for a commission in the Kings Own (Royal Lancaster) Regiment. Joined his battalion and entered France as a second lieutenant on 14th April 1916. Father applied for his medals. Memorial Ref. Pier and Face 5 D and 12 B., Thiepval Memorial, France.

HUGHES, Captain, Alexander Arbuthnott. Last seen six to eight yards from the German wire leading six to seven men forward all these men were knocked out a few yards further, 1st July 1916. Reported missing believed killed, 2nd Bn., South Wales Borderers. Aged 29. Born 20th February 1887, Woolwich, London. Elder son of Colonel Arbuthnott James Hughes and Caroline Mabel Hughes, of Presteign, Warwick Park, Tunbridge Wells. Born at Woolwich, London. Attended Clifton College and the Royal Military College as a cadet. Entered the South Wales Borderers in October 1907 as a second lieutenant, promotion in September 1909 seconded for service with the Colonial Office from July 1912 had employment with the King's African Rifles. Captain, November 1914 while still seconded to the Colonial Office. Injured by a camel in November 1915 and invalided home, he joined the battalion in April 1916. Went to France, June 1916. Remains found 3rd August 1917. Medal request sent to an address in Sussex. Memorial Ref. C. 9., Y Ravine Cemetery, Beaumont-Hamel, France.

Until The Day Break

HUMPHRIES, Second Lieutenant, Thomas. Fighting was hard and shelling heavy, machine-gun fire was intense, 1st July 1916. 15th Bn., West Yorkshire Regiment (Prince of Wales's Own). Aged 20. Born 15th November 1896. Second son of Edward Walter (Percy Lund, Humphries & Co, Ltd, printers of Bradford) and Elizabeth Humphries, of 7, Ashburnham Grove, Heaton, Bradford, Yorks. Born Bradford, Yorkshire, 1897. Educated at Bradford Grammar School (1905-1911) and St. George's, Harpenden. In October 1914, aged 17, he enlisted as a private, 2824, in C Company, 1st/6th West Yorkshire Regiment and served at Marske, Ripon and France. On the 15th April 1915, boarded a ship bound for France. 28th November 1915 he was sent for officer training and commissioned as a second lieutenant with the 15th West Yorkshire Regiment joining them in June 1916. His brother Eric was awarded the Military Cross, survived the war and took over the family business. Medals applied for by his parents. Memorial Ref. Pier and Face 2 A 2 C and 2 D., Thiepval Memorial, France.

HUNT, Second Lieutenant, John Reginald Lilly. He was killed in the advance on Gommecourt on 1st July 1916 in which 3" Stokes Mortars were introduced. The 139th Trench Mortar battery was to follow over the top with six Stokes mortars. Three more were positioned in the trenches to provide covering artillery. German artillery took most of the guns out in the trenches. Two reached enemy lines but found they were either without any ammunition or lacked sufficient men to operate them. Not one of the guns fired in action. His servant Private William Pickering wrote to John's parents, "With much regret I write these few lines of condolence to you. I was servant to your son and was with him to the last and think it is my duty to inform you of his sad but brilliant end. He was foremost in the attack and urging his men on when he was shot through the head death being instantaneous." 1st July 1916. 5th Bn., Sherwood Foresters (Notts and Derby Regiment) attached 139th Trench Mortar Battery. Aged 19. Only son of Dr. John Aspinall Hunt and Minnie Beatrice Hunt, of Woodstock, Shalford, Surrey. Born 10th September 1896 , Ockbrook, Derbyshire. Entered Epsom College Lower School in 1911 and left in 1913 was a member of the OTC. Attended University College, Reading. Member of Reading University College OTC. Obtained a commission March, 1915, 3/5th Sherwood Foresters and went to France, 10th January 1916. Attached to trench mortar batter, 29th April 1916. Father applied for his medals. Original map reference for burial 57d.E.28.a.5.0 and his grave was marked with a cross, body recovered 1917. Memorial Ref. II. E. 4., Gommecourt Wood New Cemetery, Foncquevillers, France.

HUNTRISS, Captain, Cyril John, MC. At 8.00am Captain Huntriss was killed when advancing from the British to the German trenches,'1st July 1916. 1st Bn., East Yorkshire Regiment. Aged 23. Youngest son of William Huntriss, of Mattersey Hall, Bawtry, Notts, and of Charlotte Elizabeth Huntriss, of Springfield, Newby, Scarborough. Born on 21st January 1893 at Bridlington. Cyril attended Cambridge House, Flamborough Road, Bridlington and Uppingham School in Rutland, member of the OTC. Regular hunter and hunted for the last three seasons. Enlisted 13th June 1914. He served in France with the 1st Battalion of the East Yorkshire regiment from 26th January 1915, awarded the Military Cross on 9th August 1915 at Hooge, Belgium, he had, `led four bombing parties up to the assault on the enemy's position with the greatest coolness and daring.' Mentioned in Despatches, January 1916. Wounded in action 5th May and discharged to duty 13th May 1916. Effects returned included silk scarf, drinking cup, pair of spurs, patent lighter, nail scissors, cigarette holder, pipes, compasses, grenade badge, Webley and Scott pistol, cleaning rod, photos, letters, dagger and case, ink, pocket books, MC ribbon and corkscrew. Father applied for his sons medals as two brothers were also killed in service; Captain Harold Edward Huntriss, 2nd Bn., Bedfordshire Regiment killed in action 17th July 1915 and Lieutenant William Huntriss, 9th Bn., Duke of Wellington's died on military service, 23rd October 1918. The three brothers are commemorated on a stained glass window in Mattersey Church, Nottinghamshire. Memorial Ref. Pier and Face 2 C., Thiepval Memorial, France. WO 339/19114

HUSKINSON, Captain, Frederick John. Missing, killed in action, 1st July 1916. 2nd Bn., Royal Inniskilling Fusiliers. Aged 26. Son of Charles and Georgina Huskinson, of 2, Ormiston Road, Westcombe Park, London. Husband of May Huskinson, of The Lincolns, Loughton, Essex. Attended 1910-12, Reading University College. Member of Reading University College OTC. Art teacher, Brigg Grammar School. Enlisted just before the outbreak of war and lost his brother, Shipwright 2nd Class Charles Huskinson in September 1914 aboard HMS Cressy. Frederick was wounded at Neuve Chapelle, suffered a gunshot wound to the shoulder and spent from the 4th May 1915 to the 15th May 1915 in hospital. Re-entered France, 31st January 1916. Commemorated Sir John Nelthorpe School, Brigg (formerly Brigg Grammar). Medals allocated to his widow. Memorial Ref. Pier and Face 4 D and 5 B., Thiepval Memorial, France.

HUTCHISON, Major, Edward. Died 1st July 1916. 17th (Service) Bn., Highland Light Infantry. Aged 45. Son of Robert and Marion Hutchison, of Glasgow. Born in Anderston, Glasgow on 26th February 1871, one of six sons. Edward attended Kelvinside Academy before going to the University of Glasgow to study Law in 1892, staying for two academic years. Following his time at university Edward became a Chartered Accountant, eventually becoming partner at the firm Walker & Marwick in Glasgow. Husband of Elsie K. Hutchison, of 34, Granby Terrace, Glasgow and had two sons, Archibald George and Edward Arthur. Before the war, Edward was a Major of the Volunteer Battalion of the Scottish Rifles. Upon the outbreak war he took command of the D Company, 17th Highland Light Infantry. In November 1915 he was shipped to France and by December was on the front line. Death reported 11th July 1916. Medals applied for by his wife. Memorial Ref. I. A. 12., Bouzincourt Communal Cemetery Extension, France.

HYDE, Second Lieutenant, Charles Stuart. Leading his platoon over the top, he was wounded in the arm and leg before he had gone a hundred yards. He would not go back and stated that "he would see the job through." Eventually his leg was bound and he was dragged to a shell-hole; but while sitting there with two other wounded soldiers, encouraging his men, a shell exploded, killing them all instantly. 1st July 1916. 16th Bn., West Yorkshire Regiment (Prince of Wales's Own). Aged 27. Second son of the Reverend Tom Dodsworth Hyde and Mrs. Mary Jane Hyde, of Whitechapel Vicarage, Cleckheaton, Yorks and All Saints, Matlock. Born 4th December 1890 at Street House, Dudley Hill, Bradford. Pupil at Bradford Grammar School (1902 -1904). Joining the staff of the Union of London and Smiths Bank employed at branches in Cleckheaton, Dewsbury and Leeds. He, like his brother, was involved with Whitechapel Church where their father was the vicar. Enlisted with his brother Eustace, as a private soldier, 15/494. He was commissioned into the Bradford Pals Battalion on the 27th April 1915 and went with them to Egypt in late 1915, before arriving on the Somme in May 1916. His brother, Lieutenant Eustace Emile Hyde, 4th Royal Irish Fusiliers was killed in action 12th October 1916. Commemorated on the Bradford Grammar School Roll of Honour and also on the memorials at St John's and Whitechapel Churches. (Unknown officer of the West Yorkshires buried in Serre Road Cemetery No. 3, reported buried near Hebuterne). Commemorated Sons and Daughters of the Anglican Church Clergy. His father applied for his medals. Memorial Ref. Pier and Face 2 A 2 C and 2 D., Thiepval Memorial, France.

HYDE, Second Lieutenant, James Charles. Killed near Gommecourt, died most gallantly at the head of his platoon within a few yards of the enemy parapet, reported missing, 1st July 1916. B Coy., 1st /5th Bn., Sherwood Foresters (Notts and Derby Regiment). Aged 21. Eldest son of Anne Hyde, of 36, Kidbrook Park Road, Blackheath, London, and Reverend James Bartlett Hyde, Vicar of Matlock Bank. Born 30th April, 1895 at Finsbury Park, London. Educated St. Edward's School, Oxford. Matriculated at Selwyn College, Cambridge. Enlisted 9th March 1915 in the London Scottish, private, 4489. Took part in the fighting at Loos and was wounded and returned to England. Entered France, 27th October 1915. Gazetted 24th November 1915. Back to France, 16th June 1916. Commemorated Sons and Daughters of the Anglican Church Clergy. Father applied for his medals. Memorial Ref. Pier and Face 10 C 10 D and 11 A., Thiepval Memorial, France.

HYNAM, Second Lieutenant, Walter William. Initially reported wounded and later as killed, 1st July 1916. 26th (Tyneside Irish) Bn., Northumberland Fusiliers. Resided 18 Henington Crescent, Kennington Park Road. Enlisted 12th January 1904. Married Ada Elizabeth, 9th May 1911 and had two children, Mabel Elizabeth Patricia and Phyllis Ada. Entered France, 15th August 1914. To be second lieutenant for service in the field, Squad Quartermaster Sergeant W. Hynam, 504 from 5th Lancers to Northumberland Fusiliers, 13th June 1916. His widow applied for his medals. Next of kin resided Botolph Orton, Longneville, near Peterborough. Memorial Ref. Pier and Face 10 B 11 B and 12 B., Thiepval Memorial, France. WO 339/66130

IBBITSON, Lieutenant, William Beveridge. Missing officially reported killed, he had assumed command his officers having fallen and he led his men to the third line German trench when he was hit death being practically instantaneous, 1st July 1916. 10th Bn., West Yorkshire Regiment (Prince of Wales's Own). Aged 23. Born 26th July 1893. Eldest son of Mr. and Mrs. Johanna Ibbitson, of 4, Albany Road, Bedford formerly 2 Grace Terrace, Sunderland. Husband of Fanny Agnes Ibbitson, Murrayfield, Selkirk. Nephew of Mrs. Hilson, Westend, Chirnside. Educated Chester Road and Bede School. Articled to Mr. Hugh Hedley, architect of Sunderland and went to work in the Government Land Valuation Office. Well-known figure in Chirnside. Commissioned from the Durham University OTC, 12th June 1915 and proceeded to France, 17th December 1915. Married only a few months, 12th October 1915. His widow applied for his medals. Reported killed 25th July 1916. Memorial Ref. C. 17., Fricourt New Military Cemetery, France.

In Ever Loving Remembrance Of My Dear Son Time Passes, But Love & Remembrance Remain Mother

IDE, Second Lieutenant, Thomas Norman. He fell in the trenches among his own men, officially stated 2nd July 1916. Left the assembly trenches at 8.36am and immediately encountered heavy artillery and machine-gun fire. Grave Registration Unit stated 1st July 1916. 2nd Bn., Essex Regiment. Aged 23. Eldest son of Mr. and Mrs. Thomas John Ide (glass merchant), and Jane Alexandra Ide of Henley, 175, Golders Green Road, Golders Green, London. Born at 3 Glendall Villas, Wanstead on the 4th January 1893. Educated at Wanstead College, Woodford House School, Birchington-on-Sea and at St. Paul's School from September 1908 to December 1910 where he was a member of the 3rd XI Cricket team. Thomas worked as a clerk for Kaye, Son Company Ltd, Lloyd's brokers. Following the outbreak of war, he enlisted at Westminster on the 15th September 1914 as private 5104 in the 20th (Service) Bn., Royal Fusiliers. Declared fit for active service at a medical board on the 23rd February 1915. He was discharged from the Royal Fusiliers on the 24th February 1915 when he entered RMC Sandhurst, and was commissioned as a second lieutenant in the Essex Regiment on the 11th August 1915. Embarked for France on the 29th May 1916, where he joined the 2nd Bn. End of June 1916 listed in reinforcements in the war diary. His father applied for his medals. Memorial Ref. I. H. 6., Sucrerie Military Cemetery, Colincamps, France.

To Live In Hearts We Leave Behind Is Not To Die

ILBERY, Second Lieutenant, Oscar Reginald. Killed in action, 1st July 1916. 2nd Bn., King's Own Yorkshire Light Infantry. Aged 27. Son of William Edward Ilbery. Husband of Dorothy Ilbery, of 1, Hemlock Road, Shepherd's Bush, London. Born in London. When war broke out he was in India in the tea plantations and came to England to join the army. Gazetted 24th March 1915 with the 3rd Bn. Entered France, 19th February 1916. His widow applied for his medals. Original burial map reference 57d.R.31.c.4.0 and buried as an unknown British officer, in 1928 identified through his uniform, boots, piece disc, buttons and a pocket book. Memorial Ref. XVI. K. 1., Serre Road Cemetery No.2, France.

Gone But Not Forgotten

INGLE, Second Lieutenant, Roland George. Killed at La Boisselle, 1st July 1916. 101st Brigade Trench Mortar Battery attd 10th Bn., Lincolnshire Regiment. Aged 30. Only surviving son of Robert (corn merchant) and Harriet Alice Ingle, of 92, Hills Road, Cambridge. Born 23rd May 1886. Old Boy of King's School, Ely, Cambridgeshire. Captained the cricket XI. At Queen's College, Cambridge University read the classics. Teacher, as an assistant master at the Wells House, Malvern Wells, Worcestershire Preparatory School for boys. Cadet of the OTC to be temporary second lieutenant, 14th November 1914. Served in Gallipoli with the 6th Lincolns. Embarked for France on 4th January 1916. He joined the 10th Lincolns in May 1916 after being invalided out for a period with neurasthenia. On 25th June 1916 he was at Battalion HQ, not far behind the lines, and wrote in his diary; "The men who are going to be knocked out in the push—there must be many—should not certainly be looked on with pity, because going forward with resolution and braced muscles puts a man in a mood to despise consequences. A man who is used to sport takes these things—even in the great chance of life and death—as part of the game." His family received a letter dated the 6th July 1916 from Lieutenant Colonel Kyme Cordeaux, Cmdg., 10th Bn., saying he had been killed in action and his sister sought officially communication which came on the 20th July. His father applied for his medals. Memorial Ref. I. R. 26., Becourt Military Cemetery, Becordel-Becourt, France. WO 339/1100

OFFICERS OF THE LINCOLNSHIRE REGIMENT.—Sec.-Lt. R. L. Hornsby, Lt. F. S. Cannell, Lt. A. P. Snell, Lt. H. Sargent, Lt. K. J. W. Peake, Lt. G. G. Downes, Sec.-Lt. R. G. Ingle, Sec.-Lt. D. Akenhead, Lt. Lynden-Webber, Sec.-Lt. T. D. Overton, Sec.-Lt. A. S. Hemsley, Sec.-Lt. J. C. Foster, Sec.-Lt. A. H. Bird, Sec.-Lt. L. J. Lill, Sec.-Lt. G. M. Hewart, Capt. A. Hoade (Staff Capt., 33rd Infantry Brigade), Maj. W. E. W. Elkington (Sec.-in-Command), Brig.-Gen. R. P. Maxwell (G.O.C., 33rd Infantry Brigade), Lt.-Col. M. P. Phelps (Commanding), Capt. F. G. Spring (Brigade Major, 33rd Infantry Brigade), Major A. E. Norton, Lt. H. Winslow-Woollett.

Featuring Second Lieutenant R. G. Ingle

INGOLDBY, Second Lieutenant, Roger Hugh. The 2nd Battalion, Royal Dublin Fusiliers, began to advance at 9.00am, immediately encountering heavy enfilade fire from Beaumont-Hamel. At 9.05am two runners arrived and informed Major Walsh, the commanding officer, that the attack was to be postponed. He managed to stop part of C and D companies advancing. However for the rest of the battalion, already in No Man's Land, the recall order came too late. At noon, when the order was finally received from Corps HQ to attack and consolidate the position, Walsh reported that this was impossible. Of the twenty-three officers and 480 men who had assembled that morning, fourteen officers and 311 men were now casualties. The order had to be amended and Major Walsh was now told to collect all available men to defend the British front-line. 1st July 1916. 2nd Bn., Royal Dublin Fusiliers. Born 26th April 1886. Aged 30. Son of Mr. F. J. and Mrs. M. A. Ingoldby, of Westgate House, Louth, Lincs. St Lawrence College, Ramsgate, Kent. Emmanuel College, Cambridge. B.A., 1908. Ripon Theological College. Ordained 1909. Curate of St. Thomas', Camden Town, 1909. In Canada when war broke out. Joined the Alberta Dragoons as a private, 2018, going to France, 7th February 1915, gazetted to a commission a few months later. Mentioned in Despatches. In hospital from 11th to 21st March 1916 suffering from enteritis. Father applied for his medals. Original burial map reference 57d.K.34.d.5.1 and buried as an unknown British officer, Royal Dublin Fusiliers and identified by officer's khaki, G.S boots, collar badge and watch when remains were exhumed on the 22nd September 1926. Memorial Ref. VI. H. 26., A.I.F. Burial Ground, Flers, France.

Blessed Are The Pure In Heart

Matriculation 1905 Emmanuel College

INMAN, Lieutenant, Edwin. His identification disc has been found in No Man's Land, 1st July 1916. Edwin fell leading his men when a shell burst near him and it was also reported he was hit by a machine-gun bullet. He was seen lying in the open between the first and second line German trench and a wounded private said he was badly wounded in a trench about ten yards away from him. The private reported he was still there when he left at 10 o'clock at night but he heard it took the stretcher bearers two days to get to that trench. 10th Bn., Lincolnshire Regiment. Aged 21. Son of Edwin and Alice Inman, of 5, Clifford Road, Sharrow, Sheffield formerly Knowle House, Norfolk Park Road. Born 2nd March 1895. Employed Messrs. Cammell Laird & Co, of Cyclope Works as a clerk. Worksop College OTC. Attested 15th September 1914. Applied to join the Royal Flying Corps in February 1915 and this was requested to withdrawn by his Lieutenant Colonel on the 24th September 1915 as the efficiency of the battalion would be seriously impaired. Entered France, 10th January 1916. His brother, Private Noel Inman, No. 529 was also killed on the 1st July 1916 with the 10th Lincolnshire Regiment and is commemorated Pier and Face 1C, Thiepval Memorial. His family received notification that Edwin was missing and his father wrote to the War Office on the 11th for further information and also requesting that his next of kin for his son, Noel was correct and he was assured by the War Office should anything happen he would be informed. On the 28th June 1917 his father rendered it undesirable to proceed to official acceptance of death. Edwin's name had been on the officers list in the Orderly Room as amongst those killed several weeks after the 1st July 1916. His father applied for his medals. Original map burial reference 57d.W.24.c.8.I. Memorial Ref. II. F. 8., Bapaume Post Military Cemetery, Albert, France. WO 339/15683

May He Rest In Peace And Let Light Perpetual Shine Upon Him

INNES, Lieutenant Colonel, Edgar Arthur, C.M.G. Letter received from Major Townsend stating he fell gallantly at 8.00am leading his men into action, 1st July 1916, Beaumont Hamel. He was killed whilst still inside the British lines. Commanding 1st /8th Bn., Royal Warwickshire Regiment. Son of Mr. Innes of Harborne Hill House. Resided Metchley Abbey, Metchley Lane. Principal of Messrs. Innes, Smith & Co. wine merchants, High Street, Birmingham. Took part in the campaign for National Service. Mentioned in Despatches. Formerly captain in the First (Birmingham) Volunteer Bn. Entered France, 23rd March 1915. His widow, Mrs. E. A. Innes, Morpeth, Northumberland applied for his medals and pension for two children, Edith Dorothy and John Nicholas. Memorial Ref. Pier and Face 9 A 9 B and 10 B., Thiepval Memorial, France.

INNOCENT, Lieutenant, Edward John. 3rd July 1916. Grave Registration Unit has date of death as 1st July 1916. 7th Bn., attd from 9th Bn., Queen's Own (Royal West Kent) Regiment. Reported killed locally on the 3rd July and the official date of death with the CWGC is the 3rd July 1916. Resided Elmhurst, Roydon. Cricket player. Served in the Volunteers in the South African War. Previously buried in his dug-out by the explosion of a large shell, February 1916. Original burial map reference, 62C.A.8.b.2.2 and buried with fourteen men that were killed on the 1st July 1916. Memorial Ref. VIII.D.9. Dantzig Alley British Cemetery, Mametz, France.

JACKSON, Second Lieutenant, Ernest. Led platoons of C Coy., 1st July 1916 at Thiepval Ridge. About thirty yards from the German front line he was hit in the leg and crawled into a shell hole, where his wounded was dressed. Found in the same shell hole on the 4th July, past all help. 3rd Bn. attd. 15th Bn., Lancashire Fusiliers. Aged 23. Born in 1889 at Bacup, Lancashire. Son of John and Mary Elizabeth Jackson. He arrived to study French and Flemish at Manchester University in 1906, gaining a BA in 1910, and MA and teaching diploma in 1911. After university he became assistant headmaster at Tynemouth Municipal High School until 1913 when he went to Leeds Modern to the Post of Modern Language Master. Ernest enlisted into the Rifle Brigade in April 1915 as a rifleman and on the 5th June 1915 was granted a commission into the 2nd Lancashire Fusiliers. Posted to France, 22nd May 1916. He married a E. Tunnicliffe from Leeds in late 1915 and his wife appealed for information on his death in the local papers and also applied for his medals from Burton-on-Trent. Memorial Ref. Pier and Face 3 C and 3 D., Thiepval Memorial, France.

JACKSON, Lieutenant, Henry Stewart. He was badly wounded in the neck, and fell into a shell hole, close to the neighbourhood of La Boisselle Church. Fought near Albert and was killed, 1st July 1916. 8th Bn., King's Own Yorkshire Light Infantry. Born in Bacup, 28th August 1895. Aged 20. Son of Reverend Sydney of Mitcham and Mrs. Mary Elizabeth Jackson, 86 Greyhound Lane, Streatham. He was educated at St. John's School, Leatherhead and at Whitgift School from 1907-1911 and served as a private in the OTC. Entered the Medical College in October, 1913 in London Hospital. Member of University of London, OTC. Before joining as a combatant, Henry had served for many months in the capacity of a dresser first with the Red Cross Service at Anglo-Belgian Hospital, and later at the Anglo-American Hospital, at Wimereux. Upheld the high traditions of the London Hospital. Commissioned as a second lieutenant, June 1916. Entered France, 17th June 1916 originally 25th November 1914 with the Red Cross. Commemorated Sons and Daughters of the Anglican Church Clergy. His father applied for his medals. Memorial Ref. Pier and Face 11 C and 12 A., Thiepval Memorial, France. WO 339/54193

JACKSON, Second Lieutenant, Lancelot. Went over the top from the support line, and over the first line, the bridges over the front trench having being ranged by the German machine-gunners the day previously meet with heavy losses, while crossing these bridges and passing the lanes out in the wire, reported missing believed killed, 1st July 1916. 1st Bn., Border Regiment. Son of Mr. J. Jackson, Crozier Lodge, Penrith. Reported missing but information received by his family on the 10th July leaving no doubt he was killed. Educated Penrith and St. Bee's Grammar School. Went to work as a marine engineer and when war broke out he was in Belfast. Served for a time in Egypt. Disembarked, Mudros, 22nd November 1915 on HMS Olympic. Memorial Ref. Pier and Face 6 A and 7 C., Thiepval Memorial, France.

JAGO, Second Lieutenant, Edward Arthur. Died while attacking German trenches, 1st July 1916. 3rd Bn. attd. 2nd Bn., Devonshire Regiment. Aged 20. Second son of Mr. William Henry Jago, Solicitor, Eglinton, Plymouth and Jeannie Jago. Born 12th April 1896, Bristol. His parents received intimation that he was killed on the 5th July. Previously at Plymouth College and Plymouth Preparatory School he was entered for Cambridge with the intention of entering the Church. Received his commission in July 1915. Entered France, 22nd May 1916. His brother Captain Henry Harris Jago was killed on the 24th April 1918 and was awarded the Military Cross, DSO and Bar. In their sons memory in 1919 the parents paid for a chapel in Emmanuel Church, Plymouth. Father applied for his medals. Memorial Ref. Pier and Face 1 C., Thiepval Memorial, France. WO 339/34730

JAMES, Second Lieutenant, Clement Wilbraham. Fighting was hard and shelling heavy, machine-gun fire was intense, reported wounded, missing 1st July 1916. 15th Bn., West Yorkshire Regiment (Prince of Wales's Own). Aged 26. Son of Mrs. Ella Eliza James, of 203, Sydenham Road, Durban, Natal, South Africa, and Thomas Paine Saint James. Temporary second lieutenant gazetted 28th December 1915. Application for medals by his mother, Durban, South Africa. 1915 Star to be supplied by the South African authorities. Memorial Ref. Pier and Face 2 A 2 C and 2 D., Thiepval Memorial, France.

JARMAN, Second Lieutenant, Andrew Hatch. Missing, last seen wounded in the head near La Bassee, witness believes he could not have recovered, 1st July 1916. 20th (Tyneside Scottish) Bn., Northumberland Fusiliers. Aged 34. Son of Mrs. Jarman, and brother of Miss Alice Joyce Jarman, Ivydene, 242 Antrim Road, Belfast. Born 7th January 1883. Member of the Cliftonville Cricket Club and hockey club. Member of the Queen's University, Belfast, Training Corps, 1914. One time in the service of Messrs. Workman, Clark & Co., Belfast and held commission since 10th June 1915. In was reported to relatives his body was found in October 1917, north of La Boisselle, map reference 57d.X.14 marked with a cross. Mother applied for his medals. Memorial Ref. X. D. 2., Ovillers Military Cemetery, France. WO 339/34832

JEAL, Second Lieutenant, Walter. Reported wounded, the extent of his injuries were not known, killed in action 1st July 1916. General List attd., 15th Bn., Royal Scots. Aged 24. Sixth of eight children, youngest son of Joseph (grocer) and Eliza Jeal, of Falkland Road, later Yverdon, Cliftonville, Dorking, Surrey. Born on 10th March 1892 in Dorking. Walter attended Dorking High School. Worked in Colombo, Ceylon in 1914, being a member of the Ceylon Planters' Rifle Club, lance corporal, 1942 and enlisted there in the Ceylon Force, on 2nd October 1914. Entered Egypt, 17th November 1914. After serving in the Dardanelles in April 1915 being attached to the Australians and New Zealanders, he was then commissioned, in July 1915 and attached to 4th Bn., Royal Scots. After being invalided home suffering from jaundice, September 1915, Walter then recovered and returned to the 15th Royal Scots in the Expeditionary Force in April 1916 and went to France. Four other brothers served in the army. Commemorated Dorking South Street Memorial. His father applied for his medals. Memorial Ref. Pier and Face 4 C., Thiepval Memorial, France.

JEFFCOCK, Second Lieutenant, Robert Salisbury. Killed in action, assumed command of A Company and killed near the German wire, 1st July 1916. 1st/6th Bn., South Staffordshire Regiment. Born 13th November 1877 in Wolverhampton. Aged 39. Attended Shrewsbury School. Churchill's from 1890 left in 1894. He was an artist by profession specialising in miniatures. Youngest son of Prebendary J. T. Jeffcock, rector of Wolverhampton and Mrs. Jeffcock of Harpenden. Resided Ringstead, Harpenden. Formerly Artists Rifles, private, 2908, Territorial Battalion enlisted in October 1914. Entered France, 14th February 1915. Second lieutenant, 30th May 1915 commissioned in the West Kent Regiment. After a few months service in Egypt he was sent to France. He left a wife, Marguerite Anna and a daughter, Joan Marguerite. Harpenden War Memorial. Medals to an address in Folkestone. Memorial Ref. Pier and Face 7 B., Thiepval Memorial, France.

JELLICOE, Lieutenant, Eric Maitland. He was killed outright in action during the attack on the Gommecourt Salient, in one of the latter waves of the attack, 1st July 1916. 6th Bn, Sherwood Foresters (Notts and Derby Regiment). Aged 20. Born in June 1896 at Portsea Island in Hampshire. Son of James T. Jellicoe (Indian Forest Service) and Lilian his wife. Commissoned 3rd October 1914. Promoted lieutenant, early August. Arrived in France on 28th August 1915. Attended training at Divisional School from 24th April 1916 to the 5th May 1916. Mother applied for his medals, Sinclair Road, Kensington, W14. Memorial Ref. I. B. 21., Foncquevillers Military Cemetery, France.

JESSUP, Captain, Francis Reginald. Went over the top from the support line, and over the first line, the bridges over the front trench having being ranged by the German machine-gunners the day previously meet with heavy losses, while crossing these bridges and passing the lanes out in the wire, killed 1st July 1916. 1st Bn., Border Regiment. Aged 29. Son of George James and Emma Mary Jessup, 34 Queen Anne's Garden, Enfield. Lived at Southend prior to going to British Columbia. Joined the battalion, January 1915. Saw service in Gallipoli, Egypt and France. Entered France, 19th March 1916. Promoted captain, April 1916. Father applied for his medals, Queen Anne's Gardens, Bush Hill Park, Enfield. Memorial Ref. Pier and Face 6 A and 7 C., Thiepval Memorial, France.

JEUDWINE, Captain, Spencer Henry. Battalion gained 200 yards but were forced to withdraw by 9.00am, on an attack on Ovillers-La-Boisselle. Captain Jeudwine posted as missing, 1st July 1916. Enquiries through the American Embassy failed to find any information and presumption of death, 17th October 1917. 3rd Bn., attd 2nd Bn., Lincolnshire Regiment. Aged 20. Born Grantham, Lincolnshire on the 1st September 1895. Son of Reverend George Wynne (Rector of Harlaxton, Lincolnshire) and Harriet Jeudwine. Attended Brighton College, (Junior House 1906 – 1909), one of four Brightonians killed on the 1st July 1916. Educated at Malvern College, 1909 -1914 and accepted for a place at Gonville and Caius College, Cambridge. At the outbreak of war, attested 8th August 1914 and received a commission in the Lincolnshire Regiment being promoted to lieutenant in February 1915 and captain in March 1916. May 11th 1915 shot in the right thumb by a rifle bullet and returned to England. Entered France again on the 4th October 1915.

Commemorated Sons and Daughters of the Anglican Church Clergy and stained glass, St. Mary and St. Peter, Harlaxton, Lincolnshire. Father applied for his medals whilst the Archdeacon of Lincoln, address Archdeaconry, Lincoln. Memorial Ref. Pier and Face 1 C., Thiepval Memorial, France. WO 339/18311

JOHNSON, Lieutenant, Thomas. Mown down on the left in support of B Coy., killed in action, 1st July 1916. D Coy., 16th Bn., Highland Light Infantry. Appointed lieutenant in August 1915. Entered France, 23rd November 1915. Death reported 17th August 1916. Master T. Johnson, c/o Mrs. Cormack, Caithness, Scotland applied for his medals. Memorial Ref. Pier and Face 15 C., Thiepval Memorial, France.

JOHNSON, Second Lieutenant, William Roland. Reported missing, last seen trying to get through the wire in front of the enemy trenches, gallantly led to the attack, 1st July 1916. Officer Commanding, No. 7 Platoon., B Coy., 1st/6th Bn., South Staffordshire Regiment. Aged 39. Son of John and Elizabeth Johnson, of Wolverhampton. Born 6th September 1878, Wolverhampton. Resided Brocton, Jeffcock Road, Wolverhampton. Commercial traveller for Mander Brothers varnish and colour manufacturers formerly solicitors clerk. Commissioned 5th June 1915. Entered France, 20th October 1915. Commemorated Mander Brothers Memorial. Brother received a letter from Captain H. Vivian Mander stating he was in command of his third platoon, the only hope he was a prisoner as he did not return as was not seen in a casualty clearing station. Medals to Trinity Road, Birchfield, Birmingham. Memorial Ref. Pier and Face 7 B., Thiepval Memorial, France.

JOHNSTON, Lieutenant, Adrian Alexander Hope. Died north of Montauban, stated as being killed 2nd July 1916, killed 1st July in No Man's Land with B Coy. 5th Bn. attd. 4th Bn., Middlesex Regiment. Son of Mr. A. H. Johnston, Central Hotel, Simla. Grave Registration Unit states 1st July 1916. Resided 65 Warwick Road, Earls Court, London. Enlisted 3rd March 1915 with his preference being the Indian Army as he had lived there for 12 years and was familiar with the language, second preference was the Royal Flying Corps and finally the Middlesex Regiment. Entered France, 7th October 1915. Joined battalion 12th October 1915, accidentally wounded 5th November 1915 and to Rouen 21st November 1915. Re-joined the battalion, 8th January 1916. Reported in October 1916 he was buried in the angle formed by Empress trench and a new communication trench, Montauban Trench. Sht 26. Sq. D, Contour 110 exact. Father applied for his medals. Memorial Ref. IV. L., Gordon Dump Cemetery, Ovillers-La Boisselle, France. WO 339/36144

JOHNSTON, Captain, Charles Moore. Killed in action, 1st July 1916. One runner made it back to Battalion HQ, with the message 'cannot advance without support' and the men send forward in support were wiped out. C Coy. 9th Bn., Royal Irish Fusiliers. Aged 30. Youngest son of Charles Johnston, D.L., and Marian Johnston, of Portadown. Husband of Muriel Florence Johnston, of Carrickblacker Avenue, Portadown. Born 1886. Educated at Lurgan and Campbell Colleges, and Royal School of Mines, London, and was member of the Royal Society of Music. Rowing eight and Rugby XV, 1904-05. Before enlisting in the Royal Irish Fusiliers he was a company commander in the UVF and took a prominent part in the organisation and training of the Portadown Volunteer Force. Entered France, 5th October 1915. His widow applied for his medals. Two children entitled to pension payment; Charles Collier born 4th March 1915 and Harold Moore born the 9th June 1916. Memorial Ref. III. B. 17., Mesnil Communal Cemetery Extension, France.

Earth Changes But Thy Soul And God Stand Sure

JOHNSTON, Captain, Elliott, MC. Reported missing, 1st July 1916. 13th Bn., Royal Irish Rifles. Aged 28. Second son of Samuel Johnston JP (Managing Director of the Glen Printing and Finishing Co., Newtonards) of 1, Deramore Park, Belfast. Military Cross for 'conspicuous gallantry during operations, he raided the enemy trenches and bought back thirteen prisoners including an officer.' Queen's University, Belfast, Faculty of Commerce, 1910 -1913. Captain Johnston was manager of the hem-stitching department and was also a director. Commander of one of the Newtownards companies of the 2nd Bn., UVF on the outbreak of war joined the Royal Irish Rifles. He got his first step in December 1914 and in February 1916 advanced to the rank of captain. He had been with the Ulster Division since it went to the Front in October 1915. Father applied for his medals. Memorial Ref. Pier and Face 15 A and 15 B., Thiepval Memorial, France.

JOHNSTON, Second Lieutenant, James Annandale. Missing believed killed 1st July with the 1st Bn., officially 2nd July 1916. Battalion history suggests 1st July. 3rd Bn. attd. 1st Bn., Somerset Light Infantry. Son of Lieutenant James Johnston, RN., and Mrs. A. R. Johnston. Husband of Mrs. Gladys Hobden. Johnston, of 89, Westcourt Road, Worthing. Educated at Christ's Hospital. Second lieutenant on probation, gazetted 2nd July 1915. Well known locally as a football player, volunteered for the second military contingent that Canada send to the front. Entered France, 21st May 1916. Death accepted after time period. His widow applied for his medals. Pension payment awarded to his wife and child, Annandale James Johnston. Payment was back dated to the day after his death so the authorities also took this as being the 2nd July 1916. Worthing Roll of Honour. Memorial Ref. Pier and Face 2 A., Thiepval Memorial, France.

JOHNSTON, Captain, Octavius Ralph Featherstone. Commanded the left of two leading companies. He died in a shell hole in the German second line, he was hit in the stomach and was given a morphia tabloid, 1st July 1916. B Coy., 4th Bn., Middlesex Regiment. Son of Sir Charles John Johnston, KT., and Lady Johnston, of 12, Hobson Street, Wellington, New Zealand. Born New Zealand, 21st January 1891. Resided 24 Guilford Street, W.C. Attended Wangani Collegiate School, New Zealand and St. Ignatuis College, Sydney. Novelist. Served as a lieutenant in the 5th Regiment, New Zealand from 15th January 1912 to January 1914 until leaving for England. Disembarked 9th October 1914. Body found about an hour after the first assault between the German first and second line he had been hit a few times. Originally buried Empress Trench and new communication trench Sht 26.d. Contour 110. Map reference 57d.27c.6.4. Application for 1914 Star from Miss C. F. Gathorne-Hardy, the Star being issued to the deceased mother, Lady Johnston. Three addresses listed; Reubens Hotel, Buckingham Palace Road, or c/o Messrs. John Connell, Mincing Lane, EC and finally Homewood, Wellington, New Zealand. Memorial Ref. IV. K., Gordon Dump Cemetery, Ovillers-La Boisselle, France. WO 339/11659

The Game Is Deep But I Must Play It Out I Can No Other So Away With Fear

JONES, Captain, Alfred Cotton, MC. Reported missing believed killed, official date 2nd July 1916 war diary implies 1st July 1916. Went over at 8.40am and wounded by machine gun fire. B Coy., 8th Bn., Lincolnshire Regiment. Only son of Mr. and Mrs. Mary Elizabeth Jones of 35, Carrington Street choosing the stage as his profession, acted in both England and France. Father died 22nd July 1913. He enlisted at the beginning of the war, 7th September 1914 in the 18454, Grenadier Guards and later received a commission in the Lincolns, 3rd October 1915. He won the Military Cross shortly before his death and attended investiture at Buckingham Palace. Reported wounded and in a dying condition left of Fricourt between the 1st and 2nd German line. Private King took his pocket book and watch and handed them in to Lieutenant Markham. Reported to be buried by HQ, 34th Division position X.27.c.8.3. Medals and pension payment to his mother, Upper Colwyn Bay, North Wales. Memorial Ref. Pier and Face 1 C., Thiepval Memorial, France. WO 339/44241

JONES, Lieutenant, David William Llewelyn. 10.10am Heavy barrage put up by enemy whilst to dig communication trenches, causing numerous casualties, Hebuterne, 1st July 1916. Reported to have died of wounds, 2nd July 1916 at No. 43 Casualty Clearing Station. 1st/3rd Bn., London Regiment (Royal Fusiliers). Aged 21. Only son of the Reverend Canon David Jones and Katharine Edwards Jones, of Tregarth, Penmaenmawr, Carnarvonshire. Born March 1895. Bradfield September 1908 to July 1913. Prefect 1911. Cricket in the Bradfield College XI and Football XI, St. Edward XI. Exhibitor, Magdelene College, Oxford, 1913. Gazetted in a City of London battalion in the first months of the war, received a promotion in March 1915. Medal Index Card states died of wounds, 2nd July 1916. Commemorated Sons and Daughters of the Anglican Church Clergy. Medals applied for by his mother. Memorial Ref. II. D. 2., Warlincourt Halte British Cemetery, Saulty, France.

JONES, Second Lieutenant, Horace Birchall. Initially reported wounded in action, his Major feared there was little doubt he was killed in the fighting, 1st July 1916. 1st/6th Bn., North Staffordshire Regiment. One of three children, second son of Mr. W. T. Jones, Arden Vale, Olton. Born 23rd November 1891. Educated at Stonehouse and Wellsbourne School and Wycliffe College (1905-1907) and a member of his father's firm; W. T. Jones and Co., High Street, Birmingham. Joined one of the Birmingham City Battalions at the start of the war as a private, 14/175 having been in the Birmingham University OTC. Served in the 6th King's Liverpool Regiment between 1909 to 1912. Received his commission in the North Staffordshire Regiment, 22nd September 1914. Entered France, 6th March 1916. Horace wrote his last letter home on the evening of the 30th June 1916; 'What I am going to write is intended for you all, I am not writing to you individually because it is too hard. I am leaving this behind to be posted….A big attack is coming off …in fact we are on the eve of it, and they have honoured me by selecting me and my platoon to lead the attack….many of us will not answer the roll….I thank you from the bottom of my heart for the wonderful kindness and love you have always shown me.' Confirmed killed 12th July 1916. Father applied for his medals. Memorial Ref. Pier and Face 14 B and 14 C., Thiepval Memorial, France.

JONES, Second Lieutenant, John Myddelton. Killed at Fricourt, 1st July 1916. 17th Bn., Durham Light Infantry probably attached to 15th or 18th Bn., Durham Light Infantry. Aged 25. Fifth son of Thomas Augustus Jones (solicitor) and Marian Jones of Warkworth Hall and 15, Trewsbury Road, Sydenham. Educated at Christ's Hospital, Horsham. He was in business in Calcutta and at the outbreak of war gave up six month's leave of absence to training with the Indian Army, 20th DCO Infantry, in which he obtained a temporary commission having previously held the rank of captain in the Calcutta Volunteers. Served in India from March 1915. Owing to illness he was compelled to come home, he gave up his prospects in Calcutta and joined the army being given a commission in the Durham Light Infantry and went to France in early June. Three brothers also served. Commemorated St. Bartholomew's Church, Sydenham. Miss C. M. Jones made an application for her late brother medals from Streatham Grove, Norwood. Memorial Ref. Pier and Face 14 A and 15 C., Thiepval Memorial, France.

JONES, Second Lieutenant, Kenneth Champion. At 7.28am, six leading platoons took up their position in No Man's Land, without loss. At 7.30am our front line pushed forward, they were met with very heavy artillery and machine-gun fire, some of A and B companies who did make the German front line at 7.35am were surrounded and captured by the Germans. Killed in the German trench, 1st July 1916. 1st Bn., East Lancashire Regiment. Aged 26. Fifth Son of Frederick and Rose Jones, of 15, Orchard Road, Bromley, Kent formerly Lanherne, Albemarle Road, Beckenham. Born at Sydenham on May 18th 1891, entered Oundle (School House) in May 1904 and was at the school until December 1909. In August 1914 he was articled to a firm of chartered accountants and was about to take his final examination. Joining the Artists' Rifles, private, 2011 he went out to France, 29th December 1914 and 9th July 1915 obtained a commission in the 1st East Lancashire Regiment. On July 14th , 1916, he was reported missing, believed killed near Beaumont Hamel. Medals to F. Jones, Shortlands, Kent. Memorial Ref. Pier and Face 6 C., Thiepval Memorial, France.

JONES, Major, Lewis Farewell. Missing and believed wounded from the fourth wave, there was a gap of about twenty yards in the German wire. Major Jones led a party of about eight until he fell wounded about two yards in front of the enemy's parapet and was seen to crawl into a shell hole. D Coy., 1st July 1916. 1st/12th, London Regiment (The Rangers). Aged 31. Elder son of George Farewell Jones and Anna Louisa Jones, of Brenley, Mitcham, Surrey. Born at Hampstead on 15th May 1885. Resided 13 Queen Anne's Gate. On leaving school he was articled to an architect. Educated Eastbourne College. He also became an Associate of the Surveyors' Institute, and was preparing to sit for the RIBA examination in 1914. Held the rank of captain when he was mobilised for active service in August 1914. 24th December 1914 he crossed to France with the 1st Battalion of his Regiment. Mentioned in Despatches. He was severely wounded in the Second Battle of Ypres, but was back in France in October 1915 with the rank of Major. Father applied for his medals. Exhumed 9th March 1953 from an isolated grave containing two bodies at Hebuterne and reburied 16th March 1953, identified by disc, G.S boots and equipment., the other body was that of an unknown British soldier. The CWGC reached out to the family address but received no reply, by 1953 his father, George had died without knowing his son's body had been found.

His body had been found by a German Red Cross team. Memorial Ref. Joint grave 9.J.12-13, London Cemetery And Extension, Longueval, France.

JOSEPHS, Second Lieutenant, Joseph. The remnants advanced towards Nameless Farm under withering machine-gun fire from that point. Second Lieutenant Josephs was killed whilst bravely charging a machine-gun, 1st July 1916. C Coy., 12th Bn., London Regiment (The Rangers). Aged 19 from Highbury New Park, London. Son of David and Sabina Josephs, of 206, Willesden Lane, London. Resided 72, Highbury New Park, North London. Jewish Book of Honour. Lied about his age when he enlisted. Entered France, 27th May 1916. Father applied for his medals, Crediton Hill, Hampstead. Memorial Ref. I. C. 4., Gommecourt British Cemetery No.2, Hebuterne, France.

JUPP, Second Lieutenant, Clifford Henry Oliver. Reported missing whilst serving with B Coy., 1st July 1916, 1st Bn., Newfoundland Regiment. He was seen lying wounded being hit in the chest and was not seen to move again. Aged 25. Son of William and Marion Jupp, of Pulborough, Sussex, England. Dry goods clerk. Enlisted, September 5th, 1914, No. 157. Promoted to lance corporal, June 12th, 1915 to corporal August 20th, 1915 and then to sergeant, September 13th, 1915. British Expeditionary Force, March 14th, 1916. Again promoted to acting company quartermaster sergeant, May 29th, 1916. Clifford received his commission on June 11th 1916. As an NCO he served in Gallipoli and entered the Balkans, on the 19th September 1915. Telegram confirming he had been killed delivered on the 7th July 1916 to his family. High Commission for Newfoundland confirmed entitled to medals. Memorial Ref. Beaumont-Hamel (Newfoundland) Memorial, France.

KARRAN, Second Lieutenant, John Bowler. Reported missing believed killed whilst serving as bombing officer with his battalion, 1st July 1916. 2nd Bn., South Wales Borderers. Son of Mr. George C. Karran, of Sea Mount, Castletown. Educated at King William's College, and in September 1914 received a commission in the 2nd Bn., South Wales Borderers. He spent five months at Gallipoli from September 1915, and after the British withdrawal from the Dardanelles he was posted to France. Mrs. M. M. Karran applied for medals, Isle of Man. Memorial Ref. B. 10., Y Ravine Cemetery, Beaumont-Hamel, France.

KEIGHLEY, Lieutenant, William Munkley, BSc. Killed in action, 1st July 1916. 10th Bn., West Yorkshire Regiment (Prince of Wales's Own). Aged 23. Born 11th July 1893. Family resided at 38 Russell Street, Thomaby-on-Tees, Yorkshire. Resided Thornaby. Middlesbrough High School old boy. Formerly a temporary teacher in Denmark Street Boys School, North Riding, Middlesbrough. When war broke out he joined the University College, Nottingham OTC and was gazetted as second lieutenant October 1914 securing his full lieutenancy. Entered France, 13th July 1915. Middlesbrough War Memorial. Originally buried Fricourt Sheet 62d. Sq.F.3.a.45. Row B Grave 7. Father applied for his medals, Stockton-on-Tees. Mrs. E. Keighley, 29 Dixon Street, Stockton-on-Tees choose his inscription. Memorial Ref. C. 6., Fricourt New Military Cemetery, France. WO 339/1767

Love, Laughter, Life I Laid Aside See Ye I Have Not Vainly Died

KELLY, Second Lieutenant, Percy Patrick. Died of wounds, known to be killed by 7.50am, No Man's Land, Montauban, 1st July 1916. A Coy. 8th Bn., East Surrey Regiment. Aged 27. Brother of Mr. H. M. Kelly, of 42, Moor Lane, Fore St., London. Enlisted 2nd Bn., Honourable Artillery Company, private, 3073. Commissioned East Surreys, 12th June 1915. Entered France, 17th December 1915. On the 1st July 1916 a letter from Second Lieutenant Kelly to the parents of Private H. L. Arnold appeared in The Surrey Comet telling them he died instantly and was buried with the usual burial rites, having been killed by a shell. Wallington War Memorial. Brother, E. Kelly of Moor Lane, EC2 applied for his medals. Memorial Ref. E. 30., Carnoy Military Cemetery, France.

KEMP, Second Lieutenant, Albert. First reported missing, then wounded and missing, 1st July 1916. A Coy. 10th Bn., Royal Inniskilling Fusiliers. Aged 35. Born in Audlem, in Cheshire, in 1881. Worked as an assisting brewer in 1911. Married 1915. Husband of Christine Kemp (nee Morgan), of 4, Merridale Avenue, Wolverhampton. Had a son, John. Obtained his commission 6th June 1915 and was serving with the Derry Volunteers. Wife applied for his medals. Memorial Ref. Pier and Face 4 D and 5 B., Thiepval Memorial, France.

KEMP, Second Lieutenant, Thomas. Killed close to Fricourt, 1st July 1916. Reported he was killed in the attack on Lusker Road Trench and his body lay on the ground all night being brought back for burial the following day. 20th Bn., Manchester Regiment. Aged 27. Elder son of Mr. A. C. and Mrs. A. Kemp, of 23, St. Thomas Road, Street, Anne's-on-the-Sea, Lancs. Native of Atherton, Lancs. Born 7th February 1889. Educated Leigh Grammar School and attended Denstone College. In the Cadet Corps, 1903 to 1904. Served his articles with a Manchester accountant but in 1911 accepted an engagement in Chile. Famous football player, member of Manchester RUFC and played for the Lancaster XV. When war broke out he was in Valparaiso, Chile and travelled home via the Panama Canal, enlisted 3rd April 1915 then went to France in November 1915. Effects returned were wallet, fountain pen (damaged), blank cheque, photos and papers, wrist watch and eye-glasses in case. Originally buried south of Fricourt, ESE of Albert Sht 62. Sq.F.9.d.99.10. Exhumed from map reference 62d.F.9.d.9.7 where his grave was marked with a cross and he was buried with a number of officers from his battalion also killed on the 1st July. Memorial Ref. VI. I. 7., Dantzig Alley British Cemetery, Mametz, France. WO 339/29247

He Came From Chile To Do His Duty For King And Country

KENION, Second Lieutenant, Hugh Cyril. Killed in action at Beaumont Hamel on 1st July 1916. 2nd Bn., Lancashire Fusiliers. Born on 11th December 1883, Birkenhead the fifth and youngest son of John Hamer Kenion, (solicitor, Liverpool) of Rock Ferry, Cheshire. Educated Mostyn House and Charterhouse (Saunderites 1898-1901) from Oration Quarter 1898 to Summer Quarter 1901. Member of the Cadet Corps. Solicitor with Harwood, Banner & Sons, Chartered Accountants. Referred to as 'Nipper Kenion'. Member of Royal Mersey Yacht Club and Birkenhead Park Football Club. Joined 'King Edwards Horse', 4th County of London Imperial Yeomanry (King's Colonials), he rose to the rank of sergeant, No. 31 and gained an infantry commission. Entered France 2nd June 1915. From King Edward's Horse to the Lancashire Fusiliers, 4th April 1916. Chartered Accountants and Articled Clerks Roll of Honour. War Memorial, Mostyn House School, Parkgate, Cheshire. Birkenhead Memorial. Father applied for his medals. Originally buried as an unknown British officer at map reference 57d.Q.5.a.30.40, exhumed on the 24th November 1922 and found to have H.C.K engraved on a watch, with other effects; field glasses, compass, badge, handkerchief and an additional watch. Memorial Ref. VIII. A. 6., Serre Road Cemetery No.1, France.

Birkenhead Park 1st XV for the season 1909-1910
H. C. Kenion is positioned second from right on the front row

KENNARD, Lieutenant-Colonel, Maurice Nicholl, MC. West Yorkshire Regiment. Commanding 18th Bn., formerly 6th Dragoon Guards. 8.20am message received from the Brigade to the effect that the 16th West Yorkshires were held up and ordering the CO to go to Sap 'A' to investigate. Went forward but was killed by artillery at about 8.30am, 1st July 1916. Troops had dropped on their stomachs to escape the fire whilst the Lieutenant Colonel stood upright carrying a walking stick called out 'come on boys, up you get'. Three times Mentioned in Despatches. Second son of Robert William and Rose N. Kennard, of North Leigh, Bradford-on-Avon, Wilts. Born in 1883. He was a keen polo player, a member of the Canterbury C.P.C., with a handicap of 6 goals. In South Africa he was on the side that won the Durban Tournament, and followed this up by carrying off the South African Champion Cup. In 1902 he joined the 6th Dragoon Guards from the Militia, and after holding the adjutancy of the regiment for a period from April, 1910, he became captain in 1913. Mentioned in despatches as early as October 19th, 1914. While serving with the 6th Dragoon Guards in the early days of the war, wounded, November, 1914 with a gunshot wound to the arm, in hospital from 3rd November 1914 to the 22nd December 1914. The following year, November, 1915, he was appointed temporary major and second in command of the 13th York and Lancaster Regiment, and was afterwards transferred to the command which he was holding at the time of his death. Father applied for his medals. Memorial Ref. Pier and Face 2A 2C and 2D. Thiepval Memorial, Somme, France.

KENWORTHY, Captain, Stanley. Killed at Montauban, 1st July 1916. He was seen to fall before the German first line but was not dead, later he was reported killed. There was no identity disc found but his name was on his helmet and a letter was found nearby. 17th Bn., Manchester Regiment. Aged 32. Elder son of John Dalziel Kenworthy, of Seacroft, St. Bees, Cumberland. Born 4th May 1894. Husband of Dinah T. Kenworthy of Seacroft, St. Bees. Educated at St. Bees School, 1895-1903, Captain Kenworthy obtained Fox and Grindal Exhibitions to Queen's College, Oxford, where he graduated MA, and when war broke out he was a preparatory master at Merchiston Lodge (1909 to 1914), Edinburgh. St. Bees entered the School House in and was Head of the school when he left in 1903. A good sportsman and an all-round athlete, he played in the school XI and XV, for the Cumberland XV 1903-05, for Queen's College XI and XV, and for the Cheshire XV 1907-08. As an athlete he had always taken a prominent place both for school and county, having played football and cricket for Queen's, and football for Cumberland and Cheshire. He was also an enthusiastic golfer, and well-known at Seascale, where a few years ago he won the cup for the final in the medal competition. One of the first to offer his services, and having been accepted, he was shortly afterwards gazetted as second lieutenant in the 17th City Battalion, Manchester Regiment. He soon proved himself to be a very capable and smart officer, and was promoted to the rank of lieutenant, and then to that of captain, C Coy., January 1915. Since he had been in France he had seen a good deal of fighting, and his name appeared in Sir Douglas Haig's list of those who had distinguished themselves in the field, which was published on June 16th 1915. Originally buried between Maricourt and Montauban, map reference 62C.A.9.a.7.8. Father applied for his medals. Memorial Ref. IV. U. 4., Dantzig Alley British Cemetery, Mametz, France. WO 339/19466

KERNAGHAN, Lieutenant, Graham Hemery. Killed in action, 1st July 1916. 8th Bn., King's Own Yorkshire Light Infantry. Aged 22. Born 1894. Only son of Major Thomas James and Alexandra Violet Kernaghan, of 19, Portman Street, Portman Square, London formerly The Avenue, Colchester. Born at Colchester. He attended Wellington College, 1907 – 1912 and passed into the RMA but due to illness did not complete the course. Inns of Court OTC. Enlisted 10th December 1914. Gazetted January 1915. Entered France, 22nd December 1915. Originally buried front of British line, Ovillers La Boiselle. Essex Roll of Honour. Mrs. A. V. Kernaghan, a widow by 1921 applied for her son's medals. Original burial map reference 57d.X.8.a.0.7 and identified by his disc in 1928. Memorial Ref. XIV. F. 1., Serre Road Cemetery No.2, France. WO 339/17675

Son Of Thomas James And Alexandra Violet Kernaghan Thy Will Be Done

KERR, Captain, David Bryce. Reported missing, 1st July 1916. A Coy, leading up on the right, 16th Bn., Highland Light Infantry. Aged 39. Fourth son of Robert and Margaret Kerr (nee Bryce-Buchanan). Partner in the firm of Messrs. Kerr & Co., seed merchants, 63 Queen Street, Glasgow. Formerly a member of 1st Volunteers and 5th Scottish Rifles, 7006 retiring in 1913. Territorial Force Efficiency Medal. Associated with the Boys' Brigade movement in Glasgow before the war. Father, Robert Kerr, founder Ballikinrain, Killearn and brothers in law of Mr. J. B. McLaren, chemist, Pathhead. Rejoined at the outbreak of war and proceeded to France, 5th November 1914. Returned home in March 1915 to take up his commission in the New Army, on the 1st July 1915 he was promoted to captain and returned to France, November 1915. Brother killed a few days later, on the 3rd July, Private Alexander Leopold Kerr killed with the 15th Bn., Highland Light Infantry. They two brothers had met in France accidentally three days before the advance and spent a few hours together. Executors of his will applied for his medals. Memorial Ref. Pier and Face 15 C., Thiepval Memorial, France.

KERR, Second Lieutenant, Donald. Fell in action during the 1st London Scots' assault on the Gommecourt Salient 1st July 1916. C Coy., The attack had pushed onto Fable Trench, the final objective but they believed they were in the trench prior to that, Farm Trench and pushed on further coming up against heavy machine gun fire and a counter attack, when Donald was shot and killed. 1st/14th Bn., London Regiment (London Scottish). Aged 25. Youngest son of James John (supervisor of Customs and Excise) and Anne Kerr, of 140, Albert Road, Crosshill, Glasgow. Born on 28th June 1891 in Pitlochry. In 1908, when Donald went up to the University of Glasgow to study for a degree in the Arts Faculty he enrolled for classes in Latin and Mathematics. He particularly enjoyed the sciences, and in the following three years at university he took Physics, Mathematics and Chemistry classes. He was a good student and won a chemistry prize in 1910 and a First Class Certificate in Advance Physical Laboratory in 1912. He graduated MA with Second Class Honours in mathematics and physics in October 1912, at a time when only a very small minority of students took Honours. His studies continued after graduation in arts. In October 1912 he matriculated again, this time in the Science Faculty, which awarded credits for his science classes taken in the Arts Faculty, and, after further examinations in chemistry, he was able to graduate BSc in April 1913. He went into teaching and then into the Clerical Medical and General Insurance as a trainee actuary. In early January 1915 he enlisted as a private, 4229 in London, in the 2nd London Scottish (14th London Regiment). Donald trained in London and the Home Counties before being commissioned into the battalion in December and transferred to France with a reinforcement draft to the 1st London Scottish in May 1916. He served in the trenches at Hebuterne throughout June. Mother applied for his medals. Memorial Ref. Pier and Face 9 C and 13 C., Thiepval Memorial, France.

KERR, Second Lieutenant, James. Last seen gallantly leading his platoon into the enemy trenches, missing believed killed, 1st July 1916. Leading up on the right, A Coy., 4th Bn. attd. 16th Bn., Highland Light Infantry. Aged 25. Son of James S. Kerr, (shoemaker), 3 Wellgate, Dundee, and grandson of James Kerr, (shoemaker), Keptie Street, Arbroath. Educated at the Morgan Academy and left when he was fifteen. After serving with the British Linen Bank for some years entered the employ of the International Banking Corporation, London and spent five years at the branches at Bombay, Calcutta, Singapore and Yokohama. He came to London and got a commission in August 1915 having served with the Calcutta and Singapore Volunteers as a private. On leaving the International Banking Corporation, the staff presented him with an inlaid sword. Lieutenant Kerr had two brothers in the army. He had been at the front since the 3rd June 1916. Reported missing 11th July 1916. Medals to J. S. Kerr Esq, J. P., Argyll Street, Dundee. Memorial Ref. Pier and Face 15 C., Thiepval Memorial, France.

KERSHAW, Second Lieutenant, Ellis. At 7.30am, leading sections of B, D and a bombing section dashed forward in extended order, being led by Second Lieutenants Craig, Garfunkle & Spencer, B Coy by Prescott, Edwards and Kershaw at the same moment, 1 Platoon under Lieutenant Whittam and two platoons of bombers left the trenches. The leading two lines had a moments grace and then the enemy machine-guns opened and a storm of bullets met the attack. Thiepval, 1st July 1916. B Coy., 13th Bn. attd. 1st Bn., Lancashire Fusiliers. Youngest son of James and Alice Kershaw of 23, Alexandra Road, Moss-side. Enlisted as a private, 8676, with the Lancashire Fusiliers at the beginning of the war and received his commission, 26th March 1915. Served at Gallipoli. Medals and officers' pension applied for by his mother. Memorial Ref. Pier and Face 3 C and 3 D., Thiepval Memorial, France.

KEY, Second Lieutenant, Frederick Bertram. Died as a gallant officer and gentlemen, initially reported wounded on July 2nd and then as killed on 1st July, disastrous results in attacking objectives between Beaumont Hamel and Serre. 8th Bn., Royal Warwickshire Regiment. Aged 27. Only son of Frederick (manager, Lichfield Gas Company) and Edith Key, of 30, Queen Street, Lichfield, Staffs. Educated at Lichfield Grammar School, during last year he was school captain. Then articled for three years to Mr. C. O. Rawstron, surveyor to Lichfield Rural District Council and for a year and half, assistant surveyor. Subsequently employed as a clerk of works to Lichfield's Gas Company and in the drawing office of the Dunlop Rubber Company Ltd, Aston, Birmingham. Scoutmaster of the Lichfield troop and a Sunday school teacher at Christ Church, Lichfield. Played for Lichfield Grammar School and Lichfield Cricket Club. Engaged to Miss Gwyneth. K Hall. Enlisted with some friends on the 3rd September 1914, private, 2667 and went to France, 22nd March 1915. Last home on leave in December 1915. Received his commission, 29th April 1916 after training and it was of great comfort to him that this was his own company. Last letter home read; "If you receive this you will know I have unfortunately been bowled out middle peg. However, you may be sure that I batted well. I have a sensation of fear; but think it rather funny or nice whatever happens I shall finally meet those dear to me. I have no more to say only I will hope you soon both get over it and rest assured the time will quickly pass until we meet again; but some have to die and if I am one, well I can't grumble, I have had 26 years of quite an easy life, I certainly ought to have spent it better but we all say that. I will close now. With heaps of love and kisses, your ever loving and affectionate son, Fred. PS This affair has kept any leave back." His father applied for his medals. Memorial Ref. Pier and Face 9 A 9 B and 10 B., Thiepval Memorial, France.

Photo shortly before the Battle of the Somme. Second Lieutenant Key third from left on the back row.

KING, Second Lieutenant, David Taylor. His Colonel emphasised his great bravery and his death is described as follows "shot by a sniper after he had led his men over the first and second German lines and was in the act of storming the third", 1st July 1916. Reported to be seen lying on the ground quite dead. D Coy., 2nd Bn., Gordon Highlanders. Aged 21. Son of William and Annie King, of Welney Lodge, Ravensbourne Park, Catford, London. Employed the Norwich Union Life Insurance Society, St. James Street, London described by his manager as a "splendid fellow." Enlisted 6th September 1914, 7241, Private. Entered France, 17th February 1915. Commissioned 5th December 1915. Cousin of Lieutenant Walter Taylor, Gordon Highlanders whom also fell. Originally buried 67 Support Trench 62d. F. 11c.8.3. Father applied for his medals. Memorial Ref. A. 4., Gordon Cemetery, Mametz, France. WO 339/51493

Aye In Our Thoughts

KINGSFORD, Second Lieutenant, Reginald John. Killed in action, 1st July 1916. 10th Bn., York and Lancaster Regiment. Aged 23. Son of Laura Kingsford and Philip W. Kingsford (master mariner), of 90 Addison Gardens, Kensington, London. Born December 7th 1892. Joined Latymer School on September 11th 1906, from Addison Gardens L.C.C Elementary School, and left on July 21st 1910, went on to special coaching for entry to Civil Service. Previously a master at Chatham House. Employed as schoolmaster, Arthur G. Handy, Esq. MA (Cantab). Attested 12th September 1914, 2092 6th Bn., Seaforth Highlanders. Commissioned 1st April 1915.Entered France, October 1915. His lieutenant colonel wrote: 'He was killed gallantly leading his men, a death, if it has to be, that every soldier wishes. He went forward with a dash that showed he intended to get to his objective or die in the attempt. He is buried on the field of battle.' Brother also served Philip Cave Kingsford and is named on the Latymer School War Memorial but not on the Commonwealth War Grave Commission. Commemorated on family grave in Hammersmith Margravine Cemetery. His mother applied for his medals. Memorial Ref. Pier and Face 14 A and 14 B., Thiepval Memorial, France. WO 339/38104

KIPPAX, Second Lieutenant, Arthur Haddon. Reported killed at 4.20pm, 1st July 1916. A Coy. 7th Bn., East Yorkshire Regiment. Aged 23. Elder son of John William (commercial clerk) and Sarah Emmeline Kippax, of 1, Avondale Place, Manor Drive, Halifax. Born 14th July 1892, Halifax. Educated at Rishworth Grammar School, Rishworth, Halifax and Halifax Technical College. Cadet, University of London, OTC. Journalist, on the staff of The Daily Chronicle, London. Entered France, 19th April 1916. Telegram send to his parents , 6th July 1916 and father replied for further details on the 7th July. His whistle was returned to the family and his father sought further details on his wrist watch, signet ring and photos as he thought it was usual a body was searched and anything found on a soldier returned to his relatives. Medals applied for by his father. Memorial Ref. A. 25., Fricourt British Cemetery, France. WO 339/35781

Elder Son Of John Wm. Kippax Halifax, England Res Non Verba

KIRKLAND, Second Lieutenant, Frederick William. Reported missing at Mailly Maillet, 1st July 1916 assume to be killed on that date. Reports to be shot through the head with I Coy after the captain was wounded and missing, 6th Bn., attd 3rd Bn., and later attd. I Coy., 1st Bn., Rifle Brigade. Eldest and only son of Charles Frederick (engineer and spindle maker) and Edith Kirkland of Islay Cottage, 7 Braeside Avenue, Rutherglen near Glasgow. Born Rutherglen 21st September 1895. Educated North Eastern County School and Barnard Castle where he was member of the Cadet Corps. Secured a scholarship and proceeded to Emmanuel College, Cambridge to read mechanical sciences but did not graduate. Gazetted second lieutenant, Rifle Brigade, 28th November 1914. Served in France from 8th June 1915 and was invalided home in August 1915 with endocarditis returning to France, February 1916. Reported that he was recommended for a Victoria Cross in June 1916 for staying out with a wounded man in front of the German line. His mother applied for his medals. Memorial Ref. Pier and Face 16 B and 16 C., Thiepval Memorial, France.

KLEAN, Second Lieutenant, Michael Graham. Killed in action, reported missing believed killed, 1st July 1916. 16th Bn., Northumberland Fusiliers. Aged 38. Eldest Son of Simeon and Leonora Klean of 8 Golders Green Crescent, Golders Green. Old boy of Townley Castle School, Ramsgate. Private, 2727, commissioned 22nd April 1916. Entered France, 27th April 1916. Reported wounded 26th June 1916. Unmarried. Sister applied for his medals. Jewish Book of Honour. Roll of Honour, East Ham Cemetery. Original burial map reference 57d. R.31.a.2.7. Mrs. Altshuler, Park View Road, Church End, Finchley choose his inscription. Memorial Ref. IV. T. 1., Lonsdale Cemetery, Authuille, France.

In Loving Memory Of Our Dear Michael

KNIGHT, Second Lieutenant, Philip Clifford. 1st July 1916. 1st Bn., Somerset Light Infantry attd No. 1 Section, 11th Machine Gun Company supported the 1st/8th Royal Warwicks in the attack. Aged 23. Younger son of Alexander and Josephine Knight, of Long Lynch, Child Okeford, Dorset. Born February 28th, 1892, at Wimbledon, Surrey. Educated Uppingham School. Admitted as pensioner at Trinity College, Cambridge, June 25th , 1911. BA 1914. At the outbreak of war joined as a private, 1242, Honourable Artillery Company and was gazetted in February 1915. Disembarked 14th September 1914. Wounded in April 1915. Child Okeford New Roll Of Honour. His mother applied for his medals. Memorial Ref. Pier and Face 2 A., Thiepval Memorial, France.

1912 to 1913 Hornets Hockey team
Front row reading left to right, 2nd from left Honorary Secretary P. C. Knight whilst seated on the left is Sanger Davies who would also be killed on the 1st July 1916.

KNOTT, Major, James Leadbeater, DSO. Killed in action leading his men forward, reported to be shot through the head, 1st July 1916 10th Bn., West Yorkshire Regiment (Prince of Wales's Own) formerly 9th Bn., Northumberland Fusiliers. Age 33. Son of Sir James Knott, 1st Bart., and Lady Knott, of Close House, Wylam-on-Tyne. Born 2nd December 1882. Native of Newcastle. Known in philanthropic and political circles. Educated Eton. Started as clerk before the higher offices of a ship owning business. Director, Prince Line. Travelled widely. One of the largest coal exporters on the Newcastle Quay. He declined a position in his father's company to fight at the front. Attested 8th August 1914. Entered France, 15th July 1915. James was originally buried in Row B. Grave 14. Fricourt New Military Cemetery however his brother Captain H. B. Knott also fell and was buried near where he fell in Belgium. Both brothers are buried next to each other and both headstones read 'Devoted In Life In Death Not Divided'. Left £104,350 in his will. Father, Sir James Knott applied for his medals. His remains had been moved by the 12th January 1922. Grave Ref. V. B. 15. Ypres Reservoir Cemetery, Belgium. WO 339/45395 Last letter home

My Dearest Father and Mother,

If you are reading this letter it means that this war has demanded the extreme sacrifice from me…It is not in any sense a message from the grave because whatever I may or may not doubt, I have very complete faith in the Life Eternal…Momentous events are looming and I have a premonition that I may not return to you. I have been dreaming of Basil recently… My medals are yours but I would like them destroyed when you both join me… My clothes, furniture and motor car must be immediately disposed of, everything which reminds you of my death must be removed. This is my urgent desire and wish…

Your devoted son, Jim

Devoted In Life In Death Not Divided

KNOWLES, Lieutenant, Gavin Tenison Royle. Reported missing, in the first line German trenches at Gommecourt, commanded bombing parties of the 5th South Staffs that went over the top with the leading battalion, one of the few to get in the German trenches, 1st July 1916. Commanded No. 13 Platoon, D Coy., 1st /5th Bn., South Staffordshire Regiment. Younger son of Mr. and Mrs. R. C. Knowles of Caldwell House, Wednesbury and grandson of Alderman John Knowles former Mayor of Wednesbury. Aged 21. St. Paul's Church, Wood Green, Wednesbury. Born 9th April 1895. Educated at Rossall where he was for two years in the OTC. Enlisted in August 1914 and given a commission in a territorial battalion of the South Staffordshire Regiment in October 1914. He distinguished himself in April 1916 at Vimy Ridge by defending a crater against a fierce attack by the enemy and was submitted for official recognition. Promoted to lieutenant four days before his death.

Sergeant J. Williams, D Company said, "I was in a bombing attack in the German lines with Lieutenant Knowles on July 1, 1916, when about fifteen yards away retiring from wounds and loss of blood I saw him fall, shot." Private A. Hosell, D Company added. "We went over the top at 7.30, myself, Sergeant Williams and Lieutenant Knowles. We got into the German first line when we met a party of Germans and we started bombing. There was only about 8 of us that got to the Germans, and to our surprise we found that there were only four of us in that part of the line. Being a brave and noble officer Lieutenant Knowles had no thoughts about retiring. Then we lost Sergeant Williams after being wounded three times, then we lost the Corporal wounded. There was only me and Lt. Knowles left. As we were getting short of bombs Lieutenant Knowles had my rifle, sniping at the Germans keeping them at bay. I'm sorry to say he only fired one shot when he got shot in the head and fell down. I went to him and found he was dead. When Lieutenant Knowles fell he made no sound and death was instantaneous. I remained with him about three minutes and took his head in my arms, shook him and called him by name, but there was no response. He was quite dead. I left his body where it was as the order was given to retreat." Father applied for his medals. Memorial Ref. Pier and Face 7 B., Thiepval Memorial, France.

KOHN, Second Lieutenant, Wilfrid Arthur. 1st July 1916. 11th Bn., East Lancashire Regiment. Aged 22. Only son of Arthur and Rosie Kohn, of 79, Queen's Gate, South Kensington, London. Born 31st October 1893 at Kensington. Educated Marlborough and Goville & Caius College, Cambridge. Enlisted 3rd September 1914 as private, 1720, 18th Bn., Royal Fusiliers. Appointed second lieutenant, 12th May 1915. Entered France, 11th March 1916. Jewish Book of Honour. Father applied for his medals. Memorial Ref. I. D. 13., Euston Road Cemetery, Colincamps, France.

LAING, Captain, Dudley Ogilvie. Posted as missing and feared he was killed, made the charge, he fell after being wounded on the neck but came around and went on, killed as he crossed No Man's Land, 1st July 1916. 22nd (Tyneside Scottish) Bn., Northumberland Fusiliers. Aged 26. Youngest son of Mr. and Mrs. Farquhar M. Laing, of Farnley Grange, Corbridge, Northumberland. Born 14th November 1889. Educated Aysgarth School, Yorkshire and Malvern College, 1903-1907. He had been with Messrs. Stephens, Sutton and Stephens, Prudential Buildings, Newcastle since 1908 and left to join the army at the outbreak of war. He obtained a commission soon after the outbreak of war and rapidly rose to the rank of captain. In France since January 1916. Parents received an official letter a week after his death. Two brothers also died, Captain Gerald Ogilvie Laing, 20th Northumberland Fusiliers killed 5th June 1917 and Lance Corporal Athole Ogilvie Laing died at home, 22nd February 1919. A gift of £1000 was endowed on the Royal Victoria Infirmary for a bed in memory of her youngest son. Identity disc was removed from the body and send to his family, personal effects were pocket book, cigarette case and leather case all contained photos. His mother applied for his medals. Memorial Ref. Pier and Face 10 B 11 B and 12 B., Thiepval Memorial, France. WO 339/18934

LAIRD, Second Lieutenant, Arthur Donald. Officially reported as missing and then killed on the 1st July 1916. 17th Bn., Highland Light Infantry. According to his commanding officer he died a gallant gentleman heading his platoon into battle in the most cool and capable manner. Aged 26. Son of George Holms Laird and Mary Jane Wilson Laird, of 7, Belgrave Terrace, Glasgow. He was the nephew of Dr. Laird, Cambuslang. Educated at Glasgow Academy and captain of the school in 1908. Captained the school football and cricket team and twice represented Glasgow in the inter-city team. A prominent athlete in the west of Scotland, he had an excellent record in rugby while in cricket he played for Glasgow Academy, West of Scotland and Glasgow Academicals. In civil life he was a director of the family firm of George Laird and Sons Ltd, 10 Ann Street, Bridgeton. One of the Glasgow Academicals XV that played in the final match before enlisting, from the XV, eight were killed, six wounded and one returned uninjured. At the outbreak of war he enlisted as a private, 15660 in the Commercial Bn., (17th Highland Light Infantry) and was commissioned in December 1914. Entered France, November 1915. Wounded January 1916. His eldest brother, Captain G. H. H. Laird, Highland Light Infantry was severely wounded at Gallipoli his only other brother, Captain W. W. Laird, Royal Artillery served in Egypt. Death reported 19th July 1916. Father applied for his medals. Memorial Ref. III. E. 6., Blighty Valley Cemetery, Authuille Wood, France.

He Died That We Might Live

LAMB, Lieutenant, Walter. Forster, McIntosh and Lamb got over with a party of men but the whole lot were gunned down by a machine gun, 1st July 1916. 22nd (Tyneside Scottish) Bn., Northumberland Fusiliers connected with the Machine Gun Section. Born in Christon Bank, Alnwick, Northumberland, 15th February 1890. Aged 26. Third son of Mr. James William Lamb, (brewer in Brewery Lane Warkworth) and Mrs. Minnie Lamb of Hotspur House, Warkworth, Northumberland. Father a councillor. Educated at the Dukes School, Alnwick, leaving school in 1906. Engineers pattern maker with the North Eastern Marine Engineering Co. Ltd. Enlisted into the Northumberland Hussars Yeomanry as a private, 1029 on the 18th September 1914. Entered France, 10th January 1916. Cousin also lost in a bombing accident, Second Lieutenant Thomas Lamb at Chipchase Camp died the 30th June 1916 and buried in Warkworth (St. Lawrence) Church. Walter is commemorated on the Warkworth War Memorial. Effects were advance book and cheque book. Father applied for his medals. Memorial Ref. Pier and Face 10 B 11 B and 12 B., Thiepval Memorial, France. WO 339/24488

LANCASTER, Second Lieutenant, Thomas Erwin. Majority of the casualties especially those of the officers occurred during the first two hours of fighting, 1st July 1916. 2nd Bn., Seaforth Highlanders. Aged 18. Son of Henry Percy and Elizabeth Lancaster, of 17, St. James Mansions, West Hampstead, London. Played cricket for the Highgate School eleven. Brother of Second Lieutenant P. N. Lancaster, Royal Irish Rifles. Gazetted July 1915. Entered France, 29th May 1916. Father applied for his medals. Memorial Ref. Pier and Face 15 C., Thiepval Memorial, France.

LANE, Lieutenant, Edward Alfred Joseph Ardan. Killed in action, 1st July 1916. 1st /9th Bn., London Regiment (Queen Victoria's Rifles) attd 169th Brigade Trench Mortar Battery. Aged 30. Born 9th July 1886. Son of Patrick Chaudeau Bernard Lane (deputy conductor of a choir) and Catherine Mary Ann Francis Lane of 60, Westbourne Park Villas, London. Educated College of the Sacred Heart, Wimbledon. Enlisted 19921 in the 4th Grenadier Guards, 18th September 1914 commissioned to the London Regiment, March 1915. Entered France, 1st May 1915. Promoted to lieutenant with the London Regiment, 19th April 1916. Married to Blanche Stomouth Lane and had one daughter residing at Amhurst, 21 Ditton Road, Surbiton. Medals applied for Mrs. Blanch Law, 17 Norfolk Road, Brighton and c/o Mrs. White, Lindhurst Road, Brighton. Pension payable to daughter, Eileen Ogilivy Lane born 12th May 1909. Record indicates his name on the declaration and wedding certificate was Aidan Alfred Edward Joseph Lane. Memorial Ref. Pier and Face 9 C., Thiepval Memorial, France.

LAUGHLIN, Second Lieutenant, James Courtney. Killed after 7.36am by machine gun fire, 1st July 1916. 20th Bn., The King's (Liverpool Regiment). Aged 25. Son of Robert Gardiner Laughlin and Annie Laughlin, of 129, University Street, Belfast. Member of the Queen's University, Belfast, Training Corps. In business in Ann Street and obtained a commission in the Liverpool Regiment. Three months at the Front. Entered France, 13th April 1916. One of three serving brothers. Father applied for his medals. Original Grave reference Maricourt Military Cemetery Row I Grave 13, map reference 62C.A.22.b.c.5. and reburied 1925, grave being identified by a cross. Memorial Ref. II. L. 19., Cerisy-Gailly Military Cemetery, France.

LAYTON-BENNETT, Second Lieutenant, Geoffrey Ernest. Was killed at about 8.00am on the 1st July 1916 after being struck by shrapnel and fell on the attack on Montauban. B Coy., 2nd Bn., Yorkshire Regiment. Aged 28. Born Hampstead, 4th January, 1888. Eldest son of Ernest Layton-Bennett and E. Beatrice Layton-Bennett, of 10, Belsize Grove, Hampstead, London. Educated Merchant Taylor's School. He served his articles with his father and became a member of the Chartered Accountants on 1st February 1911 admitted as a partner, 31st December 1914. Enlisted as a private, 9914 and took part in the second battle of Ypres with the 5th Bn., London Rifle Brigade and obtained his commission, 5th February 1915. Entered France, 4th November 1914. Initially buried Talus Boise British Cemetery, map reference 62C.A.18.b.5.4. Commemorated Merchant Taylors' School, Northwood. His father applied for his medals. He was buried 48 hours after his death and his ID disc was left on his grave Memorial Ref. IV. F. 32., Peronne Road Cemetery, Maricourt, France. WO 339/50652

LEACROFT, Captain, Ronald John Ranulph, MC. **Missing believed killed,** 1st July 1916. 1st Bn., Somerset Light Infantry. They advanced to attack on the 1st July in magnificent style but having entered the enemy's first line devastating fire came from the Quadrilateral and desperate fighting with bomb and bayonet followed and losses by 10.00pm amounted to 464 men. Aged 22. Younger of the two sons of Major Edward R. (former lay rector of St. Peter's, Derby) and Alice Leacroft, of Rowberrow Manor, Winscombe, Somerset. Born April 1894. Attended Blundell's School, as a "Westlake" boy during 1903-1911. Both brothers, Ronald and Geoffrey were educated at Blundell's School between 1903 and 1911, where they were known as "Romulus and Remus". Ronald was a school monitor and was a distinguished member first of the choir and then of the bugle band, winning the silver bugle twice in succession besides being twice member of the winning choir in the Glee competition. Both brothers joined the Somerset Light Infantry in which Ronald received his commission in March 1913, he went on with the Expeditionary Force at the start of the war, 21st August 1914 and was wounded at Mons in the head from a flying piece of shrapnel. 1st February 1915 he was made captain. Awarded the Military Cross, gazetted 3rd June 1916. Grandson of Bishop Leacroft. Medal Index Card implies attached York and Lancaster Regiment. Brother, Captain Geoffrey Charles Ranulph Leacroft, Somerset Light Infantry was gazetted for his Military Cross, 28th August 1916; "For conspicuous gallantry when leading a raid on the enemy's trenches. When the enemy exploded a mine he directed his parties for over two hours under heavy fire. It was mainly, owing to his coolness and personal example that his men succeeded in covering the working parties during the consolidation." Father applied for his medals. Memorial Ref. C. 40., Redan Ridge Cemetery No.1, Beaumont-Hamel, France.

Some officers of the Nth Battalion, Somerset Light Infantry.
From left to right are Captain E. T. S. de Lisle Bush (wounded), Captain R. J. R. Leacroft (killed), Lieutenant C. J. O. Danberry (wounded), Captain Harrington (wounded), Lieutenant 'Kit' Stater, Lieutenant R. Chichester (wounded), Lieutenant C. C. P. Fair (killed). A melancholy interest attaches to this photograph by reason of the fact that the officer who took it was killed in action. The Somersets have done gallant work on the Somme.

LEATHLEY, Second Lieutenant, William George. Killed in the German trenches while attacking a party of Germans coming from a dug-out, 1st July 1916. 8th Bn., Somerset Light Infantry. Aged 20. Son of William Leathley, of Grewelthorpe, Ripon, Yorks. Nephew of Miss M. Leathley of Grewelthorpe. Born 7th September 1895. Educated Drax Grammar School and up to the time of receiving his commission was assistant-master at Brynmelyn School, Weston-super-Mare, resided there. Transferred from reserve battalion, 22nd December 1914. Entered France, 20th May 1916. Effects were silk scarf, silk apron, treasury notebook, advance book, compass, gloves, five photos, fountain pen, card case, small photo, stamps, calendar, keys, drinking cup, cheque book and franc note. His aunt, Miss M. Leathley, Grewelthorpe applied for his medals. Memorial Ref. Pier and Face 2 A., Thiepval Memorial, France. WO 339/4523

LECHE, Second Lieutenant, Arthur Victor Carlton. Missing believed killed with the 1st Bn., 1st July 1916. 3rd Bn., attd 1st Bn., Somerset Light Infantry. Aged 20. Only son of Dr. Arthur Victor Carylon Leche (Medical Officer for the workhouse and Rural District Council), and Sarah Charlotte Leche of Elmcroft, Axbridge. Educated at Sexey's School, Bruton and a member of the OTC. Commissioned 15th August 1914. Entered France, 17th May 1915. On the 19th June 1915 he was in an isolation hospital suffering from German measles at Bailleul. Dr. Leche applied for his medals. Memorial Ref. I. A. 31., Serre Road Cemetery No.2, France.

From Axbridge, Somerset

LEE-WOOD, Captain, Alfred. His servant Private G. Hutton recalled that on 1st July;-"the captain was standing below the parapet, smoking a cigarette and glancing at his wrist watch. At 7:30 sharp, he leapt over the parapet followed by his men. A tornado of bullets was encountered from every side. Barely fifty yards had been covered when he was hit by a bullet which grazed his head. Without pausing he went on a little further, when a second bullet struck the captain on the head, and at that moment I was struck in the leg. Turning to me Captain Wood asked "Are you badly hit?" I replied "Yes, sir I can't go on." He then ordered me to try and get back to the trench, I begged him to come back with me but he said "No, I will get that machine-gunner." This gun was causing great losses amongst his men. Finally the gun was taken and it was found the gunner was chained to his machine and was wearing the Iron Cross. A murderous fire was coming from other machine guns, the whereabouts could not be located until it was discovered that they were hidden behind wounded Germans on stretchers, where were being used as cover. I heard the captain reached the third line of German trenches before receiving his third and fatal wound. When I last saw the captain he was lying in our trench and the colonel was with him, back in the trench his last words were "Am I dreaming?" He was a brave officer and one of the best. Amongst the men he was known as the "Gaffer" and they would have followed him anywhere."

Command of A Coy,. right half of the attacking line and had taken up a position on the south side of Oblong Wood. 1st July 1916. 15th Bn., Lancashire Fusiliers. Aged 30. Eighth son of James and Maria Anne Lee-Wood of Elm House, Bolton Road, Clifton. Born 25th May 1886 in Clifton, Salford. Father was the secretary of the Clifton & Kearsley Coal Company. His brother Percy of nearby Oakwood, became the General Manager. Educated University School, Southport and Elberfeld College, Germany (1901 – 1909) he gained a BSc at Manchester University, Electrical Engineering in 1910. His brother, Arthur was a director of the Lancashire Dynamo & Motor Co., and Alfred in Trafford Park and became the firms representative in India. Alfred enlisted at the outbreak of war, his enlistment forms specifies "Fit in all respects – he has occasionally a very slight stammer which does not affect him at all in giving orders at drill." Commissioned lieutenant, 12th October 1914, and promoted to captain, sent to France, November 1915. Member of the Institute of Electrical Engineering. His sister, Miss F. Lee-Wood applied for his medals. Author's note; It was unlikely the gunner was chained to the machine gun and probably mistaken for a lifting chain. Memorial Ref. Pier and Face 3 C and 3 D., Thiepval Memorial, France.

LEMAN, Captain, Thomas Henry. He was seen on the parapet off the second line shortly afterwards seen in the second line trench trying to organise a defensive position with Second Lieutenant A. H. Wilkins. Captain Leman saw Germans heading towards the men and shot at them with his revolver. Shot in the arm and jaw and died between the German first and second line, he continued to organise a defence until overwhelmed from both flanks and ordered his men to retire, leaving him in the German trench. Reported missing believed killed. 1st July 1916. Officer Commanding, A Coy., 1st /7th Bn., Sherwood Foresters (Notts and Derby Regiment). Born 8th February 1895. Aged 21. Son of Thomas Charles and Helena Maud Leman, of 12, Arthur Street, Nottingham. He had two sisters. Born 8th February 1895. Educated Chigwell School and in the OTC. Was at Chigwell, Essex until he was 19 and was then articled to his father's firm, Messrs. Leman and Sons, chartered accountants. Married to Helena Leman and had two daughters. Keen on cricket and golf. After the outbreak of war for some time with the OTC at the University College. Commissioned 1st October 1914 and captain, 14th October 1915. Entered France, 12th July 1915. Three officers who commanded the same company of the battalion were all killed, Major Hind and Captain J. G. Mellers. Body recovered in March 1917. One of two old boys killed from Chigwell School, his headmaster, Mr. E. H. S. Walde choose his motto for the chapel plaque; 'Fortis scit mori non cedere' translates 'he knows how to give' which also appears on his headstone. His mother applied for his medals as his father died in October 1918 and she adopted this phrase for his headstone. Memorial Ref. III. D. 10., Foncquevillers Military Cemetery, France.

Fortis Scit Mori Non Cedere

LEMON, Lieutenant, Archie Dunlap. Very gallantly led his men, and was shot by two German officers who fired their rifles at him from the top of a dug out which apparently led into the tunnel. The two German officers were afterwards killed by a bomb which exploded right at their feet, first reported missing, 1st July 1916. No. 6 Platoon under Lieutenant Lemon, were supported by a Lewis gun were to enter the Railway Sap and clear it's length and then push up the railway line to the station. B Coy. 12th Bn., Royal Irish Rifles. Aged 41. Son of A. D. Lemon, J.P., and Mrs. Lemon, of Edgcumbe House, Strandtown, Belfast. Born in County Down, Ireland in 1875. Educated Methodist College, Belfast and prior to the war was a manager of Barn Mill, Carrickfergus. Prominent member of the Royal North of Ireland Yacht Club and a regular competitor. Entered France, 5th October 1915. Miss Lemon applied for his medals. Memorial Ref. Pier and Face 15 A and 15 B., Thiepval Memorial, France.

Capt. and Adjt. F. H. M. Lewes.
Killed in action, July 1st. 1916.

LEWES, Captain, Frederick Henry Meredith. Killed near Gommecourt, reported missing 1st July 1916. He and his unit managed to reach the third line of German trenches where they were cut off and fought until they died. He was in a shell hole just in front of the German parapet and called for another attack, with men being killed as soon as they stood up. He was with Lieutenant Colonel D. D. Wilson also killed. Lieutenant M. S. Fryar provided a more accurate account as he was in the shell home with the Captain. After 12.30pm, the officers decided to give in, being in the proximity of two machine guns, Lieutenant Fryar negotiated that they could bring in the wounded and the Captain was bought in although unconscious and he died the following day. Adjutant, 5th Bn., Sherwood Foresters (Notts and Derby Regiment). Aged 29. Son of Colonel Hugh Arthur Lewes, and Mrs. Lucy Julia Perfect Lewes of Rothsay, Camelsdale, Haslemere, Surrey. Born 28th July 1887 in Kensington, London. Attended Haileybury (Trevelyan & Edmonstone 1901-1905). Civil engineer, coaching section of the Midland Railway. Married to Mrs. A. Lewes. Resided 3 Oak Hill Road, Surbiton Hill. He was commissioned second lieutenant on 11th April 1911 in the Territorial Force. He suffered trench fever in September 1915 and rejoined his battalion in November 1915. Buried by the Germans but his grave was subsequently lost after March 1917. The number of casualties was so great that they were neatly buried in common graves, but to this officer for reasons now unknown, the enemy desired to pay special honour, so they buried him alone. Frederick's remains were found in the churchyard at Essarts and subsequently lost. His mother applied for his medals and in 1921 wrote to inform a change of address to Haslemere, Surrey. Memorial Ref. Pier and Face 10 C 10 D and 11 A., Thiepval Memorial, France.

LEWIS, Lieutenant-Colonel, Harold. 37th Lancers, Indian Army commanding 20th Bn., Manchester Regiment. Advance began at 2.30pm and they came under fire from machine-guns, killed towards the bottom of the hill, 1st July 1916. Took the decision to advance with Battalion Headquarters to try and regain control of the situation, along with his pet dog. Age 35. Twice Mentioned in Despatches. Fourth son of Captain Ernest Lewis (Scots Fusiliers), of Red House, Guildford. Husband of Eleanor Mary Lewis, of 37, Hill Lane, Southampton. Born in 1880, Attended Uppingham School. Played cricket for Uppingham. He gained his first appointment in 1899, and in the following year joined the Indian Staff Corps. In 1908 he saw active service in the operations in the Zakka Khel country, and was awarded the medal with clasp. He leaves a widow in Buriton, Weybridge. Well known in Indian polo circles, he was handicapped at 5 goals by the I.P.A., and represented his regimental team in many tournaments. Brother Lieutenant-Colonel Wing Commander Donald Swain Lewis killed 10th April 1916 whilst flying over the enemy's line. Another brother killed in the South African War. Applied for medals and confirmed by India Office who had representatives in this country. Original burial map reference 62D.F.9.d.9.7 Grave Ref. VI.I.I Dantzig Alley British Cemetery, Somme, France.

LEWIS, Major, Harry Arthur, DCM. Killed with his company of men whom were decimated by machine-gun fire, 1st July 1916. 9th Bn., York and Lancaster Regiment. Aged 54. Husband of Charlotte Lewis, of 31, Port Hill, Hertford and Woburn, Beds. Born Shrivenham. Active military career originally being attached to the Grenadier Guards, whilst with them he won the DCM at the Battle of Omdurman, he also had medals for Sudan, Khartoum and one clasp for good service and conduct. He served with the Guards 21 years, moving to Woburn from the Tower of London and taking up the position of drill instructor. Trained the Woburn Boy Scouts. Training complete he took duty as a lodge porter until he left for service. Irish Guards, 5213, Sergeant. Temporary captain with the 8th Yorks and Lancs, 23rd December 1914. Entered France, 27th August 1915. Promoted to major on transferring to the 9th. Left a widow, Charlotte four sons and a daughter – Winnie. Commemorated Faculty of Engineering, King's College London Memorial. Mentioned in Despatches. A Mr. T. N. Lewis applied for his medals from Hertford. Two children on officers' payment; Frederic William and Winifred 'Winnie' Clara Louise. Memorial Ref. Pier and Face 14 A and 14 B., Thiepval Memorial, France.

LEWIS, Second Lieutenant, John Emrys. He was advancing with his company, urging his men forward when he was hit in the head by a bullet and killed instantaneously, 1st July 1916. 8th Bn., Somerset Light Infantry. John was born 16th November 1891, the son of Jenkin and Mary Anne Lewis, of Rhiwmynach, Devils Bridge, Aberystwyth. Member of the Aberystwyth OTC. He was a teacher prior to the war, and was commissioned into the Somerset Light Infantry on the 11th August 1915. John landed in France on 20th May 1916, and proceeded to join the 8th Bn., Somerset Light Infantry. His brother, Private David Lewis had been killed at Cuinchy on 18th February 1916. Originally buried Becourt-Fricourt Road. 57d.X.26.d.8.6. Reinterred 1919. Effects returned were identity disc, cap badge, cloth shoulder strap and letter. His father applied for his medals. Memorial Ref. II. M. 3., Gordon Dump Cemetery, Ovillers-La Boisselle, France. WO 339/40874

LEWIS, Second Lieutenant, Llewelyn. 17th Bn., Royal Welsh Fusiliers. Died between 1st July 1916 and 12th July 1916. Aged 25. Son of Margaret Lewis, of Bron Wylfa, Farrar Road, Bangor and Thomas Hugh Lewis. Llewelyn Lewis was born on 16th October 1891, he was educated at Ysgol y Poplars, Bangor, and King's School, Chester. In September 1908, when he was 16 years old, he went to work for National Provincial Bank of England as an apprentice at its Colwyn Bay branch. In May 1913 he transferred to Manchester branch as a clerk. Memorial Ref. Pier and Face 4A. Thiepval Memorial, France.

LEWIS, Captain, Reginald Cameron, MC. Reported missing, led the line gallantly and well, 1st July 1916. Before the attack he spoke to his men for about twenty minutes encouraging them and praising them, he got up several entertainments. B Coy., 2nd Bn., Royal Berkshire Regiment. Aged 27. Son of Charles E. (Professor of Greek at the South African College, Cape Town) and Elizabeth Tryphena Lewis, of 21, Park Road, Cape Town, South Africa. Born 12th May 1889 he was educated at the South African School and College, and graduated from Cape University with Honours in zoology in 1909. He went into residence as research student in zoology in 1911 and graduated in 1914 from Christ's College. Lewis was a good cricketer and was in the college eleven in 1912 and 1913 when his batting average was just over 30. He also rowed in the 2nd Lent boat in 1912 when it reached the 2nd Division for the first time. The War Record of Christ's College Boat Club records 2nd Lent VIII 1912- 3 and 3rd Lent VIII 1913-4. On leaving College in 1913 he received an appointment as demonstrator in the Imperial College of Science, South Kensington. Enlisted King Edward's Horse, private, 307, 23rd December 1914. Entered France, 24th April 1915. In May 1915, he was gazetted to the Royal Berkshires, and in the following May he was awarded the Military Cross. From letters received from officers of his regiment it appears he "led the first line of attack with his company and was found lying very badly wounded in a shell hole by a private who stayed by him till he died very shortly afterwards. He told the men not to attempt to move him. Lewis was a man of sterling character and high ability. He showed promise of great things and had he been spared would have gone far, both as a man and as a student and researcher. He was a type of the best product of the Colonies - sturdy, determined and capable. The world is the poorer by his loss." Death confirmed 25th November 1916. Two brothers served, Second Lieutenant P. T. Lewis, RFA and Second Lieutenant A. W. Lewis, 5th Dorsets. Close friend of High Commissioner for the Union of South Africa. Father, Professor Lewis applied for his medals from Cape Town, South Africa. Original burial map reference 57d.X.7.b. Memorial Ref. VIII. C. 3., Ovillers Military Cemetery, France. WO 339/78489

LEY, Second Lieutenant, Maurice Carew. Killed in action, 1st July 1916. 2nd Bn., Devonshire Regiment. Son of Arthur Henry and Violet Ley, of 77, Comeragh Road, West Kensington, London. Age 20. Born 26th February 1896. Educated Preparatory Church, St. Paul's. Enlisted 9th September 1914 as a private, 7th Royal Fusiliers. Commissioned 29th March 1915. Arrived in France, 24th November 1915. Effects returned were a notebook. Father applied for his medals. Originally buried as unknown officer, Devon Regiment and formally identified in 1921 with the effects being Advance Pay Book No.8844 issued by Field Cashier, VI Corps 1.6.1916, officer's cap badge, 1 officer's star, 1 pair of binoculars prismatic No. 3 marks magnification 6, No 11802, Aitchinson, London. Memorial Ref. XIII. Y. 1., Ovillers Military Cemetery, France. WO 339/48176

LIDIARD, Second Lieutenant, Richard John Abraham. 10.10am, heavy barrage put up by enemy whilst trying to dig communication trenches, causing numerous casualties, Hebuterne, killed in action whilst acting captain, 1st July 1916. 3rd Bn., London Regiment (Royal Fusiliers). Articled to his father, Herbert Lidiard, of 7 Great James Street, W.C. Mother, Kate Mary Lina Lidiard. Both 4th May 1895. Resided 23 Devonshire Terrace, Paddington. Educated St. George's School, Windsor. September 1914, second lieutenant, 3rd City of London Bn., Royal Fusiliers. Served in Gallipoli evacuated with jaundice after having malaria. Entered France, 24th April 1916. Named on family headstone, Wandsworth Cemetery. Mother applied for his medals. Memorial Ref. II. P. 1., Hebuterne Military Cemetery, France.

LIMBERY, Captain, Charles Roy, MC. Killed at as he reached Dantzig Alley, Mametz, lead his men over the top, 1st July 1916, died about the same time as Captain George White. C Coy., 1st Bn., South Staffordshire Regiment. Aged 26. Son of Thomas and Margaret Limbery, of 12, Barnpark, Teignmouth, Devon. Born 21st January 1890 at Newport, Monmouthshire. Attended Eastman's Preparatory School and Sherborne School. 1910 joined the South Staffordshire Regiment. Went to France with 1st BEF, 11th August 1914 and was twice wounded at Loos, and again in May 1916. Received his captain rank in July 1915. Admitted to hospital, 1st October 1915 with a gunshot wound to the neck and arm, discharged 7th October. Twice Mentioned in Despatches. Awarded the Military Cross in January 1916. Brother of Captain Kenneth Thomas Limbery killed 26th September 1917. Originally buried The Shrine, Mametz sheet 62d.F.5.c.1.4 with two other officers from the 1st Bn. Re-interred 1920. His mother applied for his medals whilst a Mr. Norman Limbery choose his inscription. Memorial Ref. IX. E. 8., Dantzig Alley British Cemetery, Mametz, France. WO 339/7732

O Lord, Let Light Perpetual Shine Upon Him

LINDSAY, Major, Francis Howard. Went forward under dense smoke, occupied objective assigned to him, Fame Trench by 7.45am in charge of B Coy. About 2.30pm Major Lindsay arranged with Captain Sparks to a defensive line, but was killed while walking back to Fall Trench, shot by a sniper, 1st July 1916. Captain Sparks took command and fought on until he ran out of ammunition even taking ammunition from the dead and wounded. The Major's body was covered with a waterproof sheet. A Coy., 1st/14th Bn., London Regiment (London Scottish). Aged 40. Son of William Alexander Lindsay Esq., K.C., Clarenceux King of Arms, and Lady Harriet Lindsay. Born 1876. Educated Malvern College, 1887 to 1895 and graduated from Clare College, Cambridge as a Bachelor of Arts, 1898. Employed as an examiner with the Scotch Education Department since 1899. Husband of Helen Margaret Lindsay, of 7, Emperor's Gate, South Kensington, London and father to John Stewart and Katherine Francis. Married 14th April 1910 at St. Paul's Church, Knightsbridge. Brother James also served and was wounded in 1917, brother Michael was killed in the Boer War. Entered France, 15th September 1914. Francis was severely wounded in the head, 14th November 1914 at Messines and not fit for foreign service until May 1916. Promoted to Temporary Major, 14th January 1916. Medals to address Emperor's Gate, S7. Memorial Ref. Pier and Face 9 C and 13 C., Thiepval Memorial, France.

LINTOTT, Lieutenant, Evelyn Henry. Fighting was hard and shelling heavy, machine-gun fire was intense, killed instantly, 1st July 1916. He led his men with great dash and when hit for the first time declined to take the count. Instead he drew his revolver and asked for further effort. Again he was hit but struggled on but a third shot finally bowled him over. 15th Bn., West Yorkshire Regiment (Prince of Wales's Own). Aged 33. Son of Arthur Frederick and Eleanor L. Lintott, of Hazelville, Wolseley Road, Farncombe, Surrey. Educated at the Royal Grammar School, Ilford and trained as teacher, St. Luke's College, Exeter. Former professional football player (played for Woking, Plymouth Argyle, Queens Park Rangers and Bradford City) and England international played in all International matches in 1908. In the teaching profession at Dudley Hill School, Bradford. Joined as a private and quickly given the rank of sergeant. He had been playing for Leeds when he enlisted on the 14th September 1914. One of the first professional footballers to receive a commission. Served in Egypt, disembarking 22nd December 1915. Mrs. E. A. Lintott applied for his medals. Memorial Ref. Pier and Face 2 A 2 C and 2 D., Thiepval Memorial, France.

LITTEN, Captain, Raymond. Killed whilst leading his company into action, gave the order to go over at 7.27am and killed between Bund Trench and Bund Support, 1st July 1916. B Coy., 6th Bn., Royal Berkshire Regiment. Dressed to appear as on ordinary soldier but still identifiable as an officer in the advance. Aged 32. Only son of Tobias Raphael Litten and Frances Litten, of 21, Pembridge Villas, Notting Hill, London. Born 14th August 1883, educated City of London School and in Germany. Member of the Stock Exchange 1912. Freeman of the City of London, 15th December 1915. Joined the Inns of Court OTC, 5th August 1914. Obtained commission in the Royal Berkshire, September 1914. Went to France, July 1915. Gazetted captain, October 1915. Unmarried left a mother and five sisters to mourn him. Jewish Book of Honour. His mother applied for his medals and officers pension. Memorial Ref. Q. 19., Carnoy Military Cemetery, France. WO 339/65352

All You Had Hoped For All You Had You Gave To Save Mankind

LIVERSIDGE, Second Lieutenant, Albert. Fighting was hard and shelling heavy, machine-gun fire was intense, reported wounded, 1st July officially 2nd July 1916. 15th Bn., West Yorkshire Regiment (Prince of Wales's Own). Aged 23. Born 1st July 1893 and local reports suggest he died on his birthday. Eldest son of Albert (bottle maker) and Elizabeth Ann Liversidge, of 39 Newport Street, Jack Lane, Hunslet Road, Leeds. Educated at Wheelwright Grammar School, Dewsbury, Yorkshire where he gained a scholarship to the Leeds Higher Grade School and then studied to become a teacher at Leeds Training College. At the outbreak of the war he was teaching at Hunslet Moor School, Leeds. He enlisted with the "Pals" as a private in September 1914 and because of his academic background was immediately promoted to sergeant. His commission back into the battalion as a second lieutenant came on 26th June 1915. Attached to the Machine Gun Section, he served with the Leeds Pals throughout their stay in Colsterdale, Egypt and France. Entered Egypt, 22nd December 1915. Medal Index Card has died of wounds, 2nd July 1916. Medal application by his parents. Memorial Ref. II. A. 6., Doullens Communal Cemetery Extension No.1, France.

He Died For Liberty And Right.

LIVESEY, Captain, Harry. Led the second wave of the battalion, comprising two platoons each of W and X Companies. In the early hours of 1st July 1916, the four platoons deployed in Copse Trench, killed at Serre, some 50-70 yards behind the front line. At 7.22am, Livesey - walking stick in one hand, revolver in the other – he was seen to gallantly led his men forward into No Man's Land where they lay down on the ground fifty yards behind the first wave. In the first German trench reported he shot five Germans with his revolver after one of them hurled a bomb in his direction and then an explosion grazed him in the face. 9.00am Captain Livesey reported wounded. 11.25am reported 1st wave with remnants of 2nd wave, together with 3rd wave charged German trenches led by Captain Livesey. He charged under a hail of bullets from both machine-gun and rifle fire. Reported he was hit in the arm going over the parapet, and hit in the chest half way across and finally killed by a rifle grenade. W Coy. 11th Bn., East Lancashire Regiment. Aged 35. Only son of Robert and Corrinna Livesey, of Westleigh, Blackburn. Born 25th February 1882.

Educated at Rossall and had travelled around Europe and the whole of the world on behalf of the firm of Henry Livesey Ltd, Greenbank Ironworks, Blackburn of which he was a director. Entered France, 8th March 1916. Father applied for his medals. Memorial Ref. Pier and Face 6 C., Thiepval Memorial, France.

LODGE, Second Lieutenant, Ralph Nesbit. Reported as missing, led platoons of B Coy., 1st July 1916. 3rd Bn. attd. 15th Bn., Lancashire Fusiliers. Born 22nd January 1894. Son of Charles Septimus Lodge BA a tutor, and Amelia of 43 Walmer Street, Moss Side. Member of the Manchester Staff of General Electric Company and nephew of Sir Oliver Lodge. Educated at Manchester Grammar School, joining the GEC in 1913 and was employed in the costs department. He enlisted as a private in September, 1914 in the Royal Fusiliers and a few months later received his commission, May 1915 and was sent to Camberley for training. In France, two months since 23rd May 1916. Father applied for his medals. Memorial Ref. Pier and Face 3 C and 3 D., Thiepval Memorial, France.

LOGAN, Second Lieutenant, David Herbert Hoskem. Shot as the regiment advanced from the first to the second line, Fricourt, 1st July 1916. The prior day he and some of his men were buried by the explosion of a 5.9 shell. 2nd Bn., Border Regiment. Aged 19. Son of General Logan. Born 4th August 1897. Native of Bristol. Attended Wellington College. Husband of Dora Cornilius of 119 Leinster Road, Rathmines, Dublin. Choose the Border Regiment due to ancestral claims. Entered France, 26th May 1916. Mrs. Cornilius applied for his medals. His inscription was decided by Mrs. E.M. Logan, c/o Messrs. Cox & Co., J. Dept., Charing Cross, SW. Memorial Ref. II. D. 12., Citadel New Military Cemetery, Fricourt, France. WO 339/240

At The Going Down Of The Sun And In The Morning We Will Remember Him

LOMAS, Lieutenant, Harold. Cut down leading his men forward, Fricourt sector, reported he was badly wounded and taken back and died two hours later, 1st July 1916. 20th Bn., Manchester Regiment. Born 14th September 1875 at Brooklands, Manchester. Son of G. H. Lomas. He studied at both Manchester Technical College and Manchester University graduating with an BSc in Engineering in 1895. Inns of Court OTC. Served with the East Surrey Volunteers. In 1900 he took a job with the Crocker-Wheeler Company of Baltimore, New York and emigrated to the USA. Member of the American Institute of Electrical Engineers in 1903. Younger brother of Dr. A. Lomas of Ashfield, Castleton. Played cricket for Manchester City Football Club Supporters and Wimbledon Cricket Club after going to the USA played for Baltimore and Richmond County. Left his wife and two young daughters to travel back to Britain to enlist in the 20th Bn., Manchester Regiment and was commissioned as a second lieutenant, 19th February 1915. Entered France, 9th November 1915. Promoted to lieutenant. Originally buried sheet 62. Sq.F.9.d.99.10. south of Fricourt also reported 62D.F.9.d.9.7. In his will he left an insurance policy to his wife, wrist watch to his sister-in-law, ring to his daughter, Victoria and apparel to daughter, Elaine. Effects returned were a damaged wrist watch and eye glasses. His widow applied for his medals from New York. Memorial Ref. VI. I. 4., Dantzig Alley British Cemetery, Mametz, France. WO 339/26016

LONGHURST, Second Lieutenant, Seaward. Reported missing and then killed, leading and urging his men on in the great advance, 1st July 1916. 11th Bn., Sherwood Foresters (Notts and Derby Regiment). Aged 22. Born 9th November 1893. Son of Angelo and Frances Longhurst, of 118, Venner Road, Sydenham, London. Educated Beckenham Technical Institute and Clark's College, London. Employed previously clerical work, Post Office, National Health Insurance and local government board. At the outbreak of war joined the London Scottish, private 2760. Gazetted May 1915. Father applied for his medals. Originally buried 970 yards, NW of Ovillers Church. Officially reported killed in action, October 1916 prior to this in late September Mrs. Longhurst had heard from Colonel H. Watson DSO that he was found and buried being identified by the disc that he was wearing. Memorial Ref. I. H. 56., Martinsart British Cemetery, France. WO 339/34230

LORD, Lieutenant, Henry Otto. Killed whilst leading his men, 1st July 1916. 26th Bn., Manchester Regiment. Aged 20. Son of Henry and Frieda Lord, of Kentford Lodge, Newmarket. Born 29th May 1896. Pupil at "Cheltonia" Darley Road, Eastbourne. At Felsted School he was lance corporal in the OTC from September 1911 until July 1915 when he left school, entered school September 1911 (Prefect, Football XI). Scholar, Christ's College, Cambridge. He enlisted in Newmarket. Awarded a temporary commission on 19th October 1915 he went to School of Instruction, Imperial Hydro, Hornsea, Yorkshire. He joined Base Depot at Etaples on 30th May 1916 and joined his battalion in the field on 7th June 1916. His effects, sent to his father in Kentford, were one revolver holster, a water flask and some letters. Commemorated Stained glass window, St. Mary Church, Kentford. His mother applied for his medals. Original map reference for burial 62D.F.9.d.9.7. Memorial Ref. VI. I. 6., Dantzig Alley British Cemetery, Mametz, France. WO 339/44340

Eldest Son Of Henry & Frieda Lord Kentford, Suffolk My Redeemer Liveth

LOUDOUN-SHAND, Major, Stewart Walter, VC. Killed whilst leading his company against the German trenches, under heavy machine-gun fire, 1st July 1916. B Coy., 10th Bn., Yorkshire Regiment. Victoria Cross awarded at Fricourt in the afternoon in the area of Crucifix Trench and Shelter Wood 'for most conspicuous bravery when his company attempted to climb over the parapet to attack the enemy's trenches, they were met by very fierce machine-gun fire, which temporarily stopped their progress. Major Loudoun-Shand immediately leapt on the parapet, helped the men over it and encouraged them in every way until he fell mortally wounded. Even then he insisted on being propped up in the trench, and went on encouraging the non-commissioned officers and the men until he died'. Aged 36. Son of Mr. J. L. Loudoun-Shand (tea plantation), of 27, Alleyn Park, Dulwich, London. Born on October 8th, 1879, Ceylon. Whilst at Dulwich (1891-1897) he was in the third cricket Eleven, and later he played in many parts of the world. Clerk at William Deacon's Bank. He took part in the South African War with the Pembrokeshire Yeomanry. Former tea-merchant in Ceylon, returned there in 1904 and returned to enlist being given a temporary commission as lieutenant in the 10th Bn., Yorkshire Regiment in November 1914. Promoted captain, June 1915 and major in December 1915. Went to France, September 1915 and was slightly wounded in March 1916. All four brothers served. His VC being collected by his father on the 31st March 1917. Brother of Lieutenant E. G. Loudoun-Shard, King Royal Rifles, the rugby international who was wounded in the war several times. Memorial Ref. I. C. 77., Norfolk Cemetery, Becordel-Becourt, France.

In Honoured And Loving Memory

LOW, Lieutenant, James Morrison. Wounded and missing, believed killed, 1st July 1916. Detached from 2nd Bn., Seaforth Highlanders to the 10th Bde, Machine Gun Company. Brigade machine-gun officer. Aged 24. Eldest son of Sir James Low, BT., and Lady Low, of Kilmaron Castle, Cupar, Fife. Born 14th October 1891. Educated Glenalmond and Merton College, Oxford. Attained his majority in September, 1912 whilst fresh from Oxford. Associated with his father's business. Entered France, 19th February 1915. Seconded with the Machine Gun Corps, 22nd December 1915. Memorial Ref. Pier and Face 15 C., Thiepval Memorial, France.

LUDLOW, Captain, Stratford Walter. He fell at the head of his company while gallantly leading them over the front German position in the assault on the Quadrilateral, July 1st, 1916 and although wounded was last seen with some of his men in the second line of German trenches. C Coy. 1st / 8th Bn., Royal Warwickshire Regiment. Aged 22. Second son of Brigadier General Walter Robert Ludlow, C.B., (chief recruiting officer for Birmingham) and Helen Florence Ludlow, of Lovelace Hill, Solihull. Born on 10th June 1894 and baptised at Knowle on 22nd July 1894. Worcester King's School, Worcester (1904 to 1907). Join the training ship, HMS Conway at Liverpool to train in the merchant navy. Left in April 1909 and returned to the King's School, leaving the sixth form in July 1911. Colour sergeant in the OTC. On leaving school went to work for his father's firm, Ludlow & Briscoe, Temple Street, Birmingham, intending to qualify as a surveyor. Joined the 8th Bn., Warwickshire Regiment, gazetted lieutenant in August 1913, and captain in December 1914, going to the Front with his battalion in March 1915. Initially posted as wounded and missing, which led to an appeal by his parents in the Birmingham Gazette, 14th July 1916. The article states: 'He was seen in the assault on the German position on Sunday 2 July, about 7.45 am, wounded in the arm in crossing the first of the German works, but continued in the charge until the second German trench was reached. Since then nothing has been heard of him.'

By 21st July, confirmation of his death had been received. Now reported killed;. 'Information has been received that his body has been found, and that he was interned in a shell hole on the night of 15th-16th...He fell at the head of his company, while gallantly leading them over the enemy's front position, and although wounded was last seen with some of his men in the second line of enemy trenches. Letters received from surviving officers describe him as an excellent soldier and a first-class company commander, and a more cheery and enthusiastic brother officer, his comrades say, they could not wish to have had'. Original map burial reference 57.d.K.35.a.1.5, exhumed 14th May 1931. The exhumation report showing he was 6'0", effects were pencil case, whistle, ring, card case containing gold charm (horseshoe), ORILUX lamp with case stamped Captain S. W. Ludlow 8 R.War.R, identity disc, officer's uniform and boots, leather epaulettes with three stars and Royal Warwick collar badges. The report also notes that he was shot through the head and his right arm was broken. Commemorated King's School Roll of Honour. Father applied for his medals. Memorial Ref. XXXIX. E. 12., Serre Road Cemetery No.2, France.

Dulce Et Decorum Est Pro Patria Mori

LYLE, Lieutenant Colonel, William. Fell at La Boisselle, last seen walking alive stick in hand, amongst his men about 200 yards from the German trenches, 1st July 1916. Lieutenant Colonel Shakespear's history of 34th Division says Brigadier General Ingouville Williams (known by the men as 'Inky Bill') found the bodies of Lieut-Colonels Sillery and Lyle where they had always wished to be, at the head of their battalions. The General wrote to his wife; ' I have just been reconnoitering and found poor Colonel Lyle's body, surrounded by Tyneside Scottish, all dead a most grievous site to me, who loved my faithful soldiers'. 23rd (Tyneside Scottish) Bn., Northumberland Fusiliers. Aged 40. Son of William Park Lyle. Born April 21st 1876 and educated at Mill Hill, 1888-1894. Served in South African War and awarded Queen's Medal with three clasps. Husband of Edith M. Lyle, of Springvale, Hythe, Kent. Married September 12th 1906 and left a daughter. Retired June 1914, proceeded to France, January 1916. Wife decided his inscription. Memorial Ref. I. G. 1., Bapaume Post Military Cemetery, Albert, France.

To Him That Overcometh Will I Give To Eat Of The Tree Of Life

LYNCH, Lieutenant Colonel, Colmer William Donald, DSO. Killed close to South Sausage Support Trench near Willow Patch, as he left a sap he was wounded in the left shoulder by machine gun bullets and went forward he was hit in the head and killed by a shell, 1st July 1916. Just before he was killed he spoke to Lieutenant Gordon; "Hello, Gordon are you hit?" 9th Bn., King's Own Yorkshire Light Infantry. Aged 35. Only son of Mrs. M. Florence Lynch, of Pareora, Stoke, Guildford, and Major General William Wiltshire Lynch,. Educated Eton College. Twice in Despatches. Took part in the South African War, Queen's medal with four clasps and King's medal with two clasps. Award for the DSO at the Battle of Loos for devotion to duty. At the front for nine months. Entered France, 11th September 1915. Freemason. Mrs. W.W. Lynch, Albemarle Club, Dover Street, W. decided his inscription. Memorial Ref. I. B. 87., Norfolk Cemetery, Becordel-Becourt, France.

To The Glory Of God And In Ever Loving Memory

MacBRAYNE, Lieutenant, John Burns. Reported to be lying shot through the head, he died in the most gallant manner encouraging his men to hold onto a position we had just captured, 1st July 1916. 17th Bn., Highland Light Infantry. Born 13th December 1896, Glasgow. Aged 19. Second son of Laurence MacBrayne (Retired Lieutenant Commander RNVR), and Mabel E. of 8, Park Circus, Glasgow. Educated Glasgow Academy and Aldenham School, Elstree, Herts. Commissioned lieutenant on 10th September 1914. Appointed to 'A' Company, 17th Highland Light Infantry on its formation. Crossed to France 22nd November 1915. Appointed reserve machine-gun officer. 11th February 1916 slightly wounded on the head by shrapnel. In 1927 body moved to Serre Cemetery from original map reference, 57d.R.31.c.49.09 and identified by his disc. Death reported 11th July 1916. Father applied for his medals. Memorial Ref. IX. G. 15., Serre Road Cemetery No.2, France.

They Gave All They Have Gained All

MacBRYAN, Lieutenant, Edward Crozier. Missing believed killed last seen wounded as he was leading his men through the third line of German trenches. 1st July 1916. 3rd Bn. attd. 1st Bn., Somerset Light Infantry. Aged 22. Born 1893. Second son of Dr. Henry Crawford MacBryan, of Kingsdown House, Box, Wilts. Educated at Oundle School and Jesus College, Cambridge. Entered Sidney House, Oundle School in May 1908, and was at school until July 1912 . School prefect. Captain of the school football team. He was in the Oundle Cricket Eleven in 1910 and two following seasons, being captain in 1912, and later played for Jesus College (Cambridge) and, in 1913, a little for Wiltshire. At Jesus College, Cambridge he played rugby with the position wing three quarter. By his second year he had become the Honorary Secretary of the Jesus College Rugby Football Union. Commissioned in the Somerset Light Infantry in August 1914, and later proceeded to France with them. In May 1915 at Ypres he was severely wounded in the left hip (by a shell) and was for some time in England. Making a good recovery he again went out to France in May 1916. Brother, John Crawford William MacBryan was wounded at Le Cateau and taken prisoner in 1914. Father applied for his medals. Memorial Ref. Pier and Face 2 A., Thiepval Memorial, France.

MACDONALD, Second Lieutenant, Roderick. Missing, believed killed, 1st July 1916. Two accounts; Private J. Fairless stated he bandaged an arm wound at about 7.30am and Private Walker stated he was killed shot through the heart. 23rd (Tyneside Scottish) Bn., Northumberland Fusiliers. Member of the staff of the telegraph department at Inverness Post Office and was well-known in the district. Enlisted in the Lovat Scots as a private, 3713, and received a commission in the Northumberland Fusiliers, 27th April 1915. Entered France, 9th January 1916. Telegram send 15th July 1916. William MacNab was making enquiries on the 26th July 1916. A Mrs. Watson applied for his medals, Dumbarton Road, Scotstown, Glasgow. Memorial Ref. Pier and Face 10 B 11 B and 12 B., Thiepval Memorial, France.

MacDONALD, Lieutenant, Simon. Reported missing and then killed, 1st July 1916. 23rd (Tyneside Scottish) Bn., Northumberland Fusiliers. Aged 32. Son of Simon MacDonald (retired farmer), of Drumossie, Midmills Road, Inverness. Husband of Lily Macdougall MacKenzie (formerly MacDonald), of Craiganna, 41, Harrowden Road, Inverness. Employed in the Inverness Post Office, married shortly before going to the Front. Married 17th June 1915. He had been a non-commissioned officer in the Lovat Scouts, sergeant, 5158. Attested 20th June 1908. Enlisted 21st September 1914. Commissioned 25th January 1915. Entered France, 9th January 1916. His brother, Lt. John MacDonald was wounded. Effects were field glasses, revolver, compass, flask, leather wallet containing photos. Original burial map reference 57d.X.13.b.9.1 and identified by a disc and watch. Commemorated Cavell Gardens, War Memorial. Medals to his widow, Mrs. MacKenzie who remarried, Craiganna, Harrowden Road, Inverness. Memorial Ref. II. F. 10., Cerisy-Gailly French National Cemetery, France. WO 339/24490

MacHARDY, Second Lieutenant, David Scott. Mown down on the left in support of A Coy., 1st July 1916. C Coy., 16th Bn., Highland Light Infantry. Age 20. Younger son of the Reverend J. F. MacHardy former United Free Church Minister of Kinnettles near Forfar. Previously employed in the Dundee Electricity Department. Enlisted in the City of Dundee Engineers a month after war broke out, Royal Engineers, sapper, 276, and was at the Front with that unit. Entered France, 25th June 1915. He returned and obtained a commission, gazetted 20th January 1916 in the Highland Light Infantry before again leaving for the Front. Father died two months before him and he managed to get home for the funeral and again a few weeks before his death. Death reported 19th July 1916. Elder brother joined the Mechanical Transport. Brother Mr. J. S. MacHardy applied for his medals. His sister, Elizabeth Scott MacHardy of Aberdeen claimed officers pension. Memorial Ref. Pier and Face 15 C., Thiepval Memorial, France.

MACHELL, Lieutenant Colonel, Percy Wilfrid, CMG, DSO. At 8:30am Colonel Machell gives the final order to advance towards the British front line. Colonel Machell, who survives the first lethal machine-gun fire, is killed as he climbs the parapet to advance his remaining men, shot through the head, 1st July 1916. Prior to attack wrote 'if it goes badly I shall come up and see it through.' 11th (Service) Bn. (Lonsdale)., Border Regiment. Aged 54. Son of Canon Machell of Hull and Emma Machell, sister of 8th Lord Middleton. Resided Crackenthorpe Hall. Educated Clifton College. Joined 56th (Essex Regiment) in 1882. In 1884-5 he served in the Nile Expeditionary Force (medal with clasp and bronze star). Attached to the Egyptian Army in 1886, he was in command at the capture of Fort Khor Moussa (Order of the Osmanieh, 4th class); operations round Suakin and action of Gemaizah, 1888 (clasp); Sudan, 1889-91, Toski Expedition, Brigade-Major No. 2 column; capture of Tokar (clasp, and clasp on bronze star, Medjidie, 4th class); helped to raise and commanded 12th Sudanese Battalion, 1891-95; Inspector General Egyptian Coastguard, 1896; Adviser To The Ministry Of Interior, Egypt, 1898-1906; (Grand Cordon Of The Medjidie, 1902), (CMG, 1906). Raised, trained and commanded 11th Border Regiment (Lonsdale), 1914-16. Married (1905) Lady Valda Gleichen, daughter of Admiral Prince Victor of Hohenlohe Langenbur, RN, GCB. Commemorated Sons and Daughters of the Anglican Church Clergy. Entered France, 30th December 1915. Lady Machell (widow) applied for his medals. Son Rogan Victor Machell entitled to pension. Memorial Ref. A. 17., Warloy-Baillon Communal Cemetery, France.

56 Regt. 1882 Egyptian Army 1886 C.O. XII Sudanese 1891 - 1895 Adviser Ministry Of Interior Egyptian Government 1898 - 1908 Prospice

MACINTYRE, Lieutenant, Thomas. Reported missing, 1st July 1916. 16th Bn., Northumberland Fusiliers. He was a student of agriculture and also a dietician. Resided 14 Beverley Terrace, Cullercoats. Previously private, 1102, Northumberland Fusiliers. Commissioned 17th November 1914. Gazetted 25th September 1915. Entered France, 9th March 1916. Brother Lieutenant George Duncan MacIntyre killed 10th July 1916, had biked over to meet his brother a few weeks earlier and took tea with him. Commemorated St George's Church Memorial in Cullercoats, North Tyneside. His mother applied for his medals changing address in London between Paddington and St. James Wood. Memorial Ref. Pier and Face 10 B 11 B and 12 B., Thiepval Memorial, France.

MacIVER, Lieutenant, Reginald Squarey. Reported killed in action 1st July 1916. 2nd Bn., Lancashire Fusiliers. Aged 24. Second son of David MacIver MP, and Edith Eleanor MacIver, of Wanlass How, Ambleside, Westmorland. Born 1893. Educated at Mostyn House, Parkgate and at Shrewsbury School, 1906 to 1911. Finally at Christ Church, Oxford where he held a scholarship in Natural Science where he excelled at rowing, in the college boat 1913 and 1914. He left Oxford directly to take a commission in August 1914, and was promoted in March 1915. He had been at the Front since 26th May 1915. The Salopian states; "He was universally popular and deservedly so, for he possessed in a very high degree the best of all claims to popularity, a guileless and affectionate heart and the nicest sense of honour." Brother Captain A. T. S. MacIver killed April 1916 with the Cheshire Coy., Royal Engineers. Younger brother severely wounded. His mother applied for his medals. Memorial Ref. I. H. 5., Sucrerie Military Cemetery, Colincamps, France.

MACK, Captain, Isaac Alexander. He went over the top leading his men to the attack on La Boisselle and in that inferno laid down his life, 1st July 1916. 11th Bn., Suffolk Regiment attached to the Trench Mortar Battery. Aged 24. Third son of Isaac A. and Martha S. Mack, of 44, Balliol Road, Bootle, Liverpool, two other sons in the army. Born in Bootle, Lancashire on 9th May 1892. Attended Scarborough College and the Leys School before Jesus College in October 1911. He held a History Entrance Exhibition award of £30 and graduated in 1914 having attained a 2:2 in History Tripos I (1913) and History Tripos II (1914). Fine sportsman, gaining college colours at rugby, hockey and tennis. After leaving college he had hoped to begin training for the Indian Civil Service but joined up at the outbreak of war with Suffolk Regiment from where he received his commission and subsequent promotion to captain. Straight from university to the army, and promoted captain just prior to his death. Embarked 8th January 1916. The obituary for 'Mack' in the Jesus College Cambridge Society Annual Report 1917 reveals an interesting encounter he had with Sir Douglas Haig. Apparently in the summer of 1913 Mack was on OTC manoeuvres acting as a despatch rider when he ran out of petrol, seeing a car at the roadside he asked for help. The occupant was Douglas Haig, who asked Mack to share lunch with him, presumably before getting some petrol for his motorbike. Upon Mack's death Haig wrote of "my old despatch rider… I greatly regret that he has not been spared to continue the career he had so well begun." His father applied for his medals. Special List on Medal Index Card. Original burial map reference 57d.X.20.c Memorial Ref. VI. F. 4., Gordon Dump Cemetery, Ovillers-La Boisselle, France.

Son Of Mr. & Mrs. I.A. Mack Of Bootle, Liverpool "Pass Friend, All's Well"

MACKENZIE, Second Lieutenant, Francis Ramsay. Reported wounded and missing, 1st July 1916. He was injured on the way across and was seen sheltering in a hole with a bandaged head, he could not be found by a search party. C Coy., 2nd Bn., Seaforth Highlanders. Aged 32. Born 15th February 1884 in Edinburgh to Thomas Dingwall Mackenzie and Jessie Jeffrey Mackenzie. Husband of Elizabeth Mary Stark Mackenzie, of 13, Princes Gardens, Glasgow. Educated Hillhead High School and Glasgow University. In 1915 from July until September Francis was a member of the Officers Training Corps. Drapery warehouseman, Messrs. J. W. Campbell, Ingram Street, Glasgow. He then became a second lieutenant in the 2nd Seaforth Highlanders. Married 28th December 1915 in Glasgow had one child, Frances Elma Mackenzie who died aged 19 months in May 1918. Wife and child were entitled to pension. Memorial Ref. Pier and Face 15 C., Thiepval Memorial, France.

MACKENZIE, Captain, Kenneth. Killed in action, 1st July 1916. 24th (Tyneside Irish) Bn., Northumberland Fusiliers. Born 26th June 1882. Mother resided Caragh Villa, Caragh Lake, County Kerry. Served as a private in the British Columbia Horse, in South Africa January 1901 to August 1902 with the 1st King's Royal Rifles. Captain in the 9th King's Royal Rifle Corps from May 1901 to 1906. Enlisted from being a private in Lord Strathcona's Horse and commissioned 15th January 1915, clarified by the Army Office, May 1920. Entered France, January 1916. A brother of Lieutenant-Colonel T. C. Mackenzie DSO whom applied for his medals. Two other brothers served at the Front. Memorial Ref. Pier and Face 10 B 11 B and 12 B., Thiepval Memorial, France. WO 339/497

MACKENZIE, Second Lieutenant, Noel Olliffe Compton. As leading a group of men in a vain attempt to get a fresh supply of bombs over No Man's Land, Message received 3.00pm that confirmed Lieutenant MacKenzie has been killed, 1st July 1916. Initial message 1.10pm; Shelling fearful, MacKenzie killed. Trench practically untenable, full of dead and wounded. A Coy., 1st /13th Kensington Bn., London Regiment. Aged 19. Son of Walter O. C. Mackenzie and Olliffe Augusta MacKenzie (nee Smallwood). Born 1896. Entered Upper School, Epsom College, 16th September 1909. Passed the Oxford and Cambridge School Certificate and the London Matriculation. He left in July 1914 with the intention of continuing to study medicine having passed the first examination for his medical degree but his plans were immediately interrupted by the outbreak of war. He attested for service in the army on 4th October 1914 at Guildford and joined the 54 Field Ambulance at Houslow as private, 39275 in the RAMC. He spent the following months in the UK. He was struck off the strength of the RAMC from 20th February 1915 having received his commission to be a second lieutenant in Princess Louise's, Kensington Bn. Father applied for his medals. Memorial Ref. Pier and Face 9 D 9 C 13 C and 12 C., Thiepval Memorial, France.

MacLAREN, Captain, Ernest Cecil, MC. Killed in action, 1st July 1916. Commanded D Coy., to support C Coy., on the left half of the attacking line. 15th Bn., Lancashire Fusiliers. He was the son of Frederick James MacLaren of 27 Grosvenor Road, Birkdale, and was educated at Fettes College Edinburgh. He spent some time in India and had a reputation as a skilled horseman, and was captain of the Western Cricket Club, Pendleton. His sister, Mrs. Ethel Armitage of Broad Oak Park Worsley, worked at Fairhope Red Cross Hospital, Eccles Old Road. His brother F. C. MacLaren was a Lancashire second XI cricketer and served with the Royal Scots. In October 1917 his father received Ernest's identity disk and a letter from the War Office saying that he had been buried on 30th July 1917. Captain MacLaren was awarded the Military Cross for; "conspicuous coolness and good work when reconnoitering, and later when guiding a raid on the enemies trenches. The success of the raid was largely due to his skill and forethought." In 1988 CWGC records clarified that the surname was MacLaren not McLaren. Memorial Ref. I. B. 22., Connaught Cemetery, Thiepval, France.

MACLEAN, Captain, Henry Chevers. First of all wounded in the cheek, he was in the process of getting up after writing a message when a bullet hit him in the heart, 1st July 1916. Objective was the point christened Lisnaskea in the German third line. No. 1 Coy under the command of Captain H. C. MacLean was on the right of the battalion and was supported by No. 2 Coy led by Captain P. Cruikshank. 9th Bn., Royal Inniskilling Fusiliers. Son of Henry MacLean, formerly of The Laurels, Newton-by-Chester, and grandson of Joseph Brooks (Chairman of the Bury Board of Guardians and Radcliffe District Council). Member of the Grosvenor Rowing Club. Captain MacLean before the war practised as a barrister in Liverpool and Middle Temple. Graduate of Liverpool University. Most prominent member of the Tyrone Regiment, UVF he organised the Liverpool British League. Left a wife and four month old girl. Memorial Ref. Pier and Face 4 D and 5 B., Thiepval Memorial, France.

MACNAGHTEN, Second Lieutenant, Sir Edward Harry. Missing, believed killed 1st July 1916. 1st Bn., Black Watch (Royal Highlanders) attd D Coy., 12th Royal Irish Rifles. With the front line gained but with only a small number of men the order came to retire, the Second Lieutenant encouraged his men to charge but was shot in the legs by machine gun fire and fell back into the trench. Aged 20. Born 12th February 1896. 6th Bart. Educated at Eton. Succeeded his father in the knighthood in December 1914. Eldest son of Hon. Sir Edward Charles MacNaghten, 5th Bart., K.C., D.L., of Dundarave, Co. Antrim, and of The Hon. Lady MacNaghten, of Sandhurst Lodge, Berks. Resided Bushmills, Belfast. Entered France, 5th October 1915. According to a Private Galloway, on home leave to Ballycastle a month after the 20 year-old was reported missing, Sir Harry was badly wounded on the parapet of an enemy trench. Three Germans then climbed out to take the officer a prisoner, fighting off and killing a soldier who attempted to thwart them. Sir Harry was last seen being carried towards the rear by his captors. Rumours that he was lying injured in No Man's Land inspired Rifleman Robert Quigg to leave his own trenches seven times, returning on each occasion with a wounded man, an act which earned him the Victoria Cross. His brother, Second Lieutenant Sir Arthur Douglas MacNaghten, 8th Rifle Brigade, 7th Bart also fell. The title would have passed onto Arthur but the 19-year-old former Wellington College student was himself killed on September 15th, 1916, before the fate of Sir Harry had been confirmed. Mother, Edith The Hon. Lady MacNaghten applied for his medals. Memorial Ref. Pier and Face 10 A., Thiepval Memorial, France.

MACONACHIE, Second Lieutenant, Arthur Delano. He was killed before reaching the German lines, 1st July 1916. C Coy., 9th Bn., King's Own Yorkshire Light Infantry. Aged 22. Born 19th February 1894, Tottenham. Son of Frank and Florence Edith Maconachie, of 75 Wellington Road, Bush Hill Park, Enfield, Middlesex. Husband of Muriel Maconachie of 63 Sutton Lane, Chiswick. Attended Tottenham Grammar School, London. Employed Secretaries Department, The Northern Assurance Company Ltd. Entered the company in June 1910 as a clerk. Enlisted in the HAC, 4th September 1914, No. 2176 and became a corporal, (January 1915) and onto being musketry instructor. Commissioned 4th May 1915 and afterwards a staff appointment in the bayonet fighting and physical training instructor attached to the Stockton-on-Tees Garrison. Went to France, 29th May 1916. His sister, E. M. Maconachie wrote to the War Office in August 1916 to confirm date of death and place of burial, unofficially stated as Beaucourt-Fricourt Valley. She also applied for his medals. Daughter, Audrey Mabel Maconachie received pension. Memorial Ref. Sp. Mem. B. 10., Gordon Dump Cemetery, Ovillers-La Boisselle, France. WO 339/48399

Their Glory Shall Not Be Blotted Out

MACPHERSON, Lieutenant, John. Fell whilst leading his company in the open, 1st July 1916. B Coy., 1st /7th Bn., Sherwood Foresters (Notts and Derby Regiment). Aged 25. Only son of Alexander (architect) and Mary MacPherson, of 34, Magdala Road, Nottingham formerly of Tenant Street, Derby. Born 21st January 1891. An old Cheltonian. Educated Cheltenham College passed the London Matriculation Examination, a good French and German scholar. Attended Nottingham University and a member of the OTC. He entered his father's business as an architect and at the outbreak of war joined the 6th Bn., Royal Fusiliers as a private. Obtained a commission in November 1914 and promoted lieutenant in August 1915. Prior to his death acting as captain. Went to France, 27th October 1915. Father applied for his medals. Memorial Ref. Pier and Face 10 C 10 D and 11 A., Thiepval Memorial, France.

MACWALTER, Second Lieutenant, Charles Christopher, DCM 8.41am an officer's patrol consisting of Second Lieutenant MacWalter advanced as a screen extending over the whole battalion. 8.46am directly the advance commenced the battalion came under heavy machine-gun fire and a large number of casualties occurred before reaching our own front line, 1st July 1916. 1st Bn., King's Own (Royal Lancaster Regiment) formerly corporal, 8669, The Buffs. Son of Robert and Fanny Louisa MacWalter of Dover, Kent. Educated at Dover Boys' Grammar School and enlisted in the Buffs going to France, 7th September 1914. Charles's battalion were involved in the 'Christmas Truce'. DCM awarded 30th June 1915 whilst he was a lance sergeant, for; 'conduct in performing hazardous reconnaissance as the enemy's line for which he was always ready to volunteer. On the last occasion for which he undertook this duty he was severely injured'. Commissioned 7th November 1915. Commemorated on Kent Civic War Memorial and Dover Grammar School. Captain R. MacWalter applied for his son's medals. Memorial Ref. Pier and Face 5 D and 12 B., Thiepval Memorial, France.

MacWATT, Lieutenant, Norman Ian. Reported wounded and missing, 1st July 1916. 2nd Bn., Seaforth Highlanders. Aged 24. Only son of Norman MacWatt, (Procurator-Fiscal for Clackmannanshire of Alloa). Nephew of Sheriff Substitute Hay MacWatt. Attended Wellington College. Joined the Seaforths in 1911 and had acted as a transport and requisitioning officer for his battalion since the outbreak of war. Entered France, 23rd August 1914. Gassed in May 1915 and for several months was at home, returning to the Front in February 1916. Medals applied for by his uncle, C. P. Thompson, also next of kin, Royal Chambers, West Hartlepool. Dunsfold War Memorial. Memorial Ref. Pier and Face 15 C., Thiepval Memorial, France.

MADDERS, Second Lieutenant, Hubert Franklin. Killed in action at Authuille, reported "A" Battery had been pushed to within 700 yards of the German front line for wire cutting purposes. Subjected to bombardment by heavy calibre German artillery on the opening day of the offensive, every gun in the battery was hit resulting in the deaths of Sergeant Frank Hardwick Smith plus two Gunners, one bombardier and Second Lieutenant Hubert Franklin Madders. 1st July 1916. "A" Battery, 168th Bde., Royal Field Artillery. Born at Erdington, Birmingham, 10th August 1880. Aged 35. Only son of John Messenger Madders (banker, London City and Midland Bank) and Jane Madders, Thanet Road, Westgate-on-Sea. Husband of Kate Madders (daughter of Mr. R. H. Berkeley, Lord Mayor of Birmingham in 1904), of 87, Hampstead Way, London. Educated at King Edward's School, Birmingham and obtained his degree at the University of London, 1901. From 1897 he was in the offices of Messrs. Whinney, Smith and Whinney, chartered accountants but was articled to Sharpe, Pritchard & Co. in 1901 of 12 New Court, Carey Street, W.C. At the final examination of the Incorporated Law Society in 1904 he was placed in the first class in Honours Examination. At the age of 18, Hubert enlisted in the HAC in 1899, and served in it until 1905. During Hubert's period of service in the Honourable Artillery Company, he had been amongst those who were present at the meeting of the Honourable Artillery Company of London, and the Ancient & Honourable Artillery Company of Massachusetts, which took place in Boston, Massachusetts, USA in 1903. Member of the Law Society, and a practicing solicitor, he was a partner in the firm from 1908 of Sharpe, Pritchard & Co., of 12, New Court, Carey Street, London, W.C. Married Kings Norton, Birmingham in 1911. Member of the Hendon District Council elected in the Spring of 1914. Commissioned as a second lieutenant in the Royal Field Artillery, gazetted dated 3rd December 1915. The Hubert Franklin Madders Bursary fund was founded by Mrs. Kate Madders in memory of her husband. In April 1917 it was announced a portrait of Second Lieutenant H. F. Madders was to be hung in the Council Chambers of Hendon District Council and this was carried out in July 1917. Commemorated Westgate-on-Sea War Memorial. Named on the Roll in All Saints Church, Willesden of the Garden Suburb representative of the Childs Hill Ward on the Hendon District Council. His widow applied for his medals and decided his inscription. Memorial Ref. II. B. 2., Bouzincourt Communal Cemetery Extension, France.

Whoso Takes The World's Life On Him And His Own Lays Down ...Lives

MADDISON, Lieutenant Colonel, Betram Lionel. Reported missing, believed killed, 1st July 1916. Battalion attacked Ovillers, they entered the first line and entered the second line but were driven back with heavy losses. 2nd Bn., Yorkshire Regiment. Third son of Mr. Thomas Maddison of Durham and was born on the 12th July 1881 at 6 South Bailey. Educated at Durham School and passed into the regular army from the East Surrey Militia in 1901. He served in the Boer War, 1st Bn., York and Lancasters and received the Queens Medal and four clasps becoming lieutenant in 1904 and captain in 1910. When war broke out he was attached to the reserve unit. Entered France, 26th January 1915. Wounded March 11th 1915 with a gunshot wound to the shoulder spending nine days in hospital, wounded again January 1916. Appointed commanding officer, April 1916. Medal application from W. G. Maddison, Sadler Street, Durham. Memorial Ref. I. B. 5., Blighty Valley Cemetery, Authuille Wood, France.

MAGER, Second Lieutenant, William George. Message received 11.15am that Lieutenant Mager has been killed, and that the company had not got beyond our first line, killed trying to secure Fate, Fall and Farm trenches. 1st July 1916. D Coy., 13th Kensington Bn., London Regiment. Born 4th October 1882, St. Pancras. Son of George Ludwin and Catherine Mager, 58 Penton Place, Newington, London. Educated King's College, Strand, London. Enlisted in the 12th Bn., Middlesex Volunteer Rifles, 1904. Assistant Clerk Board of Education. Gazetted 14th December 1914. Entered France, 18th April 1916. Mrs. J. P. Albrecht (sister), Kensington, SE17 applied for his medals whom was his only surviving relative. Memorial Ref. IV. M. 51., Hebuterne Military Cemetery, France.

MAITLAND, Lieutenant, Arthur Dudley. Reported wounded, 1st July 1916 and confirmed killed In January 1917. 14th Bn. attd. 16th Bn., West Yorkshire Regiment (Prince of Wales's Own). Aged 21. Son of George Arthur and Mabel Kate Maitland, of Ferndene, Canonbie Road, Forest Hill, London. Born London. Clerk at Docks Port of London Authority. Formerly gunner, 958, Royal Field Artillery. Disembarked Mudros, 22nd November 1915, HM Olympic. Commissioned 1915. Educated and commemorated Haberdashers' Aske's School in New Cross. Father applied for his medals. Memorial Ref. Sp. Mem. 4., Serre Road Cemetery No.3, Puisieux, France.

Dicemus Memores Nomina Mane Virum

MALEHAM, Captain, Stewart. At 7.30am attack on village of Serre commenced, two platoons of 'A' Company under Lieutenant Maleham (clearing up party) followed the second wave of the 11th East Lancashire Regiment. By 7.40am Major Guest and all his officers as well of those of the clearing party being killed before they reached the German first line, cut down within the first hundred yards of No Man's Land, 1st July 1916. 13th Bn., York and Lancaster Regiment. Aged 37. Son of Henry William and Elizabeth Maleham, of 15, Endcliff, Avenue, Sheffield. Formerly secretary Sheffield Wire and Rope Company. Mother applied for his medals. Memorial Ref. C. 34., Queens Cemetery, Puisieux, France.

Younger Son Of The Late Henry William Maleham And Of Mrs. Elizabeth Maleham Sheffield

MALLETT, Second Lieutenant, Eric Sydney. At 7.28am, six leading platoons took up their position in No Man's Land, without loss. At 7.30am our front line pushed forward, they were met with very heavy artillery and machine-gun fire, some of 'A' and 'B' companies who did make the German front line at 7.35am were surrounded and captured by the Germans, killed in the German trench whilst leading his platoon into action, Beaumont Hamel, 1st July 1916. 1st Bn., East Lancashire Regiment. Born 9th December 1893. South Manchester School to Manchester Grammar School 1903-04 and left to go to Dulwich College (1905-1909), and from there he went to Ecole de Commerce, Neuchatel. In 1911 he entered the Head Office of the North British and Mercantile Insurance Company, London. He joined the Artists' Rifles (28th Bn.), private, 1904 in 1914 and proceeded to France, 29th December 1914 and afterwards got a commission in the East Lancashire Regiment. Second lieutenant, 10th July 1915. On the 30th June Lieutenants Sayers and Mallett with Sergeant Redmayne made an excellent reconnaissance of the enemy wire accompanied by 2nd Lieutenant Conan Doyle, Hampshire Regiment. Mrs. H. S. Mallett, Foxley Lane, Purley, Surrey applied for his medals. Memorial Ref. Pier and Face 6 C., Thiepval Memorial, France.

MARSHALL, Lieutenant, John Woodall, MC. 1st July 1916. 27th (Tyneside Irish) Bn., Northumberland Fusiliers. Aged 24. Only child of Dr. Thomas Marshall and Mrs. Rebecca Marshall, of 5, St. Michael's Terrace, Westoe, South Shields. A law student. Native of Westoe. Educated at Ratcliffe College, at Oakham, and at Hanover and Bruges. Solicitor with Messrs., Clark and Snagg. He was a volunteer in the Northumberland Yeomanry on the outbreak of war, but being put on home service on account of eyesight, he went to Toulouse (after a vain endeavour to join the Belgian Army), and there enlisted in the Foreign Legion. During the winter of 1914-15 he suffered great hardships as a legionnaire; but in February, 1915, through the instrumentality of Lord Kitchener and Sir Edward Grey, the English legionnaires were transferred to the British Army. His experience of trench warfare procured for him a commission in the Tyneside Irish, and in December he became full lieutenant and was appointed bombing officer. Entered France, January 1916. For gallantry in action, he was the recipient of the Military Cross. His mother applied for his medals and officers pension. Originally map reference for burial 57d.26.a.14 and buried with two unknown soldiers. Memorial Ref. IX. B. 2., Gordon Dump Cemetery, Ovillers-La Boiselle, France.

Law Student Give Him Thy Divine Assistance O Lord & Grant Him Peace

MARSON, Second Lieutenant, William Henry. He died fighting gallantly for his country, caught up in the wire and killed, officer in charge section, 1st July 1916. Before the orders to advance he wrote two letters one to his father and one to his wife in which he made it clear he expected his coming fate and showed that he willing gave his life for King and country. D Coy., 1st/6th Bn., North Staffordshire Regiment. Aged 25. Son of William and Celia Marson, 105 Horninglow Street, Burton Upon Trent. Husband of Dorothy Kate Marson, of 24, Garden Walk New Rochelle, New York, USA formerly Kate Price, All Saints Road. Married five weeks. Resided 180 All Saints Road, Burton-upon-Trent. Employed brewer's foreman, Bass & Co. Going out as a non-commissioned officer, entered France, 5th March 1915 he received promotions and was commissioned on the 25th February 1916. He had only been married two days when he returned to the Front. He wrote to the 'Burton Daily Mail' on the 10th October 1915 thanking readers for the cigarettes as corporal, 2461. Local news suggested it was hoped to recover his body in April 1917 with other Burton men when the ground was retaken. Medals to his widow in New York. Memorial Ref. Pier and Face 14 B and 14 C., Thiepval Memorial, France.

MARTIN, Captain, Duncan Lenox. Killed in action, 1st July 1916. A Coy., 9th Bn., Devonshire Regiment. Aged 30. Brother of Mrs. D. L. Jeltes, of Swaylands, Brockenhurst, Hants. Born in Algiers in 1886. Son of Thomas (ostrich farmer in Cape Colony) and Anne Martin of Hailsham in East Sussex. After school near Bristol, Duncan settled in 1908 at St. Ives in Cornwall, where he joined the art school run by Elizabeth Forbes and a group of artists there. Commissioned on 29th October 1914 into 9th Bn., Devonshire Regiment. Entered France, 28th July 1915. Took part in the Battle of Loos. Mentioned in Despatches. Having been briefed on his company's part in the coming attack near Mametz, he went on leave and built a model of the terrain over which the 9th battalion would attack. It was used by 20 Brigade to help in their preparation, during which Martin became convinced that, unless it was destroyed in the barrage, a particular German machine-gun at Shrine Alley would catch his company as it advanced along the Mansel Copse track. He even pointed out to his brother officers where he and his men would fall. At 7.27am on 1st July the first line of the 9th Devons advanced, under cover of fire from sixteen Stokes Mortars, towards Mametz. Martin's fears were realised. As Duncan's No. 1 Company topped the rise and moved downhill past Mansel Copse, the machine-gun 400 yards away in Shrine Alley mowed them down. Thirty-year-old Duncan Martin was one of the first to fall, he had gone 15 yards when he was shot through the head above the right temple. He turned his head to the left, flinging out his right arm and fell dead on his back although probably from rifle fire. His plasticine model of the battlefield was displayed at the Royal United Service Institute for many years. Body discovered by Chaplain Ernest Crosse and description of the wounds would imply he was killed by rifle fire. His sister, Mrs. P. L. Jeltes, Ashdown Place, SW7 applied for his medals and also choose his inscription. Memorial Ref. A. 1., Devonshire Cemetery, Mametz, France.

Semper Fidelis

MARTIN, Lieutenant, Eldred Joseph. Killed in action, 1st July 1916. 3rd Bn. attd. C Coy. 2nd Bn., Royal Warwickshire Regiment. Aged 20. Second son of Harry and Florence Mary Martin, of Carmelwood, Chester Road, Erdington, Birmingham. Member of Ampleforth College RFC. Attended Ampleforth College. One of four brothers holding commissions. Entered France, 1st October 1915. Medals to H. A. Martin, Erdington. Memorial Ref. Believed to be buried in. I. D. 51., Norfolk Cemetery, Becordel-Becourt, France.

On Whose Soul Sweet Jesus Have Mercy R.I.P.

MARTIN, Lieutenant, George Russell Courtney. Reported wounded and missing and then killed 1st July 1916. 6th Bn., Royal Warwickshire Regiment. Only son of Mr. and Mrs. George Martin of Hartopp Court, Four Oaks. Aged 25. Educated Lickey Hill School and Repton School Memorial (1906). Obtained his commission at the outbreak of war and went to the Front, 14th February 1916. Mr. and Mrs. Martin appealed locally for information on their son, his father applying for his medals. Memorial Ref. C. 5., Miraumont Communal Cemetery, France.

MARTIN, Lieutenant, Sidney Todd. Reported missing, in the attack on Beaumont Hamel. 1st July 1916. 6th Bn. attd. 1st Bn., Royal Inniskilling Fusiliers. Elder son of Reverend W. Todd Martin and Mrs. Martin, College House, College Green, Belfast, and was in his 25th year. He was educated at Campbell College, Belfast, and Sussex College, Cambridge, (1907) where he was a member of the OTC. He entered Sidney House to read Classics in 1909 and took his BA in 1912. At the outbreak of war he was studying for the Bar in London, but at once applied for a commission. He took part in the Gallipoli operations, and was wounded at Suvla Bay in August, 1915. He was wounded about twelve hours after his arrival in Suvla Bay; when he had recovered, he was sent to Alexandria, and afterwards to France. Medals to his mother in Lewes, Sussex. Memorial Ref. Pier and Face 4 D and 5 B., Thiepval Memorial, France.

MASON, Second Lieutenant, Overton Trollope. Killed in action, 1st July 1916. B Coy., 1st/9th Bn., London Regiment (Queen Victoria's Rifles). Son of Louis Henry and S. A. Mason, of 565, Musgrave Road, Durban, Natal, South Africa. Attended Hilton College: 1884-1890. Achievements at Hilton: 1st Class English (Class 6 and 7) 1st Class French (Class 4) 1st Class Arithmetic only (Class 4), all in 1884. In 1890 2nd Class Honours. Served in South Africa, 1914, and German South West Africa, then came overseas and joined the OTC. Natal Mounted Rifles, private, 115. Gazetted to be second lieutenant, 29th December 1915. Entered France, 27th May 1916. His mother applied for his medals, c/o Messrs. Crockett Hemphill, Durban, South Africa. Memorial Ref. Pier and Face 9 C., Thiepval Memorial, France.

MASTERMAN, Second Lieutenant, Frederick Michel. 1st July 1916. 3rd Bn. attd. 10th Bn., Royal Irish Rifles. Aged 32. Born at London on 29th September 1883. Second son of Edward Masterman of Knotts Green, Essex, and Sophie Alice Masterman (daughter of Alex F. Clarke, of St. Petersburg), Harley House, Regent's Park, London. Attended Winchester College. When war broke out he was horse-ranching in Canada. He enlisted as a trooper in the 13th Regiment, Canadian Mounted Rifles on February 1st 1915 served as Lance Corporal Frederick Micheal Masterman, 118082 in the ranks of the Fort Garry Horse. Having crossed to England with the Canadian forces he transferred to the 3rd Bn., Royal Irish Rifles and then switched to the 10th Bn. He joined on 17th February, 1916, and ongoing to the front was posted to the South Belfast Volunteer Battalion. Mentioned for gallant conduct by Major Goodwin. Commemorated in Canada's National First World War 'Book of Remembrance'. Memorial Ref. Pier and Face 15 A and 15 B., Thiepval Memorial, France.

MASTERMAN, Lieutenant, Robert Chauncy. Leading his men in attack and hit before he got to the enemy's trenches, 1st July 1916. 19th Bn., Lancashire Fusiliers. Aged 20. Son of Henry Chauncy Masterman (solicitor) and Alice May Masterman, of Rough Down, Boxmoor, Herts. Educated at Harrow School. When the war broke out, Lieutenant Masterman, though still a boy at school, enlisted in the 6th Bedfordshire Regiment, private, 14403. In the following December he was discharged with a view to being given a commission, in the interval before being gazetted, he went up to Oxford and won the Harrow Scholarship at Hertford. He was given a commission in the Royal Lancashire Fusiliers and was sent to Gallipoli, 3rd October 1915 where he acted as captain. From Gallipoli he was invalided home, but again went back to the Front, this time in France. Miss M. E. Masterman his elder sister, Paulton's Square, SW3 applied for his medals. Memorial Ref. Pier and Face 3 C and 3 D., Thiepval Memorial, France.

MATTHEY, Captain, Edward Granville. Fell gallantly wounded, commanding A Coy., at Beaumont Hamel, killed 1st July 1916. At 7.30am A Coy,. south of Beaumont Road began to leave the trenches in support of B and D Coys., he had reached the road and dashed on with the men who entered near Northern End. 1st Bn., Lancashire Fusiliers. Aged 23. Only son of Cara T. Granville Matthey, of 76, Lexham Gardens, Kensington, London, and Captain G. E. Matthey (Royal Inniskilling Fusiliers). Born 1893. Educated Linton House Preparatory School, Cheltenham College and RMC Sandhurst (September 1912) and commissioned January 1913. Entered France, 5th November 1914. Wounded at Neuve Chapelle and returned to his battalion, May 1916. His mother applied for his medals, The Ladies Limited Service Club, Curzon Street, Mayfair, W1. Memorial Ref. C. 44., Redan Ridge Cemetery No.2, Beaumont-Hamel, France.

Tikkah

MAUDE, Second Lieutenant, Louis Edward Joseph. Last seen carrying ammunition to his platoon across No Man's Land, Fricourt, 1st July 1916. 11th Bn., King's Own Yorkshire Light Infantry killed with the 10th Bn. Born Oxford, 14th July 1891, only son of the Reverend Joseph Hooper Maude, Rector of Hilaray, Downham Market, Norfolk, and Louisa Frederica Grey. Educated Trinity College, Glenalmond 1905-1910. Scholar at Christ's College, Cambridge 1910-1914; pass Classics Moderations 1912; 2 Literae Humaniores 1914; BA 1915. Secretary, Hockey 1912-1913, captain 1913-1914; Secretary, Pelican Essay Club 1913; President 1913; Secretary, Owlets 1913, President 1913. Civil Service exam 1914. GPO 1915. 1915-1916, membership of the University Contingent OTC prior to 1915, (service commenced May 1915). Entered France, December 1915. Talbot House visitors book, page 33, dated 5th February 1916. From Pelican Record Vol. XIII, No. 4: 'he had a clear and trenchant literary style, and a graceful humour which made his academic work a pleasure to him and those who worked with him. His many-sided character only a complete biography could unfold to those who did not know him well, while to those who knew and loved him no words are necessary. In life he was a good friend and a pleasant comrade; in death he was a good leader and a brave officer; in such a life and death there is truly nothing to regret, but the tragedy remains that a man who could do so much that was beyond the possibilities of others should have to die for what anyone could do as well'. Mother made a donation for the College Barge, in memoriam. All Saints Church, Hilgay, Norfolk plaque reads 'Ludovicus Eduardus Iosephus Maude inter gallos pro occubuit kal: Iul:MCMXCI ann: nat: XXV Requiem aeternam dona ei Domine' translated 'Louis Edward Joseph Maude, who died in the war for freedom, first day of July 1916 aged 25. Grant him eternal rest Lord.' Reverend Maude applied for the medals. Memorial Ref. Sp. Mem. B. 7., Gordon Dump Cemetery, Ovillers-La Boisselle, France.

Their Glory Shall Not Be Blotted Out

MAUNSELL, Captain, Edwin Richard Lloyd. Killed leading his company, 1st July 1916. Assault began at 8.00am and barbed wire was cut every forty yards the Germans had their machine-guns trained on these gaps and only a few men ever got through the wire, 1st Bn., Royal Dublin Fusiliers. Aged 25. Second son of Major John Drought Maunsell and Euphemia Sullivan Maunsell (nee Bush), of Taunton, Somerset. Attended Brentwood School as boarder and from there into RMC Sandhurst, December 1909. At school in the football XI and theatricals. Attached to the Northern Nigerian Regiment and commanding troops at Kaduna when war broke out, after training went to the Cameroons and invalided home, August 1914.

His brother with the same battalion was wounded Second Lieutenant John Edmund Bush Maunsell. Major Maunsell applied for his medals. Mr. Maunsell, Station Road, Ilfracombe choose his inscription. Memorial Ref. I. A. 11., Auchonvillers Military Cemetery, France.

Honorantes Me Honorabo

MAY, Captain, Charles Campbell, Mortally wounded he gallantly continued to give orders and encourage his men, to the last, Mametz, 1st July 1916. B Coy previously A Coy., 22nd Bn., Manchester Regiment. Captain May was mortally wounded by a shell just after giving his batman a message down the line, Private Bunting nursed him as best he could. Aged 27. Only son of Major and Mrs. C. E. May, of New Zealand and London. Born New Zealand, 1888. Husband of Bessie Maude Earles (formerly May), of 1, Rue Hwys Mans, Paris lived with his wife and child at 2 Grove Mansions, Wanstead. Poet and journalist. Landed in France, 11th November 1915. After his death the soldier who carried his body off the battlefield discovered that Captain May had taken a slender notebook into battle. His last letter home written on the morning of the 1st July; ' It is a glorious morning and is now broad daylight. We go over in two hours' time. It seems a long time to wait and I think whatever happens, we shall all feel relieved once the line is launched. No Man's Land is a tangled desert. Unless one can see it one cannot imagine what a terrible state of disorder it is in.' Mentioned in Despatches. Mrs. F. J. Earles (his widow, remarried, Captain Earles a friend of Captain May), Paris 6, France applied for his medals. Officers pension to daughter, May Pauline Maude. Original map reference where body found 62d.F.6.c.1.7. Memorial Ref. II. B. 3., Dantzig Alley British Cemetery, Mametz, France. WO 339/17649

Loved In Life Let Us Not Forget Him In Death

McCLELLAN, Second Lieutenant, Allan John. Killed in action, 1st July 1916. 18th Bn. attd. 15th Bn., Royal Irish Rifles. Aged 21. Son of William and Flora McClellan, of Ballyboley, Ballynure, Belfast. On the outbreak of the war was an assistant master at Larne Grammar School. He received his commission from the 16th Royal Irish Rifles, in which he was a sergeant, being gazetted to the 18th (Reserve) Battalion. Entered France, 15th May 1916. His eldest brother served in command of a torpedo boat destroyer in the North Sea, and his youngest served with the 196th Western Universities Bn., Canada. His father applied for his medals. Memorial Ref. Pier and Face 15 A and 15 B., Thiepval Memorial, France.

McCLUGGAGE, Lieutenant, William. At zero they began to advance, and at once came under very heavy artillery and machine-gun fire. No. 4 Platoon led the attack, and were badly cut up, but what men remained entered the German front line. Missing believed killed, 1st July 1916. A Coy. 12th Bn., Royal Irish Rifles. Lieutenant McCluggage at once collected his men and tried to rush on to the German second line but was killed in the attempt. Aged 23. Son of Thomas and Annie McCluggage, of Ballyboley, Larne, Co. Antrim. BSc. (Civil Engineering). He had been taught science by Mr. John Griffiths at Larne Grammar School. After school he went on to study BSc Civil Engineering at the Queen's University of Belfast. Mr. Griffiths and William were reunited in the Larne 1st XV where they played together in the Towns Cup winning side of 1913-1914. Officer in the Larne Harbour, UVF. Useful rugby forward and played for the university and Larne. Mr. Griffiths became Captain Griffiths and was also killed in the 1st July 1916. Entered France, 5th October 1915. Father applied for his medals. Originally buried as unknown British soldier at reference 57d.Q.30.b.3.7 and in 1927 during exhumation identified as Lieutenant McCluggage by a cigarette case marked WMcC. Memorial Ref. VII. J. 3., Serre Road Cemetery No.2, France.

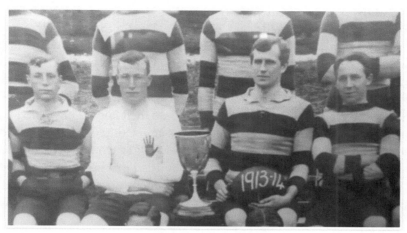

Larne First XV 1913 1914
Lieutenant McCluggage left of centre and Captain John Griffiths right of centre

McCLURE, Lieutenant, Ernest. Missing 1st July 1916. C Coy., 10th Bn., Royal Inniskilling Fusiliers. Aged 32. Son of Mrs. Mary McClure, 8 Beechwood Avenue, Derry and brother of Florence McClure. Well known in athletic circles. Lieutenant in Derry Volunteers since 23rd November 1914. Entered France, October 1915. Mentioned in Despatches and Oak Leaf. Medals to his parents address. Mother Mary McClure, Beechwood Avenue, Londonderry received his officers pension. Londonderry (Derry) War Memorial. Memorial Ref. Pier and Face 4 D and 5 B., Thiepval Memorial, France.

McCROSTIE, Second Lieutenant, Charles Hutchison. Fell 1st July 1916. 19th Bn., Highland Light Infantry attached 14th Trench Mortar Battery. Aged 31. Born in 1885. Eldest son of Hugh and Agnes Watson McCrostie, of 144, Newhaven Road, Leith. Born at Edinburgh, 1885. Attended George Watson's College, 1892-1901. He attained considerable reputation as a student of foreign languages, and had a record of five years' unbroken attendance. Entering the grain trade in Leith, his fine business instinct and his command of foreign tongues speedily brought promotion for him. He was a keen motorist and a member of the Edinburgh Motor Club. Joining the Loathian and Border Horse, lance corporal, 1549 on the outbreak of war as a motor despatch rider, he was in April 1915 gazetted to the 1/15th HLI. Entered France, 11th February 1916. He became trench mortar officer in the Bn. Records indicate 15th Bn., not 19th Bn. His mother applied for his medals. Map reference where body found 57d.X.1.a.3.2 exhumed in January 1925 and identified by officer's khaki and disc. Memorial Ref. XVIII. AA. 1., Villers-Bretonneux Military Cemetery, France.

"God Shall Wipe Away All Tears From Their Eyes" Rev. 21.V.4

McCURRACH, Second Lieutenant, George. Reported missing, and was believed killed 1st July 1916. Leading up on the right, A Coy., 13th Bn., Highland Light Infantry. Attached to the 16th Bn. Son of George McCurrach, (farm servant). Born Findochty, 16th February 1881. Educated Findochty Public School, where he was later a pupil teacher; subsequently assistant at Stewart Thomson's Business College, Aberdeen. Entering Aberdeen University in October 1905 he graduated MA in 1908 and was appointed assistant in Whitehills Public School, Banffshire. Thereafter he became assistant in the Central School, Fraserburgh, and when he joined the army was headmaster of Ruthven Public School, Cairnie, Banffshire. McCurrach enlisted in the 3rd Bn., Gordon Highlanders in April 1915, and on being commissioned, 12th September was transferred to the 13th Bn., Highland Light Infantry. After training at Richmond, Yorks, he crossed to France, 16th June 1916, just when the notable forward movement from Albert was going on. He was attached to the 16th Highland Light Infantry and had only been about fifteen days in France. As a teacher his work was of a very high order and was favourably commented on in all the schools in which he taught. His military service was very short, but he devoted himself as keenly and as scrupulously to his soldiering as he had done to the teaching work. Death reported 19th July 1916. His widow applied for his medals. Memorial Ref. Pier and Face 15 C., Thiepval Memorial, France.

McGAIN, Second Lieutenant, Ashley Waterson. Killed in action, 1st July 1916 at 8.00am on a ridge over looking the valley at La Boisselle. 11th Bn., Suffolk Regiment. Aged 23. Son of Thomas (railway guard) and Isabella McGain. From Port Erin, Isle of Man. Born 8th January 1893. Baptised 12th February 1893. Educated King William's College. Schoolmaster. Enlisted 6401, 18th Bn., Royal Fusiliers. Commissioned 22nd June 1915. Entered France, 8th January 1916. Wrote a letter on the 28th June 1916 'Within the next day or so it is possible – indeed probable – that I shall die while attacking the Germans. If I do then know I have died happy….If I ever was to be born again I should desire no other for my mother and father. Your Loving Son, Ashley, Battlefield, France'. Isle of Man Great War Roll of Honour. His mother applied for his medals. Mother applied for officers pension. Reported that he was buried on the night of the 1st July in a shell hole with Lieutenant McLean. Effects were tin of medical tabloids, pipe, cheque book, advance book, letters and photos, tube of ink tabloids and tie. Memorial Ref. Pier and Face 1 C and 2 A., Thiepval Memorial, France. WO 339/3977

McGILLICUDDY, Lieutenant, John. Reported wounded and missing 1st July 1916. Private Smith stated 'he was killed outright at La Boisselle, shot through the head by machine-gun fire. We had reached the German wire and were near their first line trench, the time was about 8.30am'. D Coy., 26th (Tyneside Irish) Bn., Northumberland Fusiliers. Born 18th December 1882 at Holloway, London. He was educated at St. Joseph's, Highgate. Served eight years with the Royal Sussex, 1900 to discharge on the 6th December 1908. Metropolitan Police Constable, PC 317, Warrant Number 96890. On joining the police on the 17th May 1909, he stated he was living at 7 Rothesay Villa's, Orpington and was a gymnastic instructor, employed at St. Joseph's Orphanage, Orpington. On the 28th February 1911 he transferred to A Division –Westminster. He very quickly moved again this time to Y Division as PC 317 Y Division on the 16th December 1911, where he remained until he applied for a commission in the army. Part of the Army reserve until 5th December 1912. Royal Humane Society award for stopping runaway horses, August 1914. Gazetted 24th March 1915, to be temporary lieutenant 12th July 1915. Entered France, 1st February 1916. Named in the service paper from a memorial service for the officers and constables who died in the Great War 17th May 1919, as PC 317 retained in Westminster Abbey. Widow applied for his medals in 1922, Clarendon Road, Holland Park, W11. Memorial Ref. I. B. 2., Bapaume Post Military Cemetery, Albert, France. WO 339/26301

Officers 3rd Bn., Tyneside Irish Brigade, 26th Bn., Northumberland Fusiliers
Lieutenant John McGillicuddy standing far right.
Also in the picture killed on the 1st July 1916 Lieutenant Fitzgerald and Captain Mullally

WO 339/55683

McGOWAN, Second Lieutenant, John Spence. The wire was cut in front of where he was, the German second line and he went through with the bombers, no-one came back, 1st July 1916. 2nd Bn., Devonshire Regiment. Aged 19. Son of Alice Clara McGowan, of Ao Tea Roa, Dormans Land, Lingfield, Surrey, and Robert Smith McGowan. Born 19th March 1897. Attended Rottingdean Preparatory School. Attended Sherborne School (Abbeylands) September 1911-July 1915 and a member of the OTC. Commissioned to 3rd Bn., in June 1915. 20th May 1916, arrived in France, attached to 2nd Bn. Buried west of the Village of Ovillers La Boisselle, 2.5 miles north of Albert. Sht 57.D. Sq.X.d.5.2. Medal Index Card points out mother entitled to all medals, Tea Room, Dormansland, Surrey. Memorial Ref. Pier and Face 1 C., Thiepval Memorial, France.

McINNES, Second Lieutenant, John Edward. In the second German line, he got up to observe what was going on in the third line German trench on a fire step the barrage having lifted from it, he was hit by a bullet in the steel helmet. He got up and looked towards the first line trench and was hit through the helmet into the brain and died immediately. Second Lieutenant Downman was with him but didn't get a chance to give him a warning. 1st July 1916. D Coy., 1st/5t Bn., Sherwood Foresters (Notts and Derby Regiment). Aged 22. Eldest son of Edward McInnes, (china manufacturer) of Hilltop, Littleover, Derby. Born Littleover, 28th October 1894. Attended Charterhouse (Weekites 1909-1913), member of the OTC. Commissioned 3rd November 1914. At the Front for the last twelve months since 12th July 1915. Parents received a letter expressing that he was taken prisoner. Memorial service held in Littleover Church, October 1916. Father applied for medals. Memorial Ref. Pier and Face 10 C 10 D and 11 A., Thiepval Memorial, France.

McINTOSH, Lieutenant, William Matthew. Died of wounds, 1st July 1916. 17th Bn., Highland Light Infantry attached Trench Mortar Battery. Aged 22. Son of John and Jane McIntosh (manager of Dailraine Distillery), of Dailraine, Carron, Morayshire. Prior to war applying for a position in the Civil Service. Previously 6th Bn., Seaforth Highlanders, corporal, 865. Commissioned 5th April 1915. Medals to his father, J. McIntosh, Dailraine. Memorial Ref. Pier and Face 15 C., Thiepval Memorial, France.

McLAREN, Captain, Robert John. Killed in action, 1st July 1916. Reported missing and then killed in action. Attached 2nd Bn., South Wales Borderers. 16th Bn., Cheshire Regiment. Born June, 1882. Eldest surviving son of Charles McLaren and grandson of John H. McLaren of the Royal Insurance Company. Attended Loretto from 1894 to 1900. Served throughout the South African campaign. Temporary lieutenant, 14th Bn., Cheshire Regiment January 29th 1915. Entered Gallipoli, 16th June 1915. His widow, Westleigh, Brook Road, Blundell Sands applied for his medals. Three children for officers pension; John Gordon, Arthur Alexander and Annie Danella McLaren. Memorial Ref. A. 48., Hawthorn Ridge Cemetery No.2, Auchonvillers, France.

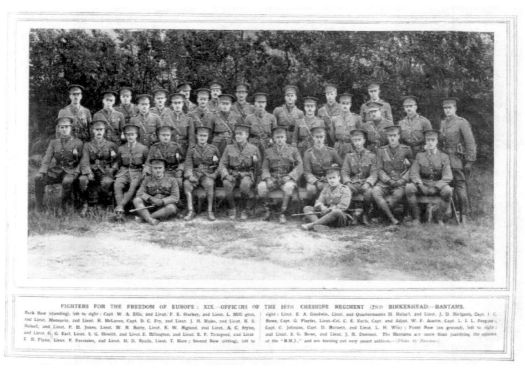

FIGHTERS FOR THE FREEDOM OF EUROPE: XIX. OFFICERS OF THE 16TH CHESHIRE REGIMENT (2ND BIRKENHEAD.—BANTAMS.

Officers of the Cheshire Regiment
Second Lieutenant R. McLaren fifth from left back row.

McLEAN, Second Lieutenant, Atholl Archibald. 1st July 1916. B Company, 11th Bn., Suffolk Regiment. Aged 23. Son of Mr. Archibald D. McLean, (manager of the Bank of Commerce, London, Ontario) and Alice McLean. Next of kin; Mrs. Ferguson (aunt), 87 Victoria Street, SW. Born in Middlesex, Ontario, Canada on 28th October 1894. Prior to enlisting at the Imperial Bank, Ontario. On 22nd September 1914, enlisted as a private with a Montreal Highland Battalion in the first contingent. When he arrived in England he received a commission and was transferred to the 11th Bn., Suffolk Regiment. He went to France on 12th September 1915. Reported that he was buried on the night of the 1st July in a shell hole with Second Lieutenant McGain. Identity disc sent to his father. Effects returned were cap badge, tobacco pouch, notebooks, letter cases, books with photos, revolver in holster and lanyard, whistle and lanyard, compass, cigarette case, photograph case, pencils, pipe lighter, cigarette holder, ammunition pouch, New Testament, advance book, purse, tin of Iodine, electric torch, bag containing shrapnel, cheque book, service book and handkerchief. Memorial Ref. I. Q. 5., Becourt Military Cemetery, Becordel-Becourt, France. WO 339/36404

Dearly Loved Son Of Archibald Duncan And Alice Mclean London, Canada

McNEILL, Second Lieutenant, Nigel Lorne. Shot through the head whilst leading his platoon in the attack, twenty yards from the German position, 1st July 1916. D Coy. 3rd Bn. attd. 2nd Bn., Gordon Highlanders. Aged 21. Youngest son of Neil and Marjorie C. McNeill, of 14, Blackwater Road, Eastbourne, Sussex formerly 45 Westbourne Gardens, Glasgow. Born 5th August 1894. Attended Glasgow Academy and Loretto School (1908-1913). Prefect. Cricket XI. Sergeant, OTC. He applied for appointment to the Special Reserve of Officers in March 1915, an application which had to be counter-signed by his mother, Marjorie C. McNeil, as he was under 21. Went to France, 2nd October 1915. The report of his death, which was sent to the War Office twenty days after he was killed, describes his place of burial as "Behind grave in '67 Support Trench', by the roadside, near Mansel Copse, just S. of Mametz" with the map reference 62d F.11.c.8.3. Mother applied for his medals. Memorial Ref. A. 2., Gordon Cemetery, Mametz, France. WO 339/42615

Their Name Liveth For Evermore

MEEKE, Captain, William Stanley. Deceased 1st July 1916. 2nd Bn., Middlesex Regiment. Aged 28. Second son of Joseph and Mary Meeke, of Sheffield. Born in 1888, educated at King's College School, Wimbledon. 1909 won the best examination in Criminal Law and Procedure. Called to the Bar at the Middle Temple on May 1st 1912. Barrister on the north-eastern circuit. Previously attached Oxford and Bucks Light Infantry. Received a special reserve commission in August 1914 and went to the Front 30th September 1914 being attached to the 2nd Bn., Munsters. Awarded the Military Cross for his work at Givenchy at Christmas 1914. Confirmed in rank, January 1915. In a letter to Second Lieutenants Phillip Maurice Elliott's parents from Reverend H. B. Burnaby (Regimental Padre) wrote; "Thus he lies where the 2nd Middlesex so splendidly opened the great attack, buried close to his brother officers who fell with him, Captain Meeke, Captain Heaton and Lieut. Van den Bok". Major R. Meeke applied for his medals. Original map reference for burial, 57d.X.13.b. Memorial Ref. XV. I. 3., Ovillers Military Cemetery, France.

MEEKING, Second Lieutenant, Norman Arthur. Wounded in the fighting and was carried to a captured dugout where he died of his wounds, 1st July 1916. B Coy., 1st/9th Bn., London Regiment (Queen Victoria's Rifles). Born 26th May 1892 at Landshire, 39 South Park, Hill Road in Croydon. Elder son of Thomas Arthur Meeking, (tea merchant), and Gertrude Mary (nee Steains) of 117 Casrellain Mansions, Maida Vale, later of Rocheford, King Edward Road in New Barnet. Christened at Croydon on the 17th of June 1892. He was educated at the Junior King's School from January 1904 and at the King's School Canterbury from April to December 1906. On the 28th of November 1907 he was apprenticed for seven years to Frank Hamilton Townend, a pewterer in London, although he did not complete his apprenticeship, instead he went to work as a clerk in the London office of Entre Rios Railways Company Ltd at River Plate House, Finsbury Circus in London. Following the outbreak of war he enlisted at Lambeth as Ordinary Seaman LZ/24 in the Royal Navy on the 1st of September 1914, posted to the Nelson Bn., Royal Naval Division on the 22nd of October as Ordinary Seaman K/860. He applied for a commission in the 2/9th (County of London) Bn., (Queen Victoria's Rifles) on the 16th of February 1915 and was commissioned as a second lieutenant in the battalion on the 1st of March 1915. He was posted to the 1/9th Bn., of his regiment and embarked for France on the 10th of July 1915 where he joined them in the field at Voormezeele, along with nine other officers, on the 14th of July where they were constructing communication trenches. He was promoted to temporary lieutenant on the 24th of March 1916. He was promoted to lieutenant which was effective from the 1st of June 1916. Commemorated Entre Rios Railway Company Roll of Honour, London Office. Reported killed 30th November 1916. His mother applied for his medals. Memorial Ref. Pier and Face 9 C., Thiepval Memorial, France.

MELLARD, Second Lieutenant, Richard 'Dick' Bartlett. During a night-time recce reported that the wire was uncut, north of Gommecourt Road, 1st July 1916. 1st/5th Bn., North Staffordshire Regiment. Aged 22. Only son of Richard Bartlett Mellard (former Mayor, Newcastle-upon-Tyne) and Annie Beatrice Mellard, of 1 Oman Mansions, Oman Road, Hampstead, London. Native of Newcastle, Staffs. Body removed from the wire, March 1917. Old boy of Newcastle High School. He was farming in Canada when war broke out and enlisted in the Canadian Contingent, Fort Garry's Horse, corporal, 14861. Shortly after arrival in England received a commission. Memorial Ref. Sp. Mem. A. 2., Gommecourt Wood New Cemetery, Foncquevillers, France.

I Thank God For Every Remembrance Of Him My Only Son Mother

MELLOR, Lieutenant, Frederick Courtney. Killed at Beaumont Hamel by a machine gun bullet as soon as the attack started, 1st July 1916. No. 7 Platoon, B Coy., 1st Bn., Newfoundland Regiment. Aged 28. Son of Reverend Thomas Crewe and Mary L. Mellor, of St Luke's Rectory, Annapolis Royal, Nova Scotia, Canada. Native of Eastern Passage, Dartmouth, Nova Scotia. Formerly Commercial Cable Company. Enlisted 2nd September 1914. Promoted second lieutenant 22nd April 1915, lieutenant 16th October 1915. Sister a war nurse in France. Certificate as instructor in signalling. Commemorated Sons and Daughters of the Anglican Church Clergy. Inscription correspondence to Lt. Col. J. L. Lambert, DGR&E, Newfoundland Contingent, Victoria St. London. Memorial Ref. B. 9., Knightsbridge Cemetery, Mesnil-Martinsart, France.

Your Life Is Hid With Christ In God

MELLOR, Lieutenant, Roy. The attack commenced at 7.30am and the leading companies reached their first objective, Bucket Trench – Dantzig Alley, with heavy casualties, and the supporting companies then pushed on towards the final objective, Fritz trench. 1st July 1916. D Coy., 22nd Bn., Manchester Regiment. Born on 16th January 1895, Macclesfield. Only son of Harriet and Richard Clowes Mellor (silk dyer), a dyer of 41 West Bond Street, Macclesfield. Educated at the Kindergarten of Macclesfield Girls High School, followed by the Modern School and Macclesfield Grammar School, where he was captain of the football team for two seasons, a member of the cricket team, and a keen athlete, winning the championship bowl for athletics in 1912. He was also a member of Macclesfield Golf Club. He had a successful scholastic career, passing the Matriculation examination when 16 years of age, and the intermediate examination for the London University BA degree. He won a County Council scholarship for three years, and also a scholarship tenable at the Manchester University. In 1913 Roy went to Manchester University to study chemistry for his BSc. degree, where he joined the University OTC. Enlisted in the Public Schools' Battalion on the 4th September 1914, and went to Leatherhead for training. In January 1915 he accepted a commission as second lieutenant in the 22nd Manchester Regiment, and underwent several more training courses: at Morecambe in January 1915, Grantham from April 1915, and at Larkhill from September 1915 onwards. Roy was musketry instructor to the battalion, and had also acted as assistant adjutant and intelligence officer. Roy was drafted to France on 11th November 1915, landing at Boulogne.

A member of the battalion wrote: "Lieutenant Mellor was in front of all…he must have been slightly hit the first time, because I was only about 150 yards behind him and he wasn't there when I went past…he got a lot of shrapnel and was killed" and a wounded officer reported "…during the advance I saw Mellor lying on the ground wounded (shot in the leg) in the act of reloading his revolver. Asked if he needed assistance, he replied in the negative…half-an-hour later I returned and found him gone." The soldier naturally concluded that he had been picked up and taken to hospital. The wife of the Colonel of the regiment, informing his parents by letter that Lieutenant Mellor's body had been found and that Lieutenant Mellor's death was due to shrapnel wounds received subsequently to the first advance. His mother applied for his medals. Memorial Ref. Pier and Face 13 A and 14 C., Thiepval Memorial, France. WO 339/23766

D Coy., Platoon No. XIII. Lieutenant Mellor seated. Also killed on the 1st July 1916 in the photo; Sergeant William Wilson, Private Alexander Gourlay, Private Herbert Connor, Private Benjamin Holt, Private George Worthington, Private Leonard Jenkins, Private Thomas Lister, Corporal Henry Rossbottom, Lance Corporal J. A. Stephenson and Private George Furness.

MELLY, Second Lieutenant, Hugh Peter Egerton Mesnard. He was killed while leading his men on to assault the second line of German trenches, 1st July 1916. 1st Bn., King's Own (Royal Lancaster Regiment). Aged 19. Son of Hon. Colonel Hugh Mesnard Melly, V.D., and Eleanor Lawrence Melly, of the Quinta, Greenheys Road, Liverpool. Born 6th October 1896. Educated at Dunchurch Hall and Malvern College from 1911 to 1914 (Army III-I) Passed into RMC Sandhurst, but did not enter. Joined the King's Own from the 3rd Bn., Liverpool Regiment. Entered France, 5th March 1915. Wounded in the foot, 27th April 1915. Commemorated St. John the Evangelist Church, Ellesmere Port. Parents applied for his medals. Memorial Ref. I. H. 11., Sucrerie Military Cemetery, Colincamps, France. WO 339/24244

Underneath Are The Everlasting Arms

MERRY, Second Lieutenant, Ralph Valentine. He was killed by machine-gun fire between the first and second line German trenches and was seen lying dead with his head over the German parapet about 2.00pm, 1st July 1916. 18th Bn., The King's (Liverpool Regiment). Aged 22. Second son of Alfred and Thora Natalie Merry, of 63, Manor Road, Liscard, Wallasey, Cheshire. He was an old Wallasey Grammar School boy and had distinguished himself in athletics. Enlisted just after outbreak of war, Liverpool Regiment, lance corporal, 18/16322 and quickly received a commission, 21st March 1915. Entered France, 7th November 1915. Prior to enlisting engaged in the Liverpool Office of a London firm of metal merchants. Originally buried Maricort-Montauban, 62C.A.9.a.8.9. Miss A. E. Merry (sister) of Wallasey applied for his medals. Memorial Ref. V. W. 10., Dantzig Alley British Cemetery, Mametz, France. WO 339/28007

MIDDLEDITCH, Lieutenant, Archibald Milne. Wounded and missing, Maillet Mailly, 1st July 1916. B Coy., 5th Platoon, 12th Bn., Essex Regiment. Aged 19. Son of Benjamin Bernard Middleditch, of 28, Bolton Street, Piccadilly, London. Born at Bardwell, Bury St. Edmunds. Educated at Merchant Taylors' and St. Paul's schools. Attended Berkhamsted School. Employed Messrs. Morton & Co., Export Merchants. Formerly 1773, Artists Rifles. Second Lieutenant 3rd December 1914. Landed in France in October 1915. His brother, Second Lieutenant Arnold Warden Middleditch died of wounds on the 19th June 1916 and is buried in New Southgate Cemetery. Commemorated Merchant Taylors' School, Northwood. His mother applied for his medals and officers pension. Body was found in May 1917. Memorial ref. I. H. 35., Serre Road Cemetery No.2, France.

This My Son Was Dead And Is Alive Again He Was Lost And Is Found

MIDDLETON, Captain, Thomas. Wounded and missing, 1st July 1916. 16th Bn., Highland Light Infantry attached Trench Mortar Battery. Aged 27. Son of Rachel Middleton, of 15, Manor Road, Gartcosh, Glasgow, and Charles Middleton. Born on the 11th April 1889 in Govan, Lanarkshire. 1906 went to the University of Glasgow to study Science. He took mathematics, natural philosophy and chemistry. 17th November 1910 he graduated BSc with a special distinction in astronomy, having won a first class certificate in the subject. Thomas had also taken classes in the arts, such as history and Latin, and on 20th June 1911 he graduated MA. Following this he took yet more classes, this time in engineering, winning prizes in engineering drawing and design and electrical engineering . On 3rd October 1911, Thomas enrolled for teacher training at the Glasgow Provincial Training College, forerunner of Jordanhill College of Education, now the University of Strathclyde. He completed the one-year course for teachers of higher subjects on 28th June 1912 to qualify as a teacher of mathematics and science. However, he never obtained a teaching post, a note in the college register of students explaining that he 'Does not desire to teach. He has taken up another profession, and if successful will give up teaching.' Commemorated Roll of Honour of the Glasgow Provincial Committee for the Training of Teachers. Entered France, 23rd November 1915. Reported wounded and missing, 12th August 1916. Mother applied for his medals. Memorial Ref. Pier and Face 15 C., Thiepval Memorial, France.

MILLAR, Captain, Stanley Gemmell. Deceased 1st July 1916. 103rd Coy., Machine Gun Corps (Infantry). Aged 29. Son of John Millar, JP, of East Knowe, Paisley. Born February 1887. Attended Paisley Grammar School and Loretto School (1899 to 1907). He played in the Loretto, Ferguslie (captained for two years) and West of Scotland Cricket XI, and was a member of the Scottish International Hockey Team. Served in the Volunteer Force at the outbreak of war he enlisted in a territorial unit and served in the battalion machine-gun section. Received his commission, September 1914. He was afterwards given a commission in The Loyal Regiment, and attained the rank of captain. In employ of Messrs. J. & P. Coats. Entered France, 26th April 1916. His mother applied for his medals. Memorial Ref. Pier and Face 5 C and 12 C., Thiepval Memorial, France.

MILLER, Second Lieutenant, Francis John. He led his men most gallantly through the hottest fire that was encountered by the battalion, and when his company was suffering heavily, killed in No Man's Land or close to Breslau Trench 1st July 1916. 7th Bn., The Queen's (Royal West Surrey Regiment). Aged 19. Youngest son of Joseph William and Eliza Miller, of Sunnycroft, Penrith Road, Boscombe, Bournemouth formerly Sunny Croft, Woodford Green. Born Buckhurst Hill, Essex, 14th October 1896. Educated Seaford College and City of London School, matriculating London University 1913. Worked for Employers' Liability Assurance Corporation Ltd. He was a very keen sportsman who started working for the company in 1913 after university. He enlisted in the London Rifle Brigade, private, 391 in August 1914 and served in France and Flanders from 24th January 1915. He was invalided home with frost bite in March 1915 and returned to the Front in March 1916 having received his commission as a second lieutenant, 16th June 1915, The Queen's, 7th Bn. His Colonel wrote: "during the comparatively short time that he was in the battalion he had shown himself to be a most excellent officer in every way. His men had the most absolute faith and confidence in him." Effects were franc notes and cheque book. His father applied for his medals. Original burial map reference, 62C.A.8.b..4.7 Memorial Ref. III. O. 5., Dantzig Alley British Cemetery, Mametz, France. WO 339/4109

MILLER, Second Lieutenant, Stanley. Reported missing, killed in action, 1st July 1916. 11th Bn., Royal Inniskilling Fusiliers. Aged 30. Son of Mr. W. F. and L. E. Miller, of Frimley Road, Camberley, Surrey. Formerly squadron corporal-major in the Royal Horse Guards, 1063. Mother applied for his medals and the application forwarded from The Imperial Institute, South Kensington. Original map reference for burial 57d.R.25.a.6.7 as an Unknown British Officer later identified via officers boots size 10, khaki officer buttons and two medal ribbons believed to be Second Lieutenant Miller. Memorial Ref. VIII. F. 5., Heath Cemetery, Harbonnieres, France.

We Loved Thee Well But Jesus Loved Thee Best

MILLIN, Captain, Edward Job. Mentioned in Despatches. Killed whilst attempting to advance between the front line and the opposing trench, 1st July 1916. C Coy. 2nd Bn., King's Own Yorkshire Light Infantry. Aged 38. Medaille Militaire (France). Son of John and Louie Millin, of Ampney St. Peter, Cirencester, Glos. Husband of Alice Maud Millin, of 89, Cammell Road, Bolsover Road, Pitsmoor, Sheffield and father to two children. Native of Gloucester. Served in the South African campaign. In August 1914 as a colour sergeant, Yorkshire Infantry, 6056 at Mons the most senior soldier left in his regiment - all the officers having been killed or taken prisoner - he refused to accept the order to retreat and kept fighting until he received a head wound (a Blighty wound) and then rode with the ammunition back through the lines to ensure that it did not fall into enemy hands. This brave action was seen by the French and the French Government awarded him their highest purely Military Medal for gallantry - the Medaile Millitaire. After treatment in Britain for his serious head injury he accepted a commission and went back to France, 2nd June 1915 where he was killed. The Sheffield Year Book records that Millin received the British Distinguished Service Medal and the French decoration for gallantry. Commemorated on a brass tablet in Ampney St Peter's Church, Gloucestershire. His widow applied for his medals. Memorial Ref. Pier and Face 11 C and 12 A., Thiepval Memorial, France.

MINOR, Second Lieutenant, Roland. Killed whilst leading his platoon, 1st July 1916, originally reported wounded. 3rd Bn., King's Own (Royal Lancaster Regiment) attd 2nd killed with the 1st Bn. Aged 21. Only son of Philip Scott Minor (solicitor) and Susan Helen Minor, of Avonmore, Alderley Edge, Manchester. Born 10th March 1895. Grandson of Mr. C. T. Saunders (former President of the Law Society) and of Mr. Samuel Minor of Stoke Park, Shropshire. Educated at Abbotsholme, Colchester Royal Grammar School and on the continent. Articled to H. W. Minor, of Manchester as an articled clerk. Joining the Public Schools Battalion on its formation in September 1914 as a private, he obtained a commission, 26th May 1915 gazetted to the King's Own Royal Lancaster and went to the Front, 21st May 1916. Shortly after his arrival he was placed on interpreter duties. His father applied for his medals. Memorial Ref. I. B. 43., Euston Road Cemetery, Colincamps, France.

The Will Of Heaven Be Done In This And All Things I Obey

Boarders at Colchester Royal Grammar School, 1911.
Roland Minor probably the older boy in the very centre at the back.

MOCKLER, Captain, Francis George Ross, MC, Mentioned in Despatches. Killed in action, 1st July 1916. 2nd Bn., Royal Irish Regiment attd 11th Machine Gun Company. Aged 26. Youngest son of Major General Edward Mockler (Indian Army), and Mrs. Mockler, of Rochford, Grange, Guernsey. Educated at Elizabeth College, Guernsey and RMC Sandhurst. Entered France, 19th December 1914. Entered on Machine Gun Corps Roll, 23rd December 1915. His sister, Mrs. S. B. Mainguy, Guernsey applied for his medals. Memorial Ref. Pier and Face 3 A., Thiepval Memorial, France.

MOCKRIDGE, Lieutenant, George Ewart. Killed in the early stages of the big advance, first posted as missing then killed, casualties sustained crossing No Man's Land, 1st July 1916. 64th Bde., Machine Gun Corps (Infantry). Born 20th September 1896. Son of Mr. Albert J. and Bertha Mockridge, Headmaster of Poole Secondary School. Educated at Clifton College and awarded a scholarship to Wadham College, Oxford University. Member of the OTC for three years. Resided 27 Starley Road, Oxford. Enlisted 21st December 1914. Gazetted 2nd January 1915. Arrived France 25th February 1916. Formerly 7th and 6th Bn., Dorset Regiment. Father wrote several times to the War Office asking for the return of his son's possessions but none returned. October 1916 ' The relief to a parent's feelings that any written paper which has been on a son's body when found must be known' and in December 1916 'If anything can be recovered I would be deeply grateful'. Father applied for his medals. Memorial Ref. Pier and Face 5 C and 12 C., Thiepval Memorial, France. WO 339/31232

MONEY, Second Lieutenant, George Russell. Killed in the first attack and fell close to the German line, 1st July 1916. A Coy., 4th Bn., Middlesex Regiment. Son of Edgar George Money and Alice Margaret Money, 25 Cadogan Square, S.W. Born 14th December 1890 in Larkspur, Douglas Country, Colorado, USA. Employed as a planter. Attended Aldenham College. Transferred to the 4th Bn., 27th January 1916 from the 1/8th London Regiment. Originally buried angle of Empress Trench and a new communication trench, Sheet 26.d. Square Contour 110. Original burial map reference 57d.27c.7.6 and in 1919 moved to 9.H.8, being originially buried as Unknown British Officer found in Lieut. Barnetts (Middlesex) grave, His father received letters from Colonel Bicknell who reported his son was killed on the 1st and also from the Reverend Dugdale that confirmed he was buried with officers killed on the 1st July as correspondence from the War Office stated 3rd July 1916. Parents applied for his medals. Moved from Plot 9.H.8 to 4.L.8 Memorial Ref. IV. L.8, Gordon Dump Cemetery, Ovillers-La Boisselle, France. WO 339/35153

MONKHOUSE, Second Lieutenant, Alfred Ernest. Battalion advanced from assembly trenches at 8.00am and came under very heavy machine-gun fire, killed in action, 1st July 1916. E Company, 11th Bn., Border Regiment. Sergeant, 1030, 1st North Field Ambulance. Gazetted second lieutenant, 5th April 1915 to 11th Border in the field, arriving 30th March 1916. Mother, Mrs. M. A. Monkhouse, Cavendish Place, Jesmond, Newcastle-on-Tyne applied for his medals. Memorial Ref. Pier and Face 6 A and 7 C., Thiepval Memorial, France.

MONTGOMERY, Second Lieutenant, Robert Taylor. He and his company reached the first line of German trenches when one of the men fell wounded and begged for a drink. He managed to reach the thirsty soldier and was about to put his bottle to the man's lips when a bullet struck him on the head, causing instant death, 1st July 1916. 9th Bn., Royal Irish Fusiliers. Son of Mr. T. J. Montgomery, (merchant) High Street, Portadown. At the outbreak of the war he was commandant of the local medical corps of the UVF, and was amongst the first to volunteer for active service. He enlisted in the 9th Royal Irish Fusiliers and received his commission in May, 1915. Lieutenant Montgomery was an enthusiastic athlete and had won several medals in competitions. Prior to the war assisted his father in the running of his business. Entered France, 5th October 1915. R. G. Montgomery applied for his medals. Memorial Ref. Pier and Face 15 A., Thiepval Memorial, France.

MOODY, Second Lieutenant, Thomas. He fell fighting gallantly for his beloved country, 1st July 1916. C Coy., 1st /4th Bn., London Regiment (Royal Fusiliers). Aged 27. Son of Mr. Thomas Riley Moody, (head postman) of Castelnau, 94, Madrid Road, Barnes. Attended Latymer Upper School. Degree (BSc) from Birkbeck College and St Mark's College and employed as a civils. Member of the London University OTC. Resided 94 Madrid Road, Castleneau, Barnes. He was gazetted in August 1914 and was wounded in April of the following year, this was when he was kicked in the mouth by a horse on the 16th at Estaires and was evacuated back to England, declared fit October 1915. Entered France, 6th January 1915. He was present at the battle of Neuve Chapelle. Malta for six months. London Council, Education Officers' Department, Central Administrative Staff. His father applied for his medals. Memorial Ref. Pier and Face 9 D and 16 B., Thiepval Memorial, France.

MOORE, Captain, Arthur Robert, MC. 11.50am message received from Captain Moore saying he was in his preliminary battle position a patrol was dispatched but found he had gone forward. At 2.30pm the front of Battalion Headquarters was blown in by a German high explosive bomb, it wounded seven and killed seven. Major Moore and his signalling officer were in the dugout at the time. Gallantly led, reinforced and reached the second German line, losing all it's officers, 1st July 1916. 'A' Company, gallantly led to the second German line by Captain A. R. Moore, MC, but 18 returned. Moore himself and one of his subalterns, Second Lieutenant F. C. Fanghangel, were killed, the other subaltern, A. G. Blunn, being captured with seven others. The rest of the company were killed. A Coy., 1st /4th Bn., London Regiment (Royal Fusiliers). Aged

32. Son of Sir John Moore, MD, FRCPI, DL, (Physician to HM The King in Ireland), and Lady Moore, of 40, Fitzwilliam Square, Dublin. Born 22nd July 1883, Dublin. Educated at the St. Stephen's Green School (formerly known as Dr. Strangway's School) and went on to Trinity College. MA, University of Dublin. He then went to study at King's Inns, being called to the Bar in 1906. He practiced on the Leinster circuit and, in 1911, was still living in his father's house at 40, Fitzwilliam Square, Dublin. Barrister-at-Law. Gazetted 29th August 1914. Military Cross gazetted 23rd June 1915 awarded at the Battle of Neuve Chappelle on the 12th March 1915; The shrapnel and machine-gun fire maintained by the Germans during the night cost a few casualties, amounting to 14 NCO's and men wounded. In addition to these was Second Lieutenant A. R. Moore, who was hit in the leg on the way up to the line. This officer, however, stuck to his duty and remained with his platoon until after relief of the battalion the next morning." Military Cross presented at Buckingham Palace on the 20th May 1916. Moore's end, like his life, was one of courageous devotion, and has been simply told by one of his own sergeants; "Captain Moore was wounded in the wrist about thirty minutes before we went over. Nevertheless he led the company, revolver in hand, and on the sunken road at the rear of Nameless Farm I saw blood flowing from his back. He still pushed on, and then I was shot through the leg and took shelter in a shell hole. The last I saw of Capt. Moore he was still going ahead". Named on the University Club Great War Memorial, Barristers' Memorial in the Four Courts in Dublin. Entered France, 6th January 1915. Sir John W. Moore applied for his medals. Memorial Ref. Pier and Face 9 D and 16 B., Thiepval Memorial, France.

MOORE, Second Lieutenant, Thomas George. Led XVI platoon, last seen in the fourth line German trench in the afternoon, holding a post when he was surrounded by Germans and either killed or taken prisoner. 1st July 1916. D Company, 17th Bn. attd. 8th Bn., Royal Irish Rifles. Born on 31st May 1892, the son of George Moore, (Head Constable) and Frances Jane Moore (nee Kent) of the Royal Irish Constabulary Barracks at 52 York Road, Belfast. Educated at Skegoniel School, the Model School, Belfast and Belfast Mercantile College and Belfast Royal Academical Institution. He was working in the linen business with Messrs. Kinnaird & Co., before enlisting in Belfast on 1st March 1915 with the 17th Bn., lance corporal, 17/2. He applied for a commission on 24th September 1915 and went to the Western Front in February 1916. Still missing 26th December 1916. His father applied for his medals. Memorial Ref. Pier and Face 15 A and 15 B., Thiepval Memorial, France.

MORGAN, Second Lieutenant, John Walter Rees. "The 2nd Bn., Royal Dublin Fusiliers, began to advance at 9.00am, immediately encountering heavy enfilade fire from Beaumont Hamel. At 9.05am two runners arrived and informed Major Walsh, the commanding officer, that the attack was to be postponed. He managed to stop part of C and D companies advancing. However for the rest of the battalion, already in No Man's Land, the recall order came too late. While leading his men to the assault on the German trenches, he was hit on the head by some shell splinters and killed instantaneously about 9.15am killed about half a mile north of Beaumont Hamel, and buried the following day. 1st July 1916. 4th Bn. attd. 2nd Bn., Royal Dublin Fusiliers. Aged 23. Younger son of Rees Powell Morgan, (solicitor of Brynhyford, Neath), and Mrs. Mary Evelyn Morgan. Born 1892. Attended Rugby School from 1905 to 1908. He then became articled clerk to his elder brother, Llewellyn Rees Morgan Solicitor, Brynhyfryd, Neath, and was preparing for his final examination when war broke out.

He enlisted in the 1st Bn., Royal Fusiliers, 8th October, 1914, as a private 281, and, after six months' training with them, obtained his commission in the 4th Bn., Royal Dublin Fusiliers, in May, 1915. He was ordered to the Front, 31st July, 1915, to join the 2nd Battalion of his regiment, and spent practically -the whole of the next year in the trenches. His captain wrote:-. The last time I saw him he was leading his men in the open under very heavy fire, in a manner in which I knew he would." His Adjutant wrote :- "I cannot say how grieved we all are to lose him, and how we all sympathise with you in your sad loss, but he gave his life for his country and what more can any of us do? I had many opportunities of seeing him. He was always bright and cheerful, setting a good example to us all, and to his men." His brother, L. R. Morgan applied for his medals. His brother, Llewellyn choose his inscription. Memorial Ref. I. D. 61., Sucrerie Military Cemetery, Colincamps, France.

Who Had It Not In Him To Fear R.I.P.

MORLEY, Lieutenant, Marmaduke Robert Hood. Made it across into the German trenches, although twice wounded whilst leading the remnants of his battalion. Despite his wounds he refused to go back. The Germans were quick to launch counter attacks and Morley, who remained with his men, was eventually killed. 1st July 1916. 8th Bn., King's Own Yorkshire Light Infantry. Aged 22. Only son of Alfred Noel and Jessie Maria I. Morley, of Lychwood, Worplesdon Hill, Woking, Surrey. Born 18th April 1894. Attended Winchester College, 1907 to 1913. He came to Winchester as an Exhibitioner from West Downs, was Head of House in his last year and a commoner prefect. He kept goal for the Soccer XI, captained second XI cricket team and, according to the Wykehamist of August 1916, developed an exceptionally fine tenor voice. He was elected to an Exhibition at Magdalene College, Cambridge to read for the History Tripos, when war broke out. He obtained a commission in 8th Bn., King's Own Yorkshire Light Infantry, and went to the France, 27th August 1915. Originally buried 800 yards, north east of Ovillers La Boisselle, 970 yards north west of Ovillers church. Effects were advance book, cheque book and letters. Father, Noel applied for his medals. Memorial Ref. V. J. 22., Blighty Valley Cemetery, Authuille Wood, France. WO 339/375

Faithful Unto Death

MORRIS, Lieutenant, Gilbert Willan. Reported at 7.30am, 'Mr. Morris pulled out his revolver, blew his whistle and said 'Over' as soon as he said it a bullet hit him between the eyes and killed him', 1st July 1916. 8th Bn., King's Own Yorkshire Light Infantry. Aged 25. Born Hampstead, 27th May 1891. Third son of Frank R. (stockbroker) and Mary Morris, of Hill House, Great Missenden, Bucks formerly Woodlands, Crofton, Orpington. District Scoutmaster of Orpington, Farnborough. Attended Bradfield College, May 1906 to March 1908. Insurance clerk. Enlisted at the outbreak of war, 29th August 1914, private, 768, 10th Bn., Royal Fusiliers. Entered France, 27th August 1915. Commissioned 30th December 1915. Memorial plaque at St. Gile's the Abott, Farnborough. Brother Second Lieutenant Clive Wilian Morris killed 9th May 1915. Originally buried 1000 yards NW of Ovillers La Boisselle, NE of Albert. Identified by the identity disc taken from his body, no other personal effects were recovered. Father applied for his medals. Memorial Ref. IV. E. 5., Blighty Valley Cemetery, Authuille Wood, France. WO 339/31233

Blessed Are The Pure In Heart For They Shall See God St.Mat.V.8

MORSE, Lieutenant, Ernest Frederick. Missing 1st July 1916, Machine Gun Corps (Infantry). Aged 27. Youngest son of Mr. A. T. and Mrs. S. A. Morse. Born 5th May 1889 at Leytonstone, Essex. Age 27. Educated at Forest School, Walthamstow and gazetted into the Border Regiment soon after the outbreak of war. Left Argentina, 1914. Temporary Second Lieutenant E. F. Morse to be temporary Lieutenant 20th October 1915. Transferred to the machine-gun regiment, January 1916. Southampton to Le Havre, 25th April 1916. Leytonstone War Memorial. Two brothers served and one wounded Second Lieutenant J. P. Morse, East Surreys. Brother, C. H. Morse, Upper Road, Plaistow, E13 applied for his medals. Original map reference where body found 57.d.X.13. Father choose his inscription address being A. T. Morse & Sons, 134 Upper Road, Plaistow. Memorial Ref. XII. J. 10., Ovillers Military Cemetery, France.

Pro Patria

MORUM, Second Lieutenant, James Pearse. Killed 1st July 1916. 6th Bn. attd. I Coy., 1st Bn., Rifle Brigade. Aged 20. Eldest son of William E. and Florence S. Morum, of Queenstown, Cape Colony, South Africa an in England, Chislehurst, Kent. Born 8th March 1896, Queenstown, South Africa. Attended Merton Court 1905 – 1910, Wellington and Pembroke College, Cambridge. Merton Court Preparatory School First World War Roll Of Honour and the Methodist Church Memorial. Commemorated London Borough of Bexley. Enlisted Cambridge. Commissioned 16th December 1914. Entered France, 5th July 1915. Father applied for his medals. Memorial Ref. I. H. 1., Sucrerie Military Cemetery, Colincamps, France.

I Go Over With Complete Trust In God

MOTT, Captain, Hugh Fenwick, MC. Killed while leading his men across, he was trying to enlarge a gap in the wire between the third and second line trench, 1st July 1916. Officer Commanding C Company, 1st/16th Bn., London Regiment (Queen's Westminster Rifles). Aged 22. Eldest child and son of Alfred Fenwick Mott and Katherine Mary Mott, of The Holt, Reigate, Surrey. Educated Hillside School in Reigate at Marlborough College and Oriel College, Oxford matriculated 1913. When war broke out in 1914 he had been at Oxford twelve months. Hugh enlisted and received a commission in the Queen's Westminster Rifles in September 1914. Hugh went to France, 24th January 1915, 3rd June 1916 he was awarded the Military Cross in the Birthday Honours List, by this time he had been promoted to captain. Father applied for his medals. Memorial Ref. Pier and Face 13 C., Thiepval Memorial, France.

MULKERN, Captain, Hubert Cowell. Deceased, 1st July 1916. Royal Army Medical Corps was the medical officer of the Tyrone Volunteer Battalion of the 9th Bn., Royal Inniskilling Fusiliers. Aged 34. Son of Alfred Courtney (doctor at Kingston-on-Thames) and Jane Mulkern. Commemorated Latymer Upper School and St. Mary's Hospital, Paddington. Entered France, 8th October 1915. A. C. Mulkern (brother) from Surrey applied for his medals. Memorial Ref. Pier and Face 4 C., Thiepval Memorial, France.

MULLALLY, Captain, Brian Desmond. Wounded on the 1st July 1916. 26th (Tyneside Irish) Bn., Northumberland Fusiliers. Aged 19. Youngest son of William Mullally, (draper, Irish Linen Warehouse, 441 Sauchiehall Street, Glasgow) of 50, Queen Mary Avenue, Crosshill, Glasgow, and Matilda Mullally. Educated at St. Aloysius's College, Glasgow, and at Mount St. Mary's College, Chesterfield. In 1914, aged 18, Mullally enrolled in his first year at the University of Glasgow as a medical student and took classes in chemistry and zoology. He was an active member of the OTC from which he received his commission. Entered France, February 1916. He never entered his second year at the university. On the 25th and 26th of June, 1916, Mullally took part in a trench raid on the German front line at La Boiselle under the command of Captain Price. Although wounded during the raid, he remained at his post, and received the Military Medal along with the other members of the 26th Battalion raiding party. He remained on duty. His father applied for his medals. Original burial map reference 57d.X.13. Memorial Ref. XI. J. 4., Ovillers Military Cemetery, France.

On His Soul Sweet Jesus Have Mercy May He Rest In Peace

MULLINS, Captain, Richard Walter. Killed gallantly leading his men into action at Fricourt, critically wounded 1st July 1916. C Coy., 10th Bn., York and Lancaster Regiment. Aged 23. Son of Mr. C. W. and Mrs. Hester Mullins. Nephew and adopted son of Mr. and Mrs. J. H, Mullins, Rosapenna. Born New Zealand, 2nd April 1893. Attended the Llandaff Cathedral School, Cardiff and later Malvern College, 1907 -1910. Clerk. Enlisted in the 2nd Bn., Welsh Regiment on the 2nd September 1914, No. 13943. Fought in the Battle of Loos. Received his commission 2nd December 1914, having served with the Cardiff Pals. Promoted captain, November 1915. Invalided home in December 1915 with jaundice and returned to the Front in May 1916. Stained glass window, St. Isans Church, Cardiff. Father applied for his medals. Original burial map reference 57d.X.26.c.3.8. reburied August 1919. Memorial Ref. II. Q. 5., Gordon Dump Cemetery, Ovillers-La Boisselle, France. WO 339/23564

MURDOCH, Second Lieutenant, John. Mown down on the left in support of B Coy., missing believed killed, 1st July 1916. He was last seen ahead of his men leading them on when a shell burst between them and he disappeared. It was hoped he was a prisoner but word came he had been buried. D Coy.' 16th Bn., Highland Light Infantry. Born in 1891 in Blantyre, Lanarkshire, where his father Peter worked as a warehouseman and manufacturer. Attended High School of Glasgow where he was known as 'Johnnie'. In the school he was in the Cadet Corps and in the shooting club winning many medals. At the age of 18 he enrolled at the University of Glasgow in September 1909 in the faculty of science. During his first year at the university, John studied mathematics. He passed his mathematics exam in October 1910 – which was the joint highest grade in his class. Over the next few years of his degree, John took a broad range of classes within the Faculty of Science, including organic and inorganic chemistry, metallurgy, and natural philosophy. By his fifth year in 1913, aged 22, John was back to studying mathematics, and passed both his mathematics and chemistry exams with high results. He did not finish his degree. Active member of the OTC. Enlisted in the Camerons, serving as a second lieutenant later transferred to the Highland Light Infantry. Gazetted in September 1914. Reported missing 11th July 1916. Original burial map reference R.21.a.6.3 reburied 1919. Memorial Ref. III. N. 3., Lonsdale Cemetery, Authuille, France.

MURPHY, Lieutenant, Johnston. Reported wounded, missing, 2nd July 1916. 6th Bn. attd. 8th Bn., Royal Irish Rifles. Aged 24. Son of Clarke Murphy, UDC, Main Street, Ballymoney. Educated Coleraine Academical Institution and Trinity where he won several scholarships. Brilliant student in the history school and played wing three-quarter at one time for the Wanderers XV. Before the war broke out he passed for the Indian Civil Service, but joined the 6th Royal Irish Rifles with whom he served in Gallipoli from 10th July 1915 where he was wounded. Rifleman Montgomery stated in an affidavit that from what he saw during the engagement he came to the conclusion that Lieutenant Murphy was shot through the heart. The War Office also came to the same conclusion that he was dead, Master of the Rolls granted the application for presuming the death. Mother applied for his medals. Memorial Ref. Pier and Face 15 A and 15 B., Thiepval Memorial, France.

MURRAY, Captain, Charles Stephenson. Died of wounds, officially recorded as 1st July 1916. In command of No 7 and No. 5 Platoon and was wounded at the very start of the attack. 12th Bn., Royal Irish Rifles. Grave Registration Report shows 2nd July 1916. Medal Index Card has died of wounds, 1st July 1916. Aged 44. Son of Colonel Alexander Murray, (4th Royal Irish Rifles) of Portrush, Co. Antrim. Commander of the UVF in Portrush. Member of the Portrush Golf Club. He joined the Matabela Mounted Police and later served in the South African War being awarded two medals. Taken prisoner during the Jameson Raid, a botched raid against the South African Republic over New Year's weekend 1985 to 1896. Entered France, 5th October 1915. Portrush War Memorial. Brother, J. P. Murray applied for his medals. Memorial Ref. I. A. 13., Warloy-Baillon Communal Cemetery Extension, France.

MURRAY, Second Lieutenant, John Claude. Missing from the 1st July, officially 9th July 1916 believed to have been killed 1st July 1916 and listed in the war diary as amongst the missing. The war diary has no officers killed on the 9th July and the battalion were positioned miles from the front line. 2nd Bn., South Wales Borderers attd. 9th Bn. Son of William and Elizabeth Murray of Treberth Farm, Saundersfoot, Pembrokeshire. Educated Greenhill Grammar School, Tenby. Member of staff, from 1908 until 1913, Bablake School, Coventry. Commissioned as a Second Lieutenant (temporary) on Christmas Day 1914 and a Lieutenant (Temporary) on the 1st April 1916. He joined the 2nd Battalion just two months before his death. Memorial Ref. Pier and Face 4A. Thiepval Memorial, Somme, France.

MURRAY, Captain, Patrick Austin. Sergeant McAndrew stated that he was killed, riddled with bullets from a machine-gun, 1st July 1916. D Coy., 25th (Tyneside Irish) Bn., Northumberland Fusiliers. Born 24th May 1882. Son of John and Annie Murray. Educated at St. Cuthbert's Grammar School, Newcastle-on-Tyne. Attended Durham University/Armstrong College, Newcastle University. Served with the Northumberland Imperial Yeomanry, 27059 in South Africa as a trooper 1901 to 1902. Queen's Medal. Discharged in 110th Coy. He was commissioned on 1st January 1915 and attained the rank of captain in June of that year in the Northumberland Fusiliers, 25th Battalion. Returned from the Gold Coast to volunteer. Entered France, 11th January 1916. Married, Dorothy May, only daughter of Mr. and Mrs. G. J. Kirkup, of Newcastle-on-Tyne. Resided 212 Westmoreland Road, Newcastle-on-Tyne formerly 4 Burnfoot Terrace, Whitley Bay. Mining engineer by profession. Originally buried a little south of La Boisselle. Mrs. G. P. Gutting (widow/remarried) applied for his medals. Mother applied for officers' pension. Memorial Ref. Pier and Face 10 B 11 B and 12 B., Thiepval Memorial, France. WO 339/26208

MUSGROVE, Lieutenant, George Henry Stuart. At the time he was hit he was leading his platoon with the utmost gallantly and coolness, known to be killed by 7.50am a few yards in front of the parapet, 1st July 1916. Coy., 8th Bn., East Surrey Regiment. Aged 27. Youngest son of (Sergeant-Major) William and Rebecca Musgrove, of 9, Suffolk Parade, Cheltenham. Old Cheltonians will remember him as the instructor for many years of the cadet corps of Cheltenham College. Received his commission on 3rd December 1914. Formerly in a Cheltenham counting house and afterwards in London. Thespian Roll of Honour. After the action some of the men from his own company asked to bring in his body and he was buried in Carnoy Cemetery on the 3rd July 1916 at 2.00pm. Formerly 2434, Artists Rifles. Entered France, September 1915. Lieutenant W. B. Musgrove applied for the medals of his late brother, from Cheltenham previously Hotel Des Families, Belle Vue, Duccant Sur Meuse. Memorial Ref. E. 30., Carnoy Military Cemetery, France.

NANSON, Second Lieutenant, Joseph. Killed leading his men in front of Mametz Wood, about 100 – 200 yards in front of Dantzig Alley and the southern section of Fritz Trench, 1st July 1916. 25th Bn., attd B Coy., 22nd Bn., Manchester Regiment. Aged 22. Born in Llangollen in 20th June 1894. Youngest son of Joseph Nanson, (slate merchant) and Jane Nanson of Bryniau, Cumberland. Member of St. Bee's OTC from 1910 to 1912. In 1910 organising of the local scout group. A fine all-round athlete. After school he spent some time, in his father's office at Llangollen, before going to London to study building construction and it was from here that he "joined up" with the Manchesters in April, 1915 and three months ago went with his regiment to France. He had a short leave in February 1916. 4th November 1916 buried near Mametz-Montauban Road. In 1920 his body was moved to Dantzig. Original burial map reference 62D.F.6.c.1.8 found with Lieutenant Peak and three privates of the 22nd Manchesters all killed 1st July. Memorial Ref. II. F. 2., Dantzig Alley British Cemetery, Mametz, France. WO 339/30668

NEAME, Captain, Gerald Tassel. Called into action on the afternoon, D Coy., and killed 1st July 1916, shot and fatally wounded along the Carnoy-Montauban Road and died whilst being carried back for medical attention. 7th Bn., The Buffs (East Kent Regiment). He had two platoons as carriers supplying designated locations. Aged 31. Eldest son of Frank and Louisa Neame, of Macknade, Queensland, Australia. Born 28th April 1885 in Horewood, Surrey. Attended Brighton College (Junior House, 1896 – 1899), one of four who died on the 1st July. Attended Cheltenham College and played cricket for the Cheltenham XI in 1900 and 1901. Received a commission and posted to France, 27th July 1915. Married Phyllis Neame in 1916. Wounded April 1916 by a shell. Originally buried north of Carnoy. Effects were, bills & keys, advance book, identity disc, spray of heather, pieces of ladies dress material, pocket wallet including photos and newspaper cuttings, gold ring, gold chain & cross, card case, wrist watch and letters & photos. Widow applied for his medals. Original map burial reference 62c.A.8.c.4.8 exhumed and concentrated from an isolated grave, December 1922 and identified by regimental cross, clothing & epaulettes. Memorial Ref. XXIII. Q. 9., Delville Wood Cemetery, Longueval, France. WO 339/12672

OFFICERS OF THE BUFFS.—Back row (left to right): Lieut. A. J. Hett, Sec.-Lieut. A. D. H. Foster, Lieut. M. Hammond, Lieut. P. G. Norbury, Lieut. G. T. Neame, Sec.-Lieut. W. L. McColl, Sec.-Lieut. E. Nightingale. Third row: Capt. A. A. Mackintosh, A.D.C., Capt. C. K. Black, Lieut. L. Wood, Lieut. E. C. Dunstan, Lieut. E. B. C. Burnside, Lieut. G. J. Neame. Second row: Brig.-Gen. J. H. V. Crowe, Maj.-Gen. F. I. Maxse, C.V.O., C.B., D.S.O., Lieut.-Col W. F. Emslie, Gen. Rt. Hon. Sir A. H. Paget, G.C.B., K.C.V.O., Major C. L. Parmiter, Brig.-Gen. A. Martyn, Major R. L. P. Birch. Front row: Sec.-Lieut. F. M. Stoop, Sec.-Lieut. H. L. Quartermaine, Sec.-Lieut. J. G. Spencer, Sec.-Lieut. G. M. Tait.

Captain Neame sat next to Lieutenant P. G. Norbury also killed on the 1st July 1916, back row fifth from left

NEEDHAM, Captain, Benjamin Llewellyn. Killed leading the men he loved and who loved him to the assault, he was seen to fall, hit through the head, by Lieutenant Lilley and several of the company, 1st July 1916. 2nd Bn., Lincolnshire Regiment. Born in Meriden, 1881. Second youngest child of Jonathan (Registrar of Births and Deaths, Coleshill District) and Catherine Louisa Needham of High Street, Coleshill. Educated at Coleshill Grammar School. On 2nd February 1910 he married Muriel May Hurst at Hounslow, Middlesex and had three children- Eric, Richard and Kenneth. He joined the army on the outbreak of the Boer War, 11th January 1901 (Awarded Queen's South African Medal) and went to Gibraltar returned from Bermuda, commissioned 1st November 1914 and landed at Le Havre on the 6th November 1914. Promoted to lieutenant but was wounded at Neuve Chapelle in spring 1915 wounded in the right arm and shoulder. After his recovery he returned to the Front in autumn 1915 and was promoted to lieutenant. He was gazetted captain in the 2nd Lincolns on 14th February 1916. Brother of Mr. H. R. Needham, Salisbury Road, Saltley another brother was a sergeant major in the RGA. Lieutenant Colonel Bastard wrote; ' I don't think even you can know what a loss he was to the regiment. The way he ran his company was beyond praise and he made it the best in the battalion. His men did splendidly the day of the attack, which was greatly due to his excellent training and I am sure he died as he would have wished, leading the men he loved and who loved him to the assault'. His widow applied for his medals. Memorial Ref. Pier and Face 1 C., Thiepval Memorial, France. WO 339/15647

The Needham Brothers;
Captain B. L. Needham, E. Needham, R.N.R, Sergeant R.G. Needham, Royal Field Artillery.

NEGUS, Second Lieutenant, Arthur George. Five officers collected their men in Etch communication trench and bombed up it and along 'Fellow' trench and then along 'Feud' until cleared and put up one of the battalion sign boards on seeing it the men came over and dropped into it, here. Second Lieutenants Yates and Negus were killed, at the junction of Fellow and Etch trench, 1st July 1916. Second Lieutenant Yates fell first, Arthur had already been wounded and was killed. C Coy., 1st /16th Bn., London Regiment (Queen's Westminster Rifles). Only son of Mr. E. M. and Mrs. C. J. Negus of 16 Cleverdon Road, Norbiton, Surrey. Chief opponent of Captain Arthur Channing Purnell in skiff racing, he was also killed 1st July. Raced chiefly in association with C. E. Chapman. Lacrosse player in the Surbiton Club. Formerly private with the 16th Bn., London Regiment. Widow, Ethel Mary Negus, Manorgate Road, Kingston Hill, Surrey applied for his medals. Memorial Ref. Pier and Face 13 C., Thiepval Memorial, France.

NEIL, Captain, Stanley Thomas Arthur. Fighting was hard and shelling heavy, machine-gun fire was intense, he was killed instantly by gallantly assisting in the battalion attack, 1st July 1916. 15th Bn., West Yorkshire Regiment (Prince of Wales's Own). Aged 27. Second son of Mr. William Warwick Neil. Born 1889. Educated King Edward VI's Grammar School and Hartley University College. A civil engineer by profession, he was employed by Messrs. Playfair and Toole, government contractors, Southampton and was the resident waterworks engineer to the Leeds Corporation under Mr. C. J. Henzell at the New Leighton Reservoir. Enlisted September 1914. Given a commission as a lieutenant and posted as second in command of 'A' Company under the command of Captain Phillip Horace Leyland Mellor. He served in Colsterdale, Egypt (entered 22nd December 1915) and France. Given seven days home leave in April 1915, he spent most of it visiting the homes and families of "Pals" that had been killed or wounded. On the 3rd June 1915, after a month away from the "Pals", (acting as an instructor, at the divisional school) he rejoined them on the day their adjutant, Captain Edward Karl Maur De-Pledge died of wounds because of his death Stanley replaced him as adjutant of the battalion. In December of 1915, he was promoted to the rank of captain. Mother applied for his medals. Memorial Ref. Pier and Face 2 A 2 C and 2 D., Thiepval Memorial, France.

NEILL, Lieutenant, James Dermot. Killed in the splendid attack, 1st July 1916. 108th Coy., Machine Gun Corps (Infantry). Aged 29. Eldest son of Sharrnan D. and Annie S. Neill, of 22 Donegal Place, Belfast and Ardmoyle, Cultra, Co. Down. Born on the 5th December 1886. Aged 29. Educated at Belfast Royal Academical Institution and Aldenham School, Herts. He attended colleges in England, Switzerland and Germany, as well as Queen's University, Belfast, where he was Member of the Queen's University, Belfast, Training Corps. 1909 – 1910. On the outbreak of war he was among the first to join the 13th Bn., Royal Irish Rifles (the Down Regiment), afterwards joining the Machine Gun Company of his Brigade. Entered France, August 1915. He was on the Committee or the Royal North of Ireland Yacht Club and a member of Holywood Golf Club, in both of which sports he was an enthusiast. He was also a director in his father's firm, a member of the UVF. Commissioned on 26th January 1916. His younger brother Robert Larmour Neill died at Fromelles in May 1915. His obituary describes; "one of those brave Ulstermen who, no any rash impulse, but after cool deliberation of all the sacrifices involved, freely and cheefully offered his services to the country." In August 1932, a French woman, Madame le Bayon, was visiting the Thiepval Memorial and found a small silver medallion in the shape of a horse shoe, with a chain. The medallion was inscribed to "Lt J D Neill, 13th R.I.R". They requested details of James's family so they could return the medallion. His father replied stating that he was most anxious to recover this memento of his son who he knew possessed and probably wore as an ID medal. Father applied for his medals. Commemorated Holywood First Presbyterian Church, Holywood and District War Memorial, Queen's University and finally the Royal Belfast Academical Institution. Memorial Ref. Pier and Face 5 C and 12 C., Thiepval Memorial, France.

NEILL, Lieutenant, Reginald (Rex) Henry. Taken command of B Coy,, after Captain Craig MP had been wounded, reported missing believe taken prisoner, 1st July 1916. Originally reported as wounded, this was subsequently changed to missing during the second week of July 1916. He was seen in a communication trench between the first and second German line, he was lying down and his wound had been dressed. 11th Bn., Royal Irish Rifles. Aged 21. Son of Reginald and Geraldine Neill, of Colingrove, Dunmurry and Sheena, Craigavad, Co. Down. Born 16th September 1894. Educated at Mourne Grange, Kilkeel, Co. Down and Malvern College (1909-1911), Worcestershire. Stock broker. Energetic member of the UVF. Embarked for France from Bordon Camp in October 1915. His father was still hopeful that he had survived having "learned from a private source that his son is slightly wounded and a prisoner." Commemorated on a plaque in St. John the Baptist Parish Church, Suffolk, Belfast erected by his fellow officers in B Company 11 RIR and on a memorial window erected by his parents. The inscription below the window reads, "Be thou faithful unto death and I will give thee a crown of life". Via the Red Cross, Captain Charles Craig wrote in November 1917 when he was interned at Freiburg; 'this officer is definitely dead, he was last seen alive by Lieutenant Salter of same company. Immediately before a counter-attack by the Germans and although not actually seen wounded or dead, he has never been heard of since, if he died he died fighting' further reports suggest he was shot in the breast and died instantaneously. Two accounts suggest his was in a held position until they were surrounded and had to surrender. His mother wrote to the War Office in October 1916 suggesting her son may have been wearing private's clothes and maybe a prisoner of war but not with the officers, his identity disc was worn on his arm. His father applied for his medals. Memorial Ref. Pier and Face 15 A and 15 B., Thiepval Memorial, France. WO 339/14586

Officers of the 11th Battalion July 1915

Top Row—Lieut. Waring, 2nd Lieut. Ellis, 2nd Lieut. P. B. Thornely, Lieut. F. G. Hull, 2nd Lieut. D. J. Brown, Lieut. E. Vance, Lieut. R. H. Neill (Assistant Adjutant), 2nd Lieut. C. C. Canning.
Second Row (standing)—Lt. and Q.M. W. L. Devoto, Lieut. R. Thompson (Transport Officer), Lieut. C. F. K. Ewart, 2nd Lieut. C. G. F. Waring, 2nd. Lieut. S. A. M'Neill, 2nd Lieut. D. S. Priestly, 2nd Lieut. W. C. Boomer, 2nd Lieut. T. H. Wilson, 2nd Lieut. G. O. Young (Scout Officer), Lieut. K. M. Moore, Lieut. M. C. Graham (Medical Officer), Captain S. D. B. Masters.
Third Row (sitting)—Captain Smyth, Capt. C. C. Craig, M.P., Capt. A. P. Jenkins, Capt. R. Rivers Smyth (Brigade Major, 108th Inf. Brigade), Major P. L. K. Blair Oliphant (2nd in Command), Lt.-Col. H. A. Pakenham (Commanding), Major W. D. Deverell (Adjutant), Capt. O. B. Webb, Capt. A. F. Charley, Capt. A. P. I. Samuels.
Two Officers sitting in front—2nd Lieut. C. H. H. Orr, 2nd Lieut. J. C. Carson.

NELSON, Second Lieutenant, John (Jack). Initially reported wounded and missing, 1st July 1916. 8th Bn., King's Own Yorkshire Light Infantry. Aged 22. Son of Thomas George and Fanny Nelson, of Sparham, Norwich. Born Sparham, Norfolk. Educated at Christ's Hospital, Horsham. Student. Next of Kin, Uncle, Reverend J. Nelson, 56 Fellowes Road, Hempstead. Attested 10th September 1914, 16726, Sherwood Foresters. Temporary second lieutenant, 11th December 1914. Entered France, 27th August 1915. Gunshot wound to the left foot, January 1916, no bone of nerve damage signed fit, 9th March 1916. Enquiries through American Embassy had no result. Three brothers also served Lieutenant Thomas Burrow Nelson, HMS Minto, Donald Horatio Nelson, HMS Talbot and Corporal Charles Davis Nelson, Canadian Infantry. Mrs. J. B. Nelson, Shrewsbury Road, Birkenhead applied for his medals and a Miss. D.N. Nelson worked at London Hospital, Whitechapel. Memorial Ref. V. G. 28., Blighty Valley Cemetery, Authuille Wood, France. WO 339/31652

NEVILL, Captain, Wilfred Percy. Hit in the head by machine-gun fire just short of German lines as he was about to bomb the German position, 1st July 1916. 1st Bn., B Coy., East Yorkshire Regiment attached 8th Bn., East Surrey Regiment. Captain Nevill bought four footballs, one for each of his platoons. The idea being that the footballs would be "kicked into No Man's Land" as far towards the German line as was possible, and the winner would receive a prize from the captain, who "kicked off" the first ball - the prize was never collected as Nevill died on the day. One of the footballs was inscribed : "The great European Cup, The Final, East Surreys v Bavarians, kick off at zero". Born Canonbury Park, London on 14th July 1894. Attended Dover College (1908 – 1913), he was head prefect and captain of the cricket and hockey teams. Attended Jesus College, Cambridge intending to study the Classical Tripos. He had been at college for just a year when war broke out. A member of the OTC he joined up in November 1914 and was promoted to captain. Entered France, 27th July 1915. Major A. P. B. Irwin wrote "He was one of the bravest men I have ever met, and was loved and trusted by his men to such a degree they would have followed him anywhere." His mother, Mrs. T. G. Nevill, Tennyson's House, Montpelier Road, Twickenham, Middlesex applied for his medals. Memorial Ref. E. 28., Carnoy Military Cemetery, France.

NEVILLE, Captain, George Henry, MC, Mentioned in Despatches. Missing believed killed 1st July officially 2nd July 1916. His batman reported he was wounded in the left arm, his attendant applied a dressing and urged him to go to the field hospital, he refused even though his wound made it impossible for him to hold his weapon, but he went on and was shot in the chest. 1st Bn., Somerset Light Infantry. Aged 35. Fourth son of Mr. and Mrs. T. Neville, of Dunchurch, Rugby. Husband of Alice Ethel Pearl (formerly Neville), of 107, Chiswell, Portland, Dorset. Recruiting officer in Bath for some time. Sergeant, 7532. Entered France, 21st August 1914. Gazetted second lieutenant 30th July 1915, to be temporary captain 21st February 1916. Military Cross awarded January 1916 in New Year's Honours List. His widow made an application for his medals. His mother applied for officers' pension for George and his brother, Captain Frank Septimus Neville killed 24th November 1917, 6th Bn., Northamptonshire Regiment. Original map reference for burial 57d.K.35.c.3.9 and buried as an Unknown British Officer (Captain) and in 1928 identified as Captain Neville, by uniform, buttons, sleeves & cuffs. Memorial Ref. XIV. G. 12., Serre Road Cemetery No.2, France.

Beloved Husband Of A. E. Neville Love Conquers All Things Even Death

NEWCOMBE, Lieutenant, Richard. Reported that he steadied his men and calmly lit a cigarette before going over the parapet, 1st July 1916. At 7.28am, six leading platoons took up their position in No Man's Land, without loss. At 7.30am our front line pushed forward, they were met with very heavy artillery and machine-gun fire, some of A and B companies who did make the German front line at 7.35am were surrounded and captured by the Germans. Killed on the way across being shot. 1st Bn., East Lancashire Regiment. Aged 23. Son of Charles Henry and Emily Newcombe, of 28, Herne Hill, London. Born 8th April 1893. In July 1913 went to work for the London County & Westminster Bank and left his job at the London West End office. Joined the Artists Rifles, private, 1873 and had been at the Front about a year since 29th December 1914. Second Lieutenant 26th May 1915. Mother applied for his medals. Memorial Ref. Pier and Face 6 C., Thiepval Memorial, France.

NEWLANDS, Second Lieutenant, Sydney Barron. Killed in action, 1st July 1916. 16th Bn., West Yorkshire Regiment (Prince of Wales's Own). Aged 20. Elder son of the Reverend R. W. and Agnes Newlands, of 5, Fairholme Avenue, Romford, Essex. The Reverend Newlands of Providence Place Chapel, Cleckheaton was also an army chaplain, and did much valuable work for the men in hospital and in the front lines in France. Former pastor of Eglington Street Congregational Church and was president of the Glasgow Christian Endeavour Union. Born at Port Byron, Illinois, USA. Sydney joined the Leeds Pals on the outbreak of war. He was a student at Glasgow High School and entered the army as a private direct from Silcoates School in Wakefield seconded to the Leeds Educational Department. The school was for the sons of Congregational Ministers and missionaries and Sydney was there as a boarder from 1912 to 1914. According to the school Roll of Honour he excelled at cricket, football and gymnastics. He became a prominent member of the Bradford Pals football team. On the 18th May 1915 he was commissioned into the 16th West Yorkshires but, due to his age, he was retained in England to assist with bombing instruction. A year later he went to the Front, 20th May 1916. After his death the Reverend Newlands funded an annual school gymnastics scholarship. Commemorated Silcoates School Roll, he also appears on the Leeds Education Department, Providence Place Chapel and St John's Church Memorials. Reverend R. W. Newlands (father) applied for his medals, Howaden Lodge, Rayleigh, Essex. Originally buried as Unknown British Officer, West Yorks in map reference 57d.k.29.c.7.8 and in 1926 identified by officer's khaki, trench boots, 3 Buckles size 8, West York collar badge and buttons, Webley '45 revolver No. 167582, photo, watch & cigarette holder. Found loose in the grave was one packet of letters addressed to 2nd/Lt Newlands, 16th West Yorks, wrapped in a piece of waterproof sheeting. Memorial Ref. VII. C. 6., Serre Road Cemetery No.2, France.

NEWTON, Lieutenant, William Trafford. Killed in action, 1st July 1916. B Coy. 1st/6th Bn., North Staffordshire Regiment. Aged 21. Youngest son of Henry Newton (cement manufacturer) and Agnes Helena, of The Cliff, Tutbury, Staffs. Born at Burton-on-Trent, January 1895. Played cricket for the Uppingham XI and three-quarter back for Burton Rugby Football Club. Attended Uppingham School. Engaged at Gresley Colliery where he was undergoing a course of mining instruction and articled to Mr. John Turner at the Moira Colliery. A month after the outbreak of war joined the King's Royal Rifles and transferred to the Rifle Brigade. Start of November, granted a commission with the North Staffs. Entered France, 12th April 1915. Major Leigh Newton DSO his elder brother served with a North Midland Howitzer Brigade. Family donated a magnificent altar to St. Mary's Priory Church, Tutbury. Father applied for his medals. Original burial map reference 57D/E. 28.a.5.0. and reburied in December 1919 his grave being marked was his means of identification. Memorial Ref. II. B. 11., Gommecourt Wood New Cemetery, Foncquevillers, France.

He Died The Noblest Death A Man May Die Fighting For God And Right

NICHOLLS, Lieutenant, John Watson. Killed in action, originally missing reported killed, 1st July 1916. At 7.25am the three leading companies of the 2nd Royal Fusiliers crossed the parapet from F Street to Bridge End. They immediately came under a heavy cross fire from machine-guns and though line after line left the parapet they failed to get as far as the enemy wire. 5th Bn. attd. (Adjutant.) 2nd Bn., Royal Fusiliers. Aged 25. Son of John Frederick and Annie Elizabeth Nicholls, of 31, Coleraine Road, Blackheath, London. Born 31st July 1890 at Hornsey, Islington. Attended Felsted School (January 1903 – July 1907). Bank clerk and worked in a bank in France, after learning in France in Rouen. Foreign correspondent at the Comptoir National D'Escompte de Paris, in Paris. Gazetted February, 1915. Served in Gallipoli and took part in the landings. Entered France, 22nd August 1915. On probation as second lieutenant, 21st January 1916. His father applied for his medals. Memorial Ref. Pier and Face 8 C 9 A and 16 A., Thiepval Memorial, France.

NICHOLSON, Lieutenant, Thomas Edward. He fell in an attack from the Tara-Usna line towards the German positions at La Boisselle, 1st July 1916 whilst in charge of the Machine Gun Section of his battalion. First reported missing believed killed and then killed, 12th July1916. 25th (Tyneside Irish) Bn., Northumberland Fusiliers. Born in Amble, 19th October 1890. Left handed cricketer for Berwick and Border district. Son of Chief Constable William, Nicholson, Berwick. Attended Berwick British School and proceeded to Grammar School (1905 -1908). Resided 34 Church Street, Berwick-on-Tweed. Chose the law as his profession and served his articles with Mr. William Weatherhead, Berwick. Admitted November 1913. Moved to Newcastle, Common Law department of Mr. Septimus Ward. Member of Berwick Debating Society. Joined 9th August 1914, as Private, No. 479, 16th Bn., Northumberland Fusiliers. Gazetted 2nd Lieutenant, 25th Bn., Northumberland Fusiliers. February 15th, 1915, promoted lieutenant September 1915. Brother of Legsby Avenue, Grimsby applied for his medals. Memorial Ref. Pier and Face 10 B 11 B and 12 B., Thiepval Memorial, France. WO 339/26884

NIELD, Lieutenant, Wilfred Herbert Everard. He had managed to cross some way over No Man's Land when he had been struck by a shot which completely severed his left wrist, but he refused to go back to the dressing station. Having had his handkerchief bound round the wound, he continued to advance, until another shot struck him in the leg and made further advance impossible. He was then carried and placed with other wounded men in a deep shell hole nearby. A few moments later a 5.9" shell burst in the hole and killed all its occupants. He fell whilst gallantly leading his company, 1st July 1916. On the left, A Coy., 11th Bn., Royal Fusiliers. Aged 25. Only son of the Right Honourable Sir Herbert Nield, K.C., M.P. (for Ealing 1906-18), and Mary Catherine, his wife, of Bishop's Mead, The Bishop's Avenue, East Finchley, London. Born 16th February 1891 in Tottenham Green, London. Educated at Winchester College 1904-10. B.A. Merton College, Oxford, 1910-13. Educated at Stanmore Park School, Middlesex, and Winchester College—where he was a House Prefect and a promising long-distance runner—before coming up to Merton in 1910. At Merton he commanded the college contingent of the Officers Training Corps. After leaving Oxford he went to Germany to learn the language and then to France to prepare for the entrance examination for the Diplomatic Service; he was there when war was declared. He obtained a commission in September 1914, and was made lieutenant in February the following year. Wounded in four places whilst serving in France from 29th December 1915, gunshot wound shoulder after 38 days in hospital he returned to the front in May 1916. Commemorated on the Westminster Hall War Memorial, London. Sir Herbert Nield applied for his medals. Original burial map reference 62C.A.7.b.3.7. Memorial Ref. III. O. 8., Dantzig Alley British Cemetery, Mametz, France.

Patriæ Quæsivit Gloriam, Videt Dei

NIVEN, Major, Allan Graham. Killed on the way across, 1st July 1916. 21st (Tyneside Scottish) Bn., Northumberland Fusiliers. Aged 38. Son of Comdr. Oswald Baylis Niven, R.N., and Rose G. Niven, of Torquay. Born 20th June 1878 at Chiddington, Buckinghamshire. Husband of Lucy Emma Niven (nee Bovet). Served in the South African Campaign with the East Lancashire Regiment, commissioned second lieutenant in the 3rd Bn., East Lancashire Regiment, 8th January 1900, and served with the regiment in South Africa. He was promoted lieutenant on 4th January 1901. Commissioned captain in the 2nd Tyneside Scottish on 18th November 1914, Niven served with his battalion in France from January 1916. Described as a 'Big, noble looking fellow'. Tea planter. Plantation Estate Manager, Boustead and Company, Malacca, Malaysia. Medals to his son, Master Michael Niven, c/o Mrs. Mary L. Bouel (grandmother), 33 Addison Gardens, W14. Pension also paid to his son, with guardian being Walter Moresby. Memorial Ref. Pier and Face 10 B 11 B and 12 B., Thiepval Memorial, France.

NIXON, Captain, William. Killed in action, 1st July 1916. 20th (Tyneside Scottish) Bn., Northumberland Fusiliers. Sergeant W. J. Waugh stated on the 1st July he passed over the captains body, at night he was asked by a German sergeant major is he knew Captain Nixon and told him he was dead, he also had some papers belonging to Captain Nixon. Reports from the Red Cross also verified killed on the 1st July 1916. Aged 32. Son of John and Jane Nixon. Naval architect by trade. Member of the Queen's University, Belfast, Training Corps. 1914. Born 29th March 1884. Attended Armstrong College. Entered France 1st December 1914. William was commissioned on 1st December 1914 as a captain in the Northumberland Fusiliers, 20th (Tyneside Scottish) Battalion. Resided 12 Harley Terrace, Gosforth, Newcastle-upon-Tyne. Next of kin, brother, J. R. Nixon, 32 Marlborough Road, Cardiff. Sir Walter Runciman Bart wrote to the Right Hon. Lloyd George MP on the families behalf. Although prior to this a special enquiry was instigated but no location of the officer could be traced. Executor of his will applied for his medals, J. R. Dixon, Esq., Marlbrough Road, Cardiff. Memorial Ref. Pier and Face 10 B 11 B and 12 B., Thiepval Memorial, France. WO 339/16901

NIXON, Lieutenant, William Gerald. As soon as the troops left the front line, heavy machine-gun fire was brought to bear on them from all directions, casualties if officers amounted to 100%. Beaumont Hamel, 1st July 1916. 3rd Bn., Hampshire Regiment attached 1st Trench Mortar Battery. Born 8th June, 1896 at Bengal, India. Only son of Mr. W. H. Nixon of Etawah, United Provinces, India and Mrs. Nixon of 9 Victoria Road, Kensington. Resided Coventry. Educated at Bedford Grammar School. Pupil at Daimler Ltd, Coventry. Enlisted August, 1914. Brother in law of Mr. Edward Manville of Coventry. After six months training he was given a commission as a second lieutenant and was at the Front since 13th July 1915. Aged 20. Address Keresley House nr Coventry and to Miss Henderson, Haddenham, Bucks. Memorial Ref. Pier and Face 7 C and 7 B., Thiepval Memorial, France.

NOBLE, Major, Thomas Gibson. Killed in action, 1st July 1916. 20th (Tyneside Scottish) Bn., Northumberland Fusiliers. Aged 28. Son of Mrs. Thomas Gibson Noble, of Brookside, Wath, Ripon, Yorks, and Thomas Gibson Noble; Born 28th February 1888. husband of Mary Ellen Noble, of 23, Albemarle Avenue, High West Jesmond, Newcastle-on-Tyne formerly 6 Kennleworth Road, Monkseaton. Commissioned 6th November 1914. Served three years with the Northumberland Hussars and three years with the Durham Light Infantry. Entered France, January 1916. Admitted in May 1916 to hospital with rubella. Widow applied for his medals. Son entitled to pension, Ian Conbrough Noble. Memorial Ref. Pier and Face 10 B 11 B and 12 B., Thiepval Memorial, France. WO 339/15015

NORBURY, Lieutenant, Philip Giesler. Killed near Fricourt, killed by a shell originally reported missing believed killed, 1st July 1916. 7th Bn., The Buffs (East Kent Regiment). Aged 21. Born at Bicester, Oxon. Son of Charles Giesler Norbury and Agnes Matilda Norbury, of Little Weirs, Sway Road, Brockenhurst, Hants. Memorial service held in September 1916 in Wadhurst attended by Captain Norbury whom was home suffering the effects of gas poisoning. Educated Eton College. Scholar Elect., Trinity College, Oxford. Gazetted temporary second lieutenant 15th September 1914. Entered France, 27th July 1915. Reported wounded November 1915. Original grave marker in the Royal Military Police Museum, Hampshire. Originally buried NW of Maricourt, NE of Bray Sur Somme, Sht 62c.Sq.A.9.a. Effects were identity disc, key, bible, pocket note book, wallet, letters, photos, franc note, advance book and cheque book. Father applied for his medals. Original burial map reference 62C.A.9.a.5.3. reburied June 1919. Memorial Ref. VII. V. 8., Dantzig Alley British Cemetery, Mametz, France. WO 339/13547

Dulce Et Decorum Est Pro Patria Mori Until The Day Break Beloved

OFFICERS OF THE 7TH BATTALION, THE BUFFS

From left to right are: Back row—2nd Lieut. A. H. White, Lieut. J. E. M. Sloan, R.A.M.C., Lieut. A. J. Hett, 2nd Lieut. A. D. H. Foster. Lieut. M. Hammond, Lieut. P. G. Norbury, Lieut. G. T. Neame, 2nd Lieut. W. L. McColl, 2nd Lieut. E. Nightingale, 2nd Lieut. I. Imbert-Terry; third row—2nd Lieut. E. V. Morse, Lieut. F. J. O. Montagu, A.D.C., Captain A. A. Mackintosh, A.D.C., Captain C. K Black, Lieut. L. Wood. Lieut. E. C. Dunstan, Lieut. E. B. C. Burnside, Lieut. G. J. Neame, 2nd Lieut. H. A. Dyson, Lieut. J. G. Whitfield, 2nd Lieut. W. H. Amos; second row—Captain A. G. Kenshington, Captain C. V. Allen, Lieut. and Adjutant F. Phillips, Brigadier-General J. H. V. Crowe, Major-General F. I. Maxse, C.V.O., C.B., D.S.O., Lieut.-Colonel W. F. Elmslie, General Right Hon. Sir A. H. Paget, G.C.B., K.C.V.O., Major C. L. Parmiter, Brigadier-General A. Martyn, Major R. L. P. Birch, Captain H. H. Hobbs, Captain G. Flemming, Captain R. T. Monier-Williams; front row—2nd Lieut. C. Morse, 2nd Lieut. F. M. Stoop, 2nd Lieut. H. L. Quartermaine, 2nd Lieut. J. G. Spencer, 2nd Lieut. G. M. Tait, 2nd Lieut. R. W. Keown.

NOYES, Second Lieutenant, Claude Robert Barton. First posted as wounded and missing as his servant had said he was wounded about an hour and half into the attack, his body was found (October 1917), 1st July 1916 assumed to have been killed on or about the date. No.1 Platoon Commander, A Coy., Killed after being hit in both knees and was killed crawling back to the Front line. 15th Bn., Lancashire Fusiliers. He was born Kingstown, Dublin 6th November 1888, the fourth son of Reverend Henry Edward Noyes. Attended St. Lawrence College, Ramsgate, Kent. Matriculated London University and took his BA at Trinity College, Dublin in 1913 with Honours in modern languages; French and German. He became a schoolmaster and taught at Rockport School, Craigavid and enlisted in Westminster 3rd September 1914. Private, Royal Fusiliers, 1914. Gazetted second lieutenant 4th January 1915. Served in France from 22nd November 1915. Brother, Captain Harry Francis Golding Noyes died in India on the 5th September 1916. Father applied for his medals. Original burial map reference 57d.R.31.c.2.7 marked as Unknown British Officer believed to be 2/Lt. Noyes. Memorial Ref. IV. G. 1., Lonsdale Cemetery, Authuille, France.

O'FLAHERTY, Captain, Douglas Hill. Struck by a shell and killed immediately, 1st July 1916. 15th Bn., Royal Irish Rifles. Aged 36. Son of Mr. and Mrs. Francis Hill Hale O'Flaherty, of Belfast. Husband of Beatrice O'Flaherty, of 31, Myrtlefield Park, Belfast later of Hampton Villa, Belmont Park, Strandtown, Belfast who he had married on 4th June 1912, at the Presbyterian Church of Ireland, Belmont. Born on 9th May 1880. Educated at Belfast Royal Academical Institution. He was a member of the Ulster Centre of the Motor Cycle Union and played cricket for the North of Ireland club. He was also a member of the UVF for 14 months, 6 as company commander. He was working as a head clerk, John Shaw Brown & Co. Ltd when he applied for a commission on 25th September 1914. He was promoted to captain on 1st February 1915. His widow applied for his medals. Memorial Ref. Pier and Face 15 A and 15 B., Thiepval Memorial, France.

O'LAND, Second Lieutenant, Valentine, MC. Fighting was hard and shelling heavy, machine-gun fire was intense, killed 1st July 1916. B Coy., 15th Bn. (formerly 14th Bn.), West Yorkshire Regiment (Prince of Wales's Own). Military Cross for conspicuous courage, 22nd May 1916, when attacked by a hostile raiding party, 2nd Lieutenant Oland jumped on the parapet rallied our wiring party who had been bombed and finally drove off the enemy who were superior in numbers. Not known in Leeds he had been gazetted to the battalion from a reserve regiment in France, he had not been with the Pals long when he gained the MC decorated by the Brigadier-General. Partly of French descent he spent the greater part of his life in Paris. Commissioned 6th August 1915. Memorial Ref. Pier and Face 2 A 2 C and 2 D., Thiepval Memorial, France.

O'NEILL, Lieutenant, Samuel. Reported as missing, 1st July 1916. General List attached Trench Mortar Battery, (Ulster Division). Native of Ballyshenan House, Borris, Co. Carlow. Employed grocery business in Londonderry. Member of Harmony Loyal Orange Lodge 858, and Temple Masonic Lodge, No. 138, Londonderry. Received his commission in the 12th Bn., Royal Inniskilling Fusiliers on the 19th April 1915. He was transferred to the Royal Irish Fusiliers and in March 1916 was transferred to a Trench Mortar Battery in conjunction with his brigade. His brother, T. O'Neill resided in Montreal. Commemorated Derry City War Memorial and registered on the memorial by his first cousin from Exeter. Memorial Ref. Pier and Face 4 C., Thiepval Memorial, France.

OAKLEY, Lieutenant, Reginald William Kennedy. Died 1st July 1916. 8th Bn., King's Own Yorkshire Light Infantry. Aged 23. Eldest son of William Henry (A journalist on editorial staff of Surrey Advertiser) and Emmeline Oakley, of Little Croft, London Road, Guildford, Surrey. Born 1st June 1893. Educated Royal Grammar School, Guildford where he was in the OTC. Journalist, Surrey Advertiser. Joined the 1/5th Queens', private, 2203 the day after war was declared and proceeded to India from 29th October 1914 with 5th Bn., Queens, Royal West Surrey Regiment to October 1915. Gazetted to 11th Reserve Bn., Kings Own Yorkshire Light Infantry, 1915. He made a special application to be sent to the Front. Reginald had been at the Front a month. Father applied for his medals. Memorial Ref. Pier and Face 11 C and 12 A., Thiepval Memorial, France WO 339/47653

OLDERSHAW, Second Lieutenant, John Joseph Fritz. They left the sap at 7.25am and were to crawl as far as possible when they got twenty five yards they were treated to a hail of machine-gun fire. 9 Platoon, C Coy., 1st July 1916. 9th Bn., King's Own Yorkshire Light Infantry. Aged 23. Son of John (farmer of Costock, Notts) and Mary Elizabeth Oldershaw, of Bunny, Nottingham. Born 3rd June 1893. Educated Loughborough Grammar School and Nottingham University College and graduated BSc. London University in 1915. Member of University College OTC and received his commission in November 1914, proceeding to France, 10th December 1915. Father applied for his medals. Memorial Ref. Pier and Face 11 C and 12 A., Thiepval Memorial, France. WO 339/2770

ORFORD, Second Lieutenant, William Kirkpatrick. Killed at Montauban on July 1st 1916, while serving with the 90th Brigade, Trench Mortar Battery. 1st July 1916. General List. Aged 21. Eldest son of Lewis Alfred (solicitor) and Frances Elizabeth Orford, of 5, Wilton Polygon, Crumpsall, Manchester. Born, Prestwich, 14th May 1895. Attended Winchester College, 1909 to 1913 from Mr. Buckland's School at Laleham, was a House prefect in his last year and was a successful bowler in Turner Cup. Member of OTC. He left to go to Clare College, Cambridge in 1913. At the outbreak of war he joined the Public Schools Battalion of the C Coy., 20th Bn., Royal Fusiliers enlisting on the 7th September 1914 and received his commission in the 17th Bn., Manchester Regiment in January 1915, C Coy., Platoon No. XII going to the front the following 14th November 1915. His great height of 6' 6" made him to conspicuous a target. Father applied for his medals. Memorial Ref. Pier and Face 4 C., Thiepval Memorial, France.   WO 339/22351

Platoon No. XII Also killed in the photograph on the 1st July 1916; Corporal Gilbert Wallwork, Private Charles Elliott, Lance Corporal Frank Andrew Jackson, Private Willoughby Mills and Private William Toole.

ORGAN, Lieutenant, Harold Percy. Signalling Officer, 1st July 1916. It was necessary to send back a message to the artillery to put out of action a machine-gun that was providing enfilading fire. He volunteered for this duty and whilst re-crossing No Man's Land he was shot in the head by a sniper and killed instantaneously. 10th Bn., York and Lancaster Regiment. Aged 22. Younger son of Thomas Arthur and Frances Helen Organ, of 23, Whitehall Park, Upper Holloway, London. Born 6th November 1894. Educated Owen's College, Islington (1905 to 1911). Entered day college at the Northampton Polytechnic Institute for Electrical Engineering. Assistant Scoutmaster 1st Muswell Hill (58th North London Troop). Member of the Institute of Electrical Engineering. Attested 2nd September 1914, No. 1882, 18th Bn., Royal Fusiliers. Commissioned 26th January 1915. Went to France 1st October 1915. Mother applied for his medals. Memorial Ref. Pier and Face 14 A and 14 B., Thiepval Memorial, France. WO 339/32551

ORMROD, Lieutenant, Harry. Hit and killed as he led his men forward, 1st July 1916. 8th Bn., King's Own Yorkshire Light Infantry. Aged 21. Youngest son of John and Alice Ann Ormrod, of 18, Alphonsus Street, Old Trafford, Born 16th December 1894 at Hulme, Manchester. Educated Bangor Street Elementary School, St. Margaret's Municipal Secondary School. Entered Manchester University in 1913 gaining a BA in 1916. Granted to him on 1st July in absentia. Training to be a teacher. Member of the University OTC and on graduation in January 1916 he enlisted and was commissioned in February 1916 as a second lieutenant in the 8th (Service) Battalion, Kings Own Yorkshire Light Infantry. Landed at Boulogne, August 1915. Commemorated on the private family gravestone in Stretford Cemetery and Stretford Borough Memorial Book. Memorial Ref. Pier and Face 11 C and 12 A., Thiepval Memorial, France. WO 339/53381

ORR, Second Lieutenant, James Kenneth. Killed in action near Beaumont Hamel, led his platoon forward, 1st July 1916. 14th Bn., attd 16th Bn., Middlesex Regiment. Aged 21. Born on May 26th, 1895, the eldest son of Dr. and Mrs. W. R. Orr, of Clydesdale, East Finchley, Middx. Educated at Queen's College, Taunton, and Highgate School. Member of University of London, OTC. Entered King's College in October 1914, where he began the study of engineering, trained until March, 1915, when he was granted a commission in the Middlesex Regiment at his own urgent request he was sent to the Front. His Colonel writes: "As you know he had only recently joined this battalion, but in this short period he had gained the respect and confidence of his men and was exceedingly popular with us all. He was one of the right sort and did his duty most nobly from start to finish." His brother, Second Lieutenant John Compton Orr, 2nd Bn. Attd 5th Bn., Royal Berkshire Regiment died on the 28th April 1917. Father applied for his medals. Memorial Ref. Pier and Face 12 D and 13 B., Thiepval Memorial, France.

OUTRAM, Second Lieutenant, Edmund. Missing believed killed, 1st July 1916. It was reported that he was seen badly wounded and later dead. Reported about 10 yards from the German trench he turned and said 'Up a bit on the left' and pitched forward, that being his last order. 26th Bn., Manchester Regiment fought with the 19th Bn. Aged 21. Only child of Edmund Outram, DSO (Capt., MM), and Agnes Young Outram, of 41, West Avenue, Filey, Yorks formerly 20 Norwich Road, Wavertree, Liverpool. Born Glasgow, 15th April 1895. Attended St. Oswald's College Lower Middle School, Glasgow High School and also at Ellesmere College in Shropshire. Commissioned 3rd April 1915. Certified from grenade school, 28th April 1916. Entered France, 29th May 1916. On the 20th March 1917 presumed killed as originally reported wounded. Father applied for his medals. Memorial Ref. Pier and Face 13 A and 14 C., Thiepval Memorial, France. WO 339/27528

PAGE, Second Lieutenant, Reginald. Fell while leading his platoon in a charge at Gommecourt Wood, 1st July 1916. 1st /6th Bn., South Staffordshire Regiment. Aged 23. Younger son of Mary Jane Page, of 3, Westland Road, Wolverhampton, and Charles Harry Page (iron trade). Wolverhampton Grammar School, 1902 to 1907. Born on February 14th 1893, emigrated to Canada, he enlisted on the day following the declaration of war, was appointed to the first Canadian contingent, and arrived in England in October 1914. After a year's work in the trenches he received a commission in the South Staffordshire Regiment, 23rd January 1916. Memorial Ref. Pier and Face 7 B., Thiepval Memorial, France.

PALK, Lieutenant-Colonel. The Hon. Lawrence Charles Walter, DSO. Commanding 1st Bn., Hampshire Regiment. Reported to have walked in front of his men, carrying only his stick and wearing white gloves, 1st July 1916. Last words reported to have been ' if you know of a better 'ole go to it'. As soon as the troops left the front line, heavy machine-gun fire was brought to bear on them from all directions, casualties if officers amounted to 100%. Killed at Beaumont Hamel. Shot early in the attack and although treated at an Advanced Dressing Station died of his wounds. Age 45. Born 28th September 1870. For his services in the retreat at Mons received the Legion of Honour and later the DSO. Son of Lawrence Hesketh Palk, 2nd Baron Haldon and Baroness Haldon (nee the Hon. Constance Mary Barrington). Polo player. He was in the Talbot 1884 – 1886, Wellington College. and enlisted in the cavalry, 8th Hussars 1890. 4th July 1894, gazetted to the Hampshire Regiment. Lieutenant 1897. Captain 1900. Major 1914. Served in the South Africa Campaign, Queens Medal with five clasps. Mentioned several times in despatches. Body recovered and buried with four battalion commanders of the 11th Infantry Brigade. Grave Ref. I. H. 4. Sucrerie Military Cemetery, Somme, France.

The Lord Gave And The Lord Hath Taken Away Blessed Be The Name Of The Lord

August 1914 Captain Hon L. C. Palk Third from left, second row

PARKER, Lieutenant, James. Previously reported missing and officially notified as killed in action, 1st July 1916. 3rd Bn., attd 26th (Tyneside Irish) Bn., Northumberland Fusiliers. Son of George Parker, of York. Husband of Ada Ethel Parker nee Clarke, of Castle Terrace, The Grove Cowes, Isle Of Wight. Resided Banks House, Haltwhistle. Attested 26th February 1891. Married 10th November 1901. Prior to war, drill instructor at Haltwhistle. Leaves a widow and four children. Served 25 years in the army enlisting in the Seaforth Highlanders. Served in the Boer War and India. Company Sergeant Major acting Regimental Sergeant Major, 6571, Northumberland Fusiliers. Commissioned 9th April 1915. Shot through the left arm suffering a compound fracture of the humerus at Loos on the 26th September 1915. Declared sound and fit for duty, February 1916. Widow applied for his medals. Memorial Ref. Pier and Face 10 B 11 B and 12 B., Thiepval Memorial, France. WO 339/26962

PARKER, Second Lieutenant, John Caird. Battalion advanced from assembly trenches at 8.00am and came under very heavy machine-gun fire, reported missing at the end of the day, and afterwards reported killed, 1st July 1916. 11th Bn., Border Regiment. Aged 20. Only son of John Caird Parker and Helen Parker, of 55, Cromartie Avenue, Newlands, Glasgow. Attended High School of Glasgow. On leaving school he entered Messrs. Weir's engineering department at Cathcart, and after some experience there took up civil engineering in Glasgow. He was for many years attached to the Boys' Brigade, in which he was serving as an officer when he obtained a commission in the Border Regiment in April, 1915. He had only been three weeks in France, and one day at the front. Mother applied for his medals. Original burial map reference 57D.X.1.b.3.6 and identified as a cross was on his grave, reburied May 1919. Memorial Ref. V. X. 4., Lonsdale Cemetery, Authuille, France.

PARKINSON, Second Lieutenant, James Herring. Killed in action in the taking of Fricourt Wood, officially 2nd July 1916, war diary implies 1st July. 8th Bn., Lincolnshire Regiment. Aged 31. Son of Ada Wellesley Parkinson, of Manscombe House, Morcombelake, Bridport, Dorset, and Walter Henshaw Parkinson formerly Headmaster House, City Schools, Brixton. Born 9th May 1885, Ilkley, Yorks. Attended St. Cyprians School, Eastbourne and Dulwich College (1899 – 1902). He went into Messrs. Donald Currie & Companies office for two years before being a superintendent of an tea plantation estate at Travancore, India. Served with the Ceylon Planter Rifle Corps. In October 1914 he enlisted in the 8th Bn., Rifle Brigade and transferred to the No. 7 Squadron, Royal Flying Corps, 2nd Class Air Mechanic, 3698 going to France, 2nd April 1915 and was with the 7th Squadron for about a year. Gazetted to Lincolns, 26th January 1916 and returned to France. Items returned to the family were letters, service pocket book, writing pad, note case, keys & chain and identity disc. Father applied for medals to go to Headmaster House. Memorial Ref. Pier and Face 1 C., Thiepval Memorial, France. WO 339/49970

PARR-DUDLEY, Second Lieutenant, John Huskisson. Between Bund Trench and Pommiers Trench, a space of some 500 yards, uncut wire was encountered by the battalion on the right of the Fusiliers, and the consequent check was seized upon by the Germans in Mametz to strike against the battalion's left flank. Second Lieutenant Parr-Dudley turned his platoon half-left and, with a vigorous charge, accounted for the small enemy party, but lost his life in the action, witnessed as being shot in the head, 1st July 1916. C Coy., 11th Bn., Royal Fusiliers. Aged 20. Eldest son of Dr. Arthur Dudley Parr-Dudley, of the Limes, East Malling, Kent. Electrical engineer. His brother Lieutenant Walter Parr-Dudley, Royal Fusiliers also fell in 1918. John was known as 'Husky'. Cricket; captain of the XI and football whilst at Cranbrook School, Kent. Joined the army start of 1915 and had been in France a year at the time of his death. Originally buried 1000 East of Mametz. Sht 62 Sq. F.6. Effects were revolver, cheque book, electric torch, whistle, fountain pen, unopened letter, metal flask, gelatin lamels, letter, certificate, scissors, compass, pocket knife and advance book. Father applied for his medals. Original burial map reference 62D.F.6.a. Writing to his parents the Company Commander stated; 'I had come to look upon him as my best subaltern, the one to trust to do any job I may give him. He was so keen and full of grit. He was the Mess President and far the cheeriest member of it – he used to look after us so well and took such a good part. I had real affection for him and knowing his worth and made him second-in-command in the advance. Quite early in the proceedings, he saw the battalion on our left was hung up. Our flank was in the air and seeing a party of some thirty Germans coming out to attack us he gallantly swung his men around on his own initiative and opened up fire on them, thus guarding our advance. Unfortunatley whilst he was organising his men in the best position to ward off this menace a machine gun came into action some 500 yards away, and the poor boy was shot in the head, but not before he got in touch with our people on the left, and ordered one of their Lewis guns, which shortly afterwards accounted for the whole party and thus secured the safety of our flank. Our attack was a tremendous success and we have the Germans on the run. But in this task that lies before me in the future advance I know I shall never be able to fill the place the loss of your son has left in my company." Memorial Ref. II. C. 4., Dantzig Alley British Cemetery, Mametz, France. WO 339/33190

I Found You Quietly Sleeping Far Out In The Tides Of Darkness

PATERSON, Lieutenant, Alan Foster. 1st July 1916. 14th., Middlesex Regiment attached to the 2nd Royal Fusiliers. Attended John Lyon School one of 59 fallen from the school. Younger son of Mr. and Mrs. J. Paterson of Harrow. Well known at the Presbyterian Church. Brother Jim died whilst of prisoner of war in Germany. Father notified authorities of change of address in 1921 from Lewes to Elsham. Memorial Ref. Pier and Face 12 D and 13 B., Thiepval Memorial, France.

PATERSON, Second Lieutenant, Frank. Killed whilst gallantly leading his platoon into the attack, 1st July 1916. 9th Bn. attd. 1st Bn., King's Own Scottish Borderers. Resided Zigzag Road, Liscard. Outbreak of war was a sergeant in the 10th Liverpool Scottish and received a commission. Secretary of the National Service League. Aged 29. Thirteen years been in the corporation service as a ledger clerk in the borough treasurer's office. Liscard High School boy, played football and cricket. Received his commission, May 1915. He was a member of St. Mary's Church, and acted for some time as the local secretary of the National Service League. Memorial Ref. Pier and Face 4 A and 4 D., Thiepval Memorial, France.

PATON, Second Lieutenant, Walter Storey. He fell in the storming of the Leipzig Redoubt, 1st July 1916. E Coy., 11th Bn., Border Regiment joined the battalion, 2nd June 1916. Aged 24. Son of John and Annie Paton, of Elder Bank, St. Boswells, Roxburghshire. Employed as a teller in the Jedburgh Branch of the British Linen Bank. He had enlisted in the Royal Scots in September 1914 and on receiving his commission he was transferred into the Border Regiment. Mother applied for his medals, also application from J. K. Ballantyne. Memorial Ref. II. F. 19., Lonsdale Cemetery, Authuille, France.

Asleep In Jesus

PATTERSON, Lieutenant, John Hylton. He was hit and found a position to encourage his men on when he was hit again, killed 1st July 1916. 23rd (Tyneside Scottish) Bn., Northumberland Fusiliers. Son of Mr. John K. Patterson, 15 William Street West, North Shields. Aged 22. Born 30th August 1894. Employed in the Labour Exchange at North Shields. Entered France, 9th January 1916. J. Patterson (brother) applied for medals. Memorial Ref. Pier and Face 10 B 11 B and 12 B., Thiepval Memorial, France. WO 339/19101

PAXTON, Second Lieutenant, Archibald Francis Campbell. Killed in No Man's Land in a gallant attack, 1st July 1916. B Coy., 4th Bn., Middlesex Regiment. Aged 19. Second son of Lucy C. Paxton, of Norfolk House, Havant, and Major Archibald Francis Pinkney Paxton Paxton (Indian Army) and his wife, Lucy Campbell. Born 25th August 1896, Edinburgh. From September 1904 until April 1907 Archie was educated at Warden House School, Upper Dea Anglican Preparatory School for boys. Entered Epsom College's Lower School Fayrer House in April 1907. He played in the college's cricket team. The new headmaster in March 1915, Reverend Barton, suggested that Archie should join the army and so Archie left Epsom College in April 1915. Joined the Middlesex Regiment, volunteering in May 1915 and immediately starting a shortened form of basic training. His time in the OTC at school had qualified him to 'Certificate A' which entitled him to enlist directly as an officer, straight to the RMC Sandhurst, joining B Company. When he passed out on 20th October, he was gazetted as a second lieutenant in the 6th Bn., Middlesex Regiment. Archie was posted to France, 29th May 1916 and went straight to the trenches on 7th June. His mother and sister worked at the military hospital at Langstone Towers, Havant and donated operating equipment to the Havant War Memorial Hospital in his memory. His mother applied for his medals. Original burial map reference 57d.27.c.7.6 and marked as an unknown officer found in Lieutenant Barnett's grave, reburied in Plot 10.E.9 in August 1919 and moved to IV.L.2 as a collective grave. Memorial Ref. IV. L.2, Gordon Dump Cemetery, Ovillers-La Boiselle, France.

And They That Are With Him Are Called And Chosen And Faithful

PAYNE, Lieutenant, Orsmond Guy. Missing from the British attack on the 1st July 1916 and it is feared his life must be despaired off. 2nd Bn., Royal Berkshire Regiment. Aged 21. Born 21st May 1895. Eldest son of Mr. and Mrs. E. Osmond Payne, of 1, Market Place, Wallingford, Berks. Grecian Scholar Christ's Hospital. From Christ's Hospital elected to a Stapleton exhibition of £50 for classics, open for this turn at Exeter College. Freshman of Exeter College, Oxford. Matriculated 1914. His father gave formal permission for him to accept a commission but added 'please note this permission does not extend to him enlisting as a private in any regiment whatsoever'. Entered Service: 7th December 1914 and later transferred to the 6th Bn., Royal West Surrey Regiment with whom he was killed at La Boisselle. To be temporary lieutenant March 1916. Entered France, 26th June 1916. His body was not found until the 28th July a letter to this effect having been received from the chaplain who performed the burial rites. Father applied for his medals. Buried Ovillers La Boisselle, 3 miles NE of Albert. Memorial Ref. Pier and Face 11 D., Thiepval Memorial, France. WO 339/2653

PEACH, Second Lieutenant, Ernest James. Reported missing, 1st July 1916. He went over with the fourth wave, with two guns and they got within 20 yards of the German front line and kept up fire until there was no-one left to operate the guns after coming under heavy fire. 7th Bn., Sherwood Foresters (Notts and Derby Regiment) attd. No. 3 Section, 139th Coy Machine Gun Corps (Infantry). Aged 28. Son of Samuel (managing director of Messrs. Wm. Gibson and Son Ltd) and Mary Ann Prudence Peach, of 24, Elm Avenue, Nottingham. Born 13th November 1888. Educated West Bridgford School and University College, Nottingham. He was hardware salesman. He was a cadet in the OTC and promoted second lieutenant on 17th September 1915. He served in France from 16th February 1916 and had been with a machine-gun company since January 1916. Parents received a telegram on the 6th July stating he was wounded. Miss M. Barker, Cambridge Road, South Farnborough applied for his medals. Memorial Ref. Pier and Face 10 C 10 D and 11 A., Thiepval Memorial, France.

PEACOCK, Lieutenant, John Luddington. Killed in action, 1st July 1916. 150th Field Coy., Royal Engineers. Aged 35. Youngest son of John Luddington Peacock and Mary Peacock, of Southery Manor, Downham Market, Norfolk. Enlisted in Belfast at the outbreak of war. Worked in Newtonards in 1910 to take a position as clerk of works and engineer for the Urban Council in sewage works, became the town surveyor in 1912. Remembered in Mayfield and Rotherfield district where he was the engineer for the drainage scheme. Received his commission, 20th January 1915 when the 3rd Field Company of Engineers in the Ulster Division was formed. Temporary lieutenant March 1915. Entered France, 6th October 1915. Commemorated stained glass, Church of England church, Little Ouse, Littleport. Stained glass in his memory in Southery, Norfolk. Miss C. Peacock, St. Anne's, Lynn, Norfolk applied for his medals and choose his inscription. Original burial map reference 57D.R.25.a.5.5 and his grave identified by a cross, reburied 1920. Memorial Ref. XI. L. 3., Connaught Cemetery, Thiepval, France.

Jesu Mercy

PEAK, Second Lieutenant, Norman. He was seen being carried on the back of Private Midwood between Bucket Trench and Fritz Trench and soon after both were witnessed being killed, 1st July 1916. B Coy., 14th Bn., Manchester Regiment. Aged 24. Son of Henry (Squadron Commander of the Southport National Motor Volunteers) and Annie Preston Peak, of 25, Shore Road, Ainsdale, Southport. Age 24. Educated King William's College, Isle of Man and Selwyn College, Cambridge. Employed John Peak and Company, Bridgewater Chemical Works, Wigan. Obtained a commission February, 1916. Was engaged in work on the south coast and as a result of a motorcycle accident changed battalion and was in France about six weeks since 29th May 1916 Originally buried Mametz-Montauban Road. Father applied for his medals. Original burial map reference 62d.F.6.c.1.8, found with Lieutenant Nanson and both reburied. Memorial Ref. II. F. 5., Dantzig Alley British Cemetery, Mametz, France. WO 339/35155

Thy Will Be Done

PEARCE, Captain, Charles Stanley. When the barrage lifted to the second Hun trench, a very heavy rifle and machine-gun fire started from our front and left, the latter coming apparently from the craters and the high ground immediately behind them. The distance which Pearce and C Company had to cross to the enemy front line was only 120 yards. Nevill was killed just before the German wire and Pearce died in No Man's Land, a few paces from the parapet, 1st July 1916, Montauban. Hand to hand fighting went on for a long time in the German trenches and news came that Captain Faltau and Pearce were killed. C Coy., 8th Bn., East Surrey Regiment. Aged 22. Born 14th April 1894 in Snaresbrook. Only son of James Stanley Pearce (chemical manufacturer) and Florence Maryan Pearce, of Priest's Mere, Tadworth, Surrey. Attended Winchester, 1907 to 1913 from Rottingdean School. At Winchester, he was Head of his House, a Commoner Prefect (three years in Sixth Book) and a member of school committee. He played in O.T.H. XV (standing on Dress for VI) and in both 2nd XI's. He went to Christ Church, Oxford in 1913 with the intention of reading for the Civil Service. On the outbreak of war he joined the Winchester OTC on Salisbury Plain and received a commission a month later in the 8th Bn., East Surrey Regiment, proceeding to the front in July 1915. Probate was granted to Charles' father of Priest's Mere, Tadworth, Surrey. He left £397-10-8. Effects were two pairs of glasses, pipes, compass, combined knife, fork & spoon, scissors, tobacco pouch, gold case for cigarette holder, advance book and knife. Father applied for his medals. Memorial Ref. E. 30., Carnoy Military Cemetery, France. WO 339/13227

PEARSE, Second Lieutenant, Frank Arthur. Missing believed killed 1st July officially 2nd July 1916. 1st Bn., Somerset Light Infantry. Aged 24. Son of Henry Charles and Clara Pearse, of 14, Eaton Place, Brighton. Born 23rd May 1892. Educated Parmiters School, Approach Road, Bethnal Green. . He joined the Accountant's Department of the Great Eastern Railway in October 1908. Formerly Honourable Artillery Company, private 1128. Enlisted in the Honourable Artillery Company in Sept 1914. Entered France 18th September 1914. Commissioned 11th July 1915. Father applied for his medals. Reported missing presumed killed at Mailly-Maillet. Memorial Ref. Pier and Face 2 A., Thiepval Memorial, France.

PEARSON, Second Lieutenant, Angus John Williams. Assault began at 8.00am and barbed wire was cut every forty yards the Germans had their machine-guns trained on these gaps and only a few men ever got through the wire, attached 1st Bn., Royal Dublin Fusiliers, 1st July 1916. 14th Bn., Royal Fusiliers. Aged 21. Son of Ernest William and Jessie Borland Pearson, of 66, Brook Green, Hammersmith, London. Born 11th June 1895.

Educated at St. Paul's School, he had been accepted for a place at Pembroke College, Oxford, but had not yet matriculated when he enlisted. Played cricket appearing at Lord's twice and picked for young amateurs of Middlesex. Promising young bowler. Pembroke Roll of Honour. Memorial Ref. II. A. 7., Auchonvillers Military Cemetery, France.

Justum Et Tenacem Propositi Virum

PELLY, Captain, William Francis Henry. 1st July 1916. 9th Bn., Royal Inniskilling Fusiliers. Born 9th April 1874, Co. Galway, Ireland. Age 42. Married to Rosa Theodora Pelly. Employed Banker. Military history twelve years Madras Volunteers as a commissioned officer. Attested 17th September 1914. Commissioned December 1914. Son of Reverend Chas H. Pelly, MA., a former rector of Killybegs, Donegal and a retired chaplain Madras Ecclesiastical Establishment and moved to Canada. Formerly sergeant, 16726, 9/Canadian Expeditionary Force. Brother of Mrs. J. Folliott Young of Dungiven. Widow applied for his medals, Portrush, Co. Antrim. Children entitled to pension, John Dennis Cavendish and Charles William Edmund Nigel Pelly. Memorial Ref. Pier and Face 4 D and 5 B., Thiepval Memorial, France.

PENNY, Captain, Arthur Hugh. At 7.28am, six leading platoons took up their position in No Man's Land, without loss. At 7.30am our front line pushed forward, they were met with very heavy artillery and machine-gun fire, some of A and B companies who did make the German front line at 7.35am were surrounded and captured by the Germans. Captain Penny killed in the German trench, Beaumont Hamel as he went off to find the rest of A Coy. 1st July 1916. A Coy., 1st Bn., East Lancashire Regiment. Son of Arthur and Charlotte Mary Penny, Bealings House, Heston, Middlesex. Born Tegpore, India, 1893. RMC Sandhurst. Commissioned 5th February 1913 and captain, 6th August 1915. Disembarked 6th November 1914. Suffered a fractured knee and in hospital from 26th September 1915 to 15th December 1915. Mother applied for his medals, Talbot Road, Highgate, N6. Memorial Ref. Pier and Face 6 C., Thiepval Memorial, France.

PEREGRINE, Lieutenant, John Pryor Puxon. He was with C Coy, 1st Bn. East Yorks in the assembly trenches between Fricourt and La Boisselle. Their first objective was the sunken Road between Fricourt and Contalmaison which they achieved. Killed in action, 1st July 1916. 1st Bn., East Yorkshire Regiment. Aged 21. Second son of the Reverend Canon David Willis Peregrine and Constance Mary Peregrine, of Branstonby-Belvoir, Grantham and formerly of Kelvedon Hatch. Born 11th February 1895 in Kelvedon Hatch, Essex. Educated at Mount Arlington House (Brighton), Hindhead, Haileybury School (Bartle Frere 1908-1913). Member of the OTC. Enlisted 15th September 1914, 3070, 21st Bn., Royal Fusiliers. RMC Sandhurst, 16th January 1915. Received his commission 29th May 1915 and went to the Front, 13th April 1916. Commemorated Sons and Daughters of the Anglican Church Clergy. Items returned were correspondence, cigarette case, drinking cup, compass, cheque book, badges, cigarette holder, and a case with two photos. Medals applied for by his father. Memorial Ref. Pier and Face 2 C., Thiepval Memorial, France. WO 339/54037

PERKIN, Second Lieutenant, Philip Kenneth. Twice wounded he continued to advance and when unable to continue was left. A private in his company reported that they advanced to the German barbed wire in front of their first line. "...was well out in front of his men and was using his revolver and shouting encouragement to them and at the same time trying to work his way through the wire when a hand bomb burst close to him. He reeled and half fell but most pluckily pulled himself together for another effort but another bomb burst which brought him down. He would have been not more than two or three yards from the German trenches and it is possible that he would have been taken in by them after nightfall." A further report suggests that he was sat on the edge of the German line calling his men on, until he was shot in the head by a machine gun. 1st July 1916. A Coy. 12th Bn., York and Lancaster Regiment. Born February 1894. Aged 22. One of three children, son of Mr. Emil Scales (headmaster of a technical science and art college) and Mrs. Isabell Lilian Perkin, of 97, Lonsdale Road, Oxford, formerly of the Wilderness, Tiverton, Devon. Education Blundell's School, from the age of 10 years 11 months as a "Day Boy"; January 1905 – Summer 1910 and some studying in France. At the outbreak of war he was shortly about to take an important post in the firm of Messrs. Huttons of Sheffield but offered his services to his country instead. Enlisted as a private, 12/213 with the Yorks and Lancaster Regiment and received his commission on 14th September 1915. Medals to his parents. Memorial Ref. Pier and Face 14 A and 14 B., Thiepval Memorial, France.

PERKINS, Second Lieutenant, George. Killed in action, 1st July 1916. 2nd Bn., West Yorkshire Regiment (Prince of Wales's Own). Aged 21. Born 8th May 1895. Son of George and Bertha Perkins, of 103, St. Mary's Mansions, Paddington, London. Formerly private, 1661, Honourable Artillery Company. Application for medals made 27th November 1920 from St. Mary's Mansion. Effects returned were letters, AB135, motor licence, cigarette case and flask. Memorial Ref. Pier and Face 2 A 2 C and 2 D., Thiepval Memorial, France. WO 339/2045

PERRY, Second Lieutenant, Charles William. 2.33pm C and D Coy's advanced over the parapet to attack but owing to heavy casualties from machine-gun fire it was found impossible to reach the enemy front line, 1st July 1916. Also reported shot by the same machine-gun were Corporal H. Lambert, Private Arthur Hill Caselton and Sergeant Varly. C Coy., 7th Bn., East Yorkshire Regiment. Aged 22. Son of Walter and Annie Elizabeth Perry, of 11, Hallam Street, West Bromwich, Staffs. Born 2nd January 1894. He is an old West Bromwich Technical School boy. BSc, Birmingham University. Connected with the OTC at Birmingham University where he was studying for the scholastic profession. He played for the Dartmouth Cricket Club last season and is a most promising batsman. Commission August 1915. Entered France, 18th April 1916. Father applied for his medals. Memorial Ref. B. 6., Fricourt New Military Cemetery, France. WO 339/35786

Greater Love Hath No Man Than This That He Lay Down His Life For His Friends

PEYTON, Second Lieutenant, Ernest N. He was leading his men to the German trenches when he was killed instantly, 1st July 1916. 4th Bn., Middlesex Regiment. Youngest son of Mr. and Mrs. Sidney Peyton of 108 Addison Road, Reading. Age 22. Native of Newbury, joined up when war broke out, 20th August 1914, Islington, London. For some time he was with Messrs. Heelas Ltd of Reading (outfitters) subsequently being employed at Barker's and Harrods' Stores, London. Member of the YMCA and the Caversham Road Presbyterian Church. He first of all joined the cavalry 3rd Hussars, private 14994 and afterwards obtained his commission in the cadets' school, 12th March 1916 with the Middlesex. Entered France, 18th October 1915. Last letter to his mother; 'By the time you get this letter you will know I have joined the great majority. If it is God's will that I will go, then I will have to, that's all. His will be done'. Buried angle of Empress Trench and new communication trench Sht 26. Sq D Contour 110. Mother applied for his medals. Original burial map reference 57d.27.c.7.6 and reburied August 1919 in Plot. 9.B.3 and later moved to IV.M.3. Memorial Ref. IV. M. 3., Gordon Dump Cemetery, Ovillers-La Boisselle, France. WO 339/58631

PIDDUCK, Second Lieutenant, Norman Andrews. Mentioned in Despatches. Killed leading his section, one of the first to fall from his company at about 9.00am, shot through the head, 1st July 1916. 102nd Coy., Machine Gun Corps (Infantry). Aged 20. Son of Mr. and Mrs. Frederick James (jewelry shop owner) and Ellen Pidduck, of Brooklyn, Sandbach Road, Alsager, Stoke-on-Trent. Born 5th August, 1895. Attended Newcastle High School and Mill Hill School, 1909 - 1913. Member of the OTC. Enlisted 28th August, 1914. Joined as a private at the outbreak of war, 5th Bn., North Staffordshire Regiment later he received a commission in the 9th Bn., North Staffs, 29th January 1916 and subsequently transferred to the Machine Gun Corps. Went to France in early 1916. Just before the attack he borrowed a watch from a fellow officer, Captain Norman Ingpen as his had stopped working. Lieutenant Rutherford wrote to the family; 'his sergeant told me that as he fell he turned towards him with a smile as much to say , 'carry on! I am quite alright'. He lay there on his back, looking upwards towards the heavens, his mouth partly open and a smile, calm, serene upon his countenance.' His father applied for his medals. In 1939 his mother's ashes were spread in an area where Norman was believed to have been killed. Memorial Ref. Pier and Face 5 C and 12 C., Thiepval Memorial, France.

PIERCE, Lieutenant Colonel, Robert Campbell. Reported killed, immediately the lines appeared on the parapet, heavy machine-gun fire brought to bear, 1st July 1916. The Forward Observation Officer, Second Lieutenant D. T. Davis, 26th Battery, 17th Brigade, Royal Field Artillery was alongside him and wounded. 1st Bn., Royal Inniskilling Fusiliers. Son of Reverend W. E. Pierce, British Guiana. Entered the Royal Inniskillings in November 1889 and took part in the operations of the Eastern Column in Burma in 1891-1892. He was also with the Peshawar Column and the 5th Brigade Tirah Expeditionary Force of the northwest frontier of India in 1897-8, obtaining the medal with clasp. To be captain, December 1897. Adjutant while the regiment was in Enniskillen in 1904-1906. Disembarked 4th September 1914. Suffered from diarrhea from the 7th October 1914 to the 22nd October 1914. He took over the 1st Bn., Royal Inniskilling Fusiliers towards the close of operations in Gallipoli. Brother in law, Captain Daniel G. H. Auchinleck killed in action, 1914. Wounded November 1914. His daughter, Doris Patricia Pierce applied for his medals and pension. Original burial map reference Q.Sq. 17.g and identified by his disc. Memorial Ref. VI. D. 18., Ancre British Cemetery, Beaumont-Hamel, France.

Lieutenant Colonel R. C. Pierce and 2nd Lieutenant A. Fortescue on board
SS Minneapolis

PILGRIM, Second Lieutenant, Henry Bastick. 1.30pm manning trench with twenty men by 4.15pm reported that he has seven men trying to hold on to 100 metres of trench. Message received 7.00pm that he has been killed by a shell. 1st July 1916. D Coy., 13th Kensington Bn., London Regiment. Aged 22. Son of Albert Ezra and Fanny Pilgrim, of Aston, Warwick. Educated Wilson's Grammar School, Wallington. One of the 120 old boys killed in the Great War. Artists Rifles. His mother wrote to the War office as only his silver apostle spoon was returned and no items of value his field glasses, cigarette case and revolver the stern reply pointed out as he was killed by shell fire these items were unlikely to have been recovered. Entered France, 31st May 1916. His mother applied for his medals, Norwood Road, SE24. His remains were exhumed on the 14th September 1920 and he was about 5ft 8" high and he had a silver spoon on his body and braces both marked H. B. Pilgrim. Khaki uniform and collar badges, 13th London Regiment also helped identification. Memorial Ref. IV. B. 14., Hebuterne Military Cemetery, France.

PINKERTON, Second Lieutenant, Eric Mikhell. Reported wounded and then killed, 1st July 1916. 15th Bn., Royal Scots. Son of E. M. Pinkerton, 83 Wentworth Road, Golders Green. Enlisted as a private, No. 495, 29th August 1914 with the 10th Bn., Royal Fusiliers in London. Listed employment as agent. Entered France 31st July 1915. Commissioned 18th March 1916 with Royal Berkshire Regiment. Golders Green Memorial. Returned to family officer's advance book and cheque book. Miss M. A. Pinkerton, (legate) applied for his medals, Golders Green. Memorial Ref. Pier and Face 6 D and 7 D., Thiepval Memorial, France. WO 339/58498

POGOSE, Second Lieutenant, Ivor Reginald. Took part in the diversionary attack on Gommecourt, died of his wounds the following day, 2nd July. Officially CWGC has the 1st July 1916. D Coy., 5th Bn., London Regiment (London Rifle Brigade). Aged 21. Son of Nicholas Pogose, of Flat 2, 2, Acre Lane, Brixton, London, and Margaret Pogose. Born on 28th May 1895 at 82 Montpelier Road, Brighton. Attended Arlington College, Chiswick from 1906 to 1911. Enlisted 5th September 1914 at Westminster. Occupation railway clerk. He was given a commission and as a 2nd lieutenant served with D company, 5th Bn., London Rifle Brigade, 56th (1st London) Division and was discharged from Kings Royal Rifles to join London Rifles on the 4th June 1915. At 11.00pm on 30th June, "Jerry" Pogose led a patrol out into No Man's Land to check the state of the German wire along the eastern edge of Gommecourt Park. He returned safely to report that the German wire had been cut enough to allow an attack on the German trenches. At noon, Captain De Cologan ordered D company to move left back down Eck towards Exe and by 1.30pm the British were in retreat, heading back across No Man's Land as best they could, but many were still trapped in the German trenches and at 4.30pm the London Rifles were still trying to extricate themselves from Eck. They withdrew, with difficulty, to Fen & Ferret where they continued to hold out until by 7.15pm they had to abandon Fen but continued to defend a short stretch of Ferret. They were down to about thirty men by 8.30pm and decided to retreat back to the British lines, reluctantly leaving the wounded behind. The officers were the last to retreat with most of them being killed as they headed out into No Man's Land and as the Germans over ran the position, Captain de Cologan, who had continued to hold the position whilst his men retreated, was captured. Late on the night of 1st July Captain Wallis of the London Rifle Brigade went out into No Man's Land in search of Ivor who had been reported as lying wounded out there. Wallis singlehandedly rescued Ivor and brought him back to the lines, but tragically Ivor died of his wounds the following day (2nd July) at the Main Dressing Station. A fact that his father, Nicholas, pointed out to the war office in a letter dated 5th December 1919. Medals applied for from Acre Lane, Brixton. Junior clerk, London & North Western Railway, Broad Street, Goods Dept. Slightly wounded at the Battle of Loos he recovered and returned to the front line where he met his death. Memorial Ref. I. C. 4., Couin British Cemetery, France.

Greater Love Hath No Man Than This

POLLOCK, Lieutenant, John. Missing since 1st July, 1916, later reported to have been killed in action on 1st July 1916. 13th Bn., Royal Irish Rifles. Aged 23. Younger son of John and Margaret Pollock, of The Priory, Marino, Co. Down. He was educated at Coleraine Academical Institution and the Royal School, Armagh, and was associated in business with his father in the firm of Lytle & Pollock, Ltd., Belfast. He was a member of the UVF, and on the formation of the Ulster Division he received a commission in the County Down Battalion. One of the best golfers in the province, he played for the Holywood Club also a promising cricketer playing for the North Ireland Cricket Club. Medal Index Card has theatre of war, France, entered 1st July 1916. Medals to Denure Street, Belfast. Memorial Ref. Pier and Face 15 A and 15 B., Thiepval Memorial, France.

PORTER, Second Lieutenant, William. Reported killed in action, immediately the lines appeared on the parapet, heavy machine-gun fire brought to bear, 1st July 1916. 6th Bn. attd. 1st Bn., Royal Inniskilling Fusiliers. Aged 31. Son of William and Mary Porter, of "Beechview," Balmoral Avenue, Belfast. Previously sergeant, Royal Munster Fusiliers. Commissioned 17th December 1914. Entered Gallipoli, 11th July 1915. His father applied for his medals. Mr. J. Porter choose his inscription. Original burial map reference 57d.R.31 and a cross marked his grave, reburied October 1919. Memorial Ref. V. E. 11., Ancre British Cemetery, Beaumont-Hamel, France.

I Am The Resurrection And The Life" St.John XI. 25

POTTER, Second Lieutenant, Francis John. Met his end serving with a French Mortar Battery, receiving a fatal head wound, 1st July 1916. General List attached 94th Light Mortar Trench Battery. Son of Charles Dalton and Annie Potter of Rhodes Villa, Barnsley. Enlisted as a private in the Royal Warwicks, 2668, was wounded and subsequently given a commission 11th August 1915, later in the York and Lancaster Regiment. Entered France, 22nd March 1915. Staff of Barclays Bank Ltd and United Counties Bank commemorated on Barclays Bank memorials and books of remembrance. Brother Private Edwin Dalton Potter, 15th Bn., Sherwood Foresters killed 17th July 1918. Last letter home dated 27th June 1916; 'My dearest Mother & Father, this is most difficult letter I have ever sat down to write. We are going into an attack tomorrow and I won't leave this to chance to be posted if I don't come back. It is a far bigger thing than I have ever been in before…Of death I havn't any fear…My Fondest love to all at home. Your loving son. Frank. Xxxxxx'. Mother of Doncaster Road, Barnsley applied for his medals. Memorial Ref. Pier and Face 4 C., Thiepval Memorial, France.

PREEDY, Captain, Alban. Killed in action, seen to be lying dead after 8.00am, 1st July 1916. 2nd Bn., Devonshire Regiment. Aged 23. Second son of the Reverend Canon Arthur Preedy and Beatrice J. Preedy, of Saltash, Cornwall. Born in Plymouth on 1st August 1892. Matriculated in 1911 after attending Allhallows School, Honiton and Plymouth College. A good middle and long distance runner and was chosen to represent the university at Cross Country. He was a valuable member of the Jesus College athletics team that met the Trinity College, Oxford athletics team that met in March 1913, winning by 8 events to 2. Preedy winning both the mile and the half mile race. He was awarded a BA in 1915 in virtue of his military service, special papers in mathematics and theology at Jesus College, Cambridge. Brother in law of the Reverend H. C. Dixon Spain, Chaplain with the forces in Egypt and Vicar of St. Nicholas, Lutton. Captain Preedy's sister died on 14th December at Lutton Vicarage.

First commission in October 1914. Suffered from a bout of influenza from 14th to the 22nd July 1915. April 1916 promoted to captain. Entered France, 18th August 1915. Father applied for his medals. Memorial Ref. Pier and Face 1 C., Thiepval Memorial, France. WO 339/28499

Possible that he appears on the 1911 Matriculation group photo

PRESCOTT, Second Lieutenant, Robert Stuart. Reported missing then killed, 1st July 1916. 10th Bn., East Lancashire Regiment attached to 1st Bn. Dunbar officer. Age 20. Third son of William Bowen Webb Prescott, Kevins Park House, Rathmines, Dublin and Mrs. Emily Joane Bowen Webb Prescott, Cairnbank, Dunbar. Two elder brothers fell in action before him. Educated at Warwick and Wellingborough, he was a member of the OTC and was gazetted in April 1915. Entered Egypt, December 1915. Medals to Merchiston Crescent, Edinburgh. Mother applied for pension. Memorial Ref. A. 78., Beaumont-Hamel British Cemetery, France.

PRICE, Second Lieutenant, Eric William Manning. As soon as the troops left the front line, heavy machine-gun fire was brought to bear on them from all directions, casualties if officers amounted to 100%. 1st July 1916. 1st Bn., Hampshire Regiment. Died of wounds received earlier in the day in the fighting near Beaumont Hamel. Aged 19. Son of Alfred Manning Price and Hannah Headley Price, of 144, Hill Lane, Southampton. Born 13th November 1896. Attended Highfield School, Liphook. Sherborne School (Abbey House) September 1911-December 1914 and RMC Sandhurst. Commissioned 14th July 1915. Entered France, 14th March 1916. Father applied for his medals. Memorial Ref. Plot 1. Row G. Grave 15., Bertrancourt Military Cemetery, France.

PRICE, Second Lieutenant, John Esmond. Killed in action, 1st July 1916. 14th Bn., Manchester Regiment. Aged 26. Son of Frank Corbyn Price, RBA., of Hillside, Mare Hill, Pulborough, Sussex. Born Islington, 15th February 1890. Clerk. Member of the Ardingley College OTC for three years. Enlisted at Westminster on the 3rd September 1914. Served with the Wiltshire Regiment, No. 11595. Gazetted November 1915. Entered Balkans, 30th June 1915. Pulborough War Memorial. Buried just south of Mametz, 1 Mile ESE of Fricourt, 4 miles ESE of Albert. Ref 62d. Sq. f. 11. C. Miss Jones wrote to the War office on the 20th April 1917 saying she had not heard of him since before the 1st July 1916. Medals applied for by his parents. Memorial Ref. Pier and Face 13 A and 14 C., Thiepval Memorial, France. WO 339/35452

PRICE, Second Lieutenant, Reginald. Serving as staff-captain in another brigade and asked to be allowed to lead his men, missing believed killed, 1st July 1916. 1st /6th Bn., Royal Warwickshire Regiment. Aged 37. Born 21st May 1878. Youngest son of Reverend Thomas Price and Anne Price, of Claverdon Vicarage, Warwickshire formerly of Selly Oak and brother of Canon Hugh Price and Stephen Price. Educated Warwick School and the Birmingham School of Art. Assistant master at Charterhouse for four years and prior to the outbreak of war was a master at Rossall School. Entered service as a private with the Royal Warwicks, private, 2459. Went to France on 22nd March 1915, before being commissioned on 24th September 1915. Commemorated Sons and Daughters of the Anglican Church Clergy. K. Francis Price application for medals due to his late brother. Memorial Ref. Pier and Face 9 A 9 B and 10 B., Thiepval Memorial, France.

PRIESTLEY, Second Lieutenant, Dyker Stanton. Wounded and last seen in the second line of German trenches with the 11th Bn., Royal Irish Rifles, missing 1st July 1916. 'A' Battery, 108th Coy., Machine Gun Corps (Infantry). Son of Mr. C. Priestley, The Crescent, Norwich Entered France, August 1915. Father applied for his medals. Memorial Ref. Pier and Face 5 C and 12 C., Thiepval Memorial, France.

PRING, Lieutenant, Basil Crompton. He fell in No Man's Land while leading his company towards the enemy. He went forward to almost certain death and by his example he inspired his men to do great things, 1st July 1916. 96th Coy., Machine Gun Corps (Infantry). One section of the 96th Brigade Machine Gun Company was allotted to the 15th Bn., Lancashire Regiment. Born September 16th 1888, in Leatherhead, Surrey. Age 27. Only son of Captain Frederick Arthur Pring of Streatham and Bexhill. He was educated at S.E. College, Kent, St. Lawrence, Ramsgate and Trinity College. Admitted as pensioner at Trinity, Cambridge, June 25th, 1906. When war broke out he was almoner and assistant secretary at the Dreadnought Seamen's Hospital, Greenwich. Enlisted in September in the 16th (Public Schools) Battalion, Middlesex Regiment as a private and in April 1915 was commissioned into the 12th Bn., Worcestershire Regiment. He was promoted to lieutenant in November 1915 and transferred to the Machine Gun Corps. Entered France, 11th March 1916. Father applied for his medals. Memorial Ref. Pier and Face 5 C and 12 C., Thiepval Memorial, France.

PRINGLE, Captain, Robert William Hay. Seen leading a column over Leeds Trench, various reports account for his death. He was dragged into a shell-hole by Private George Gransbury when a high explosive dropped right on top of them and he was blown to the opposite side of the shell hole, also killed here was Captain Donald Smith, and reported he was shot in the legs and killed by shrapnel. 1st July 1916. 16th Bn., West Yorkshire Regiment (Prince of Wales's Own). Aged 28. Son of David and Agnes Pringle, of 171a, Cromwell Road, South Kensington, London. Born on 5th April 1892. He was educated at Fettes College, Edinburgh, and went to Merton College, Oxford in 1912. A member of the OTC, he was mobilized in September 1914, and served with the battalion known as the 'Bradford Pals', in Egypt from 22nd December 1915, then in France from March 1916. His body was not found until 1936. Appointed 15th March 1915. Commemorated Fettes College, Edinburgh. His mother applied for his medals. Memorial Ref. I. A. 47., Euston Road Cemetery, Colincamps, France.

A Happy Warrior

PROCTER, Lieutenant, Arthur, MC. Killed at Beaumont Hamel, whilst still inside the British lines, 1st July 1916. Adjutant, HQ Staff, 1st /8th Bn., Royal Warwickshire Regiment. Aged 28. Second son of Mr. and Mrs. W. Procter, of 91, Trafalgar Road, Moseley, Birmingham. Educated King Edward's School, Camp Hill. Went to the Front, March 1915. Military Cross awarded for work on the night of 23rd March 1916; 'Conspicuous gallantry and good leading during a raid on enemy trenches, guided raiding party, cut the wire and ran along enemy's parapet bombing. Success due to his courage and skillful direction'. Rank of sergeant, 241 before war broke out. Commissioned March 1915. Entered France, 23rd March 1915. Brother, Frank served with the 1st Birmingham City Battalion. Twice wounded. Father applied for his medals. Memorial Ref. Pier and Face 9 A 9 B and 10 B., Thiepval Memorial, France.

PROCTOR, Captain, James Claude Beauchamp. Killed whilst gallantly leading his company on an advanced German trench in a charge of the Ulster Division, leading his company into action, 1st July 1916. 10th Bn., Royal Inniskilling Fusiliers. Aged 31. Eldest son of James Edwin (solicitor) and Frances J. Proctor, of Tullydoey, Moy, Co. Tyrone. Native of Limavady, Co. Londonderry born 21st June 1885. Educated at Reading School, Berkshire and Trinity College, Dublin (matriculated 1903). Took his MA and LLD degrees. Solicitor on the northwest circuit admitted 1907 and practiced with his father called to the Bar, 1913. Joined the South Irish Horse. On the outbreak of war, he volunteered and was gazetted captain of the 10th Service Battalion of the Royal Inniskilling Fusiliers on 21st September 1914 went to France, October 1915. Member of the Limavady Newsroom Club. Limavady Petty Sessions were adjourned as a mark of respect. Mother applied for his medals. Memorial Ref. IX. D. 9., Mill Road Cemetery, Thiepval, France.

PROWSE, Brigadier General, Charles Bertie, DSO. Reported that he left the headquarters and went forward to organise an attack, he was shot in the stomach and transferred from the trenches to the 12th Field Ambulance, Advanced Dressing Station subsequently transferred by ambulance dying at Maueux Corps Headquarters at the Casualty Clearing Station in the evening, 1st July 1916. Cdg., 11th Infantry Bde., General Staff. Aged 47. Born June 1869. Third son of Captain George James William Prowse, J.P., and Emmeline Lucy Prowse, of Bromham, Wilts. Born at West Monkton, Taunton, Somerset. Husband of Violet Stanley Prowse, of Bromham, Fleet, Hants. Resided the Minories, Colchester. Fought in South Africa. Left Colchester in August 1914 with the 1st Somerset Light Infantry. Went out to France, 22nd August 1914 with the 1st Bn., Somerset Light Infantry and later commanded it. The most senior officer to day on the first day of the Somme. Brother lost on HMS Queen Mary, 31st May 1916, Captain C. I. Prowse R.N. Charles has a cemetery named after him in France, Prowse Point. His widow applied for his medals. Two children claimed pension; Violet Muriel and Charles Anthony Stanley Prowse. Memorial Ref. Plot 1. Row E. Grave 9., Louvencourt Military Cemetery, France.

Be Thou Faithful Unto Death And I Will Give Thee A Crown Of Life

PURNELL, Captain, Arthur Channing. Killed whilst leading a special bombing company, 1st July 1916. 16th Bn., Middlesex Regiment. The bombing company were from 86 Brigade, they entered the Russian sap (tunnel) and were never seen again, this was about 6.30am. Aged 34. Son of John Alfred Purnell (upholstery) and Emily Blandford Purnell. Born Ryde, Isle of Wight on the 19th March 1881. Attended Portsmouth Grammar School, 1896. In May 1898 went to work for the National Provincial Bank of England as apprentice at its Birmingham Horsefair Branch, stayed on as a clerk and

in April 1904 moved to the London office. June 1914 appointed cashier at London Lincoln's Inn branch. Territorial soldier in the Honourable Artillery Company. Became a brigade bombing officer in August 1915. Entered France, 17th November 1915. Previously wounded. Well known skiff racer, winning the sculling championship at Teddington Beach three years in succession 1911 – 1913 and the Skiff Marathon in 1912 and 1913. One of his chief opponents Second Lieutenant A. G. Negus was also killed on the 1st July 1916. His brother, F. W. Purnell applied for his medals. Memorial Ref. Pier and Face 12 D and 13 B., Thiepval Memorial, France.

RABONE, Captain, Arthur Brian. Reported to have been one of the first to reach the German trenches killed 1st July 1916, his servant was also shot immediately afterwards. 6th Bn., Royal Warwickshire Regiment. Only son of Arthur J. and Maud Mary Rabone, of Elmwood, Handsworth, Birmingham. Husband of Jessie D. Rabone, daughter of Dr. Best. Aged 28. Educated Lickey School and Uppingham where he was a member of the OTC. Director of the firm, J. Rabone & Sons Ltd., Whitmore Street. Spoke fluent German and travelled extensively. Treasurer of the Handsworth New Church Guild. Joined the regiment as a lieutenant on the formation of the Territorials. Went to the front, March 1915. His wife remarried and on the 24th September 1919 and became Mrs. Godfrey, Oak Lodge, Surrey. She applied for his medals and officers pension. Memorial Ref. Pier and Face 9 A 9 B and 10 B., Thiepval Memorial, France.

RADCLIFFE, Second Lieutenant, George Kam. Reported missing, and then severely wounded and missing, 1st July 1916. Reported to have been killed on the 2nd July during a rescue attempt. 10th Platoon, C Coy., 14th Bn., Royal Irish Fusiliers. Incorrectly recorded by the CWGC should be Royal Irish Rifles. Educated Wilson's Grammar School, Wallington. One of the 120 old boys killed in the Great War. Played football for Surrey. His brother in law, Second Lieutenant Reginald Lambert Lack some him wounded and returned to try and to rescue him whilst being assisted by Second Lieutenant Matthew John Wright. Reginald was shot in the spine during the rescue and died of wounds on the 18th July 1916 at Dover. Second Lieutenant Wright was killed in the rescue attempt by a trench mortar bomb along with two other men. Reginald was married to Miss E. M. Radcliffe and buried at Thames Ditton Churchyard. Previously Royal Fusiliers, private, 802. Entered France, September 1915. Appeal made by George's mother; Mrs. Radcliffe, Milestones, Church Walk, Kingston-on-Thames, London. She also applied for his medals. Memorial Ref. Pier and Face 15 A., Thiepval Memorial, France.

RAIMES, Lieutenant, Leslie Robinson. Killed in action, 1st July 1916. 21st (Tyneside Scottish) Bn., Northumberland Fusiliers. Aged 22. Son of Christopher and Esther Raimes, of 21, Albury Road, Jesmond, Newcastle-on-Tyne. Trained in the office of Mr. J. Wilfred Pace, Chartered accountant, Emerson Chambers and received an appointment in the Treasury Department, Newcastle Co-Operation. Served for some time in the Northumberland Hussars Imperial Yeomanry, private, 705. Commissioned 7th December 1914. His father applied for his medals. Memorial Ref. Pier and Face 10 B 11 B and 12 B., Thiepval Memorial, France.

RAM, Second Lieutenant, Percival John. Killed in action, 1st July 1916. A Coy, commanded the group following the 22nd Manchesters and was killed after reaching Black Trench. 26th Bn., Manchester Regiment. Aged 19. Second son of the Reverend Canon Stephen Adye Scott Ram (St. Mary's, Lowgate, Hull) and Margaret King Ram, of 8, St. Peter's Grove, York. Born 13th July 1896. Attended Haynes College, Hull and Haileybury (Lawrence 1910-1915). Inns of Court OTC, lance corporal, 5609. Scholar of Pembroke College, Cambridge. Enlisted 15th August 1915. Entered France on 27th May 1916. Joined the battalion, 5th April 1916, previously 21st Bn. Originally buried ESE Fricourt and ESE of Albert sht 62d sq. F.11.c . Plaque in St. Mary's, Lowgate dedicated in October 1929 to Percival and his father. Commemorated Sons and Daughters of the Anglican Church Clergy. His father applied for his medals. Memorial Ref. Pier and Face 13 A and 14 C., Thiepval Memorial, France. WO 339/46275

RANSOME, Lieutenant, Cecil Talbot. Last seen by Second Lieutenant Laxton after crawling into a shell hole, served as a machine-gun officer, 1st July 1916. Adjutant, 16th Bn., West Yorkshire Regiment (Prince of Wales's Own). Aged 26. Son of William Fenn Ransome, of Norwich. Attended Thetford Grammar School. Employed Head Office, Norwich Union Life Assurance Society having started work for them as a junior clerk in 1909. A member of the Territorials he received his full commission in the Spring of 1915 and obtained his full lieutenancy. Entered Egypt, 19th December 1915. For some time he was acting adjutant of his battalion. Father applied for medals to be sent to Miss M. A. Ransome, Nurse's Home, St. Bartholomew Hospital, London.

A Mr. H. G. Ransome, Norwich choose his inscription. Memorial Ref. I. B. 8., Euston Road Cemetery, Colincamps, France.

Went The Day Well? He Died, And Never Knew But-Well Or Ill- England, He Died For You

RATCLIFFE, Lieutenant, Alfred Victor. Fell in action in the third line, German trenches at Fricourt near Albert whilst gallantly leading his company. Missing, believed, wounded, Fricourt, 1st July 1916. 10th Bn., West Yorkshire Regiment (Prince of Wales's Own). Aged 29. Third son of Frederick and Florence Brotherton Ratcliffe, of 15, Sloane Gardens, Chelsea, London. Born 1st February 1887 in Gravesend, Kent brought up in Harrogate, Yorkshire. Educated Dulwich College (1903 – 1907), London, Framlington College and Sidney Sussex College (1907), and took his BA in modern languages and law in 1914 at Cambridge. He was a student of the Inner Temple to be a barrister when he joined the army. War poet and had published a poetry book prior to the war. A friend of the war poet, Rupert Brooke. Engaged to Pauline Benson Clough, sister of the poet Dorothy Una Clough and was due to marry on his next leave. One of his war poems was 'Optimism', his last publication entitled "A Broken Friendship and other Poems." Commissioned 1914 and joined his battalion, March 1916. Nephew of Colonel E. A. Brotherton and brother of Mr. Charles F. Ratcliffe managing director of Messrs., Brotherton and Company (Ltd). His brother, B. L. Ratcliffe was wounded and taken prisoner in September, 1914. A fellow officer wrote to his mother: 'Your son's work was very highly thought of by his company officer and "Ratters", as we called him, was very popular with everyone. His senior officer having been killed early on, your son was commanding the company at the time of his death. From where he body was found he must have led it pluckily and well'. Entered France, 9th March 1916. His mother applied for his medals. Memorial Ref. C. 8., Fricourt New Military Cemetery, France. WO 339/1053

The World Was Sweeter For His Life And Life Lives .. Poorer By A Friend.A.V.R.

RATCLIFFE, Second Lieutenant, William Henry. Reported wounded in the shoulder about 600 yards beyond the German first line and reported missing, later it was confirmed his death was a result of a shell as he had been buried by Private Barton of his platoon, 1st July 1916. No. 9 Platoon, 4th Bn. attd. C Coy., 1st Bn., South Staffordshire Regiment. Aged 19. Son of Thomas Snodgrass Ratcliffe, of The Sheiling, Cyprus Road, Tavistock Drive, Mapperley Park, Nottingham. Born in Greenock, Renfrewshire on the 10th February 1897. Wife, Mary Arundel Ratcliffe. He was educated at High Pavement School. The family attended St. Andrew's Presbyterian Church, Nottingham. He was a member of University College OTC under Captain Trotman and received his commission in 1915. He was employed by the Boots Company. In 1911 William's father's occupation was described as accountant, wholesale chemists, possibly Boots Company. Family received notification wounded on July 6th. Reported buried where he fell in Dantzig Trench. Father appealed for news with articles appearing in the 'Daily Sketch' and 'Daily Express'. Father applied for his medals. Memorial Ref. Sp. Mem. 7., Dantzig Alley British Cemetery, Mametz, France. WO 339/47889

In My Father's House Are Many Mansions

RAWES, Lieutenant, Joscelyn Hugh Russell. In the very front wave of the assault, leading B Company out into No Man's Land. He left the trench at 7.28am and immediately came under machine-gun fire but made it all the way across No Man's Land at the head of his men. He fell as he arrived at the first line of German trenches, just before 8.00am, this was about 10 yards from the German front line when a bomb exploded next to him he doubled over and fell, 1st July 1916. 7th Bn., Bedfordshire Regiment. Born 4th August 1895, youngest son of the Reverend and Mrs. F. Russell Rawes, 140 Cherry Hinton Road, Cambridge. Educated at the grammar school in Bury St. Edmunds and Perso School, Cambridge, where he was captain of the Rugby Team, Head boy between 1913 and 1914 as well as being the colour sergeant in the OTC. He also won an exhibition at St. Catherine's College, Cambridge and had just left school when war was declared. Enlisted September 1914, at which time his father was the vicar of Sandy, Bedfordshire and lived at Hatley Street, George Rectory in Sandy. After training, he became a second lieutenant and went to France with the 7th battalion in July 1915. On the 5th June 1916; Assumed command of D Company pending the return of Captain T. E. Lloyd from leave. Lieutenant Rawes' runner, Private 13944 N. Faulkner wrote from hospital a few days later that he was just behind Lieutenant Rawes as they tried to get through the German barbed wire, around ten yards from the German front lines, when a bomb exploded next to him and the Lieutenant doubled up and fell to the ground. Lieutenant Rawes' body was recovered from the battlefield. Memorial Ref. F. 32., Carnoy Military Cemetery, France.

RAYNER, Second Lieutenant, Harold Leslie. Killed in action whilst in command of his company, reported to have been killed by machine-gun fire in a German sap in their front line trench, 1st July 1916. He was hit in the body and placed in a shell hole, he spoke several times to the man he was with and then fell asleep, this was about 8.00am and died soon afterwards. C Coy., 9th Bn., Devonshire Regiment. Second and younger son of Edward (director of Maples and Co) and Louisa Rayner, of The Haven, Blatchington Road, Tunbridge Wells. Born Hampstead, London 19th January 1890. Educated Heddon Court, Tonbridge Public School (Entrance Scholar), Kent 1904-1909 where he was a scholar, prefect, captain of boats and captain of school, in 1908. Won an open classical scholarship at Corpus Christi College, (1909-1913) Oxford where he was a sergeant in the OTC and President of the Corpus College Boat Club. Scholar; 1 Classics Moderations 1911; 2 Literae Humaniores 1913; BA 1913. College captain 1911-1913; Secretary, Boat Club 1910-1911, captain 1911-1913; Secretary, Pelican Essay Club 1911, President 1911. Read for Geography Diploma, Oxford 1913-1914. In September 1911 his father died, leaving an estate totalling £82,000. While his brother Edward trained to become a doctor, Harold travelled the world. He returned on the outbreak of war and joined the army. He was commissioned into the 9th Bn., Devonshire Regiment on 22nd December 1914. When war broke he was travelling and returned, gazetted 22nd

December 1914 and served in France from July 1915 and took part in the Battle of Loos. Buried in a trench at Mansel Copse, near Mametz with his men and many friends. On 9th July 1917, Harold's brother Edward, a Royal Navy surgeon, was killed at Scapa Flow aboard HMS Vanguard when the ship exploded. Memorial Ref. A. 5., Devonshire Cemetery, Mametz, France. WO 339/17743

REID, Second Lieutenant, Robert. 1st July 1916. 9th Bn. attd. 1st Bn., King's Own Scottish Borderers. Aged 26. Son of John and Elizabeth Reid, of 5, Ferguslie Buildings, 77, Maxwellton Road, Paisley. Born in Paisley, 1st February, 1890. Robert enrolled at the University of Glasgow in the Faculty of Arts in 1908, aged 18. During his first year, Robert studied Latin and Greek, both of which he passed in the May 1909 exams. He then went on to take a variety of subjects including logic and mathematics and graduated from the university on the 16th November 1912 with a degree in Social Economics and Political Philosophy, aged 22. Student of Divinity in the U. F. College when he enlisted shortly after the outbreak of war. Served first in the Dardanelles. A brother Private John Reid, Argyll and Sutherland Highlanders was killed 8th June 1915. Memorial Ref. F. 53., Knightsbridge Cemetery, Mesnil-Martinsart, France.

Faithful Unto Death

REID, Lieutenant, Robert. Shot by a sniper whilst wounded, 1st July 1916. 15th Bn., Royal Scots. The son of Mr. F. F. Reid, Edinburgh. Born 31st May 1880. Attended George Watson's College, 1888-97. After receiving business training in Leith, he entered the service of the Straits Trading Coy., in 1903, and held several important posts in the Federated Malay States and Siam. Home on furlough when war broke out, he enlisted in the Sportsman's Bn., Royal Fusiliers, 8th December 1914, was gazetted to the Royal Scots, 13th February 1915. Entered France, January 1916. Interested in soldiering and shooting, he had been a NCO in the 1st Merchants' Coy. of the Old' Queen's, Edinburgh Rifles, and in the Penang Volunteers and the Malay States Volunteer Rifles. Effects returned were advance book and cheque book. A stretcher bearer witness saw Lieutenant Reid lying on the ground about twenty yards away as if he was dead. Private C. Elmore his observer and another man went to go the fallen officer but both were shot as machine-gun fire was playing over Lieutenant Reid. A shell went over and buried all three of them. Private Rowley, climbed out of cover and tied him up but your son was killed as he lay wounded deliberately shot by a German sniper. He fell near La Boisselle and is buried there. Father applied for his medals. Memorial Ref. Pier and Face 6 D and 7 D., Thiepval Memorial, France. WO 339/22916

REID, Second Lieutenant, Robert Bruce. He was killed on July 1st 1916, while he was gallantly leading his men, near Beaumont Hamel, in the first attack despite the fact he had been wounded and very few of his men were left he went straight on and was seen to fall again near the German barbed wire. 1st Bn., Newfoundland Regiment. Aged 21. Eldest son of Sir William Duff Reid (President of the Reid Newfoundland Railway and Steamship Co., of St. Johns, Newfoundland) and Lady Reid, of "Bartra", Circular Road, St. John's. Grandson of Sir Robert Gillespie Reid, of Montreal. Trinity College, Cambridge. Born in Montreal. Attended Harrow. Enlisted as a private in August, 1914, in the 1st Newfoundland Regiment, and received his commission in 1915. He was sent to Gallipoli, 19th September 1915, where he served until the end of the campaign, taking part in the evacuation of Suvla Bay and Cape Helles, acting as machine-gun officer. Commissioned 16th August 1915. He was then sent to Egypt, and from there to France, in March, 1916. Memorial Ref. Beaumont-Hamel (Newfoundland) Memorial, France.

RETTIE, Second Lieutenant, William Philip. Reported wounded and missing, was hit in the thigh about ten yards in front of the firing line and was advised to drop back into the trench and get his wound dressed, replied that he would try to carry on and assumed he was hit fatally, 1st July 1916. 10th Bn., attd. 1st Bn., Border Regiment. Aged 24. Born 4th November 1892. Youngest son of Mr. William and Mrs. Annie Low Rettie, of Balcairn, Dundee. Attended Seafield House, Broughty Ferry and Fettes College and later entered the offices of Messrs. Pattullo & David as a law apprentice. Two of his brothers served one in the army (Captain James L. Rettie) and one in the navy, (Lieutenant Archibald Rettie). His father applied for his medals. Memorial Ref. Pier and Face 6 A and 7 C., Thiepval Memorial, France.

REW, Second Lieutenant, John Frederick George. Came under machine gun fire near Mansel Copse, 1st July 1916. 8th Bn., Devonshire Regiment. Aged 25. Elder son of Harry and Lina Rew, of Elmdale, Uxbridge Road, Hampton Hill, Middx. Born 26th November 1891. Attended Isleworth & Syon School. Warehouseman, tapestry in business with father. Enlisted 16th February 1909 with 1st Bn., Queens Westminster Rifles, lance corporal, No. 733. Gazetted 11th Bn., 14th August 1915. Remembered on the stained glass memorial window in Newton St Cyres Church. Hampton Hill Roll of Honour. Father applied for his medals. Memorial Ref. B. 3., Devonshire Cemetery, Mametz, France. WO 339/43923

RICE, Second Lieutenant, Fred. Died 1st July 1916. 8th Bn. attd. 2nd Bn., South Wales Borderers. Son of Mr. and Mrs. C. Rice of Wylde Green and before the war in the employ of Charles Wade and Co. Ltd, iron and steel manufacturers, Aston Road, Birmingham. Educated Green Lane Schools, Wylde Green was a member of the congregational church and of the Early Morning School. Aged 25 and married to Effie in May 1915. He enlisted at the outbreak of war in the Oxford and Bucks and progresses through the ranks, getting a commission in May 1915 in the Borderers. Served in Gallipoli from 30th August 1915 and sprained his tendons in his leg. Parents applied for his medals. Memorial Ref. Sp. Mem. A. 3., Y Ravine Cemetery, Beaumont-Hamel, France.

Their Glory Shall Not Be Blotted Out

RICHARDSON, Second Lieutenant, William Turner. He was one of the first to leave his trench on the opening day of the "big advance", but had only reached the parapet when he was shot through the head, 1st July 1916. 108th Machine Gun Corps formerly 12th Bn., Royal Irish Rifles. Aged 34. Youngest son of Thomas and Mary Richardson, of St. Doloughs, Raheny, Co. Dublin. Well known athlete, and for a number of years was a prominent member of the Old Wesley Rugby Football Club. Popular official of the Midland Great Western Railway, Broadstone. Early in March, 1915, he obtained his commission in the 12th Bn., Royal Irish Rifles, and having completed his training left for the front with his regiment some ten months ago, but was attached to the Infantry Brigade (Ulster Division) at the time of his death. Entered France, 26th January 1916. Brother, T. Richardson applied for his medals. Mother applied for officers pension. Memorial Ref. Pier and Face 15 A and 15 B., Thiepval Memorial, France.

RIDDELL, Second Lieutenant, William. Killed with the 16th Platoon, D Coy., 9th Bn., reported to have been shot in the head, 1st July 1916. At 7.40am Lieutenant Colonel Storey ordered to take D Company to the hollow at the foot of a copse, before reaching the hollow he was killed. 11th Bn., Devonshire Regiment. Aged 29. Husband of Hilda Elizabeth Riddell, of Maysville, Babbacombe, Torquay married 28th September 1915. Only son of Mr. and Mrs. Riddell, of The Lodge, Calverleigh, Tiverton, Devon. He held a responsible commercial position (drapery business) in Jamaica, but on the outbreak of war threw this up, and, returning to England, was given a commission, November 1914, in the Devonshire Regiment. He had been at the Front in Flanders and France since 5th October, 1915. Three weeks prior to his death home on leave. Originally buried Mansel Copse, 1 mile ESE of Fricourt, 4 miles ESE of Albert. His mother applied for his medals. Memorial Ref. A. 3., Devonshire Cemetery, Mametz, France. WO 339/933

Esto Fidelis Usque Ad Mortem Et Dabo Tibi Coronam Vitae R.I.P.

RIDPATH, Lieutenant, Geoffrey Lionel Chevalier. He was in front of his men, leading them in a very gallant manner at a very critical period of the action, 1st July 1916. Lewis gun officer, 4th Bn., Middlesex Regiment. Aged 19. Only son of Alexander Lionel (diamond merchant) and Anna Madeleine Ridpath, of 5, Pembroke Road, Kensington, London. Attended Harrow. RMC Sandhurst, 1914. On leaving Sandhurst Lieutenant Ridpath was gazetted to the Middlesex Regiment. He went to the Front in 21st June 1915. He had one very narrow escape, a bullet going through his hair and leaving a furrow of its track along his head on the 27th September 1915 but after a few days in hospital and short leave in England he went back to France. Second lieutenant 17th April 1915. Lieutenant, 18th December 1915. Originally buried angle of Empress Trench and new communications trench Sht 26d. Sq. 110. Original burial map reference 57d.27c.6.4 as unknown 4th Middlesex Regiment buried in Lieutenant Barnett's grave. His mother applied for his medals. Memorial Ref. IV. K., Gordon Dump Cemetery, Ovillers-La Boisselle, France. WO 339/45862

RILEY, Captain, Henry Davison. Command of the fourth wave, advanced at 7.29am, he was hit in the head when gallantly leading his men against the German trenches, led Burnley Company, 1st July 1916, Serre. 11th Bn., East Lancashire Regiment. Aged 34. Only son of Mr. and Mrs. W. J. Riley, of Hawks House, Brierfield, Burnley. Attended Shrewsbury School. Chance's (now Severn Hill); from 1895 left in 1898 to become a member of the family firm selling fancy clothes, Messrs. W & A. Riley, Houlker Street Mill, Colne. Also director of Messrs. R. J. Elliott & Co., cigar manufacturers of Huddersfield, and well known on the Manchester Exchange. After an association with the Ancoats' Lad's Club in 1905, founder of the Burnley Lads' Club and taking a great interest in the industrial school movement, he was appointed County Magistrate in 1912. In September 1914 volunteered for 'D' Burnley Company, seventy Lads' Club members enlisted with him. Gazetted to captain in 1915 and went to France, 8th March 1916. An extract from 'The Manchester Guardian', 10th July 1916 states, "Courageous and full of high spirits himself, he could sympathise…with the high spirited lads he had to deal with… Let a boy meet with an accident, suffer from some slight illness, he must be told at once, and usually it was by leader and friend that the boy was attended… War, and all that stands for war, was hateful to him, but he said to me, 'How can I let my lads go and not go myself?' And so he joined the battalion in which so many of his lads were serving, and soon came to be loved by all." Father applied for his medals. Memorial Ref. Pier and Face 6 C., Thiepval Memorial, France.

ROBERTON, Second Lieutenant, Charlie Drinnan. Hit before reaching our own front line, 1st July 1916. The Roman road running northwest from Beaumont Hamel was reached at 9.00am. "Up till then no casualties had been incurred. But a few minutes later the first serious barrage was met, and thereafter casualties became frequent." Signalling officer, attached to the 2nd Bn., 4th Bn., Lancashire Fusiliers. Aged 23. Eldest son of Mrs. J. R. Roberton, of 31, Elgin Terrace, Dowanhill, Glasgow, and Mr. C. G. Roberton, O.B.E., (submarine designer at the shipyard and an inventor) of Barrow In Furness. Educated Scot's Public School, Clifton Bank, St. Andrews. Shipyard apprentice in engineering with Vickers. Mentioned in an account of the 2nd Bn., Lancashire Fusiliers. The Barrow School's magazine noted: "The Somme Battle had just commenced when we heard that Charlie Roberton had fallen leading his men against the enemy." During sixth form studies at Barrow, he was the Fell Essay Prizeman and was captain of the cricket team. The Barrovian magazine noted: "High-minded and honourable, he was the type of our English manhood which in these days has so gloriously upheld British traditions." Entered France, 27th November 1915. His father applied for his medals. Memorial Ref. V. E. 10., Euston Road Cemetery, Colincamps, France.

ROBERTSON, Captain, (adjutant from April 1916) George. Killed in action, 1st July 1916. 21st (Tyneside Scottish) Bn., Northumberland Fusiliers. Aged 24. Son of George and Jane Robertson, of 7, Balmoral Terrace, Gateshead-on-Tyne. Born 28th April 1892, Gateshead. Clerk. Enlisted 6th September 1914. Miss A. Robertson, Balmoral Terrace applied for his medals. Memorial Ref. Pier and Face 10 B 11 B and 12 B., Thiepval Memorial, France. WO 339/14342

Last letter home was dated the 27th June 1916.
My Own Dearest Dad,
I go into the fight on Thursday with those words of yours just received strong in my heart. I believe what you say absolutely but I am anxious if I should fall you should know that I would so much like to lift that heaviness of heart which must be yours. Death for me has no terror. But the thought of separation brings the blinding tears. Dad, Mother, Annie and Dorothy, my world of affection. Dad dearest in the world, I shall if I fall, be nearer to you than ever before. I like those words of Ogden's ….not that I acclaim myself a hero – 'Better a dead hero than a living coward'. So I go into the trenches tonight for the adventure on Thursday. God is very near. May he sustain and keep my own loved ones.
George.

ROBERTSON, Captain, Maxwell Alexander. Reported wounded and missing and later killed on that date, 1st July 1916. B Coy. 10th Bn., Royal Inniskilling Fusiliers. Aged 42. Husband of Ethel Louise Robertson, of Wickham, Hants. A barrister-at-law. Member of the Inner Temple. Enlisted 1914. Born in October 1874, attended Loretto School (1889 to 1894). On going up to Oxford (Trinity College, 1894) he got his Rugby Blue his first term, and played for two years in the Varsity XV. He took his degree with Honours in 1897, and was called to the Bar in 1899. Obtained his captaincy in 1915. Son of Mr. Robert A. Robertson, Glasgow and Mrs. Robertson, Limavady. Entered France, October 1915. His widow applied for his medals and officers pension. Memorial Ref. Pier and Face 4 D and 5 B., Thiepval Memorial, France.

ROBERTSON, Second Lieutenant, Walter Raymond. Killed in action, 1st July 1916. 2nd Bn., Border Regiment. Son of Joseph Robertson, of Abbey Road, Llangollen, Denbighshire. Popular local athlete. On the death of his mother went to live in Godalming with his aunt, Miss Robertson of Langham. Attended Godalming Grammar School, played football for Godalming and Farncombe football clubs. When war broke out he was rubber planting in Straits Settlements and coming home from Singapore was given a commission in the Border Regiment. Enlisted 12th July 1915 and served in the Inns of Court OTC, private, 5082. He visited Godalming on leave on Whit-Sunday and went to the Front a day or two later. Joined the battalion on the 17th June 1916. Brother Rifleman D. A. Robertson, Queen's Westminster Rifles died of wounds in France, 1917 and Private Herbert Robertson was wounded with the RAMC. Father applied for his medals. Memorial Ref. II. D. 9., Citadel New Military Cemetery, Fricourt, France. WO 339/51407

ROBINSON, Lieutenant, Benjamin Stanley. Killed gallantly leading his men in the assault, reported to have been hit by machine gun fire, about 300 yards into No Man's Land, he led the company with a private's equipment and bayonet fixed saying "I'll make up for one of the boys." 1st July 1916. C Coy, IX Platoon, 2nd Bn., Royal Berkshire Regiment. Aged 21. Born 8th June 1895. Younger son of Harry and Annie Robinson, of Avenue Terrace, Spilsby, Lincs. Attended Oakham School, 1906-1909, Sherborne School (Harper House) January 1910-July 1913. Student. Enlisted 15th September 1914 and attended RMC Sandhurst. Second lieutenant in Princess Charlotte of Wales's (Royal Berkshire Regiment), 2nd Bn. Passed out of Sandhurst in May 1915. Promoted lieutenant in November 1915. Entered France, 7th December 1915. Presumed dead, 22nd March 1917. Original burial map reference 57d.X.7.b and noted as Private B. S. Robinson. Father applied for his medals. Memorial Ref. VIII. D. 3., Ovillers Military Cemetery, France. WO 339/52019

ROBINSON, Lieutenant, Eli. Lieutenant Colonel W. Burnett and 2nd Lieutenants Read and Robinson went forward to the advance trench, tried to reorganise and push on. Lieutenant Robinson's party moved forward but he and most of his men were killed. 1st July 1916. A Company, 1st /5th Bn., North Staffordshire Regiment. Lieutenant Colonel W. Burnett died of wounds on the 3rd July. Son of Mrs. Robinson, Freehold Street, Basford. Educated National and Middle School, Newcastle-under-Lyme. Joined as a private, 3169 in September 1914 and promoted to second lieutenant, 16th April 1915 and lieutenant in May 1916. Entered France, 28th October 1915. Teacher at Rycroft School and a choirmaster at St. Paul's Church. Mother applied for his medals. Memorial Ref. Pier and Face 14 B and 14 C., Thiepval Memorial, France.

ROBINSON, Lieutenant, Harold Fletcher. Killed leading his men forward, 1st July 1916. Led platoons of D Coy in support of C Coy., and took command of the remnants of C Coy when he came up, encouraging the men with 'Come on, boys!' 15th Bn., Lancashire Fusiliers. Aged 24. Younger son of Thomas Fletcher Robinson (silk waste silk merchant) and Emma Robinson, of 117, Claremont Road, Pendleton, Salford. Born 16th April 1892, Moston. Educated at Manchester Grammar School. He left the school to go to the University of Manchester, where he joined up with the OTC and got his full commission in October 1914. He became a full lieutenant in September 1915. Entered France, 22nd November 1915. A Sunday school teacher at the Unitarian Sunday School, Cross Lane, he served on the governing body of the District Association of Unitarian Churches. He was a member of Swinton Park Hockey Club, Barrfield Tennis Club and

West Salford young Liberals, and worked in the Portland Street offices of Ashton Brothers & Co., cotton manufacturers. Eight months in France.

Sergeant Lawless wrote " Lieutenant Robinson was always anxious for the welfare of his men, whose confidence he gained, and was one of the bravest officers. For instance one night, in the same sector from which we went into action, we had a patrol out and the Germans turned their machine-guns on them and wounded three of our patrol. As soon as Lieutenant Robinson heard of it he dashed over the top and brought in two of the wounded, his orderly Private Watson bringing the third man." His father applied for his medals. Original burial map reference 57d.R.25.b.2.6. Memorial Ref. III. E. 7., Connaught Cemetery, Thiepval, France.

Peace Perfect Peace The Fruit Of Victory Nobly Won

ROBINSON, Second Lieutenant, John. Reported missing, killed in action, 1st July 1916. 3rd Bn. attd. 2nd Bn., South Wales Borderers. Aged 29. Son of Richard Syer Robinson and Alice Louise Robinson, of 8, Vicarage Terrace, Kendal, Westmorland. Born at Barry, Glam. Joined the battalion, 8th June 1916. Father applied for his medals. Memorial Ref. B. 74., Hawthorn Ridge Cemetery No.2, Auchonvillers, France.

ROBINSON, Second Lieutenant, John Holdsworth. Reported missing, took command off Captain Alan Clough's company when he was killed and he himself was killed shortly afterwards, 1st July 1916. 16th Bn., West Yorkshire Regiment (Prince of Wales's Own). Son of Mr. John Holdsworth Robinson, the president of the Bradford Chamber of Commerce. Educated Woodhouse Grove School, Bradford. Gazetted Temporary second lieutenant, 21st October 1914. Resided Bisley. Commissioned 26th October 1914. Formerly private 3092, Dragoons. Will notes that he left £277 (effects) to John Holdsworth Robinson (his father). Medals applied for by his father, Bingley, Notts. Memorial Ref. Pier and Face 2 A 2 C and 2 D., Thiepval Memorial, France.

ROBINSON, Second Lieutenant, Percival Bewman Palmer. Reported wounded and then as missing, 1st July 1916. 8th Bn., King's Own Yorkshire Light Infantry. Son of George Robinson. Attended Newland Avenue School and was an Old Hymerian (Hymers College, Hull), before the war was on the commercial staff of Messrs. Reckitt where he worked since 1910. His home was 135 Newland Avenue, Hull being born there on the 18th June 1894. Joined the Yorkshire Light Infantry, lance corporal, 3415 and transferred to the Kings Own Yorkshire Light Infantry and worked his way through the ranks being given a temporary second lieutenant, 1st October 1915 and took up a position with the 11th Battalion in November 1915. Entered France, 3rd August 1915. He qualified as a Brigade Signalling Instructor and on the 16th June 1916 went to France and joined the 8th Bn. In March 1917 he father wrote to the War Office, stating that his if his son was wounded in the spine, it may have caused a lapse of memory and that if his tunic was cut away for the purpose of dressing his wounds, there would be nothing to identify him by. In April 1917 the War Office replied in deference to your wishes no further action will be taken at present in connection with official acceptance of death. Enquiries by the American Embassy had been without result. On the 7th March 1919 the War Office wrote that they were constrained to conclude that Second Lieutenant Robinson was dead. Medals to his address his address in Hull. Memorial Ref. Pier and Face 11 C and 12 A., Thiepval Memorial, France. WO 339/43360

RODGER, Lieutenant, Douglas, MB, FRCSE. Died of wounds, working in an advanced dressing station, 1st July 1916. 90th Field Ambulance, Royal Army Medical Corps. Age 32. Born 3rd September 1883 in Cheetham Hill, Manchester. Youngest son of Dr. and Mrs. Rodger, West Kirby. Educated at Trent College at Edinburgh and at Owen's College, Manchester former student of medicine, Manchester University entered in 1902 and graduated in 1907 taking up the post of Assistant Medical Officer at Barnes Convalescent Hospital, Cheadle. Fellowship of the Royal College of Surgeon in 1912. After acting as House Surgeon of the Royal Eye Hospital, Manchester he went to Australia as whole time ophthalmic inspector of schools in Queensland. In July 1915 wrote a technical article on eye infections in Western Australia. Took a temporary commission in September 1915. Memorial Ref. V. C. 3., Warloy-Baillon Communal Cemetery Extension, France.

ROGERS, Lieutenant, George Murray. No. 10 & 12 platoons went in support of A Coy & No. 9 Platoon was following as a carrying platoon. No. 12 Platoon crossed the first line and almost reached the wire of the second line trench, when they were held up by a strong point on their left, which appeared to be a bomb store & also a machine-gun post. Just about this time Lieutenant Rogers was mortally wounded after having given the order for bombers to go to the left flank, 1st July 1916. 13th Bn., Royal Irish Rifles (1st County Down Volunteers),. Aged 24. Only son of George M. (prominent figure in the flax trade) and Nellie Rogers, of Dalkeith, Hawthornden Road, Knock, Belfast. Native of Banbridge, Co. Down. Lieutenant Rogers, who had been prominently identified with the Down Volunteers, was in Courtrai in charge of his father's business when the war broke out, but succeeded in getting away before the German invasion. On returning he joined the Ulster Division, and received his commission as second lieutenant on the 12th November, 1914. Entered France, 31st October 1915. His mother applied for his medals. Memorial Ref. II. D. 5., Mill Road Cemetery, Thiepval, France.

ROOPE, Second Lieutenant, Charles Francis. Killed in action, 1st July 1916. 16th Bn., attd 2nd Bn., Royal Fusiliers. Aged 32. Only son of Charles and Millicent Matilda Roope, of Briar Knoll, Lake, Sandown, Isle Of Wight. Born 24th December 1883 at Bognor, Sussex. He was educated at St. Augustine's, Ramsgate, and received his commission in August 1915. Entered France 26th March 1916. His mother applied for his medals. Memorial Ref. B. 57., Hawthorn Ridge Cemetery No.2, Auchonvillers, France.

R.I.P.

ROOS, Captain, Gustaf Oscar. He was posted as missing having seen to enter a German trench by Serre village, 1st July 1916 long afterwards it was discovered he died of wounds in a German hospital. 14th Bn., York and Lancaster Regiment. A Coy., under Captain Roos with Second Lieutenants Hirst, Anderson and Kell in file in front end of Nairne Trench and along Traffic Trench from Nairne to John Copse. To proceed in file across No Man's Land immediately following assaulting waves. Many casualties were also caused by machine-gun and rifle fire to which A and B companies were

much exposed owing to levelling of Nairne Trench etc. Aged 47. Born London, 21st August 1868. Younger son of Gustaf and Annie Roos, of 7, Queen's Gate Terrace, London. Educated Westminster School and Balliol College, Oxford. He was admitted in 1882, became a Queen's Scholar in 1883. In 1887 left the school and was admitted to Balliol College Oxford where he took a first-class in jurisprudence in 1891. As a law student in London he took a very active part in organising and managing working boys' clubs in the East End which were managed as a charitable endeavour. He became a solicitor and often worked as a 'Poor Man's Solicitor' at Toynbee Hall. In the Boer War joined Thorneycroft's Mounted Infantry. He was twice wounded, severely at the Battle of Spion Kop in 1900, and obtained the King's Medal and the Queen's Medal with six clasps. He then remained in Johannesburg practicing once again as a solicitor. He was initially buried in the Fremicourt Communal Cemetery by the German forces in 1916.

The Elizabethan records that: 'He came to England for the war, and though at first refused a commission on the ground of his age obtained it by his importunity. He had boundless energy and great capacity, and was the most unselfish of men. He lived, as he died, for the good of others.' His body exhumed on 26th June 1924 for reburial in a Commonwealth War Graves Cemetery identified by khaki shirt, officer's underclothing, certified report and plan. Father applied for his medals. Memorial Ref. III. D. 10., Douchy-Les-Ayette British Cemetery, France.

M.A., B. C. L. Of Balliol College, Oxford
The Dearly Loved Son Of Gustaf And Annie Roos

ROSE, Second Lieutenant, Reginald Vincent. Reported killed, Beaumont Hamel, 1st July 1916. B Coy. 1st/6th Bn., Royal Warwickshire Regiment. Aged 19. Son of Ethelbert Rose and Louise Rose, of 58, Gillott Road, Edgbaston, Birmingham,. Born 19th April 1897. Educated Five Ways Grammar School and King Edwards High School, New Street, Birmingham. Entered service of Lloyds Bank at Colmore Row branch. Enlisted outbreak of war, corporal, 2665, entered France, 22nd March 1915 and obtained commission, 6th May 1916. Home on leave, June 1916. His father applied for his medals. Memorial Ref. Pier and Face 9 A 9 B and 10 B., Thiepval Memorial, France.

ROSE-CLELAND, Lieutenant, Alfred Middleton Blackwood. Assault began at 8.00am and barbed wire was cut every forty yards the Germans had their machine-guns trained on these gaps and only a few men ever got through the wire, 1st July 1916. 3rd Bn., attd 1st Bn., Royal Dublin Fusiliers. Aged 21. Only child of Henry Somerville Rose Cleland (linen manufacturer) and Elizabeth A. Rose-Cleland, of Redford House, Moy, Co. Tyrone, Ireland. Born about 1895 in County Tyrone. Alfred was educated at Dungannon Royal School and Columba's College, Dublin. Employed building firm of McLaughlin and Harvey on a contract in Essex when the war started. Alfred returned home to enlist in the 9th Royal Inniskilling Fusiliers, private. Lance corporal when gazetted as second lieutenant, 10th February 1915. Father applied for his medals. Memorial Ref. II. B. 3., Auchonvillers Military Cemetery, France.

Called And Chosen And Faithful REV.XVII. 14

ROSS, Lieutenant, Douglas Stuart. Reported as missing, 1st July 1916. Eye witnesses report him killed at the beginning of the attack. 2nd Bn., Lincolnshire Regiment. Aged 20. Son of Alexander and Annie Ross, of 36, Fellows Road, Hampstead, London. Born 13th August 1895. Attended Rossall School and later served in the Royal Naval Division, LZ970. Posted as missing 22nd July 1916. Joined the Lincolns on the 1st January 1915. Entered France, 1st June 1915. Confirmed in rank, 3rd Battalion on 22nd July 1915. Wounded at Gallipoli. On the 19th September 1916 his mother wrote to the War Office saying she had made every enquiry possible, the reply pointed out letters had gone to the American Embassy. On the 28th October 1917 the War Office reported they had found his body at Ovillers La Boisselle but they could not tell her how he had been identified. Parents applied for his medals. Original burial map reference 57d.X.7.b. Memorial Ref. VIII. O. 2., Ovillers Military Cemetery, France. WO 339/31154

ROSS, Lieutenant, Frederic Gordon. Killed near Fricourt in the Great Push, 1st July 1916. 20th Bn., Manchester Regiment. Aged 46. Son of F. B. Ross, of Alderley Edge, Cheshire; Born 1870. Husband of Kathleen Ross, of Colwood Hill, Cuckfield, Haywards Heath, Sussex formerly Oakleigh, Alderley Edge. Employed Stalybridge Mill Director. Had three children, Sheila, David and Olive. Married 29th April 1897. Educated Clifton College. Enlisted as a private in January 1915 in the Public Schools Battalion, Royal Fusilier and in May, 1915 given a commission in the Manchester Regiment, promoted lieutenant 8th June 1916. Entered France, 9th November 1915. Originally buried Sheet 62. F.q.d.99.10. and grave identified by a memorial cross. Reinterred 1920. His wife applied for his medals. Memorial Ref. V. I. 10., Dantzig Alley British Cemetery, Mametz, France. WO 339/29263

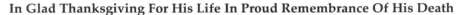

In Glad Thanksgiving For His Life In Proud Remembrance Of His Death

ROSS, Lieutenant, George Munro. Reported missing and then killed, 1st July 1916. Army Cyclist Corps. Aged 24. Son of James Ross and Lydia A. Ross, of 12, Day St., Newcastle-on-Tyne. Born 27th February 1892. Enlisted Northern Cyclist Battalion, 5th April 1909, No. 387. Commissioned 8th April 1915 into the 20th Bn., Northumberland Fusiliers. Records show to the Army Cyclist Corps on the 3rd November 1915, attd. to 20th Bn. Entered France, 11th January 1916. His mother read that he was missing in the Newcastle Chronicle, enquiries to the War Office revealed that two telegrams had been send to the wrong addresses, one in Liverpool and one in Whitley Bay. His mother applied for his medals and three children his pension. Memorial Ref. Pier and Face 12 C., Thiepval Memorial, France. WO 339/27543

ROSS, Captain, Peter. Reported killed, near La Boisselle, 1st July 1916. A Coy., 16th Bn., Royal Scots. Aged 39. Son of Peter and Margaret MacLeod Ross, of Thurso, Caithness. Husband of Alice M. Jones Ross, MA, Hons. (Edinburgh, teacher of Modern Languages), of 20, Inverleith Gardens, Edinburgh BSc. (Edinburgh), 1897 – 1903, MA (Hons. Mathematics and Natural Philosophy). A schoolmaster and author. Thurso F. C. School. Born 16th January 1876. Married, Dundee, 31st July 1907. Second Lieutenant, December 1914. Lieutenant, February 1915. Captain May 1916. Politician and teacher of mathematics in Edinburgh. Left three children, Alice Margaret, Margaret McLeod and John McLeod. His widow applied for his medals. Memorial Ref. Pier and Face 6 D and 7 D., Thiepval Memorial, France. WO 339/18299

ROSS, Second Lieutenant, Robert Wallace. Killed in action, 1st July 1916. 1st Bn., Newfoundland Regiment. Aged 22. Second son of Hector and Elizabeth Ross, of Victoria Street, Toronto, Ontario, Canada. Enlisted Church Lad's Brigade Armoury, St. John's, Newfoundland. Employee with the Reid Newfoundland Company. Attested 8th March 1915. Commissioned 27th November 1915. Graduate, Machine Gun School. Resided 14 Victoria Street, St. John's. Brother Lieutenant Hector Ross. Inscription via Lt. Col. Nangle, D.G.R&E, Newfoundland Contingent, Victoria St., SW1. Memorial Ref. A. 51., Hawthorn Ridge Cemetery No.2, Auchonvillers, France.
Glory Only In The Cross Of Christ

ROTHON, Second Lieutenant, Charles Francis. Reported wounded and then killed, killed in action in the assault on the Leipzig Redoubt. 1st July 1916. 1st Bn., Dorsetshire Regiment. Aged 26. Only son of Francis John Rothon and E. E. P. Rothon, of Vectis Lodge, 49, Geraldine Road, Wandsworth, London. Educated Mercer's School. Employers' Liability Assurance Corporation Ltd and had been on their staff since at least 1911. Joined the London University OTC in January 1915 and gazetted to Dorsetshire Regiment, February 1915. Went to the Front on New Year's Day, 1916. Father applied for his medals. Memorial Ref. Pier and Face 7 B., Thiepval Memorial, France.

ROUND, Captain, William Haldane. Killed in action, just after 8.00am buried by a shell and killed, the shell coming from Adinfer Wood, 1st July 1916. Officer Commanding, D Coy., 7th Bn., Sherwood Foresters (Notts and Derby Regiment). Aged 23. Only son of Reverend William and Edith Hornby Round, of East Drayton Vicarage, Redford, Notts. In charge of "D" company, which was the carrying and digging company that followed the attacking waves of "A", "B" and "C" companies. The company suffered heavy casualties as they climbed over the parapet and moved through the wire. It was at this point in the attack that William Round was buried by a shell and killed and his two subalterns wounded. Very few of the company advanced beyond the old fire trench. Born 4th May 1893. Attended Chesterfield School. Educated St. John's, Leatherhead in the Cricket XI in 1911 and two following years, being captain in 1913. Attended Downing College, Cambridge. Resided 58, Forest Road West, Nottingham. Commissioned 26th August 1914. Entered France, 28th February 1915. Commemorated Sons and Daughters of the Anglican Church Clergy. His father, Reverend W. Round, East Drayton Vicarage, Retford applied for his medals. Memorial Ref. I. L. 18., Foncquevillers Military Cemetery, France.

ROWATT, Second Lieutenant, David. His battery had just taken up its new advanced position when a shell landed right on top of it, killing him and two other officers instantaneously, as well as mortally wounding a fourth, 1st July 1916. "A" Bty. 10th Bde., Royal Field Artillery. Aged 26. Born at Waterloo, 12th April 1890. Eldest son of Mr. and Mrs. David Crawford Rowatt (tobacco merchant), of The Coppice, Abbey Road, Rhos-on-Sea. Husband of Sadie Williams (Formerly Rowatt, Nee Harvey-Gibson.) the daughter Robert John Harvey-Gibson, Professor of Botany at Liverpool University. Married at St. Bride's Church of England Church, Liverpool on the 21st August 1913. Left two children, David Lawrie Rowatt born on the 6th December 1914, and Alison Mary Rowatt born in 1916. Employed as a Secretary of Rowatt & Lyon Ltd. Brother Second Lieutenant Edmund Rowatt killed 20th July 1916. Old boy of Merchant Taylors' School. Lieutenant Rowatt joined Lord Derby's County Palatine Artillery in July 1915 and had been at the front from 30th November 1915. Four brothers served, two were killed, one severely injured and one died in the flu pandemic. Left £6,354 in his will. Medals to Mrs. Williams (widow remarried), Leamington Spa. Original burial map reference 62C.A.21.a.2.9. Memorial Ref. II. E. 36., Peronne Road Cemetery, Maricourt, France.

The Eleven Rowatt Children shortly before WW1

ROWLEY, Captain, Hugh Travers. Hit as he was advancing across No Man's Land, wounded in the leg pretty badly, offered to be bandaged but told his men to go on, reported to be lying dead by one of the men of his regiment, 1st July 1916. 9th Bn. attd. 2nd Bn., Royal Berkshire Regiment. Aged 23. Born 30th January 1893. Elder son of The Reverend Herbert Seddon Rowley, MA, and Mrs. F. L. Rowley, of Wretham Rectory, Thetford. Norfolk. Educated Worcester Cathedral Choir School and King's School Worcester (on memorial) leaving in 1910 to start engineering. Worcester OTC. Enlisted in the London Regiment at the outbreak of war and obtained a commission in the Royal Berkshire, December 1914. Promoted lieutenant June 1915 and made captain, April 1916. Entered France 25th October 1915. His father wrote to the War Office in August 1916; 'I would be glad to hear if possible if his body was identified and his grave marked'. Father applied for his medals. Memorial Ref. Pier and Face 11 D., Thiepval Memorial, France. WO 399/29877

ROWLEY, Second Lieutenant, Joseph. Signal officer, killed in action, 1st July 1916. 1st Bn., King's Own (Royal Lancaster Regiment). Only surviving son of W. Bryan Rowley (pit sinker/engineering contractor) and Mrs. Davies (formerly Rowley), of 24, Havelock Street, Bowerham, Lancaster formerly Crossgates, Leeds. Completed fourteen years of service in November 1915 and served in India for seven years, sergeant, 6943. Entered France, 23rd August 1914. Aged 29. Left a widow who he married in November 1913 and baby girl, Joan Grace at 10 Ivydene, Nicholl Road, Hastings. Attended Seaforth School and Bowerham School. His widow applied for his medals and pension. Memorial Ref. Pier and Face 5 D and 12 B., Thiepval Memorial, France.

RUPP, Lieutenant, Frederick Albert. Reported wounded and missing, 1st July 1916 in April 1917 reported killed on that date. 6th Bn. attd. 11th Bn., Border Regiment. Aged 23. Son of Frederick Michael and Barbara Rupp, of 4, St. Bedes, East Boldon, Co. Durham. Born 1893. Newcastle University. Educated Armstrong College, BSc in Pure Sciences. Gazetted 5th December 1914. He served at Gallipoli and France from 1915 to 1916 and was wounded twice in 1915. In hospital with a gunshot wound to the thigh, 10th to 24th September 1915. He was posted to France on recovery attached 11th Borders in 1916. The Grave Registration Unit reported they had found his body in October, 1917, northeast outskirts of Authuille Wood. Medals applied for by his parents. Memorial Ref. Pier and Face 6 A and 7 C., Thiepval Memorial, France.

Lieutenant Frederick Albert Rupp Far right Middle row

RUSHTON, Second Lieutenant, Frank Gregson. 53 Trench Mortar Battery, he had fired his last four rounds trying to kill a German officer when he stood up to use his revolver and was killed by the German officer, 1st July 1916. The sniper was killed by Second Lieutenant Lancelot Sayer whom died of wounds on the 11th July 1916. General List and 2nd Bn., Wiltshire Regiment. Trench Mortar Battery. He had worked with Captain Fenner to a German strong point, attacked with the Stokes mortars and a Lewis gun, whilst the defensive bombers were killed the German officer remained. Aged 30. Son of Mrs. Martha A. Crompton, of 22, Gillibrand St., Darwen, Lancs. His mother was visiting friends in Hull when notification received of his death and his father had to journey there. Journalist after leaving school with the Darwen Gazette and Daily Dispatch and came to be a reporter at the House of Commons. Joined as 3391, Artists Rifles. Associated with St. Cuthbert's Church and Sunday school. Several years employed on the Manchester Literary Staff of Messrs. E. Hulton and Co and subsequently went to London to represent the Daily Dispatch in the lobby of the House of Commons. A single man he gave up the opportunity of a wonderful career to join the army. Soon after securing his commission he was engaged in Howitzer work. Second lieutenant 12th May 1915. Mother applied for his medals. Memorial Ref. Q. 25., Carnoy Military Cemetery, France.

And His Spirit Returned To The God Who Gave It Pro Patria

His mother wrote a letter to Major Higham enclosing a photo.

Dear Sir,

I now have the liberty of sending this small photo he was not fond of having his picture taken and I could not induce him to be taken in uniform. What I have lost no words of mine can express – But I hope this small token will supply your wants

I remain yours,

His Sorrowing Mother

M. A. Crompton

PS I may just shake as he was my only son

RUSSELL, Lieutenant, Edward. Reported wounded and missing, reported to have been killed instantly by machine gun fire, having reached the German barb wire, 1st July 1916. D Coy., 11th Bn., Sherwood Foresters (Notts and Derby Regiment). Aged 20. Born 24th September 1895. Son of John Russell MA, (President of the Bromley House Library) and Edith Russell, of 328, Mansfield Road, Carrington, Nottingham. Bank clerk, employed the British Bank of South America. Educated at Trent College, after training in the Inns of Court OTC, private 1126 he obtained his commission early in the war, 26th November 1914. Promoted lieutenant in August 1915 and had been at the Front since September 1915. Presumed killed on the 1st July on the 29th June 1917. His mother applied for his medals. Lance Corporal W. H. Booth reported that his body was recovered one month later when they took the line, Nab trenches on the left of Albert and buried just behind the trenches in a cemetery close by, a photo was shown to Lance Corporal Booth and he immediately recognised it. He also believed his body was bought in with that of Second Lieutenant Longhurst, unknown British soldiers are buried next to Second

Lieutenant Longhurst. Brother G. H. Russell was an assistant paymaster in the Royal Navy. Memorial Ref. Pier and Face 10 C 10 D and 11 A., Thiepval Memorial, France. WO 339/1713

RUSSELL, Second Lieutenant, George Smith. Fell in action near Contalmaison, managed to get a party of men across four lines of trenches, first reported missing than killed, 1st July 1916 in the attack at La Boisselle. C Coy., 9th Platoon, 16th Bn., Royal Scots. Youngest son of Mr. and Mrs. George Russell, 14, Howe Street, Edinburgh. Born 22nd July 1895. Age 21. Banker. Enlisted Edinburgh, 19th December 1914 as private, 18905 in the Royal Scots. Gazetted 14th June 1915. Witness accounts vary, one stated he was seen lying dead and another that he had his head blown off by a shell. In October 1916 his father received an unofficial letter saying he had been buried and asked for clarification the War Office requested where this information came from, however they were able to recover and send his identity disc. In 1922 Kathleen Black Russell his mother stated she was entitled to two sets of war medals, George's and another son Lieutenant W. B. Russell who was killed at Gallipoli on the 19th June 1915. Mother applied for pensions. Entered France, 20th April 1916. His father applied for his medals. Memorial Ref. Pier and Face 6 D and 7 D., Thiepval Memorial, France. WO 339/38916

RUTLEDGE, Captain, John Bedell. 2.33pm C and D Coy's advanced over the parapet to attack but owing to heavy casualties from machine-gun fire it was found impossible to reach the enemy front line, killed in action, 1st July 1916. C. Coy., 7th Bn., East Yorkshire Regiment. Aged 33. Eldest son of the Reverend Lawrence William Rutledge and Alicia Maud Rutledge of Steeple Aston, Oxford. Born 14th September 1882 in Co. Fermanagh. Educated St. John's, Leatherhead (1892 – 1897). Husband of Theodora Bracebridge Rutledge, of Cheltenham, formerly of Alejandro, Argentine. Saw prior service second lieutenant 1901 and lieutenant 1902, 4th Bn., Royal Garrison Regiment. Married 14th June 1910. Returned from Argentina to rejoin the forces. Attested 9th January 1915. Captain 21st January 1915. Entered France, 14th July 1915. Suffered from septicaemia from the 12th to the 18th December 1915. His widow applied for his medals. Pension for daughter Theodora Elizabeth Patricia Bedell Rutledge. Inscription chosen by Miss M. Bose, Tivoli Lawn, Tivoli Road, Cheltenham. Originally buried Fricourt Grave 33. Memorial Ref. B. 4., Fricourt New Military Cemetery, France. WO 339/22502

Into Thy Hands O Lord I Commend My Spirit

RUTTLEDGE, Captain, John Forrest, MC, Mentioned in Despatches. Had the honour to go first over the parapet, 1st July 1916, though wounded he carried on and past the first trench at the head of his men and in the open he was hit in the head and died instantly. A Coy. 2nd Bn., West Yorkshire Regiment (Prince of Wales's Own). Aged 21. Eldest son of Lieutenant Colonel Alfred Ruttledge, of The Woodlands, Castleconnell, Co. Limerick. Born at Birr, King's County (now Offaly), Ireland on 1st August 1894. Educated Dr. Lynams Oxford Preparatory, Arnold House, Llandullas also Clifton College, Wellington College and RMC Sandhurst. Gazetted on 24th February, 1914, to his father's old regiment, the 2nd Bn., Prince of Wales's Own (West Yorkshire) Regiment. Disembarked 5th November 1914. Military Cross; ' For coolness and gallantry on 19th December 1914 near Neuve Chapelle when his company was moving over open ground under very heavy fire, many casualties occurred he remained to the last helping the wounded away to cover.' Received his MC at Buckingham Palace, 1st March 1916. A thorough sportsman. His father applied for his medals, address c/o Messrs. Cox & Co., 10 Charing Cross, London. Memorial Ref. Pier and Face 2 A 2 C and 2 D., Thiepval Memorial, France. WO 339/9580

RYALL, Second Lieutenant, William Thomas. Killed, Beaumont Hamel, 1st July 1916. Newfoundland Regiment. Aged 28. Son of Robert and Elizabeth Ann Ryall, of 40, Hayward Avenue, St. John's. Jeweller at T. J. Duley & Co. Brilliant musician and a member of the C.L.B Band. Enlisted 2nd September 1914. Second lieutenant, 27th November 1915. Attended course of instruction at the Lothian School and also in grenades at Troon. His brother, Private Robert Ryall, Newfoundland Regiment was killed, 12th October 1916, neither were found. Memorial Ref. Beaumont-Hamel (Newfoundland) Memorial, France.

SACH, Second Lieutenant, Charles Burleigh. Killed in action, Gommecourt, 1st July 1916. Reported killed by noon, 1st /13th Kensington Bn., London Regiment. Aged 19. Elder son of Charles Frederick and Emily Hannah Sach, of 155, Victoria Street, Westminster, London. Born 18th May 1897. Attended Emanuel School and Wandsworth School, London and City of London School. Insurance clerk, Clerical, Medical and General Assurance Company. Enlisted 15th September 1914, Inns of Court OTC. Commissioned 24th December 1915. Resided 76 Lebanon Gardens, Wandsworth. Entered France, 25th May 1916. Memorial Ref. Pier and Face 9 D 9 C 13 C and 12 C., Thiepval Memorial, France.

SADLER, Second Lieutenant, Charles Edward. Killed whilst leading his men at Beaumont Hamel, At 7.28am, six leading platoons took up their position in No Man's Land, without loss. At 7.30am our front line pushed forward, they were met with very heavy artillery and machine-gun fire, some of 'A' and 'B' Coys who did make the German front line at 7.35am were surrounded and captured by the Germans. Killed on the way across, 1st July 1916. 10th Bn. attd. 1st Bn., East Lancashire Regiment on the 20th June 1916. Commissioned 2nd September 1915. Entered France, 9th June 1916. Aged 21. Son of William E. and Sarah Sadler, of Heath Road, Holmewood, Chesterfield. Borough Road College now part of Brunel University London. Member of University of London, OTC. Memorial Ref. Pier and Face 6 C., Thiepval Memorial, France.

SAFFERY, Second Lieutenant, Leslie Hall. Died 1st July 1916. 4th Bn., Royal Dublin Fusiliers. Aged 23. Son of F. J. Saffery, of 10, Clifton Gardens, Maida Vale, London. Gazetted 4th April 1915 served as a cadet in the OTC. Seconded for service with a Trench Mortar Battery, June 1916. Entered France, 10th October 1915. Memorial Ref. Pier and Face 16 C., Thiepval Memorial, France.

SALTMARSHE, Lieutenant, Oliver Edwin. Fell as he lived, a very gallant officer, leading his men to the attack, killed in No Man's Land or close to Breslau Trench 1st July 1916. 7th Bn., The Queen's (Royal West Surrey Regiment). Aged 20. Eldest son of Edwin William and Isabel Saltmarshe, of 62, Avonmore Road, Kensington, London. Member of the staff of the Torquay Constitutional Club prior to the war, being trained for a political career by Mr. H. G. Levenson Hallewell. Formerly in the offices of the Torquay Division Unionist Association and a member of the Torquay Cricket Club. Gazetted 16th September 1914. Lieutenant, 27th November 1915. Previously private, 2045. Entered France, 27th July 1915. Original burial map reference 62C.A.8.c.8.9 with four other officers also killed on the 1st July, Lieut. Cloudesley, Lieut. Goss, 2nd Lieut. Baddeley and Captain Scott. Memorial Ref. VIII. R. 5., Dantzig Alley British Cemetery, Mametz, France.

Ad Astra Virtus

SAMPSON, Second Lieutenant, Arthur Henry Winn. Killed in No Man's Land, 1st July 1916. 4th Bn., Middlesex Regiment. Aged 30. Born 27th June 1886. Only son of Lieutenant Colonel Francis Robert Winn Sampson and Mrs. Winn Sampson, of 115, Tannsfield Road, Sydenham, London formerly of Old Calabar, Nigeria. Attended St. Winifred's Preparatory School, Henley and Sherborne School (Harper House) May 1901-December 1904. Enlisted as 1542, Honourable Artillery Company, 26th August 1914. Entered France, 18th September 1914. Suffered a gunshot wound to the left leg on the 26th November 1914 and returned to England. Commissioned 12th June 1915. He wrote his will in the field on the 27th June 1916 and left his money to his mother, any books to the Reverend Montague Summer and to his father and sister (Mrs. Eric Roper) anything they want of his other things. He also left instructions for all his debts to be paid and the receipts were in the right hand chest of drawers in his bedroom. Sherborne School, UK, Book of Remembrance. Original burial map reference 57d.27.c.7.6 and was marked as an unknown officer from Lieutenant Barnett's grave. Memorial Ref. IV. L., Gordon Dump Cemetery, Ovillers-La Boisselle, France. WO 339/54471

B Coy., 4th Bn., Middlesex Regiment photographed 26th June 1916
2nd Lt A.H. Winn-Sampson (killed 1st July 1916), 2nd Lt W. John Wood (killed 1st July 1916), 2nd Lt. A. A. Johnston (killed 2nd July 1916), 2nd Lt. A.F. C Paxton (killed 1st July 1916), Lt. D. Cutbush killed 10th April 1917, Lt. H.M. Williams, 2nd Lt. A. Branch killed 1st July 1916, Captain O. R. F. Johnston Centre killed 1st July 1916

SANBY, Second Lieutenant, William Worthington. Killed attacking La Boisselle, gallantly leading and cheering his men on when he fell mortally wounded, 1st July 1916. 20th (Tyneside Scottish) Bn., Northumberland Fusiliers. Aged 21. Youngest son of Arthur Hill Sanby and Ellen Sanby, of The Gables, Stratford-on-Avon formerly Hartopp Road, Four Oaks, Birmingham. Born 9th August 1895. Attended King Edward VII School, Birmingham. Auctioneers pupil with F. Matthews & Co. Joined as private, 14th Bn., Royal Warwickshire Regiment, 10th September 1914 to lance corporal, 764 and second lieutenant, 16th April 1915. Admitted to hospital, May 1916 with slight influenza. His brother Lance Sergeant Harold Ernest also fell on the 9th August 1915. Two other brothers served. Father wrote to the War office advising only his identity badge was received and also advised the War Office to write to his business address to save his and family's feelings. Memorial Ref. Pier and Face 10 B 11 B and 12 B., Thiepval Memorial, France. WO 339/27762

SANDERSON, Lieutenant, Geoffrey Evian. At about 3.30pm the right flank were being bombed by the Germans and his men ran out of bombs. He seized a rifle from a man and called for the men to charge, he rushed forward, turned around, waved to the men and immediately fell dead, 1st July 1916. 107th Coy., Machine Gun Corps (Infantry). Aged 27. Youngest son of Alderman W. J. and Amy Sanderson, of Eastfield Hall, Warkworth, Northumberland. Born 3rd April 1889, Newcastle-upon-Tyne. Attended Marlbrough College and Jesus College, Cambridge, 1907 - 1910, BA Theology. The first scoutmaster in Northumberland. Assisted in recruiting miners. His captain reported that "on the day of his death he, his party and his gun were wiped out while gallantly holding an important point." Seen in action in the southern part of the German fourth line where he was killed. Warkworth War Memorial. Memorial Ref. Pier and Face 5 C and 12 C., Thiepval Memorial, France.

SANDERSON, Second Lieutenant, Walter Ker. Reported missing believed killed, bravely leading his men into the thickest of action, 1st July 1916. 1st Bn., Border Regiment. Aged 35. Only son of Dr. Sanderson and E. A. Sanderson, of Fairfield, Penrith, Cumberland. Born 19th August 1881. Educated Sedbergh (1895 to April 1899). He read medicine at Edinburgh (1899 – 1901) but went to work away from medicine. Officer of the Vote Office, House of Commons served for eleven years. At the outbreak of war he enlisted in the Public Schools Battalion gazetted to the Royal West Kent Regiment, but afterwards transferred to the Honourable Artillery Company, private, 3849 and later the Borders. Commissioned 22nd April 1916. Entered France 18th August 1915.

Major Meiklejohn wrote; ' Your son died as gallant a death as any officer or man could. He was leading his platoon right up to the German lines, and never faltered or checked when caught in the terrible fire. He died encouraging his men in the most gallant manner.' House of Commons, Book of Remembrance. Memorial Ref. Pier and Face 6 A and 7 C., Thiepval Memorial, France.

SANGER, Second Lieutenant, Thomas Rudolph. Missing, killed in action, D Party, 4th wave, 1st July 1916, his parents had worse fears confirmed in April 1917. Last seen lying face down covered with earth from British shells. 1st/5th Bn., South Staffordshire Regiment. Only son of Thomas and Ellen Theresa Sanger, Ryde, Isle of Wight. Born 20th September 1889, Isle of Wight. Educated St. Mary's College Training College, Hammersmith. Had a very successful scholastic career at the Upper Grade School and Sandown Secondary Schools and after leaving college he obtained a teaching appointment at St. Johns Road Boys School before training and going to Walsall. He was a teacher at St. Mary's (The Mount) Schools, Walsall. Obtained his commission from the ranks of the battalion. Joining as a private 1/8th Bn., No. 8883, South Staffordshire Regiment. He had risen to sergeant when after about eleven months active service he came home to take up a commission and was soon drafted out again. Participated in the capture of Hohenzollern Redoubt. Mother applied for his pension. Education Department, Walsall Corporation Roll of Honour. Entered 5th March 1915. Commissioned 17th February 1916. Memorial Ref. Pier and Face 7 B., Thiepval Memorial, France.

SANGER-DAVIES, Captain, Llewelyn Herbert. Killed leading his company, 1st July 1916. 15th Bn., Durham Light Infantry. Aged 22. Born September 13th , 1893, in Canterbury, Kent. Son of Reverend Joseph Sanger-Davies and Harriet A. Sanger-Davies, of 3, Albany Road, St. Leonard's-on-Sea. BA. (Cantab). Attended Marlbrough College and admitted as Entrance Exhibitioner at Trinity College, Cambridge, June 25th , 1912. BA 1915. Played hockey and in the team was Philip Clifford Knight also killed on the 1st July 1916. Intended to be a clergyman. His brother, Florian Morgan Sanger-Davies served with the Royal Sussex Regiment and was seriously wounded. Entered France, 11th September 1915. Mother applied for his medals. Memorial Ref. Pier and Face 14 A and 15 C., Thiepval Memorial, France. WO 339/59938

SAPTE, Captain, Anthony. Killed in action, 1st July 1916. A Coy. 4th Bn., Middlesex Regiment. Aged 19. Son of Fitzroy and Edith Frances Courtney Sapte, of 21, Crediton Hill, Kilburn, London. Born 10th August 1896. Attended Haileybury (Colvin 1910- 1913). Attended Edinburgh House School, Ballard School, Hampshire. Choose the Middlesex Regiment as he had two uncles in the regiment and his parents owned property in the county. Entered France on 16th October 1914. Gazetted 30th September 1914 and 6th April 1916. Commemorated St. John, Hampstead Parish Church. Originally buried Empress Trench and angle of new communications trench sht 26. Sq. 110. 57d.X.26.d.8.6. Memorial Ref. IV. M. 1., Gordon Dump Cemetery, Ovillers-La Boisselle, France.

Faithful Unto Death

SAUNDERS, Second Lieutenant, Charles. Fighting was hard and shelling heavy, machine-gun fire was intense, 1st July 1916. 15th Bn., West Yorkshire Regiment (Prince of Wales's Own). Barclays Bank Roll of Honour. Register entitled "Barclay & Company Limited – Staff on Active Service" includes, in the section for Great Yarmouth local head office, the name C. Saunders, with branch given as Beccles. His rank/regiment was recorded as 2nd Lieut., 13 Batt W Yorks Regt. (Sergt., Reserve Cavalry Bucks., had originally been written and then crossed out.) He was described as being single, his normal full salary was £110 per annum, his army pay per annum was £41 12s, and his net salary paid by the bank was £68 8s per annum. Memorial Ref. Pier and Face 2 A 2 C and 2 D., Thiepval Memorial, France.

SAVAGE, Second Lieutenant, William Howard. Pommiers Redoubt had still to be taken Captain Johnson was held in Black Alley by a machine-gun, and could not approach that way. He then attempted to take the redoubt from the rear. Second Lieutenant Savage accounted for the snipers in Beetle Alley, on the northwest, and Johnson was able to bring his machine-guns up to enfilade the front of the redoubt. With this assistance the Bedfordshires were able to advance frontally, and the obstacle was won at 9.30am. Beetle Alley was rushed shortly afterwards. Shot by a sniper after leading his platoon through terrific fire, 1st July 1916. 11th Bn., Royal Fusiliers. Aged 31. Eldest son of William F. and Edith M. Savage, of 70, Park Drive, Port Elizabeth, South Africa formerly of Mapperly House, Halylud, Woodford. Grandson of Mr. and Mrs. J. W. Thomas of Hale End, Woodford Green. Gazetted 8th November 1915. Previously private, 1 & 2 M. R, private, 181. Originally buried ENE of Mametz and East of Albert, Sht 62d. Sq. F.6. Effects note book, advance book, New Testament, card case and cigarette holder. Medals to be issued by South African authorities. Original map burial map reference 62D.F.6.a. Memorial Ref. II. D. I., Dantzig Alley British Cemetery, Mametz, France. WO 339/47590

That Life Is Long Which Answers Life's Great End

On the left, Frederick 53rd Bde, Trench Mortar Battery who survived the 1st July and
William Howard seated in the middle

SAYCE, Captain, George Ben. Asked his Commanding Officer to allow him to lead and led his men to splendidly capture the enemy's front line trench, he was about to jump into the second line trench when he was hit by a sniper's bullet in the head, 1st July 1916. Witness saw him lying dead on the 2nd and witnessed him being buried in what was a German Trench with his Commanding Officer and three other officers. 26th (Service) Bn., Manchester Regiment. Aged 29. Son of George and Elizabeth Sayce. Born at Rock Ferry. Attended Denstone College. Husband of Dilys Kirkby (formerly Sayce), of 67, Bridge Street, Manchester and they had a son. Married November 1914. Joined the Manchesters in November 1914, promoted captain, January 1915, 20th Bn., E Coy. Commissioned 7th November 1914. Previously 4th Bn., Cheshire Regiment, private, 726. Entered France, 27th March 1916. Originally buried south of Fricourt and ESE of Albert, 62d. Sq. F.d.99.10. Effects returned were a wrist watch, cigarette case, silver flask, leather purse, cheque book, wallet with photo, tobacco pouch and photos. Pension to two children, Peter Ben and Ben Caradoc Sayce, a note was made in the log that Ben died on the 18th February 1917. Original burial map reference 62D.F.9.d.9.7. Memorial Ref. VI. I. 2., Dantzig Alley British Cemetery, Mametz, France. WO 339/17230

SAYRES, Captain, Hugh Wingfield. Commanded C Coy. on the attack on Beaumont-Hamel and fell leading his men, hit before reaching our own front line, 1st July 1916. 1st Bn. attd. 2nd Bn., Lancashire Fusiliers. Aged 27. Only son of William Borrett Sayres and Ellen Harriet Sayres, of 60, Longridge Road, Earl's Court, London. Born 2nd December 1888. Educated Allen House, Guildford and Army House, Bradfield College (September 1902 to July 1904), Westgate. RMC Sandhurst 1908. In November 1910 during the coal strikes in South Wales and at the riots there where he received commendation for his tactful handling of several difficult situations. In 1912 he was sent to India and in 1915 was shot in the right shoulder while landing in Gallipoli. Entered Gallipoli, 25th April 1915. Captain Sayres died alongside his dog Nailer while leading his company in an attack on Beaumont-Hamel. His 1912 Webley Revolver was discovered in a bag of clothes donated to a charity shop in Earl Shilton, Leicestershire. Sergeant Matlock said: "Hugh Winfield Sayres was a remarkable officer who excelled at everything he did including boxing, hockey, steeplechase and cricket." Served as a Brigade Major for three months in France. His mother applied for his pension. Memorial Ref. I. I. 71., Sucrerie Military Cemetery, Colincamps, France.

The Lord Gave And The Lord Hath Taken Away Blessed Be The Name Of The Lord

SCHNEIDER, Second Lieutenant, Stewart Spearing. Killed in action, 1st July 1916. 9th Bn. attd. 2nd Bn., Royal Berkshire Regiment. Aged 21. Son of Stewart and Alice Schneider, of Flixton, Queens Road, Haywards Heath, Sussex. Was well-known in mid-Sussex cricket. Previously private, 954, Royal Sussex Regiment. Wrote his will in the field, 19th June 1916 leaving all money and goods to his dear mother, Alice with the exception of his sword he left to dear Amy Leverson and the life sized photo of himself to be framed and given to Ada Austen. On receipt of the telegram informing the family of his death his father replied via telegram on the 10th July 1916; 'If he was identified after death if so by whom?' Effects returned were cheque book, officers advance book and identity disc. Memorial Ref. Pier and Face 11 D., Thiepval Memorial, France. WO 339/32634

SCOTT, Lieutenant, Dudley Holme. Reported to have died from wounds, 2nd July 1916. He led 'A' Coy into action on the right of the line evacuated to a military hospital at Cerisy and died of his wounds. A Coy., 17th Bn., The King's (Liverpool Regiment) most successful battalion of the day. Aged 38. Youngest son of George and Frances Scott, of Oxton, Cheshire. Educated Birkenhead School. Cotton salesman. Played cricket and hockey being awarded an international cap in 1904, England vs Ireland. Gazetted 1st September 1914 to 1st Bn., formerly private, 15187. Commemorated Royal Liverpool Golf Club. Left his estate to his two brothers. Entered France, 11th March 1916. W. H. Scott his brother applied for his medals. Burial return states he died on the 1st July, and original burial map reference 62d.Q.2.d.8.6. Reburied 1923. Grave Registration form also states he died on the 1st July. Memorial Ref. IX. D. 3., Heath Cemetery, Harbonnieres, France. WO 339/66465

SCOTT, Captain, George Henry Hall. Gained and held objective, Montauban, at 8.30am went forward in an attempt to find the battalion and assess the situation, the outcome he was spotted in No Man's Land and killed, 1st July 1916. C Coy. 7th Bn., The Queen's (Royal West Surrey Regiment). Aged 34. Younger son of Sir Henry Hall Scott and Henrietta, of Ellanreach, Co. Inverness. His wife, of 17, Stratton Street, Piccadilly, London. Native of Ainham House, Whittingham, Northumberland. Born 18th June 1882. Educated Aysgarth and Charterhouse (Verites 1896 – 1900). Consulting mining engineer and director of Bolsover and Blackwell Collieries, Derby and Newbiggin Colliery, Northumberland. Outbreak of war volunteered, gazetted lieutenant September 1914 and went to France, 26th July 1915. Keen sportsman, salmon fisher and deer-stalker when at the country residence in Inverness. Since September 1915 he commanded his company which up to that point was commanded by his brother-in-law, Captain Roland Hebeler was killed on that date, 16th September 1915. Resided with his mother at Down Place, Guildford. Buried in the battlefield at Carnoy. His mother applied for his medals. Original burial map reference 62C.A.8.c.8.9 with four other officers also killed on the 1st July, Lieut. Cloudesley, Lieut. Goss, Lieut. Saltmarshe and 2nd Lieut. Baddeley. Memorial Ref. VIII. R. 3., Dantzig Alley British Cemetery, Mametz, France. WO 339/133

In Proud & Fairest Memory So Sweet To Live Magnificent To Die

SCOTT, Lieutenant, Gordon. Reported wounded and missing and then killed in action, 1st July 1916. 2nd Bn., Middlesex Regiment. Aged 19. Third son of Henry Steele Scott and Janet Keith Scott, Montrose, Winchmore Hill Road, Winchmore Hill. Entered France, 4th January 1916. His father applied for his medals. Originally buried Mash Valley Cemetery, 57d.X.13.b.8.7. Collar and badge returned to father. Henry felt there should have been more and wrote to the War Office in October 1916, the reply stated ' it is impossible under the present conditions attaching to active service to guard entirely against losses which sometimes occur.' Memorial Ref. Pier and Face 12 D and 13 B., Thiepval Memorial, France. WO 339/35752

SCOTT, Second Lieutenant, Ian Archibald Sawers. Killed in action, 1st July 1916. 2nd Bn. attd. 1st Bn., King's Own Scottish Borderers. Aged 19. Youngest son of William Sawers Scott, M.D., of Manchester, and of Margaret S. Scott, of 28, Romilly Road, Barry, Glam. He went from South Manchester School/Manchester Grammar School to Fettes College, where he had won a scholarship. When his brother, Norman, was killed at Ypres he had been awarded a university scholarship and he applied at once for a position in the Kings Own Scottish Borderers and joined the University OTC. He spent some time in Egypt and was put in sole charge of a contingent for France. Second Lieutenant Norman Sawers Scott, 2nd Bn., King's Own Scottish Borderers died 23rd April 1915. Father applied for his medals. Memorial Ref. G. 9., Knightsbridge Cemetery, Mesnil-Martinsart, France.

SCOTT, Second Lieutenant, William Francis. Fell gallantly leading his men amid a perfect hail of bullets, 1st July 1916. 8th Bn., Somerset Light Infantry. Aged 31. Second son of Francis Henry Scott. Born on the 24th February 1885 at Tiverton, Bath. He attended St. Mark's College, Chelsea before coming up to St. Catharine's College in 1909. B.A Degree at Cambridge awarded 15th June 1912. Member of the OTC. One of the masters of Hendon County School. Appointed to the county school in September 1914, before Hendon was master at Waggston School, Leicester. Enlisted as a private in the 9th Bn., Queen Victoria Rifles in 1914 and obtained commission in June 1915 in the Somersets. Moved from reserve 24th June 1915. Husband of Gertrude Violet Scott, of 40, Voltaire Road, Clapham, London married, 6th October 1915. Entered France, 25th December 1915. Three brothers served with the Canadians. Originally buried Becourt –Fricourt Road, 57D.X.26.d.8.6. His brother, Staff Sergeant E. J. Scott was notified of his death and was shocked he had to inform Gertrude, she only received communication in the casualty list. Effects returned were letters, wrist watch, gold ring and photos. Memorial Ref. II. M. 2., Gordon Dump Cemetery, Ovillers-La Boisselle, France. WO 339/5496

In Proud & Fairest Memory So Sweet To Live Magnificent To Die

St. Catharine's 1909 Matriculation Photo

SCOTT-HOLMES, Second Lieutenant, Henry Favil. 1st July 1916. 208th Field Coy., Royal Engineers. Aged 22. Only son of Robert and Eleanor Scott-Holmes, of 127, Rosary Road, Norwich formerly Neville Street, Norwich. Grandson of Major Holmes of Wacton House. Born 15th March 1893. Attended Gresham School left 1907, entered 1905. Enlisted August, 1914 when he was about to be employed with the Norwich Electric Tramway Company. Joined the transport section of the 6th Norfolks at the outbreak of war and obtained a commission in the 10th. He transferred to a battalion of the Royal Engineers raised by the Lord of Norwich. Mother applied for his medals. Memorial Ref. Pier and Face 8 A and 8 D., Thiepval Memorial, France.

SEGGIE, Second Lieutenant, Alexander. Reported missing, believed killed and then reported killed leading his platoon, 1st July 1916. B Coy. 3rd Bn., attd 9th Bn., Royal Irish Fusiliers. Aged 24. Son of William Fergusson Seggie and Janet Seggie, of 28, Prince's Street, Prospect Road, Tunbridge Wells. Born 1893, Dublin. Attended Kendrick School and University College, Reading. Trainee teacher. Member of Reading University College OTC. Obtained BA (1st Class in Philosophy) in 1913. Member of Debating Society and Student Union Representative Council. Entered Public School Battalion, September 1914. Received commission, May 1915. Medal Index Card unusually has theatre of war, November 15 to 1st July 1916. Father applied for his medals. Memorial Ref. VIII. A. 86., Ancre British Cemetery, Beaumont-Hamel, France.

Your Memory Is Hallowed In The Home You Loved

SEWELL, Major, William Tait. Reported missing, believed killed, 1st July 1916. 11th Bn., Royal Inniskilling Fusiliers. Aged 34. Second child and eldest son of William Sewell, M. Inst. C.E (agent for Sir Hedworth Williamson Bart., and managing director of the Fulwell Lime Works Ltd.) and Elizabeth Janet Sewell of High Croft, Whitburn, Sunderland and manor offices, Monkwearmouth. Born 1882, Garmondsway, Durham. Studied at St. Andrews University, Newcastle-upon-Tyne. Educated Wellingborough Grammar School and afterwards Newcastle College of Medicine taking his degree of M.D at Durham in 1908 and the degree of D.Ph. at Newcastle in 1909. He was for some time medical officer at the Fleming Memorial Hospital, Newcastle and later pathologist at Newcastle Royal Infirmary and Fleming Memorial Hospital, and assistant medical officer to the Durham County Sanatorium at Stenhope. He had been conducting research at Freiburg University, Germany five months prior to the outbreak of war. Pathological lecturer. Unmarried. He was captain in the OTC and on outbreak of war became the adjutant. Member of the Pathological Society of Great Britain. Two brothers also fought, Lieutenant Sydney E. Sewell and Second Lieutenant T. R. Sewell. Father applied for his medals. Memorial Ref. I. C. 22., Mill Road Cemetery, Thiepval, France.

SHANN, Lieutenant, John Webster. Killed in action, 1st July 1916. Adjutant, 10th Bn., West Yorkshire Regiment (Prince of Wales's Own). Aged 22. Elder son of Silvanus and Ann Elizabeth Shann, of 19, Well Close Place, Carlton Hill, Leeds. Born Leeds. Went to Leeds Grammar School and to Christ Church, Oxford in 1913 as an Exhibitioner. Outbreak of war, he joined the 10th West Yorkshire Regiment. Twice wounded, once on the 14th January 1916 and returned to duty. Entered France, 13th July 1915. Memorial Ref. C. 13., Fricourt New Military Cemetery, France. WO 339/17745

The Memory Of The Just Is Blessed Call It Not Death 'Tis Life Begun

SHAPLEY, Lieutenant, Alfred Edwin. Report that the officer was sat down and looked like he had been hit, position X.13.d.45.85 Sheet Ovillers 57D.5.E.4 and was not seen again, led his men most gallantly in the direction of the German trenches. 1st July 1916. 23rd (Tyneside Scottish) Bn., Northumberland Fusiliers. Aged 28. Only son of Edwin Maynard Shapley and Annie Shapley, of 3, Jesmond Vale Terrace, Heaton, Newcastle-on-Tyne. Born Liverpool, 12th November 1888. Husband of H. Constance Shapley (Nee Fisher), of 10, Larkspur Terrace, Jesmond, Newcastle-on-Tyne. He was assistant surveyor to Whickham Council and at the outbreak of war to the Manchester Corporation. Attested 4th September 1914. 20th Bn., Royal Fusiliers, quartermaster sergeant, 5622. Enlisted Manchester Grammar School. Two years as a territorial he joined the Manchester Battalion of the Public Schools Corps, and later gained a commission, 6th January 1915. Entered France, 9th January 1916. It was not possible to recover effects for eight days as the Germans had patrolled for two to three nights after the 1st July 1916. Memorial Ref. Pier and Face 10 B 11 B and 12 B., Thiepval Memorial, France. WO 339/23259

SHARP, Second Lieutenant, Leon Owen. He died magnificently close up to the enemy's parapet, 1st July 1916. 2nd Bn., Lincolnshire Regiment. Aged 22. Youngest son of Thomas and Ada Annie Sharp, of Oakdale, Regent Street, Leamington Spa. Born 26th October 1893. Educated at King's School, Warwick and Grantham School, being a member of the OTC. He originally belonged to the Royal Flying Corps but transferred to the Lincolnshire Regiment. He had been at the Front about eighteen months. Before enlisting in the RFC on the second day of the war he was on the staff of the London City and Midland Bank at Moreton-in-the-Marsh. Arrived France, 3rd April 1915. Received his commission 23rd April 1916 from 1st Class Air Mechanic, 1618. Two brothers in the Garrison Artillery. About a week before his death he was taken from the regiment to the new Stoke mortars battery in which he had been trained and said as soon as he could he would make his way to his old company, on his arrival he gathered a group of men about eight and organised a desperate attack on a very strong point on the German line, he was seen walking slowly and suddenly put his hand to his left side and his throat fell on his face and lay still. Private Caffing tried to reach him but got close enough to know he was dead. Leamington Spa War Memorial. North Leamington School. Stained glass Holy Trinity Church. On the 7th July 1916 his father wrote to the War Office asking would it be possible for his body to brought home as his mother was broken hearted and by the 22nd August 1916, replied in frustration 'no-one can say what became of him or where he was buried.' The family looked for effects but they were send from the field on the 7th July 1916 but noted in his record no effects were received by those in England. Original burial map reference 57d.R.32.c.9.1 and his grave was marked by a cross. Memorial Ref. X. E. 3., Lonsdale Cemetery, Authuille, France. WO 339/59709

SHARP, Second Lieutenant, Lewis Frederick. Died 1st July 1916. 10th Bn., King's Own Yorkshire Light Infantry. Born in Bermondsey, London on 12th March 1879, the son of Edward (manager of factory manufacturing helmets and hats) and June Sharp. Employed Field, Son & Co., who made hats and helmets. Sportsman and played cricket and football. Resided Adswood Lane, Stockport. Enlisted into the army on 4th September 1914, at the age of 41, joining the 2/6th Bn., Manchester Regiment, No. 2529, promoted to lance corporal and, in March 1915, he applied for a commission, received 7th April 1916. In June, he was taken ill with rheumatism in his right foot, left knee, hip and back and was sent on sick leave for a month. On returning to duty, he was under canvas at Strenshall when he got wet and this caused the problem to flare up again. This time he was not fit enough to return until 23rd November 1915. Lewis was again ill in April 1916 whilst attached to the 11th Bn.,Light Infantry and only went overseas to join the 10th as a 2nd lieutenant on 19th June when he joined the 10th Bn. Widower. Effects were identity disc and letters. Memorial Ref. Pier and Face 11 C and 12 A., Thiepval Memorial, France. WO 339/32895

SHARP, Lieutenant, Stephen Oswald. Killed whilst leading his men, near Serre, 1st July 1916. A Coy. 13th Bn., York and Lancaster Regiment. Aged 26. Elder son of Mr. and Mrs. H. J. Sharp, of Kenilworth, Avenue Road, Doncaster. B.A. (Cantab.), June 1912. Born 8th June 1890, Rotheram. Educated Retford Grammar School and Pembroke College, Cambridge. Played Rugby for Doncaster RFC. Cricket played for Retford Grammar School and Rotherham Town. Articled clerk with a firm of solicitors in Rotheram, Mr. J. H. Cockburn, of Messrs. Parker, Rhodes & Co. Well-known as a cricket and football player. On the outbreak of war, 11th September 1914 he joined 12th Bn., York and Lancaster Regiment as a private, 1048 and obtained a commission, 20th November 1914 getting his second star in June 1915. Memorial Ref. V. Q. 3., Euston Road Cemetery, Colincamps, France.

B.A. (Cantab) Son Of Mr. & Mrs. H.J. Sharp Avenue Road, Doncaster

SHAW, Captain, Alexander James McIntosh. 14th Bn., Kings Royal Rifle Corps attd 1st Bn., Kings Own Scottish Borderers. Reported missing, believed killed 9th July 1916. War diary states he was one of 11 officers killed with the 1st Bn., all other officers were given a date of death of the 1st July 1916. Grave Registration Unit also states 1st July 1916. Reported killed locally on the 28th July 1916. Temporary second lieutenant, 6th January 1915. Lieutenant, February 1915. Temporary captain, March 1915. Original burial location Y Ravine Cemetery, Q.17.a.4.9. Grave Ref. I. A. 18. Ancre British Cemetery, Somme, France.

SHAW, Lieutenant, Clarence Gordon. Missing 1st July 1916. 1st Bn., Lincolnshire Regiment, war diary states 2nd Bn. Son of Samuel and Lydia Emma Shaw of Ferns Hollow, Ilkeston. Student in the elementary training department at Nottingham University College from 1911 to 1913. It was on the recommendation of Captain S. R. Trotman that he received his commission. Belonged to the Notts and Derby Regiment, Special Reserve and then attached 1st Lincolns and onto 2nd Bn. Second lieutenant, January 1914. Disembarked 26th October 1914. Gazetted in February 1915. Treated on the 19th March 1915 for neurasthenia at No. 5 Casualty Clearing Station, Hazebrouck. His mother tried to get further details from injured officers but he was presumed to be killed on the 1st July 1916 in March 1917. University College Nottingham OTC War Memorial. Mrs. Dorothy Mellor Shaw his wife applied for his medals and pension, Burns Street, Ilkeston. Memorial Ref. Pier and Face 1 C., Thiepval Memorial, France. WO 339/9539

SHAW, Lieutenant, Robert Ramsay Stuart. Adjutant killed with Major C. E. Boote, went forward with one of the leading waves, 1st July 1916. 1st/6th Bn., North Staffordshire Regiment. Aged 20. Born 29th January 1896. Only son of Dr. Thomas David Stuart Shaw and Daisy Stuart Shaw, of 8, Bore Street, Lichfield, Staffs. Educated at Uppingham, 1909 to 1913 and was a member of the OTC. Visited France to learn the language. He joined the Lichfield Territorials in March 1914 as a subaltern. In October 1915 a severe wound necessitated a return to England and he rejoined the battalion in March. Three weeks prior to death acting as adjutant. Entered France, 3rd March 1915. Adjutant, 26th June 1916. His father applied for his medals. Body recovered after the war. Memorial Ref. Sp. Mem. A. 3., Gommecourt Wood New Cemetery, Foncquevillers, France.

Requiescat In Pace

SHAW, Second Lieutenant, William. Killed in action in the heavy fighting, 1st July 1916. Majority of the casualties especially those of the officers occurred during the first two hours of fighting, 2nd Bn., Seaforth Highlanders. Son of Mr. William Shaw, 27 Inglis Street, Dunfermline and Mrs. Christina Shaw (nee Wilson), 30 East Back Street. Born Elgin. Enlisted Fort George. Age 37. Joined the Seaforths as a private in January 1897. Husband of Mrs. Ellen Shaw, Cherry Cottage, Elgin. Memorial Ref. Pier and Face 15 C., Thiepval Memorial, France.

SHEPARD, Second Lieutenant, Cyril Harry. Killed whilst capturing Danube Trench and Shrine Alley in front of the village of Mametz, 1st July 1916 and died in the German lines. 9th Bn., Devonshire Regiment. Aged 39. Born in St. John's Wood on the 20th December 1877, the elder son of Ernest Henry Dunkin Shepard FRIBA, an architect, and Harriette Jessie (née Lee) Shepard of 3 Boscobel Place. Educated Colet Court and St. Paul's School. Previous employed as an underwriter's clerk for A.C. Brown Esq. and others at Lloyd's. He was married to Rosemary in March 1916. Enlisted as private 123 in the Inns of Court OTC on the 18th of April 1908 and was discharged on the 17th of April 1912. Rejoined and commissioned as a second lieutenant in the 11th (Reserve) Bn., Devonshire Regiment on the 3rd May 1915. He was posted to the 9th Battalion of his regiment on the 18th of May 1916. Embarked for France on the 22nd May. Joined the 9th Bn., for duty on the 24th May 1916. Member of the Blackheath Lawn Tennis Club, Blackheath Dramatic Society and Barnehurst Golf Club. Originally buried Mansel Copse. Sheet 62d. Sq. F.11.c. His widow, Stuart Terrace, Stoke, Plymouth applied for his medals. Inscription chosen by Mr. F. P. Shepard, Stuart Terrace, Stoke, Devonport. Memorial Ref. B. 6., Devonshire Cemetery, Mametz, France. WO 339/41142

I Am The Resurrection And The Life

SHIRREFF, Second Lieutenant, Francis Gordon. At 7.30am the three assaulting companies advanced to attack the German line. They were met by intense rifle and machine-gun fire which prevented any of the waves reaching the enemy lines. A little group on the left of the battalion succeeded in getting in, but were eventually bombed out. 2nd Lieutenant F.G. Shirreff was listed as missing, reported to have died leading his platoon like a gallant soldier, 1st July 1916. His servant, Private E. Neale, 14840, saw him wounded and later saw him die. Private E. Tedder also confirmed this before he died in hospital at Southampton on the 15th July 1916. Private A. Jackson states he was severely wounded and rolling over and over on the ground being peppered by the Germans, with Private Eyre stating he was stuck in the chest, he turned over to get his field dressing out of his pocket and thinks a sniper saw the white of the bandage and shot him twice. B Coy. 2nd Bn. formerly 3rd Bn., Royal Berkshire Regiment. Aged 34. Son of Reverend F.A. P. Shirreff, Vicar Of Sparsholt-Cum-Kingstone Lisle, Berks, and of E. L. Shirreff (nee Davidson). MA (Oxon). Born 10th October 1881. Attended St. Lawrence College, Ramsgate, Kent. Merchant Taylors' School. Exhibitioner. Exeter College, Oxon. Exhibitioner, Exeter College matriculated 1900, Oxford. Honours history. Oxford University Rifle Volunteers, 1900 – 1903. Inns of Court OTC, January 1915. Some years assistant in Bodlean Library and Historical Medical Museum and gave this up to enlist. Gazetted second lieutenant, Royal Berkshire Regiment, June, 1915. Entered France, 22nd March 1916. In the latter part of July, Captain H. C. Harvey, Royal Engineers picked up some of Second Lieutenant Shirreff's papers in a shell hole, there was no indication of rank or regiment or where the body had been taken or if it was buried this was at location map sheet 57.D.S.E.X.7.D.7.7. He send these papers back to his wife, and they contained the address of Mrs. E. L. Shirreff she forwarded them on explaining where they had come from. With this knowledge and from speaking to the sergeant involved in the attack, Mrs. Shirreff wrote to the War Office asking if it was possible that her son was picked by the Germans, although she had the accounts of his death she was led to conclude he was concussed and was a prisoner. She also pointed out that no body was found by the search party. The War Office replied that it was the rule that they would search the body of an officers should he have valuable papers on him and that they had no grounds for believing he was a prisoner as no information had been received. Commemorated Merchant Taylors' School, Northwood. Medal Index Card death accepted as being the 1st July. His mother applied for his medals, c/o Jotcham & Sons, solicitors. Memorial Ref. Pier and Face 11 D., Thiepval Memorial, France. WO 399/6221

SHORTALL, Lieutenant, Richard Aloysius. Beaumont Hamel, 1st July 1916. 1st Bn., Newfoundland Regiment. Son of Richard and Catherine Shortall, of Cross Roads, St. John's, Newfoundland. Enlisted September 1914 and commissioned April 1915. Employed engineer at Reid-Newfoundland Company. Gazetted 22nd April 1915. Wounded at Suvla, Gallipoli in November 1915, left Malta Hospital for Alexandria in February 1916 and rejoined his battalion in March 1916. Entered the Balkans, 19th September 1915. Contact for headstone inscription, Lt. Col. T. Nangle, Newfoundland Contingent. Memorial Ref. C. 44., Y Ravine Cemetery, Beaumont-Hamel, France.

He Died In The Service Of God And Humanity

 **SHORTER,** Second Lieutenant, Alfred George. Killed in action, 1st July 1916. 16th Bn., Durham Light Infantry probably attached to 15th or 18th Bn. Aged 27. Born in 1888 at Clifton, Bristol and was the youngest son of Alfred John and Eliza Shorter. He was a Unionist agent for North West Durham. Lieutenant Shorter was employed at the offices of Consett Iron Company, previous to the war and enlisted in the Royal Field Artillery on September 3rd 1914, acting bombardier receiving a commission in the Durham Light Infantry a few months later, March 1915. Entered France, 24th May 1916. Bell ringer at Christ Church, Consett. His mother of Derwent Street, Co. Durham applied for his medals. Memorial Ref. Pier and Face 14 A and 15 C., Thiepval Memorial, France.

SHUTTLEWORTH, Second Lieutenant, Ernest Ronald. Reported wounded, killed at Beaumont Hamel, 1st July 1916. 1st/8th Bn., Royal Warwickshire Regiment. Aged 22. Son of Thomas Ernest (Accountant) and Mary Edith Shuttleworth, of 5, Park Avenue, Riverdale Road, Sheffield. Born Sheffield 21st June 1894. Initially in Royal Navy, ordinary seaman, LZ/987 then second lieutenant, Royal Warwickshire Regiment commissioned 10th April 1915. Educated in Oxenford House School, St. Lawrence, Jersey, and then articled to a chartered accountant. University of Sheffield. Father applied for his medals. Memorial Ref. Pier and Face 9 A 9 B and 10 B., Thiepval Memorial, France.

Back Row Second Lieutenant Shuttleworth taken June 1916

 **SIBBIT,** Major, Henry. Killed in action, 1st July 1916. 22nd (Tyneside Scottish) Bn., Northumberland Fusiliers. Aged 27. Son of Thomas Henry and Janet Elizabeth Fisher Sibbit, of 26, Rothbury Terrace, Heaton, Newcastle-on-Tyne. Born January 1st, 1889. He was educated at Rutherford College, then Armstrong College, Newcastle University, 1909/1910 where he trained to be a teacher. He later became a teacher at West Jesmond County School. He was made temporary lieutenant on 18th November 1914. By 1916, Henry had risen to the rank of Major. He was wounded on 8th February 1916 and returned to duty within a week. Originally buried fifty yards south of La Boisselle. Effects returned were cheque book, card case and diary. Brother, Lieutenant George Bertrand Sibbit, also died in the war on the 27th September 1918. His father wrote to the War Office and enquired about Henry's oilskin coat, binoculars, cigarette case, compass, two flasks, gold signet ring, two watches and his revolver. His father applied for his medals. Memorial Ref. Pier and Face 10 B 11 B and 12 B., Thiepval Memorial, France. WO 339/18948

 **SILLARS,** Second Lieutenant, Harry Frederick Lionel. 1st July 1916. Majority of the casualties especially those of the officers occurred during the first two hours of fighting, served with 2nd Bn., Seaforth Highlanders according to the war diary. 4th Bn., Argyll and Sutherland Highlanders. Aged 21. Son of H. J. Sillars, J. P. and Mrs. Sillars, of Garden Cottage, Grove Road, Richmond, Surrey, formerly of Saltcoats, Ayrshire. Pupil at Ardrossan Academy. He entered the theatre of war on May 24th , 1915 and on leave 3rd to 11th June 1916. Commemorated Saltcoats War Memorial and Ardrossan Academy Roll of Honour. His father applied for his medals. Memorial Ref. Pier and Face 15 A and 16 C., Thiepval Memorial, France.

SILLERY, Lieutenant Colonel, Charles Cecil Archibald. Killed 1st July 1916. Commanding 20th (Tyneside Scottish) Bn., Northumberland Fusiliers. Aged 54. Born 15th October 1862 in Tasmania. Husband of Edith. Sillery, of the Grange, Scalby, Scarborough and father of Anthony and Charles. Eldest child of Major General Charles Jocelyn Cecil Sillery. Charles was Honorary Queen's Cadet, commissioned from the Royal Military College as a lieutenant in 5th Dragoon Guards on 10th March 1883 and moved from the Suffolk Regiment to the Madras Staff Corps on 14th August 1884. He was promoted captain on 10th March 1894 and major on 10th July 1901, becoming commandant of the Chindit Hills Battalion, Burma Military Police. Charles retired from the Indian Army on 10th March 1907. In 1908 his novel, 'A Curtain of Cloud' was published. By December 1915 Charles Sillery was brought out of retirement to lead the volunteers of Kitchener's new army. 20th Battalion Northumberland Fusiliers (1st Tyneside Scottish) was raised in October 1914 in Newcastle-upon-Tyne. They trained at Alnwick and on Salisbury Plain and underwent a week's musketry training in Hornsea in August 1915.

Their Commanding Officer was Lieutenant Colonel C. H. Innes Hopkins, who had to resign owing to ill health in December, and Charles Sillery replaced him. At Christmas 1915 the battalion were at Sandhill Camp, Longbridge Deverill near Warminster and on 9th January 1916 they embarked from Southampton for Le Havre, in France. On 26th January they marched to the trenches in the Fleurbaix sector. Scarborough Mercury of 14th July 1916 reports, "Colonel Sillery, of The Croft, Scalby, was killed in action on 1st July The gallant officer, better known as Major Sillery, was promoted Lieutenant Colonel about six months ago. Colonel C. C. A. Sillery, who was 52 years of age, and son of the late Major-General Sillery, served with the Punjab Frontier Force and went through the Burma war, being wounded and Mentioned in Despatches. He was for ten years commandant of the Chin Hills (Burma) and had served on the staff in South Wales before retiring. He, however, rejoined at the beginning the war and was second in command of the 11th York and Lancasters, but was transferred to the 1st Tyneside Scottish Northumberland Fusiliers. Lieut-Colonels Sillery and Lyle where were they had always wished to be, at the head of their battalions. They are buried side by side in Bapaume Post Military Cemetery, Albert.'

An extract from a letter written by Inky Bill, published in the North Western Courier on 29th November 1916, written to his wife, Edith, says "It may be some small consolation to you to be told by me how much I regret the loss of Colonel Sillery. He is a loss to the army and a great loss to the 34th Division in the 20th Northumberland Fusiliers. He died splendidly, leading his men over a shell swept zone – the admiration of everyone. He was with the last line of our battalion. He had not gone far before he was seriously wounded, but still gallantly struggled on, cheering his men, until hit again. He fell, never to rise. He died a gallant soldier, a fine type of English gentleman." Two brothers; Trooper Alfred Cyril Walter Sillery, died in the second Boer War on 21st October 1899. The other, Major John Jocelyn Doyne Sillery of 11th Bn., Manchester Regiment, died at Suvla Bay, Gallipoli, on 7th August 1915. Scalby War Memorial. His widow applied for his medals. Memorial Ref. I. G. 2., Bapaume Post Military Cemetery, Albert, France.

SIMMONDS, Second Lieutenant, Percy Grabham. After the death of Captain Cunningham he was left as the only remaining officer, and this was his first time he led his men into battle. He was organising a party of bombers in a communication trench before storming the German third line when a sniper's bullet hit him. Simmonds was killed instantly, Gommecourt, 1st July 1916. 'A' Company, 1st /9th Bn., London Regiment (Queen Victoria's Rifles). Aged 30. Born 4th July 1886 at Southend-on-Sea. Younger son of Harry and Eliza Mary Simmonds, of Holland Road, Clacton-on-Sea. Grandson of Thomas Dowsett JP, first Mayor of Southend. Passed through London University and Queen's College, Oxford a member of the OTC. At Mansfield College, Theology student in preparations for the congregational ministry when he joined the army. He became a Sunday school teacher, ran a club for boys and was a superintendent of a school in Saffron Walden. He was commissioned into the London Regiment in August 1915. Entered France, 4th March 1916. His brother, H. D. Simmonds, Clacton-on-Sea applied for his medals. Memorial Ref. Pier and Face 9 C., Thiepval Memorial, France.

Entry into the 'The Battle of the Somme Memories Souvenir and Roll of Honour, 1920' has the following poem;

He hated war, his soul abhorred
Even the thought of it.
But through it came the Master's call,
He faced the cost, not feared to fall,
So cheerfully he gave his all,
And called it "just his bit."

SIMPSON, Lieutenant, Thomas. He was seen to fall gallantly leading his men against the German trench, his men took the trench and held on to it for three days and two nights until relieved by fresh troops. 1st July 1916. 27th (Tyneside Irish) Bn., Northumberland Fusiliers. Aged 34. Son of Thomas Simpson and of Annie Simpson, of 74, Fern Avenue, Newcastle-on-Tyne. Born Newcastle-on-Tyne, 1882. Educated at Dame Allan's School. A gun maker's manager. Memorial Ref. Pier and Face 10 B 11 B and 12 B., Thiepval Memorial, France.

SLACKE, Captain, Charles Owen. He was "moving forward leading A company" this was the last I ever heard from him, killed in the third line of German trenches, 1st July 1916. Hoped he was a prisoner. 14th Bn., Royal Irish Rifles. Aged 44. Eldest son of Sir Owen Randal Slacke. Husband of Catherine Anne Slacke (nee Lanyon). Born Carrick-on-Suir on 21st January 1872. Volunteered with the Ulster Division on the outbreak of war. He married Kate Dixon, daughter of Sir Daniel Dixon, in 1902. Slacke was a businessman with premises at 16-18 Ashton Street and his company manufactured galvanised hollowware. Proprietor of Slacke & Co. Manufacturers, lived Wheatfield, Crumlin Road, Belfast. College of St. Columba Roll of Honour 1914 – 1918. For official purposes his death declared in October 1916 as 1st July, his pension paid to his wife and his two children; Randal Charles and Edith Avril Slacke.   Original burial map reference R.25.a.4.9. Inscription chosen by Mr. D. C. Slacke, c/o Messrs. Ross Kelly & Son, Solicitors, Donegal Street, Belfast. Memorial Ref. IV. A. 9., Connaught Cemetery, France.

I Have Fought A Good Fight II Timothy 4.7

SMITH, Captain, Donald Charnock. Killed between Leeds Trench and the front line, 1st July 1916. Reported wounded and missing and originally in hospital believed to be suffering from shock at Le Cateau or Landrecies. Badly wounded in the back, reported to be killed by a high explosive dropped right on top of the men finding shelter in a shell hole, 1st July 1916. B Coy. 16th Bn., West Yorkshire Regiment (Prince of Wales's Own). Aged 23. Only son of Mrs. Smith, of Grange House, Westgate Hill, Bradford, Yorks, and Edward James Smith (Chairman of the Health Committee, Bradford Corporation). Born 1st November 1893. Educated Mill Hill School, 1907 to 1911. Member of Batley RFC. He was engaged in his father's business and was about to set up his own account in the Bradford trade. Commissioned September 1914. Appointed 29th November 1915. Entered Egypt, 22nd December 1915. His mother applied for his medals. Memorial Ref. Pier and Face 2 A 2 C and 2 D., Thiepval Memorial, France.

SMITH, Captain, Douglas Wilberforce. Attached 20th Manchesters killed near Bois Francais, 1st July 1916. Royal Army Medical Corps attached 6th Bn., Manchester Regiment. Aged 39. Son of William Wilberforce Smith. Husband of Alice Wilberforce Smith (Butcher), of Castilla, Plaistow Lane, Bromley, London. Medical education at Guy's Hospital, 1898-1901, King's College, London. He was assistant house-surgeon to Sir Charters Symonds in 1901, and passed his Final FRCS in 1911. He was a civil surgeon with the South African Field Force. He was for a time Emden scholar in the Cancer Research Laboratory of the Middlesex Hospital, and wrote two reports on squamous cell carcinoma in respect of Alltmann's granules in the archives of the Middlesex Hospital cancer reports. He had also held the office of registrar of the Samaritan Free Hospital for Women. Entered France, 22nd July 1915. British Medical Association War Memorial. His widow applied for his medals, Bickley Park Road, Bickley, Kent. Children entitled to pension, Gwendolen Wilberforce and Brian Wilberforce. Original burial map reference 62D.F.9.d.9.7. Memorial Ref. VI. I. 3., Dantzig Alley British Cemetery, Mametz, France.

SMITH, Captain, George De Ville. Waited in reserve at zero hour 9.00am orders were received for D Coy., (Captain Smith) to advance to & hold the first & second German line respectively as a support to our first four waves who were then thought to have succeeded in reaching the German fourth line, led his company in the advance across the open, in face of heavy shell and machine-gun fire 1st July 1916. While moving forward they received verbal orders from the Brigadier that all the preceding waves had been decimated and consequently not reached their objective, the order to retire came a little too late. He was hit by a piece of shrapnel and died instantly, struck down by the side of Captain Normansell. 13th Bn., York and Lancaster Regiment. Educated St. David's College, Lampeter. Ordained St. Anne's Church, Birkenhead. Curate at St. Thomas's Church, Worsbrough. Commissioned 28th September 1914. H. Blundell Esq, Derby Road, Nottingham applied for his medals. Mother Annie Smith of Leicester applied for his pension. Memorial Ref. I. A. 15., Euston Road Cemetery, Colincamps, France.

SMITH, Second Lieutenant, Leonard George. Killed gallantly leading his platoon, 1st July 1916. Reports suggest he was either killed by a bomb or shrapnel when rounding a corner in the German second line trenches clearing the enemy out. His death occurred about noon and his body was covered by an overcoat. Died on his 20th birthday. B Coy. 2nd Bn., Essex Regiment. Aged 20. Eldest son of Alexander and Alice B. Smith, of Verulam, London Road, Pitsea, Essex. Native of Stoke Newington, London. Old boy of Southend High School for boys (1906 to 1908). Educated Central Foundation School, London and Southend Technical School. Employed as a motor engineer. Enlisted 30th September 1914 and commissioned on the 1st May 1915 as a second lieutenant in the 16th Bn., Middlesex Regiment but transferred to the 2nd Bn, Essex Regiment. Entered France, 13th April 1916. His Command Officer wrote 'The platoon reached the German lines but were unable to make progress. They made every effort to maintain their position and your son directed their operations with great coolness and gallantry. He was unfortunately struck on the head by a piece of shrapnel and was killed instantly. His death was deeply regretted.' Wickford War Memorial. Parents applied for his medals. Memorial Ref. Pier and Face 10 D., Thiepval Memorial, France.

SMITH, Second Lieutenant, Norman McNeill. Signalling Officer, reported missing and believed killed, 1st July 1916. 21st (Tyneside Scottish) Bn., Northumberland Fusiliers. Spotted by a private when he got to the wire lying dead. Aged 21. Younger son of Rupert and Annie Ellis O'Hara Smith, of 38, Greenhill Gardens, Edinburgh. Born 3rd February 1895. Educated Merchiston Castle, 1909 – 1911 in the Cadet Corps, 1909 to 1911. Edinburgh University and in the OTC. Second lieutenant, March 1915. Entered France February, 1916. Father applied for his medals. Memorial Ref. Pier and Face 10 B 11 B and 12 B., Thiepval Memorial, France. WO 339/26294

SMITH, Second Lieutenant, Percy Claud Jacomb. Killed in action, 1st July 1916. 1st Bn., East Yorkshire Regiment. Aged 19. Younger son of Sydney Smith, of Endwood, 18, Grassington Road, Eastbourne, Sussex and the Grand Hotel, Eastbourne. Born 20th October 1896 in Wimbledon. Educated Cheam School, St. Wilfred's, Bexhill, 1907 to 1911, and Malvern College, 1911 to 1914. Member of the OTC. Enlisted 29th December 1914. Gazetted second lieutenant from Royal Military College, 15th June 1915. Entered France, April 1916. Left £5,580 in his will to his father, Sydney. Member of the Stock Exchange. Effects were safety razor, fountain pen, badges, cheque book, advance book, pipe and razor. Parents applied for his medals. Memorial Ref. Pier and Face 2 C., Thiepval Memorial, France. WO 339/54050

SMITH, Second Lieutenant, Quintin Livingstone. Reported as missing 1st July 1916. 13th Bn. attd. 15th Bn., Lancashire Fusiliers. Aged 26. Son of Robert and Agnes Livingstone Smith, of 77, Davenport Street, Bolton. Born 24th July 1889. An old boy of Bolton Grammar School (1902-1904). He attended Manchester University 1907 to 1910 and obtained a BA and a Diploma in Education and a Teaching Diploma in 1911. Whilst at university he was an active member of the Debating Society, and a member of the OTC. He became a teacher at Latymer School, Edmonton, London. He was the first casualty master at the school. Commissioned November 1915 following OTC membership at Victoria University, Manchester. Entered France, 15th June 1916. Attached 15th Bn, 19th June 1916. His mother applied for his medals and officers pension. Memorial Ref. Pier and Face 3 C and 3 D., Thiepval Memorial, France.

SMITH, Captain, Raymond. Battalion advanced from assembly trenches at 8.00am and came under very heavy machine-gun fire, one of ten officers killed, 1st July 1916. A Company, 11th Bn., Border Regiment. Aged 27. Son of Mr. Francis Paul Smith, of Haltwhistle, Northumberland. Born 23rd May 1889. Formerly, worked in the family firm in South Africa and commanded the Haltwhistle Company of the 4th Northumberland Fusiliers. His brother also served with the Border Regiment. Attended Malvern College, 1903 to 1906. Entered France, 23rd November 1915. His father wrote to the Military Secretary on the 18th July 1916; 'I do not know what you think about this sort of thing but I call it absolutely inhuman, you have evidently made no enquiries whatsoever…if so you would know that the Commanding Officer was killed and all the officers either killed or wounded'. Two soldiers had reported him killed, one by a shell the other after being shot and fell and was breathing heavily. Effects returned were a pair of field glasses, revolver, electric pocket lamp, compass, whistle, platoon roll book, note book and a pencil. Father applied for his medals. Memorial Ref. Pier and Face 6 A and 7 C., Thiepval Memorial, France. WO 339/21844

SMITH, Captain, Rex Johnston. Died 1st July 1916. 15th Bn., York and Lancaster Regiment. Aged 34. Son of Cecilia Johnston Smith, of Morningside, Barnstaple Road, Ilfracombe, and Timothy Smith. Served in the South African Campaign with Lumsden's Horse. Admitted Queen Alexandra's Military Hospital At Millbank on the 30th October 1915 to 11th January 1916. Formerly Army Service Corps, 2nd Lieutenant. Embarked 4th November 1914. Mother applied for his medals and officer pension. Memorial Ref. III. H. 6., Blighty Valley Cemetery, Authuille Wood, France.

Faithful Unto Death

SMITH, Second Lieutenant, Robert. 1st July 1916. 2nd Bn., King's Own Yorkshire Light Infantry. Aged 35. Second son of Robert (Messrs. Plimpton and Smith, oil merchant of The Avenue, High Street) and Gertrude Smith, of 76, Trinity Road, Bridlington. He had been in France about three months. Partner in the firm of Messrs. Smith Bros., timber merchants, Queens' Dock and was a bachelor. Old Hymerian and former director of the Old Hymerians Club and East Riding Club. Memorial Ref. Pier and Face 11 C and 12 A., Thiepval Memorial, France.

SMITH, Lieutenant, Samuel Donard Irvine. Killed whilst leading his men in a charge on the third line of German trenches. Witness said he was wounded in the second line German trench by a bayonet in the breast and kept fighting and throwing bombs and killed by machine gun fire at the third line, 1st July 1916. 5th Bn. attd. D Coy., XIII Platoon, 1st Bn., Royal Irish Rifles. Initially reported missing and killed in August 1916 as a burial report has been received. Aged 25. Born 14th February 1891. Son of Mrs. M. Irvine-Smith, of Annesley Mansions, Newcastle, Co. Down, and J. Irvine Smith, B.L of 53 Leinster Square, Bayswater. Grandson of Reverend J. A. McMordie, of Seaforde, Co. Down. Educated Campbell College and St. Andrew's College. Served in the militia in Canada as a private from June 1913 to June 1914. Attested 22nd August 1914 Entered France, 19th May 1915. His mother applied for his medals. Body recovered from a point, Ovillers La Boiselle, 7 miles north east of Albert, sheet 57d. sq. X. 7. b.0.8 and reburied. Memorial Ref. III. J. 8., Blighty Valley Cemetery, Authuille Wood, France. W0339/1183

Beloved By All Who Knew Him

SMITH-MASTERS, Captain, Bruce Swinton, MC. 1st July 1916. D Coy., 2nd Bn., Essex Regiment. Aged 24. Third son of Reverend John Ernest (Vicar of South Banbury) and Eliza Margaret Smith-Masters, of Warren Lodge, near Newbury. Native of Kidmore End, Oxon. Born 31st January 1892 in Kidmore End, Oxfordshire. Reported killed on July 2nd, aged 24. Educated Eversley and Haileybury. At Haileybury he was in the second eleven, and subsequently he played in regimental cricket and for the Band of Brothers. Fine athlete. Came of an old Kent family and belonged to the Band of Brothers Cricket Club. Entered RMC Sandhurst in February 1911 and received commission in February 1912. Entered France on 22nd August 1914 with the 4th Division and at Le Cateau, Marne, Meteren, Le Bizet, Auchonville, Ypres and Tourvent Farm. He had been wounded twice in the autumn of 1914 and been awarded the Military Cross, 1916 in the Birthday Honours List. Brother Second Lieutenant George Arthur Smith-Masters also fell in August 1915. Commemorated Sons and Daughters of the Anglican Church Clergy. His father applied for his medals. Memorial Ref. I. H. 9., Sucrerie Military Cemetery, Colincamps, France.

Obedient Unto Death For God, King And Country Requiescat In Pace

SMITH-MAXWELL, Lieutenant, Archie Findlay. Killed in action leading his platoon and died like a very gallant gentleman, 1st July 1916. 17th Bn., Highland Light Infantry. Aged 18. Elder son of James Edward Smith and Mrs. Edith Smith-Maxwell, of Merksworth, Renfrewshire previously Old Town Lodge, Formby, Lancashire. Educated Holmwood School, Formby, Lancashire and Fettes College, Edinburgh where he was prominent in rugby football and a member of the OTC. Accepted a commission in the Highland Light Infantry, November 1914 whilst he was still at Fettes. February 1915 gazetted temporary second lieutenant with E. A. Gallie both of whom were in the Fettes College XV. Went to the Front, November 1915 when he was promoted to the rank of lieutenant. Death reported 11th July 1916. Medals applied for by his mother. Original burial map reference 57d.R.31.c.50.13 and identified by a disc and signet ring, reburied 1927. Memorial Ref. IX. E. 12., Serre Road Cemetery No.2, France.

To His Loved & Honoured Memory

SMYTH, Captain, William Haughton. No. 9 Platoon came on under the command of Captain W. H. Smyth who was killed almost immediately. They were the carrying platoon and some of them reached the first line with material, which after dumping there or carrying to second line was not required, as all the time was spent consolidating, holding the line and helping the fighting platoons. 1st July 1916. C Coy. 13th Bn., Royal Irish Rifles. Aged 37. Son of John and Florence Haughton Smyth, of Milltown House, Banbridge, Co. Down. Director of the firm, William Smyth & Co., Ltd., Banbridge. Prominently identified with the local Unitarian Church, treasurer of the congregation. Entered France, October 1915. Commemorated First Presbyterian Church, Banbridge and Banbridge War Memorial. Memorial Ref. Pier and Face 15 A and 15 B., Thiepval Memorial, France.

SOAMES, Lieutenant, Robert Eley. As a platoon commander, he took part in the famous football charge of the East Surreys against Montauban, over a mile and a quarter of open ground. In the course of the attack he was shot through the heart and killed next to his captain, known to be killed by 7.50am, close to the German wire, 1st July 1916. 8th Bn., East Surrey Regiment. Age 21. Born on 19th February 1895, the only son of Alfred Soames, (electrical engineer), of Grafton, Weybridge, and of Florence Soames. Educated at Rugby School from 1909 to 1913 (played on the VI) and at Oriel College, Oxford from 1913. Enlisted in the Public Schools Brigade in August 1914. Commissioned as a second lieutenant in September 1914. Went to France with the 8th (Service) Bn, East Surrey Regiment on 27th July 1915. Invalided to the UK in October 1915 with a wound to the head. Returned to France in February 1916. The record of his year at Oxford was summed up in these words-" A thoroughly good man in all relations of life; he did not make an enemy but many attached friends." Father applied for his medals. Memorial Ref. E. 30., Carnoy Military Cemetery, France.

SOMERS-SMITH, Captain, John Robert, MC. Prisoners taken and sent across by orders by 6.00pm nothing had been seen of the captain or Lieutenant Baker, reported killed in action in the enemy's trenches at Gommecourt, 1st July 1916. By 8.20pm the officers consisting of Captain Somers-Smith, (London Regiment), Lieutenant Petley, (London Rifle Brigade), Captain Leys Cox (Queen Victoria's Rifles), Second Lieutenant Arthur, (Cheshire Regiment), Captain Harvey (London Rifle Brigade) and Second Lieutenant Bovill (Queens Westminster Rifles) admitted they would be forced to return to the British lines and provided covering fire for the men. Making a run for the nearest shell holes, the only officer who returned was Lieutenant Petley, five officers being killed. Officer Commanding B Coy., 1st/5th Bn., London Regiment (London Rifle Brigade). Second son of Robert Vernon and Mary Getrude Wellington Somers-Smith. Born 15th December 1887 in Surrey lived at Deans Lane, Walton on the Hill, Surrey. Age 29. Educated Eton and Magdalen College, Oxford where he was a keen rower. Gazetted second lieutenant, 1906 and captain June 1914. Went to France, 3rd November 1914 injured 3rd June 1915 and rejoined 24th October 1915. Mentioned in Despatches. Military Cross awarded May 1915, for services at the Battle of Ypres. Married on the 25th July 1914 and had one son with Marjorie Duncan. Talbot House visitors book, page 4, dated 18th December 1915. His widow applied for his medals and pension to his child, Henry Cecil Willingdon Somers-Smith. His brother, Second Lieutenant Richard Wilingdon Somers-Smith was killed with the 7th Kings Royal Rifle Corps on the 30th June 1915. Memorial Ref. Pier and Face 9 D., Thiepval Memorial, France.

SOUPER, Second Lieutenant, Noel Beaumont. He met his death showing the courage he always showed, advancing on machine-gun positions at Casino Point alongside the Montauban-Mametz Road. 1st July 1916. 6th Bn., Royal Berkshire Regiment. Aged 40. Born on 20th December 1877, Eastbourne. Son of the Reverend Francis Abraham & Fanny Emmeline Souper, of Grantchester Meadows, Cambridge. Received his early education under his father at St. Andrew's, Eastbourne. Between 1893 and 1897 Noel was in Canada where he tried his hand at being a farmer and schoolmaster, returning to the UK in June 1897 where his father and step-mother were now living at the Vicarage, Hilton his father being the Vicar. Noel studied at St. John's 1899 – 1902 Pembroke College, Cambridge with the intention of joining the clergy, before returning to Canada as a schoolmaster in June 1905, here he later met and married Rosalie Frances Noire in April 1910 of 54, Fitz James Avenue, London. Resided Cowichan, Vancouver Island. Enlisted 23rd September 1914 into the 15th Gordon Highlanders as part of the Canadian Expeditionary Force, 28675 and following his transfer back to the UK, was re-commissioned into the 6th Bn. Royal Berkshire Regiment going to the Front in December 1915. Appointed temporary second lieutenant, December 1914. Commemorated Hilton Lychgate Memorial and Newnham War Memorial. Known as 'Old soup-can'. His widow applied for his medals. Memorial Ref. Pier and Face 11 D., Thiepval Memorial, France.

SPALDING, Second Lieutenant, Albert Goodwill. He had gallantly descended to bomb an enemy dug-out about 8.00am and with this accomplished he was shot and killed at short range, 1st July 1916. 10th Bn., Royal Inniskilling Fusiliers. Aged 25. Adopted son of Albert Goodwill (businessman and former baseball player) and Elizabeth Spalding (nee Churchill). Born in Illinois. Worked at the Paris office of his father's sporting goods company and returned at the outbreak of war. Originally rejected at the recruiting office due to be an American he then enlisted as a Canadian. Attested in Chelsea. Joined the 5th Dragoon Guards on the 29th August 1914 and transferred to the Coldstream Guards where he became a lance-corporal, 13808 on the 27th April 1915. In 3rd Bn., Coldstream Guards, and after the Battle of Loos obtained his commission, 6th December 1915. He took part in the fighting at Festubert, Hill 70, Hulluch and Loos and also formed one of Sergeant Brooke's, VC bombing party in November 1915. Reported to be buried in trench where he died and grave subsequently lost. K. Spalding applied for his medals, Pasadena, California, USA. Memorial ref. Pier and Face 4 D and 5 B., Thiepval Memorial, France.

SPATZ, Second Lieutenant, Walter Rudolf Carl. Killed after being driven out of the German front line trench and his body was seen in No Man's Land, 1st July 1916. 2nd Bn., Middlesex Regiment. Enlisted 6th August 1914. Second lieutenant, 23rd April 1915. Formerly 1546, Artists Rifles. Son of Otto Friedrich Spatz and Jenny Spatz, 11 Lyndhurst Road Hampstead London. Born 2nd March 1894, Germany Apia former German Samoa. Brother R. Spatz, Colet House, Giddon Road, West Kensington. Attended St. Paul's School and a member of the OTC. Memorial Ref. Pier and Face 12 D and 13 B., Thiepval Memorial, France. WO 339/29444

SPENCER, Second Lieutenant, Arthur. Reported missing, Ovillers near Albert, 1st July 1916 and three months later reported killed on that date. Gallantly led his men in the assault against overwhelming fire. 15th Bn., York and Lancaster Regiment. Aged 25. Only son of Squire Radcliffe (coal factor) and Kate Spencer, of 54, Gawber Road, Barnsley. Born Barnsley 11th May 1891. Educated High School and New College, Harrogate. Served indentures with Messrs. Needham & Co. Engineers and commenced motor and cycle engineer at Goldthorpe. Trained with Yorkshire Dragoons for four years prior to outbreak of war obtained a commission in February 1915. Served in France from 5th December 1915. Father applied for his medals. Memorial Ref. V. B. 30., Blighty Valley Cemetery, Authuille Wood, France.

"The Greatest...... Is Love" 1.Cor.13.13

SPROAT, Lieutenant, Gerald Maitland. His battalion was detailed to attack the village of Montauban and having captured their objective, were awaiting the enemy's counter-attack. Lieutenant Sproat was struck by a shell while walking up and down the line under heavy fire directing his men where to dig themselves in. His brother James Sproat survived attack but was killed on the 11th July. 1st July 1916. 11th Bn. attd. 17th Bn., Manchester Regiment. Aged 22. Eldest son of Thomas and Mary Caroline Sproat, of 1, Rock Park, Rock Ferry, Cheshire. Attended Winchester College, 1906 to 1912. He entered college third on the Roll from The Leas, Hoylake, and showed a special aptitude for ancient history. He became a prefect, played in college XV and in 1912 won a scholarship to Magdalen College, Oxford. He obtained a commission in the 11th Bn., Manchester Regiment in September 1914 and in July 1915 sailed for the Dardanelles. He took part in the landing at Suvla Bay in August but was invalided home that September. In May 1916 he went to France with 17th Bn., Manchester Regiment. His Medal Index Card states theatres of war of Montauban, Gallipoli, France. Medals to be sent to his father. Memorial Ref. Pier and Face 13 A and 14 C., Thiepval Memorial, France. WO 339/12041

STACK, Captain, John Masfen. Killed in action, 1st July 1916. 1st/6th Bn., North Staffordshire Regiment. Aged 26. Second son of Col. Edward Churchill Stack, RAMC, FRCSI, BD and Susan of the Soho, Burton-on-Trent. Born on 28th August 1889 at Stanningley, Pudsey, Yorkshire. Entered Epsom College, 21st September 1905. He was a member of the 2nd Volunteer Battalion, North Staffordshire Regiment and served as a drummer between 28th August 1906 and 31st January 1908. He obtained a commission and was promoted to second lieutenant in the 6th North Staffordshires on 1st February 1908 and lieutenant on 15th July 1909. He resigned from the regiment on 25th November 1911. He applied for a commission in the Auxiliary Forces on 14th May 1913 and rejoined the army on the 19th May. He went to France on 4th March 1915 and served in 3/6 Staffordshires from 22nd April 1915 until he was wounded in the attack on the Hohenzollern Redoubt on 13th October 1915 with a gunshot wound to the right leg. He was made temporary captain 13th January 1916. He applied for a commission in the regular army on 22nd February 1916. Second Lieutenant Wilfred Arthur Lawrence provides an eye-witness account: "After going about 100 yards through the smoke cloud, Captain Stack dropped and rolled over. I said, 'Are you hurt badly?' and he replied, 'I think so. You go and take charge of the men'. I went off and hadn't gone ten yards when I was sent down with shrapnel in the leg. I crawled back to Stack and asked, 'Where have you got it?' and he said, 'I think I have got it badly in the stomach'. I asked if I could do anything for him and he said, 'No thank you, Lawrence'. Played for Burton Rugby Football Club. John's father went out to the front with the 6th North Staffordshires in February 1915 as the Medical Office. His mother applied for his medals. Original burial map reference 57D.E.28.a.3.0. identified as a cross was erected, reburied 1919. Memorial Ref. II. B. 20., Gommecourt Wood New Cemetery, Foncquevillers, France.

STAINTON, Second Lieutenant, Robert Meres. 1st July 1916. 10th Bn., York and Lancaster Regiment. Aged 22. Only son of Walton and Annie Alice Stainton, of Hill Crest, 37, Mount Pleasant, Barrow-in-Furness, Lancs. He was a former pupil at Barrow's Municipal Secondary School for boys and Nottingham College. Signed up as a private soldier with the King's Own Royal Lancaster Regiment and rose through the ranks, lance corporal, 17693. Entered France, 18th May 1915. The Barrow School's magazine the Barrovian noted: "Bob Stainton was looked upon as one of the bravest of the brave. He often took work which brought him into the greatest peril to save his men and he seems to have been a shining example of the fearless officer associated with our great British regiments." His pocket book and silver watch had stopped a bullet in January 1915. Gazetted 3rd October 1915. Member of Nottingham University OTC. Lieutenant-Colonel Ridgway, the battalion commanding officer said: "His death is a great loss to me, as he was an officer who showed great promise of doing good work in the times that are coming. His company was one of the first over the parapet on the memorable occasion and I feel sure that he was one of the first to get over." Reported he was buried in the field of battle along with other men of his company. London County Council, Education Officers Department, Teaching Staff. Medals applied for by his father. Memorial Ref. Pier and Face 14 A and 14 B., Thiepval Memorial, France. WO 339/44272

STEAD, Second Lieutenant, Ralph. Stead was in the front line with a few men scraped together for a rush, having been wounded in the knee, mown down by machine-gun fire and found dead in a shell hole, by Second Lieutenant Laxton, 1st July 1916. C Coy., 16th Bn., West Yorkshire Regiment (Prince of Wales's Own). Aged 31. Youngest son of Arthur Charles Stead, of Necton, Swaffham, Norfolk. Attended Thetford Grammar School. Enlisted, 4th September, 1914 at Norwich with the Public Schools Battalion. Gazetted to the 22nd Manchesters as second lieutenant on the 3rd April 1915 transferred to the West Yorks in July 1915 and qualified as company commander in the spring 1916, rejoining his battalion in May. Entered France, 24th May 1916. Schoolmaster at Paignton College, Devon. Wrote to his parents 28th June 1916; "The advance has come at last and early tomorrow we shall attack. If I come through I shall be able to tell you about our part in the greatest battle that ever shall be. If I should be killed you must not fret as it is the finest death to die, and I have no fear of meeting it. I must stop now. With love, Ralph." His father applied for his medals. Memorial Ref. I. E. 53., Serre Road Cemetery No.1, France.
Enlisted In Royal Fusiliers U.P.S. Sept.1914

STEPHENSEN, Second Lieutenant, Olaf Stephen. Reported wounded 22nd July 1916 later changed to missing, 1st July 1916. Informant stated that he was killed as he was in the same shell hole as him. 8th Bn., King's Own Yorkshire Light Infantry. Aged 29. Born 19th May 1897, Cottingham, East Riding Yorkshire. Husband of Kathleen F. Stephensen, of Nokomis, Saskatchewan, Canada. Homestead farmer previously clerk. Enlisted 30th June 1915, Saskatoon, Saskatchewan in the Princess Patricias Canadian Light Infantry, No. 476041. Commissioned 24th January 1916. Intended address was 31 Salisbury Street, Hull. His widow, Kathleen applied for his medals. Memorial Ref. Pier and Face 11 C and 12 A., Thiepval Memorial, France. WO 339/53824

STEPHENSON, Second Lieutenant, Erik. Reported wounded 22nd July 1916 later changed to missing, 1st July 1916. 3rd Bn., York and Lancaster Regiment. To be second lieutenant 16th July 1915. Medal Index Card has surname amended in 1922 to be Stephensen. Memorial Ref. V. B. 38., Blighty Valley Cemetery, Authuille Wood, France.

STEVENSON, Lieutenant, Leonard William Hugh, MC. Killed, whilst leading his men in the famous charge of the Ulster Division, fell in the firing line at the head of his men, killed taking the second line of German trenches, 1st July 1916. 9th Bn., Royal Inniskilling Fusiliers. Born 25th June 1896. Younger son of Mr. Isaac Stevenson, Hampstead Hall, Londonderry, and nephew of Mr. J. M. MacCaw, M.P. Educated at Foyle College, Londonderry, and Eastman's RVA School, Winchester, Hampshire. Sherborne (1910 – 1914), where he was in the OTC. He entered Trinity College, Dublin, June, 1914, and passed his Junior Fresh whilst awaiting his commission. He received his commission in October, 1914, and went to France with the regiment, 5th October, 1915. He was awarded the Military Cross in May, 1916, 'for conspicuous gallantry and promptness during a successful raid on the enemy's trenches. His quickness at a critical moment saved two minutes, and the enemy were actually issuing from their dug-outs as his party entered their trenches. Later he organised a party, and brought in a wounded man under fire.' His brother Lieutenant M. M. Stevenson served with the Indian Army.

Father applied for his medals, c/o W. J. M. Law Esq., Eaton Square, SW. Londonderry (Derry) War Memorial. Memorial Ref. Pier and Face 4 D and 5 B., Thiepval Memorial, France.

STEWART, Second Lieutenant, Robert. Killed in action, 1st July 1916. 1st Bn., King's Own Scottish Borderers. Aged 26. Eldest son of James and Mary Stewart, of Hawthorn Cottage, Station Road, Kelty, Fife. Educated Dunfermline High School. Graduated with an MA from Edinburgh University, 1912. Assistant teacher at Kelty Public School for three years prior to enlisting. Enlisted Royal Scots, September, 1914. France, November, 1914. Invalided, February 1915. Gazetted 1st KOSB, May 1915. Sent to Egypt to join battalion and transferred to France, March 1916. Memorial Ref. Pier and Face 4 A and 4 D., Thiepval Memorial, France.

STEWART, Captain, Robert Colin. He was in the attack near Ovillers after leading his company with the utmost coolness and gallantry under a terrific fire was seen to fall, mortally wounded. He led his men in the most gallant way and died taking part in the biggest battle, 1st July 1916. 8th Bn., York and Lancaster Regiment. Aged 24. Younger son of John and Mary Stewart, of Thornleigh, Huddersfield. Born at Peebles, Scotland. Educated at Mr. Roscoe's School, Harrogate and Uppingham leaving 1910. He shot at Bisley for his school in 1908 and 1909. At the outbreak of war he enlisted in the ranks. A few months later he obtained a commission in the York and Lancaster Regiment and was gazetted captain before going to the Front in August 1915. His elder brother, Captain Ian Stewart was wounded. Commemorated St. Stephen's Church, Lindley, Huddersfield. Memorial Ref. V. A. 17., Blighty Valley Cemetery, Authuille Wood, France

STEWART, Second Lieutenant, William Johnston. Reported missing, 1st July 1916. 10th Bn. attd. 9th Bn., Royal Irish Fusiliers. Only son of Mr. and Mrs. Robert Stewart, 9 Queen's Park Avenue, Crosshill, Glasgow. Born in Glasgow in 1893. Age 23. In 1913 he enrolled at the University of Glasgow in the Faculty of Arts, aged 20. He studied Moral Philosophy and Latin. During his first year of study. Enlisted September 1914. Argyll and Sutherland Highlanders, private, 2113. Entered France, 1st May 1915. On the 6th January 1916, made a temporary second lieutenant, on probation. Twice wounded. Still missing 26th December 1916. Nephew of Misses Johnston, High Street, Enniskillen. Father applied for his medals. Memorial Ref. Pier and Face 15 A., Thiepval Memorial, France.

STIMPSON, Second Lieutenant, John Crockett. Seriously wounded on the 1st July after 4.00pm and officially reported death as the 2nd July 1916. School records indicate 1st July 1916. 1st /8th Bn., West Yorkshire Regiment (Prince of Wales's Own). Aged 19. Second son of Mr. and Mrs. Alfred Stimpson, of Cheyne Walk, Northampton. OTC Leeds University. Born at Northampton on May 1897. He came to Oundle in September 1911, entering School House and remaining at school until July 1913. Stimpson joined the West Yorkshire Regiment in August 1915 as an lieutenant from the Leeds University OTC, and went to France with them, 25th May 1916. Father applied for his medals. Medal Index Card has missing, 2nd July 1916. Memorial Ref. Pier and Face 2 A 2 C and 2 D., Thiepval Memorial, France.

STOCKS, Major, Harris Laurance, DSO. Reported wounded, three times, when the enemy gathered for the counter attack he was lost sight off in the darkness, 1st July 1916. Reported to have been wounded in the arm and carried on encouraging his men, he was then shot through the body and reported to have been taken prisoner. He was bandaged by Private Bishop whom himself was later mortally wounded. 15th Bn., Royal Scots. Aged 45. Son of Provost J. T. Stocks, of Kirkcaldy. Steamship owner. Resided St. Katherine's, Kirkcaldy, head of the firm, Messrs. Stocks, Turnbull & Co. Kirkcaldy and London Shipping Company. Leader, Kirkcaldy Boys' Brigade and Boy Scouts. Captain, 4th Kirkcaldy Coy,. Boys Brigade. Entered France, 9th January 1916. Telegram was received by Mr. Robert Stocks his brother, he wired for information and got no reply so he went to London and found a captain of the battalion who had seen Major Stocks in action who had informed him he was shot through the arm, but did not know he was missing. A more accurate report came from his man-servant.

In his will left £25,000 to the Kirkcaldy Boy's Brigade. Mr. R. Stocks applied for his brother's medals, Kirkcaldy. Body not found until 1917. Memorial Ref. III. D. 11., Bouzincourt Communal Cemetery Extension, France. WO 339/15563

Son Of Provost J.T. Stocks Captain 4th Kirkcaldy Company, The Boy's Brigade Steamship Owner

STONEHOUSE, Lieutenant, Charles. Killed near German lines, Serre, 1st July 1916. He was wounded in the wrist, and as his orderly Private Roland Banks from Accrington was dressing his wound, he was killed, a few moments later Lieutenant Stonehouse was killed. 11th Bn., East Lancashire Regiment. Born 15th May 1882 at Blackburn. Third son of Francis and Mary Ann Stonehouse; lived at Irving Place, Blackburn. Enlisted 17th September 1914 as private, 15360, East Lancashire Regiment; Appointed lance corporal 4th December 1914; Second lieutenant, 18th January 1915; Lieutenant 20th June 1915. Entered France, 8th March 1916. Served his apprenticeship with Messrs. Briggs and Wolstenholme, architects and before enlisting was with a Manchester firm. His mother applied for his medals. Private Banks and Lieutenant Stonehouse have no known grave. Memorial Ref. Pier and Face 6 C., Thiepval Memorial, France.

STONOR, Second Lieutenant, Cuthbert Anthony. Reported missing, 1st July 1916. 1st Bn., Royal Inniskilling Fusiliers. Born in 1887, the youngest son of Mr. and Mrs. Charles J. Stonor, of Llanvair, Ascot. He was educated at Downside College, and then spent some years in the East. He was on his way home, and had reached Colombo on August 4th 1914, where he heard that war had just been declared. Soon after his return home he enlisted in the Public Schools Battalion, 16th Middlesex Regiment, private and on June 27th, 1915, he was given his commission in the 3rd Bn., Royal Inniskilling Fusiliers. He was sent to the Front on May to last, and was reported as "missing" on July 1st. His body was recovered some weeks later, and was identified by a letter from his mother which was found on him. The officer who discovered him said :—" He must have fallen leading his men into action, as many bodies of men in his own regiment were found around him'. His mother applied for his medals. Medal Index Card has Cuthbert Mary Anthony Stonor as the contact. Memorial Ref. D. 99., Y Ravine Cemetery, Beaumont-Hamel, France.

STRANGE, Second Lieutenant, William Frederick. Killed by machine gunners whilst he tried to pass through a narrow gap in the wire and cross Fern Trench, the German front line . 1st July 1916. Attached B Coy., 1/16th London Regiment from the 1st /2nd Bn., London Regiment (Royal Fusiliers). Son of Joseph James and Mary Ann Strange of St. Dunstan's School. Born 16th January 1889. Educated St. Dunstans' College. Managing clerk. Resided 142, Inderwick Road, Stroud Green. Formerly, private 2208 and had recently returned form Gallipoli. Prior to the war was a member of the 1st Cadet Battalion, King's Royal Rifle Corps. Memorial Ref. Pier and Face 9 D and 16 B., Thiepval Memorial, France.

STROUD, Second Lieutenant, Reginald Gordon. Killed in action, 1st July 1916. C Coy. 9th Bn., York and Lancaster Regiment. Aged 20. Son of George Gordon and Hannah Stroud, of "Jarrowville," Lowther Hill, Forest Hill, London. Gazetted April 1915. Entered France, 27th August 1915. H. N. Stroud applied for medals due to his late brother, Barclays Bank, Stock Office, George's Yard. Memorial Ref. V. J. 12., Blighty Valley Cemetery, Authuille Wood, France.

Tranquil You Lie Your Knightly Virtue Proved Your Memory Hallowed

STRUGNELL, Second Lieutenant, Alfred Charles. Killed in the attack on Montauban as they crossed No Man's Land, 1st July 1916. 2nd Bn., Yorkshire Regiment. Born Aldershot, 9th March 1889. Attended Watford Grammar School, 1903 to 1906. Son of Mr. and Mrs. Alfred Charles and Dora Strugnell, New Road, Croxley Green. Enlisted in the 16th Lancers 23rd June 1906, No. 5568 at London and rose to the rank of sergeant, (August 1913) and transferred to the 2nd Bn., being commissioned 14th June 1916. Went to France, 17th August 1914. Watford Grammar School Book of Remembrance. Father listed as next of kin and applied for his medals. Mother Dorothy Eileen Strugnell claimed officers pension an additional note made that she was the widow of Bandmaster & Warrant Officer A. C. Strugnell. Memorial Ref. Pier and Face 3 A and 3 D., Thiepval Memorial, France. WO 339/66152

STUBBS, Second Lieutenant, Cecil Arthur. Suffered a small wound in his stomach and another in his back, he was shot by a bullet clean through his body, five minutes after being made comfortable he passed away, officially 2nd July 1916. His batman, R. Bastick wrote I was with him up to the point of being hit, nobody could have acted in a more courageous manner then he did when he led his platoon out of the trench across the open under a terrible storm of lead and shell. Died at No. 43 Casualty Clearing station. D Coy., 2nd Bn ., London Regiment (Royal Fusiliers) attached support D Coy., 1st/16th London Regiment (Queen's Westminster Rifles). Aged 22. Son of Arthur and Martha Ann Stubbs, of 26, Grafton Road, Worthing, Sussex. Born 1894. Pupil at Shoreham College, 1906. Entered France, 5th June 1916. Father applied for his medals. Memorial Ref. II. D. 1., Warlincourt Halte British Cemetery, Saulty, France.

God Bless Our Boy

SUTCLIFFE, Second Lieutenant, Herbert Richard Charles. 1st July 1916. 24th (Tyneside Irish) Bn., Northumberland Fusiliers. Transferred for service for Trench Mortar Battery, 30th May 1916. Born 19th August 1891. Enlisted 3rd September 1914 with the 9th Bn., Northumberland Fusiliers, served in ranks. Commissioned 1st March 1915. Entered France, 12th January 1916. Next of kin; Father, F. C. Sutcliffe, 46 Wingrove Road, Newcastle-on-Tyne. Enquiries received from Mrs. J.E. Sutcliffe, 15 Burns Street, Nottingham. Originally buried 650 yards SW of La Boisselle Church in November 1916. Reburied January 1920. Date of death changed from the 2nd to the 1st July. Father applied for his medals. Original burial map reference 57d.X.19.b. and grave marked by a cross. Memorial Ref. V. A. 2., Ovillers Military Cemetery, France. WO 339/24495

Northumberland Fusiliers 24th Battalion Officers Included Byrne, Sutcliffe, Thompson, MacKenzie, Horrox and Howard

SUTTON, Second Lieutenant, Cyril John. Wounded as soon as he went over the top with Second Lieutenant R. T. Hardman and Lieutenant Swann, 1st July 1916. Second Lieutenant Hardman tried to bring him in but was killed by machine gun fire. In the same action Sergeant Potts was awarded the DCM for conspicuous gallantry and devotion. During a retirement which had become necessary owing to casualties, he remained to pick up, and ultimately carried back under heavy fire a wounded comrade. He also made a gallant effort to succour two officers (Second Lieutenant Hardman & Sutton) who unfortunately were found to be dead. Royal Field Artillery. Aged 25. Only son of John (schoolmaster) and Sarah Ann Sutton, Of "Pittville," 11, Milton Avenue, East Ham, London. Born on 11th May 1891 in East Ham, Essex. After attending Mile End Pupil Teachers Secondary School and Birkbeck College, he matriculated as a non-collegiate student in 1911, migrating to Pembroke College, Oxford in 1912. Entered France, 30th January 1916. Father applied for medals in respect of deceased. Memorial Ref. Pier and Face 1 A and 8 A., Thiepval Memorial, France.

SWAINSON, Captain, Francis Gibbon, MC. Killed shortly after leaving the second line German trench (Feint Trench), reported as missing, he was waiting to get through the gap in the barb wire, 1st July 1916. Commanding A Coy. 1st /16th Bn., London Regiment (Queen's Westminster Rifles). Aged 21. Younger son of Mrs. Eliza Prowse Swainson (wealthy Preston tea merchant), of Rosebank,"Knowsley, Prescot, Lancs, and G. A. Swainson. Born on 2nd October 1894 at 49, Watling Street Road, Fulwood, Preston. Repton School Memorial. (1909). Resided 101, Lee Road, Blackheath, Kent. Entered France, 1st November 1914. Talbot House visitors book, page 11, dated 28th December 1915. At first he was only reported as missing and his mother Eliza spent the next year trying to find out what had happened to him. Eventually the army wrote to Eliza at her home at Breeze Hill, Cadley, Preston, to inform her that all hope was lost. Military Cross awarded 1916. His mother applied for his medals. Memorial Ref. Pier and Face 13 C., Thiepval Memorial, France.

Officers of the 16th Queens Westminster Rifles
Back Row third from left Captain Swainson

SWAN, Second Lieutenant, George Grieve. Killed by machine-gun fire near Mametz, at about 11.00am, whilst trying to organise his platoon, 1st July 1916. 4th Bn. attd. 22nd Bn., Manchester Regiment. Elder son of Mr. and Mrs. T. Swan (Messrs. Swan, Mackie & Co), Anfield, Kirkcaldy. 27 years of age, served his apprenticeship with Mr. W. Lockhart, civil engineer, and afterwards was engaged in the civil engineers' department of the North British Railway, Edinburgh. He, along with his brother Tom, enlisted in the 15th Bn., Royal Scots when it was formed shortly after war broke out. They had been members of Kirkcaldy High School Cadet Corps, and after serving for some time in the ranks obtained commissions, George being appointed to the Manchester Regiment, while his brother went to the 7th Border Regiment. Lieutenant George Swan was in the reserve of officers, and was sent out to France, 29th May 1916. Thomas Swan applied for medals due to his late brother. Memorial Ref. Pier and Face 13 A and 14 C., Thiepval Memorial, France. WO 339/46252

SWEETNAM, Captain, Richard Rodney Stephen. Died 1st July 1916. 125th Bty., Royal Field Artillery. Attended Berkhamsted School. Cadet of the OTC to be Temporary Second Lieutenant, 19th January 1915. To be temporary captain whilst employed with the Trench Mortar Battery, entered France, 16th April 1916. Born Pembroke. Planter. Seremban Estate, N. Sembilan, Malaya. Father, J. L. Sweetnam, Esq., RN., MD., York Avenue, Hove, Sussex applied for his medals. Unable to act as best man for his step-brother, Captain Lionel Berkeley Harbord in December 1915 as he was uable to get leave, the place being filled by Lieutenant Boileau, Gurkha Rifles. Memorial Ref. I. I. 70., Sucrerie Military Cemetery, Colincamps, France.

SWIFT, Second Lieutenant, William. 8th Bn., Lincolnshire Regiment Died between 1st July 1916 and the 3rd July 1916. Date of death on Grave Registration form has the 13th July although other officers on the same form have the 1st July. Reported locally as killed on the 2nd July. Archive record has the 1st to 3rd July 1916. Eldest son of Mr. and Mrs. G. H. Swift of Morton, Bourne, Lincoln. Born 2nd April 1889. Closely associated with the Bourne Council School as a pupil teacher. During his apprenticeship he matriculated at London University. Career at Peterborough Training College was very successful. In residence at St. Catharine's College, Cambridge University and named on the memorial. Married 12th December 1915 to May Swift. Commissioned 23rd January 1915. Daughter born 2nd November 1916 and named Regan Fricourt Smith. Effects were pocket book, pipe, fountain pen, protractor, identity disc and shoulder strap. Original burial map reference 57d.X.26.d.8.4 Reinterred 1919. Memorial Ref. II.M. 9. Gordon Dump Cemetery, Ovillers La Boisselle, Somme, France. WO 339/40260

St. Catharine's College

SYKES, Lieutenant, Charles. 1st July 1916. General List. 63rd Trench Mortar Battery detached from the 10th Bn., York and Lancaster Regiment. Medal Index Card states date of death as the 1st July 1916 and forename as Claude. CWGC has been amended from the 2nd July to the 1st July 1916. Entered France, 3rd January 1916. Next of kin; Mrs. L. Sykes, Seaview, Arnside, Westmorland. Memorial Ref. Pier and Face 4 C., Thiepval Memorial, France.

SYMINGTON, Lieutenant, Percy George. Killed instantaneously on the Somme, whilst leading his platoon at Thiepval, 1st July 1916. D Coy. 17th Bn., Highland Light Infantry. Aged 20. Third son of George Elder Symington and Mary Jane C. Symington, of Windyhaugh, Troon, Ayrshire. Born Paisley 31st March 1896. Educated Loretto, Musselburgh and was due to enter King's College, Cambridge. Member of Troon Golf Club and promising golfer. His cousin, Captain Boyd was killed with him. Enlisted, August 1914. Granted a commission with the battalion on its formation, D Coy. Entered France, October 1915. Death reported 11th July 1916. Father applied for his medals. Original burial map reference 57d.R.31.c.04.61 and buried as an unknown British officer, Lieut. HLI and later identified as Lieutenant Symington, reburied 1927. Memorial Ref. XVI. K. 14., A.I.F. Burial Ground, Flers, France.

For His King His Country And His God

SYMONDS, Second Lieutenant, Frank James. Blew his whistle and was one of the first up the scaling ladder with his revolver in one hand and his cigarette in the other, 'Come on, boys'. Reported missing, last seen fatally wounded in a shell hole, killed in action, 1st July 1916. Scouting officer, No. 7 Platoon, 16th Bn., West Yorkshire Regiment (Prince of Wales's Own). Aged 20. Born 27th October 1895. Son of Ernest and Annie Mary Symonds, of Brookmead, The Rise, Sheringham, Norfolk formerly Crown Street, Bury St. Edmunds. Educated at Thetford Grammar School and obtained a commission through Captain T. H. Russell, West Yorks Regiment. After a short time he was made scouting officer previously being in the scouting movement. Member of the Bury Hockey Club. Joined the 17th Royal Fusiliers. Appointed 11th May 1915. Father applied for his medals. Memorial Ref. Pier and Face 2 A 2 C and 2 D., Thiepval Memorial, France.

Entry into the 'The Battle of the Somme Memories Souvenir and Roll of Honour, 1920' has the following poem;

He died the noblest death a man can die,

Fighting for God, and Right, and Liberty,

And such a death is Immortality.

TANQUERAY, Lieutenant, Frederic Baron. Seen going forward about midday shouted to his friend, 'Good luck' at Beaumont Hamel, reported "wounded and missing and believed to have died" on that day 1st July 1916. B Coy. 16th Bn., Middlesex Regiment. Aged 24. Younger son of Frederic Thomas (solicitor) and Catherine Tanqueray, of Woburn, Beds. Attended Sherborne, 1905 to 1908 entered the school from The Knoll, Woburn Sands. Cadet Corps. He was for fifteen months with a London firm at the end of his articles, and having passed the final Law Examination in January, 1914, was shortly afterwards admitted solicitor and joined his father in business some six months before the outbreak of war. Promptly enlisted in the Public Schools Battalion (Middlesex Regiment) and was soon promoted to sergeant, No. 117. Early in 1915 he was offered, and accepted, a commission as temporary second lieutenant in the same battalion and went to France in the following November. He was with his regiment at the Front all through the winter of 1915 and the spring of 1916, and came home on short leave at Whitsuntide, 1916. The Chaplain of the regiment wrote of him that he 'was a splendid fellow and had endeared himself to all as a cheery, unselfish comrade.' Father applied for his medals. Body recovered 1917. Memorial Ref. B. 62., Beaumont-Hamel British Cemetery, France.

God Proved Them And Found Them Worthy For Himself Wisdom III. 5

TAPLIN, Second Lieutenant, Albert William. The company had suffered more casualties before going over than any other; its leading wave had considerable difficulty in getting through their own wire, and reached the German lines only to find themselves confronted with a broad belt of wire, through which possibly 2nd Lieutenant Taplin – certainly Sergeant King and some men of the leaving wave – found a gap and reached temporarily the German line, but from which the remainder were beaten back by a withering fire of bombs, machine-guns and rifles, 1st July 1916. No. 5 Platoon, B Coy., 1st /12th Bn., London Regiment (The Rangers). Aged 24. Son of William James and Sarah Taplin, of 12, North Side, Paddington, London. Born 8th June 1892. Resided 12, Wharf House, North Wharf Road, Paddington. Educated Paddington Technical Institute. Cashier with Public Trustee Office, The Strand. Private, 3021. 14th London Regiment. Commissioned 28th November 1915. Marylebone lad associated with St. Mary's, Bryanstone Square. Entered France, 8th March 1915. Medals to his fiancee, Miss M. Bluck. Memorial Ref. Pier and Face 9 C., Thiepval Memorial, France.

TART, Second Lieutenant, Cyril James. Killed by shell fire, Thiepval, 1st July 1916. 219th Field Coy., Royal Engineers. Aged 26. Eldest son of James (clerk, Estates Committee, Birmingham Corporation) and Harriet Matilda Tart, of 18, Charleville Road, Handsworth, Birmingham. Born in West Bromwich Staffordshire, 14th November 1889. Attended King Edward's School, Birmingham. Entered France, 8th March 1916. Father applied for his medals. Original burial map reference 57d.R.31.c.4.0 and identified by a disc and locket. Exhumed 28th September 1931, breeches with leather strappings, officer's ankle boots and covered in waterproof sheet. Memorial Ref. XL. J. 14., Serre Road Cemetery No.2, France.

TATE, Captain, Charles Bernard. Reported wounded and missing, badly wounded in the shoulder when left at the third line of German trenches, assumed killed 1st July 1916. 15th Bn., Royal Irish Rifles. Aged 27. Son of John Tate, of Rantalard, Whitehouse, Belfast, a well-known member of the Belfast Rural Council. Born 29th December 1888. Attended St. Lawrence College, Ramsgate, Kent. Before the war in the service of Messrs. Richardson, Sons & Owden Ltd. Entered France, 3rd October 1915. Father applied for his medals. Memorial Ref. Pier and Face 15 A and 15 B., Thiepval Memorial, France.

TAYLOR, Second Lieutenant, George Hayward. Missing in France, 1st July 1916. Machine Gun Detachment, Newfoundland Regiment. Aged 24. Son of Eugene F. (employed H. M. Customs) and Mary Taylor, of 5, Maxse Street, St. John's. Clerk at Ayres & Sons Ltd. Commissioned 13th September 1915. Served at Gallipoli from 1st December 1915. Two brothers in the Newfoundland Regiment whom were both killed on the 14th April 1917; Private Richard H. Taylor and Private Eugene Fred Taylor. Memorial Ref. Beaumont-Hamel (Newfoundland) Memorial, France.

TELFER, Lieutenant, Henry Adam. Killed in action, 1st July 1916. 9th Bn. attd. 64th Trench Mortar Bty., King's Own Yorkshire Light Infantry. Son of William Telfer Leviansky of 90 & 91 Queen Street, London. Articled to his father. Joined September 1914, as private, Public Schools Bn., and subsequently gazetted second lieutenant, 9th Bn., King's Own Yorkshire Light Infantry, promoted lieutenant 1916 and acting captain, May 1916. Joined Trench Mortar Battery 1916. Served in France from 10th December 1915. His brother, Lieutenant Claude William also fell on the 8th November 1918. Father applied for his medals. Medal Index Card has date of death as 5th July 1916. Original burial map reference 57D.27c.8.9 and exhumed 31st July 1919. Memorial Ref. II. N. 9., Gordon Dump Cemetery, Ovillers-La Boisselle, France.

No. 11 Lieutenant Henry Adam Telfer

THICKNESSE, Lieutenant Colonel, John Audley. Killed leading his men before our trenches were passed, 1st July 1916. Commanding 1st Bn., Somerset Light Infantry. Aged 46. Youngest son of the Right Rev. Dr. Francis Henry Thicknesse, D.D., Bishop of Leicester, and Anne Thicknesse. Husband of Phyllis Margaret Thicknesse, of Bishops Hull, near Taunton. Born at Middleton Cheney, Northants on 8th November 1869. Charterhouse (Gownboys 1882 – 1885). In 1890 he was commissioned into the Somerset Light Infantry. He served on the northwest frontier of India, including the Chitral Expedition of 1895, and in the South African War in 1902. At the outbreak of the Great War he was acting as Brigade Major to the Kent Territorial Brigade. He was appointed to command of 1st Bn., Somerset Light Infantry in August 1915. Mentioned in Despatches. Entered France, 13th August 1915. He left two sons, Henry John Anthony & Ralph Neville and a daughter, Cicely Ann Holme. Commemorated Sons and Daughters of the Anglican Church Clergy. Buried on the evening of the 3rd July in the Military Cemetery close to the Sucrerie with three other commanders of the 11th Infantry Brigade. Memorial Ref. I. H. 15., Sucrerie Military Cemetery, Colincamps, France.

God Proved Them And Found Them Worthy For Himself

255

THOMAS, Captain, Heinrich William Max. At 7.28am, six leading platoons took up their position in No Man's Land, without loss. At 7.30am our front line pushed forward, they were met with very heavy artillery and machine-gun fire, some of 'A' and 'B' Coys who did make the German front line at 7.35am were surrounded and captured by the Germans. Captain Thomas killed on the way across. 1st July 1916. C Coy., 1st Bn., East Lancashire Regiment. Aged 24. Eldest son of Max and Helena Thomas, of 31, Wolseley Road, Crouch End, London. Second lieutenant 11th June 1915 and lieutenant September 29th 1915. Formerly Artists Rifles, 28th London Regiment, private, 1217. Entered France, 26th October 1914. Shipping clerk. Father applied for his medals. Memorial ref. A. 12., Munich Trench British Cemetery, Beaumont-Hamel, France.

He Was But Words Fail To Say What Think What A Good Son Should Be,
And He Was That

THOMAS, Second Lieutenant, Sidney. Fell in action, 1st July 1916, telegram received 4th July 1916. 11th Bn., Suffolk Regiment. Aged 23. Son of Thomas and A. Thomas, of 149, Cowbridge Road, Cardiff. Locally reported "So far as is at present known, one of the first Cardiff officers to fall in the "great push" is Second Lieutenant Sidney Thomas, of the Suffolk Regiment, who was a son of Mr. Thomas Thomas, of Carmarthen Dairy, Cowbridge Road, Cardiff. Educated Severn Road Council School and the secondary school, Canton, Cardiff. In private life he was a bank clerk at Caerphilly with the London Provincial Bank and after three years at the Barry branch had transferred. At the outbreak of war he joined the Honourable Artillery Company as a private, 3982 enlisting 5th July 1915, he was the best shot in the battalion receiving a commission, 6th May 1916 after service in France from the 10th October 1915." Father applied for his medals. Effects were flask, identity disc, small photos, letters, picture postcards, shoulder bag and pocket case. Memorial Ref. Pier and Face 1 C and 2 A., Thiepval Memorial, France. WO 339/135870

THOMAS, Second Lieutenant, Wilfrid Patrick Otto. Killed in action, 1st July 1916. 9th Bn., York and Lancaster Regiment. Aged 20. Son of Harry Otto Thomas and Maggie Ramsay Thomas, of Byways, Harpenden, Herts. Attended Hurstpierpoint College. Commissioned 22nd December 1914. Previously corporal, 12th Bn., Royal Fusiliers. Entered France, 28th December 1915. Father applied for his medals. Memorial Ref. IV. E. 1., Blighty Valley Cemetery, Authuille Wood, France.

He Hath Outsoared The Shadow Of Our Night

THOMPSON, Captain, Arthur. Deceased 1st July 1916. 24th (Tyneside Irish) Bn., Northumberland Fusiliers. Two brothers wounded in the same action with the Northumberland Fusiliers. Second son of Mr. Matthew J. Thompson of Spital Tongues, Newcastle. Born Hexham. Assistant secretary to Salford Hospital. Original burial map reference 57d.X.20.a and marked as Captain Thompson 11/Suffolks later changed to Northumberland Fusiliers, reburied November 1919. Memorial Ref. V. B. 2., Ovillers Military Cemetery, France.

THOMPSON, Second Lieutenant, Fendall Powney. As soon as the troops left the front line, heavy machine-gun fire was brought to bear on them from all directions, casualties if officers amounted to 100%. Killed in action, Beaumont Hamel, 1st July 1916. 1st Bn., Hampshire Regiment. Aged 19. Only son of Lieutenant Colonel C. Powney Thompson (Indian Army) and grandson of Lieutenant General Clifford, C.B., Carn Cottage, Belturbet. When war broke out the doctors refused to pass him as fit for service owing to a slight stiffness of the left arm, the result of an accident in childhood, but being resolved to serve in some capacity he offered himself as a chauffeur, without pay, to St. John Ambulance Society, was accepted, and spent two months in France. On Colonel Thompson's return from India the facts were represented to Lord Kitchener's secretary, who said "a boy like that is worth having", and Lieutenant Thompson was eventually posted to the 3rd Bn., Hampshire Regiment, from which he joined the 1st Battalion. Entered France, 6th June 1916. His father applied for his medals. Memorial Ref. I. H. 7., Sucrerie Military Cemetery, Colincamps, France.

Killed In Action Only & Dearly Loved Son Of Col. Powney Thompson, I.A.

THOMPSON, Second Lieutenant, Herbert William. 11.25am reported first wave with remnants of second wave, together with third wave charged German trenches led by Captain Livesey. Lieutenant. Thompson also entered German trenches, 1st July 1916 reported wounded and missing. His servant, Private Riley was also missing at the same time. 10th Bn. attd. 11th Bn., East Lancashire Regiment. Aged 21. Son of Albert William Thompson and Florence Augusta Thompson, of 67, Kenyon Street, Fulham Palace Road, London. Born 2nd September 1894 at Chelsea. Enlisted 23rd September 1912 as rifleman, 1464, 16th Bn., London Regiment, (Queen's Westminster Rifles); Appointed second lieutenant 10th Bn., East Lancashire Regiment 9th/10th June 1915; attached 11th Bn., East Lancashire Regiment 17th June 1916. Memorial Ref. Pier and Face 6 C., Thiepval Memorial, France.

THOMSON, Lieutenant, Frederick Stanley. During the morning leading the 1/14th London Scottish from the 168th Brigade Machine Gun Company managed to get a Vickers machine-gun to 'A' Company, with the crew killed he disabled the Vickers gun in Fancy Trench picked up a German rifle and whilst running back across No Man's Land, as he tried to return fire he was killed, a head shot proving fatal, 1st July 1916. Two machine gun teams had set off from a sap in the front line at 10.20am. 1st /14th Bn., London Regiment (London Scottish). Aged 34. Son of W. E. S. Thomson (Admiralty Registry and Treasury). A civil servant. (Admiralty Registry). Second Lieutenant December 1914. War memorial erected in the Royal Courts of Justice, engraved brass plate by his colleagues and legal friends. Father applied for his medals. Memorial Ref. Pier and Face 9 C and 13 C., Thiepval Memorial, France.

Officers of the 14th Battalion London Regiment
Lieutenant Thomson fourth from right middle/standing row

THORMAN, Second Lieutenant, Alan Marshall. Deceased 1st July 1916. 1st /2nd Bn., London Regiment (Royal Fusiliers). Aged 20. Son of John Marshall Thorman and Eleanor Reed Thorman, of Witton Castle, Witton-Le-Wear, Co. Durham. Born 23rd July 1895. Attended Charterhouse, Pageites 1909-1912. Coal exporter. Commissioned 16th January 1915. Served in Malta, Gallipoli and Egypt. Entered France, 24th April 1916. Father applied for his medals. Memorial Ref. Pier and Face 9 D and 16 B., Thiepval Memorial, France.

THORNE, Lieutenant, John Parry. Reported missing, in command of a bombing party was seen to enter a hostile trench with his men, and nothing heard of him, reported as missing, 1st July 1916. 1st /5th Bn., South Staffordshire Regiment. Born 7th November 1888. Younger and second son of George Rennie Thorne, MP for East Wolverhampton and Susan May Thorne. Educated Tettenhall College, Wolverhampton. He joined the Colours as a private, 9394 in the early days of the war and was given a commission, 13th June 1915. Made lieutenant October 1915. Entered France, 5th March 1915. Engaged with his father as a solicitor in London. Wounded in a bombing accident in February 1916. Appeal from the Mayor for news, 15th July 1916 in the hope he had been taken prisoner. House of Commons, Book of Remembrance. Memorial Ref. Pier and Face 7 B., Thiepval Memorial, France.

THORNTON, Second Lieutenant, Frank. 2.33pm C and D Coy's advanced over the parapet to attack but owing to heavy casualties from machine-gun fire it was found impossible to reach the enemy front line, 1st July 1916. C Coy. 7th Bn., East Yorkshire Regiment. Aged 23. Son of William and Martha Thornton, of Nuneham House, 12, South Parade, Llandudno formerly Ashfield, Lepton near Huddersfield. Born 3rd April 1893, Birkby, Huddersfield. Educated Almondbury Grammar School and The Leys School, Cambridge where he was in the OTC. Enlisted 7th September 1914. Employed as a traveller with his father's business, Messrs. Woodhead and Barker, woollen merchants. Rugby player for Huddersfield Old Boys. Gazetted November, 1914. He had been at the Front about six months. St. John's Church, Kirkheaton; Waterloo Rugby Union Football Club and Birkby War Memorial. Originally buried Fricourt New Military Cemetery Grave 32. Memorial Ref. B. 5., Fricourt New Military Cemetery, France. WO 339/1520

Beloved Son Of William And Martha Thornton Huddersfield

TODD, Captain, John George. Died at La Boiselle, fell before he reached the British wire. 1st July 1916. 23rd (Tyneside Scottish) Bn., Northumberland Fusiliers. Aged 33. Only son of James Todd, of Overdale, Newcastle-upon-Tyne formerly of Darlington. Husband of Florence Todd, married 2nd June 1910 at Darlington and father to two sons, Raymond Thorman and John Thorman Todd. Prominent member of the Corporation of Durham. Born at Hetton-le-Hole, Co. Durham, 4th January 1883 and educated at Durham School. Matriculated at Jesus College, Cambridge 1901 - 1904 where he took degrees of B.A and L.L.B. Member of the first boat in Lent 1902, Lent 1903 and May 1903. Adopted the law as his profession, served his articles with Messrs. Lucas, Hutchinson and Meek, Darlington becoming a partner, firm of Maughan and Hall solicitors in Newcastle. Held a commission with the 1st Volunteer Battalion, Durham Light Infantry and three years with the Cambridge University Rifle Volunteers. Enlisted as a private in the Public Schools Battalion, 18th Bn., Royal Fusiliers, August 1914. Commissioned 31st December 1914. His widow applied for his medals and sons entitled to pension. Original burial map reference 57d. X.13.b.3.6. reburied 1919. Memorial Ref. I. I. 13., Bapaume Post Military Cemetery, Albert, France. WO 339/18729

TOLSON, Lieutenant, Robert Huntriss. Fighting was hard and shelling heavy, machine-gun fire was intense, reported wounded, missing 1st July 1916. No. 2 platoon, A Coy. 15th Bn., West Yorkshire Regiment (Prince of Wales's Own). Aged 31. Son of Whiteley (cotton manufacturer) and Mrs. Jessy Tolson, of Oaklands, Dalton, Huddersfield. Born 6th November 1884, Kirkheaton, Huddersfield. Educated at Aysgarth, and King Williams School Isle of Man. When war broke out was living with his wife Zoe at 78 Holly Bank, Leeds, and working at Beckett's Bank, Leeds from 1910. Married 9th October 1909. He enlisted into the Public Schools battalion, as a private. Given a commission into the Kings Own Yorkshire Light Infantry. In September 1915, he was transferred to the "Pals" whilst they were at Ripon. Served with them in Egypt from 22nd December 1915 to March 1916. He immediately became commander of 2 Platoon, 'A' company where his Commanding Officer was Captain Phillip Horace Leyland Mellor. Reported locally "wounded and in hospital, but his father has no news of his whereabouts, and is very anxious." Body found March 1917. On the 20th October 1918, brother James Martin Tolson aged 20, was killed in action, 2nd Lieutenant in "A" Battery, 74th Brigade the Royal Field Artillery. On the death of the brothers a house was donated to Huddersfield Corporation now known as Tolson Museum. Commemorated Huddersfield Parish Church and St. John's, Kirkheaton. Widow, Zoe Annie residing in Scarborough applied for his medals and pension. Widows pension awarded less pay at pension rates already issued. Memorial Ref. I. B. 52., Serre Road Cemetery No.1, France.

Husband Of Zoe Tolson And Son Of Whiteley Tolson Of Huddersfield

TOMLINSON, Second Lieutenant, Charles Valentine. Killed in the attack on Moquet Farm, reported missing 1st July 1916. 11th Bn., Sherwood Foresters (Notts and Derby Regiment). Born 14th February 1895. Son of Edward and Isabelle Tomlinson, The Limes, Crofwell Butler, Notts. Electrician. Commissioned 7th November 1915. Originally buried 970 yards NW of Ovillers Church after being found by the Colonel Adjutant and Padre. Commemorated Holy Trinity Church, Tithby. Memorial Ref. II. I. 8., Blighty Valley Cemetery, Authuille Wood, France. WO 339/46892

TOMPKINS, Second Lieutenant, Harold Arthur. At 7.28am, six leading platoons took up their position in No Man's Land, without loss. At 7.30am our front line pushed forward, they were met with very heavy artillery and machine-gun fire, some of 'A' and 'B' Coys who did make the German front line at 7.35am were surrounded and captured by the Germans. Killed on the way across, 1st July 1916. 10th Bn. attd. 1st Bn., East Lancashire Regiment from 20th June 1916. Son of Arthur Thomas and Mary Gertrude Tompkins. Born 1892 at Stockwell, Surrey. Educated at Hampton Grammar School. Clerk of 35 Sandycoombe Road, Twickenham. Camerons, private, 2174. Entered France, 19th February 1915. Gazetted 27th November 1915. Teddington War Memorial. Medal application by H. A. Tompkins, Twickenham. Daughter Josephine Mary Tompkins entitled to pension born 31st January 1917. Memorial Ref. Pier and Face 6 C., Thiepval Memorial, France.

TOOLIS, Lieutenant, James Hollingworth. Missing believed killed 1st July 1916. Seen to fall at the assaulting position, Sergeant Carter (also killed) went over and raised his head and then dropped it, he then gave the order to advance. Lieutenant Colonel Bastard wrote; 'killed gallantly leading his men that loved him to the assault'. X Coy., 2nd Bn., Lincolnshire Regiment, 1st Bn., attd to 2nd Bn. Only son of Mr. Thomas Smith Toolis (barrister at law) and Mrs. Toolis, Lincoln's Inn, The Lodge, Gatton Point, Redhill. Age 22. Born 22nd July 1893. Educated at the Grange, Stevenage, Perse School, Cambridge and Clare College, Cambridge. Passed to RMC Sandhurst, 1914 and received his commission in the Lincolns, November 1914. In June 1915, thirteen teeth were extracted which required a trip back to the UK and the fitting of dentures, in hospital from 22nd April to 15th May 1915. Entered France, 3rd October 1915. On his death, Reverend J. E. Hamilton wrote to the family saying that he had known Toolis for 11 months and reports say he was shot in the heart. The wife of Captain Needham (killed 1st July 1916) also wrote and reported that Captain Needham's servant had explained that he had buried Lieutenant Toolis next to Captain Needham just outside La Boisselle. Other witnesses stated they had seen the two officers lying next to each other dead. Neither men have a known grave. Cambridge Guildhall Memorial. His father applied for his medals. Memorial Ref. Pier and Face 1 C., Thiepval Memorial, France. WO 339/2447

TOPP, Second Lieutenant, Richard William. He fell severely wounded by shell fire, reported wounded and missing, 1st July 1916. Unofficially stated he went out with his platoon and was afterwards seen lying in a trench. 6th Bn. attd. 11th Bn., Royal Inniskilling Fusiliers. Aged 18. Eldest son of Richard W. (Bank of Ireland official) and Emily G. Topp, of Newry, Co. Down. He attended Galway Grammar School and then the Cork Grammar School where he joined the OTC. Entered the service of the bank. Commissioned 6th February 1915 and the following June was sent to France for the purpose of completing his course of instruction behind the lines. His parents spent many months looking for him after the Battle of the Somme. His father applied for his medals. Address Bank of Ireland, Newry. Memorial Ref. Pier and Face 4 D and 5 B., Thiepval Memorial, France.

TOUGH, Captain, Arnold Banatyne. At 07.20am he blew his whistle and led "X" company into the attack. He advanced 100 yards into No Man's Land, but was wounded twice before being shot in the head and killed. Serre, 1st July 1916. 7.20am the first wave crossed and the Germans opened immediately with machine-gun and rifle fire. 11th Bn., East Lancashire Regiment. Aged 26. Son of Dr. William Robb Tough and Margaret Tough, of 34, Delamere Road, Ainsdale, Southport. Born at Crook, Co. Durham, 31st March 1890. Educated Accrington Municpal Secondary School. Studied dentistry at Manchester University graduating in 1911 and returning home to set up practice in Accrington. Renowned amateur boxer and trained at Burnley Boys Club. On 17th September 1914 he joined the battalion with the rank of lieutenant. After serving three months in Egypt the battalion was returned to France. Promoted captain 5th May 1915. Entered France, 8th March 1916. In his last letter home to his sister Christina in June 1916 Arnold wrote: "We have been more than busy & I hardly know whether I am on my head or my heels. Probably won't be able to write for some time so don't worry – will write as soon as possible – you'll know why." Lieutenant Colonel Rickman wrote to Arnolds father: "…as our men left the front line trenches they came under a hail of machine-gun and rifle fire; and an intense artillery barrage was put on our front line. Nevertheless, without the slightest hesitation, your son moved forward according to orders received from Higher Command, and the men never wavered under him, but with the utmost gallantry carried out the role allotted…" Brother Captain John Tough killed with the RAMC, 6th October 1918. His father applied for his medals. Memorial Ref. D. 62., Queens Cemetery, Puisieux, France.

A Loved And Loving Son And Brother

TOWERS-CLARK, Lieutenant, John William. Killed as he led his men, Montauban, 1st July 1916. Reported that about 8.00am he was shot in the stomach and crawled in a 'Jack Johnson' hole and died. A Coy. 2nd Bn., Royal Scots Fusiliers. Aged 20. Only son of Major Alex Towers-Clark (Middlesex Regiment) and Mirabel Towers-Clark, of The Beach House, Bembridge, Isle of Wight. Born 23rd May 1896. Educated Marlborough College and RMC Sandhurst. Severely wounded 16th June 1915 1915. Nephew of Mr. William Towers-Clark, writer, Glasgow and a grandson of Mr. William Towers-Clark, Dean of the Faculty of Procurators in Glasgow. Effects were pocket book, spirit flask, wrist watch and leather cigarette case. Father applied for his medals. Memorial Ref. Pier and Face 3 C., Thiepval Memorial, France. WO 339/15752

TOWNSEND, Lieutenant, Richard Stapleton Barry. Missing believed killed 1st July 1916. 9th Bn., Royal Irish Fusiliers. Aged 32. Fourth and youngest son of Norman Lionel Townsend (Resident Magistrate), and Annabella Harriett Townsend, of Cathedral Close, Armagh. Received his commission September, 1914. In November, 1915, he was attached to the 10th (Reserve) Battalion at Lurgan, and subsequently at Newtownards. In February, 1916, he rejoined the 9th Battalion at the Front. Parents applied for his medals. Original burial Hamel Military Cemetery, Plot 1 Row D Grave 5 and grave marked with a cross. Memorial Ref. VIII. A. 18., Ancre British Cemetery, Beaumont-Hamel, France.

TRAILL, Lieutenant, Kenneth Robert. Killed in action, by 7.45am in the taking of Pommiers Trench, 1st July 1916. 6th Bn., Royal Berkshire Regiment. Previously injured when he and Lieutenant Remnant were hurdled through the doors of a dug-out by the explosion of a trench bomb, February 1916 and rejoined his battalion in March. Age 22. Born on 9th January 1893. Younger son of Dr. Cecil Traill (surgeon) and Mrs. Mary Traill of Cooralee, Sunningdale. Educated at Sunningdale School (Smith &Crabtree), Bradford College, matriculated London University and entered Guy's Hospital as a medical student in 1911. He joined the Inns of Court OTC on the outbreak of war, private, 1044 and received a commission in September 1914 being promoted in December 1914. Sent to France in July 1915. He was slightly wounded in the arm in February 1916 and returned to his regiment in March 1916. His sisters, Ethel and Cecil worked in military hospitals and his brother, Captain Charles Harold Traill won a Military Cross whilst serving with the RFA. His father applied for his medals. Memorial Ref. Q. 24., Carnoy Military Cemetery, France.

TREASURE, Second Lieutenant, William Herbert. Missing believed killed, he was in command of Trench Mortar Battery when he fell, 1st July 1916. 1st Bn., Somerset Light Infantry. Aged 19. Only son of Herbert George and Grace Georgina Treasure, of 2, Hyde Lodge, Bristol formerly 196, Redland Road, Bristol. Born March 1897 he was educated at Merchant Taylors School and in Sutton Courtenay. He passed into RMC Sandhurst in December 1914 and received his commission in July 1915. He went to the Front, 4th May 1916. On the eve of the attack he took a fatigue party with 39 buckets to bale trenches. Reported killed 18th August 1916. Father applied for his medals, c/o Lloyds Bank Limited, Bristol. Memorial Ref. Pier and Face 2 A., Thiepval Memorial, France.

TREGELLES, Captain, Geoffrey Philip. Mentioned in Despatches. Directed by Lieutenant Colonel Storey to reinforce in between the 9th Devons and the 2nd Gordons, led his company out onto No Man's Land at 10.00am and his body was seen lying in the field, killed by machine gun fire, 1st July 1916. A Coy. 8th Bn., Devonshire Regiment. Aged 23. Only son of Mr. George F. and Mrs. Marion S. Tregelles, of 5, Clarence Place, Barnstaple. Born at Penzance, 1892. Educated at Clifton College (1904 -1911) Undergraduate of Caius College, Cambridge. Commissioned 26th August 1914 and went abroad October 1915. His Medal Index Cards states joined unit 5th October 1915. Originally buried Mansel Copse. Father applied for his medals. Memorial Ref. B. 6., Devonshire Cemetery, Mametz, France. WO 339/11523

Blessed Are The Pure In Heart

TREVOR-JONES, Second Lieutenant, Evan Edward. Killed by a shell a couple of yards from the front trench whilst returning, carrying a wounded soldier, 1st July 1916. Reported he was wounded in the upper part of the left arm, during next three hours was wounded twice more, he found a wounded man who was injured in the right arm and between them bringing in a wounded man a shell burst and killed him the other two men being uninjured. 6th Bn. attd. 1st Bn., Rifle Brigade. Aged 20. Elder son of Lieutenant Colonel E. J. Trevor Cory, OBE., TD, of 38, Hyde Park Gate, South Kensington, London. Educated at Downside School and at the outbreak of war was in residence at Clare College, Cambridge, and a member of the University OTC. He obtained his commission in December, 1914, and in the July following went to the Front, 5th July 1915 where he acted as bombing officer for some time. Step-grandson of Mr. Richard Cory JP, Oscar House, Cardiff. Grandson of Rear Admiral Messin. Resided Aberdare. His brother Captain Eric Trevor-Jones MC, 6th attd 1st Bn., Rifle Brigade was killed on the 22nd April 1918. Father applied for his medals. Memorial Ref. Pier and Face 16 B and 16 C., Thiepval Memorial, France.

TROUTON, Lieutenant, Edmund Arthur. "Hardly were they across, German front line trench when the German barrage fell upon 'No Man's Land', upon the rear companies of the first line battalions, and upon those of the second line. However, they pressed on and reached their objective but it was at this point that Trouton was last seen, leading his men to the capture of the third enemy line." 1st July 1916. 3rd Bn. attd. No. 3 Coy., 9th Bn., Royal Inniskilling Fusiliers. Aged 24. Son of Edmund Arthur Trouton, CBE. Born 27th November 1891 in Orange, New Jersey, USA. Son of Edmund Arthur Trouton, of Fern Hill, Kilgobbin, Co Dublin. From Bilton Grange attended Winchester College, 1905 to 1909. Admitted as pensioner at Trinity, June 25th, 1910. He graduated from Trinity College, Cambridge in 1913 and, volunteering his services as soon as war broke out, was given a commission in 3rd Bn., Royal Inniskilling Fusiliers. Early in 1915 he joined 1st Battalion in Gallipoli, 11th July 1915 as a machine-gun officer and took part with them in the general assault on 21st August, when the unit suffered very badly. He was subsequently invalided home with dysentery and on his recovery attended a course at the Staff College, RMC Sandhurst, joining 9th Battalion of his regiment in France in the Spring of 1916. Father applied for his medals. Memorial Ref. Pier and Face 4 D and 5 B., Thiepval Memorial, France.

TUCKER, Second Lieutenant, Lionel Louis Clerici. Reported missing, believed killed, 1st July 1916. 20th (Tyneside Scottish) Bn., Northumberland Fusiliers. Aged 21. Only son of Francis G. Tucker (Manageress of the King Street Club, South Shields), of 18, King Street, South Shields, and Albert Tucker. Born in France, 21st June 1894. Apprentice engineer at Messrs. Readhead's, South Shields prior to the war and joined the Northumberland Fusiliers as a private, 16/176, 9th September 1914, 16th Bn. Obtained his commission April 1915. Entered France, January, 1916. Mother applied for his medals. Memorial Ref. Pier and Face 10 B 11 B and 12 B., Thiepval Memorial, France. WO 339/30319

TUCKER, Second Lieutenant, William Henry. Deceased 1st July 1916, seen to be wounded after being shot in the knee. 1st/12th Bn., London Regiment (The Rangers). Born 20th October 1881. Educated All Saints Residents Choir School. Accountant. Husband of Gladys A. Tucker, Woodbury Grove, Finsbury Park, London. Enlisted 2504, rifleman, 16th London Regiment, 31st August 1914. To be second lieutenant, 6th January 1916. Entered France, 24th January 1915. Widow, Mrs. W. H. Tucker, Holmleigh Road, Stamford Hill, N16 applied for his medals. Memorial Ref. Pier and Face 9 C., Thiepval Memorial, France.

TULLIS, Captain, William. Experienced officer and acting adjutant when he fell, 1st July 1916. Royal Scots Fusiliers. Aged 32. Third son of Mr. and Mrs. Robert Tullis, of Strathenry, Leslie, Fife. Attended Fettes College. Entered France, 27th August 1914. Seriously injured in the early part of the war. Three brothers also served. A service was held in Leslie Parish Church in his and his brother's memory. He was one of the first to be wounded and his brother Captain John D. Tullis died of wounds, November 1914. Two other brothers served. Medal Index Card implies adjutant role with the Northumberland Fusiliers. Father applied for his medals. Memorial Ref. Pier and Face 3 C., Thiepval Memorial, France.

TWEEDALE, Second Lieutenant, Eric. Killed within yards of the British Lines at Serre, 1st July 1916. 13th Bn. attd. 16th Bn., West Yorkshire Regiment (Prince of Wales's Own). Son of W. H. (an Engine Waste Dealer) and Emma Tweedale, of Serre, Cliff Place, Bispham, Lancs. Born at Bispham, Blackpool, Lancashire. He entered Manchester University in 1913 to study electrical engineering. Eric joined the university OTC and when war broke out was still at university. He enlisted in May 1915 and was commissioned in the 13th Bn., West Yorkshire Regiment. He was attached to the 16th Battalion shortly before they departed for Egypt to defend the Suez Canal in late 1915, and was still with the battalion when it was recalled to France in March 1916. Application for his medals, who renamed their address as 'Serre', Cliff Place, Blackpool. Memorial Ref. Pier and Face 2 A 2 C and 2 D., Thiepval Memorial, France.

TWENTYMAN, Captain, Denzil Clive Tate. Fell after successfully attacking German Front, while gallantly leading his men 1st July 1916 being shot by a sniper shortly after entering a vacated German trench. A Coy., 10th Bn., York and Lancaster Regiment. Aged 26. Elder son of Alderman James Robert Twentyman, J.P., of Kirby-Misperton Hall, Yorkshire. Born at Maplehurst, Bubbling Well Road, Shanghai on the 27th June 1890. Husband of Sybil Twentyman, of Kirby-Misperton Hall. Educated at Bromsgrove; B.A. Cambridge, 1913 at St. John's College. Member of OTC at Bromsgrove and Cambridge. Good sportsman. Joined the Hong Kong and Shanghai Banking Corporation prior to enlisting. He got a commission in September 1914 and was made full lieutenant in December and promoted to captain in May 1915. He was married on 30th June 1915 to Mildred Sybil Josephine, eldest daughter of Mr. and Mrs. Percy Hall of Cambridge. He went to the Front in September 1915 and was the only officer unscathed in his battalion at the Battle of Loos, known as 'Twenty'. Buried 3rd July 1916 near Fricourt Village, original burial map reference 57d.X.27.d.1.2. Reinterred 1920. His widow applied for his medals. Memorial Ref. II. Q. 4., Gordon Dump Cemetery, Ovillers-La Boisselle, France. WO 339/20050

Till The Day Dawns And The Shadows Flee Away

TYTLER, Lieutenant, William Boyd. Only officer of his battalion to reach the third line German trenches and although wounded continued to wave his men on, missing believed killed, 1st July 1916. Officer Commanding stated he went over in the advance and nothing has been seen or heard of this officer since. 22nd (Tyneside Scottish) Bn., Northumberland Fusiliers. Aged 22. Son of J. M. Tytler, Grenville House, Newtonmore, Invernesshire. Educated at Kingussie Grammar School. Student at Moray House Training College, Edinburgh. Intended to be a teacher when war broke out and planned to finish his training at Edinburgh University. He had received an offer for appointment of the staff of Dornoch Academy when war broke out. Jesmond Presbyterian Church. Being a private in the 4th Royal Scots, 1478 he was mobilised, receiving a commission. Went to France, 9th January 1916. Buried by the 34th Division. His ID disc was found on the body of 2nd Lt. B.C. de B. White also killed 1st July 1916. Brother Lieutenant J. H. Tytler also killed on the 16th September 1916. His father applied for his medals. Memorial Ref. Pier and Face 10 B 11 B and 12 B., Thiepval Memorial, France. WO 339/17234

UPRICHARD, Major, Henry Albert. Went down at the head of his men, killed by machine-gun fire, 1st July 1916. D Coy., 13th Bn., Royal Irish Rifles. Aged 36. Second son of Henry Albert and Emily Green Uprichard, Elmfield, Gilford, Co. Down. He was educated at Leighton Park School, Reading from 1893-1898. Keen sportsman, having won many point-to-point races. He was a member of the Co. Down Staghounds, and in 1914 was elected Master of the Iveagh Harriers on the resignation of his brother, Mr. W. F. Uprichard. He received his majority in February 1915. Managing Director of the Belfast Company, Forster Green & Co. his late grandfather's business. Resided Bannvale House. Keen polo player. Prior to the start of the war was Commander of the 2nd Battalion, West Regiment of the UVF. Played polo and hockey for North of Ireland. One of 28, Old Leightonians whom died for great ideals. His son, Captain F. G. Uprichard was injured in August 1916. His Commanding Officer wrote; 'His men worshipped him as they were his first thought, and he could not do enough for them'. W. F. Uprichard applied for his medals. Original burial map reference R.24.d.4.6 and reburied May 1919. Memorial Ref. X. C. 8., Mill Road Cemetery, Thiepval, France.

VAN DEN BOK, Second Lieutenant, Frederick. Killed in the opening phase of the Somme offensive at La Boisselle, reported wounded and missing and then killed, 1st July 1916. A Coy. 2nd Bn., Middlesex Regiment. Aged 22. Son of Mr. Adrianus and Mrs. N. Van Den Bok, of Crescent Moor House, Sydenham Hill, London. He was born 6th May 1894, at Hackney, the son of Dutch-born merchant Adrianus and his wife Nelly Isabel Van den Bok, of Australia. Educated at Dulwich College (1907-1910), finished education at Bruges, Belgium. Enlisted in September 1914, in the Public Schools' Battalion of the 16th Royal Fusiliers as private, No. 120. He obtained a commission in April 1915, in the 6th Bn., Middlesex Regiment. Went to France, 29th May 1916 with the 2nd Bn. Father wrote a letter in requesting more details that ended ' apologies for troubling you but my great and lasting loss is my excuse'. Items returned were mirror in case, identity disc, knife, cheque book and letters. Buried sq. X.12.B.9.7 Mash Valley Cemetery. In a letter to Second Lieutenant's Phillip Maurice Elliott's parents from the Reverend H. B. Burnaby (Regimental Padre); "Thus he lies where the 2nd Middlesex so splendidly opened the great attack, buried close to his brother officers who fell with him, Captain Meeke, Captain Heaton and Lieut. Van den Bok". Father applied for his medals. Memorial Ref. Pier and Face 12 D and 13 B., Thiepval Memorial, France. WO 339/55302

VASSIE, Second Lieutenant, Charles Edward. Killed in action, 1st July 1916. A Coy., 9th Bn., King's Own Yorkshire Light Infantry. Aged 21. Son of Henry James, Regimental Sergeant Major, Royal Garrison Artillery and Mary Ann Vassie, of The Standards, Boat House, Dunbar. Born 15th May 1895. Previous to the outbreak of war he was studying for the ministry in connection with the Episcopal Church and for some time was in the OTC at Durham University. Enlisted whilst a student at St. Chad's, Durham on the 19th October 1914. Commissioned 28th November 1915. Entered France, 16th June 1916. Shoulder strap and letters returned to family. Originally buried near the Beaucourt-Fricourt Road. Father applied for his medals. Original burial map reference 57d.X.26.d.8.6 reburied 1919. Memorial Ref. II. M. 7., Gordon Dump Cemetery, Ovillers-La Boisselle, France. WO 339/52494

R.I.P.

VAUDREY, Captain, Norman. He was in Command of the 2nd Company in the advance on Montauban, went forward to ascertain the cause of the halt in advance when he was hit in the stomach by a bullet from a German machine-gun by 9.10am, and died in thirty seconds in the arms of a sergeant who was himself killed later. Shot, whilst gallantly leading his men, 1st July 1916. B Coy., 17th Bn., Manchester Regiment. Aged 33. Younger son of Sir William Henry and Lady Eleanor Vaudrey, of 33, Mount Avenue, Ealing, London formerly The Gables, Manchester Road, Buxton. Born at Eccles, Lancs. Before the war he was a civil engineer with Messrs. Edmund Nuttall, Trafford, Manchester. Educated Bilton Grange and entered Rugby School in 1897 and left in 1901. After leaving Rugby he became a civil engineer, and before the outbreak of war he was engaged on Railway Work and Bridge Building with Messrs. Edmund Nuttall & Co., of Trafford Park, Manchester. In September, 1914, he obtained a commission in the 17th Manchesters and went with them to the Front in France in November, 1915. His elder brother, Captain C. H. S. Vaudrey died while on service in Mesopotamia from cholera, on May 2nd, 1916. His Colonel, who was wounded on July 1st, wrote from hospital :- "Your son Norman was a most excellent Officer. He knew his work well. I could always rely on him." His body was found a few days later in our trench and properly buried. His father applied for his medals. Original burial map reference 62C.A.9.d.7.1. Memorial Ref. IX. O. 3., Dantzig Alley British Cemetery, Mametz, France. WO 339/15409

A Loving Son Who Gave His Life For His Country All You Had You Gave

Pictured with his platoon whilst a Lieutenant N. Vaudrey Platoon No. VI also killed in the group were Corporal Arthur Worrall, Private Frank Byrne, Private Cyril Trueman and Private William Ernest Walton.

VAUSE, Lieutenant, John Gilbert. Fighting was hard and shelling heavy, machine-gun fire was intense, reported as one of the missing, 1st July 1916. Reported he was hit in the elbow and then in the thigh and whilst taking cover was hit again in the chin and back, he made the remark 'this has just about finished me off' and died. No. 15 Platoon, D Coy. 15th Bn., West Yorkshire Regiment (Prince of Wales's Own). Aged 23. Youngest son of Frederick William (Firm Thomas Vause and Sons Ltd (Manufacturers), Low Road, Hunslet) and Sarah Vause, of Meadowfield, Chapel Allerton, Leeds. Educated Leeds Grammar School and later at Leeds University. Apprentice with the firm of Messrs. Mortimer & Co. woollen manufacturers, Morley. Acting captain. Served in Egypt from 22nd December 1915 and went to France, 1916. Asking for clarification his father received a note from the War Office; 'Reported missing this does not mean wounded or killed'. Played for Headingly RFC. Father applied for his medals. Memorial Ref. Pier and Face 2 A 2 C and 2 D., Thiepval Memorial, France.

VENUS, Second Lieutenant, Frederick Arthur. Missing believed killed, 1st July 1916. 20th (Tyneside Scottish) Bn., Northumberland Fusiliers. Aged 21. Eldest son of Frederick Robert and Hannah Elizabeth Venus, of 10, Park Avenue, North Shields. Born 25th August 1894. Uncle Mr. W. B. Venus received news that he was missing via a telegram. Attached to the Tynemouth Garrison Artillery, stationed at Tynemouth Castle from the 25th November 1912 and left for the Front in June 1916. His grave was found by the Grave Registration Unit in June 1917 and identified by a visiting card taken from his body. Body located at La Boisselle. Father applied for his medals. Original burial map reference 57d.X.14.A.&.C., originally buried as unknown and later identified. Memorial Ref. XII. N. 3., Ovillers Military Cemetery, France. WO 339/50118

Greater Love Hath No Man Than This

VERNON, Captain, Frederick Lewis. Killed in action, 1st July 1916. 26th (Tyneside Irish) Bn., Northumberland Fusiliers. Aged 30. Born 2nd December 1884, Newport, Monmouthshire. Son of David and Martha Vernon, of Newcastle-on-Tyne. Educated at Thornaby School. Husband of Evelyn Davidson (formerly Vernon) of 203, Park Road, Blackpool. Had six children. Clerk, Engineering Department. Enlisted Northumberland Fusiliers, 11th March 1912, sergeant, 265065, previously served 1st Volunteer Battalion, Durham Light Infantry. Commissioned 25th January 1915. His widow, Central Avenue, Blackpool applied for his medals. Pension for five children, Edna Clifford, Dorothy, Marjorie, Frederick Clive, Patricia Lillian and Sydney Morton who was born 24th December 1916. Wife choose his inscription. Memorial Ref. Sp. Mem. 8., Ovillers Military Cemetery, France. WO 339/30962

Loved By Us All

VIGERS, Second Lieutenant, Lancelot Leslie. Died 1st July 1916. 30th Field Coy., Royal Engineers attd No 1. Section, 80th Field Coy. He arrived at Carnoy Valley at 11.45am with four pack animals, by 1.15pm three horse drawn wagons loaded with bridging materials were unloaded over No Man's Land. At 2.00pm the party were subjected to Howitzer shells and Lancelot was killed, with five men wounded and two horses. Aged 25. Son of Leslie Robert and Rosa May Vigers, of 5, Eaton Terrace, Eaton Square, London. Born 20th December, 1890 at Sydenham, London. Attended Horton School. Resided Seymour Lodge, Sydenham Hill Road, Lewisham. Engineering student. Elected member of the Royal Aero Club of the United Kingdom, 1911. Gazetted 27th August 1915. Entered France, 25th November 1915. Member of the Institution of Civil Engineers. Studied under Professor W. E. Dalby M. Inst. C.E and Mr. Basil Mott M. Inst. C.E. Father applied for his medals. Memorial Ref. J. 29., Carnoy Military Cemetery, France.

VOLKERS, Second Lieutenant, Frederick Cyril Stowell. Missing, 1st July 1916. I Coy., 1st Bn., Rifle Brigade. Aged 20. Son of Robert Charles Francis Volkers, C.I.E., of 5, Lovelace Road, Dulwich, London, and of Ellen Volkers. Born 16th June 1896. Attended Dulwich College (1907-1914). Enlisted in the 5th Bn., London Regiment, private, 110 and went to France, 4th November 1914. Invalided home, April 1915 and returned to the Front in August. In November 1915 entered the cadet school at St. Omer and gazetted in the 1st Bn., Rifle Brigade, 5th December 1915. Captain R. C. F. Volkers applied for his medals. Memorial Ref. Pier and Face 16 B and 16 C., Thiepval Memorial, France.

WALKER, Second Lieutenant, Henry Gerald. He had been previously wounded but refrained to go back continued to lead his men and jumping over the parapet shouted to his men to come on when he was instantly killed, 1st July 1916. C Coy., 2nd Bn., King's Own Yorkshire Light Infantry. Aged 25. Son of J. Henry and Emily Walker, of Highgorth, Mirfield, Yorks. Enlisted August, 1914, 21st Bn., Royal Fusiliers, private, 3374. Commissioned 17th May 1915. Entered France, 11th March 1916. Educated at Dollar Academy and Fettes. Headingley RFC. Yorkshire Rugby Football Union "In Memoriam" 1914-1919". Brother Surgeon Lieutenant Godfrey Alan Walker killed 14th November 1916. Father applied for his medals. Memorial Ref. Pier and Face 11 C and 12 A., Thiepval Memorial, France.

WALKER, Second Lieutenant, John. He was in charge at Fricourt and one of the first out of the trenches, from that moment nothing has been heard of him and posted as missing, 1st July 1916. 14th Bn., Northumberland Fusiliers. Aged 21. Son of Mr. and Mrs. John Sharp Walker, of 19, St. Andrew's Drive, Pollokshields, Glasgow. Born in 1895. Attended the High School of Glasgow. Glasgow University OTC, where he was a cadet between 1912 and 1914. Enlisted in the army and was assigned to the 14th Bn. of the Northumberland Fusiliers. In this regiment, he was gazetted to second lieutenant. Recorded on the Glasgow University Chapel's Roll of Honour, the High School of Glasgow and Pollokshields' Church of Scotland, in a Remembrance Book. Memorial Ref. Pier and Face 10 B 11 B and 12 B., Thiepval Memorial, France.

WALKER, Second Lieutenant, Turner Russell. Died of wounds, 97 Field Ambulance, 1st July 1916. 18th Bn., The King's (Liverpool Regiment). On the day of his advance his dearest wish was to be fulfilled, being placed in charge of his own platoon with the men he trained and by their side he fell. Aged 22. Only son of Captain James Watt and Mary Frances Walker, of "Yenda", Eastham, Cheshire. Grandnephew of John Stuart Blackie and descendant of James Watt, the famous engineer. Born at Birkenhead. Enlisted 3rd September 1914. Private, 17007. Commissioned 7th April 1915. Entered France, 11th March 1916. Joined his battalion 18th March 1916. Death officially reported 10th August 1916. Originally buried Talus Boise British Cemetery. Effects were locket, silver chain, cheque book, pocket book and platoon roll. Father applied for his medals. Original burial map reference 62C.A.14.b.5.4. identified as a cross was on his grave. He was buried by a chaplain of the Wiltshire regiment along with 14 others, at the foot of a little wood on the side of a hill, in happier times it would have been a beautiful spot. Memorial Ref. IV. C. 39., Peronne Road Cemetery, Maricourt, France. WO 339/29713

Teach Us The Joy Of Duty Done

WALKER, Captain, William. Killed by machine-gun fire, at the top of the parapet, Russian Sap, 1st July 1916, his body was passed by Lieutenant B. L. Gordon. C Coy., 9th Bn., King's Own Yorkshire Light Infantry. Son of James D. Walker, of 17, St. Andrew Square, Edinburgh formerly 13, Brights Crescent, Edinburgh. Born 25th June 1878. Edinburgh Academy; Students of Arts; 1896 to 1900. MA 1900. Served in Queen's Rifle Volunteer Brigade, Royal Scots and University OTC. Enlisted 29th December 1914 . Second lieutenant 1915. Captain, August 1915. Head of the firm of J. D. Walker, stockbroker. Memorial Ref. I. B. 91., Norfolk Cemetery, Becordel-Becourt, France. WO 339/19235

WALKER, Captain, William Eaton Guy. Signaller officer reported killed, 1st July 1916. 7th Bn., Sherwood Foresters (Notts and Derby Regiment). Aged 23. Eldest son of William Eaton Walker (the manager of Clifton Colliery), and Adeline I. Walker, of Rock House, Old Basford, Nottingham. Born 29th September 1892. His younger brother, Second Lieutenant Harry Cullis Steele Walker was killed on 12th March 1915 at Neuve Chapelle. Attended Worksop College after the High School, presumably as a boarder to finish his education, being a member of the OTC. He was articled to C. H. Williams of Nottingham. Entered France, February 1915. Treated at hospital from the 22nd October 1915 to 4th November 1915 from pyrexia of unknown origin. Captain Walker's body was recovered from the German wire at Gommecourt in March 1917, from where it had lain since 1st July 1916, and he was buried on 21st March 1917. Medals to Major W. E. Walker (father). Memorial Ref. III. E. 6., Foncquevillers Military Cemetery, France.

Hi Mortui In Aeturnum Nos Viventes Morimur

WALPOLE, Captain, John Robert. Killed in action, in No Man's Land or close to Breslau Trench, 1st July 1916. 7th Bn., The Queen's (Royal West Surrey Regiment). Aged 34. Second son of Sir Charles (Chairman of the Surrey Quarter Sessions) and Lady Walpole, of 4, Kensington Court, London. Native of Chobham, Surrey. Born 1882. Attended Eagle House School. Received his commission in January 1901 in the Lancashire Artillery Militia and subsequently in 1904 a commission as second lieutenant in the Queens. In 1910 he sent in his papers and spent three years rubber planting in Malaya and in 1914 purchased a small estate in Antigua. He abandoned this at the outbreak of war and obtained a commission as lieutenant in his old regiment being gazetted as captain in December 1914. He went to the Front, 28th July 1915.

Educated at Eton and unmarried. Cousin of Bishop Wapole, Edinburgh. Originally buried battlefield at Carnoy. Effects were receipt, leather note case, photo cases, silver cigarette case, silver watch, chain, seal and pencil. Medals to be sent to his father. Unusually his Medal Index Card has 'K.I.A Somme'. Original burial map reference 62C.A.8.b.3.2 Memorial Ref. VIII. N. 3., Dantzig Alley British Cemetery, Mametz, France. WO 339/5938

Son Of Sir Charles Walpole Of Broadford Chobham

WALTON, Second Lieutenant, Francis John George. Killed in action, 1st July 1916 reported August 1916. 18th Bn., West Yorkshire Regiment (Prince of Wales's Own). Aged 25. Son of Francis James and Annie M. Walton. Husband of Christina Frances Walton, of 13, First Avenue, Hendon, London. Born at Hampstead, London. Enlisted private, 9th Bn., London Regiment, 5190. Gazetted 5th November 1915. Attended Haberdashers' School. Building contractors assistant. His widow applied for his medals. Son, Francis William Walton entitled to pension. Original burial map reference 57d.K.24.d.3.7 and identified by his disc. Memorial Ref. IV. B. 11., Serre Road Cemetery No.1, France.

His Gain, Our Loss Till We Meet Chris & Frank Mother & Dad

WARD, Second Lieutenant, Dacre Stanley. Missing 1st July 1916. 1st/12th Bn., London Regiment (The Rangers). Aged 33. Son of Alfred and Alice Ward, of 67, Westcombe Park Road, Blackheath, London. Husband of Marion Ethel Ward, of 16, Alexandra Court, Queen's Gate, Kensington, London getting married on the 16th June 1915. Spice merchant. Enlisted, 4689, private, Inns of Court OTC, 8th July 1915. To be second lieutenant 27th November 1915. Entered France, 1st June 1916. His widow applied for his medals and pension. Memorial Ref. Pier and Face 9 C., Thiepval Memorial, France.

WARD, Second Lieutenant, George Cecil. Killed by the explosion of a shell that threw up a stone injuring Lieutenant Colonel J. W. Alexander, 1st July 1916. B Coy. 8th Bn., West Yorkshire Regiment (Prince of Wales's Own). Aged 23. Fourth son of William George and Ada Anne Ward, of Frogmore, Town Street, Upper Armley, Leeds. Born Cromolin near Newport, Monmouthshire, Wales. George and brother Donald both went to the Town Hall in September 1915 and enlisted into the 15th Bn., West Yorkshire Regiment Joined the Leeds Pals Battalion on its formation he received a commission in the Rifles six months later and joined the regiment in France. Educated at Upton School, Slough and the Leeds Boys Modern School. Articled to Messrs. Murphy and Lonsdale, analytical chemists. Donald (left) and George Cecil Ward photographed. Donald was badly wounded and invalided home surviving the war. George entered France, September 1915. His father applied for his medals. Memorial Ref. I. C. 29., Connaught Cemetery, Thiepval, France.

Nobly Fought Love Eternal And Triumphant

WARDEN, Captain, Walter George. Attacked near Fricourt, 1st July 1916, gains were being consolidated by just 100 men at the west end of Lozenge Wood, Fricourt. Reported to be hit by a machine-gun bullet and died from the effects, led the attack and last words reported to be; 'I want to see my boys advancing'. C Coy., 8th Bn., Somerset Light Infantry. Aged 30. Son of G. F. and J. B. Warden, of Elmbridge Road, Gloucester. Husband of Constance S. Warden, of 12, Highbury Road, Weston-Super-Mare. Born August 1885, in Gloucester. Educated Crypt Grammar School and attended Blundell's, Tiverton (1901 – 1903). Member of the Blundell's Cadets for three years. When war broke out he came over with the first Canadian contingent. Formerly private 9258, 3rd Bn., 1st Brigade Canadians, he attested at Valcartier on 23rd September 1914, transferred to a commission in the Somerset Light Infantry in March 1915. He fought in the battles of La Bassee and Neuve Chapelle and went into the Battle of Loos as a second lieutenant. Promoted captain, 12th October 1915. Previously employed civil engineer. Originally buried Fricourt, Sheet 57a Sq. X.27a. Effects returned were letters, pocket book, advance book, map and photos. He was originally posted as missing, a letter to his wife from Reverend Longdean confirmed he was killed and had been laid to rest.

The Reverend removed from his body, a compass and an identity disc that he send to his wife. Original burial map reference 57d.X.27.c.3.3 and exhumed August 1919. Memorial Ref. II. Q. 2., Gordon Dump Cemetery, Ovillers-La Boisselle, France. WO 339/38491

The Noblest Death A Man Can Die For God And Right And Liberty

WARDILL, Second Lieutenant, Charles Henry. Killed in action, 1st July 1916. 15th Bn. attd 12th Bn., York and Lancaster Regiment. Aged 39. Husband of Edith E. Wardill, of 18, Violet Bank Road, Nether Edge, Sheffield. One of six brothers of whom all volunteered. His family were connected with the Cemetery Road Baptist Church. Commissioned 25th October 1915. Leaves a widow, and one son, Reginald. Originally in the City Defence Corps. Edith applied for medals due to her late husband. Son entitled to pension. His brother, Private Sidney G. Wardill was also killed on the 1st July and has no known grave. Memorial Ref. Pier and Face 14 A and 14 B., Thiepval Memorial, France.

WARE, Captain, Francis Henry. C Coy strength ninety ranks were to move forward as soon as the attack was started and to occupy trenches left by 'A' Company. 7.50am displayed great gallantry in getting a carrying party over assisting London Scottish with small arms and grenades. 9.00am A Coy and one platoon of C Coy had gone forward and disappeared. Captain Ware had led one party and believed to have been hit by shell fire in taking bombs across for the London Scottish. By 9.15am reported wounded and missing. 1st July 1916, C Coy., 1st/13th Kensington Bn., London Regiment. Born September 12th , 1873, in London. Youngest son of Charles Tayler and Zillah Ware of 11 Phillimore Gardens, Kensington. Educated at Mr. C. A. Ford's School & Winchester, 1886 to 1891and Trinity College, Cambridge took the Law Tripos and afterwards practiced as a solicitor with Messrs. Foster, Spicer and Foster. Admitted as pensioner at Trinity, June 15th, 1891. Matric. Michs. 1891; BA and LL.B 1894; MA 1898. Admitted as a solicitor, 1898. Practiced at 7 Queen Street Place, London, E.C. Served in the South African War (4th Middlesex Volunteer Rifle Corps). Joined November 12th, 1914, as captain, 13th (Princess Louise's Kensington) Bn., London Regiment. Went to the Front in September 1915. Memorial Ref. Pier and Face 9 D 9 C 13 C and 12 C., Thiepval Memorial, France.

WAREHAM, Lieutenant, Frederick William. Killed in action, Beaumont Hamel, 1st July 1916. 1st /8th Bn., Royal Warwickshire Regiment. Aged 25. Eldest son of Frederick (headmaster of Leigh Sinton School) and Harriett Wareham, of Lydgate, Carlton Road, Malvern Link, Malvern Worcs. Troop Leader Malvern Link 1st Troop. Brother Second Lieutenant Lawrence John Wareham, Worcester Regiment also killed 21st July 1916. Educated Worcester Grammar School (1904 to 1908), student teacher at Malvern Link County Council School and onto Saltley Training College (1911-1912) and possessed diplomas in physical training and hygiene. When war broke out he was a teacher for London County Council at at St Matthews Boys School, Westminster and as a corporal, 1524 in the 12th Bn., London Regiment, he proceeded to Flanders, 24th December 1914 and was wounded in March 1915. He obtained a commission in the Warwicks, 25th June 1915 becoming lieutenant in November 1915. He went to the Front in Easter week. London County Council, Teaching Staff. Memorial Ref. Pier and Face 9 A 9 B and 10 B., Thiepval Memorial, France.

SATURDAY, 16 JUNE, 1917.

An Historic Battlefield Picture.

Taken in the Field just before the Battle of the Somme. Lieutenant Wareham
Back row fifth from left

WARNER, Second Lieutenant, Archibald. Killed near Gommecourt, early in the attack on July 1st a big shell came through the parapet of an advanced British trench and killed him by its concussion, other reports suggest killed trying to go forward from a shell hole. 1st July 1916. 5th Bn., London Regiment (London Rifle Brigade). Aged 32. Born 13th February, 1884 at Waddon. Son of John Warner (iron founder) and Alice, of Waddon House, Croydon. Husband of Norah E. Marriage (formerly Warner), of the Parsonage, Broomfield, Essex. Born 13th February 1884. Educated 'The Limes', Croydon, Whitgift Grammar School, Leighton Park School, Reading 1899-1902, and Queens' College, Cambridge. Captain of the Queens' College boat. Solicitor by profession and served his articles with Messrs. Trinder, Capron & Co., 68 Coleman Street, London. Admitted January 1910 and joined staff of Messrs. Bennett and Ferris, solicitors. Keen sportsmen. Member of the Society of Friends. Member of the Reigate Priory Football Club for many seasons. In September 1914 married Norah E. Goodbody. Joined June 4th, 1915, as a private in the 3rd Bn., Artist Rifles. Obtained his commission in the Artists' Rifles, 3997, October 28th, 1915 and gazetted to the regiment his brother was killed in December 1914, Sergeant Evan Warner. Entered France, 27th May 1916, so had only been in France a few weeks when he fell. "He showed great confidence at the Front and used to go into No Man's Land as though he was looking at flowers in his front garden." One of 28, Old Leightonians whom died for great ideals. His widow applied for his medals. Memorial Ref. IV. D. 7., Hebuterne Military Cemetery, France.

They Shall Shine As The Stars For Ever & Ever

WARNER, Second Lieutenant, Douglas Redston. Assault began at 8.00am and barbed wire was cut every forty yards the Germans had their machine-guns trained on these gaps and only a few men ever got through the wire, originally posted as missing, then seriously wounded and believed killed, 1st July 1916. He fell mortally wounded and his corporal offered to carry him back but he refused to allow this and bade his men to go on, when hit he was gallantly leading his men. 4th Bn. attd. 1st Bn., Royal Dublin Fusiliers. Aged 28. Only son of William Redston Warner and grandson of Isaac Redston Warner, Captain 3rd Dragoon Guards and John Haig of Braycourt, Maidenhead and brother of Rubie Drummond-Nairne Warner. Born January 1888. Educated at Woodcote House, Windlesham and Bradfield College, September 1901 to April 1906. He after trained as an engineer at Messrs. Marshalls, Gainsborough and left in 1912 for Vancouver. At the outbreak of war he returned home and enlisted in the 1st Sportsman's Battalion but in April 1915 he was given a commission in the Dublin Fusiliers. Gazetted 20th April 1915. In August 1915 he went to the Dardanelles where he stayed until the evacuation.

Confirmed killed, September 1916. His sister, Rubie applied for his medals to go to Wellington Square, Oxford. Memorial Ref. B. 7., Hawthorn Ridge Cemetery No.1, Auchonvillers, France.

WARR, Second Lieutenant, William Charles Samuel, DCM. Killed in Bulgar Alley by a sniper and died at once, 1st July 1916. He was going forward as an observation officer, directing the laying of telephone wire towards the line which our infantry had captured and he fell, 22nd Bde., Royal Field Artillery. Throughout the day he had directed fire and killed whilst establishing a new position. Awarded the DCM, 17th December 1914 whilst a corporal in the 106th Battery as a sergeant; 'for conspicuous gallantry in assisting to serve a single gun until and after all of the sub section had been killed or wounded' and Russian Cross of St. George. Resided Chew Stoke. Came back from South Africa to join his old regiment, sergeant, 31652. Entered France, 6th October 1914. Gained his commission, 12th April 1915 and the Military Cross in 1916. Original burial map reference 62d.F.5.d Memorial Ref. V. B. 4., Dantzig Alley British Cemetery, Mametz, France.

WARREN, Second Lieutenant, Fred Langford. Killed in action, 1st July 1916. 4th Bn. attd. 2nd Bn., West Yorkshire Regiment (Prince of Wales's Own). Second lieutenant on probation, 25th June 1915. Entered France, 18th May 1916. Miss L. C. Warren, Ardsley-on-Hudson, New York, USA applied for his medals. Memorial Ref. Pier and Face 2 A 2 C and 2 D., Thiepval Memorial, France.

WATERHOUSE, Second Lieutenant, Gilbert. His company was ordered to capture communication lines around Serre. He was in the second wave to attack. 1st July 1916. C Coy., 2nd Bn., Essex Regiment. Born 22nd August 1883 to John and Louisa Waterhouse, Forest Drive, Woodford Green. Attended Bancroft's School as a day boy between 1894 and 1900. He became a ship's draftsman and subsequently qualified as an architect (R.I.B.A.).and a member of the Town Planning Institute. At the outbreak of war, he enlisted in the 18th Bn., Royal Fusiliers. He was commissioned second lieutenant in the 3rd Bn., Essex Regiment in May 1915, later posted to the 2nd Bn. He had written some poetry at school, however his first wartime poem, possibly influenced by his training around Harwich, "Coming in Splendour through the Golden Gate", was published in the English Review in October 1915. By February 1916, his battalion occupied the Somme front line near Serre. Here on 22nd February 1916 he received an injury to his left arm, hospitalised for a spell but by April was back in the line, south of Serre. Private Adkins gave the following account of Waterhouse's fate. "We had got over one German trench and was advancing to a second when I was shot. I caught sight of Lieutenant Waterhouse about thirty yards ahead. He had a revolver in his hand and he stood out, a solitary figure. I saw him drop and begin to crawl. I thought at the time he was avoiding enemy fire, but he may have been hit". His body was not discovered until the summer of 1917. After his death his poems were published in a volume entitled, "Rail-head" and other poems. Entered France, 4th December 1915. His mother applied for his medals. Memorial Ref. I. K. 23., Serre Road Cemetery No.2, France.

WATKIN, Second Lieutenant, Alfred Charles. He got out his trench to investigate why there was a delay and was immediately killed, 1st July 1916. A Coy., 1st/5th Bn., North Staffordshire Regiment. Born 27th January 1889, Aged 27. Youngest son of Albert And Clara Martha Watkin, of 83, Peel Street, Dresden, Stoke-on-Trent. Educated Queensberry Road Elementary School. Received scholastic training at Longton and afterwards went to Saltley Training College. Formerly a teacher under the Birmingham Education Committee at Conway Road Council School and joined the Warwicks at the outbreak of war as a private becoming corporal, 2786. He was transferred to the North Staffordshire and given a commission, 21st December 1915. Entered France, 22nd March 1915. Brother, J. Watkin applied for his medals. Engaged to Miss Winifred Vickerstaff of Small Heath. Memorial Ref. I. L. 51., Foncquevillers Military Cemetery, France.

WATSON, Second Lieutenant, Charles Edward Stephens. At 7.28am, six leading platoons took up their position in No Man's Land, without loss. At 7.30am our front line pushed forward, they were met with very heavy artillery and machine-gun fire, some of 'A' and 'B' Coys who did make the German front line at 7.35am were surrounded and captured by the Germans. Killed on the way across, 1st July 1916. 1st Bn., East Lancashire Regiment. Aged 29. Born 19th September 1895. Son of William Stephens Watson and Alice Maude Watson, of Cape Town, South Africa. Educated at the High School, Rondebosch, Cape Province. Kent College, Canterbury began to board, 1911; Wicket keeper for the first XI 1912. Served with the Royal Naval Reserve at Simonstown, 1914 returned to England for RMC Sandhurst. Gazetted July, 1915. Entered France, 25th May 1916. Memorial Ref. Pier and Face 6 C., Thiepval Memorial, France.

1912 Cricket Team Far Right Back Row

WATSON, Captain, Cyril Pennefather. At 7.28am, six leading platoons took up their position in No Man's Land, without loss. At 7.30am our front line pushed forward, they were met with very heavy artillery and machine-gun fire, some of 'A' and 'B' Coys who did make the German front line at 7.35am were surrounded and captured by the Germans. Killed on the way across, 1st July 1916. 3rd Bn. attd. 1st Bn., East Lancashire Regiment. Cyril was away from the battalion at the Third Army School and finding themselves short of officers for the upcoming attack, he was recalled on an urgent basis. Aged 32. Eldest son of Brigadier General A. G. Watson (East Lancashire Regiment) and Mrs. Watson, of Sheringham, Norfolk. Employed Simmer & Jack mines, Transvaal. Enlisted in King Edward's Horse and later received a commission, 9th January 1915. 29th June 1916, Commanding Officer received a letter from OC 3rd Army School, Lieutenant Colonel Brownlow in which he referred to the excellent services tendered by 2nd Lieutenant C. P. Watson whilst an instructor in Lewis gun and bombing at the school in which he states "We appreciate it very much, the way in which you and your battalion has helped this school is indeed splendid. I can truly say you helped us more than the rest of the army put together'. Captain Watson rejoined his battalion on the 28th June 1916 following an urgent appeal as the battalion were short of officers for the forthcoming attack. Entered France 7th July 1915. Seconded as Brigade Machine Gun Officer on 27th August 1915. Suffered a gunshot wound to the shoulder and in hospital from 27th September 1915 to the 8th October. Father applied for his medals. Memorial Ref. Pier and Face 6 C., Thiepval Memorial, France.

WATSON, Lieutenant, Frank. Wounded and missing between Serre and Beaumont Hamel, 1st July 1916. Part of a trench raid on the morning of the 30th June 1916 to capture a German prisoner and obtain information. Lieutenant Watson and Second Lieutenant John William Worsnop did not return from this raid. Second Lieutenant Worsnop was given a date of death of the 30th June 1916 and is commemorated on the Thiepval Memorial. 18th Bn., West Yorkshire Regiment (Prince of Wales's Own) attached to the 93rd Trench Mortar Battery. Last entry referenced in the war diary refers to the 30th June. Appointed 1st August 1915. Unusually Medal Index Card has death accepted as 1st July 1916. His widow (remarried), Mrs. A. Chisholm, Woodview Terrace, Bradford applied for his medals. Memorial Ref. Pier and Face 2 A 2 C and 2 D., Thiepval Memorial, France.

WATSON, Second Lieutenant, Stanley Meredith. Died of wounds, heaving casualties sustained crossing No Man's Land, 1st July 1916. 64th Bde., Machine Gun Corps. Attached from Leinster Regiment. Employee of Central Cordoba Railway left 1914. Argentina in the Great War. Medals to Hamlins, Grammer and Hamlin solicitors, Surbiton, Surrey with no name on the Medal Index Card. Original burial map reference 57d.27.c.7.6. reburied 8th August 1919. Memorial Ref. VII. D. 4., Gordon Dump Cemetery, Ovillers-La Boisselle, France.

WATSON, Second Lieutenant, Sydney Towers. Reported killed at Fricourt on the 5th July died 1st July 1916. 16th Bn. attd. 15th Bn., Durham Light Infantry. Aged 21. Youngest of three sons of Henry Towers Watson and Catherine Elizabeth Devereux Watson, of 27, Burgoyne Road, Harringay Park, London. A civil servant (board of agriculture and fisheries). Two brothers served. Nephew of Mr. Robert Locke of Aylesbury. Gazetted 28th July 1915. Entered France, June 1916. Father applied for his medals. Memorial Ref. Pier and Face 14 A and 15 C., Thiepval Memorial, France.

WATTS, Captain, Talbot Hamilton. Killed whilst gallantly leading his company, 1st July 1916. 'A' Coy., 16th Bn., Middlesex Regiment. A survivor Lionel Renton describes 'I saw the acting company commander lying half in and half out of a shell-hole, his body and his head in the hole, his legs sticking out. He was dead. I couldn't see where he was hit but blood was trickling out of his mouth.' Aged 27. Younger son of Dr. Fred Watts and Dorothea H. Watts of 13, Argyll Road, London. Attended West Buckland School between 1897 and 1903. Played regularly for Notts County Football Club when he left school. He had been a school master after leaving West Buckland but had to give up this career as well as the football due to heart trouble. Belonged to the firm, Messrs. Killick, Nixon & Co and was home from Bombay when war broke out. He immediately joined the Public Schools Battalion and received his commission in September 1914. He went to the Front in November 1915 and in January 1916 was gazetted captain. Described in his obituary in the School's Register of November 1916 as, 'one of the finest all-round athletes in the history of the school. It is hard to draw comparisons, but looking back he has strong claims for the title of the best all-round cricket player'. His brother, J. Watts Esq., c/o Australian United Steam Navigation Coy Ltd., Port Adelaide, South Australia applied for his medals. Memorial Ref. Pier and Face 12 D and 13 B., Thiepval Memorial, France.

WEATHERHEAD, Second Lieutenant, Andrew. Originally reported as missing, 1st July 1916. 3rd Bn. attd. 1st Bn., King's Own (Royal Lancaster Regiment). Son of Canon Robert Johnston and Anna Bagot Weatherhead. Vicar of Seacombe. Reported missing in the early stage of the big advance, is now officially placed among the killed. He had the distinction of being twice Mentioned in Despatches during the last six months. When war broke out he was home on a holiday from Calcutta and joined the 10th Bn., Liverpool Scottish, private, 3167. Entered France, 1st November 1914. He was wounded by a sniper in February, 1915, and during his convalescent obtained a commission in the King's Own Lancaster Regiment, in which his brother, had been. Captain G. E. Weatherhead was killed on the 9th May 1915 with the 2nd King's Own Royal Lancaster Regiment. Birkenhead Park Football Club. Commemorated Sons and Daughters of the Anglican Church Clergy. Mrs. J. C. Gill (sister), Horbourne, Birmingham applied for his medals. Memorial Ref. Pier and Face 5 D and 12 B., Thiepval Memorial, France.

WEBBER, Second Lieutenant, Stanley Albert. Killed in action, 1st July 1916. 1st Bn., South Staffordshire Regiment. Aged 21. Only son of William and Maria Camillia Webber, of 5, St. Lawrence Road, Plymouth. Born 15th April 1895. Attended Taunton College. Clerk with the Western Counties Acquisitional Coy. Joined as a territorial in the 7th Devons on the 3rd April 1913, private, 828. He was on service on the East Coast of England until the spring, and was given a commission in the South Staffs. Gazetted March 1915.

His last letter to his father was dated 30th June 1916; ' My dear father – Tomorrow we are going to make another big attempt to drive the enemy back. I have a feeling I shall come out of it safely. But the risks of a big battle are considerable. I am going into with perfect confidence in the success of our arms, and feel, as everyone else here does that the end is not far off. While out at the Front I have been upheld, strengthened and made happy by all the love at home. This has sustained me all through the trials and dangers of warfare, and I only wish I could repay you for your devotion. If it should be my fate to go under, do not grieve for me. For love stretched over death and makes it only a temporary separation. I have no fear of death. I am going into the fight with the assurance of God's goodness and I will submit myself to his care. If it be His will to call me to the higher existence, I shall leave this world without regret, and be glad to have died doing my duty to you all and to my country. My gratitude for all the love from home is deeper than it is possible for me to say. It has been my greatest incentive to duty. There are many to whom I would like to say farewell personally. But, that being impossible, I will be glad if you would give my love to all my friends. Well, dear father, it be God's will that I should fall, do not be sorrowful. But thank Him that I have had the privilege of dying for my country. With the greatest of love to you all. Your most affectionate son, Stanley'. Originally buried 'The Shrine', Mametz, Sht 62d. Sq.F.5c.1.4 and reinterred 1920, identified as there was a cross on the grave. His father applied for his medals. Memorial Ref. IX. E. 10., Dantzig Alley British Cemetery, Mametz, France. WO 339/41536

Do Not Grieve But Thank God I Die For My Country

WEBSTER, Lieutenant, Michael Harold. 1st July 1916. 13th Bn. attd. 16th Bn., West Yorkshire Regiment (Prince of Wales's Own). Father, Mr. R. Webster lived at The Hollies, Wesley Road, Armley. Age 22. Educated at the West Leeds High School and took his BA degree at Leeds University joining the OTC. He enlisted as a private, 22878 in the Highland Light Infantry on June 14th 1915 and served in France from 23rd August 1915 before he received a commission dated 21st January 1916. He returned to the Front on June 15th being passed to West Yorks. Brother, Willie served with the RFA. His father applied for his medals. Memorial Ref. Pier and Face 2 A 2 C and 2 D., Thiepval Memorial, France.

WEDGWOOD, Lieutenant, Gilbert Colclough. He fell when approaching the German trenches and died instantaneously, 1st July 1916. 109th Coy., Machine Gun Corps (Infantry). Aged 22. Son of Reverend George Ryles Wedgwood (Methodist Minster) and Elizabeth Wedgwood, of "Egerton," 76, North Road, Bloomfield, Belfast formerly Methodist Church, University Road. Born in Dublin, 1893. After leaving school went to work for the Ulster Bank and left in October 1914 to join the army. Brother of Second Lieutenant, Philip Egerton Wedgwood also killed 1st July 1916. Old M.C.B Boy and was an officer in the Young Citizen Volunteers. Official wire described him as 10th Bn., Royal Irish Rifles posted to the Machine Gun Corps, March 1916. Mother later placed a notice in the Belfast Evening Telegraph: 'In loving memory of my dear sons, Gilbert and Philip Wedgwood, killed in action at the Somme on July 1, 1916. Elizabeth Wedgwood' and applied for both sons medals and officers pension. Memorial Ref. Pier and Face 5 C and 12 C., Thiepval Memorial, France.

WEDGWOOD, Second Lieutenant, Philip Egerton. Treacherously murdered by a German whose life he had spared, 1st July 1916. 16th Bn., Royal Irish Rifles. Brother of Lieutenant, Gilbert Colclough Wedgwood also killed 1st July 1916. Third son of Reverend George Ryles Wedgwood and Elizabeth Wedgwood, of Egerton, 76, North Road, Bloomfield, Belfast. Canon King a chaplain of the Ulster Division wrote to his father and explained, "he was in the German trenches and was taking prisoners in the dugout, his party had bombs with them and the Germans were at their mercy. He came to a dug out where there were twenty Germans, he could have killed them but offered their lives if they came out and surrendered, they did so he turned his back for a moment and one of them shot him dead." Educated Methodist College and received his commission 19th October 1914. His mother applied for both sons medals and officer pensions. Original burial map reference 57d.R.19.c.5.4, cross found on grave and identified as 2/Lt. Weagood, 14 R.I.R. reburied and corrected May 1919. Memorial Ref. IV. A. 4., Mill Road Cemetery, Thiepval, France.

WEIR, Captain, John. Fell gallantly leading his platoon, who would have followed him anywhere. He was hit just at the German wire and was killed instantly, 1st July 1916. He had a few hours before the assault put out tapes to enable our columns to get the correct direction. 9th Bn., Royal Inniskilling Fusiliers. Aged 50. Son of John and Elizabeth Weir, of Frendraught, Ballindrait, Co. Donegal. Member of the firm, Alex Weir of Carrickbrack, Convoywoollen Mills a well-known auctioneer. Lieutenant Colonel Ricardo wrote to his brother, Alexander Weir. Entered France, 26th September 1915. Was home in February 1916. He had taken part in a raid in May 1916 and made the subject of a special order by Major General Nugent DSO. A. Weir, (brother), Convoy, Co. Donegal applied for his medals. Memorial Ref. Pier and Face 4 D and 5 B., Thiepval Memorial, France.

WELCH, Lieutenant, James Stanley Lightfoot. Died gallantly leading his platoon against the enemy. He was wounded first of all by a bullet and fell, but he was killed immediately afterwards by a shell, 1st July 1916. His last words to his platoon were :-'Never mind me; carry on'. 197 all ranks including one officer killed and three wounded. 12th Bn., King's Own Yorkshire Light Infantry. Aged 20. Only son of the Reverend Edward Ashurst and Edith Marion Welch, of Southchurch Rectory, Southend-on-Sea. Born at Toronto, Canada in 1896. Attended Upper College, Canada. Was at Lawrence Saunders School and Rugby School. He entered Rugby School with a Scholarship in 1910, and left in July 1914. On the outbreak of war he applied for a commission, and, while waiting for it, he went into residence at King's College, Cambridge, where he had won a Scholarship in history and classics. He was only there for a week before being gazetted to the Yorkshire Light Infantry. Enlisted October 1914, promoted lieutenant in the following May. His battalion went to Egypt, 22nd December, 1915, and thence to France, in March, 1916. Mentioned in Despatches of January 4th, 1917. He was buried on the field by a party of his men. Father applied for his medals. Memorial Ref. D. 66., Queens Cemetery, Puisieux, France.

Being Made Perfect In A Little While He Fulfilled Long Years

WELLS, Second Lieutenant, Thomas William Maurice. Reported missing, then killed, he fell in an attack on the German entrenchments, last seen gallantly leading his men in a maze of craters near the German wire, 1st July 1916. A wounded soldier who crawled back to the British lines said he had been hit three times in the head and in the back and thigh and when a search party went to look for him they could find no trace, 2nd Bn., South Wales Borderers. From Claudius Road, Colchester. Elder son of Thomas Wells (sanitary inspector for the Borough of Colchester). Age 28. He was one of the 'Deathless Army' that fought at Mons. He was formerly employed in the Army Ordnance Corps at Colchester and enlisted in the Essex Regiment, lance corporal, 8796. He was called up with the reserve at the outbreak of war, served in France from the 22nd August 1914 and rendering gallant service for the retreat from Mons he was promoted to sergeant. Served for four years in India. He was badly gassed but recovered and gazetted in the South Wales Borderers from the 2nd Essex in May 1916. Engaged five weeks before his death to Miss Bell. Father applied for his medals. Memorial Ref. Pier and Face 4 A., Thiepval Memorial, France.

WESTAWAY, Second Lieutenant, Leslie Thomas. Missing believed killed leading his men near Beaumont Hamel, 1st July 1916. 2nd Bn., Royal Fusiliers. Aged 22. Son of John and Sarah Westaway, of 120, Melrose Avenue, Cricklewood, London. Attended Kilburn Grammar School, obtained a scholarship, 1910. Member of University of London, OTC. Goldsmith's College. Enlisted HAC, No. 4199, private. Entered France, 10th November 1915. Commissioned 22nd April 1916. Death confirmed September 1916. Medals applied for 25th November 1920 by his father. Memorial Ref. B. 98., Hawthorn Ridge Cemetery No.2, Auchonvillers, France.

WESTMORE, Second Lieutenant, Lawrence Arthur. As soon as the troops left the front line, heavy machine-gun fire was brought to bear on them from all directions, casualties if officers amounted to 100%. Beaumont Hamel, 1st July 1916. 1st Bn., Hampshire Regiment. Aged 22. Son of Arthur Sydney and Gertrude Mary Westmore, of 9, Wimborne Road, Bournemouth. Educated at Radley. Exhibitioner of Wadham College, Oxford. Received his commission, December 1915. Memorial Ref. I. I. 72., Sucrerie Military Cemetery, Colincamps, France.

WESTON, Second Lieutenant, John Douglas. Reported missing 1st July 1916. Captain J. H Brett provided a report "Between half past three and four on the afternoon of July 1st. 2nd Lt. Weston was in action at La Boisselle and he was missing. Most careful search was made for him by search parties, but without success. I was one of the search party. We were attacking at the time; very furious fighting was going on. He was undoubtedly killed by shell fire and buried in the debris." 13th Bn. attd. 11th Bn., Suffolk Regiment. Aged 19. Son of Frederick James and Annie Weston. Born 6th December 1896 in Islington, son of Frederick and Annie Weston. In 1911 he lived with his parents in Tetherdown Downs, Court Road, Purley, Surrey. Clerk with Bankers Guarantee Trust. Enlisted 6th Bn., London Regiment, private, 1956. 3rd August 1915 admitted to a Casualty Clearing Station and returned to England. Commissioned 30th November 1915. Joined battalion, 23rd April 1916. The family were visited by a fellow officer and asked the War Office to issue a death certificate but death was not presumed until 8th March 1917. Father applied for his medals. Memorial Ref. Pier and Face 1 C and 2 A., Thiepval Memorial, France. WO 339/48119

WHARTON, Second Lieutenant, Sidney, Alfred. Died of wounds, 1st July 1916. 8th Bn., Norfolk Regiment. Aged 20. Son of Mrs. Arthur P. Wharton, of Bircham Tofts, King's Lynn and nephew of Mr. W. D. Wharton of Wellingborough. Deceased was an old Wellingburian. Father prominent member of the Docking District council, condolences received by his uncle, Mr. H. E. Wharton. Army Service Corps (Territorial Force), driver, 1528. Commissioned 23rd January 1915. Entered France, 4th December 1915. Father applied for his medals. Memorial Ref. II. B. 26., Dive Copse British Cemetery, Sailly-Le-Sec, France.

Officers of the 8th Battalion Norfolk Regiment
Second Lieutenant Wharton far right middle row also includes Captain B. P. Ayre far right bottom row also killed 1st July 1916.

WHEELER, Second Lieutenant, William Pierce. Reported missing believed killed 1st July officially 2nd July 1916. Medal Index Card has 1st July 1916. 1st /6th Bn., Royal Warwickshire Regiment. Aged 20. Eldest son of Edward (agent to Mr. Steel-Maitland M.P) and Edith Wheeler, of Westbourne, Beech Hill Road, Wylde Green, Gravelly Hill, Birmingham. Educated privately, joined the ranks shortly after the outbreak of war, private, 2649 and became a corporal. Entered France, 22nd March 1915. He received his commission, 6th May 1916. In civilian life was an engineering pupil at Wolseley Motors Ltd. A brother was in the Scottish Borderers. Father applied for his medals. Memorial Ref. Pier and Face 9 A 9 B and 10 B., Thiepval Memorial, France.

WHITAKER, Captain, George Clifford. Fighting was hard and shelling heavy, machine-gun fire was intense, led his company over the parapet and was soon hit, he got up and continued to lead his men until hit a second time, 1st July 1916. C Coy., 15th Bn., West Yorkshire Regiment (Prince of Wales's Own). Aged 28. Born Leeds, 20th January 1888. Youngest Son of Matthew Whitaker (stone mason and railway contractor), of The Prospect, Horsforth, Leeds. Educated at Ilkley Grammar School, Leeds University and on leaving school chose engineering as his profession. He also served for two years with the 5th Bn., (Territorial), The Kings Own Light Infantry. Played as a forward for Headingley Rugby Union Football Club. When war broke out he enlisted as a private was given a temporary commission as a lieutenant with the battalion. He was promoted to captain on 1st May 1915 and placed in command of the recruiting party. This included 2nd Lieutenant Major William Booth, Roy Kilner and Arthur Dolphin, three well known Yorkshire and England Cricketers. He was engaged to Miss Mary Hamilton, youngest daughter of Mr. J. B. Hamilton, the Leeds Tramways Manager. Entered France, 22nd December 1915. On the 28th February 1917, when the Germans abandoned Serre, the opportunity was taken to search the 1st July battleground. Among the officers they identified were Captain Whitaker and 2nd Lieutenant M. W. Booth. In his memoirs, after the war, Private Arthur V. Pearson Wrote: "Months afterwards, when he (the Germans) had abandoned Serre, a party of "Old Boys" were sent up to the old sector we had attacked over and we identified several bodies. One was our company commander (Captain Whitaker). We put what was left of him into a sandbag and carried him down to a cemetery. We had the Padre with us and he read the burial service as we buried him." Father applied for his medals. Memorial Ref. I. A. 1., Sailly-Au-Bois Military Cemetery, France.

WHITBY, Second Lieutenant, Ernest Victor. Killed in action, 1st July 1916. 4th Bn., Middlesex Regiment. Aged 25. Son of Philip And Harriet Whitby, of 5 Church Row, High Street, Wandsworth, London. Attended Wandsworth School. Plantation manager. Enlisted 3rd September 1914. Served with the Royal Naval Volunteer Reserve. Joined battalion, France 23rd January 1916. Originally buried Empress Trench and angle formed by new communication trench Sht 26. Sq. d. Contour 110. Father applied for his medals. Originally buried as unknown officer 57d.X.27c.7.6 and later identified in collective grave. Memorial Ref. IV. L., Gordon Dump Cemetery, Ovillers-La Boisselle, France. WO 339/54377

Rest Well Brave Heart

WHITE, Second Lieutenant, Aubrey Cecil. Killed while leading his men, 1st July 1916. 8th Bn., York and Lancaster Regiment. Aged 20. Second son of Richard and Anna M. White (nee Croly), of Gowran, Co. Kilkenny. Educated Castle Park, Dalkey, Co. Dublin, and Trent College, Derbyshire. He was gazetted second lieutenant in October, 1914, and went out to France, 28th December 1915. Father applied for his medals. Original burial map reference 57D.R.32.c.2.7 and reburied May 1919. Miss D. I. White, Gowran House, Kilkenny choose his inscription. Memorial Ref. II. B. 10., Lonsdale Cemetery, Authuille, France.

He Giveth His Beloved Sleep Psalm 127.2

WHITE, Lieutenant, Bernard Charles De Boismaison. His platoon was amongst the first to leave the trenches and he was last seen standing on German parapet throwing bombs, 1st July 1916. Reported he was placed in a dug-out and buried. 20th (Tyneside Scottish) Bn., Northumberland Fusiliers. Aged 29. Son of Bernard White and Louie Stamp White, of 15, West End Avenue, Pinner, Middlesex. Born 9th October 1886, Harlesden. Educated at home. 1909 various positions in printers including Hutchinsons, 1912 moved to the publicity department of Marconi Company and became assistant editor of the Wireless News. London University OTC. Gazetted temporary second lieutenant, 22nd December 1914, Yorks and Lancashire, February 1915 and to France January, 1916. War poet; Remembrance and Other Verses published in 1917 Next of kin was his step-mother, Mrs. L. M. Hoseford, Chowringhill, Hammerton Road, Bromley. Commemorated St Mary's Church, Bromley. Miss. D. H. White (sister) applied for his medals. Memorial Ref. Pier and Face 10 B 11 B and 12 B., Thiepval Memorial, France. WO 339/4864

WHITE, Second Lieutenant, Edward Beadon. In charge of four guns to stop a counter attack and was hit by a rifle bullet about 4.00pm, died of wounds, 1st July 1916. 11th Bn., Yorkshire Regiment attd 92nd Machine Gun Company. Born St. Paul's, Bristol in 1879. Served in the 2/1 North Somerset Yeomanry from 1902, Regimental Quarter Master Sergeant, 554. Married to Jeannie in 1912 and had one daughter, Maria Young White. Resided 11, Boyton Avenue, Cathcart, Glasgow. Employed HM Customs and Excise. Commissioned 26th September 1915. Joined Machine Gun Corps 1916. Entered France, 17th May 1916. Youngest son of Mr. John White, Deanery Road. Unusually Medal Index Card has two addresses for Mrs. E. B. White with instructions one for before the 2nd September 1922 and the other one for after; both were in Glasgow. Daughter received pension. Memorial Ref. V. G. 7., Euston Road Cemetery, Colincamps, France.

WHITE, Captain, George. Slightly wounded in the neck in the morning but continued at the head of his section and received a fatal bullet in the head, 1st July 1916. Reported to have said 'Come on boys. I will lead you down' and was immediately killed about the same time as Captain Limbery. B Coy., 1st Bn., South Staffordshire Regiment. Aged 29. Eldest son of John White (Councillor) and Mrs. John White, of 95, Paris St., Exeter. Gazetted in May 1915 and promoted to the rank of temporary captain the following December. Entered France, 28th July 1915. Married and left a son. Originally buried The Shrine, Mametz, Sht 62d.sq.F.5. Re-interred 1920. Mother applied for his medals. Original burial map reference 62D.F.5.c.1.4 and grave marked with a cross. Brother Victor was a second lieutenant in the same battalion. Memorial Ref. IX. E. 9., Dantzig Alley British Cemetery, Mametz, France. WO 339/46283

WHITE, Second Lieutenant, Herbert Robert. Reported missing at Mailly-Maillet, 1st July 1916. Went over in the second wave, 8.00am to 8.15am, he got three-quarters of the way between the Front line and the German front line. He turned as if to shout to his men when he was shot and died instantly. 3rd Bn. attd. 2nd Bn., Essex Regiment. Aged 39. Son of William Henry and Sara White (nee Brookes of East Ham, Essex. Born 23rd July 1878. Enlisted 1st Bn., Essex Regiment, 1895, Quarter Master Sergeant, 4515. Served in the South African campaign Queen's Medal and King's Medal and seven clasps. Served in France and Flanders from 22nd August 1914. Gazetted second lieutenant, 9th May 1915. Husband of Marguerite Blanche Emmeline White (nee Twiss), of St. Margaret's, Kiltegan, Co. Wicklow married 1910 and had three children, Vivian Sara Godfrey, Marguerite Valerie Twiss and Iris Claire Anita White. End of June 1916 in the list of reinforcements. Widow applied for his medals. Memorial Ref. Pier and Face 10 D., Thiepval Memorial, France.

WHITE, Second Lieutenant, John (Jack) Lindsay. He was in the bombing section and attacked by a party of the enemy and though he drove them off he was wounded in the leg. He was unable to walk and was being assisted back when he was shot in the head and died instantly, 1st July 1916. 3rd Bn. attd. 2nd Bn., Gordon Highlanders. Aged 23. Younger son of John and Lily White, of 53, East Claremont St., Edinburgh. Born 2nd October 1893. Educated Edinburgh Institution. When war broke out he was sheep farming at his father's extensive farm, Kerarabury, New South Wales. Returning he enlisted as a private in January 1915 and was promoted to corporal, 5th Cavalry Reserve Regiment, corporal, 9787, he applied for a commission and got it in the 3rd Gordon Highlanders dated 18th August 1915. He had been at the Front for six weeks since 27th May 1916. Buried 67 Support Trench near Mansel Copse 62d. Sq.F.11.c.8.3. Father applied for his medals. Memorial Ref. A. 5., Gordon Cemetery, Mametz, France. WO 339/62561

Until We Meet Again

WHITE, Captain, John Vernon. Killed in action, Fricourt Farm, 1st July 1916. C Coy., 20th Bn., Manchester Regiment. Aged 24. Eldest son of Dr. John Hall and Mary Louise White, of Bournemouth formerly Hesketh Park, Southport. Born at Shaw, Lancashire in 12th November, 1891. Attended Denstone College. Played for Waterloo Rugby F.C. Played for the Southport Cricket Club. One of the most popular members of the Southport and Birkdale Cricket Club, with whom he played in matches against most of the prominent clubs in the Liverpool district. He was also a member of the Southport Olympic and Waterloo Rugby Football Clubs. Shortly after the war broke out he joined the Manchester "Pals," received a commission as lieutenant in November, 1914, and as captain in January last.

He had been in France for the past six months. Worked for William Deacon's Bank at it's Formby and Southport branches. Resided 44 Park Road, Southport. Originally buried King George's Hill, 1000 yards SW of Mametz, sht 62d. F.9.d.5.5. Memorial Ref. VI. A. I., Dantzig Alley British Cemetery, Mametz, France. WO 339/17236

I Thank My God For All My Remembrance Of Thee Mother

WHITE, Lieutenant, Malcolm Graham. Missing believed killed, 1st July 1916. 6th Bn. attd. A Coy., 1st Bn., Rifle Brigade. Youngest son of John Arnold White, of Mere Cottage, Birkenhead. Captain, Shrewsbury School. OTC. Master at Shrewsbury School. Joined in 1909, graduate of King's College, Cambridge. For the first six months of the war he remained at school, and was gazetted captain (OTC) 13th February 1915. He joined up in the summer of 1915 and left for the Front, 9th February 1916. A memoir containing his letters and other writings with those of Captain Evelyn Herbert Lightfoot Southwell, another Master, was published in 1919 under the title of 'Two Men'. In his final letter to Southwell on 27th June 1916, White wrote: "Oh Man, I can't write now. I am too like a coach before the Bumping Races or Challenge Oars. So, Man, good luck. Our New House and Shrewsbury are immortal, which is a great comfort." Brother H. G. White applied for his medals. Captain Southwell was killed on the 15th September 1916 and with no known grave is also commemorated on the Thiepval Memorial. Memorial Ref. Pier and Face 16 B and 16 C., Thiepval Memorial, France.

WHITE, Second Lieutenant, Nathan. Killed in the advance, 1st July 1916. 29th (Tyneside Scottish) Bn., Northumberland Fusiliers. Age 31. Born in Jarrow 1885. Only son of Martha and Joseph White (Manager of the Palmer Company gas works) of 18 Caroline Street, Jarrow. Age 30. Succeeded his father. When the King called one of the first to offer to serve. Obtained his commission at Christmas 1915. 'His death removes a young fellow of much promise.' Mother applied for his medals and officers pension, c/o Messrs. Newland & Newland, Grange Road, Jarrow-upon-Tyne. Memorial Ref. Pier and Face 10 B 11 B and 12 B., Thiepval Memorial, France.

WHITGREAVE, Second Lieutenant, Henry Egerton. Missing, 1st July 1916. 1st Bn., Somerset Light Infantry. Aged 34. Eldest son of Robert Whitgreave and Marion Whitgreave, of Bushbury, Clevedon, Somerset formerly of Moseley Court, Staffordshire Born at Stafford. Educated Radford House School, Coventry and Beaumont College, Old Windsor. Enlisted on the outbreak of war, Somerset Light Infantry, lance sergeant, 12029 and was commissioned 6th August 1915, 1st Bn., and went to France, 21st May 1915. His commanding officer, writing to his parents, says :—"It is with very great regret that I have to tell you that there is no longer any hope that your son is alive. I have received a letter from another battalion saying that his body was found outside our parapet, and has been buried there. Your son was a most capable officer, and he is a great loss to us." L. Whitgreave, (brother) applied for his medals. Memorial Ref. A. 51., Redan Ridge Cemetery No.1, Beaumont-Hamel, France.

May He Rest In Peace

WHITTAM, Second Lieutenant, Francis Joseph. At 7.30am, leading sections of B, D and a bombing section dashed forward in extended order, being led by Second Lieutenants Craig, Garfunkle & Spencer, B Coy by Prescott, Edwards and Kershaw at the same moment, 1 platoon under Lieutenant Whittam and two platoons of bombers left the trenches. The leading two lines had a moments grace and then the enemy machine-guns opened and a storm of bullets met the attack. 1st July 1916. 3rd Bn. attd. 1st Bn., Lancashire Fusiliers. Second son of Major and Mrs. James Whittam, of Prestwich Park, Manchester. Aged 38. Educated at Ampleforth College and Ushaw, he returned from Canada in 1914 to offer his services. In Gallipoli, where he went through the campaign he acted as adjutant to the Lancashire Fusiliers. Left a widow and a son, Francis Joseph Richie Whittam whom was educated at Stonyhurst College. Well known in catholic circles. His Colonel wrote; 'he led them forward nobly and was hit when close up to the German trenches. I know his servant went out to him as soon as he heard but he never got back. Our battlefield was large and we tried for three nights to find your husband but never succeeded.' Parents applied for his medals. Memorial Ref. Pier and Face 3 C and 3 D., Thiepval Memorial, France.

WILKINS, Second Lieutenant, Alfred Henry. Reported missing believed killed, known to have been wounded in the arm, 1st July 1916. He fought in the second line German trench with Captain Leman and assisted in trying to organise a defensive position until the were overwhelmed. No. 5 Platoon. B Coy., 1st/7th Bn., Sherwood Foresters (Notts and Derby Regiment). Son of Mr. Henry and Julia Wilkins of 14, Forest Road, Nottingham. Educated at High Pavement School. He had seen a good deal of military service. A resident of South Africa he served in the Boer War and held the star for the siege of Kimberley. When war broke out he rejoined the service and went through the German South West Africa campaign being a sergeant in the Imperial Light Horse, he came home with a view to joining the forces and was given a commission. Commissioned 9th October 1915. Arrived in France, May 1916. Well known in local Masonic circles. Brother fought with the Canadians. Father applied for medals, to be issued by South African authorities. Memorial Ref. Pier and Face 10 C 10 D and 11 A., Thiepval Memorial, France.

WILKINSON, Second Lieutenant, Gordon Frederick Noble. 1st July 1916. 10th Bn., King's Own Yorkshire Light Infantry. Aged 23. Born 20th September 1892. Son of Robert Daniel and Kate Wilkinson, of 10 Granville Road, Blackheath, London. Educated at Westminster School arrived in 1906. Clerk, Stock Exchange Memorial. In August 1914, he enlisted in the 10th Bn., Royal Fusiliers (City of London Regiment) No. 282 as a private and later became a second lieutenant in the King's Own Yorkshire Light Infantry, 3rd June 1916. In the field from 31st July 1915. In response to the War Office telegram his mother wrote asking for further details, where he fell, where he is buried and officers she could contact. R. P. Wilkinson applied for medals in respect of his late brother. Memorial Ref. Pier and Face 11 C and 12 A., Thiepval Memorial, France. WO 339/65228

WILLEY, Second Lieutenant, Thomas Arthur Raymond Robert Ellicott. He was killed on July 1st, 1916, whilst leading his men in the Battle of the Somme, near Hebuterne. Fighting was hard and shelling heavy, machine-gun fire was intense. No. 13 Platoon, D Coy. 15th Bn., West Yorkshire Regiment (Prince of Wales's Own). Aged 19. Born 1897, Leeds. Elder son of Arthur Willey (solicitor), of Calverley Chambers, Victoria Square, Leeds. Attended Roscoes College, Harrogate and Harrow. Was articled to his father as a solicitor. Lieutenant Willey joined the 15th West Yorkshire Regiment as a private in August, 1914, and was given a commission in the same Regiment in the following December. He went to Egypt with the Battalion, 22nd December 1915 and in the following April was sent to France. On leaving Harrow he and his younger brother became articled clerks in their father's firm. Enlisted as a private in the "Pals" September 1914 and on December 4th 1914 was offered and accepted a commission as temporary 2nd lieutenant. Best boxer of the battalion at his weight. He served at Colsterdale, Egypt and France. 2nd Lieutenant Tom Willey and 2nd Lieutenant Arthur Norman Hutton (Commander of C Company, 10 Platoon) were to have the distinction of leading the first waves over the top. Willey's childhood friend and fellow "Pals" Officer Lieutenant John Gilbert "Jackie" Vause, Commander of No. 15 Platoon D Company was in the second wave. At about 7.15am Mr. Willey passed down the order, 'Get ready 13,' as casually as though on an ordinary parade. We then filed out, up the scaling ladder, through the gap in our own wire and to our place as the first wave (the post of honour) in advance of our wire, Mr. Willey said, 'Ten paces interval boys' and it was done just as though on manoeuvers." "At 7:30am, Young Willey jumped up, and waving his revolver, shouted "Come on 13. Give Them Hell", "Willey lost his legs when he was hit by a shell" . He was killed a few minutes after Zero hour. That night a few unwounded survivors from No. 10 platoon crawled out into No Man's Land trying to find 'young Willeys' body but to no avail. Father applied for his medals. Memorial Ref. Pier and Face 2 A 2 C and 2 D., Thiepval Memorial, France.

WILLIAMS, Second Lieutenant, Leslie. He was killed instantly, 1st July 1916. Private Hunter stated 'he was in front of Albert and he saw him hit. I am afraid he was killed. I believe he came from Kent. He was a splendid fellow'. 23rd (Tyneside Scottish) Bn., Northumberland Fusiliers. Aged 25. Born 29th January 1891. Engineer. Son of W. A. and Ada M. Williams, of Copper Beeches, Tower Road, Orpington, Kent. Educated Devonshire House School, Orpington and Elstow School, Bedford. Played cricket for Bedford County and hockey for Kent. In October 1914 joined the Sportsmans Battalion and promoted. Commissioned 11th May 1915. Entered France,

9th January 1916. Originally reported wounded and then confirmed as killed 10th July. Miss L. Williams wrote into say she had been informed he was killed but his name appeared in the list of the missing, the War Office wrote back on the 22nd July; 'Regret to inform killed on the 1st'. Originally buried as unknown British Officer at location 57d.X.13.d.2.3 and exhumed in 1930 identified by officers uniform, boots, buttons, whistle, matchbox engraved L.W, medallion engraved L. W, advance pay book and ring with Tyneside Scottish crest, officer's revolver holster and map case. Memorial Ref. XXXIII. E. 10., Serre Road Cemetery No.2, France. WO 339/29913

WILLIAMSON, Second Lieutenant, Harold Godwin. Killed in action, Gommecourt, 1st July 1916. 1st/6th Bn., North Staffordshire Regiment. Born 17th February 1896. Third son of Mr. A. W. Williamson, Oxnaford, New Romney, Kent. Joined the Queen Victoria Rifles in September 1914, private, 3039, and proceeded to France, 20th January 1915. Gazetted 13th November 1915. In the choir school of All Saints and entered St. Edwards School, Oxford playing cricket and rugby and a member of the OTC. Student of the Society of the Sacred Mission, Kelham. He was in the cricket Eleven whilst at St. Edward's School, Oxford. Requiem sang in memory at All Saints, Margaret Street, London. Memorial Ref. Pier and Face 14 B and 14 C., Thiepval Memorial, France.

WILLIAMSON, Second Lieutenant, John. Killed whilst leading his men in the greatest gallantry in the attack in which the battalion took part and was shot. 2nd Bn., Seaforth Highlanders. Aged 19. Eldest son of Reverend James Alexander and Martha W. Williamson, of the Manse, Alva, Clackmannanshire. Body was side by sided in a large British cemetery, 200 yards NW of the Sucrerie. Enlisted although he had not attained military age at the start of the war. Promoted February 1916. The bodies of Captain Alison, 2nd Lieutenants Williamson, Broom, Buchanan and Blackwood with 25 others were side by sided. 'Nothing could have exceeded his braveness and devotion to duty and in dying such a splendid and heroic death he is every way proved himself worthy of the traditions and record of the 2nd Highlanders.' Educated Dollar Academy and left in 1913. Memorial Ref. I. H. 22., Sucrerie Military Cemetery, Colincamps, France.

WILLIS, Captain, Samuel. Message received at 4.00pm that he was hanging on but hard pressed. Reported missing, and hoped he had fallen into the hands of the enemy, 1st July 1916. D Coy., 14th Bn., Royal Irish Rifles. Aged 43. Son of Jacob and Mrs. Willis of Mountcharles, Donegal. Husband of Mary Christina Willis, of Lynncrest, Coleraine Road, Portrush, Co. Antrim. Teacher in the Coleraine Academical Institution. Member of the Portstewart Golf Club and a member of the council for many years. Captain Willis wrote a letter of sympathy to the family of Sergeant William Stephenson who was killed in April 1916. Wife appealed for information on him whilst residing at 250 Antrim Road, Belfast. Still missing 26th December 1916. Memorial Ref. Pier and Face 15 A and 15 B., Thiepval Memorial, France.

WILSON, Lieutenant, Arthur Desmond Lloyd. Officially reported missing, Beaumont Hamel, 1st July 1916. 9th Bn., Queen's Own (Royal West Kent Regiment). Joined the 1st Bn., Royal Inniskilling from the Royal West Kent on the 3rd March 1916 joining in Egypt. Gazetted 18th March 1915. Awarded a testimonial on vellum by the Royal Humane Society in recognition of gallant conduct in saving a life in France on the 3rd April 1916. Appeal for info on the fate of her son by Lady Wilson, Fernleigh Hospital, Larkfield, Kent. Lady Wilson applied for the medals of her son. Memorial Ref. D. 42., Y Ravine Cemetery, Beaumont-Hamel, France.

WILSON, Lieutenant Colonel, Denis Daly. Shot during the attack, after the attack, reported missing, 1st July 1916. He was in a shell hole just in front of the German parapet and another attack was ordered, with men being killed as soon as they stood up. 17th Indian Cavalry att. 1/5th Sherwood Foresters. He and his father had served in the Boer War. He had been made a second lieutenant in the 1st (Oxford University) Volunteer Battalion, Oxford Light Infantry on 4th March 1899 and was transferred into the York and Lancaster Regiment as a University candidate on 29th November 1899. Served with it the operations round Ladysmith and Spion Kop, also in the operations in Natal and Transvaal 1899-1901. He was promoted lieutenant on 29th July 1902 with effect from 5th February 1901 transferred to Indian Army in 1902. His father was Colonel John Gerald Wilson, 3rd

York and Lancaster Regiment and Denis Wilson appears to have served in the same unit. He and his father both served in the Boer War, his father dying of wounds received at Tweebosch on 8th March 1902. Lieutenant Wilson was promoted captain into the 17th Indian Cavalry on 29th November 1908. At some point he attended Staff College and, prior to his appointment as Commanding Officer of the 5th Sherwoods on 29th March 1916, he had been a GSO3 attached to the 46th Division's Staff. Adjutant April 1906 to April 1909. Squadron Commander, 10th October 1913. Proceeded to Staff College, Camberly, December 1913. Appointed to the General Staff, 46th Division on the outbreak of war and served with it in France. Subsequently appointed in March 1916 to command 5th Battalion, Sherwood Foresters. Twice Mentioned in Despatches. Queens South African Medal with seven clasps. Captain to be temporary major April 5th 1916 whilst commanding a battalion of the Notts and Derby. Brother of Lieutenant-Colonel M. J. Wilson who commanded the Sherwood Foresters. Born 22nd October 1878. He married Mary Henrietta Franks on 17th December 1911. Three children. Medals issued by Indian authorities. Memorial Ref. Panel 6., Neuve-Chapelle Memorial, France.

WILSON, Second Lieutenant, Eric Maurice. He fell in action whilst gallantly cheering on his men in the attack, 1st July 1916. 17th Bn. attd. 10th Bn., Royal Irish Rifles. Aged 20. Younger son of the Reverend W. M. (Methodist Minister) and Rosalie S. Wilson, of L'abri, Newtown Butler, Co. Fermanagh. Born Fermoy, Co. Cork, July 10th, 1895. Educated at Wesley College, Dublin, The Grammar School, Youghal, and the Methodist College, Belfast, and was studying at Queen's University, Belfast, (Faculty of the Arts, 1914 – 1915) when he joined the OTC in January, 1915. In the following August he received his commission, and was in training attached to the 17th Bn., Royal Irish Rifles in Ballykinlar Camp till he was sent to France in the middle of June, 1916. Memorial Ref. Pier and Face 15 A and 15 B., Thiepval Memorial, France.

WILSON, Second Lieutenant, George Frederick. Gallantly met his death in the big advance on the Western Front, 1st July 1916. 21st Bn., Manchester Regiment. Aged 27. Elder Son of George and Ellen Ravenscroft Wilson, of 32, Worbeck Road, Anerley, London. Attested 1st December 1914, No. 1287, Private. Promoted corporal 30th January 1915 and acting sergeant 27th February 1915. Received his commission from the Rifle Brigade. In the field, 3rd March 1916. News of his death was received by his widowed mother. Originally buried Mametz, Sht 62.d Sq. F.11.a, 62d.F.5.d.1.4 reinterred 1920. Advance book returned to next of kin. Memorial Ref. II. C. 10., Dantzig Alley British Cemetery, Mametz, France. WO 339/37608

He Died To Make Men Free

WILSON, Second Lieutenant, John. Killed in action 1st July 1916. 2nd Bn., Middlesex Regiment. Aged 20. Son of John Parker and Louisa Edith Wilson, of 36, South Grove, Highgate, London formerly St. Michael's School, Highgate. Enlisted as a private No. 3784, Artists Rifles. Commissioned 5th December 1915, joined the Middlesex regiment on the 11th December 1915. Memorial Ref. Pier and Face 12 D and 13 B., Thiepval Memorial, France. WO 339/51518

WINKLEY, Second Lieutenant, Sydney Joseph. Reported killed near Gommecourt, 1st July 1916. 1st /6th Bn., Royal Warwickshire Regiment. Youngest son of Mr. and Mrs. Winkley of Darnel Hurst, Hartopp Road, Four Oaks. Obtained his commission at the outbreak of war and had been at the Front from 24th March 1916. Educated Warwick School where he was a member of the Cadet Corps. With his father in business. Mother applied for his medals from Bournemouth. Memorial Ref. Pier and Face 9 A 9 B and 10 B., Thiepval Memorial, France.

WINSTANLEY, Second Lieutenant, George Clement. Missing 1st July officially 2nd July 1916. 1st Bn., Somerset Light Infantry. Married to Ethel Winstanley. Born 1888. Appeals for information to go to 71, Grove Street, Derby. Previously Army Service Corps, private, MS/3411. Entered France August 1914. On the eve of the attack he reconnoitred the enemy's wire and stated it was cut but could not get near the area known as the Quadrilateral. His wife from Derby applied for his medals. Pension for children; Gordon George and Ethel. Record has for official purposes death accepted and pension issued from the 3rd July 1916. Two addresses Trinity Road, Birmingham and Haddon Street, Derby. Memorial Ref. Pier and Face 2 A., Thiepval Memorial, France.

WISEMAN, Captain, Willingham Franklin Gell. Missing believed killed, 1st July 1916. He was killed outright shot through the head by a bullet, he turned around and fell on his face, Mr. Anstee went to him and asked him if he was OK, he got no reply and stated 'the captains done for'. Z. Coy., 2nd Bn., Lincolnshire Regiment. Son of the Reverend Henry John Wiseman and Eleanor Elizabeth Franklin Gell Wiseman. Born 28th January 1892 in Bitterne, Hampshire. The Reverend Wiseman was later chaplain at Clifton College, Bristol. Aged 25 years. In 1902 to 1906, boarder at Packwood Haugh School. He left to attend Clifton College, 1906 to 1910, cadet at the Royal Military Academy, Woolwich. Commissioned lieutenant, and later promoted captain, in the 2nd Bn., Lincolnshire Regiment. Suffered gunshot wound to the right thigh on the 10th March 1915 at Neuve Chapelle and returned to England, 13th March to the 7th April 1915 in hospital. Promoted lieutenant 6th November 1912. Disembarked 5th November 1914. He was Mentioned in Despatches in June 1915. Temporary captain, March 1915. Brothers also enlisted. John served in Canada and England as an army chaplain with the Canadian Infantry. Philip enlisted in the army and was commissioned lieutenant with the Loyal North Lancashire Regiment dying of wounds on 27th October 1917 near Ypres. Willingham was originally buried 800 yards NW of Ovillers La Boisselle Cemetery. E. F. Gell applied for his medals. Memorial Ref. Pier and Face 1 C., Thiepval Memorial, France. WO 339/7978

Packwood School

WITHERS, Second Lieutenant, Frank Dean. Killed leading his men into action, 1st July 1916 the captain having fallen a few minutes earlier. When the German machine gun went silent from reloading, Frank and a number of NCO's took the opportunity and he got as far as Empress Trench and was leading the assault to the next line when he was shot in the temple by a rifleman and killed. 8th Bn., Somerset Light Infantry. Born on 4th November 1893 in Street, Somerset. Aged 22. Youngest son of Mr. William Patient Withers and Sarah Mary (nee Knight) Withers, Cranhill Road, Street, Somerset. Builder. Attended Sexey's School, Bruton, to the University College, Reading. Member of the Reading OTC 1912-1914. Attested 16th November 1914. Went to France on 6th October 1915. He won his Military Cross at Armentieres the award was gazetted on 21st January 1916. " For conspicuous gallantry near Armentieres on the night of 15th /16th December 1915. He was in command of the leading party of his battalion in a successful raid on the Germans, and was the first man to jump into their trench. He shot the German sentry and behaved with such cool bravery that the remainder of his party were able to accomplish their task." He received his Military Cross from the King at Buckingham Palace on 1st April 1916.

Effects returned were tiepin, shoulder strap, miniature medal star, cheque book, photo and identity disc. Brother applied for his medals. Memorial Ref. Pier and Face 2 A., Thiepval Memorial, France. WO 339/1585

WOOD, Lieutenant Colonel, Donald. Killed 1st July 1916. He was running across the open to speak to Lieutenant Colonel William Hodgson Franklin, 1st/6th Royal Warwickshire Regiment when he was shot. Commanding 1st Bn., Rifle Brigade. Youngest son of Mr. Arthur Hardy Wood J.P, and Annis Wood of Theddon Hall, Uckfield. Born 4th April, 1878. Served in South Africa. Played regimental cricket. Married to Irene, née Thornton, Ross. Gazetted second lieutenant, 9th March 1899. He joined the 2nd Battalion in Crete that Autumn and proceed to serve in the South African Wars. He participated in the Defence of Ladysmith 1899 and took part in the destruction of the Boer howitzer on 10th December. He saw action at Lombards Kop and took part in the attack on Wagon Hill, 6th January 1900. He was awarded the Queen's Medal with clasp. He was gazetted lieutenant, 3rd June 1904. He was gazetted Brigade Major, 15th December 1914 and Lieutenant Colonel 1916. Memorial Ref. Pier and Face 16 B and 16 C., Thiepval Memorial, France.

WOOD, Second Lieutenant, Harry Douty. Reported, wounded and missing, 1st July 1916. Accounts state he was in the fourth line but the fourth line had caught up with the first line by the time the German trench was reached and he was seen lying underneath the German wire shot by machine-gun fire. 3rd Bn. attd. 2nd Bn., Middlesex Regiment. Aged 19. Youngest and second son of John Thomas (long manager to the racing stud of Mr. Leopold de Rothschild) and Alice Wood, of Aynsford Lodge, Boscombe Cliff, Bournemouth formerly Elms House, Hammersmith. Born 29th December 1896. Educated at Ovingdean School, Brighton and Bradfield College (September 1910 to December 1914), where he was captain of the shooting VIII in the OTC. He entered RMC Sandhurst in 1914 and was gazetted in May 1915 and left for the Front in June. In September 1916 reported he was buried at the angle of Empress Trench and a new communication trench. However on the 26th November 1916 this was changed as Reverend R. W, Dugdale reported he buried 2nd Lieutenant W. J. Wood of the 4th Middlesex and in 1918 the position was changed to 57.D.X.1.D.7.6 NW of Ovillers Le Boisselle, 200 yards SW of road from Ovillers La Boisselle to Athiulle. Reported to have been buried by the Life Guards. Father applied for his medals. Memorial Ref. Pier and Face 12 D and 13 B., Thiepval Memorial, France. WO 339/49725

WOOD, Second Lieutenant, Wilfred John. killed in action near Fricourt, 1st July 1916. 4th Bn., Middlesex Regiment. Aged 25. Son of Robert and Isabel Wood, of 125, Hindpool Road, Barrow-in-Furness. Born 9th May 1891. Higher Grade School boy and went into the teaching profession. Teacher at St. Jame's School for a while and afterwards studied at Cheltenham Training College. Obtained an appointment at Acton Boys School and proceeded to Birkbeck College. University of London OTC. Preparing to sit his final examination for his BSc when war broke out. Joined his battalion, 24th November 1915. In September 1916 reported that 2nd Lt. H. D. Wood was buried at the angle of Empress Trench and a new communication trench. However on the 26th November 1916 this was changed as Reverend R. W, Dugdale reported he buried 2nd Lieutenant W. J. Wood of the 4th Middlesex. Originally buried Sheet 26. Sq D. Contour 110, Montauban Trench map/ 57d.27c.6.4. Memorial Ref. IV. K., Gordon Dump Cemetery, Ovillers-La Boisselle, France. WO 339/38370

Until The Resurrection Morn

B Coy., 4th Bn., Middlesex Regiment photographed 26th June 1916

2nd Lt A. H. Winn-Sampson (killed 1st July 1916), 2nd Lt W. John Wood (killed 1st July 1916), 2nd Lt. A. A. Johnston (killed 2nd July 1916), 2nd Lt. A. F. C Paxton (killed 1st July 1916), Lt. D. Cutbush killed 10th April 1917, Lt. H. M. Williams, 2nd Lt. A. Branch killed 1st July 1916, Captain O. R. F. Johnston Centre killed 1st July 1916

WOODSTOCK, Lieutenant, Walter Percy. Seen to fall about ten yards from the German trench parapet, killed at La Boisselle, 1st July 1916. 8th Bn., York and Lancaster Regiment. Aged 29. Elder son of Walter and Victoria Caroline Woodstock, of 30, Whitehall Gardens, Acton Hill, London formerly 76 Creffield Road, Acton. Educated at Colet Court and Cranleigh School. Employed Employers' Liability Assurance Corporation Ltd. Liked to be known as Percy. At the outbreak of war he enlisted in the London Rifle Brigade, private, 467 and gazetted in January 1915. Went to France, 27th August 1915. Member of the choir of St. Martin's Church, West Acton. Member of the Marlborough Lawn Tennis Club and Horsenden Hill Golf Club. Father applied for his medals. Memorial Ref. Pier and Face 14 A and 14 B., Thiepval Memorial, France.

WRAGG, Major, Frederick William. Mentioned in Despatches, January 1916. Led his company and was shot in the shoulder when he reached the German lines, he attempted to silence a German machine-gun and was again shot falling in the German line, killed at Gommecourt in the second wave, 1st July 1916. Reported missing. Officer Commanding C Coy on the left of the attack, 1st/5th Bn., Sherwood Foresters (Notts and Derby Regiment). Aged 34. Third son of Mr. John D. Wragg, J.P. and Mrs. Wragg, of Eureka Lodge, Swadlincote, Derbyshire. Born 14th November 1881. Entered the family business eventually becoming Work's Manager and Director, Messrs. T. Wragg & sons and Messrs. James Woodward Ltd. Keen mason, and played rugby for the Burton Club. Served with the Territorial Force. Captain, 1st April 1914 and Temporary Major, 1st April 1916. Entered France, 25th February 1915. The Brigadier-General wrote; 'I am sure that it will be some small comfort for you to know he fell gallantly leading his men after he had been wounded. He was a very gallant officer.' His Commanding Officer wrote; ' The only news I have of him, was he was gallantly leading his men when he was shot down by a machine gun. It is the death we know he would have preferred and he did gloriously.' Brother W. Wragg applied for his medals, whilst another brother, Lieutenant Norman John Wragg, 3rd Bn., attd 1st Bn., South Staffordshire Regiment died of wounds on the 18th July 1916. Memorial Ref. Pier and Face 10 C 10 D and 11 A., Thiepval Memorial, France.

WRIGHT, Lieutenant, Clarence Harris. A few minutes before Zero he crept along Hammerhead Sap and the North Side of Oblong Wood to within a hundred yards of Thiepval. One of a small section that jumped over the parapet along left half of attacking line was Private Alfred Walsh; 'We had advanced to about 100 yards of the enemy's first line under a heavy shower of shrapnel and machine-gun fire when I saw Lieutenant Wright drop to his knees with a bullet through his forehead. The last words I heard him say were "Go on boys." The last of the officers to fall, 1st July 1916. C Company, 15th Bn., Lancashire Fusiliers. Aged 22. Born 14th February 1894. Son of William Harris Wright and Elizabeth Wright, of Haddon Hall Hydro, Buxton, Derby. Educated at Rossall School and Manchester Grammar, where he was in the OTC and a friend of Captain Geoffrey Heald, also killed 1st July 1916. He became an assistant at George Fraser & Co., Portland St., Manchester. He applied for a commission in the Salford Battalion, 24th September 1914 and was commissioned 1st February 1915. Entered France, 22nd November 1915. Commemorated St. Clement's Church Memorial. A grave marker was found by Lieutenant Norman Blackett which bore the following inscription; RIP Lieutenant C. H. Wright, 15th Lancashire Fusiliers, Killed in action 1st July 1916.' Mother applied for his medals. Memorial Ref. Pier and Face 3 C and 3 D., Thiepval Memorial, France.

WRIGHT, Second Lieutenant, Matthew John. Killed by a trench mortar bomb along with two other men whilst trying to rescue, Second Lieutenant George Radcliffe. 1st July 1916. C Coy. 14th Bn., Royal Irish Rifles. Aged 28. Fourth son of the Reverend William Wright, D.D. and Charlotte MCW. Wright, of Newtownards, Co. Down. Born on 23rd February 1888. Employment of Messrs. James P Corry Ltd, Belfast, and formerly in the employment of Messrs. John Stevenson Ltd., Coalisland. Enlisted as a private, 19833, 6th October 1914. For a time was engaged instructing in the bomb throwing school. Commissioned as a second lieutenant in January 1915. He met with a rather serious accident in May 1915 and was sent home to recuperate. Entered France, 30th October 1915. He received permission to extend his home leave, but he refused to accept the privilege, preferring as he stated, to be with the boys at the front. Reported to have been killed on the 2nd July 1916. Second Lieutenant Reginald Lambert Lack saw his brother in law, Second Lieutenant George Radcliffe wounded and returned to try and to rescue him whilst being assisted by Second Lieutenant Matthew John Wright. Reginald was shot in the spine during the rescue and died of wounds on the 18th July 1916 at Dover. Mother applied for his medals. Memorial Ref. Pier and Face 15 A and 15 B., Thiepval Memorial, France.

WRIGLEY, Lieutenant, Joseph. He and his orderly were hit by a shell, 1st July 1916. 1st/5th Bn., York and Lancaster Regiment. Aged 23. Son of John and Hannah Wrigley, of 425, Langsett Road, Hillsborough, Sheffield. Father and five sons all served. Qualified Civil Service and worked in the Labour Exchange, Sheffield. Teacher at the Sunday school. One time employed at the 'Sheffield Independent' office. Formerly, private, 3rd Bn. Entered France 27th July 1915. His brother, Private Ernest Wrigley King's Own Yorkshire Light Infantry was wounded the same day and received treatment in Durham. Commemorated memorial to the Staff of the Ministry of Labour, Board of Trade - Labour Department (Yorkshire & East Midlands Division). Parents applied for his medals. Memorial Ref. Pier and Face 14 A and 14 B., Thiepval Memorial, France.

WRONG, Lieutenant, Harold Verschoyle. Last seen crossing the German front line wounded in the hand, led platoons of D Coy., killed at Thiepval and buried there, 1st July 1916. 15th Bn., Lancashire Fusiliers. Aged 23. Second son of George MacKinnon Wrong (Professor of History at the University of Toronto and author) and Sophia Hume Wrong (daughter of the late Hon Edward Blake MP), of 73, Walmer Road, Toronto, Canada. Born 1st December 1891 in Toronto. He attended St. Andrew's College, (1902 to 1907), Ridley College, St. Catherine's, University College at University of Toronto (1909 to 1913) where he took First Class Honours in classics, English and history and won a Flavelle Scholarship to Christ Church College, Oxford University for two years. Arrived in the UK from Canada in October 1913 to continue his education at Christ Church, Oxford. He was back in Canada when war broke out, but returned to England and was commissioned into the 15th Lancashire Fusiliers on 14th of December. Arrived in France, 21st November 1915. Father applied for his medals. Memorial Ref. Pier and Face 3 C and 3 D., Thiepval Memorial, France.

YATES, Second Lieutenant, Arthur Gerald Vavasour. Five officers collected their men in 'Etch' communication trench and bombed up it and along 'Fellow' trench and then along 'Feud' until cleared and put up one of the battalion sign boards on seeing it the men came over and dropped into it, here 2nd Lieutenant Yates and Negus were killed at the junction of Fellow and Etch Trench, 1st July 1916. C Coy., 1st/16th Bn., London Regiment (Queen's Westminster Rifles). Aged 29. Third son of Hercules Campbell Yates (Coroner for Macclesfield), and Annie Yates, of The Lower Beech, Tytherington, Macclesfield. Gerald was educated at the Macclesfield Grammar School, which he entered in September 1898 at twelve years of age. He left in December 1903, having been a prominent member of the cricket and football elevens, and in May 1904 was articled to Mr. Charles Blunt, solicitor, of the firm of Messrs. Blunt and Brocklehurst, King Edward Street, Macclesfield, passing his final examination in early 1909 with Second Class Honours. Admitted November 1912. Gerald remained with the firm of Messrs. Blunt and Brocklehurst until the outbreak of war, when he immediately enlisted as a private in the Artists' Rifles. In 1915 he received a commission in the Queen's Westminster Rifles, and was drafted to France in March 1916. Commemorated Roll of Honour of the Macclesfield Grammar School. Father applied for his medals. Memorial Ref. Pier and Face 13 C., Thiepval Memorial, France.

YOUNG, Captain, Arthur Cecil. He came out of the trench when his company was in sore straits and took command, urging his men forward. Unfortunately he was hit by a machine-gun bullet, 1st July 1916. A Coy. 16th Bn., Northumberland Fusiliers. Aged 24. Younger son William Young J.P and Mrs. Selina Young, of Aldersyde, Alnwick, Northumberland. Born 5th July 1891. Educated at Sedbergh, (1906 – July 1909) and prior to the war was studying at Armstrong College, where he took his degree of BSc, in pure sciences. Analytical chemist. At the outbreak of the war he enlisted as a private, and within the year was promoted to the rank of captain. He was a keen golfer and also took a very great interest in ornithology. Young was a member of the Bamburgh Golf Club, and was well known on the Bamburgh and Alnmouth courses, where his loss will be much regretted. Named on the Alnwick Memorial. Entered France, 23rd November 1915. Will £3632 granted to his sister Miss Constance Jane Young. Captain Ritson wrote 'He worked very hard and very gallantly, amidst a storm of bullets and shell for over three hours, until he was hit'. Wall of St. Michael's Church, Alnwick as brass plaque to memory of William Lawrence Young, Charles Edward Young and Arthur Cecil Young who gave their lives in the service of the country, paid for by their mother. Private William Lawrence was killed the 30th December 1917 and Lieutenant Charles Edward Young died the 17th December 1918. Mother applied for his medals. Memorial Ref. Pier and Face 10 B 11 B and 12 B., Thiepval Memorial, France.

YOUNG, Captain, John Ferrers Harington. He fell at the head of his company, leading his men in the attack of the German trenches, 1st July 1916. 1st Bn., King's Own (Royal Lancaster Regiment). Aged 19. Son of Mrs. Patrick Stewart (formerly Young), of 8, Vicarage Gate, Kensington, London, and Captain J. E. H. Young (R.A.). Born 1897. He was in the Beresford 1910 – 1914, Wellington College and passed to RMC Sandhurst, September 1914. Commissioned 11th November 1914. Entered France, 9th December 1914. Made temporary captain whilst under the age of nineteen, 28th January 1916. Mrs. Mildred Stewart applied for medals of her son. Memorial Ref. I. G. 41., Sucrerie Military Cemetery, Colincamps, France.

He Sleeps In Peace May God Remember Him For Ever

YOUNG, Second Lieutenant, James Vincent. Led his men in an attack near Fricourt, 1st July 1916. 9th Bn., attd. B Coy. 8th Bn., Somerset Light Infantry. Aged 24. Son of the Reverend Vincent and Eleanor Young, of Charleton Rectory, Kingsbridge, Devon. Born 20th August 1892. Attended Marlbrough College and Selwyn College, Cambridge and took his degree in 1914. Entered France, 7th October 1915. Father applied for his medals. Original burial map reference 57d.X.26.d.8.6. Memorial Ref. II. M. 6., Gordon Dump Cemetery, Ovillers-La Boisselle, France.

Fling Open Wide The Golden Gates And Let The Victors In

YOUNGER, Second Lieutenant, David George. Shot dead by machine-gun fire, 1st July 1916. 17th Bn., Highland Light Infantry. Aged 23. Son of John Younger, (ironbroker), of Overbridge, 1, Dumbreck Road, and of Mrs. Younger, of 17, Fotheringay Road, Pollokshields, Glasgow. Born in March 1893. Educated Glasgow High School, Glasgow Academy and at Loretto (1907 to 1910). Shortly after the outbreak of war he enlisted as a private in the Highland Light Infantry, 15741, and later was commissioned. Entered France, 29th May 1916. Death reported 11th July 1916. Mother applied for his medals. Original burial map reference 57d.R.31.c.5.4. Memorial Ref. VI. H. 6., Lonsdale Cemetery, Authuille, France.

Eldest Son Of Mrs. John Younger Overbridge, Dumbreck, Glasgow Dearly Beloved

Appendix 1
Order of Battle

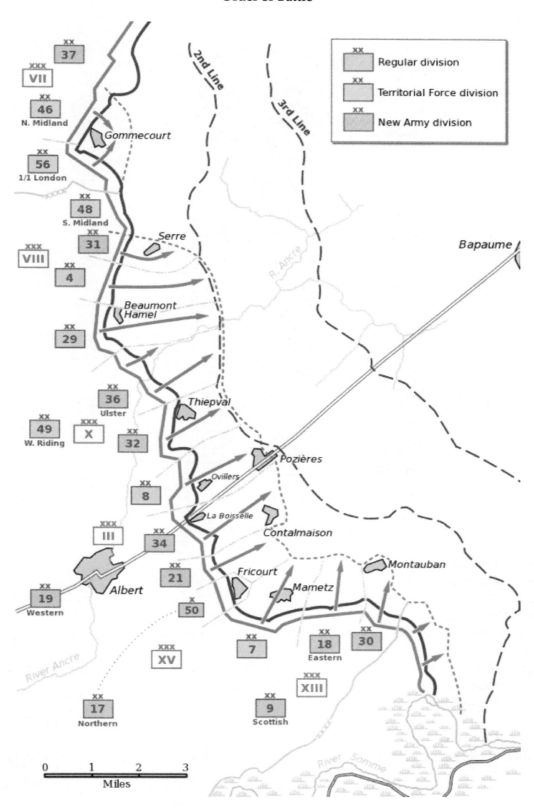

Anglo-French Objectives 1st July 1916

In relation to the map Divisions are listed down from Gommecourt to Montauban

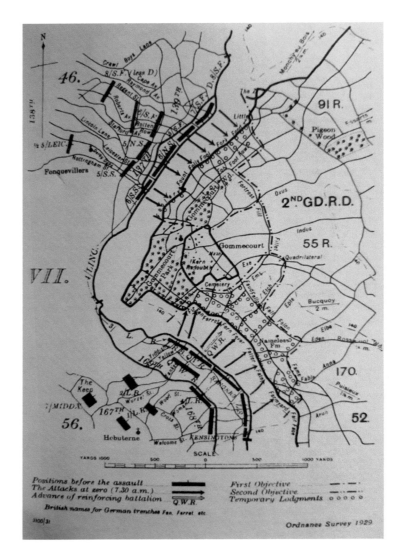

VII Corps attack on Gommecourt 1st July 1916

VII Corps (Gommemcourt)
46th Division (Gommemcourt)
137th Brigade; 1/5th South Staffs, 1/6th South Staffs, 1/5th North Staffs, 1/6th North Staffs, 137th Machine Gun Coy, 137th Trench Mortar Battery
138th Brigade; 1/4th Lincolns, 1/5th Lincolns, 1/4th Leicesters, 1/5th Leicesters, 138th Machine Gun Coy, 138th Trench Mortar Battery
139th Brigade; 1/5th Sherwood Foresters, 1/6th Sherwood Foresters, 1/7th Sherwood Foresters, 1/8th Sherwood Foresters, 139th Machine Gun Coy, 139th Trench Mortar Battery
Pioneers; 1/1st Monmouths

56th Division (Gommemcourt)
167th Brigade; 1/1st London, 1/3rd London, 1/7th Middlesex, 1/8th Middlesex, 167th Machine Gun Coy, 167th Trench Mortar Battery
168th Brigade; 1/4th London, 1/12th London, 1/13th London, 1/14th London, 168th Machine Gun Coy, 168th Trench Mortar Battery
169th Brigade; 1/2nd London, 1/5th London, 1/9th London, 1/16th London, 169th Machine Gun Coy, 169th Trench Mortar Battery
Pioneers; 1/5th Cheshires

37th Division In Reserve

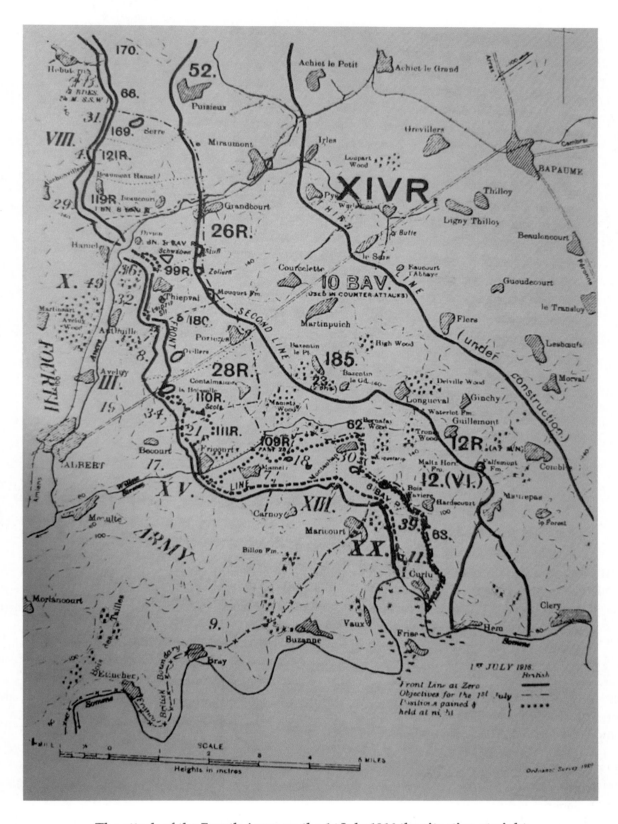

The attack of the Fourth Army on the 1st July 1916 the situation at night

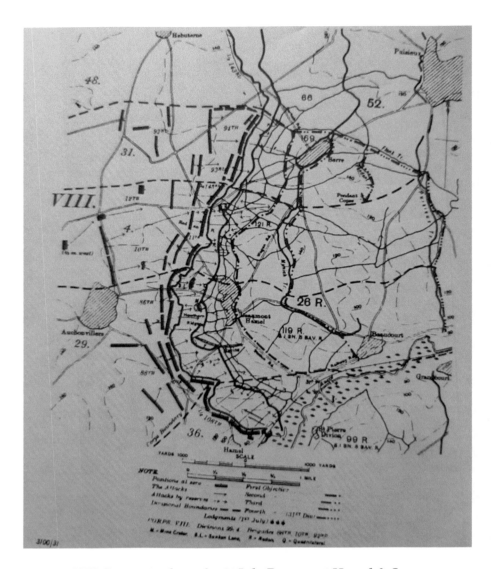

VIII Corps attack on the 1st July Beaumont Hamel & Serre

VIII Corps (Serre, South of Serre, North of Beaumont Hamel, Beaumont Hamel)
48th Division (In Reserve)
143rd Brigade; 1/5th Royal Warwicks (In reserve), 1/7th Royal Warwicks (In reserve), 1/8th Royal Warwicks (In reserve), 1/6th Royal Warwicks (In reserve), 143rd Machine Gun Coy, 143rd Trench Mortar Battery
* 1/8th Royal Warwicks and 1/6th Royal Warwicks in attack South of Serre and North of Beaumont Hamel
144th Brigade; 1/4th Gloucesters (In reserve), 1/6th Gloucesters (In reserve), 1/7th Worcesters (In reserve), 1/8th Worcester (In reserve), , 144th Machine Gun Coy, 144th Trench Mortar Battery
145th Brigade; 1/5th Gloucesters (In reserve), 1/4th Oxford and Bucks (In reserve), 1st Bucks (In reserve), 1/4th Royal Berks (In reserve), 145th Machine Gun Coy, 145th Trench Mortar Battery
Pioneers; 1/5th Royal Sussex (In reserve)

31st Division (Serre)
92nd Brigade; 10th East Yorks, 11th East Yorks, 12th East Yorks, 13th East Yorks, 92nd Machine Gun Coy, 92nd Trench Mortar Battery
93rd Brigade; 15th West Yorks, 16th West Yorks, 18th West Yorks, 18th Durham Light Infantry, 93rd Machine Gun Coy, 93rd Trench Mortar Battery
94th Brigade; 11th East Lancs, 12th York and Lancs, 13th York and Lancs, 14th York and Lancs, 94th Machine Gun Coy, 94th Trench Mortar Battery
Pioneers; 12th King's Own Yorkshire Light Infantry

4th Division (South of Serre, North of Beaumont Hamel)
10th Brigade; 1st Royal Irish Fusiliers, 2nd Royal Dublin Fusiliers, 2nd Seaforth, 1st Royal Warwicks, 10th Machine Gun Coy, 10th Trench Mortar Battery
11th Brigade; 1st Somerset Light Infantry, 1st East Lancs, 1st Hampshires, 1st Rifle Brigade, 11th Machine Gun Coy, 11th Trench Mortar Battery
12th Brigade; 1st King's Own Royal Lancaster, 2nd Lancashire Fusiliers, 2nd Duke of Wellingtons, 2nd Essex
Pioneers; 21st West Yorks, 2nd Machine Gun Coy, 2nd Trench Mortar Battery

29th Division (Beaumont Hamel)
86th Brigade; 2nd Royal Fusiliers, 1st Lancashire Fusiliers, 16th Middlesex, 1st Royal Dublin Fusiliers, 86th Machine Gun Coy, 86th Trench Mortar Battery
87th Brigade; 2nd South Wales Borderers, 1st King's Own Scottish Borderers, 1st Royal Inniskillings, 1st Border, 87th Machine Gun Coy, 87th Trench Mortar Battery

88th Brigade; 1st Essex, 1st Newfoundland, 4th Worcesters, 2nd Hampshires
Pioneers; 1/2nd Monmouths

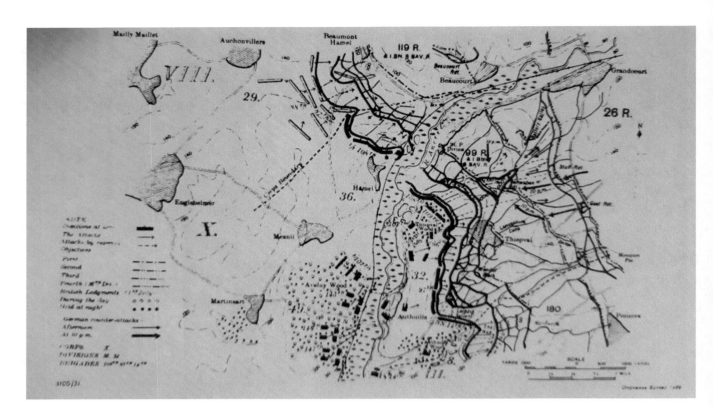

X Corps attack on the 1st July Thiepval

X Corps (North of Thiepval, Thiepval)
36th Ulster Division (North of Thiepval)
107th Brigade; 8th Royal Irish Rifles, 9th Royal Irish Rifles, 10th Royal Irish Rifles, 15th Royal Irish Rifles
108th Brigade; 11th Royal Irish Rifle, 12th Royal Irish Rifles, 13th Royal Irish Rifles, 9th Royal Irish Fusiliers
109th Brigade; 9th Royal Inniskillings, 10th Royal Inniskillings, 11th Royal Inniskillings, 14th Royal Irish Rifles
Pioneers; 16th Royal Irish Rifles

49th Division (In Reserve)
146th Brigade; 1/5th West Yorks, 1/6th West Yorks, 1/7th West Yorks, 1/8th West Yorks
147th Brigade; 1/4th Duke of Wellingtons, 1/5th Duke of Wellingtons, 1/6th Duke of Wellingtons, 1/7th Duke of Wellingtons
148th Brigade; 1/4th York and Lancs, 1/5th York and Lancs, 1/4th King's Own Yorkshire Light Infantry, 1/5th King's Own Yorkshire Light Infantry
Pioneers; 1/3rd Monmouths

32nd Division (Thiepval)
14th Brigade; 19th Lancashire Fusiliers, 1st Dorsets, 2nd Manchesters, 15th Highland Light Infantry
96th Brigade; 16th Northumberlands, 2nd Royal Inniskillings, 15th Lancashire Fusiliers, 16th Lancashire Fusiliers
97th Brigade; 11th Border, 2nd King's Own Yorkshire Light Infantry, 16th Highland Light Infantry, 17th Highland Light Infantry
Pioneers; 17th Northumberlands

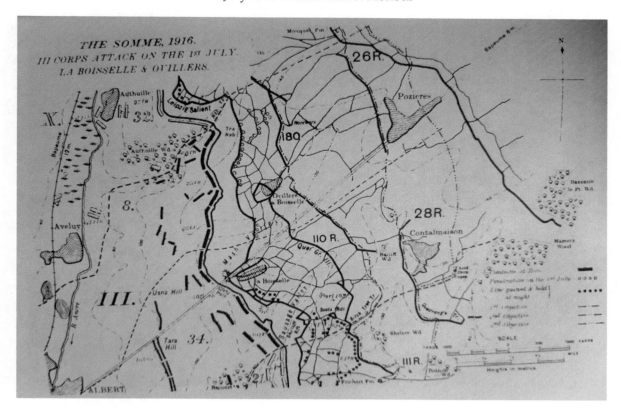

III Corps attack on the 1st July La Boisselle & Ovillers

III Corps (Ovillers, La Boisselle)
8th Division (Ovillers)
23rd Brigade; 2nd Devons, 2nd Middlesex, 2nd West Yorks, 2nd Scottish Rifles
25th Brigade; 2nd Lincolns, 2nd Royal Berks, 1st Royal Irish Rifles, 2nd Rifle Brigade
70th Brigade; 11th Sherwood Foresters, 8th King's Own Yorkshire Light Infantry, 8th Yorks and Lancs, 9th York and Lancs
Pioneers; 22nd Durham Light Infantry

34th Division (La Boisselle)
101st Brigade; 15th Royal Scots, 16th Royal Scots, 10th Lincolns, 11th Suffolks
102nd Brigade; 20th Northumberland, 21st Northumberland, 22nd Northumberland, 23rd Northumberland
103rd Brigade; 24th Northumberland, 25th Northumberland, 26th Northumberland, 27th Northumberland
Pioneers; 18th Northumberlands

19th Division (All In Reserve)
56th Brigade; 7th King's Own, 7th East Lancs, 7th South Lancs, 7th Loyal North Lancs
57th Brigade; 10th Royal Warwicks 8th Gloucesters, 10th Worcesters, 8th North Staffs
58th Brigade; 9th Cheshires, 9th Royal Welsh Fusiliers, 9th Welsh, 6th Wiltshire
Pioneers; 5th South Wales Borderers

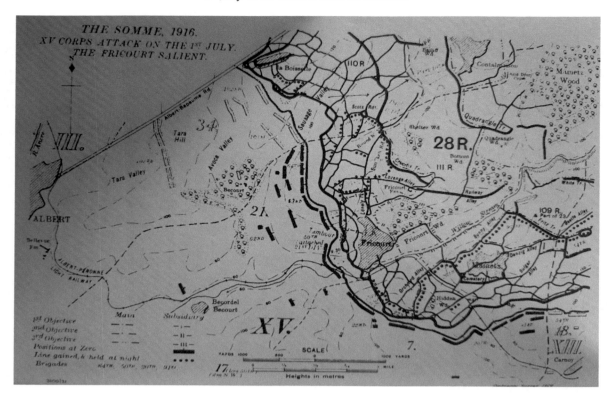

XV Corps attack on the 1st July The Fricourt Salient

XV Corps (South West of Contalmaison, Mametz, Fricourt)
21st Division (South West of Contalmaison)
62nd Brigade; 12th Northumberlands, 13th Northumberlands, 1st Lincolns, 10th Green Howards
63rd Brigade; 8th Lincolns, 8th Somerset Light Infantry, 4th Middlesex, 10th York and Lancs
64th Brigade; 9th King's Own Yorkshire Light Infantry, 10th King's Own Yorkshire Light Infantry, 1st East Yorks
15th Durham Light Infantry
Pioneers; 14th Northumberlands

7th Division (Mametz)
20th Brigade; 8th Devons, 9th Devons, 2nd Border, 2nd Gordon Highlanders
22nd Brigade; 2nd Royal Warwicks, 20th Manchesters, 1st Royal Welch Fusiliers, 2nd Royal Irish
91st Brigade; 2nd Queens, 1st South Staffs, 21st Manchesters, 22nd Manchesters
Pioneers; 24th Manchesters

17th Division (Fricourt)
50th Brigade; 10th West Yorks, 7th East Yorks, 7th Green Howards, 6th Dorsets
51st Brigade; 7th Lincolns (In reserve), 7th Border (In reserve), 8th South Staffs (In reserve), 10th Sherwood Foresters (In reserve)
52nd Brigade; 9th Northumberlands (In reserve), 10th Lancashire Fusiliers (In reserve), 9th Duke of Wellingtons (In reserve), 12th Manchesters (In reserve)
Pioneers; 7th York and Lancs

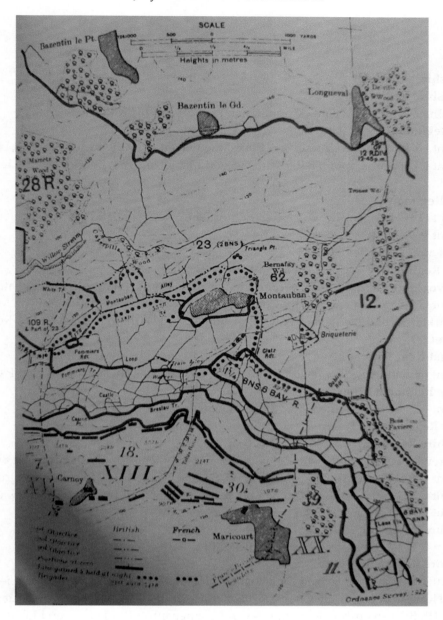

XIII Corps attack on the 1st July The Capture of Montauban

XIII Corps (East of Mametz & West of Montauban, Montauban)
18th Division (East of Mametz & West of Montauban)
53rd Brigade; 8th Norfolks, 6th Royal Berks, 10th Essex, 8th Suffolks
54th Brigade; 11th Royal Fusiliers, 7th Bedfords, 6th Northamptons, 12th Middlesex
55th Brigade; 7th Queens, 7th Buffs, 8th East Surreys, 7th Royal West Kents
Pioneers; 8th Royal Sussex

30th Division (Montauban)
21st Brigade; 18th King's Liverpool, 19th Manchesters, 2nd Wiltshire, 2nd Green Howards
89th Brigade; 17th King's Liverpool, 19th King's Liverpool, 20th King's Liverpool, 2nd Bedfords
90th Brigade; 2nd Royal Scots Fusiliers, 16th Manchesters, 17th Manchesters, 18th Manchesters
Pioneers; 11th South Lancs

9th Division In Reserve

Appendix 2
Fallen officers regimental list

2nd Bn., Bedfordshire Regiment
7th Bn., Bedfordshire Regiment
9th Bn. attd. 7th Bn. Second Lieutenant J Cunningham, Lieutenant J H R Rawes,

1st Bn., Border Regiment
Second Lieutenant J Y Baxendine, Captain T H Beves, Lieutenant H L Cholmeley, Second Lieutenant A W Fraser, Second Lieutenant L Jackson, Captain F R Jessup, Second Lieutenant W P Rettie, Second Lieutenant W K Sanderson

2nd Bn., Border Regiment
Second Lieutenant D H H Logan, 11th Bn., North Staffordshire Regiment attd 2nd Bn., Lieutenant P N Fraser, Second Lieutenant W R Robertson

7th Bn., Border Regiment (In Reserve)
11th Bn., Border Regiment
Captain C S Brown, 1st Bn. attd. 11th Bn. Second Lieutenant G Coe, Captain A E Corbett, attd to 97th Brigade, Second Lieutenant G P Dunstan, Lieutenant Colonel P W Machell, Second Lieutenant A E Monkhouse, Second Lieutenant J C Parker, Second Lieutenant W S Paton, 6th Bn. attd. 11th Bn Lieutenant F A Rupp, Captain R Smith,

1st Bucks (In Reserve)
7th Bn. Buffs (East Kent Regiment)
Second Lieutenant J F Baddeley, Lieutenant E H A Goss, Captain G T Neame, Lieutenant P G Norbury

5th Bn., Cheshire Regiment (Pioneer)
Second Lieutenant G S Arthur, Lieutenant P B Bass, Lieutenant F A Davies

9th Bn., Cheshire Regiment (In Reserve)
2nd Bn. Devonshire Regiment
Captain J A Andrews, Second Lieutenant C V Beddow, Second Lieutenant L A Carey, 3rd Bn. attd. 2nd Bn. Second Lieutenant G S D Carver, 3rd Bn. attd. 2nd Bn. Second Lieutenant F B Coldwells, 3rd Bn. attd. 2nd Bn. Second Lieutenant E M Gould, 3rd Bn. attd. 2nd Bn. Second Lieutenant E A Jago, Second Lieutenant M C Ley, Second Lieutenant J S McGowan, Captain A Preedy

8th Bn. Devonshire Regiment
Second Lieutenant R H W Davidson, Second Lieutenant J F G Rew, Captain G P Tregelles

9th Bn. Devonshire Regiment
Second Lieutenant T F Adamson, Second Lieutenant P J F Dines, 8th Bn. attd 9th Second Lieutenant C P Hirst, Lieutenant W N Hodgson, Second Lieutenant R B Holcroft, Captain D L Martin, Second Lieutenant H L Rayner, 9th Bn attd from 11th Bn. Devonshire Regiment Second Lieutenant W Riddell, Second Lieutenant C H Shepard,

1st Bn. Dorsetshire Regiment
Second Lieutenant C F Rothon

6th Bn., Dorsetshire Regiment
2nd Bn. Duke Of Wellington's (West Riding Regiment)
Second Lieutenant C H Bowes, Captain N W Hadwen, 2nd Bn attd from 3rd Bn., Captain C L Hart

4th Bn. Duke Of Wellington's (West Riding Regiment) (In Reserve)
5th Bn. Duke Of Wellington's (West Riding Regiment) (In Reserve)
6th Bn. Duke Of Wellington's (West Riding Regiment) (In Reserve)
7th Bn. Duke Of Wellington's (West Riding Regiment) (In Reserve)
9th Bn. Duke Of Wellington's (West Riding Regiment) (In Reserve)
15th Bn. Durham Light Infantry
Second Lieutenant R O Cormack, Captain J East, Captain D H J Ely, Second Lieutenant C S Haynes, Second Lieutenant M L Huddleston, Captain L H Sanger-Davies, 15th Bn., attd from 16th Bn., Second Lieutenant S T Watson

16th Bn. Durham Light Infantry
Second Lieutenant A G Shorter
17th Bn. Durham Light Infantry
Second Lieutenant J M Jones
18th Bn. Durham Light Infantry
22nd Durham Light Infantry (Pioneers)

1st Bn. East Lancashire Regiment Lieutenant T E C Fisher, Second Lieutenant K C Jones, Second Lieutenant E S Mallett, Lieutenant R Newcombe, Captain A H Penny, 1st Bn attd from 10th Bn. Second Lieutenant R S Prescott, 10th Bn attd 1st Bn., Second Lieutenant, C E Sadler, Captain H W M Thomas, 10th Bn. attd. 1st Bn. Second Lieutenant H A Tompkins, Second Lieutenant C E S Watson, 3rd Bn. attd. 1st Bn. Captain C P Watson

7th Bn., East Lancashire Regiment (In Reserve)

11th Bn. East Lancashire Regiment

10th Bn. attd. 11th Bn. East Lancashire Regiment Second Lieutenant A Beacall, 10th Bn., attd 11th Second Lieutenant H N Davies, 10th Bn., attd 11th Lieutenant J F Hitchon, Second Lieutenant W A Kohn, Captain H Livesey, Captain H D Riley, 10th Bn., attd 11th Bn., Second Lieutenant H W Thompson, Lieutenant C Stonehouse, Captain A B Tough

8th Bn. East Surrey Regiment

Second Lieutenant T E Evans, Captain A T Flatau, Second Lieutenant P P Kelly, Lieutenant G H S Musgrove, 8th Bn attd from 1st Bn., East Yorkshire Regiment Captain W P Nevill, Captain C S Pearce, Lieutenant R E Soames

1st Bn. East Yorkshire Regiment Second Lieutenant 9th Bn., attd 1st Bn., B R Boncker, Second Lieutenant A H Eames, 3rd Bn., attd 1st Bn., Lieutenant R J H Gatrell, Captain C J Huntriss, Lieutenant J P P Peregrine, Second Lieutenant P C J Smith

7th Bn. East Yorkshire Regiment

Second Lieutenant A H Kippax, Second Lieutenant C W Perry, Captain J B Rutledge, Second Lieutenant F Thornton

10th Bn. East Yorkshire Regiment

11th Bn. East Yorkshire Regiment

12th Bn. East Yorkshire Regiment

13th Bn. East Yorkshire Regiment

1st Bn. Essex Regiment

Second Lieutenant W R Cheshire, 3rd Bn attd 1st Bn., Second Lieutenant R B Horwood

2nd Bn. Essex Regiment

Second Lieutenant G A Allen, Lieutenant T Fraser, Second Lieutenant S C Goodchild, Second Lieutenant A Holmes, Second Lieutenant T N Ide, 3rd Bn. Essex Regiment Lieutenant A M Middleditch attd from 12th Bn killed with the 2nd Bn.,Second Lieutenant L G Smith, Captain B S Smith-Masters, Second Lieutenant G Waterhouse, 3rd Bn attd 2nd Bn, Second Lieutenant H R White

10th Bn. Essex Regiment

Captain H E Hawkins

1st Bn. Gloucestershire Regiment

Brevet Major G B Bosanquet

4th Gloucesters (In Reserve)

5th Gloucesters (In Reserve)

6th Gloucesters (In Reserve)

8th Gloucesters (In Reserve)

2nd Bn. Gordon Highlanders

Second Lieutenant W Fearnley, Second Lieutenant G Giles, 3rd Bn. attd to 2nd Bn., Second Lieutenant C G Gordon, Second Lieutenant D T King, 3rd Bn. attd. 2nd Bn. Second Lieutenant N L McNeill, 3rd Bn. attd. 2nd Bn. Second Lieutenant H R White, 3rd Bn. attd. 2nd Bn. Second Lieutenant J White

2 Green Howards

7 Green Howards

10 Green Howards

1st Bn. Hampshire Regiment

Lieutenant H I Adams, Second Lieutenant H T Alexander, 3rd Bn. attd 1st Bn., Second Lieutenant N H Bell, 3rd Bn. attd 1st Bn., Captain A T Bonham Carter, 3rd Bn. attd. 1st Bn. Second Lieutenant G H J Bramble, Second Lieutenant R S Cane, Lieutenant C J H Goodford, Lieutenant Colonel L C W Palk, Second Lieutenant E W M Price, Second Lieutenant F P Thompson, Second Lieutenant L A Westmore

2nd Bn., Hampshire

15th Bn., Highland Light Infantry

16th Bn. Highland Light Infantry

Second Lieutenant R S Brown, Second Lieutenant J A Gemmill, Lieutenant T Johnson, Captain D B Kerr, 4th Bn. attd. 16th Bn. Second Lieutenant J Kerr, Second Lieutenant D S Machardy, 16th Bn., attd from 13th Bn Second Lieutenant G McCurrach, Second Lieutenant J Murdoch

17th Bn. Highland Light Infantry

Second Lieutenant W M Alexander, Captain G V M Boyd, Second Lieutenant H Brunton, Second Lieutenant J N Carpenter, Captain R W Cassels, Lieutenant E A Gallie, Major E Hutchison, Second Lieutenant A D Laird, Lieutenant J B MacBrayne, Lieutenant W M Mcintosh, Lieutenant A F Smith-Maxwell, Lieutenant P G Symington, Second Lieutenant D G Younger

11th Infantry Bde.

Cdg. General Staff Brigadier General C B Prowse

17th Bn. King's (Liverpool Regiment)

Lieutenant D H Scott

18th Bn. King's (Liverpool Regiment)

Captain A De B Adam, Captain C N Brockbank, Lieutenant G M Dawson, Second Lieutenant E Fitzbrown, Second Lieutenant G B Golds, Second Lieutenant G A Herdman, Second Lieutenant R V Merry, Second Lieutenant T R Walker

19th Bn. King's (Liverpool Regiment)

20th Bn. King's (Liverpool Regiment)

Second Lieutenant J C Laughlin

22nd Bn. The King's (Liverpool Regiment)

Second Lieutenant F F Barnes

1st Bn. King's Own (Royal Lancaster Regiment)

Major J N Bromilow, Second Lieutenant P Clegg, Second Lieutenant G R Hablutzel, Second Lieutenant A H W Hudson, Second Lieutenant C C Macwalter, Second Lieutenant H P E M Melly, 2nd Bn. King's Own (Royal Lancaster Regiment) attd from 3rd Bn Second Lieutenant R Minor, Second Lieutenant J Rowley, Captain J F H Young, 3rd Bn. attd. 1st Bn. Second Lieutenant A Weatherhead

7th Bn. King's Own (Royal Lancaster Regiment) (In Reserve)

1st Bn. King's Own Scottish Borderers

12th Bn. attd. 1st Bn. Second Lieutenant P T Bent, Second Lieutenant H F B Cooper, , 9th Bn. attd. 1st Bn. Second Lieutenant W Dickie, Second Lieutenant J H Glennie, 9th Bn. attd. 1st Bn Second Lieutenant J L Gow, , 9th Bn. attd. 1st Bn. Second Lieutenant J A S Graham Clarke, 9th Bn. attd. 1st Bn. Second Lieutenant F Paterson, 9th Bn. attd. 1st Bn. Second Lieutenant R Reid, 2nd Bn., attd 1st Bn., Second Lieutenant I A S Scott, Captain A J M Shaw, Second Lieutenant R Stewart

2nd Bn. King's Own Yorkshire Light Infantry

10th attd 2nd Bn., Captain C K Butler, Second Lieutenant O R Ilbery, Captain E J Millin, Second Lieutenant R Smith, Second Lieutenant H G Walker

4th Bn. King's Own Yorkshire Light Infantry

5th Bn. King's Own Yorkshire Light Infantry

8th Bn. King's Own Yorkshire Light Infantry

Second Lieutenant P G Boswell, Lieutenant E M B Cambie, 3rd Bn. attd. 8th Bn. Lieutenant H S Drury, Lieutenant A H Hack, Lieutenant W I S Hartley, Lieutenant H S Jackson, Lieutenant G H Kernaghan, Lieutenant M R H Morley, Lieutenant G W Morris, Second Lieutenant J Nelson, Lieutenant R W K Oakley, Lieutenant H Ormrod, Second Lieutenant P B P Robinson, Second Lieutenant O S Stephensen

9th Bn. King's Own Yorkshire Light Infantry

Second Lieutenant N L Alexander, 3rd Bn. attd. 9th Bn. Lieutenant C W Ellis, Second Lieutenant G H Featherstone, Second Lieutenant F A Golding, Captain G E Griffin, Captain G Haswell, Captain L D Head, Second Lieutenant C W Howlett, Lieutenant Colonel C W D Lynch, Second Lieutenant A D Maconachie, Second Lieutenant J J F Oldershaw, Second Lieutenant C E Vassie, Captain W Walker

10th Bn. King's Own Yorkshire Light Infantry

3rd Bn. attd. 10th Bn. Second Lieutenant J Andrew, Second Lieutenant K J P Asher, Lieutenant J W Bamber, 6th Bn. attd. 10th Bn Lieutenant R S M Beatson, 11th Bn. attd. 10th Bn. Second Lieutenant A C Cockcroft, Second Lieutenant J A A Fountain, 2nd Bn. attd. 10th Bn. Captain C R Heygate, 11th Bn. Killed with the 10th Bn., Second Lieutenant L E J Maude, Second Lieutenant L F Sharp, Second Lieutenant G F N Wilkinson,

12th Bn. King's Own Yorkshire Light Infantry

Lieutenant J S L Welch

1st Bn. Lancashire Fusiliers

4th Bn. attd. 1st Bn. Second Lieutenant A F D Anderson, 3rd Bn. attd. 1st Bn. Second Lieutenant F W Anderton, Second Lieutenant H N Grant, 13th Bn. attd. 1st Bn. Second Lieutenant E Kershaw, Captain E G Matthey, 2nd Bn. attd. 1st Bn. Second Lieutenant I A S Scott, 3rd Bn. attd. 1st Bn. Second Lieutenant F J Whittam, ,

2nd Bn. Lancashire Fusiliers

4th Bn. attd. 2nd Bn. Second Lieutenant B Farrow, Captain M P Gamon, Second Lieutenant H C Kenion, Lieutenant R S MacIver, 2nd Bn attd from 4th Bn. Lancashire Fusiliers Second Lieutenant C D Roberton, 1st Bn. attd. 2nd Bn. Captain H W Sayres

10th Bn. Lancashire Fusiliers (In Reserve)

15th Bn. Lancashire Fusiliers

15th Bn., attd from 13th Bn., Second Lieutenant J G Aird, Formerly 13th Bn. Lancashire Fusiliers Second Lieutenant E C Audaer, Second Lieutenant A Clegg, Second Lieutenant C Crossley, 15th Bn., attd from 13th Bn., Second Lieutenant R I Doncaster, Captain G Y Heald, 3rd Bn. attd. 15th Bn. Second Lieutenant E Jackson, Captain A Lee-Wood, 3rd Bn. attd. 15th Bn. Second Lieutenant R N Lodge, Captain E C Maclaren, Second Lieutenant C R B Noyes, Lieutenant H F Robinson, 13th Bn. attd. 15th Bn. Second Lieutenant Q L Smith, Lieutenant C H Wright, Lieutenant H V Wrong

16th Bn. Lancashire Fusiliers

16th attd from 15th Bn., Lieutenant E Hampson

19th Bn. Lancashire Fusiliers

9th Bn. attd. 19th Bn. Second Lieutenant E D Ashton, Second Lieutenant E C E Chambers, 4th Bn. attd. 19th Bn. Second Lieutenant A N Dussee, Second Lieutenant F H Freeman, Lieutenant R C Masterman

4th Bn. Leicestershire Regiment

5th Bn. Leicestershire Regiment

Second Lieutenant W K Callard

1st Bn., Lincolns

1st/4th Bn., Lincolns

Second Lieutenant W H Geliot

2nd Bn. Lincolnshire Regiment

Second Lieutenant J Anstee, 1st Bn. (War diary shows 2nd Bn.,)Second Lieutenant G W H Applin, ,Lieutenant H G F Clifford, 3rd Bn attd 2nd Bn., Captain S H Jeudwine, Captain B L Needham, Lieutenant D S Ross, Second Lieutenant L O Sharp, 1st Bn., (War diary shows 2nd) Lieutenant C G Shaw, 1st Bn., attd 2nd Bn., Lieutenant J H Toolis, Captain W F G Wiseman,

7th Bn. Lincolnshire Regiment (in Reserve)

8th Bn. Lincolnshire Regiment

Second Lieutenant R L Courtice, Second Lieutenant J F Cragg, Captain A C Jones, Second Lieutenant J H Parkinson, Second Lieutenant W Swift

10th Bn., Lincolnshire Regiment

Captain T Baker, Second Lieutenant L Cummins, Lieutenant R P Eason, 101st Brigade, Trench Mortar Battery attd 10th Bn., Second Lieutenant R G Ingle, Lieutenant E Inman

1st Bn. London Regiment (Royal Fusiliers)

Lieutenant H W Cundall

1st/2nd Bn. London Regiment (Royal Fusiliers)

Second Lieutenant B R Buxton, Captain J R Garland, Second Lieutenant H C Gosnell, Second Lieutenant J S Grainger, Captain P J A Handyside, Second Lieutenant A M Thorman,

1st/3rd Bn. London Regiment (Royal Fusiliers)

Second Lieutenant R A Calder-Smith, Lieutenant D W L Jones, Second Lieutenant R J A Lidiard

1st/4th Bn. London Regiment (Royal Fusiliers)

Second Lieutenant F R C Bradford, Second Lieutenant F C Fanghanel, Second Lieutenant T Moody, Captain A R Moore

1st/5th Bn. London Regiment (London Rifle Brigade)

Second Lieutenant C V Balkwill, Second Lieutenant A L Benns, Lieutenant G E Clode-Baker, Second Lieutenant C B Doust, Captain B S Harvey, Second Lieutenant I R Pogose, Captain J R Somers-Smith, Second Lieutenant A Warner

1st/9th Bn. London Regiment (Queen Victoria's Rifles)

Second Lieutenant R H Cary, Captain H E L Cox, Captain R W Cunningham, , Second Lieutenant F W Fielding, Captain P S Houghton, Second Lieutenant O T Mason, Second Lieutenant N A Meeking, Second Lieutenant P G Simmonds

1st/12th Bn. London Regiment (The Rangers)

Lieutenant R E K Bradshaw, Second Lieutenant W R Davey, Captain R L Hoare, Major L F Jones, Second Lieutenant J Josephs, Second Lieutenant A W Taplin, Second Lieutenant W H Tucker, Second Lieutenant D S Ward,

1st/13th Kensington Bn. London Regiment

Second Lieutenant H B Pilgrim, Second Lieutenant N O C Mackenzie, Second Lieutenant W G Mager, Second Lieutenant C B Sach, Captain F H Ware

1st/14th Bn. London Regiment (London Scottish)

Second Lieutenant R A Brown, Lieutenant J C Brown Constable, Second Lieutenant H A Coxon, Second Lieutenant W E F Curror, Second Lieutenant D Kerr, Major F H Lindsay,

1st/16th Bn. London Regiment (Queen's Westminster Rifles)

Second Lieutenant E H Bovill, Second Lieutenant F A Farley attd from 1st/16th, Second Lieutenant J A Horne, Captain H F Mott, Second Lieutenant A G Negus, attd from the 1st/2nd Bn., Second Lieutenant W F Strange, , Second Lieutenant C A Stubbs attd from 1st/2nd, Captain F G Swainson, Second Lieutenant A G V Yates

7th Loyal North Lancs (In Reserve)

Machine Gun Corps (Surname order)

10th Bde, Machine Gun Company attd from 2nd Bn., Seaforth Highlanders Captain G N Alison, Machine Gun Corps (attd from 3rd Bn. Essex Regiment) Lieutenant K F Barratt, 101st Coy. Machine Gun Corps (Infantry) Second Lieutenant G R Bible, 93rd MGC attd from 14th Bn. Middlesex Regiment Second Lieutenant P E O Booth, 87th Machine Gun Corps (attd from 1st Bn., Royal Warwickshire Regiment) Lieutenant T F Breene, 10th Bde., Machine Gun Coy (attd from 2nd Bn., Seaforth Highlanders) Lieutenant C R Buckworth, 25th Company, 6th Bn, Machine Gun Corps (Infantry),attd from 6th Bn., Rifle Brigade Second Lieutenant J M V Buxton, 64th Bde. Machine Gun Corps (Infantry) Second Lieutenant J P A Callaghan, MGC from 3rd Bn. Royal Sussex Regiment Lieutenant H A F V Catmur, MGC from 3rd Bn. Royal Inniskilling Fusiliers Lieutenant E W Costello, 108th Bde, Machine Gun Officer attd from 13th Royal Irish Rifles) Captain J S Davidson, 93rd Machine Gun Corps attd from 4th Bn. Royal Warwickshire Regiment Second Lieutenant R F M Dean, 101st Bn. Machine Gun Corps Second Lieutenant A C Dore, 109th Bn., Machine Gun Corps (Infantry) attd from 15th Bn. Middlesex Regiment Second Lieutenant N D Edingborough, 169 Infantry Bde, Machine Gun Corps (attd from 1st/16th London Regiment) Second Lieutenant J S Engall, 169 Infantry Bde, Machine Gun Corps (attd from 1st/2nd London Regiment) Second Lieutenant K M C Fradd, 22nd Coy., Machine Gun Corps, attd from 2nd Bn., Royal Warwickshire Regiment Second Lieutenant C S Gibson, 70th Bn., Machine Gun Corps attd from 3rd Bn. Norfolk Regiment Second Lieutenant W O Hampton, Machine Gun Corps (Infantry) Second Lieutenant G Harrison, 109th Bn. Machine Gun Corps Lieutenant A C Hart, 109th Bn. Machine Gun Corps (Infantry) Lieutenant H M Hewitt, , 1st Bn., Somerset Light Infantry attd 11th Machine Gun Company Second Lieutenant P C Knight, 10th Bde, Machine Gun Company attd from 2nd Bn., Seaforth Highlanders Lieutenant J M Low, 103rd Coy. Machine Gun Corps (Infantry) Captain S G Millar, 11th Machine Gun Company attd from 2nd Bn. Royal Irish Regiment Captain F G R Mockler, 64th Bde. Machine Gun Corps (Infantry) Lieutenant G E Mockridge, Machine Gun Corps (Infantry) Lieutenant E F Morse, 108th Coy. Machine Gun Corps (Infantry) Lieutenant J D Neill, 139th Coy Machine Gun Corps (Infantry) attd from 7th Bn. Sherwood Foresters (Notts And Derby Regiment) Second Lieutenant E J Peach, 102nd Coy. Machine Gun Corps (Infantry) Second Lieutenant N A Pidduck, 108th Coy. Machine Gun Corps (Infantry) Second Lieutenant D S Priestley, 96th Coy. Machine Gun Corps (Infantry) Lieutenant B C Pring, 108th Machine Gun Corps formerly 12th Bn., Royal Irish Rifles Second Lieutenant W T Richardson, 107th Coy. Machine Gun Corps (Infantry) Lieutenant G E Sanderson, 168th Brigade Machine Gun Company attd from 1/14th London Regiment Lieutenant F S Thomson, 64th Bde. Machine Gun Corps (attd from Leinster Regiment) Second Lieutenant S M Watson, 109th Coy. Machine Gun Corps (Infantry) Lieutenant G C Wedgwood, 92nd Machine Gun Corps from 11th Bn. Yorkshire Regiment Second Lieutenant E B White.

2nd Manchesters

12th Manchesters (In Reserve)

14th Bn. Manchester Regiment
Second Lieutenant N Peak, Second Lieutenant J E Price

16th Bn. Manchester Regiment
Second Lieutenant S R Allen

17th Bn. Manchester Regiment
Second Lieutenant T H Clesham, Captain R J Ford, Captain S Kenworthy, 11th Bn. attd. 17th Bn. Manchester Regiment Lieutenant G M Sproat, Captain N Vaudrey

18th Manchesters

19th Bn. Manchester Regiment
Second Lieutenant A W Atkinson

20th Bn. Manchester Regiment
Second Lieutenant F S Brooks, Second Lieutenant J W Eaton, Second Lieutenant T Kemp, 37th Lancers (Baluch Horse), Indian Army attd 20th Manchesters, Lieutenant Colonel H Lewis, Lieutenant H Lomas, Lieutenant F G Ross, Captain D W Smith 6th Bn to 20th Bn., (attd from RAMC), Captain J V White

21st Bn. Manchester Regiment
Second Lieutenant H H Cowin, Second Lieutenant G F Wilson

22nd Bn. Manchester Regiment
Captain A E Bland, Second Lieutenant W E Brunt, 4th Bn. attd. 22nd Bn. Second Lieutenant C T Gill, Lieutenant W E Gomersall, Captain C C May, Lieutenant R Mellor, 22nd attd from 25th Bn Second Lieutenant J Nanson, 4th Bn. attd. 22nd Bn. Second Lieutenant G G Swan,

24th Manchesters

26th Bn. Manchester Regiment
Lieutenant H O Lord, Second Lieutenant E Outram, Second Lieutenant P J Ram, Captain G B Sayce

2nd Bn. Middlesex Regiment
5th Bn. attd. 2nd Bn. Second Lieutenant C S Davis, 2nd Bn., attd from 3rd Bn. Second Lieutenant P M Elliott, Second Lieutenant W F Forge, Second Lieutenant A I Frost, Second Lieutenant R E Grundy, Captain C S Hilton, Captain W S Meeke, Lieutenant G Scott, Second Lieutenant W Spatz, Second Lieutenant F Van Den Bok, Second Lieutenant J Wilson, 3rd Bn. attd. 2nd Bn. Second Lieutenant H D Wood,

4th Bn. Middlesex Regiment
Second Lieutenant P Barnett, Second Lieutenant A Branch, Second Lieutenant A G Chambers, 5th Bn. attd. 4th Bn. Lieutenant A A H Johnston, Captain O R F Johnston, Second Lieutenant G R Money, Second Lieutenant A F C Paxton, Second Lieutenant E Peyton, Lieutenant G L C Ridpath, Second Lieutenant A H W Sampson, Captain A Sapte, Second Lieutenant E V Whitby, Second Lieutenant W J Wood,

7th Bn., Middlesex Regiment

8th Bn., Middlesex Regiment

12th Bn., Middlesex Regiment
Attd from 14th Bn., Second Lieutenant, H R Hudlestone

16th Bn. Middlesex Regiment,
Second Lieutenant H E Asser, Lieutenant H W Barker, Lieutenant H D Goodwin, Lieutenant H J Heath, 14th Bn. attd. 16th Bn. Second Lieutenant E R Heaton, Second Lieutenant H C Hertslet, Captain G H Heslop, Second Lieutenant J K Orr, Captain A C Purnell, Lieutenant F B Tanqueray, Captain T H Watts

1 Monmouthshire (Pioneers)

2 Monmouthshire (Pioneers)

3 Monmouthshire (Pioneers)

1st Bn. Newfoundland Regiment
Captain E S Ayre, Second Lieutenant G W Ayre, Second Lieutenant W D Ayre, Second Lieutenant J R Ferguson, Lieutenant H C Herder, Second Lieutenant C H O Jupp, Lieutenant F C Mellor, Second Lieutenant R B Reid, Second Lieutenant R W Ross, Second Lieutenant W T Ryall, Lieutenant R A Shortall, Second Lieutenant G H Taylor

8th Bn. Norfolk Regiment
Second Lieutenant J H Attenborough, Captain B P Ayre, Second Lieutenant S A Wharton

1st/5th Bn. North Staffordshire Regiment Second Lieutenant A D Chapman, Captain G H Fletcher, Second Lieutenant R B Mellard, Lieutenant E Robinson, Second Lieutenant A C Watkin

1st/6th Bn. North Staffordshire Regiment Lieutenant Colonel C E Boote, Lieutenant A Evershed, Second Lieutenant W H Heath, Second Lieutenant H B Jones, Second Lieutenant W H Marson, Lieutenant W T Newton, Lieutenant R R S Shaw, Captain J M Stack, Second Lieutenant H G Williamson

8th Bn. North Staffordshire Regiment (In Reserve)

6th Northamptonshire

Northumberland Fusiliers

Royal Scots Fusiliers attd to Northumberland Fusiliers Captain W Tullis,

9th Northumberland (In Reserve)

12th Northumberland

13th Northumberland Fusiliers

Attd from 36th Jacob's Horse, Indian Cavalry Lieutenant Colonel H Allardice

14th Bn. Northumberland Fusiliers

Second Lieutenant J Walker

15th Bn Northumberland Fusiliers

Second Lieutenant C Ashley

16th Bn. Northumberland Fusiliers

Lieutenant F C Arnaud, Second Lieutenant W E Avery, Lieutenant R W Falconer, Captain P G Graham, Second Lieutenant M G Klean, Lieutenant T Macintyre, Captain A C Young

17th Bn. Northumberland Fusiliers

18th Bn. Northumberland Fusiliers (Pioneers)

20th (Tyneside Scottish) Bn. Northumberland Fusiliers

Second Lieutenant N A Arkle, Second Lieutenant C S Binns, Second Lieutenant A Coleman, Lieutenant G E Cope, Lieutenant R C Davidson, Second Lieutenant J J Donaldson, Lieutenant A E Head, Second Lieutenant A H Jarman, Captain W Nixon, Major T G Noble, 20th Bn., attd from Army Cyclist Corps Lieutenant G M Ross, Second Lieutenant W W Sanby, Lieutenant Colonel C C A Sillery, Second Lieutenant L L C Tucker, Second Lieutenant F A Venus, Lieutenant B C D White

21st (Tyneside Scottish) Bn. Northumberland

Captain J M Charlton, Lieutenant R J Dougal, Second Lieutenant J M Hall, attd from Leinster Regiment Lieutenant Colonel F C Heneker, , 21st attd from 29th Bn. Captain D D Horne, Major A G Niven, Lieutenant L R Raimes, Captain G Robertson, Second Lieutenant N M Smith, 21st attd from 29th Bn. Second Lieutenant N White

22nd (Tyneside Scottish) Bn. Northumberland Fusiliers

Lieutenant Colonel A P A Elphinstone, Captain J P Forster, Second Lieutenant J W Fryer, Captain D O Laing, Lieutenant W Lamb, Major H Sibbit, Lieutenant W B Tytler

23rd (Tyneside Scottish) Bn. Northumberland Fusiliers

Captain H A Bolton, Major M Burge, Captain J B Cubey, Lieutenant Colonel W Lyle, Second Lieutenant R Macdonald, Lieutenant S Macdonald, Lieutenant J H Patterson, Lieutenant A E Shapley, Captain J G Todd, Second Lieutenant L Williams

24th Bn. Northumberland Fusiliers

Second Lieutenant L F Byrne, Second Lieutenant H M Horrox, Lieutenant Colonel L M Howard, Captain K Mackenzie, Captain A Thompson

25th Bn. Northumberland Fusiliers

Second Lieutenant T S Charlesworth, Major W H Edmond-Jenkins, Captain J Foley, Captain P A Murray, Lieutenant T E Nicholson

26th Bn. Northumberland Fusiliers

Second Lieutenant J L Beavon, Lieutenant G Fitzgerald, Second Lieutenant C W Flint, Second Lieutenant W W Hynam, Lieutenant J McGillicuddy, Captain B D Mullally, 3rd Bn attd 26th Bn., Lieutenant J Parker, Captain F L Vernon

27th Bn. Northumberland Fusiliers

Lieutenant J R C Burluraux, Second Lieutenant H R H Evered, 30th (Tyneside Irish) Bn. attd. 27th Bn. Captain R Falkous Lieutenant J W Marshall, Lieutenant T Simpson

4th Oxford and Bucks Light Infantry (In Reserve)

2nd Bn. Queen's (Royal West Surrey Regiment) Captain T P Brocklehurst Second Lieutenant W Crees, Second Lieutenant J M Foord-Kelcey, Second Lieutenant L S Ford, Second Lieutenant J Gillies, Second Lieutenant E Hobbs

7th Bn. Queen's (Royal West Surrey Regiment)
 Lieutenant H Cloudesley, Second Lieutenant G S Dandridge, Second Lieutenant R C Herbert, Second Lieutenant F J Miller, Lieutenant O E Saltmarshe, Captain G H H Scott, Captain J R Walpole

1st Bn. Rifle Brigade
Captain W H Beever, Captain G T Cartland, 5th Bn. attd. 1st Bn. Second Lieutenant C A Clark, 5th Bn. attd 1st Bn., Second Lieutenant A G Clarke, Lieutenant G C L Dewhurst, 6th Bn. attd. 1st Bn. Captain R Fraser, Captain A W Henderson, Second Lieutenant F W Kirkland, 6th Bn. attd. 1st Bn. Second Lieutenant J P Morum, 6th Bn. attd. 1st Bn Second Lieutenant E E Trevor-Jones, Second Lieutenant F C S Volkers, , 6th Bn. attd. 1st Bn. Lieutenant M G White, Lieutenant Colonel D Wood,

2nd Rifle Brigade
Royal Army Medical Corps
RAMC formerly 9th Bn., Royal Inniskilling Fusiliers. Captain H C Mulkern, 90th Field Amb. Royal Army Medical Corps Lieutenant D Rodger

2nd Bn. Royal Berkshire Regiment
Second Lieutenant S H Bedford, Second Lieutenant B H Belcher, Second Lieutenant H Godfrey, Lieutenant A J G Goodall, Second Lieutenant M I Heming, Captain R C Lewis, Lieutenant O G Payne, Lieutenant B S Robinson, 9th Bn. attd. 2nd Bn. Captain H T Rowley, 9th Bn. attd. 2nd Bn. Second Lieutenant S S Schneider 2nd Bn. Formerly 3rd Bn. Second Lieutenant F G Shirreff

4th Bn., Royal Berkshire Regiment (In Reserve)
6th Bn. Royal Berkshire Regiment
Second Lieutenant E C Bayly, Second Lieutenant T A Collot, Second Lieutenant G M Courage, Second Lieutenant C K Howe, Captain R Litten, Second Lieutenant N B Souper, Lieutenant K R Traill

1st Bn. Royal Dublin Fusiliers
1st Bn attd from 9th Bn. The Queen's (Royal West Surrey Regiment) Second Lieutenant C F Greenlees, Captain E R L Maunsell, 14th Bn, Royal Fusiliers attd 1st Bn., Second Lieutenant A J W Pearson, 3rd Bn., attd 1st Bn., Lieutenant A M B Rose-Cleland, 4th Bn. attd. 1st Bn. Second Lieutenant D R Warner

2nd Bn. Royal Dublin Fusiliers
Second Lieutenant R H Ingoldby, 4th Bn. attd. 2nd Bn. Second Lieutenant J W R Morgan

4th Bn. Royal Dublin Fusiliers
Second Lieutenant L H Saffery

Royal Engineers
1st Edinburgh Field Coy. Royal Engineers Second Lieutenant S Angus, Field Engineer, Iv Corps Royal Engineers Captain D Fraser, No. 1 Mortar Company, 5th Mortar Bn., Special Bde, Royal Engineers Second Lieutenant R T Hardman, 150th Field Coy. Royal Engineers Lieutenant J L Peacock, 208th Field Coy. Royal Engineers Second Lieutenant H F Scott-Holmes,
219th Field Coy. Royal Engineers Second Lieutenant C J Tart, 30th Field Coy. Royal Engineers Second Lieutenant L L Vigers

Royal Field Artillery, Royal Garrison Artillery & Trench Mortar Batteries
114th Heavy Bty. Royal Garrison Artillery Second Lieutenant R G Bagnall, 5th Bty. 3rd North Midland Bde. Royal Field Artillery Second Lieutenant E H L Clark, "A" Bty. 96th Bde. Royal Field Artillery Second Lieutenant A C Colmer, 150th Bde. Royal Field Artillery Second Lieutenant J Cotton, Second Lieutenant B T Craven," North Midland Div. Ammunition Col Royal Field Artillery Lieutenant T A M Davies,
Second Lieutenant P F Fenwick, "A" Bty. 150th Bde. Royal Field Artillery Major J F Graham,
175th Bde. Royal Field Artillery Second Lieutenant W C Hickman, 168th Bde. Royal Field Artillery Second Lieutenant H F Madders, "A" Bty. 10th Bde. Royal Field Artillery Second Lieutenant D Rowatt, Second Lieutenant C J Sutton, 125th Bty. Royal Field Artillery Captain R R S Sweetnam,
22nd Bde. Royal Field Artillery Second Lieutenant W C S Warr

Trench Mortar Batteries
Second Lieutenant K Bemrose seconded to 139th Trench Mortar Battery from 1st/5th Sherwood Foresters, 93rd Trench Mortar Battery (attd from 18th Bn Durham Light Infantry) Second Lieutenant S F Bobby, 101st Trench Mortar Battery from General List Second Lieutenant G J Brand, 86th Trench Mortar Battery (attd from 13th Bn., Lancashire Fusiliers) Second Lieutenant S McD Campbell, Trench Mortar Battery (attd from Royal Field

Artillery) , 63rd Trench Mortar Battery Second Lieutenant S P Churchfield, B" Bty. 68th Bde. Royal Field Artillery Second Lieutenant A L Dagge (Burial records has TMB), Light Trench Mortar Battery from 11th York and Lancasters Second Lieutenant H C Dalby, Lieutenant L T Day, 102nd Trench Mortar Battery attd from 21st Northumberland Fusiliers Second Lieutenant W H Furse, 139 Trench Mortar Battery attd from 1st/7th Bn., Sherwood Foresters Second Lieutenant F B Gamble, 55th Trench Mortar Battery attd from 7th Bn. Queen's Own (Royal West Kent Regiment) Captain B H Glover, 139th Trench Mortar Battery attd from 5th Bn., Sherwood Foresters (Notts and Derby) Regiment Second Lieutenant J R L Hunt, Lieutenant E A J A Lane 1st/9th London Regiment attd 169th Brigade Trench Mortar Battery, 14th Trench Mortar Battery attd from 19th Bn. Highland Light Infantry Second Lieutenant C H McCrostie,Trench Mortar Battery attd from, 16th Bn., Highland Light Infantry Captain T Middleton, Trench Mortar Battery formerly Royal Irish Fusiliers General List Lieutenant S O'Neill, 90th Brigade, Trench Mortar Battery from General List Second Lieutenant W K Orford, 1st Trench Mortar Battery attd from 3rd Bn. Hampshire Regiment Lieutenant W G Nixon, 94th Light Mortar Trench Battery attd from General List Second Lieutenant F J Potter, 53 Trench Mortar Battery, General List And 2nd Bn. Wiltshire Regiment Second Lieutenant F G Rushton, Trench Mortar Battery from 24th Bn. Northumberland Fusiliers Second Lieutenant H R C Sutcliffe, 63rd Trench Mortar Battery detached from the 10th Bn., York and Lancaster Regiment. Lieutenant C Sykes, 9th Bn. attd. 64th Trench Mortar Bty. King's Own Yorkshire Light Infantry Lieutenant H A Telfer, 93rd Trench Mortar Battery from 18th West Yorkshires Lieutenant F Watson,

2nd Bn. Royal Fusiliers

Attd from 16th Bn., Second Lieutenant C Blackwell, Lieutenant F M Drinkill, 6th Bn. attd. 2nd Bn Lieutenant A M Haycraft, 5th Bn. attd. (Adjt.) 2nd Bn. Royal Fusiliers Lieutenant J W Nicholls, Middlesex Regiment attd 2nd Bn., Lieutenant A F Paterson, Second Lieutenant C F Roope, Second Lieutenant L T Westaway,

11th Bn. Royal Fusiliers

Lieutenant W H E Nield, Second Lieutenant J H Parr-Dudley, Second Lieutenant W H Savage

1st Bn. Royal Inniskilling Fusiliers

1st Bn., Royal Inniskilling Fusiliers attd from 9th Bn. Queen's Own (Royal West Kent Regiment) Lieutenant F M S Bowen, 1st Bn attd from 15th Bn. The King's (Liverpool Regiment) Captain B St. G French, 3rd Bn. attd. 1st Bn. Lieutenant G A L Harbord, 6th Bn. attd. 1st Bn. Lieutenant S T Martin, Lieutenant Colonel R C Pierce, 6th Bn. attd 1st Bn., Second Lieutenant W Porter, Second Lieutenant C A Stonor, 9th Bn., Queen's Own (Royal West Kent Regiment) Lieutenant A D L Wilson,

2nd Bn., Royal Inniskilling Fusiliers

Captain, F J Huskinson.

9th Bn. Royal Inniskilling Fusiliers

Captain E N F Bell, Lieutenant W M Crozier, Captain P Cruickshank, Second Lieutenant F P Fox, Second Lieutenant J S M Gage, 12th Bn. attd. 9th Bn. Second Lieutenant A H Gibson, Second Lieutenant W A Hewitt, Captain H C Maclean, Captain W F H Pelly, Lieutenant L W H Stevenson, , 3rd Bn. attd. 9th Bn. Lieutenant E A Trouton, Captain J Weir,

10th Bn. Royal Inniskilling Fusiliers

Second Lieutenant A Kemp, Lieutenant E McClure, Captain J C B Proctor, Captain M A Robertson, Second Lieutenant A G Spalding

11th Bn. Royal Inniskilling Fusiliers

Captain J Ballintine, Second Lieutenant J A T Craig, 6th Bn. attd. 11th Bn. Second Lieutenant F D Gunning, Second Lieutenant J Hamilton, Second Lieutenant S Miller, Major W T Sewell, 6th Bn. attd. 11th Bn Second Lieutenant R W Topp

2nd Royal Irish Regiment

1st Bn., Royal Irish Fusiliers

9th Bn. Royal Irish Fusiliers

Major T J Atkinson, Lieutenant A C Hollywood, Captain C M Johnston, Second Lieutenant R T Montgomery, 3rd Bn., attd 9th Bn., Second Lieutenant A Seggie, 10th Bn. attd. 9th Bn. Second Lieutenant W J Stewart Lieutenant R S B Townsend

1st Bn. Royal Irish Rifles

Captain D A Browne, 5th Bn. attd. 1st Bn. Second Lieutenant H M Glastonbury, 5th Bn. attd. 1st Bn Second Lieutenant W H Gregg, 5th Bn. attd. 1st Bn. Royal Irish Rifles Lieutenant S D I Smith,

8th Bn. Royal Irish Rifles

Captain H P Beggs, Second Lieutenant A E Coote, attd from 17th Bn. Second Lieutenant T G Moore, 8th Bn., attd from 6th Bn., Royal Irish Rifles Lieutenant J Murphy

9th Bn. Royal Irish Rifles

Second Lieutenant W M Campbell, Major G H Gaffikin, Second Lieutenant R V Hamilton, 3rd Bn. attd. 9th Bn. Lieutenant J F Healy, 3rd Bn. attd. 9th Bn. Lieutenant N F Hone, 6th Bn. attd. 8th Bn. Lieutenant J Murphy,

10th Bn. Royal Irish Rifles

, Royal Scots Fusiliers attd 10th Bn. Second Lieutenant M L Adamson, Colonel H C Bernard, 3rd Bn. attd. 10th Bn. Second Lieutenant W Dean, Second Lieutenant T B Elliott, Second Lieutenant W O Green, Captain B Hill, 3rd Bn. attd. 10th Bn. Second Lieutenant F M Masterman, 17th Bn. attd. 10th Bn. Second Lieutenant E M Wilson

11th Bn. Royal Irish Rifles

Captain C F K Ewart, Lieutenant R H Neill

12th Bn. Royal Irish Rifles

Lieutenant L B Campbell, Captain J Griffiths, Lieutenant T G Haughton, 18th Bn. attd. 12th Bn. Second Lieutenant J Hollywood, Lieutenant A D Lemon, 1st Bn. Black Watch (Royal Highlanders) attd 12th Bn., Second Lieutenant E H MacNaghten, Lieutenant W McCluggage, Captain C S Murray

13th Bn. Royal Irish Rifles

5th Bn. attd. 13th Bn Second Lieutenant E G Boas, Second Lieutenant N S Hatch, Captain E Johnston, Lieutenant J Pollock, Lieutenant G M Rogers, Captain W H Smyth, Major H A Uprichard,

14th Bn. Royal Irish Rifles

Second Lieutenant W J W Carson, Second Lieutenant B C Harley, Second Lieutenant G K Radcliffe, Captain C O Slacke, Captain S Willis, Second Lieutenant M J Wright,

15th Bn. Royal Irish Rifles

Captain W H Chiplin, Second Lieutenant E W G Hind, 18th Bn. attd. 15th Bn. Second Lieutenant A J Mcclellan, Captain D H O'Flaherty, Captain C B Tate,

16th Bn. Royal Irish Rifles

Second Lieutenant P E Wedgwood

15th Bn. Royal Scots Second Lieutenant J L Brough, Major J R Bruce, Second Lieutenant J B Dougal, Second Lieutenant A Elder, 14th Bn. attd. 15th Bn. Second Lieutenant W Gibson, Second Lieutenant J Grant, Lieutenant W A Hole, 15th Bn., Royal Scots from General List Second Lieutenant W Jeal, Second Lieutenant E M Pinkerton, Lieutenant R Reid, Major H L Stocks

16th Bn. Royal Scots

Captain L G Coles, 3rd Bn. attd 4th killed with 16th Royal Scots Second Lieutenant W L Crombie, Captain P Ross, Second Lieutenant G S Russell,

2nd Bn. Royal Scots Fusiliers

Second Lieutenant V Godfrey, 3rd Bn. attd. 2nd Bn. Second Lieutenant J L H Grierson, Lieutenant J W Towers-Clark,

5th Royal Sussex

8th Royal Sussex

1st Royal Warwicks

1st/6th Bn. Royal Warwickshire Regiment

Second Lieutenant J Balkwill, Captain C T M Davies, Captain J E B Dixon, Second Lieutenant H L Field, Lieutenant G R C Martin, Second Lieutenant R Price, , Captain A B Rabone, Second Lieutenant R V Rose, Second Lieutenant W P Wheeler, Second Lieutenant S J Winkley

6th Bn. Royal Warwickshire Regiment

1st/8th Bn. Royal Warwickshire Regiment

Lieutenant R Adams, Major A A Caddick, Second Lieutenant F B Freeman, Lieutenant J G Fussell, Lieutenant C Hoskins, Lieutenant Colonel E A Innes, Second Lieutenant F B Key, Captain S W Ludlow, Lieutenant A Procter, Second Lieutenant E R Shuttleworth, Lieutenant F W Wareham

8th Bn. Royal Warwickshire Regiment

2nd Bn. Royal Warwickshire Regiment

Lieutenant A Hodgkinson, 3rd Bn. attd. 2nd Bn. Lieutenant E J Martin

5th Royal Warwicks (In Reserve)

7th Royal Warwicks (In Reserve)

10th Royal Warwicks (In Reserve)

1st Bn., Royal Welch

9th Bn Royal Welch (In Reserve)

17th Bn., Royal Welsh Fusiliers

Second Lieutenant L Lewis

7th Bn., Royal West Kent

7th attd from 9th Bn. Queen's Own (Royal West Kent Regiment) Lieutenant E J Innocent

2nd Bn. Cameronians (Scottish Rifles)

Second Lieutenant M G Fraser

2nd Bn. Seaforth Highlanders

Captain C E Baird, Second Lieutenant M H Blackwood, Second Lieutenant F J Broom, Second Lieutenant D Buchanan, Second Lieutenant F A Conner, Second Lieutenant S A Crum, Second Lieutenant J N Gourlay, Second Lieutenant J Harvey, Second Lieutenant T E Lancaster, Second Lieutenant F R Mackenzie, Lieutenant N I MacWatt, Second Lieutenant W Shaw, 2nd Bn. attd from 4th Bn. Argyll And Sutherland Highlanders Second Lieutenant H F L Sillars, Second Lieutenant J Williamson

6th Bn. Sherwood Foresters (Notts And Derby Regiment)

Lieutenant M E Jellicoe

1st/5th Bn. Sherwood Foresters (Notts And Derby Regiment)

Second Lieutenant W G W Barber, Second Lieutenant A N Bates, Second Lieutenant D Callow, Second Lieutenant R B Cecil, Second Lieutenant H S Dornton, Second Lieutenant H F Godfrey, Second Lieutenant H M Hibbert, Second Lieutenant J C Hyde, , Captain F H M Lewes, Second Lieutenant J E McInnes, 17th Indian Cavalry attd 1/5th Bn., Lieutenant Colonel D D Wilson, Major F W Wragg, From South Staffordshire Regiment (attd from RAMC) Captain J L Green

1/6th Sherwood

1st/7th Bn. Sherwood Foresters (Notts And Derby Regiment)

Second Lieutenant C H Burton, Second Lieutenant A Charles, Second Lieutenant J H C Fletcher, Second Lieutenant W E Flint, Captain R M Gotch, Lieutenant Colonel L A Hind, Captain T H Leman, Lieutenant J MacPherson, Captain W H Round, Captain W E G Walker, Second Lieutenant A H Wilkins

1/8 Sherwood

10th Sherwood (In Reserve)

11th Bn. Sherwood Foresters (Notts And Derby Regiment)

Second Lieutenant W A Davis, 13th Bn. attd. 11th Bn. Captain H S Harris, Second Lieutenant S Longhurst, Lieutenant E Russell, Second Lieutenant C V Tomlinson

1st Bn. Somerset Light Infantry

Lieutenant V A Braithwaite, Lieutenant T M Dodington, Second Lieutenant R E Dunn, Second Lieutenant G P C Fair, Captain C C Ford, 3rd Bn. attd. 1st Bn. Second Lieutenant J A Hellard, 3rd Bn. attd. 1st Bn. Second Lieutenant J A Johnston, Captain R J R Leacroft, 3rd Bn. attd from Devonshire Regiment killed with 1st Bn., Second Lieutenant A V C Leche, 3rd Bn. attd. 1st Bn. Lieutenant E C Macbryan, Captain G H Neville, Second Lieutenant F A Pearse, Lieutenant Colonel J A Thicknesse, Second Lieutenant W H Treasure, Second Lieutenant G C Winstanley, Second Lieutenant H E Whitgreave

8th Bn. Somerset Light Infantry

Second Lieutenant J R T Chalmers, Second Lieutenant H Dalrymple, Captain A B Hatt, Second Lieutenant W G Leathley, Second Lieutenant J E Lewis, Second Lieutenant W F Scott, Captain W G Warden, Second Lieutenant F D Withers, 9th Bn., attd. "B" Coy. 8th Bn. Somerset Light Infantry Second Lieutenant J V Young

7th Bn. South Lancashire Regiment (In Reserve)

Lieutenant J B Hoyle

11th Bn. South Lancashire Regiment

Lieutenant R W Garton

1st Bn. South Staffordshire Regiment

Second Lieutenant P H Emberton, Lieutenant W Hall, Captain C R Limbery, 4th Bn. attd. 1st Bn. Second Lieutenant W H Ratcliffe, Second Lieutenant S A Webber, Captain G White

1st/5th Bn. South Staffordshire Regiment

Second Lieutenant H Allen, Captain F Eglington, Second Lieutenant S J Ellison, Second Lieutenant F A Fawcett, Lieutenant G T R Knowles, Second Lieutenant T R Sanger, Lieutenant J P Thorne

1st/6th Bn. South Staffordshire Regiment

Second Lieutenant T A Dickinson, 1st Bn. attd. 4th Bn. Captain C W Evans, Second Lieutenant A E Flaxman, Captain A D Harley, Second Lieutenant R S Jeffcock, Second Lieutenant W R Johnson, Second Lieutenant R Page

8th Bn. South Staffordshire Regiment (In Reserve)

Second Lieutenant A C Brown,

2nd Bn. South Wales Borderers

2nd Bn., attd from 15th Bn., The King's (Liverpool Regiment) Captain F S Blake, Second Lieutenant G H Bowyer attd 87th Machine Gun Company, 2nd Bn., attd from 14th Bn. Sherwood Foresters (Notts And Derby Regiment) Second Lieutenant D F Don, Lieutenant H P Evans, Captain A A Hughes, Second Lieutenant J B Karran, 2nd Bn., attd from 16th Bn. Cheshire Regiment Captain R J Mclaren, Second Lieutenant J C Murray, 8th Bn. attd. 2nd Bn. Second Lieutenant F Rice, 3rd Bn. attd. 2nd Bn. Second Lieutenant J Robinson, Second Lieutenant T W M Wells

5th South Wales Borderers

7th Bn. Suffolk Regiment

Second Lieutenant A G Horsnell

8th Suffolk

11th Bn. Suffolk Regiment

Second Lieutenant D J Darley, Lieutenant R Q Gilson, Captain I A Mack, Second Lieutenant A W McGain, Second Lieutenant A A McLean, Second Lieutenant S Thomas, 13th Bn. Attd. 11th Bn Second Lieutenant J D Weston

9 Welsh (In Reserve)

2nd Bn. West Yorkshire Regiment (Prince Of Wales's Own)

Second Lieutenant E G Brophy, Second Lieutenant R A R Campbell, Lieutenant E R Cholmeley, Captain P Y Harkness, Second Lieutenant G Perkins, Captain J F Ruttledge, 4th Bn. attd. 2nd Bn. Second Lieutenant F L Warren

1/5 West Yorkshire (In Reserve)

1st/6th Bn. West Yorkshire Regiment (Prince Of Wales's Own) (In Reserve)

Second Lieutenant N Dodd, Second Lieutenant C G Higgins

1/7 west Yorkshire (In Reserve)

1st/8th Bn. West Yorkshire Regiment (Prince Of Wales's Own) (In Reserve)

Second Lieutenant J C Stimpson, Second Lieutenant G C Ward

10th Bn. West Yorkshire Regiment (Prince Of Wales's Own)

Lieutenant H D Allen, Captain A J Anderson, Captain G G Blackburn, Second Lieutenant R H Blatherwick, 1st Bn., South Lancashire Regiment attd. 10th Bn.Lieutenant Colonel, A Dickson, 13th Bn. attd. 10th Bn. Second Lieutenant F J Hicking, Lieutenant W B Ibbitson, Lieutenant W M Keighley, Major J L Knott, Lieutenant A V Ratcliffe, Lieutenant J W Shann,

15th Bn. West Yorkshire Regiment (Prince Of Wales's Own)

Lieutenant S M Bickersteth, Second Lieutenant M W Booth, Second Lieutenant J P Everitt, Second Lieutenant T Humphries, Second Lieutenant C W James, Lieutenant E H Lintott, Second Lieutenant A Liversidge, Captain S T A Neil, Formerly 14th Bn. Second Lieutenant V O'Land, Second Lieutenant C Saunders, Lieutenant R H Tolson, Lieutenant J G Vause, Captain G C Whitaker, Second Lieutenant T A R R E Willey

16th Bn. West Yorkshire Regiment (Prince Of Wales's Own)

Captain A Clough, 2nd Bn., Royal Fusiliers killed leading 16th Bn., Lieutenant Colonel G S Guyon, Second Lieutenant C S Hyde, 14th Bn. attd. 16th Bn. Lieutenant A D Maitland, Second Lieutenant S B Newlands, Captain R W H Pringle, Lieutenant C T Ransome, Second Lieutenant J H Robinson, Captain D C Smith, Second Lieutenant R Stead, Second Lieutenant F J Symonds, 13th Bn. attd. 16th Bn. Second Lieutenant E Tweedale, 13th Bn. attd. 16th Bn. Lieutenant M H Webster,

18th Bn. West Yorkshire Regiment (Prince Of Wales's Own)

Lieutenant J R Akam, Second Lieutenant H Colley, Second Lieutenant R I Derwent, Lieutenant H E Foizey, Lieutenant Colonel M N Kennard, Second Lieutenant F J G Walton

21st Bn, West Yorkshire

2nd Bn., Wiltshire Regiment

6th Bn., Wiltshire Regiment (In Reserve)

4th Bn., Worcesters

7th Bn., Worcesters (In Reserve)

8th Bn., Worcesters (In Reserve)

10th Bn., Worcesters (In Reserve)

4th Bn. York And Lancaster Regiment (In Reserve)

1st/5th Bn. York And Lancaster Regiment (In Reserve)

Lieutenant J Wrigley

3rd Bn. York And Lancaster Regiment

Second Lieutenant E Stephenson

6th Bn. York And Lancaster Regiment

Lieutenant G G Hicking

7th Bn. York And Lancaster Regiment

8th Bn. York And Lancaster Regiment

Second Lieutenant J H Baker, 11th Bn. Lieutenant W C Bolton, attd. 8th Bn. Lieutenant H S Booth, Captain O R Cuthbert, Lieutenant S Dawson, Captain C R E Edmundson, Second Lieutenant J Ekin Second Lieutenant L M Ekin, Second Lieutenant A M Herapath, Captain R C Stewart, Second Lieutenant A C White, Lieutenant W P Woodstock

9th Bn. York And Lancaster Regiment

Lieutenant Colonel A J B Addison, Second Lieutenant S A Bryan, Lieutenant B B Geake, Major H A Lewis, Second Lieutenant R G Stroud, Second Lieutenant W P O Thomas

10th Bn. York And Lancaster Regiment

Second Lieutenant R J Kingsford, Captain R W Mullins, Lieutenant H P Organ, Second Lieutenant R M Stainton, Captain D C T Twentyman

11th Bn. York And Lancaster Regiment

Lieutenant W A D Goodwin

12th Bn. York And Lancaster Regiment

Second Lieutenant A J Beal, Second Lieutenant E M Carr, Captain W S Clark, Captain W A Colley Second Lieutenant F Dinsdale, Lieutenant C Elam, Second Lieutenant P K Perkin, 15th Bn. attd 12th Bn. Second Lieutenant C H Wardill

13th Bn. York And Lancaster Regiment

Captain H Dart, Captain E H Firth, Major T H Guest, Captain S Maleham, Lieutenant S O Sharp, Captain G De V Smith

14th Bn. York And Lancaster Regiment

Second Lieutenant R D B Anderson, Lieutenant D Fairley, Lieutenant H B Forsdike, Second Lieutenant W Hirst, Captain F N Houston, Captain G O Roos

15th Bn. York And Lancaster Regiment

Second Lieutenant C H Godwin, Captain R J Smith, Second Lieutenant A Spencer

2nd Bn. Yorkshire Regiment

Lieutenant C B Brooke, Second Lieutenant P D Denman, Second Lieutenant G E Layton-Bennett, Lieutenant Colonel B L Maddison, Second Lieutenant A C Strugnell

7th Bn. Yorkshire Regiment

Second Lieutenant J H F Clarke, Second Lieutenant H B Coates, Second Lieutenant L A D David, Second Lieutenant H G Hornsby, 11th Bn. attd. 7th Bn. Lieutenant H A M Hillman,

10th Bn. Yorkshire Regiment

Major S W Loudoun-Shand

Appendix 3
Known 1st July 1916 Burials

A.I.F. Burial Ground, Flers

Second Lieutenant **Clarke**, Arundel Geoffrey; Lieutenant **Elam**, Charles; Second Lieutenant **Hatch**, Nicholas Stephen; Second Lieutenant **Ingoldby**, Roger Hugh; Lieutenant **Symington,** Percy George;

Adanac Military Cemetery, Miraumont

Captain **Edmundson** Charles, Robert Ewbank; Second Lieutenant **Elliott,** Philip Maurice

Albert Communal Cemetery Extension

Major Edmond-Jenkins, William Hart

Ancre British Cemetery, Beaumont-Hamel

Major **Atkinson**, Thomas Joyce; Captain **Ayre**, Eric S.; Lieutenant **Bowen**, Francis Moull Storer; Second Lieutenant **Cooper**, Howard Frank Byrne; Captain **French**, Bertram St. George; Second Lieutenant **Graham Clarke**, John Altham Stobart; Captain **Griffiths**, John; Second Lieutenant **Horwood**, Ronald Bentall; Lieutenant Colonel **Pierce**, Robert Campbell; Second Lieutenant **Porter,** William; Second Lieutenant **Seggie,** Alexander; Captain, **Shaw,** A. J. McIntosh; Lieutenant **Townsend**, Richard Stapleton Barry;

Auchonvillers Military Cemetery

Captain **Beves,** Trevor Howard; Lieutenant **Drinkill**, Frederick Maurice; Second Lieutenant **Greenlees**, Charles Fouracres; Second Lieutenant **Hertslet**, Harold Cecil; Captain **Maunsell**, Edwin Richard Lloyd; Second Lieutenant **Pearson**, Angus John Williams; Lieutenant **Rose-Cleland**, Alfred Middleton Blackwood

Aveluy Communal Cemetery Extension

Second Lieutenant **Ashton**, Edward Deakin; Lieutenant **Goodall**, Albert James Gill

Bailleul Road East Cemetery, St. Laurent-Blangy

Second Lieutenant Ellison, Stanley John

Bapaume Post Military Cemetery, Albert

Captain **Baker,** Tom; Lieutenant **Fitzgerald**, Gerald; Second Lieutenant **Furse,** William Henry; Lieutenant **Inman,** Edwin; Lieutenant Colonel **Lyle,** William; Lieutenant **Mcgillicuddy**, John; Lieutenant Colonel **Sillery**, Charles Cecil Archibald; Captain **Todd**, John George

Beaumont-Hamel (Newfoundland) Memorial

Second Lieutenant **Ayre**, Gerald W.; Second Lieutenant **Ferguson,** J. Roy; Second Lieutenant **Jupp,** Clifford Henry Oliver; Second Lieutenant **Reid**, Robert Bruce; Second Lieutenant **Ryall**, William Thomas; Second Lieutenant **Taylor**, George Hayward

Beaumont-Hamel British Cemetery

Second Lieutenant **Anderson**, Arthur Furneaux Dalgaims; Second Lieutenant **Campbell**, S. Mcd.; Second Lieutenant **Prescott**, Robert Stuart; Lieutenant **Tanqueray**, Frederic Baron

Becourt Military Cemetery, Becordel-Becourt

Lieutenant Colonel **Addison**, Arthur Joseph Berkeley; Lieutenant **Gilson**, Robert Quilter; Second Lieutenant **Ingle,** Roland George; Second Lieutenant **Mclean**, Atholl Archibald

Bertrancourt Military Cemetery

Captain **Dart**, Hugh; Second Lieutenant **Hirst**, William; Second Lieutenant **Price,** Eric William Manning

Blighty Valley Cemetery, Authuille Wood

Captain **Cuthbert**, Olaf Ranson; Second Lieutenant **Davis**, Walter Arthur; Lieutenant **Dawson**, Sydney; Second Lieutenant **Ekin**, Leslie Montrose; Lieutenant **Geake**, Boyd Burnet; Lieutenant **Goodwin**, William Alexander Dunlap; Lieutenant **Hack**, Adrian Henry; Captain **Harris,** Hamilton Snow; Lieutenant **Hartley**, William Ismay Spooner; Second Lieutenant **Laird**, Arthur Donald; Lieutenant Colonel **Maddison**, Betram Lionel; Lieutenant **Morley**, Marmaduke Robert Hood; Lieutenant **Morris**, Gilbert Willan; Second Lieutenant **Nelson,** John (Jack); Captain **Smith**, Rex Johnston; Lieutenant **Smith,** S. Donard Irvine; Second Lieutenant **Spencer**, Arthur; Second Lieutenant **Stephenson,** Erik; Captain **Stewart**, Robert Colin; Second Lieutenant **Stroud**, Reginald Gordon; Second Lieutenant **Thomas**, Wilfrid Patrick Otto; Second Lieutenant **Tomlinson**, Charles Valentine

Bouzincourt Communal Cemetery Extension

Second Lieutenant **Bagnall**, Richard Gordon; Second Lieutenant **Brophy**, Ernest Gordon; Second Lieutenant **Chambers**, Edward Chandos Elliot; Second Lieutenant **Dussee**, Arthur Norman; Major **Hutchison,** Edward Second Lieutenant **Madders**, Hubert Franklin; Major **Stocks**, Harris Laurance

Bray Vale British Cemetery, Bray-Sur-Somme

Major Gaffikin, George Horner

Carnoy Military Cemetery

Captain **Ayre** Bernard Pitts; Second Lieutenant **Bayly,** Erskine Cochrane; Second Lieutenant **Collot,** Thomas Alexander; Second Lieutenant **Courage,** Godfrey Michell; Second Lieutenant **Craven,** Brian Thornthwaite; Second Lieutenant **Dines,** Percy John Francis; Second Lieutenant **Evans,** Tudor Eglwysbach; Captain **Flatau,** A Theodore; Captain **Hawkins,** Herbert Edwin; Second Lieutenant **Howe,** Charles Kingsley; Second Lieutenant **Hudlestone,** Harold Robert; Second Lieutenant **Kelly,** Percy Patrick; Captain **Litten,** Raymond; Captain **Nevill,** Wilfred Percy; Captain **Pearce,** Charles Stanley

Lieutenant **Musgrove,** George Henry Stuart; Lieutenant **Rawes,** Joscelyn Hugh Russell; Second Lieutenant **Rushton,** Frank Gregson; Lieutenant **Soames,** Robert Eley; Lieutenant **Traill,** Kenneth Robert; Second Lieutenant **Vigers,** Lancelot Leslie

Cerisy-Gailly French National Cemetery

Second Lieutenant **Fenwick,** Percival Fenwick; Second Lieutenant **Freeman,** Francis Basil; Second Lieutenant **Laughlin,** James Courtney; Lieutenant **Macdonald,** Simon

Citadel New Military Cemetery, Fricourt

Lieutenant **Fraser,** P. Neill; Second Lieutenant **Logan,** David Herbert Hoskem; Second Lieutenant **Robertson,** Walter Raymond

Connaught Cemetery, Thiepval

Second Lieutenant **Craig,** John Arnott Taylor; Second Lieutenant **Dagge,** Albert Lima; Lieutenant **Hart,** Andrew Chichester; Captain **Maclaren,** Ernest Cecil; Lieutenant **Peacock,** John Luddington; Lieutenant **Robinson,** Harold Fletcher; Captain **Slacke,** Charles Owen; Second Lieutenant Ward, George Cecil

Couin British Cemetery

Second Lieutenant **Pogose,** Ivor Reginald

Dantzig Alley British Cemetery, Mametz

Second Lieutenant **Baddeley,** John Frederick; Second Lieutenant **Barnes,** Francis Frank; Captain **Bland,** Alfred Edward; Captain **Brockbank,** Charles Norman; Captain **Brocklehurst,** Thomas Pownall; Second Lieutenant **Brooks,** Frank Smith; Second Lieutenant **Brown,** Andrew Cranstoun; Second Lieutenant **Brunt,** William Edward; Second Lieutenant **Clarke,** James Henry Fisher; Lieutenant **Cloudesley,** Hugh; Second Lieutenant **Coates,** Harold Brearley; Second Lieutenant **Cowin,** Henry Hampton; Second Lieutenant **Dandridge,** George Sidney; Second Lieutenant **David,** Lionel Adolf David; Second Lieutenant **Eaton,** James Willcox; Second Lieutenant **Emberton,** Percival Harvey; Second Lieutenant **Foord-Kelcey,** John; Captain **Ford,** Reginald James Captain **Glover,** Ben Hilton; Second Lieutenant **Golds,** Gordon Brewer; Lieutenant **Goss,** Edouard Herbert Allan; Lieutenant **Hall,** Warwick; Second Lieutenant **Herbert,** Ronald Crouch; Lieutenant **Hillman,** Harold Alexander Moore; Second Lieutenant **Hirst,** Cecil Pollock; Second Lieutenant **Hobbs,** Eric; Lieutenant **Hodgkinson,** Alan; Lieutenant, **Innocent,** E. J., Second Lieutenant **Kemp,** Thomas; Captain **Kenworthy,** Stanley; Lieutenant Colonel **Lewis,** Harold; Captain **Limbery,** Charles Roy; Lieutenant **Lomas,** Harold; Lieutenant **Lord,** Henry Otto; Captain **May,** Charles Campbell; Second Lieutenant **Merry,** Ralph Valentine; Second Lieutenant **Miller,** Francis John; Second Lieutenant **Nanson,** Joseph; Lieutenant **Nield,** Wilfred Herbert Everard; Lieutenant **Norbury,** Philip Giesler; Second Lieutenant **Parr-Dudley,** John Huskisson; Second Lieutenant **Peak,** Norman; Second Lieutenant **Ratcliffe,** William Henry; Lieutenant **Ross,** Frederic Gordon; Lieutenant **Saltmarshe,** Oliver Edwin; Second Lieutenant **Savage,** William Howard; Captain **Sayce,** George Ben; Captain **Scott,** George Henry Hall; Captain **Smith,** Douglas Wilberforce; Captain **Vaudrey,** Norman; Captain **Walpole,** John Robert; Second Lieutenant **Warr,** William Charles Samuel; Second Lieutenant **Webber,** Stanley Albert; Captain **White,** John Vernon; Captain **White,** George; Second Lieutenant **Wilson,** George Frederick

Dartmoor Cemetery, Becordel-Becourt

Lieutenant Colonel **Allardice,** Harry; Second Lieutenant **Colmer,** Arthur Cecil

Delville Wood Cemetery, Longueval

Captain Neame, Gerald Tassel

Devonshire Cemetery, Mametz

Second Lieutenant **Adamson,** Travers Farrant; Second Lieutenant **Davidson,** Robert Henry Walter; Lieutenant **Hodgson,** William Noel; Second Lieutenant **Holcroft,** Raymond Boycott; Captain **Martin,** Duncan Lenox; Second Lieutenant **Rayner,** Harold Leslie; Second Lieutenant **Rew,** John Frederick George; Second Lieutenant **Riddell,** William; Second Lieutenant **Shepard,** Cyril Harry; Captain **Tregelles,** Geoffrey Philip

Dive Copse British Cemetery, Sailly-Le-Sec

Second Lieutenant Cotton, John; Second Lieutenant Wharton, Sidney

Douchy-Les-Ayette British Cemetery

Captain Roos, Gustaf Oscar

Doullens Communal Cemetery Extension No.1

Second Lieutenant Liversidge, Albert

Ecoivres Military Cemetery, Mont-St. Eloi

Captain Fraser, Donald

Euston Road Cemetery, Colincamps

Second Lieutenant **Beacall**, Arthur; Second Lieutenant **Booth**, Percival Edward Owen; Second Lieutenant **Dean**, Rosser Fellowes Marriott; Second Lieutenant **Derwent**, Robert Ivor; Lieutenant **Fairley**, Duncan; Captain **Firth**, Ernest Hartley; Lieutenant **Foizey**, Harold Egbert; Second Lieutenant **Herapath**, Alfred Maltravers; Second Lieutenant **Kohn**, Wilfrid Arthur; Second Lieutenant **Minor**, Roland; Captain **Pringle**, Robert William Hay; Lieutenant **Ransome**, Cecil Talbot; Second Lieutenant **Roberton**, Charlie Drinnan; Lieutenant **Sharp,** Stephen Oswald; Captain **Smith,** George De Ville; Second Lieutenant **White**, Edward Beadon

Foncquevillers Military Cemetery

Second Lieutenant **Bates**, Alfred Neville; Second Lieutenant **Callard**, William Kingsley; Captain **Fletcher**, Gilbert Harding; Second Lieutenant **Flint**, Wilfred Ernest; Second Lieutenant **Gamble**, Frank Burfield; Second Lieutenant **Geliot**, William Henry; Captain **Green**, John Leslie; Lieutenant **Jellicoe**, Eric Maitland; Captain **Leman**, Thomas Henry; Captain **Round**, William Haldane; Captain **Walker**, William Eaton Guy; Second Lieutenant **Watkin**, Alfred Charles

Fricourt British Cemetery

Lieutenant **Allen**, Humphrey Decius; Captain **Anderson**, Archibald Joseph; Captain **Blackburn,** Geoffrey Gaskell; Second Lieutenant **Blatherwick**, Robert Hugh; Lieutenant Colonel **Dickson,** Arthur; Second Lieutenant **Hicking**, Francis Joseph; Second Lieutenant **Hornsby**, Harold Gibson; Lieutenant **Ibbitson**, William Beveridge; Lieutenant **Keighley**, William Munkley; Second Lieutenant **Kippax**, Arthur Haddon; Second Lieutenant **Perry**, Charles William; Lieutenant **Ratcliffe**, Alfred Victor; Captain **Rutledge**, John Bedell; Lieutenant **Shann**, John Webster; Second Lieutenant **Thornton**, Frank

Gommecourt British Cemetery No.2, Hebuterne

Second Lieutenant **Arthur**, George Stuart; Lieutenant **Brown Constable**, John Cecil; Lieutenant **Clode-Baker**, George Edmund; Second Lieutenant **Curror**, William Edwin Forrest; Second Lieutenant **Davey**, William Roy; Lieutenant **Davies**, Frank Arnold; Lieutenant **Davies**, Trevor Arthur Manning; Second Lieutenant **Fielding**, Francis Willoughby; Captain **Garland,** James Richard; Captain **Handyside**, Percy James Alexander; Captain **Hoare**, Richard Lennard; Second Lieutenant **Horne,** James Anthony; Second Lieutenant **Josephs**, Joseph

Gommecourt Wood New Cemetery, Foncquevillers

Lieutenant Colonel **Boote**, Charles Edmund; Second Lieutenant **Hunt**, John Reginald Lilly; Second Lieutenant **Mellard**, Richard Bartlett; Lieutenant **Newton**, William Trafford; Lieutenant **Shaw**, Robert Ramsay Stuart; Captain **Stack**, John Masfen

Gordon Cemetery, Mametz

Second Lieutenant **Fearnley**, William; Second Lieutenant **Giles**, Geoffrey; Second Lieutenant **Gordon**, Colin Graham; Second Lieutenant **King**, David Taylor; Second Lieutenant **Mcneill**, Nigel Lorne; Second Lieutenant **White**, John

Gordon Dump Cemetery, Ovillers-La Boisselle

Second Lieutenant **Alexander**, Noel Legard; Second Lieutenant **Andrew**, John; Second Lieutenant **Barnett,** PhillipLieutenant **Bamber,** John Walton; Lieutenant **Beatson**, Roger Stewart Montresor; Brevet Major **Bosanquet**, Graham Bromhead; Second Lieutenant **Branch**, Albert; Second Lieutenant **Byrne**, Louis Frederick; Second Lieutenant **Chambers**, Anthony Gerald; Second Lieutenant, **Charlesworth**, Thomas Stephens; Second Lieutenant **Churchfield**, Sidney Percival; Second Lieutenant **Cockcroft**, Arthur Clarence; Captain **Coles,** Lionel George; Second Lieutenant **Dore**, Alfred Clarence; Lieutenant **Eason**, Raymond Praed; Second Lieutenant **Elder,** Alexander; Lieutenant **Ellis**, Clifford Walker; Second Lieutenant **Fountain**, John Alfred Arnott; Second Lieutenant **Golding**, Frank Alfred; Captain **Hatt**, Arthur Beach; Lieutenant **Head**, Albert Everest; Captain **Head**, Leslie Dymoke; Captain **Heygate**, Claud Raymond; Second Lieutenant **Huddleston**, Maurice Louis; Lieutenant **Johnston**, Adrian Alexander Hope; Captain **Johnston**, Octavius Ralph Featherstone; Second Lieutenant **Lewis,** John Emrys; Second Lieutenant **Maconachie**, Arthur Delano; Captain **Mack**, Isaac Alexander; Lieutenant **Marshall**, John Woodall; Second Lieutenant **Maude**, Louis Edward Joseph; Second

Lieutenant **Money**, George Russell; Captain **Mullins**, Richard Walter; Second Lieutenant **Paxton**, Archibald Francis Campbell; Second Lieutenant **Peyton**, Ernest; Lieutenant **Ridpath**, Geoffrey Lionel Chevalier; Second Lieutenant **Sampson**, Arthur Henry Winn; Captain **Sapte**, Anthony; Second Lieutenant **Scott**, William Francis; Second Lieutenant **Swift**, William; Lieutenant **Telfer**, Henry Adam; Captain **Twentyman**, Denzil Clive Tate; Second Lieutenant **Vassie**, Charles Edward; Captain **Warden**, Walter George; Second Lieutenant **Watson**, Stanley Meredith; Second Lieutenant **Whitby**, Ernest Victor; Second Lieutenant **Wood**, Wilfred John; Second Lieutenant **Young**, James Vincent

Hamel Military Cemetery, Beaumont-Hamel

Lieutenant Haughton, Thomas Greenwood

Hawthorn Ridge Cemetery No.1, Auchonvillers

Lieutenant **Heath**, Henry James; Second Lieutenant **Heaton**, Eric Rupert; Captain **Heslop**, George Henry; Lieutenant **Goodwin**, Harold Desborough; Second Lieutenant **Warner**, Douglas Redston

Hawthorn Ridge Cemetery No.2, Auchonvillers

Second Lieutenant **Baxendine**, John Young; Second Lieutenant **Fraser**, Arthur William; Lieutenant **Haycraft**, Alan Montague; Captain **Mclaren**, Robert John; Second Lieutenant **Robinson**, John; Second Lieutenant **Roope**, Charles Francis; Second Lieutenant **Ross**, R. Wallace; Second Lieutenant **Westaway**, Leslie Thomas

Heath Cemetery, Harbonnieres

Second Lieutenant **Miller**, Stanley, Lieutenant **Scott**, Dudley Holme

Hebuterne Military Cemetery

Second Lieutenant **Fradd**, Kingsley Meredith C.; Second Lieutenant **Lidiard**, Richard John Abraham; Second Lieutenant **Mager**, William George; Second Lieutenant **Pilgrim**, Henry Bastick; Second Lieutenant **Warner**, Archibald

Knightsbridge Cemetery, Mesnil-Martinsart

Second Lieutenant **Ayre**, Wilfrid D.; Second Lieutenant **Cheshire**, William Robert; Second Lieutenant **Glennie**, John Herbert; Second Lieutenant **Gow**, James Lightfoot; Lieutenant **Mellor**, Frederick Courtney; Second Lieutenant **Reid**, Robert; Second Lieutenant **Scott**, Ian Archibald Sawers

London Cemetery And Extension, Longueval

Major **Jones**, Lewis Farewell

Lonsdale Cemetery, Authuille

Lieutenant **Arnaud**, Frederick Cooper; Second Lieutenant **Baker**, James Henry; Captain **Brown**, Colin Selwyn; Second Lieutenant **Brown**, Robert Stanley; Captain **Cassels**, Robert Wilson; Second Lieutenant **Doncaster**, Robert Ivan; Second Lieutenant **Dunstan**, Guy Peirce; Second Lieutenant **Ekin**, James; Captain **Heald**, Geoffrey Yates; Lieutenant **Gallie**, Edward Archibald; Second Lieutenant **Gemmill**, John Adshead; Second Lieutenant **Hampton**, William Orr; Second Lieutenant **Klean**, Michael Graham; Second Lieutenant **Murdoch**, John; Second Lieutenant **Noyes**, Claude Robert Burton; Second Lieutenant **Parker**, John Caird; Second Lieutenant **Paton**, Walter Storey; Second Lieutenant **Sharp**, Leon Owen; Second Lieutenant **White**, Aubrey Cecil; Second Lieutenant **Younger**, David George

Louvencourt Military Cemetery

Brigadier General **Prowse**, Charles Bertie

Martinsart British Cemetery

Colonel **Bernard**, Herbert Clifford; Second Lieutenant **Longhurst**, Seaward

Mesnil Communal Cemetery Extension

Captain **Johnston**, Charles Moore

Mill Road Cemetery, Thiepval

Captain **Ballintine**, Joseph; Captain **Proctor**, James Claude Beauchamp; Lieutenant **Healy**, John Frederick; Lieutenant **Hewitt**, Holt Montgomery; Lieutenant **Rogers**, George Murray; Major **Sewell**, William Tait; Major **Uprichard**, Henry Albert; Second Lieutenant **Wedgwood**, Philip Egerton

Miraumont Communal Cemetery

Lieutenant **Martin**, George Russell Courtney

Munich Trench British Cemetery, Beaumont-Hamel

Captain **Thomas**, Heinrich William Max

Neuve-Chapelle Memorial

Lieutenant Colonel **Wilson**, Denis Daly

Norfolk Cemetery, Becordel-Becourt

Second Lieutenant **Asher**, Kenneth John Penrith; Captain **Haswell**, Gordon; Second Lieutenant **Howlett,** Charles Wilfred; Major **Loudoun-Shand**, Stewart Walter; Lieutenant Colonel **Lynch**, Colmer William Donald Lieutenant **Martin**, Eldred Joseph; Captain **Walker**, William

Ovillers Military Cemetery

Lieutenant **Burluraux**, John Rene Cornelius; Lieutenant **Clifford** Hugh, Gilbert Francis; Captain **Cubey,** Joseph Berkeley; Second Lieutenant **Davis**, Charles Stewart; Second Lieutenant **Freeman**, Francis Hubert; Second Lieutenant **Grundy**, Ronald Edwin; Second Lieutenant **Harrison**, Geoffrey; Lieutenant Colonel **Heneker,** Frederick Christian; Second Lieutenant **Hickman**, William Christie; Lieutenant Colonel **Howard**, Louis Meredith; Lieutenant **Hoyle**, John Baldwin; Second Lieutenant **Jarman**, Andrew Hatch; Captain **Lewis**, Reginald Cameron; Second Lieutenant **Ley**, Maurice Carew; Captain **Meeke**, William Stanley; Lieutenant **Morse**, Ernest Frederick; Captain **Mullally**, Brian Desmond; Lieutenant **Robinson**, Benjamin Stanley; Lieutenant **Ross**, Douglas Stuart; Second Lieutenant **Sutcliffe**, Herbert Richard Charles; Captain **Thompson**, Arthur; Second Lieutenant **Venus**, Frederick Arthur; Captain **Vernon**, Frederick Lewis

Pargny British Cemetery

Second Lieutenant **Balkwill**, John; Second Lieutenant **Gourlay**, John Norman

Peronne Road Cemetery, Maricourt

Lieutenant **Brooke**, Charles Berjew; Second Lieutenant **Crees**, William; Second Lieutenant **Denman**, Percy Darrell; Second Lieutenant **Gill**, Charles Treverbyn; Second Lieutenant **Gillies**, James; Major **Graham**, John Frederick; Second Lieutenant **Layton-Bennett**, Geoffrey Ernest; Second Lieutenant **Rowatt**, David; Second Lieutenant **Walker**, Turner Russell

Point 110 New Military Cemetery, Fricourt

Second Lieutenant **Gibson**, Charles Sydney

Queens Cemetery, Puisieux

Second Lieutenant **Beal**, Arnold James; Lieutenant **Bickersteth**, Stanley Morris; Second Lieutenant **Dinsdale**, Frank; Lieutenant **Hitchon**, James Foldys; Captain **Maleham**, Stewart; Captain **Tough**, Arnold Banatyne; Lieutenant **Welch**, James Stanley Lightfoot

Redan Ridge Cemetery No.1, Beaumont-Hamel

Second Lieutenant **Holmes**, Aubrey; Captain **Leacroft**, Ronald John Ranulph; Second Lieutenant **Whitgreave**, Henry Egerton

Redan Ridge Cemetery No.2, Beaumont-Hamel

Second Lieutenant **Alexander**, Henry Talbot; Second Lieutenant **Anderson**, Reginald Dudley Bawdwen; Second Lieutenant **Anderton**, Frank Westall; Second Lieutenant **Grant**, Henry Norman; Captain **Matthey**, Edward Granville

Sailly-Au-Bois Military Cemetery

Captain **Whitaker**, George Clifford

Serre Road Cemetery No.1

Lieutenant **Adams**, Ralph; Second Lieutenant **Booth**, Major William; Major **Bromilow**, John Nesbit; Second Lieutenant **Farrow**, Brian; Second Lieutenant **Kenion**, Hugh Cyril; Second Lieutenant **Stead,** Ralph; Lieutenant **Tolson**, Robert Huntriss; Second Lieutenant **Walton**, Francis John George

Serre Road Cemetery No.2

Captain **Andrews**, James Allfrey; Captain **Baird**, Charles Edward; Second Lieutenant **Beddow**, Cecil Victor; Second Lieutenant **Belcher,** Basil Henry; Captain **Bonham-Carter**, Arthur Thomas; Second Lieutenant **Bowes,** Cyril Hulme; Lieutenant **Buckworth**, Charles Raymond; Captain **Cartland**, George Trevor; Captain **Clark**, William Spencley; Second Lieutenant **Crum**, Stewart Alexander; Captain **Davidson**, James Samuel; Lieutenant **Dewhurst**, George C. L; Captain **Dixon**, James Evelyn Bevan; Second Lieutenant **Dodd**, Neville; Second Lieutenant **Field**, Henry Lionel; Captain **Gamon**, Maurice Partridge; Second Lieutenant **Hellard**, John Alexander; Second Lieutenant **Ilbery**, Oscar Reginald; Lieutenant **Kernaghan**, Graham Hemery; Second Lieutenant **Leche**, Arthur Victor Carlton; Captain **Ludlow**, Stratford Walter; Lieutenant **Macbrayne**, John Burns Lieutenant **Mccluggage**, William; Lieutenant **Middleditch**, Archibald Milne; Captain **Neville**, George Henry; Second Lieutenant **Newlands**, Sydney Barron; Lieutenant **Smith-Maxwell**, Archie Findlay; Second Lieutenant **Tart,** Cyril James; Second Lieutenant **Waterhouse**, Gilbert; Second Lieutenant **Williams**, Leslie

Serre Road Cemetery No.3, Puisieux

Lieutenant **Maitland**, Arthur Dudley

Sucrerie Military Cemetery, Colincamps

Lieutenant **Adams,** Hugh Irving; Captain **Alison,** George Newdegate; Second Lieutenant **Blackwood,** Miles Harry; Second Lieutenant **Broom,** Frederick Jordan; Second Lieutenant **Buchanan,** David; Second Lieutenant **Clegg,** Percy; Second Lieutenant **Fair,** George Patrick Conroy; Captain **Ford,** Charles Clement; Lieutenant **Goodford,** Charles James Henry; Captain **Hart,** Cecil Lyon; Second Lieutenant **Ide,** Thomas Norman; Lieutenant **Maciver,** Reginald Squarey; Lieutenant Colonel **Palk,** The Hon. Lawrence Charles W.; Second Lieutenant **Melly,** Hugh Peter Egerton Mesnard; Second Lieutenant **Morgan,** John Walter Rees; Second Lieutenant **Morum,** James Pearse; Captain **Sayres,** Hugh Wingfield; Captain **Smith-Masters,** Bruce Swinton Captain **Sweetnam,** Richard Rodney Stephen; Lieutenant Colonel **Thicknesse,** John Audley; Second Lieutenant **Thompson,** Fendall Powney; Second Lieutenant **Westmore,** Lawrence Arthur; Second Lieutenant **Williamson,** John; Captain **Young,** John Ferrers Harrington

Tincourt New British Cemetery

Lieutenant **Hone,** Nathaniel Frederick

Villers-Bretonneux Military Cemetery

Second Lieutenant **Mccrostie,** Charles Hutchison

Warlincourt Halte British Cemetery, Saulty

Lieutenant **Jones,** David William Llewelyn; Second Lieutenant **Stubbs,** Cecil Arthur

Warloy-Baillon Communal Cemetery Extension

Captain **Murray,** Charles Stephenson; Lieutenant **Rodger,** Douglas

Warloy-Baillon Communal Cemetery

Lieutenant Colonel **Machell,** Percy Wilfrid

Y Ravine Cemetery, Beaumont-Hamel

Lieutenant **Herder,** Hubert Clinton; Captain **Hughes,** Alexander Arbuthnott; Second Lieutenant **Karran,** John Bowler; Second Lieutenant **Rice,** Fred; Lieutenant **Shortall,** Richard A.; Second Lieutenant **Stonor,** Cuthbert Anthony; Lieutenant **Wilson,** Arthur Desmond Lloyd

Ypres Reservoir Cemetery

Major **Knott,** James Leadbitter

Appendix 4

Thiepval Memorial

Captain **Adam**, Arthur De Bels; Second Lieutenant **Adamson**, Maurice Leslie; Second Lieutenant **Aird**, James Gilbert; Lieutenant **Akam**, James Rhodes; Second Lieutenant **Alexander**, William Mercer; Second Lieutenant **Allen**, Geoffrey Austin; Second Lieutenant **Allen,** Herbert; Second Lieutenant **Allen**, Sydney Raymond; Second Lieutenant **Angus,** Stewart; Second Lieutenant **Anstee,** Joseph; Second Lieutenant **Applin,** Geoffrey Walter Henry; Second Lieutenant **Arkle**, Norman Armitage; Second Lieutenant **Ashley**, Claude; Second Lieutenant **Asser**, Harold Edward; Second Lieutenant **Atkinson**, Arthur Wilfrid; Second Lieutenant **Attenborough**, John Haddon; Second Lieutenant **Audaer**, Ernest Clifford; Second Lieutenant **Avery**, William Ernest; Second Lieutenant **Balkwill**, Charles Vince; Second Lieutenant **Barber,** William Geoffrey Wright; Lieutenant **Barker**, Harold William; Lieutenant **Barratt**, Kenneth Franklin; Lieutenant **Bass,** Philip Burnet; Second Lieutenant **Beavon**, John Leonard; Second Lieutenant **Bedford**, Seaton Hall; Captain **Beever**, William Henry; Captain **Beggs**, Henry Parker; Second Lieutenant **Bell**, Norman Henderson; Captain **Bell**, Eric Norman Frankland; Second Lieutenant **Bemrose**, Karl; Second Lieutenant **Benns**, Arthur Lionel; Second Lieutenant **Bent**, Percy Temple; Second Lieutenant **Bible**, Geoffrey Roskell; Second Lieutenant **Binns,** Clement Stanley; Second Lieutenant **Blackwell**, Cyril; Captain **Blake**, Francis Seymour; Second Lieutenant **Boas**, Ernest George; Second Lieutenant **Bobby**, Sidney Fitzgerald; Lieutenant **Bolton**, William Curtis; Captain **Bolton,** Henry Albert; Second Lieutenant **Boncker,** Barry Robert; Lieutenant **Booth**, Harold Stanley; Second Lieutenant **Boswell**, Percy George; Second Lieutenant **Bovill**, Edward Henry; Second Lieutenant **Bowyer,** George Henry; Captain **Boyd**, George Vallance Mckinlay; Second Lieutenant **Bradford**, Frederick Reith Campbell; Lieutenant **Bradshaw**, Richard Edward Kynaston; Lieutenant **Braithwaite**, Valentine Ashworth; Second Lieutenant **Bramble**, Gerald Henry Joseph; Second Lieutenant **Brand**, Geoffrey Jermyn; Lieutenant **Breene**, Thomas Frederick; Second Lieutenant **Brough**, James Lindsay; Second Lieutenant **Brown**, Ralph Adair; Captain **Browne**, Dominick Augustus; Major **Bruce**, John Russel; Second Lieutenant **Brunton**, Hereward; Second Lieutenant **Bryan**, Sydney Arthur; Major **Burge**, Montague; Second Lieutenant **Burton,** Cyril Henry; Captain **Butler,** Charles Kingstone; Second Lieutenant **Buxton**, Bertie Reginald; Second Lieutenant **Buxton**, Jocelyn Murray Victor; Major **Caddick**, Alfred Armstrong; Second Lieutenant **Calder-Smith**, Raymond Alexander; Second Lieutenant **Callaghan**, Joseph Patrick Aloysious; Second Lieutenant **Callow**, Donald; Lieutenant **Cambie**, Edward Maurice Baldwin; Lieutenant **Campbell**, Lawford Burne; Second Lieutenant **Campbell**, Robert Alexander Rankine; Second Lieutenant **Campbell,** William Mackenzie; Second Lieutenant **Cane**, Reginald Shapland; Second Lieutenant **Carey**, Leonard Arthur; Second Lieutenant **Carpenter**, John Neilson; Second Lieutenant **Carr**, Eric Marcus; Second Lieutenant **Carson**, William John White; Second Lieutenant **Carver,** George Sholto Douglas; Second Lieutenant **Cary**, Richard Harry; Lieutenant **Catmur**, Harry Albert Frederick; Second Lieutenant **Cecil**, Rotheram Bagshawe; Second Lieutenant **Chalmers**, John Robert Thorburn; Second Lieutenant **Chapman**, Arthur Donald; Second Lieutenant **Charles,** Albert; Captain **Charlton**, John Macfarlan; Captain **Chiplin**, William Henry; Lieutenant **Cholmeley**, Eric Randolph; Lieutenant **Cholmeley**, Harry Lewin; Second Lieutenant **Clark**, Eric Henry Lloyd; Second Lieutenant **Clark**, Charles Augustus; Second Lieutenant **Clegg**, Alexander; Second Lieutenant **Clesham**, Thomas Henry; Captain **Clough**, Alan; Second Lieutenant **Coe,** George; Second Lieutenant **Coldwells**, Francis Baker; Second Lieutenant **Coleman**, Arthur; Captain **Colley**, William Arthur; Second Lieutenant **Colley**, Harold; Second Lieutenant **Conner,** Frederic Attenborrow; Second Lieutenant **Coote**, Arthur Eyre; Lieutenant **Cope**, George Eric; Captain **Corbett**, Alfred Edward; Second Lieutenant **Cormack**, Reginald Ormiston; Lieutenant **Costello**, Edward William; Second Lieutenant **Courtice**, Reginald Leyster; Captain **Cox**, Harold Edward Leys; Second Lieutenant **Coxon**, Herbert Archibald; Second Lieutenant **Cragg**, John Francis; Second Lieutenant **Crombie**, William Lauder; Second Lieutenant **Crossley**, Cyril; Lieutenant **Crozier**, William Magee; Captain **Cruickshank**, Philip; Second Lieutenant **Cummins**, Leslie; Lieutenant **Cundall**, Hubert Walter; Captain **Cunningham**, Robert William; Second Lieutenant **Cunningham**, James; Second Lieutenant **Dalby**, Herbert Charles; Second Lieutenant **Dalrymple**, Hew; Second Lieutenant **Darley**, Desmond John; Lieutenant **Davidson**, Roland Cooper;

Second Lieutenant **Davies**, Harry Noel; Captain **Davies**, Cyril Thomas Morris; Lieutenant **Dawson**, Gerald Moore; Lieutenant **Day**, Leslie Terrett; Second Lieutenant **Dean**, William; Second Lieutenant **Dickie**, William; Second Lieutenant **Dickinson**, Thomas Arthur; Lieutenant **Dodington**, Thomas Marriott; Second Lieutenant **Don**, David Fairweather; Second Lieutenant **Donaldson**, John James; Second Lieutenant **Dornton**, Harold Shafto; Lieutenant **Dougal**, Robert Joseph; Second Lieutenant **Dougal**, John Braes; Second Lieutenant **Doust**, Charles Bowden; Lieutenant **Drury**, Harold Strickland; Second Lieutenant **Dunn**, Ralph Ellis; Second Lieutenant **Eames**, Arthur Horwood; Captain **East**, John; Second Lieutenant **Edingborough**, Noel Duncan; Captain **Eglington**, Ferdinand; Second Lieutenant **Elliott**, Thomas Brignall; Lieutenant Colonel **Elphinstone**, Arthur Percy Archibald; Captain **Ely**, Denis Herbert James; Second Lieutenant **Engall**, John Sherwin; Captain **Evans**, Charles William; Lieutenant **Evans**, Humphrey Pennefather; Second Lieutenant **Evered**, Henry Robert Hastings; Second Lieutenant **Everitt**, John Paxman; Lieutenant **Evershed**, Albury; Captain **Ewart**, Cecil Frederick Kelso; Lieutenant **Falconer**, Robert Whitfield; Captain **Falkous**, Robert; Second Lieutenant **Fanghanel**, Frederick Charles; Second Lieutenant **Farley**, Frederick Albert; Second Lieutenant **Fawcett**, Frank Aldridge, Second Lieutenant **Featherstone**, George Herbert; Lieutenant **Fisher**, Thomas Edward Coney; Second Lieutenant **Fitzbrown**, Eric; Second Lieutenant **Flaxman**, Alfred Edward; Second Lieutenant **Fletcher**, John Harwood Cash; Second Lieutenant **Flint**, Charles William; Captain **Foley**, John; Second Lieutenant **Ford**, Lawton Stephen; Second Lieutenant **Forge**, William Frederick; Lieutenant **Forsdike**, Harold Brooke; Captain **Forster**, John Percival; Second Lieutenant **Fox**, Francis Parker; Captain **Fraser**, Rowland; Lieutenant **Fraser**, Thomas; Second Lieutenant **Fraser**, Malcolm Goulding; Second Lieutenant **Frost**, Alfred Ingo; Second Lieutenant **Fryer**, James Whaley; Lieutenant **Fussell**, James Gerald; Second Lieutenant **Gage**, John Stewart Moore; Lieutenant **Garton**, Reginald William; Lieutenant **Gatrell**, Reginald James Hurst; Second Lieutenant **Gibson**, Albert Henry; Second Lieutenant **Gibson**, William; Second Lieutenant **Glastonbury**, Harold Mynett; Second Lieutenant **Godfrey**, Hugh; Second Lieutenant **Godfrey**, Harry Frederick; Second Lieutenant **Godfrey**, Victor; Second Lieutenant **Godwin**, Colin Harold; Lieutenant **Gomersall**, William Ellis; Second Lieutenant **Goodchild**, Stanley Cecil; Second Lieutenant **Gosnell**, Harold Clifford; Captain **Gotch**, Roby Myddleton; Second Lieutenant **Gould**, Eric Melville; Captain **Graham**, Percy Gordon; Second Lieutenant **Grainger**, John Scott; Second Lieutenant **Grant**, John; Second Lieutenant **Green**, William Osmond; Second Lieutenant **Gregg**, William Henry; Second Lieutenant **Grierson**, John Livingston Hailes; Captain **Griffin**, George Edward; Major **Guest**, Thomas Heald; Second Lieutenant **Gunning**, Frank Douglas; Lieutenant Colonel **Guyon**, George Sutherland; Second Lieutenant **Hablutzel**, George Rudolph; Captain **Hadwen**, Noel Waugh; Second Lieutenant **Hall**, John Mcrobb; Second Lieutenant **Hamilton**, John; Second Lieutenant **Hamilton**, Robert Victor; Lieutenant **Hampson**, Edgar; Lieutenant **Harbord**, George Alfred Lionel; Second Lieutenant **Hardman**, Robert Taylor; Captain **Harkness**, Percy Yarborough; Captain **Harley**, Arthur Darent; Second Lieutenant **Harley**, Benjamin Chapman; Captain **Harvey**, Bernard Sydney; Second Lieutenant **Harvey**, James; Second Lieutenant **Haynes**, Clifford Skemp; Second Lieutenant **Heath**, William Hutsby; Second Lieutenant **Heming**, Maurice Ivory; Captain **Henderson**, Andrew William; Second Lieutenant **Herdman**, George Andrew; Second Lieutenant **Hewitt**, William Arthur; Second Lieutenant **Hibbert**, Howard Morley; Lieutenant **Hicking**, George Graham; Second Lieutenant **Higgins**, Cuthbert George; Captain **Hill**, Barry; Captain **Hilton**, Clarence Stuart; Lieutenant Colonel **Hind**, Lawrence Arthur; Second Lieutenant **Hind**, Ernest William Gayles; Lieutenant **Hole**, William Arthur; Lieutenant **Hollywood**, Arthur Carson; Second Lieutenant **Hollywood**, James; Captain **Horne**, David Douglas; Second Lieutenant **Horrox**, Henry M.; Second Lieutenant **Horsnell**, Alick George; Lieutenant **Hoskins**, Cyril; Captain **Houghton**, Philip Squarey; Captain **Houston**, Fredrick Neville; Second Lieutenant **Hudson**, Arthur Henry William; Second Lieutenant **Humphries**, Thomas; Captain **Huntriss**, Cyril John; Captain **Huskinson**, Frederick John; Second Lieutenant **Hyde**, Charles Stuart; Second Lieutenant **Hyde**, James Charles; Second Lieutenant **Hynam**, Walter William; Lieutenant Colonel **Innes**, Edgar Arthur; Lieutenant **Jackson**, Henry Stewart; Second Lieutenant **Jackson**, Ernest; Second Lieutenant **Jackson**, Lancelot; Second Lieutenant **Jago**, Edward Arthur; Second Lieutenant **James**, Clement Wilbraham; Second Lieutenant **Jeal**, Walter; Second Lieutenant **Jeffcock**, Richard Salisbury; Captain **Jessup**, Francis Reginald; Captain **Jeudwine**, Spencer Henry; Lieutenant **Johnson**, Thomas; Second Lieutenant **Johnson**, William Roland; Second Lieutenant **Johnston**, James Annandale; Captain **Johnston**, Elliott; Captain **Jones**, Alfred Cotton; Second Lieutenant **Jones**, Horace Birchall; Second Lieutenant **Jones**, John Myddelton; Second Lieutenant **Jones**, Kenneth Champion; Second Lieutenant

Kemp, Albert; Lieutenant Colonel **Kennard**, Maurice Nicholl; Captain **Kerr**, David Bryce; Second Lieutenant **Kerr**, Donald; Second Lieutenant **Kerr**, James; Second Lieutenant **Kershaw**, Ellis; Second Lieutenant **Key,** Frederick Bertram; Second Lieutenant **Kingsford**, Reginald John; Second Lieutenant **Kirkland,** Frederick William; Second Lieutenant **Knight**, Philip Clifford; Lieutenant **Knowles**, Gavin Tenison Royle; Captain **Laing,** Dudley Ogilvie; Lieutenant **Lamb**, Walter; Second Lieutenant **Lancaster**, Thomas Erwin; Lieutenant **Lane**, Edward, Alfred Joseph Ardan; Second Lieutenant **Leathley**, William George; Captain **Lee-Wood**, Alfred; Lieutenant **Lemon**, Archie Dunlap; Captain **Lewes**, Frederick Henry Meredith; Major **Lewis**, Harry Arthur; Second Lieutenant, **Lewis**, Llewelyn; Major **Lindsay**, Francis Howard; Lieutenant **Lintott**, Evelyn Henry; Captain **Livesey**, Harry; Second Lieutenant **Lodge**, Ralph Nesbit; Lieutenant **Low**, James Morrison; Lieutenant **Macbryan**, Edward Crozier; Second Lieutenant **Macdonald**, Roderick; Second Lieutenant **Machardy**, David Scott; Lieutenant **Macintyre,** Thomas; Captain **Mackenzie**, Kenneth; Second Lieutenant **Mackenzie**, Francis Ramsay; Second Lieutenant **Mackenzie**, Noel Olliffe Compton; Captain **Maclean**, Henry Chevers; Second Lieutenant **Macnaghten**, Sir Edward Harry; Lieutenant **Macpherson**, John; Second Lieutenant **Macwalter**, Charles Christopher; Lieutenant **Macwatt**, Norman Ian; Second Lieutenant **Mallett**, Eric Sydney; Second Lieutenant **Marson**, William Henry; Lieutenant **Martin**, Sidney Todd; Second Lieutenant **Mason**, Overton Trollope; Lieutenant **Masterman**, Robert Chauncy; Second Lieutenant **Masterman**, Frederick Michel; Second Lieutenant **Mcclellan**, Allan John; Lieutenant **Mcclure**, Ernest; Second Lieutenant **Mccurrach**, George; Second Lieutenant **Mcgain**, Ashley Waterson; Second Lieutenant **Mcgowan**, John Spence; Second Lieutenant **Mcinnes**, John Edward; Lieutenant **Mcintosh**, William Matthew; Second Lieutenant **Meeking**, Norman Arthur; Lieutenant **Mellor**, Roy; Captain **Middleton**, Thomas; Captain **Millar**, Stanley Gemmell; Captain **Millin**, Edward Job; Captain **Mockler**, Francis George Ross; Lieutenant **Mockridge** George,Ewart; Second Lieutenant **Monkhouse**, Alfred Ernest; Second Lieutenant **Montgomery**, Robert Taylor; Second Lieutenant **Moody,** Thomas; Captain **Moore**, Arthur Robert; Second Lieutenant **Moore**, Thomas George; Captain **Mott**, Hugh Fenwick; Captain **Mulkern**, Hubert Cowell; Lieutenant **Murphy**, Johnston; Second Lieutenant John Claude Murray; Captain **Murray**, Patrick Austin; Captain **Needham**, Benjamin Llewellyn; Second Lieutenant **Negus** Arthur George; Captain **Neil**, Stanley Thomas Arthur; Lieutenant **Neill**, James Dermot; Lieutenant **Neill**, Reginald Henry; Lieutenant **Newcombe**, Richard; Lieutenant **Nicholls**, John Watson; Lieutenant **Nicholson**, Thomas Edward; Major **Niven**, Allan Graham; Captain **Nixon**, William; Lieutenant **Nixon**, William Gerald; Major **Noble**, Thomas Gibson; Lieutenant **Oakley**, Reginald William Kennedy; Captain **O'Flaherty**, Douglas Hill; Second Lieutenant **O'Land**, Valentine; Second Lieutenant **Oldershaw**, John Joseph Fritz; Lieutenant **O'Neill**, Samuel; Second Lieutenant **Orford**, William Kirkpatrick; Lieutenant **Organ**, Harold Percy; Lieutenant **Ormrod**, Harry; Second Lieutenant **Orr**, James Kenneth; Second Lieutenant **Outram**, Edmund; Second Lieutenant **Page**, Reginald; Lieutenant **Parker**, James; Second Lieutenant **Parkinson**, James Herring; Lieutenant **Paterson**, Alan Foster; Second Lieutenant **Paterson**, Frank; Lieutenant **Patterson,** John Hylton; Lieutenant **Payne**, Orsmond Guy; Second Lieutenant **Peach**, Ernest James; Second Lieutenant **Pearse**, Frank Arthur; Captain **Pelly**, William Francis Henry; Captain **Penny**, Arthur Hugh; Lieutenant **Peregrine**, John Pryor Puxon; Second Lieutenant **Perkin**, Philip Kenneth; Second Lieutenant **Perkins**, George; Second Lieutenant **Pidduck**, Norman Andrews; Second Lieutenant **Pinkerton**, Eric Mikhell; Lieutenant **Pollock**, John; Second Lieutenant **Potter**, Francis John; Captain **Preedy**, Alban; Second Lieutenant **Price**, John Esmond; Second Lieutenant **Price**, Reginald; Second Lieutenant **Priestley**, Dyker Stanton; Lieutenant **Pring**, Basil Crompton; Lieutenant **Procter**, Arthur; Captain **Purnell**, Arthur Channing; Captain **Rabone**, Arthur Brian; Second Lieutenant **Radcliffe**, George Kan; Lieutenant **Raimes**, Leslie Robinson; Second Lieutenant **Ram**, Percival John; Lieutenant **Reid,** Robert; Second Lieutenant **Rettie**, William Philip; Second Lieutenant **Richardson**, William Turner; Captain **Riley**, Henry Davison; Captain **Robertson**, George; Captain **Robertson**, Maxwell Alexander; Lieutenant **Robinson**, Eli; Second Lieutenant **Robinson**, John Holdsworth; Second Lieutenant **Robinson**, Percival Bewman Palmer; Second Lieutenant **Rose**, Reginald Vincent; Captain **Ross**, Peter; Lieutenant **Ross**, George Munro; Second Lieutenant **Rothon**, Charles Francis; Captain **Rowley**, Hugh Travers; Second Lieutenant **Rowley**, Joseph; Lieutenant **Rupp**, Frederick Albert; Lieutenant **Russell**, Edward; Second Lieutenant **Russell**, George Smith; Captain **Ruttledge**, John Forrest; Second Lieutenant **Sach**, Charles Burleigh; Second Lieutenant **Sadler**, Charles Edward; Second Lieutenant **Saffery**, Leslie Hall; Second Lieutenant **Sanby**, William Worthington; Lieutenant **Sanderson**, Geoffrey Evian; Second Lieutenant **Sanderson**, Walter Ker; Second Lieutenant **Sanger**,

Thomas Rudolph; Captain **Sanger-Davies**, Llewelyn Herbert; Second Lieutenant **Saunders**, Charles; Second Lieutenant **Schneider**, Stewart Spearing; Lieutenant **Scott**, Gordon; Second Lieutenant **Scott-Holmes**, Henry Favil; Lieutenant **Shapley**, Alfred Edwin; Second Lieutenant **Sharp**, Lewis Frederick; Lieutenant **Shaw**, Clarence Gordon; Second Lieutenant **Shaw**, William; Second Lieutenant **Shirreff**, Francis Gordon; Second Lieutenant **Shorter**, Alfred George; Second Lieutenant **Shuttleworth**, Ernest Ronald; Major **Sibbit**, Henry; Second Lieutenant **Sillars**, Harry Frederick Lionel; Second Lieutenant **Simmonds**, Percy Grabham; Lieutenant **Simpson**, Thomas; Captain **Smith**, Donald Charnock; Captain **Smith**, Raymond; Second Lieutenant **Smith**, Robert; Second Lieutenant **Smith**, Leonard George; Second Lieutenant **Smith**, Norman McNeill; Second Lieutenant **Smith**, Percy Claud Jacomb; Second Lieutenant **Smith**, Quintin Livingstone; Captain **Smyth**, William Haughton; Captain **Somers-Smith**, John Robert; Second Lieutenant **Souper**, Noel Beaumont; Second Lieutenant **Spalding**, Albert Goodwill; Second Lieutenant **Spatz**, Walter; Lieutenant **Sproat**, Gerald Maitland; Second Lieutenant **Stainton**, Robert Meres; Second Lieutenant **Stephensen**, Olaf Stephen; Lieutenant **Stevenson**, Leonard William Hugh; Second Lieutenant **Stewart**, William Johnston; Second Lieutenant **Stewart**, Robert; Second Lieutenant **Stimpson**, John Crockett; Lieutenant **Stonehouse**, Charles; Second Lieutenant **Strange**, William Frederick; Second Lieutenant **Strugnell**, Alfred Charles; Second Lieutenant **Sutton**, Cyril John; Captain **Swainson**, Francis Gibbon; Second Lieutenant **Swan**, George Grieve; Lieutenant **Sykes**, Charles; Second Lieutenant **Symonds**, Frank James; Second Lieutenant **Taplin**, Albert William; Captain **Tate**, Charles Bernard; Second Lieutenant **Thomas**, Sidney; Second Lieutenant **Thompson**, Herbert William; Lieutenant **Thomson**, Frederick Stanley; Second Lieutenant **Thorman**, Alan Marshall; Lieutenant **Thorne**, John Parry; Second Lieutenant **Tompkins**, Harold Arthur; Lieutenant **Toolis**, James Hollingworth; Second Lieutenant **Topp**, Richard William; Lieutenant **Towers-Clark**, John William; Second Lieutenant **Treasure**, William Herbert; Second Lieutenant **Trevor-Jones**, Evan Edward; Lieutenant **Trouton**, Edmund Arthur; Second Lieutenant **Tucker**, William Henry; Second Lieutenant **Tucker**, Lionel Louis Clerici; Captain **Tullis**, William; Second Lieutenant **Tweedale**, Eric; Lieutenant **Tytler**, William Boyd; Second Lieutenant **Van Den Bok**, Frederick; Lieutenant **Vause**, John Gilbert; Second Lieutenant **Volkers**, Frederick Cyril Stowell; Second Lieutenant **Walker**, Henry Gerald; Second Lieutenant **Walker**, John; Second Lieutenant **Ward**, Dacre Stanley; Second Lieutenant **Wardill**, Charles Henry; Captain **Ware**, Francis Henry; Lieutenant **Wareham**, Frederick William; Second Lieutenant **Warren**, Fred Langford; Captain **Watson**, Cyril Pennefather; Lieutenant **Watson**, Frank; Second Lieutenant **Watson**, Sydney Towers; Second Lieutenant **Watson**, Charles Edward Stephens; Captain **Watts**, Talbot Hamilton; Second Lieutenant **Weatherhead**, Andrew; Lieutenant **Webster**, Michael Harold; Lieutenant **Wedgwood**, Gilbert Colclough; Captain **Weir**, John; Second Lieutenant **Wells**, Thomas William Maurice; Second Lieutenant **Weston**, John Douglas; Second Lieutenant **Wheeler**, William Pierce; Lieutenant **White**, Bernard Charles De; Lieutenant **White**, Malcolm Graham; Second Lieutenant **White**, Herbert Robert; Second Lieutenant **White**, Nathan; Second Lieutenant **Whittam**, Francis Joseph; Second Lieutenant **Wilkins**, Alfred Henry; Second Lieutenant **Wilkinson**, Gordon Frederick Noble; Second Lieutenant **Willey**, Thomas Arthur Raymond R. E.; Second Lieutenant **Williamson**, Harold Godwin; Captain **Willis**, Samuel; Second Lieutenant **Wilson**, Eric Maurice; Second Lieutenant **Wilson**, John; Second Lieutenant **Winkley**, Sydney Joseph; Second Lieutenant **Winstanley**, George Clement; Captain **Wiseman**, Willingham Franklin Gell; Second Lieutenant **Withers**, Frank Dean; Lieutenant Colonel **Wood**, Donald; Second Lieutenant **Wood**, Harry Douty; Lieutenant **Woodstock**, Walter Percy; Major **Wragg**, Frederick William; Lieutenant **Wright**, Clarence Harris; Second Lieutenant **Wright**, Matthew John; Lieutenant **Wrigley**, Joseph; Lieutenant **Wrong**, Harold Verschoyle; Second Lieutenant **Yates**, Arthur Gerald Vavasour; Captain **Young**, Arthur Cecil.

Appendix 5 Informal Names of Battalions

11th Border	Lonsdales
18th Durham Light Infantry	Durham Pals
11th East Lancs	Accrington Pals
10th East Yorks	Hull Commercials
11th East Yorks	Hull Tradesmen
12th East Yorks	Hull Sportsmen
15th Highland Light Infantry	Glasgow Tramways
16th Highland Light Infantry	Glasgow Boys Brigade
17th Highland Light Infantry	Glasgow Commercials
17th, 18th, 19th & 2nd King's Liverpool	Liverpool Pals (1st, 2nd, 3rd & 4th)
12th King's Own Light Infantry	Halifax Pals
15th, 16th, & 19th Lancashire Fusiliers	Salford Pals (1st, 2nd, 3rd)
10th Lincolns	Grimsby Chums
5th London	London Rifle Brigade (1st)
9th London	Queen Victoria's Rifles
12th London	Rangers
13th London	Kensington
14th London	London Scottish
16th London	Queen's Westminster Rifles
16th , 17th , 18th , 19th , 20th , 21st, 22nd	1st 2nd 3rd 4th 5th 6th 7th
Manchesters	Manchester Pals
24th Manchesters	Oldham Pals
16th Middlesex	Public Schools Battalion
16th Northumberland Fusiliers	Newcastle Commercials
17th Northumberland Fusiliers	Newcastle Railway Pals
18th Northumberland Fusiliers	Tyneside Pioneers
20th, 21st, 22nd, 23rd	1st, 2nd, 3rd, 4th
Northumberland Fusiliers	Tyneside Scottish
24th, 25th, 26th, 27th	1st, 2nd, 3rd, 4th
Northumberland Fusiliers	Tyneside Irish
9th Royal Inniskilling Fusiliers	Tyrone
10th Royal Inniskilling Fusiliers	Derry
11th Royal Inniskilling Fusiliers	Donegal &Fermanagh
9th Royal Irish Fusiliers	Armagh, Monaghan & Cavan
8th Royal Irish Rifles	East Belfast
9th Royal Irish Rifles	West Belfast
10th Royal Irish Rifles	South Belfast
11th Royal Irish Rifles	South Antrim
12th Royal Irish Rifles	Central Antrim
13th Royal Irish Rifles	Down
15th Royal Irish Rifles	North Belfast
16th Royal Irish Rifles	Down (2nd)
15th Royal Scots	Edinburgh City (1st)
16th Royal Scots	Edinburgh City (2nd)
7th Sherwoods	Robin Hood Rifles
11th Suffolks	Cambridge
15th West Yorks	Leeds Pals
16th & 18th West Yorks	Bradford Pals (1st & 2nd)
2nd Yorks	Green Howards (2nd)

7th Yorks	Green Howards (7th)
10th Yorks	Green Howards (10th)
12th York & Lancs	Sheffield City Battalion
13th & 14th York and Lancs	Barnsley Pals (1st & 2nd)

Appendix 6 National Archives Files Consulted

WO 339/24888, Captain, A De B, Adam **WO 339/4694,** Second Lieutenant, T F, Adamson **WO 339/14817,** Second Lieutenant, N L, Alexander **WO 339/25468,** Second Lieutenant S R, Allen **WO 339/17068,** Lieutenant, H D, Allen **WO 339/25041,** Captain, A J, Anderson **WO 339/64499,** Second Lieutenant, J, Andrew **WO 339/7366,** Captain, J A, Andrews **WO 339/45226,** Second Lieutenant, J, Anstee **WO 339/29451,** Second Lieutenant, G W H, Applin **WO 339/17201,** Second Lieutenant, N A, Arkle **WO 339/3650,** Second Lieutenant, K J P, Asher **WO 339/20790,** Captain, B P, Ayre **WO 339/5267,** Second Lieutenant, J F, Baddeley **WO 339/15871,** Captain, T, Baker **WO 339/17207,** Lieutenant, J W, Bamber **WO 339/36352,** Second Lieutenant, F F, Barnes **WO 339/61644,** Second Lieutenant, P, Barnett **WO 339/1596,** Second Lieutenant, E C, Bayly **WO 339/5268,** Lieutenant, R S M, Beatson **WO 339/56460,** Second Lieutenant, J L, Beavon **WO 339/37152,** Second Lieutenant, C V, Beddow **WO 339/62156,** Second Lieutenant, S H, Bedford **WO 339/53785,** Second Lieutenant, B H, Belcher **WO 339/5248,** Second Lieutenant, C S, Binns **WO 339/13171,** Captain, G G, Blackburn **WO 339/19222,** Captain, A E, Bland **WO 339/38240,** Second Lieutenant, R H, Blatherwick **WO 339/17244,** Captain, H A, Bolton **WO 339/47635,** Second Lieutenant, B R, Boncker **WO 339/6698,** Brevet Major, G B, Bosanquet **WO 339/44267,** Second Lieutenant, P G, Boswell **WO 339/47898,** Second Lieutenant, A, Branch **WO 339/65375,** Captain, C N, Brockbank **WO 339/804,** Captain, T P, Brocklehurst **WO 339/17246,** Second Lieutenant, F S, Brooks **WO 339/50505,** Second Lieutenant, E G, Brophy **WO 339/23127,** Second Lieutenant, J L, Brough **WO 339/7134,** Captain, D A, Browne **WO 339/55464,** Major, J R, Bruce **WO 339/65925,** Second Lieutenant, W E, Brunt **WO 339/7715,** Captain, C K, Butler **WO 339/15322,** Second Lieutenant, L F, Byrne **WO 339/20197,** Lieutenant, E M B, Cambie **WO 339/39759,** Second Lieutenant, R A R, Campbell **WO 339/59701,** Second Lieutenant, L A, Carey **WO 339/31056,** Second Lieutenant, G S D, Carver **WO 339/41195,** Second Lieutenant, J R T, Chalmers **WO 339/56804,** Second Lieutenant, A G, Chambers **WO 339/28849,** Captain, J M, Charlton **WO 339/1685,** Second Lieutenant, P H, Chase **WO 339/11155,** Lieutenant, E R, Cholmeley **WO 339/54353,** Second Lieutenant, S P, Churchfield **WO 339/5477,** Second Lieutenant, J H F, Clarke **WO 339/23626,** Lieutenant, H G F, Clifford **WO 339/4696,** Second Lieutenant, H B, Coates **WO 339/4245,** Second Lieutenant, A C, Cockcroft **WO 339/32420,** Second Lieutenant, F B, Coldwells **WO 339/36597,** Second Lieutenant, A, Coleman **WO 339/23539,** Captain, L G, Coles **WO 339/29740,** Lieutenant, G E, Cope **WO 339/47208,** Second Lieutenant, R O, Cormack **WO 339/54326,** Second Lieutenant, R L, Courtice **WO 339/65241,** Second Lieutenant, H H, Cowin **WO 339/5166,** Second Lieutenant, J F, Cragg **WO 339/60960,** Second Lieutenant, W, Crees **WO 339/52800,** Second Lieutenant, W L, Crombie **WO 339/17248,** Captain, J B, Cubey **WO 339/17900,** Second Lieutenant, L, Cummins **WO 339/49146,** Second Lieutenant, J, Cunningham **WO 339/2818,** Second Lieutenant, H, Dalrymple **WO 339/21739,** Second Lieutenant, D J, Darley **WO 339/663,** Second Lieutenant, L A D, David **WO 339/40009,** Second Lieutenant, R H W, Davidson **WO 339/17203,** Lieutenant, R C, Davidson **WO 339/66843,** Second Lieutenant, C S, Davis **WO 339/45777,** Second Lieutenant, P D, Denman **WO 339/30256,** Second Lieutenant, P J F, Dines **WO 339/30491,** Second Lieutenant, J J, Donaldson **WO 339/39446,** Second Lieutenant, J B, Dougal **WO 339/48393,** Lieutenant, H S, Drury **WO 339/28245,** Second Lieutenant, A H, Eames **WO 339/15682,** Lieutenant, R P, Eason **WO 339/29823,** Captain, J, East **WO 339/66160,** Second Lieutenant, J W, Eaton **WO 339/9625,** Major, W H, Edmond-Jenkins **WO 339/38819,** Second Lieutenant, A, Elder **WO 339/27781,** Second Lieutenant, P M, Elliott **WO 339/47850,** Lieutenant, C W, Ellis **WO 339/30823,** Captain, D H J, Ely **WO 339/65217,** Second Lieutenant, P H, Emberton **WO 339/31115,** Second Lieutenant, J P, Everitt **WO 339/65134,** Second Lieutenant, W, Fearnley **WO 339/33876,** Second Lieutenant, G H, Featherstone **WO 339/27343,** Lieutenant, G, Fitzgerald **WO 339/52034,** Second Lieutenant, C W, Flint **WO 339/26003,** Captain, J, Foley **WO 339/33773,** Second Lieutenant, J M, Foord-Kelcey **WO 339/19067,** Captain, R J, Ford **WO 339/30172,** Second Lieutenant, L S, Ford **WO 339/18932,** Captain, J P, Forster **WO 339/35576,** Second Lieutenant, J A A, Fountain **WO 339/40134,** Second Lieutenant, A W, Fraser **WO 339/32928,** Second Lieutenant, A I, Frost **WO 339/25932,** Second Lieutenant, J W, Fryer **WO 339/41091,** Second Lieutenant, W H, Furse **WO 339/23885,** Lieutenant, R W, Garton **WO 339/43170,** Lieutenant, R J H, Gatrell **WO 339/39912,** Second Lieutenant, W, Gibson **WO 339/27917,** Second Lieutenant, G, Giles **WO 339/45911,** Second Lieutenant, C T, Gill **WO 339/64249,** Second Lieutenant, J, Gillies **WO 339/29720,** Lieutenant, R Q, Gilson **WO 339/30831,** Second Lieutenant, H M, Glastonbury **WO 339/49362,** Captain, B H, Glover **WO 339/53210,** Second Lieutenant, H, Godfrey **WO 339/27787,** Second Lieutenant, V, Godfrey **WO 339/47645,** Second Lieutenant, F A, Golding

WO 339/23785, Lieutenant, W E, Gomersall **WO 339/33446**, Lieutenant, A J G, Goodall **WO 339/64133**, Second Lieutenant, C G, Gordon **WO 339/20784**, Lieutenant, E H A, Goss **WO 339/55679**, Second Lieutenant, E M, Gould **WO 339/51794**, Second Lieutenant, W H, Gregg **WO 339/2439**, Captain, G E, Griffin **WO 339/56437**, Second Lieutenant, R E, Grundy **WO 339/31224**, Lieutenant, A H, Hack **WO 339/23581**, Lieutenant, W, Hall **WO 339/22996**, Second Lieutenant, J M, Hall **WO 339/28607**, Captain, P Y, Harkness **WO 339/34207**, Captain, H S, Harris **WO 339/52056**, Lieutenant, W I S, Hartley **WO 339/20283**, Captain, G, Haswell **WO 339/36466**, Captain, A B, Hatt **WO 339/30905**, Captain, H E, Hawkins **WO 339/54360**, Second Lieutenant, C S, Haynes **WO 339/14708**, Captain, L D, Head **WO 339/15016**, Lieutenant, A E, Head **WO 339/62160**, Second Lieutenant, M I, Heming **WO 339/6585**, Captain, C R, Heygate **WO 339/34251**, Second Lieutenant, F J, Hicking **WO 339/5494**, Second Lieutenant, C P, Hirst **WO 339/43015**, Second Lieutenant, E, Hobbs **WO 339/19422**, Lieutenant, W N, Hodgson **WO 339/18678**, Second Lieutenant, R B, Holcroft **WO 339/16924**, Lieutenant, W A, Hole **WO 339/36975**, Second Lieutenant, H G, Hornsby **WO 339/40407**, Second Lieutenant, H M, Horrox **WO 339/20453**, Lieutenant Colonel, L M, Howard **WO 339/43090**, Second Lieutenant, C K, Howe **WO 339/4450**, Second Lieutenant, C W, Howlett **WO 339/35950**, Second Lieutenant, M L, Huddleston **WO 339/19114**, Captain, C J, Huntriss **WO 339/66130**, Second Lieutenant, W W, Hynam **WO 339/1100**, Second Lieutenant, R G, Ingle **WO 339/15683**, Lieutenant, E, Inman **WO 339/54193**, Lieutenant, H S, Jackson **WO 339/34730**, Second Lieutenant, E A, Jago **WO 339/34832**, Second Lieutenant, A H, Jarman **WO 339/18311**, Captain, S H, Jeudwine **WO 339/11659**, Captain, O R F, Johnston **WO 339/36144**, Lieutenant, A A H, Johnston **WO 339/44241**, Captain, A C, Jones **WO 339/1767**, Lieutenant, W M, Keighley **WO 339/29247**, Second Lieutenant, T, Kemp **WO 339/19466**, Captain, S, Kenworthy **WO 339/17675**, Lieutenant, G H, Kernaghan **WO 339/51493**, Second Lieutenant, D T, King **WO 339/38104**, Second Lieutenant, R J, Kingsford **WO 339/35781**, Second Lieutenant, A H, Kippax **WO 339/45395**, Major, J L, Knott **WO 339/18934**, Captain, D O, Laing **WO 339/24488**, Lieutenant, W, Lamb **WO 339/50652**, Second Lieutenant, G E, Layton-Bennett **WO 339/4523**, Second Lieutenant, W G, Leathley **WO 339/40874**, Second Lieutenant, J E, Lewis **WO 339/78489**, Captain, R C, Lewis **WO 339/48176**, Second Lieutenant, M C, Ley **WO 339/7732**, Captain, C R, Limbery **WO 339/65352**, Captain, R, Litten **WO 339/240**, Second Lieutenant, D H H, Logan **WO 339/26016**, Lieutenant, H, Lomas **WO 339/34230**, Second Lieutenant, S, Longhurst **WO 339/44340**, Lieutenant, H O, Lord **WO 339/24490**, Lieutenant, S, Macdonald **WO 339/497**, Captain, K, Mackenzie **WO 339/48399**, Second Lieutenant, A D, Maconachie **WO 339/17649**, Captain, C C, May **WO 339/3977**, Second Lieutenant, A W, Mcgain **WO 339/26301**, Lieutenant, J, Mcgillicuddy **WO 339/55683**, Second Lieutenant, J S, Mcgowan **WO 339/36404**, Second Lieutenant, A A, Mclean **WO 339/42615**, Second Lieutenant, N L, Mcneill **WO 339/23766**, Lieutenant, R, Mellor **WO 339/24244**, Second Lieutenant, H P E M, Melly **WO 339/28007**, Second Lieutenant, R V, Merry **WO 339/4109**, Second Lieutenant, F J, Miller **WO 339/31232**, Lieutenant, G E, Mockridge **WO 339/35153**, Second Lieutenant, G R, Money **WO 339/375**, Lieutenant, M R H, Morley **WO 339/31233**, Lieutenant, G W, Morris **WO 339/23564**, Captain, R W, Mullins **WO 339/26208**, Captain, P A, Murray **WO 339/30668**, Second Lieutenant, J, Nanson **WO 339/12672**, Captain, G T, Neame **WO 339/15647**, Captain, B L, Needham **WO 339/14586**, Lieutenant, R H, Neill **WO 339/31652**, Second Lieutenant, J, Nelson **WO 339/26884**, Lieutenant, T E, Nicholson **WO 339/16901**, Captain, W, Nixon **WO 339/15015**, Major, T G, Noble **WO 339/13547**, Lieutenant, P G, Norbury **WO 339/47653**, Lieutenant, R W K, Oakley **WO 339/2770**, Second Lieutenant, J J F, Oldershaw **WO 339/22351**, Second Lieutenant, W K, Orford **WO 339/32551**, Lieutenant, H P, Organ **WO 339/53381**, Lieutenant, H, Ormrod **WO 339/27528**, Second Lieutenant, E, Outram **WO 339/26962**, Lieutenant, J, Parker **WO 339/49970**, Second Lieutenant, J H, Parkinson **WO 339/33190**, Second Lieutenant, J H, Parr-Dudley **WO 339/19101**, Lieutenant, J H, Patterson, **WO 339/2653**, Lieutenant, O G, Payne **WO 339/35155**, Second Lieutenant, N, Peak **WO 339/13227**, Captain, C S, Pearce **339/54037**, Lieutenant, J P P, Peregrine **WO 339/2045**, Second Lieutenant, G, Perkins **WO 339/35786**, Second Lieutenant, C W, Perry **WO 339/58631**, Second Lieutenant, E, Peyton **WO 339/58498**, Second Lieutenant, E M, Pinkerton **WO 339/28499**, Captain, A, Preedy **WO 339/35452**, Second Lieutenant, J E, Price **WO 339/46275**, Second Lieutenant, P J, Ram **WO 339/47889**, Second Lieutenant, W H, Ratcliffe **WO 339/1053**, Lieutenant, A V, Ratcliffe **WO 339/17743**, Second Lieutenant, H L, Rayner **WO 339/22916**, Lieutenant, R, Reid **WO 339/43923**, Second Lieutenant, J F G, Rew **WO 339/933**, Second Lieutenant, W, Riddell **WO 339/45862**, Lieutenant, G L C, Ridpath **WO 339/14342**, Captain, G, Robertson **WO 339/51407**, Second Lieutenant, W R, Robertson **WO 339/52019**, Lieutenant, B S, Robinson **WO 339/43360**, Second Lieutenant, P B P, Robinson **WO 339/29263**, Lieutenant, F G, Ross **WO 339/18299**, Captain, P, Ross **WO 339/27543**, Lieutenant, G M, Ross

WO 339/31154, Lieutenant, D S, Ross **WO 399/29877**, Captain, H T, Rowley **WO 339/7411**, Captain, D T C, Rowley **WO 339/1713**, Lieutenant, E, Russell **WO 339/38916**, Second Lieutenant, G S, Russell **WO 339/22502**, Captain, J B, Rutledge **WO 339/9580**, Captain, J F, Ruttledge **WO 339/54471**, Second Lieutenant, A H W, Sampson **WO 339/27762**, Second Lieutenant, W W, Sanby **WO 339/59938**, Captain, L H, Sanger-Davies **WO 339/47590**, Second Lieutenant, W H, Savage **WO 339/17230**, Captain, G B, Sayce **WO 339/32634**, Second Lieutenant, S S, Schneider **WO 339/133**, Captain, G H H, Scott **WO 339/5496**, Second Lieutenant, W F, Scott **WO 339/66465**, Lieutenant, D H, Scott **WO 339/35752**, Lieutenant, G, Scott **WO 339/17745**, Lieutenant, J W, Shann **WO 339/23259**, Lieutenant, A E, Shapley **WO 339/59709**, Second Lieutenant, L O, Sharp **WO 339/32895**, Second Lieutenant, L F, Sharp **WO 339/9539**, Lieutenant, C G, Shaw **WO 339/41142**, Second Lieutenant, C H, Shepard **WO 399/6221**, Second Lieutenant, F G, Shirreff **WO 339/18948**, Major, H, Sibbit **WO 339/1183**, Lieutenant, S D I, Smith **WO 339/21844**, Captain, R, Smith **WO 339/26294**, Second Lieutenant, N M, Smith **WO 339/54050**, Second Lieutenant, P C J, Smith **WO 339/29444**, Second Lieutenant, W, Spatz **WO 339/12041**, Lieutenant, G M, Sproat **WO 339/44272**, Second Lieutenant, R M, Stainton **WO 339/53824**, Second Lieutenant, O S, Stephensen **WO 339/15563**, Major, H L, Stocks **WO 339/66152**, Second Lieutenant, A C, Strugnell **WO 339/24495**, Second Lieutenant, H R C, Sutcliffe **WO 339/46252**, Second Lieutenant, G G, Swan **WO 339/40260**, Second Lieutenant, W, Swift **WO 339/135870**, Second Lieutenant, S, Thomas **WO 339/1520**, Second Lieutenant, F, Thornton **WO 339/18729**, Captain, J G, Todd **WO 339/46892**, Second Lieutenant, C V, Tomlinson **WO 339/2447**, Lieutenant, J H, Toolis **WO 339/15752**, Lieutenant, J W, Towers-Clark **WO 339/11523**, Captain, G P, Tregelles **WO 339/30319**, Second Lieutenant, L L C, Tucker **WO 339/20050**, Captain, D C T, Twentyman **WO 339/17234**, Lieutenant, W B, Tytler **WO 339/55302**, Second Lieutenant, F, Van Den Bok **WO 339/52494**, Second Lieutenant, C E, Vassie **WO 339/15409**, Captain, N, Vaudrey **WO 339/50118**, Second Lieutenant, F A, Venus **WO 339/30962**, Captain, F L, Vernon **WO 339/19235**, Captain, W, Walker **WO 339/29713**, Second Lieutenant, T R, Walker **WO 339/5938**, Captain, J R, Walpole **WO 339/38491**, Captain, W G, Warden **WO 339/41536**, Second Lieutenant, S A, Webber **WO 339/48119**, Second Lieutenant, J D, Weston **WO 339/54377**, Second Lieutenant, E V, Whitby **WO 339/17236**, Captain, J V, White **WO 339/46283**, Captain, G, White **WO 339/62561**, Second Lieutenant, J, White **WO 339/4864**, Lieutenant, B C D, White **WO 339/65228**, Second Lieutenant, G F N, Wilkinson **WO 339/29913**, Second Lieutenant, L, Williams **WO 339/37608**, Second Lieutenant, G F, Wilson **WO 339/51518**, Second Lieutenant, J, Wilson **WO 339/7978**, Captain, W F G, Wiseman **WO 339/1585**, Second Lieutenant, F D, Withers **WO 339/38370**, Second Lieutenant, W J, Wood **WO 339/49725**, Second Lieutenant, H D, Wood

Appendix 7
Fallen Officer 2nd July 1916

ADDINGTON, Second Lieutenant, Cyril John Flintan. Died of wounds, 2nd July 1916 received at Beaumont-Hamel the previous day. 16th Bn., Middlesex Regiment, attd 24th Bn. Aged 22. Born 1894. Son of Paul Flintan Addington and Mary Louisa Addington, of 49, Merton Hall Road, Wimbledon, Surrey. Native of Merton, Surrey. Gazetted temporary lieutenant 11th September 1915 transferred from Res. Bns, 1st July 1916. Commemorated Kings College School Memorial, Wimbledon. Memorial Ref. II. E. 11., Auchonvillers Military Cemetery, France.

The Dead In Christ Shall Rise First

ALLEN, Second Lieutenant, Lawrence John Maynard. Killed when attack commenced 2nd July 1916. 6th Bn., Wiltshire Regiment. Aged 19. Only son of William and Jane A. Allen, of 51, West Side, Clapham Common, London. Attended Emanuel School, London. He went from school into the army as a Private, No. 3137, 2nd London Regiment. 6th Bn., not involved on the 1st July but on the 2nd. Father applied for his medals. Memorial Ref. Pier and Face 13 A., Thiepval Memorial, France.

BAINES, Second Lieutenant, John Hugh. Died 3rd July 1916. 10th Bn., Lincolnshire Regiment. War diary implies the 1st July, five other casualties were given date of death of the 1st July 1916. Archive file has the 3rd July and Medal Index Card. Son of Thomas Baines, 58 Holywell Road, Putney. Born 11th August 1892. Memorial Digby Stuart College, University of Roehampton. Attended Wimbledon College. Attested 7th June 1915 as private, 4062. Member of the Inns of Court OTC. Commissioned 21st October 1915. Gazetted 6th November 1915. Entered France, 10th January 1916. Brothers killed Captain Joseph Baines, Middlesex Regiment, 29th July 1916 and Second Lieutenant George Baines, Royal Flying Corps, 3rd June 1917. Grantham Roll of Honour. Memorial Ref. Pier and Face 1C. Thiepval Memorial, Somme, France. WO 339/44442

BENSON, Second Lieutenant, William Roy Gwyn. Acting Lewis gun officer at the time of his death, 2nd July 1916. During a terrific shelling he left the dug-out and went round the front line trenches to visit the Lewis guns, whilst doing so he came across, a wounded sentry who was half buried through the explosion of a shell and pinned down by a box of ammunition. Whilst releasing the man a shell burst over him a piece of shrapnel entering his back and he sank down unconscious and never recovered. 2nd Bn., South Staffordshire Regiment. Born near Cowbridge, S. Wales, March 16th 1895. Aged 21. Eldest son of W. T. Benson (Manager of the London and Provincial Bank, Pontypridd formerly Ilford) and Mary Benson, of 79, Merthyr Road, Pontypridd, Glam. Educated the Grocers' Company School, Hackney Downs and entered the service of the Standard Bank of South Africa in March 1911. Transferred to the Bank of Montreal in 1912 and served in the London Office for two years. Served as a trooper with the Westminster Dragoons, 1912 – 1914. Sailing to Montreal in May, 1914 he returned to enlist in the University and Public Schools Brigade of the Royal Fusiliers, company quartermaster-sergeant, 1269. Obtained a commission in May, 1915 and proceeded to the Front, 1st October. Held the vellum certificate of the Royal Humane Society for gallantry in saving a life from drowning. Father applied for his medals. Memorial Ref. I. A. 17. Cabaret-Rouge British Cemetery, Souchez, France.

Beloved Son Of William Tyler & Mary Benson Of Pontypridd

BIGGS, Second Lieutenant, Arthur Ridley. Last seen gallantly leading his men, killed in action 2nd July 1916. 6th Bn., Wiltshire Regiment. Born 14th October 1894, Middlesex, Lower Edmonton. Son of James and Ellen Biggs. Attended University College, Reading (1912). Member of the Reading University College Officers' Training Corps. Admitted as an Associate of University College Reading in 1915. 6th Bn., not involved on the 1st but on the 2nd July. Entered France 22nd April 1916. Father applied for his medals. Original burial map reference 57dX.20.a. Memorial Ref. V. D. 9., Ovillers Military Cemetery, France.

BOWERS, Lieutenant, William Aubrey. He died on July 2nd 1916, at Warlincourt, of wounds received the day before at Gommecourt. William had been assisting one of his men carry a load of barbed wire when a shell exploded overhead and he was hit by shrapnel. C Coy., 1st/5th Bn., North Staffordshire Regiment. Born at Barlaston Hall. Aged 29. Only son of William Eli Bowers J.P and Alice Bowers nee Blagg (of Barlaston Hall, Barlaston), of Caverswall. Attended Winchester College, 1900 to 1906. Entered Culverlea from Sandroyd School. He became Head of his House and a member of Senior Divison, Sixth Book; he played in Commoner VI in 1905 and kept goal for the school his last two years. He went up to New College, Oxford in 1906 and graduated with Honours in classics and history. Member of University OTC and gained a Master's degree. Enjoyed playing cricket and football whilst at Winchester. Member of North Staffordshire hunt. Soon after leaving College he was elected a member of Staffordshire County Council and when war broke out obtained a commission in the 5th Battalion. Married 1913, Vera Aimee Bowers (Latham), of Caverswall Castle, Stoke-on-Trent and left one daughter, Penelope Vera, born 15th January 1915. Joined the regiment in April 1915. Entered France, 10th May 1916. He studied law but did not study further with his legal studies due to the death of his father when he succeeded to the estates. Founded the Caverswall Cricket Club with his father. Wife was staying at Eastbourne when she heard the news. Family had mining interests. Widow applied for his medals. Memorial Ref. I. E. 1., Warlincourt Halte British Cemetery, Saulty, France.

His Servants Shall Serve Him

BROTHERS, Captain, Arthur Stanley. Killed in action, 2nd July 1916. 178th Coy., Royal Engineers. Aged 34. Son of William H. and Marie A. Brothers, of Peckham Rye, London. Gazetted 23rd October 1915. Entered France, 19th November 1915. His sister, Mrs. Leatherbarrow, Peckham Rye applied for his medals and choose his inscription. Memorial Ref. I. A. 86., Norfolk Cemetery, Becordel-Becourt, France.

On Whose Soul Sweet Jesus Have Mercy R.I.P.

BROWN, Second Lieutenant, John Arbuckle. B Coy leading on the left. 16th Highland light Infantry. 3rd July 1916. Age 24. War Diary states 1st July 1916. Son of Caroline L. H. Brown, of 4, Hamilton Terrace East, Patrick, Glasgow, and John Arbuckle Brown. Born 26th March 1892. Reported in the Daily Record on the 8th July 1916 to have died of wounds. Grave Registration documents also state died of wounds received 1st July. Joined the Highland Light Infantry at the outbreak of war receiving the rank of Company Quartermaster Sergeant. September 1915 received his commission and went to France, 10th February 1916. His cousin also died in the war Lieutenant James T. Lyall, reported died of wounds 19th July 1916. Hutchesons' Boys' Grammar School. Mother applied for his medals and officer payments. Grave Ref. II.B. 6. Bouzincourt Communal Cemetery Extension, Somme, France.

CASEBOURNE, Lieutenant, Rowland Telford. Lieutenant and Adjutant Casebourne with a small party of the 1/5th Bn., West Yorkshire Regiment reached the Schwaben Redoubt on the 1st July 1916, the remainder of the battalion moving to Johnstone's Post. Died, killed in action 2nd July 1916. 3rd Bn., Yorkshire Regiment. Aged 39. Son of Charles Townsend Casebourne and Eliza Jane Casebourne, of Greatham House, Greatham, Co. Durham; Husband of Eva Gertrude Casebourne, of Hartburn, Stockton-on-Tees, second daughter of Mr. R. W. Brydon and Mrs. Brydon of The Cottage, Greatham. Served in the South African Campaign with the Imperial Yeomanry. An old member of Hartlepool Rovers Football Club he sometimes played for Durham County. His wife was overcome with grief and could not attend his memorial service. Entered France, 27th August 1915. His widow applied for his medals. Memorial Ref. Pier and Face 3 A and 3 D., Thiepval Memorial, France.

CATHER, Lieutenant, Geoffrey St. George Shillington, VC. He heard a man calling and went over the parapet in broad daylight, gave him water, called out to see if there was anyone else within hail, saw a hand waving feebly, went on and was shot through the head by a machine-gun and killed instantaneously, 2nd July 1916. Adjt. 9th Bn., Royal Irish Fusiliers. Aged 25. Elder son of Mr. Robert Gabriel Cather Cather (merchant) and of Mrs. Margaret Matilda Cather, of Limpsfield, Surrey. Educated Hazelwood School. Attended Rugby School.

He entered the school in 1905, and left, on his father's death, in 1908. He then entered the business of Messrs. Joseph Tetley and Co., Tea Merchants, in which his father had been Director, and, in 1912, was sent by them to America and Canada, returning in May, 1914. On the outbreak of War he enlisted in the 19th (2nd Public Schools) Battalion of the Royal Fusiliers. He obtained a Commission in the Royal Irish Fusiliers in May, 1915, and went with his Battalion in the Ulster Division to France, 5th October, 1915. He became Assistant Adjutant in November, and was appointed Adjutant in December, 1915. He was awarded the Victoria Cross on September 9th, 1916 for most conspicuous bravery on the 1st/2nd July 1916; 'From 7.00pm. till midnight he searched "No Man's Land", and brought in three wounded men. Next morning, at 8 o'clock, he continued his search, brought in another wounded man, and gave water to others, arranging for their rescue later. Finally, at 10.30am, he took out water to another man, and was proceeding further on when he was himself killed. All this was carried out in full view of the enemy, and under direct machine-gun fire and intermittent artillery fire. He set a splendid example of courage and self-sacrifice'. He was buried where he fell, south of Beaumont Hamel. The Chaplain wrote :- "He has left behind with us all the happiest of memories, and by his noble self-sacrificing death, the highest of examples. "We all very much hope that his name will be added to the list of gallant heroes who have gained the VC." His mother applied for his medals. Memorial Ref. Pier and Face 15 A., Thiepval Memorial, France.

COOMBS, Lieutenant, Henry Whitaker. Wounded whilst leading a platoon into action, died of wounds, 2nd July 1916 at No. 5 Casualty Clearing Station, Albert. He was shot in a communication trench between supports and front line. 'C' Company, 18th Bn., Northumberland Fusiliers. Aged 23. Only son of the Reverend Arthur Henry (Baptist Minister, of Sale, Manchester) and Mary Sophie Whitaker Coombs, of The Manse, Bratton, Wiltshire; and of Keyford School, Frome, Somerset. BA, C.C.C., Oxon. Born Frome, Somerset, 7th January 1893. Educated Kingsmead School, Hoylake and Manchester Grammar School 1909-1911. Educated at Corpus Christie College, Oxford University where he obtained a scholarship for mathematics. Scholar; 1 Mathematics Moderations 1912; 2 Mathematics 1914; BA 1914. Secretary, Association Football Club 1912-1913, captain 1913-1914; Secretary, Cricket 1913, captain 1914. He also rowed in the Torpids. Assistant Mathematics Master, Wellington College, Berkshire 1914. Also enlisted in August 1914, service commenced January 1915. Fiancé of Phyllis Hope (Taunton). Mathematical master at Wellington College when the war broke out, went to the Front, 7th January 1916. His mother received the news on the 3rd July. Effects were gold wrist watch and strap, prayer book, note book, field service pocket book, photo case and photos, identity disc, field message and some money. Commemorated Downton War Memorial and Bratton War Memorial. Father applied for his medals. Memorial Ref. Plot 1. Row B. Grave 8., Corbie Communal Cemetery Extension, France. WO 339/22304
B.A. C.C.C. Oxon In Christo Vivificabitur

COY, Second Lieutenant, Alfred Reginald. Killed in action, 2nd July 1916. 7th Bn., West Yorkshire Regiment (Prince of Wales's Own). Aged 22. Son of Nathan James Coy, of 7, Gloucester Road, Kingston Hill, Surrey. Gazetted 13th November 1915. Only casualty from 7th Bn. Previously 28th London Regiment, private, 4026. Entered France, 8th January 1916. Father applied for his medals. Memorial Ref. Pier and Face 2 A 2 C and 2 D., Thiepval Memorial, France.

DAMIANO, Second Lieutenant, Walter Henry Alexander. "The 2nd Battalion, Royal Dublin Fusiliers, began to advance at 9.00am, immediately encountering heavy enfilade fire from Beaumont-Hamel. At 9.05am two runners arrived and informed Major Walsh, the commanding officer, that the attack was to be postponed. He managed to stop part of C and D companies advancing. However for the rest of the battalion, already in No Man's Land, the recall order came too late. At noon, when the order was finally received from Corps HQ to attack and consolidate the position, Walsh reported that this was impossible. Of the twenty-three officers and 480 men who had assembled that morning, fourteen officers and 311 men were now casualties. The order had to be amended and Major Walsh was now told to collect all available men to defend the British front-line." Died of gunshot wounds after being shot in the chest, 2nd July 1916. 2nd Bn., Royal Dublin Fusiliers. Aged 19. Born 11th February 1897. Son of Nicholas and Enid Damiano, of 2, Church Lane, Calcutta, India. Baptised 2nd April 1897 at Holy Trinity, Bedford. Came to London, aged 2. Attended Ripley Court School, Surrey, 1910 to 1911, Cheltenham college 1911 to 1914 and RMC Sandhurst. Cheltenham OTC. Gazetted 15th June 1915. Entered France, 10th October 1915. Major T. W. Bartlett, applied for his medals on behalf of his parents who were in India. Memorial Ref. A. 9., Beauval Communal Cemetery, France.
Heart And Soul Of A Boy Simple & Cheery Never Now To Grow Old Never Grow Weary.

DAVIDSON, Second Lieutenant, William Adrian. He was mortally wounded in action near Mametz, and died on 2nd July 1916. 2nd Bn., Gordon Highlanders. Aged 21. Eldest son of Alexander Davidson, of Blythewood, Inverurie, Aberdeenshire. Born Aberdeen, 28th December 1894. Educated at the Grammar School and Robert Gordon's College, Aberdeen, and later at Trinity College, Glenalmond. Commenced the study of Medicine at Aberdeen University in 1912. In January 1915 he entered the RMC Sandhurst, and after a few months of training was gazetted to the Gordon Highlanders, 2nd Battalion, with which he served in France till the following September, when, having been wounded in action near Hulluch, he was invalided home. On recovery, and after a short period of home service (at Stoneywood Wireless Station) he rejoined his regiment in France. Officers and men alike testify to the bravery with which Davidson led his men in the face of terrible odds ; his gallantry and pluck are praised by all who knew him under the difficult conditions. Memorial Ref. A. 30., Morlancourt British Cemetery No.1, France.

Of Blythewood, Inverurie Aberdeenshire

DEAKIN, Second Lieutenant, Charles Joseph John King. As the leading lines came out of the trenches came under terrific machine-gun fire and crumpled up the attack, died of wounds, 2nd July 1916 wounded at Beaumont Hamel. 16th Bn., Middlesex Regiment. Aged 25. Son of Charles Frank and Ellen Louise Deakin, of Burton-on-Trent. Admitted June 1914. In the legal profession in Shropshire as Managing clerk with Messrs. Onion & Davies of Market Drayton. Joined September 1914 as a private, 66 in the Public Schools Bn., promoted sergeant January 1915. Gazetted 2nd lieutenant May 1915. Served at home September 1914 to May 1915. Named on the War Shrine at St Mark's Church, Kennington 1916, London. Played cricket for Aldenham School 1906 to 1908. Only brother of Miss Gladys E. Deakin, Hollis Wood, Faraham and she applied for his medals and choose his inscription. War diary states 2nd July 1916. Memorial Ref. II. A. 5., Doullens Communal Cemetery Extension No.1, France.

His Life Was Fine His Death Glorious.

·⚬ O. A. F. C. ⚬·

Standing—G. D. HERRON, J. W. HUNTER, W. E. GOODYEAR, E. N. MATHIESON, F. J. BIDDLE, and L. LEAGE.
Sitting—C. F. ETHERIDGE, F. H. W. HIRSCH, A. F. WHITE, C. J. J. K. DEAKIN, and C. H. GIMINGHAM.

DICKINSON, Captain, George Sidney. Killed in the Great Advance, 2nd July 1916 with 19 other ranks being wounded. 7th Bn., Lincolnshire Regiment. Received his commission as a second lieutenant, 18th September 1915 and proved himself a very capable officer. Formerly in the office, Messrs. Oakden & Co. and when war broke out he joined the Artists' Rifles shortly after the outbreak of war and was Sir John French's bodyguard, and was granted a commission. June promoted to captain. Native of London. Married Miss Suzanne Marie Estelle Chevassus of Eastbourne in March 1916 service carried out by his uncle, the vicar of Long Sutton the Reverend Dixon Spain. Marie was born in Mons, France. Only son of Mr. and Mrs. J. Dickinson of Pallmer's Green. Educated at Stationers' School. Entered France, 22nd January 1915. Widow applied for his medals. Original burial map reference 62C.A.15.c.5.C. Memorial Ref. III. B. 25., Peronne Road Cemetery, Maricourt, France.

FAVELL, Second Lieutenant, William Reginald. 2nd July 1916. 4th Bn., York and Lancaster Regiment. Aged 34. Second son of Richard (surgeon) and Ada Favell, of Belmont House, Glossop Road, Sheffield. Born 18th June 1885. Attended Oakham School between 1896 and 1900, and during this time was a prefect and rugby Colour. He went out to Canada and worked as a rancher and joined the local militia. On 8th December 1914 he attested for the Canadian Army but instead of joining up there he came home and was commissioned. Entered France, 19th October 1915. Brother served, Captain Richard Vernon Favell, RAMC. His sister applied for his medals. Memorial Ref. F. 4., Authuile Military Cemetery, France.

HEARD, Captain, Geoffrey Richard, L.R. C.P. (Lon)., M.R.C.S (Eng.). Killed in action near La Boisselle, 2nd July 1916 at the time of his death he was attending to a wounded man, when a piece of shrapnel passed through his chest. Royal Army Medical Corps attached 10th Bn., Royal Warwickshire Regiment. Aged 30. Elder son of Richard William and Annie Louisa Heard, of 7, Osborne Villas, Devonport. Married. Educated Plymouth College, studied at University of London, qualified as M.R.C.S and L.R.C.P. (London) in 1909. Joined the RAMC as a temporary lieutenant on December 18th 1914 and became a captain after a year. Held House Surgery at Newark Hospital obtained a Ship-Surgeoncy on SS Herefordshire and made two voyages to Rancoon. Followed by an appointment with Essex Council and offered his services. Entered France, July 1915. Application by Mr. Edward J. Tozer on behalf of his daughter, Mrs. A. J. Tozer the late Mrs. Heard. Memorial Ref. I. C. 5., Bapaume Post Military Cemetery, Albert, France.

HUNTER, Second Lieutenant, Archibald. Reported locally to have been killed on the 1st July 1916 officially 2nd July 1916. Reported killed by machine-gun fire whilst taking a trench. 14th Bn. attd. 9th Bn., Cheshire Regiment. Aged 41. Son of Daniel Munchie Hunter and Mary Hunter. Husband of C. E. F. Hunter, of 33, St. George's Road, Kilburn, London. Born 1875, Clapham, Surrey. Employed as an estate agent and eventually an auctioneer. Widow applied for his medals. Memorial Ref. Pier and Face 3 C and 4 A., Thiepval Memorial, France.

HUNTER, Second Lieutenant, John Maurice. Killed near La Boisselle in a dangerous task for which he had volunteered, bombing officer who gave magnificent aid but was killed, displaying the greatest gallantry possible, 2nd July 1916. 6th Bn., Wiltshire Regiment. Aged 31. Born 17th April 1885. Elder son of Reverend John Hunter, D.D. Educated Kelvinside Academy, Glasgow and University College School, London and Balliol College. Formerly employed publishing house and the Board of Education. Entered France, 4th October 1915. Original burial map reference 57d.26.b. Memorial Ref.

Believed to be buried in. X. C. 2., Gordon Dump Cemetery, Ovillers-La Boisselle, France.

The Eternal God Is Our Refuge And Underneath Are The Everlasting Arms

JACKSON, Captain, Thomas Leslie, MC. The advance was stuck up by a deep and wide communication trench, the trench was entered and occupied, bombing parties were formed, good work indeed was done by Captain Jackson, afterwards killed. Locally reported as being killed on the 1st July 1916, officially 2nd July 1916. 9th Bn., Cheshire Regiment. Killed instantly after being shot in the head leading his men. Aged 23. Born 1893, Holbeach, Lincolnshire. Son of Dr. Thomas Jackson and Mrs. Lucy Jackson of Greystoke, Cumberland. Educated St. Bees Grammar School and Glasgow University. In 1909 he came to the University of Glasgow for the first time, taking the Physical Laboratory class. He then came back in 1911-1914 and took subjects such as chemistry and natural philosophy with the intention of earning a degree in Naval Architecture although he never graduated. During his time at university he was a member of the OTC. The regiment trained on Salisbury Plain and in Basingstoke before landing in Boulogne on 19th July 1915. He took part in diversionary action at Pietre during the Battle of Loos. Awarded Military Cross in February 1916 for rescuing a dangerously wounded fellow officer under heavy fire, and close to the enemy lines. Entered France, 20th July 1915. Father applied for his medals. Original burial map reference 57d.20.a. Memorial Ref. X. H. 2., Gordon Dump Cemetery, Ovillers-La Boisselle, France.

In His Keeping

JAMESON, Lieutenant, James Leslie, MC. His death was instantaneous, 2nd July 1916. 1st /5th Bn., West Yorkshire Regiment (Prince of Wales's Own). Aged 20. Youngest son of the Reverend Thomas E. Jameson, (Vicar of St. Stephens, Leeds) of Thornton-Le-Dale, Pickering, Yorks. Yorkshire Rugby Football Union. Headingley RFC. Attended Ripon Grammar School and gained the De Grey Scholarship at Leeds University 1914 and was a member of the OTC: Played for Leeds University at hockey and cricket, and has been chosen as vice-captain at the latter game for next season. Awarded Military Cross at the start of 1916 for bravery during a German gas attack on the British lines at Ypres. Youngest of six brothers. He wrote ' Before another day is over we hope to go over the parapet in the biggest scrap the world has ever known....I consider it an honour to be able to take part in so glorious a battle'. On the 1st July, battalion withdrawn and ordered to occupy Schwaben Redoubt which was reached by a small party. Entered France, 15th April 1915. Father applied for medals for his two sons, the remaining brother, Major Horace Armytage Jameson killed 24th March 1918. Memorial Ref. Pier and Face 2 A 2 C and 2 D., Thiepval Memorial, France.

JOHNSON, Captain, William Morton. On July 1st , 1916, he and his company captured Montauban, but he was killed next day at Faure, 2nd July 1916. C Coy., 16th Bn., Manchester Regiment. He was probably the first man into the village and had the honour of chalking the regiment's name on the abandoned German field gun. Reported that he was shot in the head leading his men against a counter attack, as he passed ammunition to a machine gunner. Aged 34. Elder son of William Henry Johnson, BSc, (Ironmaster, Chairman of Messrs. R. Johnson, Clapham and Morris, Ltd., Manchester) and Agnes Morton Johnson, of Woodleigh, Altrincham, Cheshire. Born 4th September 1884, at Altrincham, Cheshire. Educated at Summer Fields, Harrow and Trinity College, Cambridge. MA, F.R.G.S. Admitted as pensioner at Trinity, College, Cambridge, June 25th 1900. Trinity B.A. 1903, MA 1908, F.R.G.S. Entered his father's business and, on his father's death, succeeded him as Chairman of the firm in 1914, Johnson, Clapham and Morris Ltd. He was an original member of the Institute of Metals, of which his father had been one of the founders. Captain Johnson joined the Public Schools Battalion as a private in August, 1914, and was given a commission in the Manchester Regiment in the following October, being promoted captain in March, 1915. He went to the Front 8th November 1915. A student of history and a collector of historical works. He was buried where he fell with the men of his company who fell with him. In his will left his estate to the Reverend Alan Douglas Johnston and Arthur Laurence Johnston, his brothers. His effects were purse, cheque book, advance book, field message book, German bomber tassles, identity disc, letters, cigarette case, whistle, pair of compasses, leather wallet, fountain pen, pencils, case with knife, fork, spoon, hankerchiefs, pair field glasses and flash light. His family made enquiries about his watch. Mother applied for his medals. Known as 'Morton'. Memorial Ref. Pier and Face 13 A and 14 C., Thiepval Memorial, France. WO 339/19465

JONES, Second Lieutenant, Eric. Struck in the chest with a piece of shell which killed him instantly. The trenches were being bombarded and a dug-out had been blown in by a shell. Lieutenant Jones took a rescue party to dig the men out when he was killed. 2nd July 1916. 1st /9th Bn., The King's (Liverpool Regiment). Aged 20. Son of George Henry and Annie Jones, of 48, Strathcona Road, Wallasey, Cheshire. Native of Liverpool. Father applied for his medals. Memorial ref. I. E. 3., Wailly Orchard Cemetery, France.

Waiting In A Holy Stillness Wrapt In Sleep Mother And Father

JONES, Captain, Ernest Kerrison. He took part in the forward movement which began on July 1, and lost his life on the second day, 2nd July 1916. On Sunday afternoon we were called upon to assault the German trenches opposing us, near the village of La Boisselle (near Albert). This involved a charge over some 150 yards of ground swept by machine-guns. Commanding A Company, 8th Bn. attd. 9th Bn., Royal Welsh Fusiliers. Aged 24. Born 16th April 1892, Wrexham. Second son of John Kerrison Jones (assistant overseer and chief collector), of Glasfryn, Wrexham. Educated at Grove Park, Wrexham, where he carried off the Mayor's gold medal before leaving for Oxford. Won a scholarship. He was a student at University College, Oxford, and passed First Class Mods, He was at the university when war broke out, and, as a member of the OTC, he at once offered his services to the country. He was given a commission, and was posted to the 8th Royal Welsh Fusiliers. He went to the Dardanelles with his battalion, April 1915 and quickly secured company rank. Whilst in Gallipoli, he was slightly wounded, and early this year was invalided home suffering from dysentery. On his recovery, he went to France. Father applied for his medals. Memorial Ref. Pier and Face 4 A., Thiepval Memorial, France.

KEAY, Lieutenant, James Gordon. Died of wounds, at London Brigade Casualty Clearing Station 2nd July 1916 received in action near Neuve Chapelle the previous day. 2nd /5th Bn., Royal Warwickshire Regiment. Aged 20. Younger son of Ernest Charles (Ironmaster and Engineer) and Edith Helen Keay of Longmynd, 28, Westfield Road, Edgbaston, Birmingham. Born Edgbaston, Warwick, 25th August 1895; Educated Aldro School, Eastbourne; Charterhouse (Gownboys) (where he was a member of the OTC., passing the examination for promotion), and at Clare College, Cambridge, leaving after one term in residence to take a commission in the 2/5th Bn.,Royal Warwickshire Regiment; Gazetted 2nd Lieutenant 4th January 1915, and promoted Lieutenant 3rd August following; trained at Northampton, Essex, and on Salisbury Plain; served with the Expeditionary Force in France and Flanders from 21st May 1916; was seconded for duty with the 182nd Trench Mortar Battery in June. He was fond of all sport, and while at Aldro School was in the first football and cricket elevens, and at Charterhouse (Gownboys 1909 – 1914) he obtained his House Football and Swimming Colours. St. Augustine's Edgbaston War Memorial. Captain E. D. Keay applied for medals on behalf of James's mother. Memorial Ref. VII. A. 20., Merville Communal Cemetery, France.

Greater Love Hath No Man Than This That A Man Lay Down His Life To Save His Friends

KELLY, Lieutenant, Charles Patrick. Killed in action whilst commanding the stretcher-bearer division of his field ambulance, 2nd July 1916. 96th Field Ambulance, Royal Army Medical Corps. Aged 26. Brother of Mr. A. P. Kelly, of the Chalet, Arranmore Road, Herbert Park, Dublin. Third son of Mr. T. P. Kelly and Mrs. Kelly, 63 Northumberland Road, Dublin. He was educated at Woburn Park, Weybridge, Surrey, Ushaw (1903), Trinity College, Dublin, where he took his BA in December, 1913, and his M.B., B.A.O., B.Ch. in April, 1914. He went to Southport Infirmary as medical officer and later took over charge of the fever hospital at Fazakerley, near Liverpool. When released from command there, in August, 1915, he took a commission in the RAMC and proceeded to France with the 96th Field Ambulance. Entered France, 8th November 1915. Mother applied for his medals. Memorial Ref. I. A. 29., Dive Copse British Cemetery, Sailly-Le-Sec, France.

KIRK, Second Lieutenant, Thomas James. Died of wounds, 2nd July 1916. D Coy. 2nd Bn., Essex Regiment. Twenty casualties were caused on the 2nd July 1916. Previously sergeant, 6 Devon's, 5448. Commissioned 5th March 1916. Entered France 16th December 1914. Application for medals from Dulwich. His step-mother Elizabeth Mary Kirk of Brentwood, Essex received his pension. Memorial Ref. Pier and Face 10 D., Thiepval Memorial, France.

LAMAISON, Lieutenant, Leonard William Henry. Killed by a sniper being shot through the head, whilst trying to bring in a wounded man from the open, 2nd July 1916. 2nd /5th Bn., Royal Warwickshire Regiment. Aged 40. Eldest son of William Englebert and Marian Lamaison, of Southwold, Kenley, Surrey. Husband of Charlotte Florence Barton (Formerly Lamaison), of Esmeryl, Dehra Dun, India. Born 29th June 1876 at 17, The Waldrons, Croydon. Attended Hazelwood School and Harrow. Elder son of William Lamaison (O.H.), Barrister-at-Law, of Southwold, Kenley, Surrey, and of his wife, Marian Lamaison. Married, in 1904, Charlotte Florence May. Became a Solicitor with Powell, Burt and Lamaison. Lieutenant Lamaison joined the Inns of Courts OTC in September, 1914, and was subsequently given a commission in the Royal Warwickshire Regiment, 14th March 1915. He went to the Front in May, 1916, and was killed by a sniper, on July 2nd, 1916, in Moated Grange, near Neuve Chapelle, while endeavouring to answer a cry for help from one of his men. Solicitor. In France, three weeks. Widow, Mrs. C. P. Barlow applied for medals from India. Memorial Ref. I. J. 7., Rue-Du-Bacquerot No.1 Military Cemetery, Laventie, France.

Blessed Are The Pure In Heart

LEE, Second Lieutenant, Arthur Basil. Reported that he was leading his men along a trench that had just been taken when a German officer from a dug-out shot him with a revolver, 2nd July 1916. 5th Bn., West Yorkshire Regiment (Prince of Wales's Own). Aged 20. Only son of Charles Arthur (manager of the Ilkley branch of the Bank of Liverpool) and Sarah Lee, of 1, Wells Walk, Ilkley, Yorks. Member of Ilkley RFC. Employed Messrs. Sutherland, Parker & Co. stuff merchants, Bradford. He joined the West Riding Divisional Ammunition column early in the war and after three months service secured a commission. Went to the Front, 8th July 1915 and was accidentally wounded. On the 1st July, battalion withdrawn and ordered to occupy Schwaben Redoubt which was reached by a small party. Father applied for his medals. Memorial Ref. Pier and Face 2 A 2 C and 2 D., Thiepval Memorial, France.

LORENZEN, Second Lieutenant, Otto Hans Herman. Mortally wounded close to the enemy's front line trench where the wire was uncut, died 2nd July 1916 at No. 20 Casualty Clearing Station, of wounds received. The attack had started at midnight. 7th Bn., Middlesex Regiment attacked with the 5th Bn., Lincolnshire Regiment. Aged 22. Born in 1893 at Aldgate, London. Resided East Finchley with his wife. Son of Danish-born Christian Carl, a chronometer maker, and Ellen Elizabeth Lorenzen, of Dalkeith, The Bishops Avenue. London. Employed as a clerk. Enlisted as an other rank on 3rd September 1914, in the 3/9th (City of London) Battalion (Queen Victoria's Own), The London Regiment, with which he eventually attained the rank of acting corporal. He obtained a commission in September 1915, in the 4/7th Bn., Middlesex Regiment and arrived on the Western Front in May 1916. Memorial Ref. I. E. 2., Warlincourt Halte British Cemetery, Saulty, France.

MEYER, Lieutenant, Constant Clifford William. Lincolnshire Regiment. Died of wounds, 3rd July 1916 a note in the war diary states died of wounds against the 1st July entry. Shot in the stomach in the German trench after gallantly leading his platoon that loved him dearly to the assault, died of wounds from internal hemorrhage. When at the dressing station he said to the doctor "Don't mind me, dress the men." Age 20. Second son of Mr. and Mrs. H.C.F. Meyer of Wise House, Dacca, Bengal, India. Born 3rd March 1896. Estate agent. Next of kin, 170 Worpole Road, Wimbledon. Attended Beaumont College 1905 to 1912 a member of the OTC. Wimbledon College 1912 to 1914. A fine tennis player and won three open tournaments in France. Enlisted 24th September 1914. Attended RMC Sandhurst. Treated for 13 days at 2nd General Hospital from 1st April 1916 with an injury to the forearm. Commissioned May 1915 and to lieutenant just before his death. Private R. W. Clarke, 2nd Lincolns was awarded the Military Medal when he carried the wounded officer of his platoon from the German trenches to the British Line the officer later dying in hospital. Mr. S. C. H. Meyer , brother of the deceased, presented Private Clarke with a gold watch on behalf of the parents living in India. The watch was inscribed "R. W. Clarke in grateful remembrance of heroic gallantry to Lieut. C. W. Meyer of the 2nd Lincoln Regt. on the July 1st 1916." Father applied for his medals. Memorial Ref. Daours Communal Cemetery, Somme, France WO 339/47302

I Plucked It In All Its Fresh Beauty Before The Scorching Breeze Had Tarnished Its Purity

MURPHY, Second Lieutenant, Philip Frederick. Killed in action, by a shell burst whilst consolidating, 2nd July 1916. 201st Field Coy., Royal Engineers. Tottenham Grammar School Roll of Honour (1895 – 1900). Formerly in the surveyors department of the Leyton Urban Council. Leaves a wife and one child. Born 24th November 1885. After gaining experience under Mr. W. H. Prescott M.Inst. C.E, he became in 1904 Chief Engineering Assistant to Mr. William Dawson M.Inst C.E, Leyton where he was engaged on the construction of the tramway track, car depot, new roads etc. as well as revising the ordnance survey. Associate Member of the Institute of Chartered Engineers, 10th January 1911. Entered France, 6th December 1915. Son, Philip Arthur Murphy born 25th November 1915. Widow, Humberstone Road, Cambridge applied for his medals. Memorial Ref. Pier and Face 8 A and 8 D., Thiepval Memorial, France

NOWELL, Second Lieutenant, Francis Percival. Died in a field ambulance hospital from wounds received the previous day, 2nd July 1916. 18th Bn., West Yorkshire Regiment (Prince of Wales's Own). Son of Mr. David Oldham Nowell and Elizabeth Ann Kenworthy of Westfield, Victoria Park, Shipley, Yorks. Aged 22. Educated Bradford Grammar School. Commissioned as a Second Lieutenant 26th February 1915, appointed 9th June 1915. Captain Francis M. Horner wrote 'if there was a vote as to which officer would get the Military Cross, Frank would get it'. Entered Egypt, 22nd December 1915. Mother applied for his medals. Memorial Ref. I. C. 20., Couin British Cemetery, France.

RAINE, Second Lieutenant, George Kenneth. Wounded in an attack on the village of Serre, he died of his wounds the following day on 2nd July 1916. 16th Bn. attd. 18th Bn., Durham Light Infantry. Aged 19. Son of George and Elizabeth J. Raine, of 61, Percy Park, Tynemouth. Born 17th December 1896. He was educated at Tynemouth School then Epworth College, Rhyl. Attended Armstrong College Newcastle University. Attended University's OTC. George was commissioned in November 1914 just before his 18th birthday from the University's OTC. Previously wounded at Hooge in 1915, whilst attd. to 2nd Bn., Durham Light Infantry. He was seriously wounded on this attachment and in September 1915 was sent home. He then returned to the Western Front on Good Friday April 21st 1916. Entered France, 17th August 1915. Father applied for his medals. Memorial Ref. I. A. 11., Gezaincourt Communal Cemetery Extension, France.

Wounded 1915. Mortally Wounded Somme July 1st. Aged 19 Deeds Not Years.

RAPER, Major, Robert George. Gallantly superintending an operation by two companies and had just succeeded in carrying out his objective, when a machine-gun swept the whole front and he was killed instantaneously, 2nd July 1916. 8th Bn., South Staffordshire Regiment. Third Son of Mr. and Mrs. William Augustus Raper of Battle, Sussex. Husband of Mrs. I Raper of Richards Hill, Battle, Sussex. Aged 39. Attended Tonbridge, 1891 - 1894 and joined the Cadet Corps. Solicitor with his father's office and then, on passing his Final Law Examination, became managing clerk to Mr. T. V. Pearse, of Wiveliscombe, in Somerset. Retired 1912 and rejoined received captaincy, November 1914. Promoted Major, May 1915.

He took a prominent part in Conservative electioneering campaigns in the Eye Division of Sussex, being a speaker on Tariff Reform, amongst other subjects. Attended Cranleigh. Soon after leaving school he joined the Volunteers, with a commission in the 5th (Cinque Ports) Bn., Royal Sussex Regt. In the Boer War he volunteered for foreign service, but was attached to the 8th (Militia) Bn., Royal Sussex Regt. for garrison duty at Shorncliffe, where he remained during the whole of the war, and was promoted to his captaincy. After the war he returned to command B Company of the Cinque Forts Battn. and, when the territorial scheme was introduced and they became a territorial battalion, he remained with them as a captain.

Major Raper was twice invalided home early in 1916, but finally rejoined his Regiment at the Front at the end of February. On February 4th , 1916, their Commanding Officer, Lieut.-Colonel G. N. Going, was promoted to Brigadier, and Major Raper became second in command. On July 2nd , as the Commanding Officer stated, Major Raper "was gallantly superintending an operation by two companies and had just succeeded in carrying out his objective, when a machine-gun swept the whole front and he was killed instantaneously. Earlier in the day," he added. " I had occasion to notice several pieces of excellent work that he did, and I intend sending in his name to the higher authorities." Major Raper was mentioned in Sir Douglas Haig's Despatch dated November 13th , 1916.

His old Commanding Officer, then in command of another Brigade, said :— " I always looked on him as a man of the highest character and principles, absolutely brave himself and inspiring courage in others. It win indeed be hard to replace him in the Regiment." The Brigadier of the 51st Brigade also wrote to Major Raper's widow as follows:— " I know all the Brigade joins me in offering you my deep sympathy in your great loss. I know it will be a comfort to you to know that he suffered no pain at all, and that he knew that his countrymen were winning and that his own gallant Regiment was covering itself with glory'. The main street in Fricourt is named after him 'Rue du Major Raper'. Son William Augustus Raper born 3rd July 1916, Pamela Ross born 20th October 1912 and Josephine Ellis Baxter. His widow applied for his medals but returned the Victory Medal for a replacement. Original burial map reference 62D.F.9.a.77.95 in a piece of land measuring 7 by 5 metres purchased by the next of kin in an isolated grave at Fricourt. On the 28th June 1965 his remains were exhumed and he was reburied in Fricourt British Cemetery. Memorial Ref. B. 24A., Fricourt British Cemetery, France.

ROWLEY, Captain, Dalbiac Thomas Cotton. Died of wounds No. 92 Field Ambulance, at Warloy-Baillon, 2nd July 1916 of wounds sustained 1st July. C Coy., 2nd Bn. attd. 4th Bn., Middlesex Regiment. Aged 28. Son of Richard Cotton Rowley and Margaret Rowley, of Harpenden, Herts. Born 7th April 1889 at Kinpton. Attended Haileybury College (Batten 1903-1908). Husband of Olive Marie Gower Rowley, of 94, High St., Kensington. Father of Olive Margaret Cotton Rowley. Captain 15th March 1915. Married 23rd June 1915. He entered France on 1st January 1915. July 21st 1915 wounded by gunshot to the right thigh and slight head wound, by the 22nd in the Royal Hospital, Woolwich. Effects were handkerchief, pipe, cigarette case, tobacco pouch, wrist watch, pencil, badges, buttons, wallet containing photos, letters, photograph, advance book and cheque book. Medal Index Card has the 1st July 1916. Widow applied for his medals and daughter Olive Margaret Cotton Rowley entitled to his pensions. Memorial Ref. I. B. 18., Warloy-Baillon Communal Cemetery Extension, France. WO 339/7411

Until The Day Break

THE OFFICERS OF THE 2ND BATTALION, MIDDLESEX REGIMENT

From left to right are : Back row—2nd Lieutenant R. S. Lindsell, 2nd Lieutenant R. J. Young, 2nd Lieutenant H. B. W. Savile, 2nd Lieutenant T. L. Mills, Lieutenant J. J. Macartney ; middle row—Lieutenant and Quartermaster H. A. Wiemers, 2nd Lieutenant C. M. Harvey (killed), Lieutenant F. A. H. Castberg (killed), Lieutenant H. A. O. Hanley, Captain A. H. Hooper (killed), Lieutenant A. Fergusson, Captain D. C. Owen, Captain H. L. Homan (killed), Lieutenant D. T. C. Rowley, ——, Captain C. A. S. Page ; front row—Captain and Adjutant A. G. Wordsworth (killed), Captain F. W. Ramsay, Major W. C. C. Ash, Lieut.-Colonel R. H. Hayes, Lieut.-General Hon. H. Kent, Brigadier-General Heath, Major J. H. Hall, Captain H. P. F. Bicknell, Captain R. M. Heath, D.S.O.

SERNBERG, Captain, Allan. Reported amongst the fallen, 2nd July 1916. Listed locally as being killed on the 1st July killed on the 2nd July when the attack was made in the afternoon on La Boisselle. 9th Bn., Cheshire Regiment. Born 1873. Son of William and Annabella Sernberg. Seen considerable amount of service with the Colours, home and abroad having joined the army, March 1895. Served in India. At the start of the war he was a non-commissioned officer and obtained his commission, December 1914 being gazetted captain April 1915. Been at the front a considerable time, leaves a widow (Martha) and three children, Allan Rowland, Ada Amelia and Donald Theodore. Memorial Ref. Pier and Face 3 C and 4 A., Thiepval Memorial, France.

SHEARMAN, Lieutenant, Herbert Henry. Died of wounds, 5th July 1916. 2nd Entrenching Bn., formerly 1st Bn., Lincolnshire Regiment. A note in the war diary against the 1st July 1916 has died of wounds. Age 26. Son of Charles and Louise Shearman of Tynemouth. Local papers report 5th died of wounds. Attested 10th August 1914 with the Royal Engineers, No. 28218. Commissioned 31st October 1914. Surveyor. Married Dora Lambert on the 8th February 1916. Effects were cigarette case, cheque book, tobacco pouch, pipes, photo case, card case, wrist watch/strap (damaged), card case, snap shots and bullets. Sister resided in Sutton Coldfield. Two telegrams went to his sister, the first on the 7th July stated died of wounds on the 5th July, the second on the 8th stated missing believed killed. In hospital with fractured ankle from 18th April 1915 to the 10th May 1915. Miss E. R. Shearman , Chelsea SW3 choose his inscription. Grave Ref. Plot. 1. Row B. Grave 44. Corbie Communal Cemetery Extension, Somme, France. WO 339/15057

Dimicans Pro Patria

SIMPSON, Second Lieutenant, George Arnold. Died of wounds from the 1st on the 2nd July 1916. Reported wounded locally. Wounded establishing guns to support and protect the Division's left flank. 5th Bn., Leinster Regiment. Gazetted 16th April 1915. Appointed to Leinster Regiment, January 1916. Seconded for service with the 64th Machine Gun Corp. Formerly 13th Bn., London Regiment, private, 2314. Entered France, 11th February 1915. Memorial Ref. Pier and Face 16 C., Thiepval Memorial, France.

SPENCER, Lieutenant, Arthur Egerton. When he fell was in charge of a wire cutting party at Fricourt Wood, 2nd July 1916 during a burst of machine-gun fire he dropped into a trench on the enemy's side and was killed by bombs. 3rd Bn. attd. 10th Bn., Sherwood Foresters (Notts and Derby Regiment). Aged 20. Son of Dr. Edward Macready Spencer, of Builth Wells, Breconshire. Born Black Torrington, Devon on 24th March 1896. Educated Kelly College, Tavistock, Devon. Won an open scholarship at Sidney Sussex College, Cambridge with war preventing him from his residence where he intended to study history. A relative of General Sir Neville Macready, Adjutant of the Forces. Kelly College War Memorial, and a brass plaque in Tavistock church, Devon. Colonel Gilbert hoped to place a cross to mark the spot where he fell. Father applied for his medals. Memorial Ref. Pier and Face 10 C 10 D and 11 A., Thiepval Memorial, France.

St. JOHN, Second Lieutenant, Thomas, DCM. Died of wounds, 2nd July 1916. 1st Bn., East Lancashire Regiment attd No. 2 Section, 11th Machine Gun Company supported the 1st B., Hampshire Regiment in the advance. Aged 24. Son of John and Catherine St. John, of Longsight, Manchester. Gazetted 1st April 1915 for DCM whilst Acting Sergeant Major, 1st Bn, No. 9555, for conspicuous gallantry at Le Gheer on 15th January 1915, in voluntarily going a distance of 35 yards in front of his trench in daylight and assisting in the rescue of a wounded man (who was still being fired at) and conveying him to cover, whilst exposed to heavy fire. Formerly East Lancashire Regiment, sergeant, 9555. Entered France, 22nd August 1914. Commissioned 25th July 1915. Seconded to Machine Gun Company, 23rd December 1915. Medals to Mrs. D. M. Craig, Sheffield. Memorial Ref. II. E. 37., Auchonvillers Military Cemetery, France.

STOW, Lieutenant Colonel, Montague Bruce. Died of wounds in No. 34 Casualty Clearing Station of wounds received earlier in the day, officially, 2nd July 1916. War diary states 1st July 1916. 1st Bn., East Yorkshire Regiment. Aged 32. Son of Montague Haslam and Mrs. Margaret Jane Stow. Born Hampstead, 22nd May 1884. Educated Repton and RMC Sandhurst. Cricket in the Repton XI in 1901. Repton School Memorial (1898). Husband of Gladys M. C. Doughty (formerly Stow), of Napier House, Sidcup, Kent. Married 23rd February 1914. ADC to Governor of Bengal, 1913. Gazetted 1903, 1906, 1914, 1915 and Lieutenant Colonel, 3rd June 1916. Served with his regiment in Burma and India and rejoined his regiment in August 1915. Entered France, 17th August 1915. Left a son. Mrs. G. M. C. Doughty applied for her late husband's medals, Napier House, Sidcup, Kent. Admision and discharge book states he was admitted on the 1st July with a fracture of the femur and died on the 2nd July although the 1st July has been crossed through. Pension payments to his son, James Montague Stow started 3rd July so these records also took 2nd July as date of death. Memorial Ref. II. A. 7., Daours Communal Cemetery Extension, France.

Splendid He Passed Into The Light That Nevermore Shall Fade

THOMPSON, Major, Frederick Charles. Posted as missing, 2nd July 1916. 1st /5th Bn., West Yorkshire Regiment (Prince of Wales's Own). Aged 42. Son of W. and A. J. Thompson, of York. Husband of D. Thompson, of 6, Edinburgh Terrace, Acomb, York. . On the 1st July, battalion withdrawn and ordered to occupy Schwaben Redoubt which was reached by a small party. Entered France, 15th April 1915. H. Davis Thompson Esq. (solicitors) applied for medals on behalf of his widow. Memorial Ref. Pier and Face 2 A 2 C and 2 D., Thiepval Memorial, France.

TRECHMANN, Second Lieutenant, Kuno Griffith. He fell about 1.00pm on Sunday, 2nd July 1916. He fell while bravely leading his men in the storming of Fricourt. He was shot through the head and died instantaneously. 12th Bn., Northumberland Fusiliers. Aged 20. Elder son of Dr. Emil J. and Marian N. Trechmann, of 27, Langland Gardens, Hampstead, London late of Sydney, New South Wales. Attended University College School, Hampstead. Commissioned 1914. His platoon gave touching proof of there devotion to him, it so happened that we had to retire from the place where he fell and so it was impossible to bring him away. However when darkness fell some of his men stole away from our line and brought him in. He was buried in Becordel Valley. Father applied for his medals. Memorial Ref. Pier and Face 10 B 11 B and 12 B., Thiepval Memorial, France.

SOME OF THE OFFICERS OF THE 12TH SERVICE BATTALION, NORTHUMBERLAND FUSILIERS

Mentioned in General Sir Douglas Haig's recent despatch for excellent work in the field

From left to right are: Back row—2nd Lieut. G. P. Stirling, 2nd Lieut. R. F. Woodhouse; middle row—2nd Lieut. K. G. Trechmann, Interpreter M. Preton, 2nd Lieut. P. R. Cowell, 2nd Lieut. R. C. Hobson, Lieut. E. A. Malcolm, 2nd Lieut. J. C. Wrench, Lieut. J. Brunton, 2nd Lieut. A. McArthur, 2nd Lieut. C. N. G. Koch; front row—2nd Lieut. J. L. Hay, Lieut. G. M. Philip, 2nd Lieut. L. Borrell, Captain E. H. Griffin, Colonel H. B. Warwick, Lieut. and Adjutant G. White, Captain J Locke, Captain H W. Gush, Lieut. J. Bailey; seated in front—Lieut. D. E. Waight

WALCOTT, Lieutenant, Lyons George Edmund. Led his platoon to within a few yards of the German wire when he was shot in the head, 2nd July 1916. At midnight the front line of platoons went forward and very heavy rifle and machine-gun fire was opened up while Verey lights and flares lit the whole front line. 5th Bn., Lincolnshire Regiment. Aged 25. Son of Lyons Roden Sympson Walcott, J.P., and Jean Cleland Walcott. He was originally a member of the London Scottish, but on appointment to the Land Valuation Scheme in Lincolnshire joined the territorial regiment. His Colonel said that in a night attack, " Walcott led his platoon in a most gallant manner to within a few yards of the German wire, where he was shot through the head." Sergeant T. G. Goodchild went out to find the body but was unsuccessful for this and other acts he was awarded the DCM. Entered France, 25th June 1915. Medals to Mrs. L. Walcott, St. George's Square, SW. After the action, Sergeant T. G. Goodchild went out in an attempt to find the body but was unsuccessful. Original burial map reference 57.DE.28.B.18. Inscription chosen by Mrs. Lyons Walcott, The Ladies Army & Navy Club, Burlington Gardens, London. Memorial Ref. I. H. 26., Gommecourt Wood New Cemetery, Foncquevillers, France.

This Gallant But Gentle Youth He Helped

WHEATCROFT, Lieutenant, Ronald Duncan. At 8.45am., Lieutenant Wheatcroft at head of his platoon crossed our wire, all but Sergeant Wagg being hit and withdrew to old sap, almost at once badly wounded. The left platoon of A Coy got over the parapet under Lieutenant Wheatcroft, the barrage was very heavy and Lieutenant Wheatcroft was almost at once badly wounded. Sergeant Dick Wagg carried him back to the trenches and he died of wounds, 2nd July 1916. 6th Bn., Sherwood Foresters (Notts and Derby Regiment). Aged 26. Sixth and youngest son of George Hanson Wheatcroft J. P., and Ada Maria Wheatcroft, of Waltham House, Wirksworth. Derbyshire. Rugby School entered in 1903 and left in 1908. He then went up to New College, Oxford, where he took his degree with Honours. He became a member of the Inner Temple, and had just passed the Final Bar Examination when War was declared. While living in London, he had become a member of the Cavendish Club, and worked for the Oxford Mission and for the Rugby Club at Notting Hill, where he served on the Staff. A sergeant in the Inns of Court OTC at the outbreak of war, he received his commission in September, 1914, and was promoted lieutenant in the following December. He went to the Front in France 26th February, 1915, and saw much active service there. An Officer wrote ;- "He died the best of deaths, at the head of his platoon, leading a forlorn hope. He was the bravest of the brave. Only a few days before, he did a most gallant action. He went out into' No Man's Land' under machine-gun fire to render aid to a covering party of the 7th Battalion, who had been wounded by that fire. He died as he had lived, brave, fearless, cheerful, a very gallant gentleman." Brothers, Second Lieutenant G. H. Wheatcroft was killed near Mailly-Maillet, on August 11th, 1915 by a bursting shell. Father applied for his medals. Memorial Ref. I. F. 14., Warlincourt Halte British Cemetery, Saulty, France.

He Died The Nobled Death Fighting For God And Right And Liberty

WILLIAMSON, Second Lieutenant, Cyril George. On July 2nd the 10/Warwicks took over the front line from Keats Redan to Argyll Street, west and northwest of La Boisselle, with three companies in the line. Orders were received that a major attempt to capture La Boisselle would be made at 2.15am on July 3 with the battalion in brigade reserve. Before that there was heavy shelling with one officer and five other ranks killed and two officers and thirty-four other ranks wounded and nine missing, six of whom were known to be buried alive. One of those killed was Second Lieutenant Cyril Williamson from Selly Park, Birmingham, 2nd July 1916. 10th Bn., Royal Warwickshire Regiment. Aged 22. Only son of Sarah Elizabeth Williamson and Arthur Williamson, of Newlyn, Selly Park Road, Selly Park, Birmingham. Born in Birmingham in 1894. Attended Solihull Grammar School and joined its OTC and received his education at the University of Birmingham, BSc. Institute of Chemistry. Cricket XI at St. Edward's School, Oxford. Wrote a letter of sympathy in March 1916 to the relatives of Coventry man, Private George Clifford. Gazetted to the 13th Battalion and transferred. Gazetted 14th August 1915. Entered France, 10th February 1916. Memorial Ref. Pier and Face 9 A 9 B and 10 B., Thiepval Memorial, France.

WITHY, Lieutenant, Basil. Fatally wounded in the abdomen and left hand, in action with No. 4 Company on the 1st July and admitted to 96 Field Ambulance. He died from the effects of his wounds in 21 Casualty Clearing Station (Corbie) the following day, 2nd July. Private, 16400, S. R. Steele described how he found what he thought was the dead body of Lieutenant Withy some thirty minutes after the battle started, motionless, with a broken glass morphine vial in his hand. He had lapsed into unconsciousness and was bought to the Casualty Clearing Station. 18th Bn., The King's (Liverpool Regiment). Aged 30. Born in West Hartlepool, 31st January 1886. Third and youngest son of Henry (shipbuilder, Furness, Withy and Co. Ltd.) and Mary Forrest Withy, Of Brantford House, West Hartlepool. Educated Uppingham and Strathclyde University. Served apprenticeship with his father's shipping firm which qualified him as a naval architect. Employed Messrs. Denny Brothers, Leven Shipyard, Dumbarton and prior to the war was engaged in the scientific department of that firm. Sometime after the outbreak of war did excellent work with the Dumbarton Red Cross organisation. Enlisted in Liverpool on the 1st September 1914 as Private No. 15140 and posted to the 18th Bn., King's Liverpool Regiment excelled until receiving his commission. Appointed machine-gun officer before crossing to France on the 6th November 1915. November 1916, father Mr. Henry Withy J.P paid £500 for a cot in Cameron Hospital, West Hartlepool in memory of his son. Commemorated on the West Hartlepool War Memorial, the war memorial in All Saints Church, Stranton, Hartlepool and on the memorial board in Hartlepool Rugby Football club. Father applied for his medals. Memorial Ref. I. A. 47., La Neuville British Cemetery, Corbie, France.

Bibliography

A memorial records of Watsonians who served in the Great War 1914 – 1918. Edinburgh 1920.

Adcock, A St. John For Remembrance Soldier poets who have fallen in the war.

Adler, Michael Rev. British Jewry Book of Honour. (1922)

Allardyce, Desborough Mabel. University of Aberdeen. Roll of Service in the Great War. 1914 – 1919 (1921)

Allinson, John. Smith, Charlotte. Great Ideas; Leighton Park School and the First World War (2014)

Arbroath and District Roll of Honour 1914 1919 (1921)

Arscott, David. Floreat Lewys 500 Years of Lewes Old Grammar School. (2012)

Artists Rifles. Regimental Roll of Honour and War Record 1914-1919

Baker, Allan C. Allen Civil TD. Bagnalls of Stafford: Builders of Locomotives for the World's Railways: the Firm and Its Folk 2008

Bank of Ireland Staff Service Record, Great War 1914 - 1918

Barton, Peter. The Somme. A New Panoramic Perspective. (2006)

Bell, Ernest W. Soldiers killed on the First Day of the Somme. (1977)

Beresford, Charles. The Bath at War. A Derbyshire Community and the Great War.

Bickersteth, John. The Bickersteth Diaries 1914 – 1918 (1998)

Blaney, Rob. Alsager in the Great War. (2016)

Bosher, J. F. Imperial Vancouver Island. Who was who 1850 1950 (2010)

Bostrom, Alex. An Oxford College at War: Corpus Christi College, 1914-18 (2018)

Bradfield College Register Sixteenth Edition (1924)

Brown, Malcolm. The Imperial War Museum Book of the Somme (1997)

Brown, S. W. Leighton Park. A History of the School (1952)

Brett-James, Norman. Gifford, John. Mill Hill Book of Remembrance and War Record. (1922)

Brett-James, Norman. G. Mill Hill. 1938

British Roll of Honour. The Roll of Honour of the Empire's Heroes. Privated circulation

Clan Donald Roll of Honour. The Clan Donald Roll of Honour Committee (1931).

Clayton, Derek. From Pontefract to Picardy. The 9th King's Own Yorkshire Light Infantry in the First World War. (2004)

Cockman, C. R. Thomas, C. L.R. Roll of Honour and War List, 1914-1918 of University College School, Hampstead

Colchester Royal Grammar School in the Great War

Cooksey, Jon. Murland, Jerry. The First Day of the Somme. Gommecourt to Marricourt. A Visitors Guide. (2016)

Cooksey, Jon. Barnsley Pals. The 13th and 14th Battalions York and Lancaster Regiment. A History of the two battalions raised by Barnsley in World War One. (1996)

Cooper, Stephen. After the Final Whistle. The First Rugby World Cup and the First World War (2015)

The Regimental Roll of Honour and War Record of the Artists Rifles (1922)

Cornwell, John. Hear Their Footsteps. King Edward VII School, Sheffield and the Old Edwardians in the Great War 1914 1918 (2016)

Croydon and the Great War. The Official History of the War Work of the Borough and its citizens from 1914 to 1919 together with the Croydon Roll of Honour. Edited by H. Keatley Moore. (1920)

Dixon, Herbert A. Tootal Broadhurst, E. A Record of the Manchester City Battalions of the 90th and 91st Infantry Brigades. Book of Honour (1916) Drum, Neil. Dowson, Roger. God's Own 1st Salford Pals 1914 1916 An account of the 15th (Service) Battalion Lancashire Fusiliers. (2003)

Dover College Register Centenary Edition October 1871 to July 1971 (1972)

Dulwich College War Record (1923)

Duncan, Leland L. Colfe's Grammar School and The Great War 1914-19 (1920)

Dunfermline High School Roll of Honour of the Pupils and Staff (1920)

Edwards, C. E. Merchiston Caste School. Roll of Honour 1921

Evans, Gareth. A Century in the Life of Merton Court School, Sidcup. 1899 – 1999. (1999)

Ewing, J. C. Major. The Royal Scots 1914 - 1919 (1920)

Firth, David. The Golden Age of Cricket 1890 – 1914.

Galloway, David. In Splendid Manner. The Prestwich Roll of Honour 1914 – 1918.

George Heriot's School Roll of Honour 1914 1919 (1921)

Glasgow Academy Roll of Honour 1914 – 1918 (1918)

Grayson, Richard S. Belfast Boys. How Unionists and Nationalists fought and died together in the First World War (2010)

Green, Edward, Downton and the First World War. (2002)

Griffiths, Ann. The Great War of 1914 to 1918. Havant's Roll of Honour (2014)

Grimwade, Captain F. Clive. The War History of the 4th Battalion The London Regiment (Royal Fusiliers) 1914 1919. (1922)

Gunn, Dr. The Book of Remembrance for Tweeddale

Hallport, D. H. Camberwell Grammar School. A Short History of the Foundation, under Royal Charter of Edward Wilson, Clerk, in Camberwell in the County of Surrey, commonly called Wilson's Grammar School including an account of the former Greencoat School (1964)

Halstead, Timothy. A School in Arms. Uppingham and the Great War. (2017)

Hampshire Regimental Journal

Harkin, Trevor. City of Coventry. Roll of the Fallen (2011)

Harkin, Trevor. Polo and the Great War, (2016)

Harkin, Trevor. Brighton and the Great War (2014)

Harkin, Trevor. Bablake School and the Great War (2009)

Highland Light Infantry Chronicle

Hildrey, Trevor W. To Answer Duty's Call. Remembering the Old Crosbeians who fell in World War 1.

Hillhead High School War Memorial Volume (1921)

Hills, J. D. Captain MC, Croix de Guerre. The Fifth Leicestershire. A Record of the 1/5th Battalion the Leicestershire Regiment during the war 1914 1919 (1919)

History of the King's Regiment (Liverpool) 1914-1919

Hodgson, Linda & Sarah Lee. The Stars of Night. Roll of Honour. Old Boys of Carlisle Grammar School who fell in the war 1914 1918 ((2014)

Hurst, Steve. The Public Schools Battalion in The Great War. 'Goodbye Picadilly'. (2007)

Iles, Lesley. Baker. John. (2008). They Rest From Their Labours. The stories behind the names on the Southend High School for Boys Roll of Honour 1914 – 1918

Jamaicas Part in the Great War 1914 1918

Jarvis, Jeffrey. The Southend & District. Roll of Honour 1914 -1921. (1998)

Kempster, F. Brigadier General. Westropp. H.C.E Brigadier General. Manchester City Battalions of the 90th & 91st Infantry Brigades. Book of Honour. 1916

Lancashire Fusiliers Annual

Lancing Register The Third Edition Revised and Continued to 1932 (1933)

Last, Simon. Aldeburgh War Memorial The Story Behind the Names 1914 1918 (2014)

Lavery, Felix. Irish Heroes in the War (1917 Reprint)

Lethbridge, J. P. Birmingham in the First World War (1993)

Linge, Pam and Ken. Missing but not Forgotten. Men of the Thiepval Memorial, Somme. (2015)

Linnell, Reverend C. L. S Gresham's School History and Register 1555 - 1954

London County Council. Record of Service in the Great War 1914 – 1918 by Members of the Council Staff. (1922).

Loretto Roll of Honour 1914 – 1920 (1921)

Lloyd, Mark. The London Scottish in the Great War. (2001)

Lowe, W. D. Lieut-Col. DSO, MC. War History of the 18th Battalion Durham Light Infantry (1920)

Lyon, Neil. Four Centuries. The History of Wellingborough School. 2nd Ed. (2001)

MacDonald, Lyn. Somme. (1993)

MacDonald, Alan. A Lack of Offensive Spirit? The 46th (North Midland) Division at Gommecourt, 1st July 1916 (2008)

MacDonald, Alan. Pro Patria Mori. The 56th (1st London) Division at Gommecourt, 1st July 1916 (2008)

Mace, Martin. Grehan, John. Slaughter on the Somme 1st July 1916. The complete war diaries of the British Army's worst day. (2016)

MacKenzie, John E. Major. University of Edinburgh Roll of Honour (1921)

Maddocks, Graham. Liverpool Pals. 17th, 18th, 19th, 20th Battalion. The King's (Liverpool Regiment). (1991)

Majendie, V.H.B Major, DSO. A History of the 1st Battalion The Somerset Light Infantry. July 1st 1916 to the end of the war. (1921)

McCrery, Nigel. The Final Season. The footballers who fought and died in the Great War. (2014)

McPherson, Eric. Remembered with Honour. The Old Boys and staff of Bolton School who died in two world wars. (2009)

Merchiston Castle School Roll of Honour 1914 1919 (1921)

Merckx, Elaine. Rigby, Neal. Some other and wider destiny. Wakefield Grammar School Foundation and the Great War. (2017)

Middlebrook, Martin. The First Day on the Somme. Revised Edition. (2016)

Middleton, Ian. Hillfoots Armed Forces Fatalities 1914 – 1919

Milner, Laurie. Leeds Pals. A History of the 15th (Service) Battalion (1st Leeds)

Moller, F. S. Alumni Felstedienses Being a list of boys entered at Felsted School May 1564 – September 1931. (1931)

National Union of Teachers War Record 1914 – 1919

Prince of Wales's Own (West Yorkshire Regiment) 1914 1918 (1998)

Morris, J. A. A History of the Latymer School at Edmonton. (1975)

Munro, I. S. Arthur. John W. The Seventeenth Highland Light Infantry (Glasgow Chamber of Commerce Battalion). (1920)

Northridge, Richard. Portora and Portorans in the Great War (2014)

O'Neill, H.C. The Royal Fusiliers in the Great War. (1922)

Pegum, Michael. Our Fallen Members The War Casualties of the Kildare Street and Dublin University Clubs

Pendrill, Colin. And we were young. Oundle School and the Great War. (2017)

Porter, Jonathon. Zero Hour Z Day 1st July 1916. XIII Corps Operations between Maricourt and Mametz. (2017)

Porter, Jonathon. Zero Hour Z Day 1st July 1916 XV Corps between Mametz and Fricourt Volume Two (2020)

Quinn, Anthony. Wigs and Guns. Irish Barristers in the Great War (2006)

Raw, David. Bradford Pals. A Comprehensive History of the 16th – 18th & 20th (Service) Battalions of the Prince of Wales Own West Yorkshire Regiment 1914 1918 (2006)

Record of Service of service of solicitors and Articled Clerks with His Majesty's Forces 1914 1918

Risman, Ann. Penrith Remembers 1914 – 1918. Heroism, Hardship… and Victory. (2017)

Roberts, Andrew. Elegy. The First Day on the Somme. (2015)

Robertson, George, Captain. Letters of a Temporary Gentleman. The family correspondence of Captain George Robertson 21st (Service Battalion) Northumberland Fusiliers, 2nd Tyneside Scottish 1915 – 1916.

Rogers, Mark. All the King's Men. King's School. (2018)

Rogers, Mark. In Dedication to a Future World. The lives & deaths of the men on the Royal Grammar School Worcester War Memorials (2014)

Samuels, Arthur Purefoy Irwin and Dorothy Gage Samuels. With the Ulster Division in France. A Story of the 11th Battalion Royal Irish Rifles. From Bordon to Thiepval .

Sandall, T. E. Colonel. A History of the 5th Battalion. The Lincolnshire Regiment. 1922

Short History of the London Rifle Brigade (1916) Compiled regimentally

Simpson, C. R. Major General. The History of the Lincolnshire Regiment 1914 1918 Compiled from war diaries, Despatches, Officers' Notes and other sources. 1931

Sparrow, Chris. No Time to Spare? Our Boys who went to war…(2006)

Spurrell, Jonathan. None Have Done Better: The lives of the Old Colchestrians who died in the First World War 2018

Stansfield, Margaret J. Huddesfield's Roll of Honour 1914 – 1922. (2012)

Steers, David. First World War Roll of Honour of the Non-Subscribing Presbyterian Church of Ireland (2018)

Stewart, Graham & Sheen, John. Tyneside Scottish 20th, 21st, 22nd & 23rd (Service) Battalions Northumberland Fusiliers (2014)

Stott, Godfrey. A History of Chigwell School. 1960

The Lawyers List. A Selected List of General Practitioners, Corporation and Trial Lawyers of the United States (1913)

The Leys and the War. Record of 1914 1918. Supplement Directory Leys School 1920

The Sedbergh School Register 1875 to 1928 (1930)

The Stock Exchange Memorial of those who fell in the Great War. MCMXIV-MCMXIX

The War Record of the Northern Assurance Co. Ltd 1914 1918 (1919)

Thornicroft, Nick. Dauntless Courage on the Somme; Officers of the 19th Division who fell at La Boisselle 1-10 July 1916 (2016)

Thornicroft, Nick. Gloucestershire and North Bristol Soldiers on the Somme (2007)

Tonbridge School and the Great War of 1914 to 1919 A Record of the services of Tonbridgians in the Great War of 1914 to 1919 (1923)

Ussher, Richard. Roll of the Sons and Daughters of the Anglican Church Clergy throughout the world and of the Naval and Military Chaplains of the same who gave their lives in the Great War

Vaughan, Edward Littleton. List of Etonians who fought in the great war, 1914-1919 (1921)

Venn, John and J. A. Venn, Alumni Cantabrigienses. A Biographical list of all known students, graduates and Holders of Office at the Univeristy of Cambridge, from the Earliest times to 1900. Volume 2. (2011)

Walsall and District. The Roll of the Great War 1914 - 1918

Ward, R. V (1937). A Register of Old Wycliffians 1882 – 1937.

Weetman, W. C. C. Captain. The Sherwood Foresters in the Great War. 1/8th Battalion. 1914 -1 1919. (1920)

Wheeler-Holohan, Captain A. V. and Wyattt, G M. G, Captain. The Rangers' Historical Records. From 1859 to the conclusion of the Great War (1921)

Whitney. C. E. We Will Remember Them. Old Decanians Who Lost Their Lives as a Result of Conflict. (2014)

Williams, Ricard et al. The New Forest and The Great War 1916. Jutland and the Somme. (2016)

Wykehamist War Service Roll Fifth Edition July 1918

BV - #0003 - 191021 - C0 - 297/210/20 [22] - CB - 9780957299832 - Gloss Lamination